四川统计年鉴
Sichuan Statistical Yearbook

2019

（总第37期 No.37）

四川省统计局
国家统计局四川调查总队 编

Statistical Bureau of Sichuan
NBS Survey Office in Sichuan

中国统计出版社
China Statistics Press

图书在版编目（CIP）数据

四川统计年鉴. 2019 : 汉英对照 / 四川省统计局，国家统计局四川调查总队编. -- 北京 : 中国统计出版社，2019.10
ISBN 978-7-5037-8872-7

Ⅰ. ①四… Ⅱ. ①四… ②国… Ⅲ. ①统计资料—四川—2019—年鉴—汉、英 Ⅳ. ①C832.71-54

中国版本图书馆 CIP 数据核字（2019）第 153342 号

四川统计年鉴—2019

作　　者 / 四川省统计局　国家统计局四川调查总队
责任编辑 / 佘竞雄　且淑芬
执行编辑 / 宋　兰
装帧设计 / 李雪燕
出版发行 / 中国统计出版社有限公司
通信地址 / 北京市丰台区西三环南路甲 6 号　邮政编码 /100073
电　　话 / 邮购（010）63376909　书店（010）68783171
网　　址 / http://www.zgtjcbs.com
印　　刷 / 河北鑫兆源印刷有限公司
经　　销 / 新华书店
开　　本 / 880mm×1230mm　1/16
字　　数 / 1128 千字
印　　张 / 37　彩页 1
版　　别 / 2019 年 10 月第 1 版
版　　次 / 2019 年 10 月第 1 次印刷
定　　价 / 420.00 元　Price: 420.00 yuan(RMB)

本书附同版本 CD-ROM 一张，光盘内容以书面文字为准。
如有印装差错，由本社发行部调换。

《四川统计年鉴－2019》

编委会和编辑出版人员

SICHUAN STATISTICAL YEARBOOK - 2019

Editorial Board and Staff

编 者 说 明

一、《四川统计年鉴－2019》是一部全面反映四川省经济和社会发展情况的综合性统计资料年刊。本年鉴收录了全省和各市（州）、县（市、区）2018年经济和社会发展各方面的大量统计数据，以及历史重要年份和近年来的全省主要统计数据。

二、本年鉴正文内容分为22个篇章，即：1. 综合；2. 国民经济核算；3. 人口；4. 就业和工资；5. 固定资产投资；6. 能源；7. 资源和环境；8. 财政和物价；9. 人民生活和社会保障；10. 城市发展；11. 民族自治地方概况；12. 县（市、区）概况；13. 农业；14. 工业；15. 建筑业；16. 交通运输和邮电业；17. 国内贸易；18. 对外经济贸易和旅游；19. 金融和保险；20. 教育、科技和专利；21. 文化、体育和卫生；22. 其他社会活动。为帮助读者理解和使用统计数据，部分统计表下作了简要注释，并在各篇末附有主要统计指标解释。

三、与《四川统计年鉴－2018》比较，在本年鉴第一章“综合”中增加了四川经济社会发展70年主要指标的总量、速度、比例和构成资料；在第五章“固定资产投资”中将全社会固定资产投资及构成的绝对值调整为增长速度；在第六章“能源”中，将“各市（州）单位地区生产总值能耗”、“各市（州）单位工业增加值能耗”调整为“各市（州）单位地区生产总值能耗指数”、“各市（州）单位工业增加值能耗指数”；在第九章“人民生活和社会保障”中删减了“离退休、退职人员数和离退休金及退职人员生活费”；在第二十二章“其他社会活动”中删减了“检察机关直接立案侦查职务犯罪案件情况”和“各市（州）检察机关直接立案侦察职务犯罪案件情况”。

四、本年鉴中，涉及的部门统计资料均由省级相关部门提供。

五、本年鉴对过去发表的统计资料重新进行了核实，凡与本年鉴数据有出入的，以本年鉴为准。

六、本年鉴中所使用的度量衡单位均采用国际统一标准计量单位。

七、本年鉴中部分数据合计数或相对数由于单位取舍不同而产生的计算误差，均未做机械调整。

八、本年鉴表中的符号使用说明：“空格”表示该项统计指标数据不足本表最小单位数、数据不详或无该项数据；“#”表示其中的主要项。

Preface

Ⅰ. *Sichuan Statistical Yearbook 2019* is an annual statistics publication to reflect various aspects of Sichuan's economic and social development, which covers very comprehensive data series in 2018 and some selected data series in historically important years and the most recent years at provincial level, local levels of prefecture and level of county.

Ⅱ. The text of this Yearbook contains the following 22 parts: 1. General Survey, 2.National Accounts, 3.Population, 4.Employment and Wages, 5.Investment in Fixed Assets, 6.Energy, 7.Resources and Environment, 8.Local Government Finance and Price, 9. People's Living Conditions and Social Security, 10.Urban Development, 11.Survey of Minority Nationality Autonomous Areas, 12.Survey of County (City, District), 13.Agriculture, 14.Industry, 15.Construction, 16.Transportation and Post, 17.Domestic Trade, 18.Foreign Trade and Economic Cooperation and International Tourism, 19.Finance and Insurance, 20.Education, Science, Technology and Patents, 21.Culture, Sports and Public Health, 22.Other Social Activities. Explanatory Notes on Main Statistical Indicators is attached to the end of each chapter to help the readers to understand and use the statistical data in this book.

Ⅲ. Compared with *Sichuan Statistical Yearbook 2018*, the Yearbook adds data on the aggregate, speed, proportion and composition of the main indicators of national economic and social development in the 70 years in Chapter 1"General Survey"; adjusts absolute value of total investment in fixed assets and its composition to growth rate in Chapter 5 "Investment in fixed assets"; adjusts "energy consumption of unit GDP by region" into "the growth of energy consumption of unit GDP by region" and "energy consumption of unit added value of industry by region" into "the growth of energy consumption of unit added value of industry by region" in Chapter 6 "Energy"; delete "number of retired and resigned staff and workers and retirement pay of retirees and living expenses of resigned staff and workers" in Chapter 9 "People's livelihood and social welfare"; delete "cases under direct investigation by procurator's offices" and "duty crime cases under direct investigation by procurator's offices by region" in Chapter 22 "Other social activities".

Ⅳ. In this yearbook, the relevant department statistics are provided by relevant departments at the provincial level.

Ⅴ. The statistics data published in the past is re-verified in this book. Any discrepancy between the data of this book, it prevails.

Ⅵ. The units of measurement used in this book are international standard measurement units.

Ⅶ. Statistical discrepancies on totals and relative figures due to rounding are not adjusted in the yearbook.

目 录

CONTENTS

一、综 合
Chapter 1 General Survey

二、国民经济核算
Chapter 2 National Accounts

三、人 口
Chapter 3 Population

四、就业和工资
Chapter 4 Employment and Wages

五、固定资产投资
Chapter 5　Investment in Fixed Assets

六、能源
Chapter 6 Energy

七、资源和环境
Chapter 7 Resources and Environment

八、财政和物价
Chapter 8　Local Government Finance and Price

九、人民生活和社会保障
Chapter 9　People’s Living Conditions and Social Security

十、城市发展
Chapter 10 Urban Development

十一、民族自治地方概况
Chapter 11 Survey of Minority Nationality Autonomous Areas

十二、县（市、区）概况
Chapter 12 Survey of County(City, District)

十三、农 业
Chapter 13 Agriculture

十四、工 业
Chapter 14 Industry

十五、建筑业
Chapter 15 Construction

十六、交通运输和邮电业
Chapter 16　Transportation and Post

十七、国内贸易
Chapter 17　Domestic Trade

十八、对外经济贸易和旅游
Chapter 18 Foreign Trade and Economic Cooperation and Tourism

十九、金融业
Chapter 19 Financial Intermediation

二十、教育、科技和专利
Chapter 20 Education, Science, Technology and Patents

二十一、文化、体育和卫生
Chapter 21 Culture, Sports and Public Health

二十二、其他社会活动
Chapter 22 Other Social Activities

年末户籍人口

（万人）
7000
6000
5000
4000
3000
2000
1000
0
366 4263
568 4521
536 4152
689 5364
784 6288
830 6325
1102 6791
1565 6843
2355 6646
2998 6140
3116 5997
3272 5850
1952年 1957年 1962年 1970年 1978年 1980年 1990年 2000年 2010年 2016年 2017年 2018年
城镇人口 乡村人口

就业人员

（万人）
5000
4000
3000
2000
1000
0
2028
2258
2102
2738
3087
3260
4265
4658
4773
4860
4872
4881
1952年 1957年 1962年 1970年 1978年 1980年 1990年 2000年 2010年 2016年 2017年 2018年

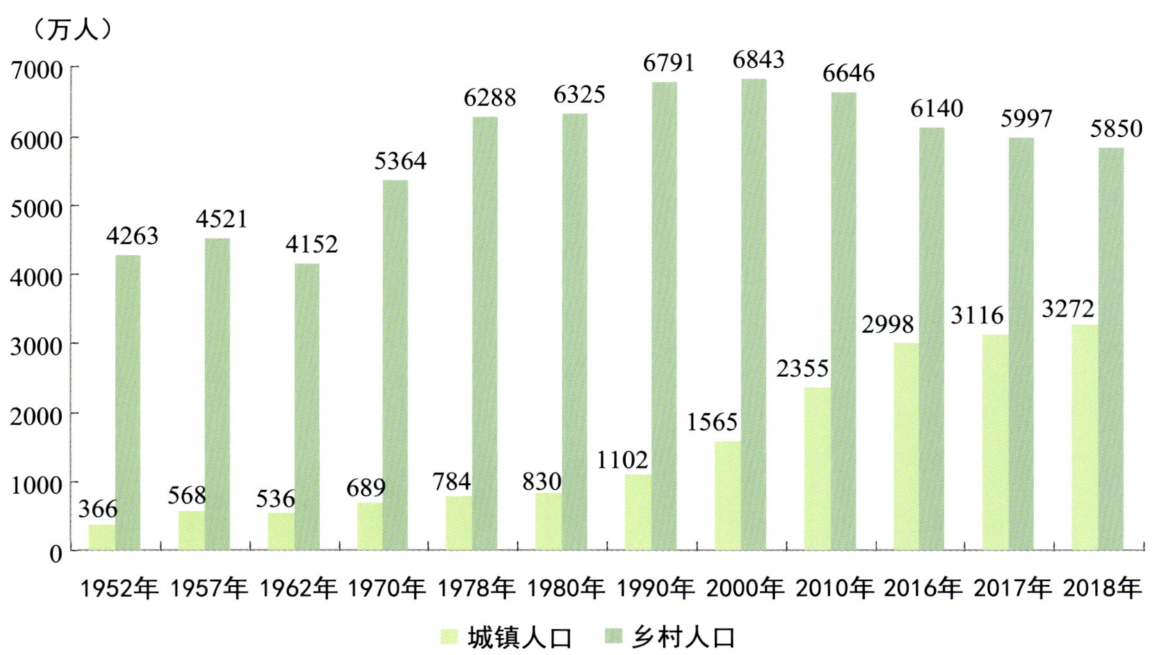

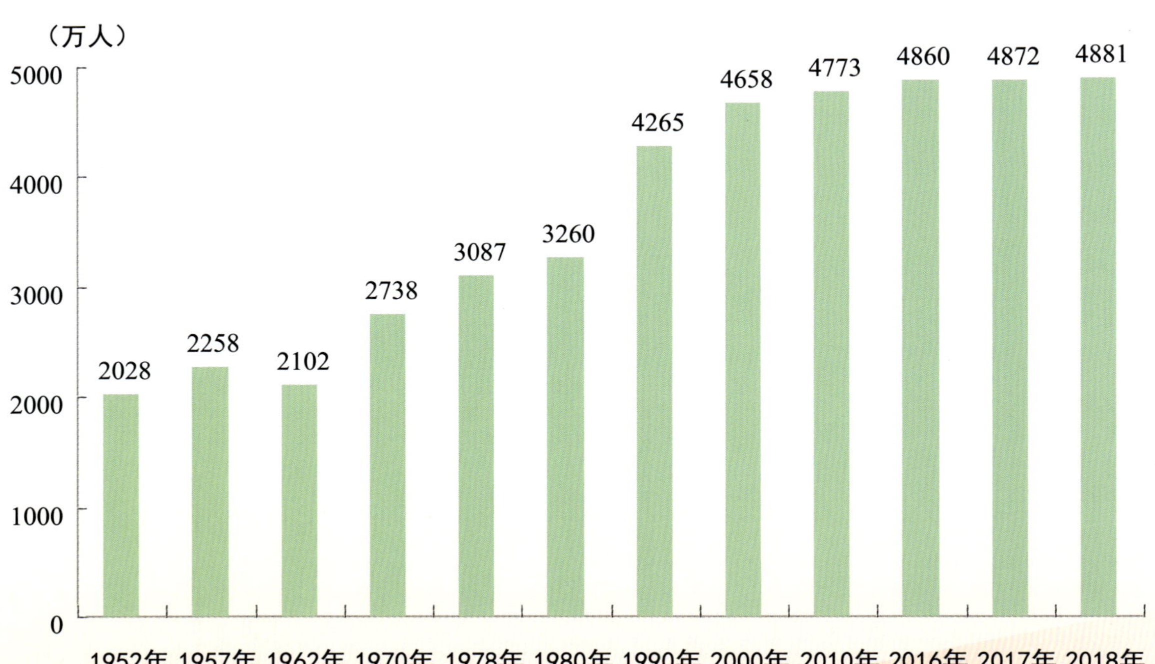

三次产业就业人员构成

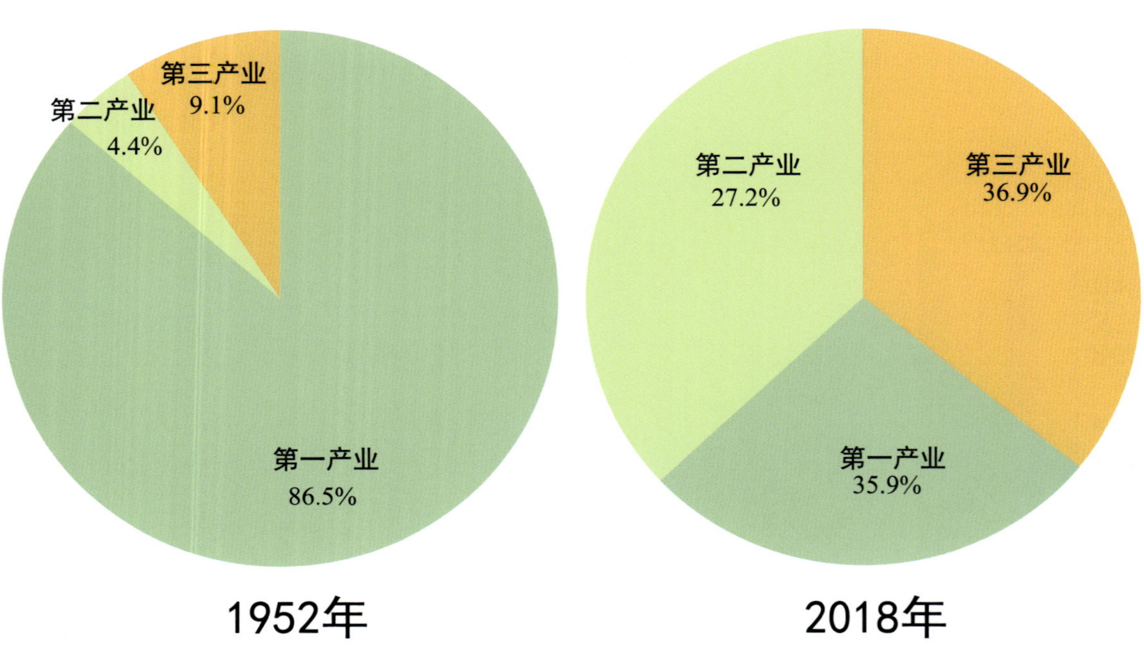

地区生产总值和增长速度

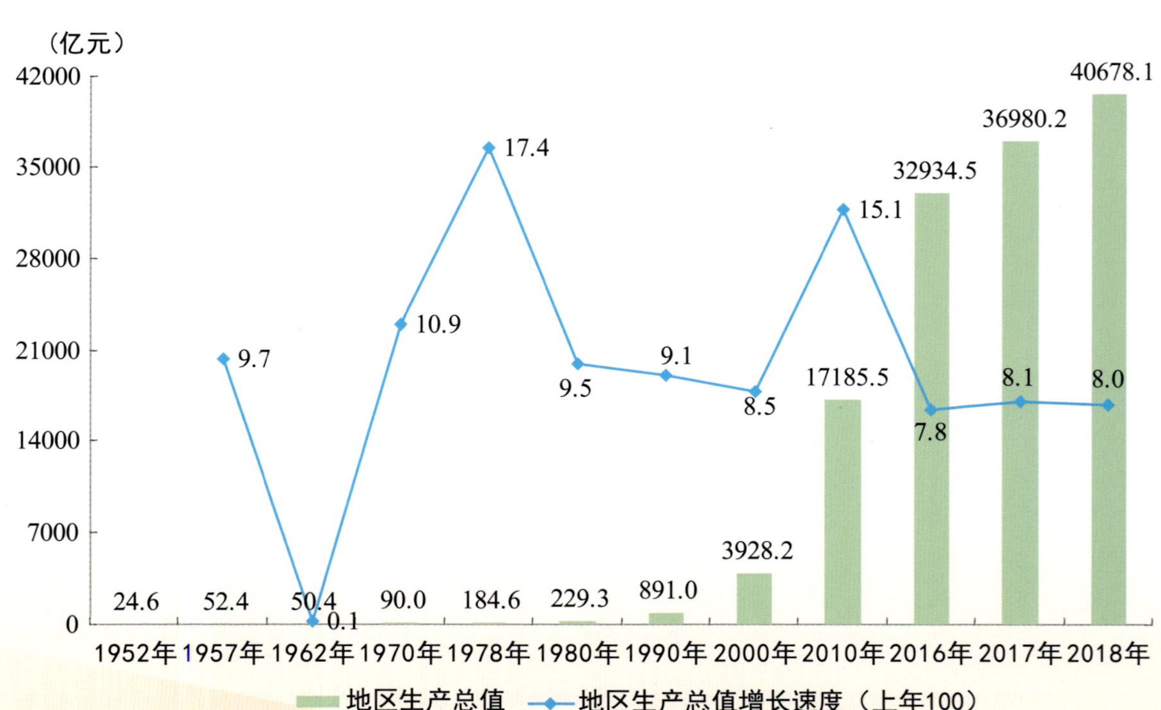

地区生产总值构成

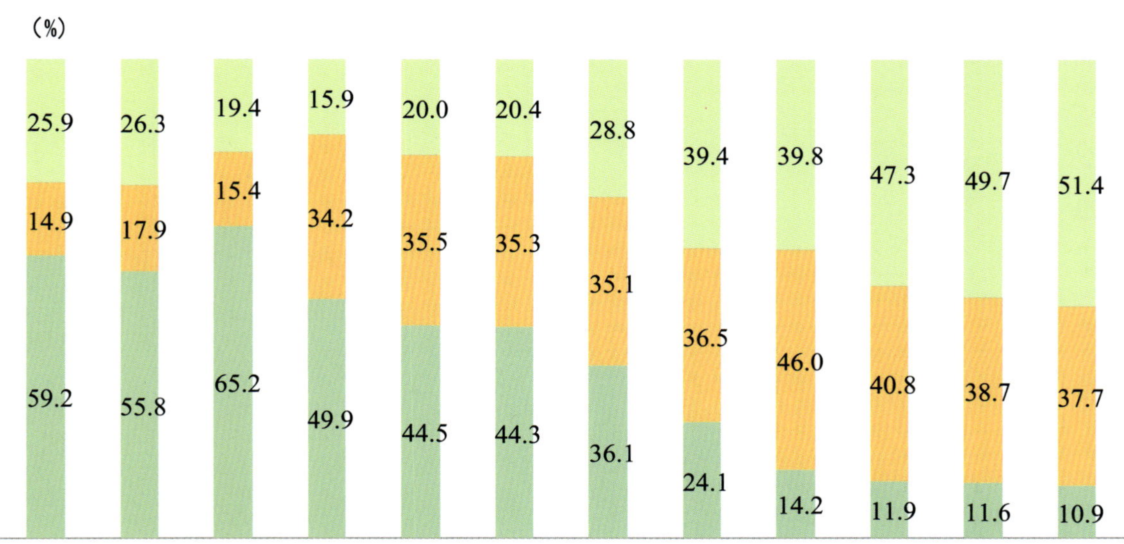

人均地区生产总值

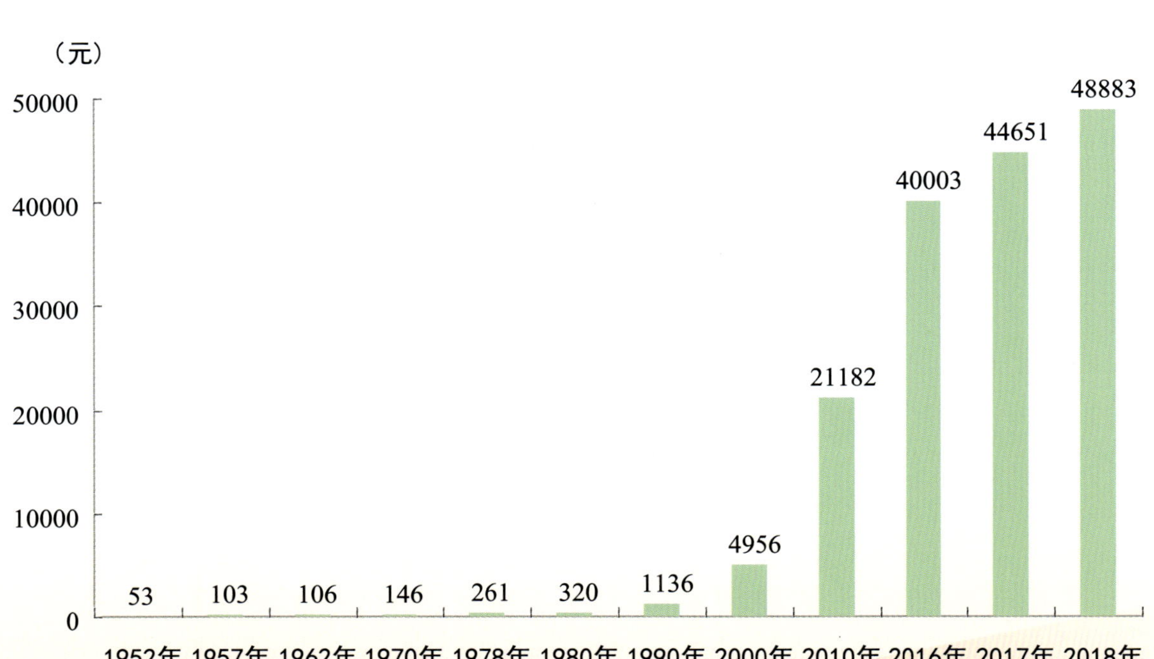

农林牧渔业总产值

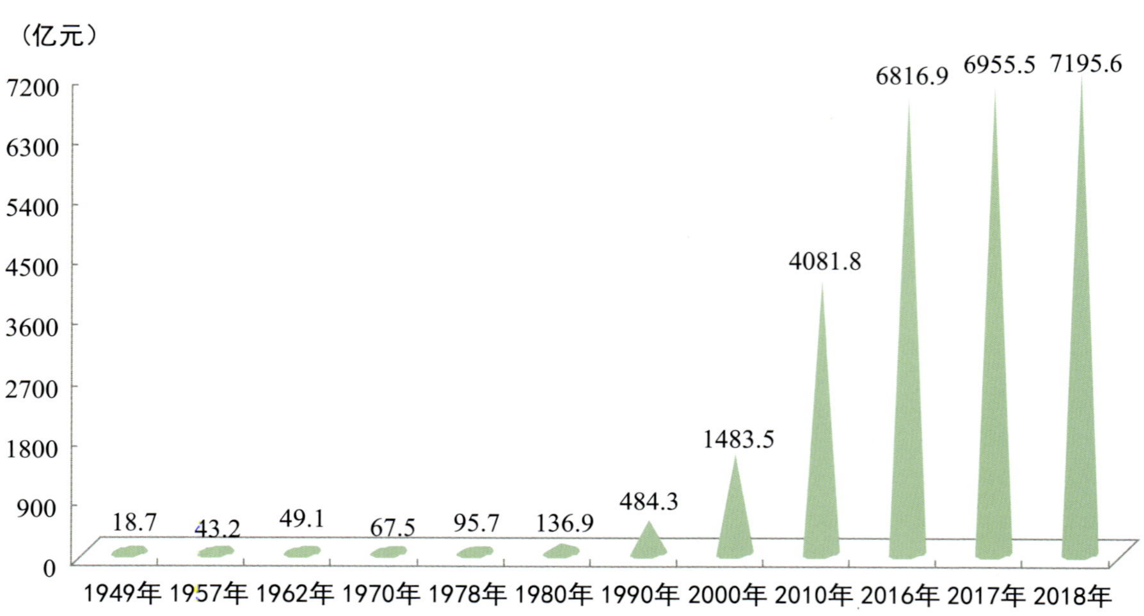

粮食作物和油料作物播种面积

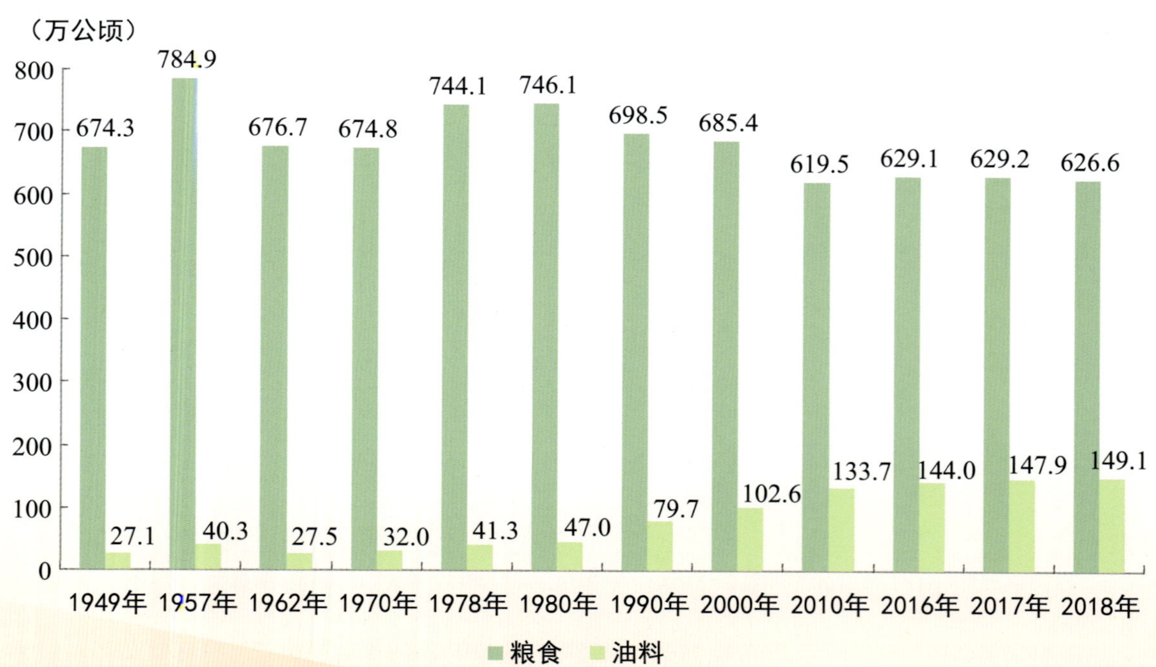

粮食产量和油料产量

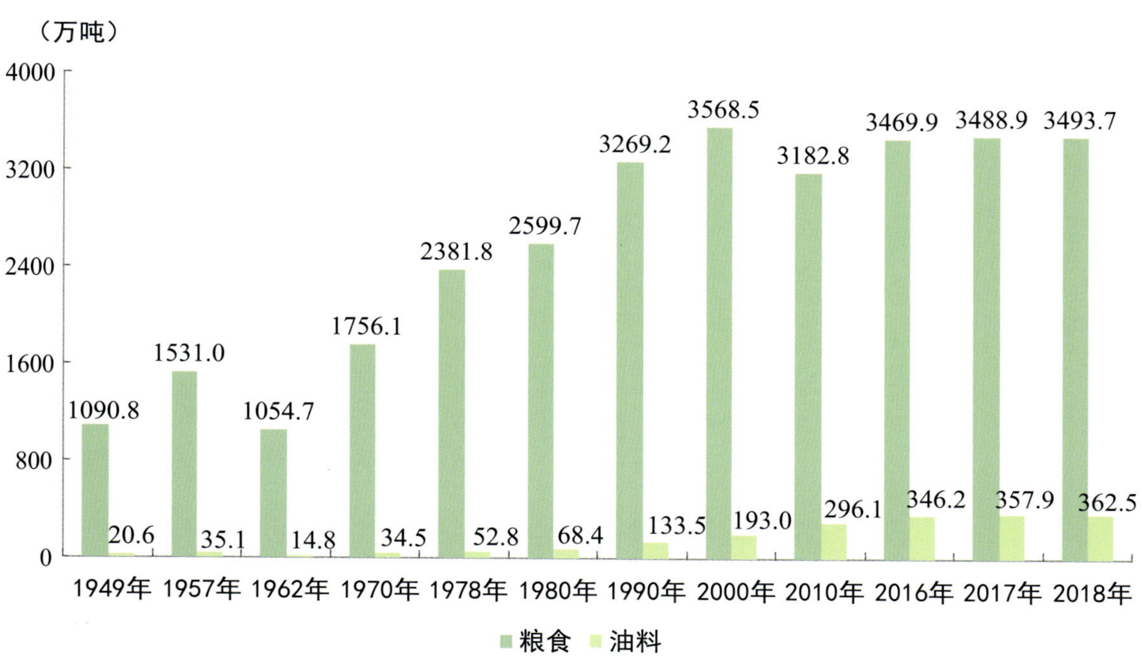

肉类总产量

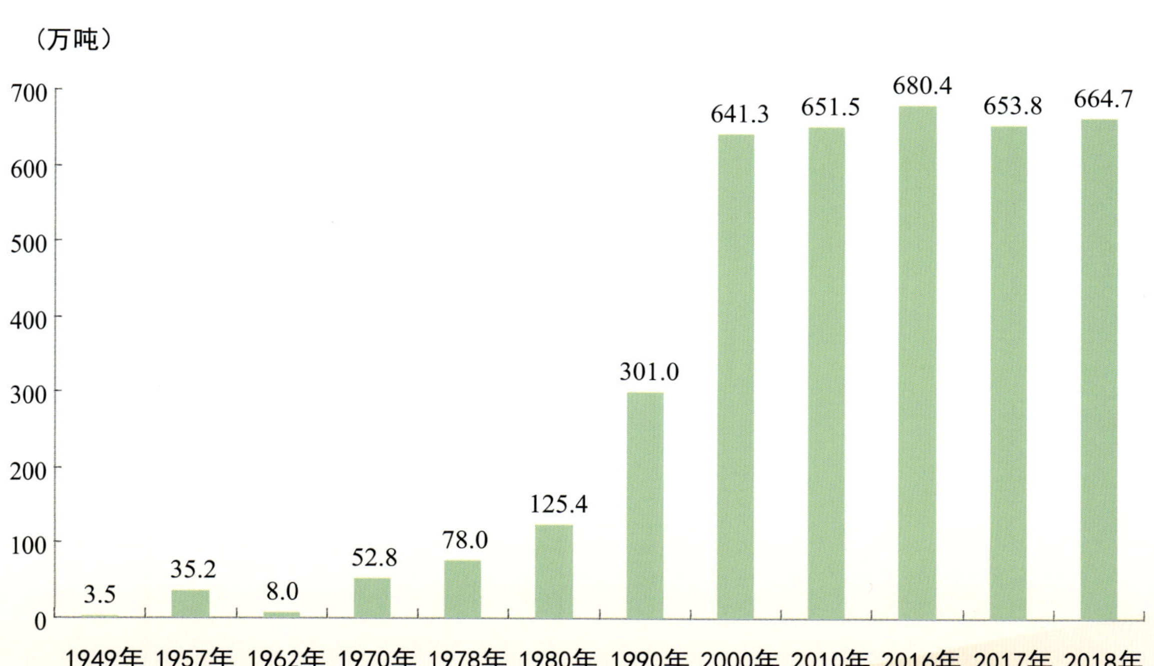

化肥施用量

（万吨）
280
240
200
160
120
80
40
0
0.1
1.0
4.0
11.5
62.5
80.4
143.9
212.6
248.0
249.0
242.0
235.2
1950年
1957年
1962年
1970年
1978年
1980年
1990年
2000年
2010年
2016年
2017年
2018年

农村用电量

（亿千瓦时）
200
160
120
80
40
0
2.2
7.7
9.4
19.3
33.0
61.2
82.8
112.9
141.7
183.1
188.4
198.6
1971年
1978年
1980年
1985年
1990年
1995年
2000年
2005年
2010年
2016年
2017年
2018年

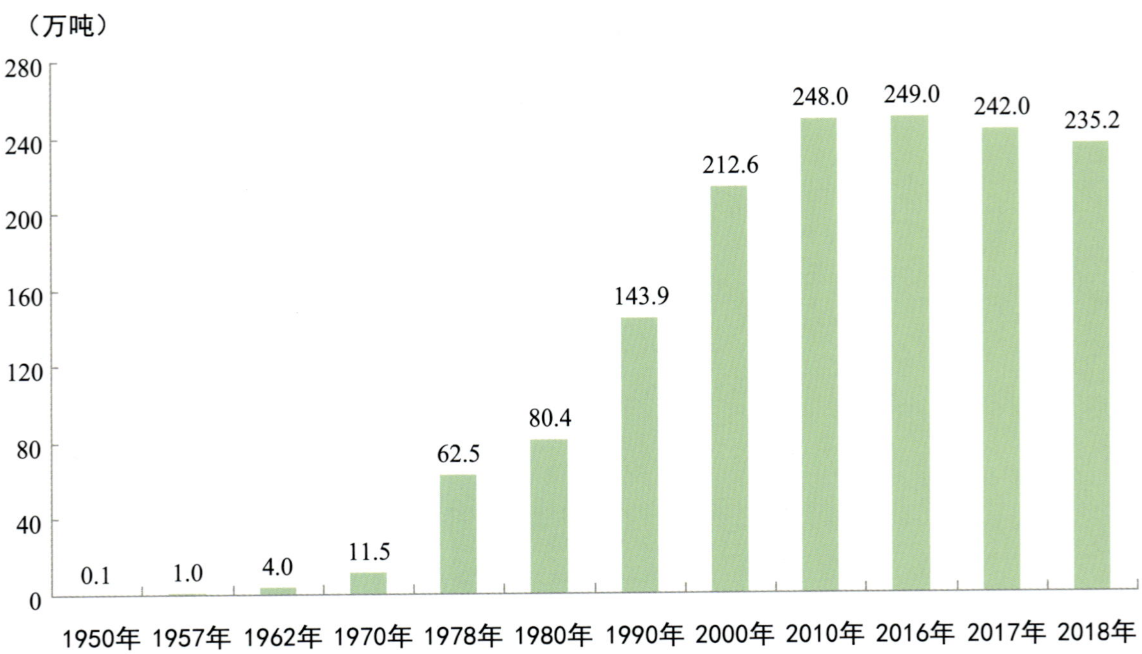

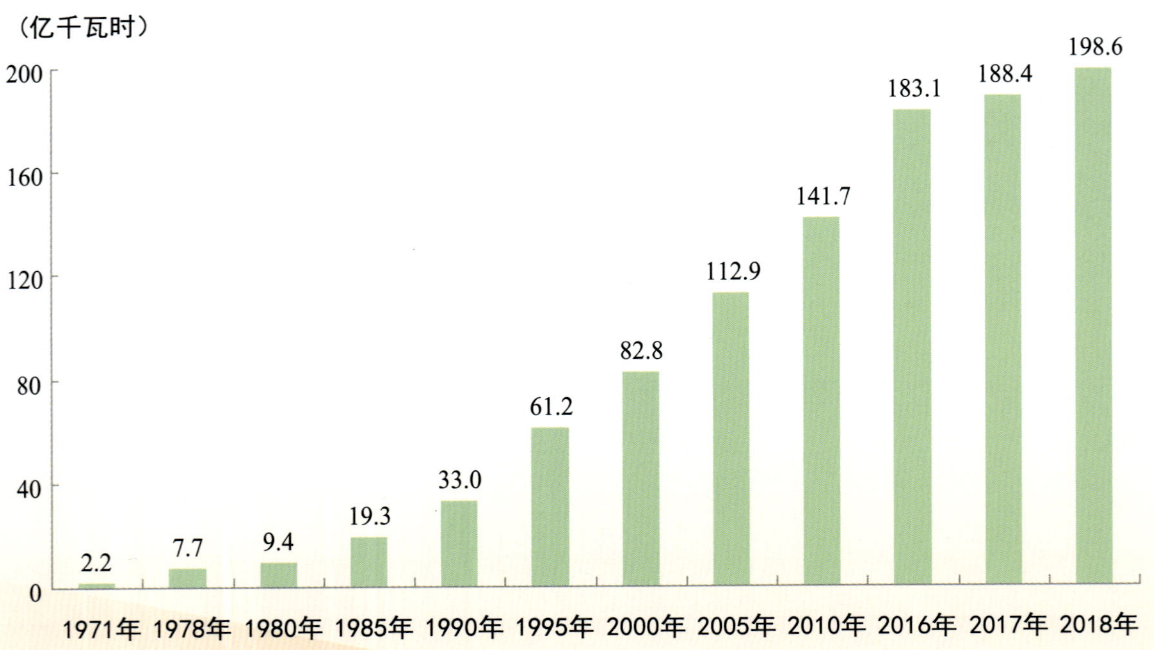

工业增加值

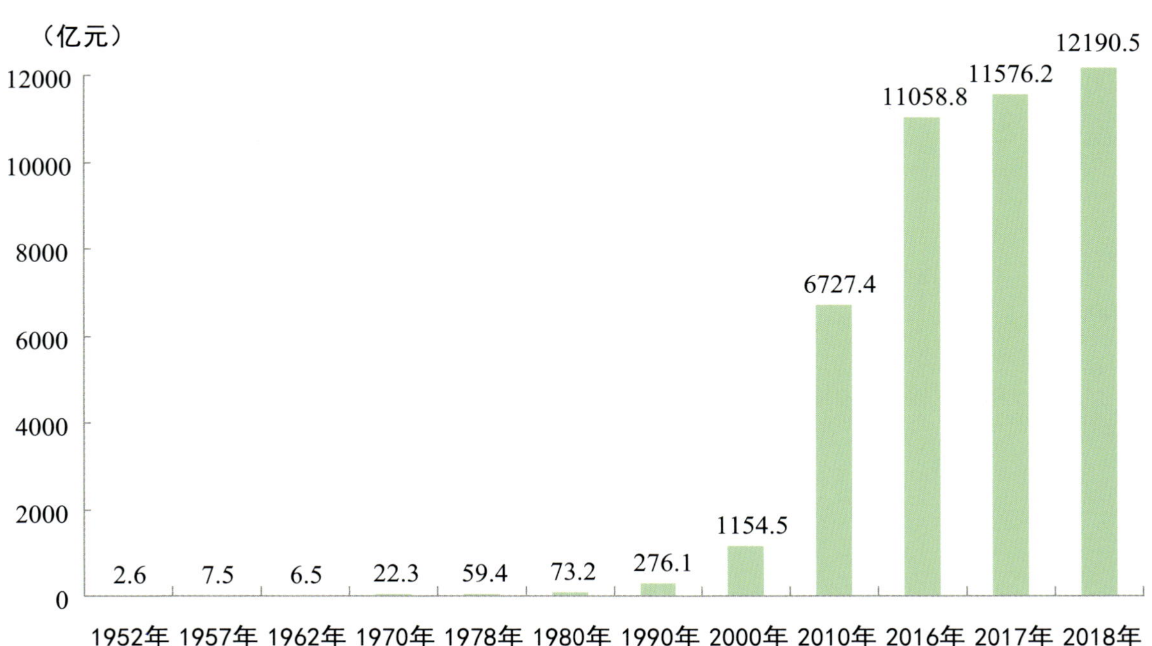

规模以上工业企业利润总额

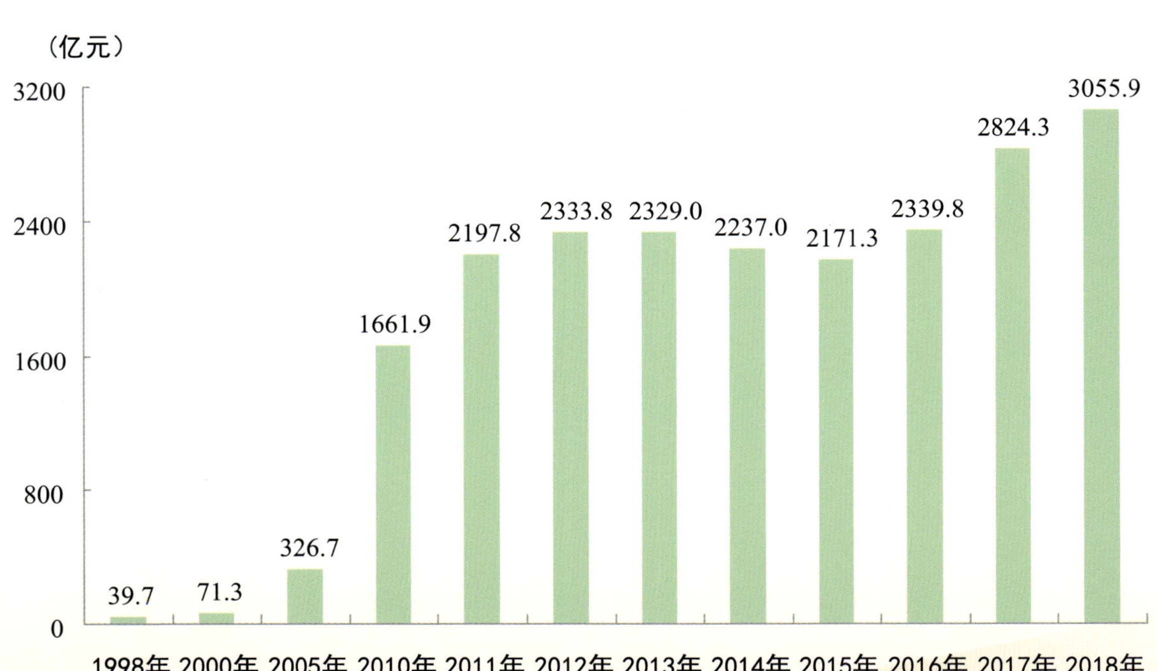

发电量

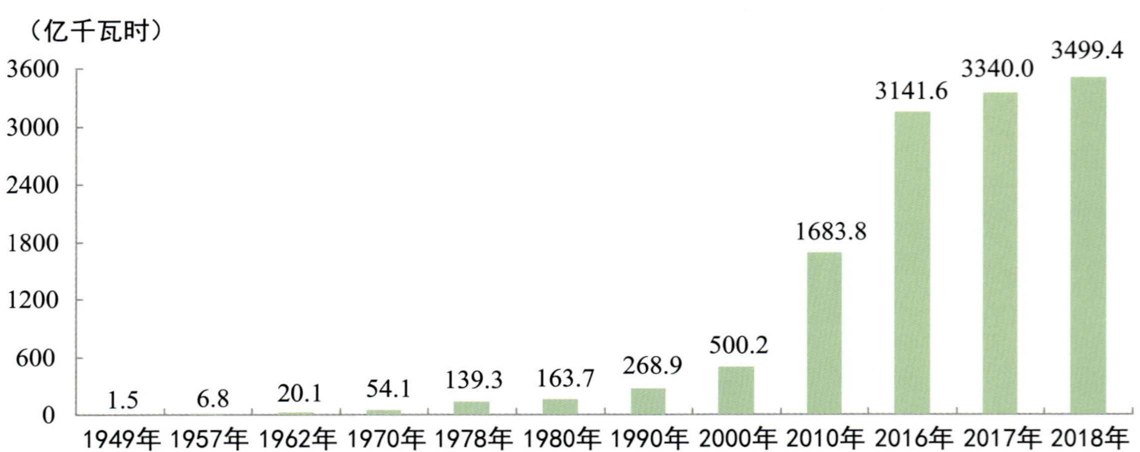

水泥和成品钢材产量

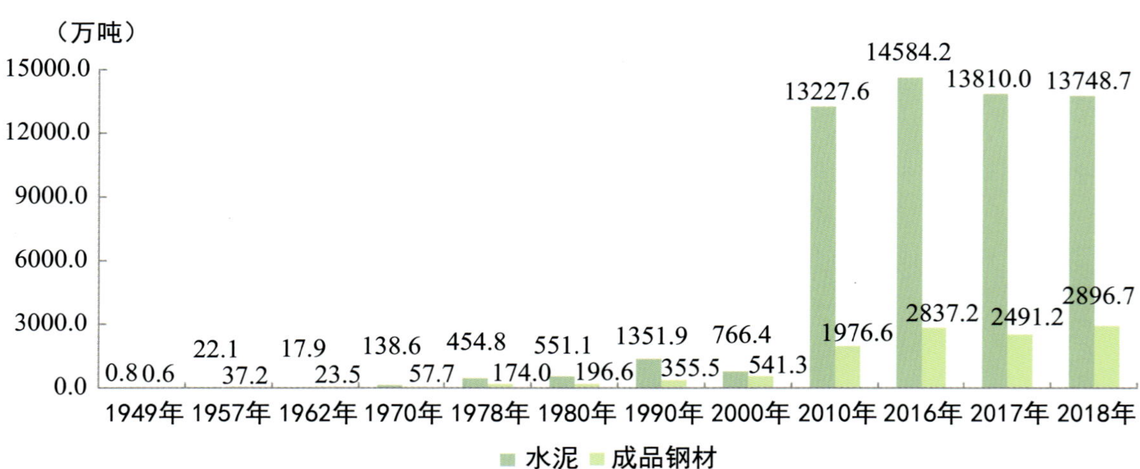

汽车产量

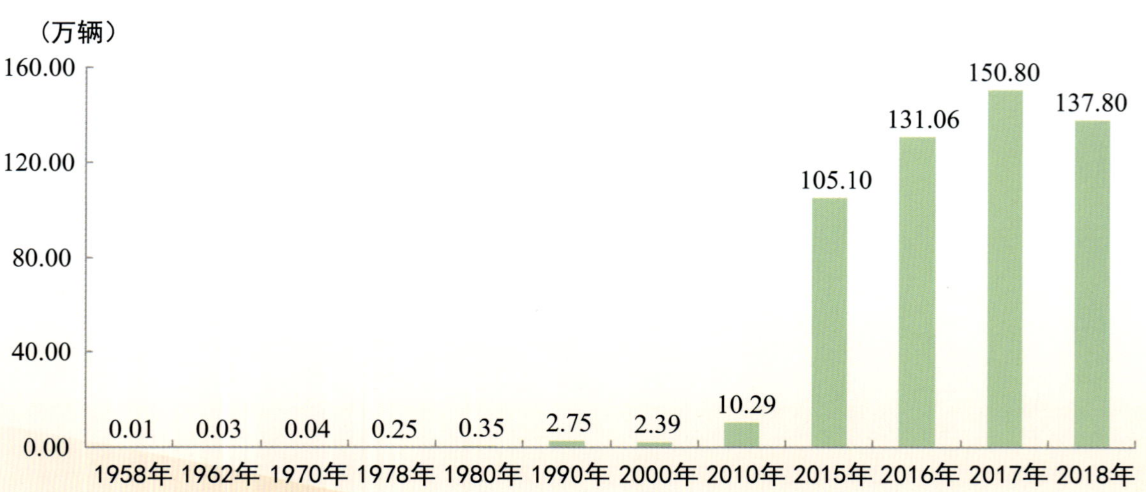

全社会固定资产投资增长速度
（上年 =100）

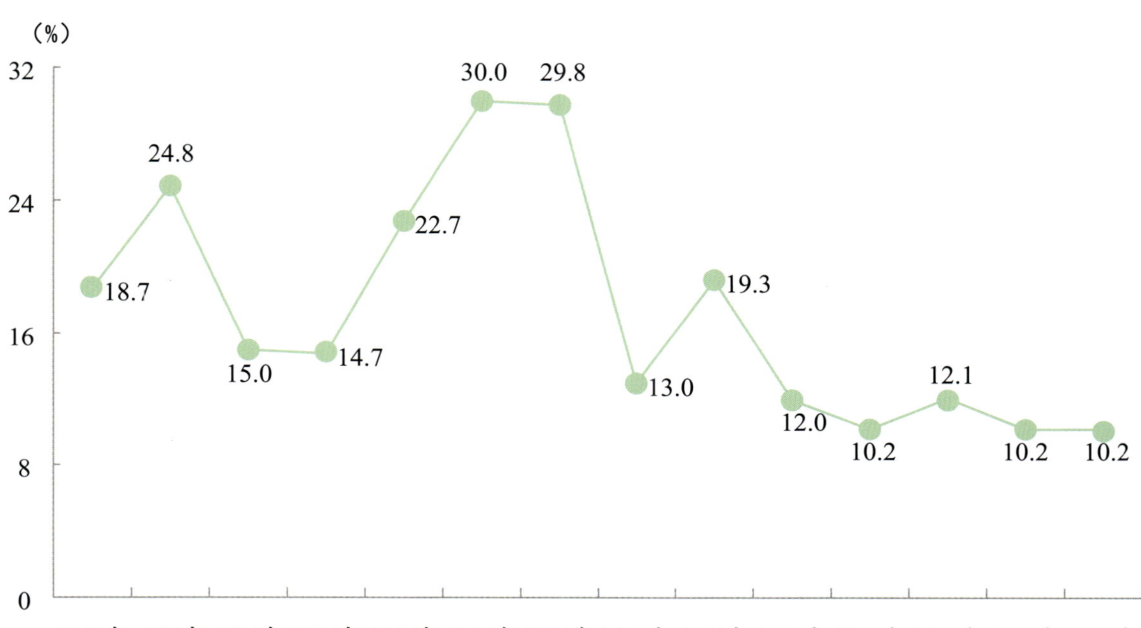

全社会固定资产投资构成

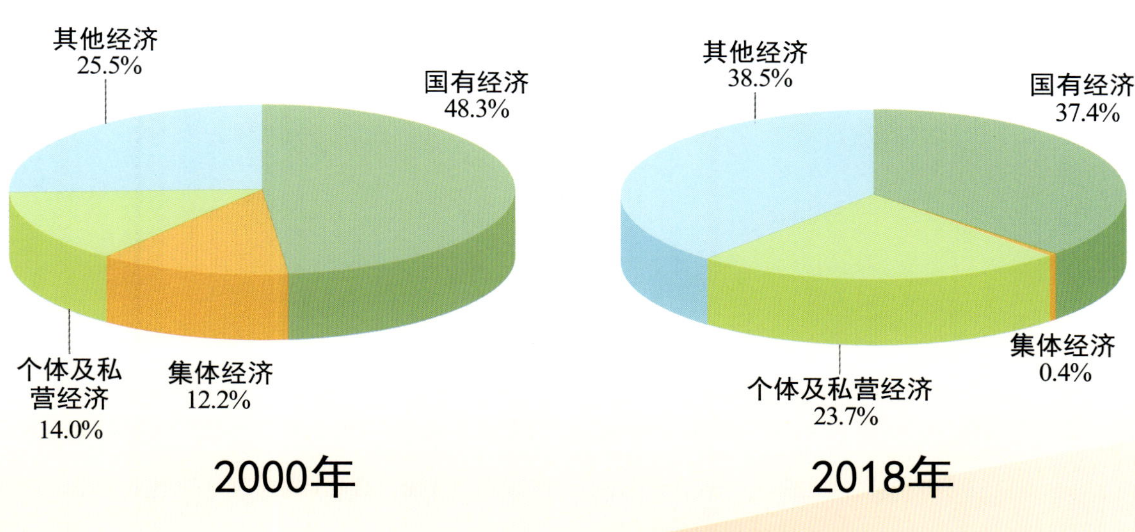

房地产开发投资增长速度
（上年 =100）

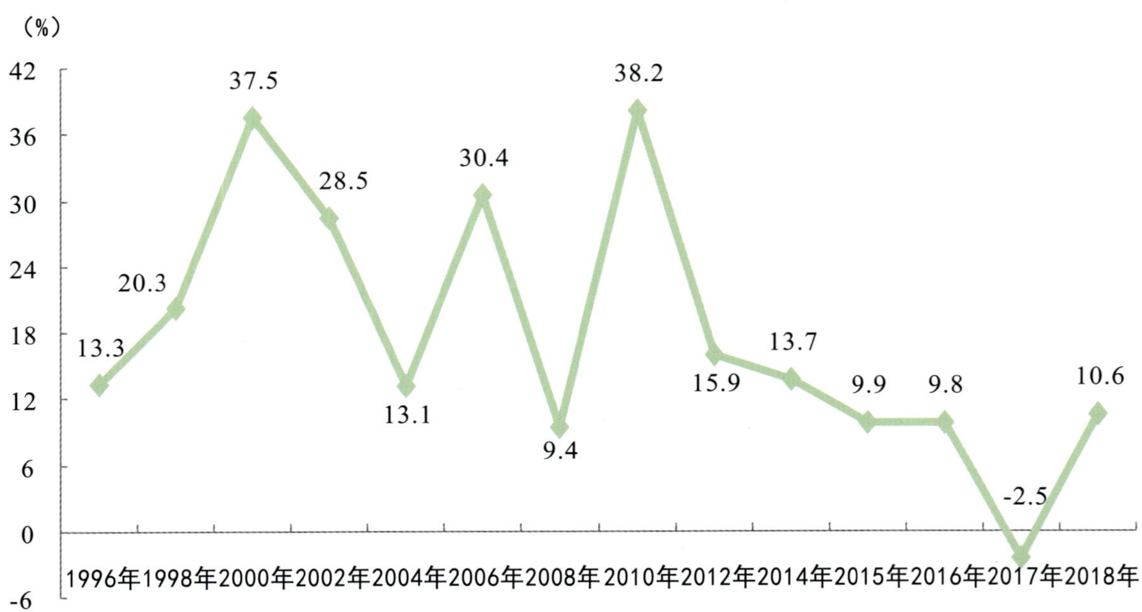

能源生产量和消费量

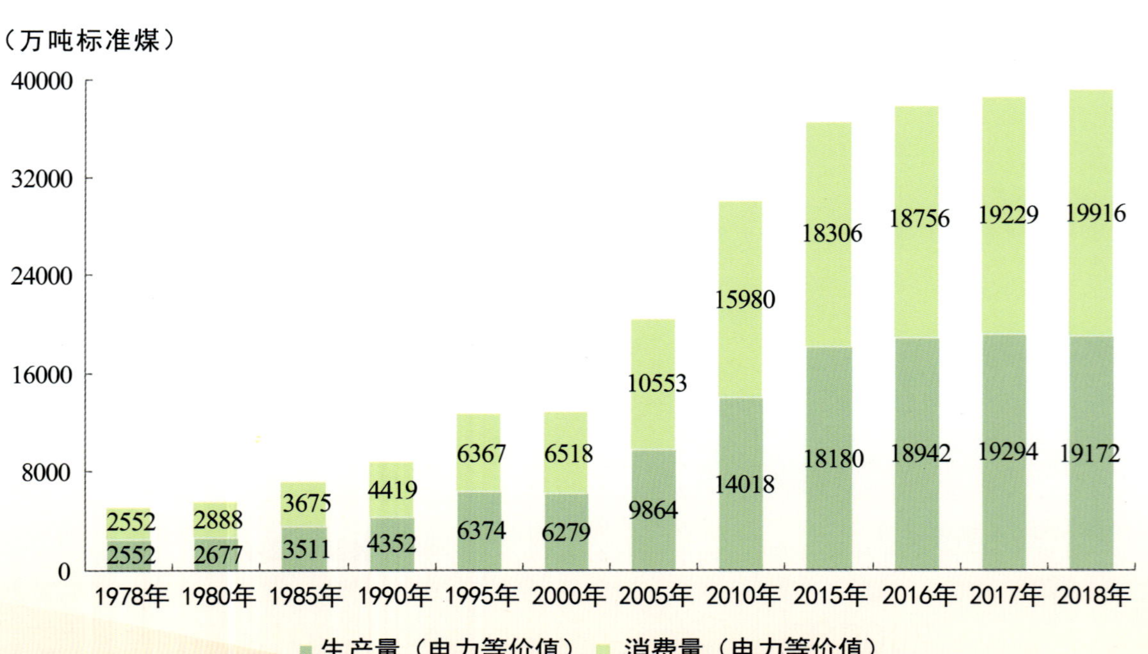

社会消费品零售总额

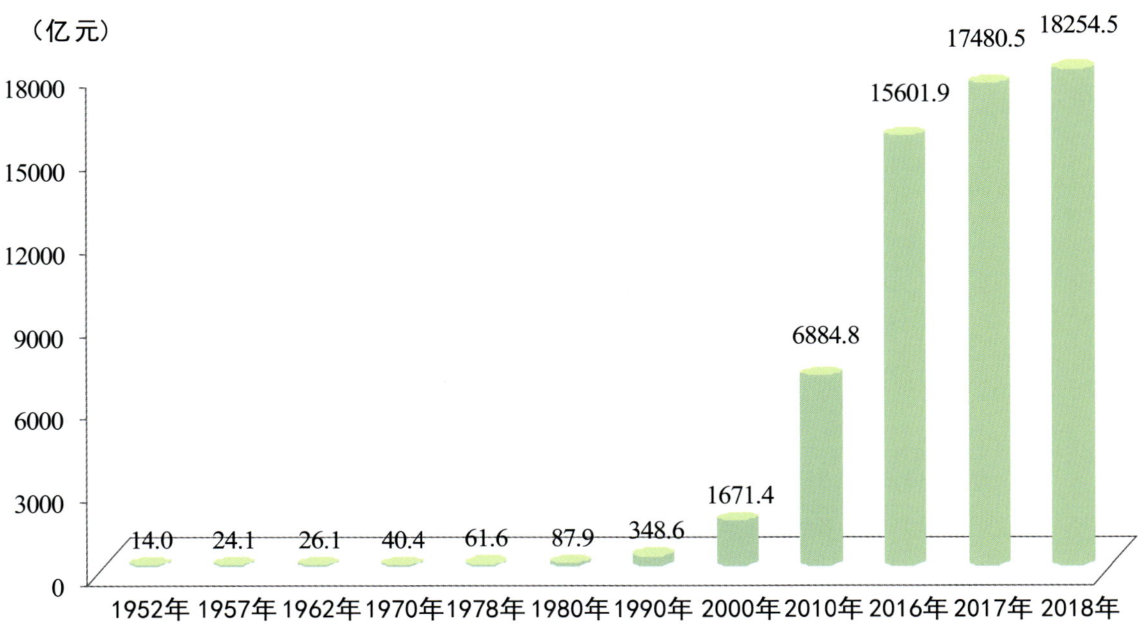

进口额和出口额

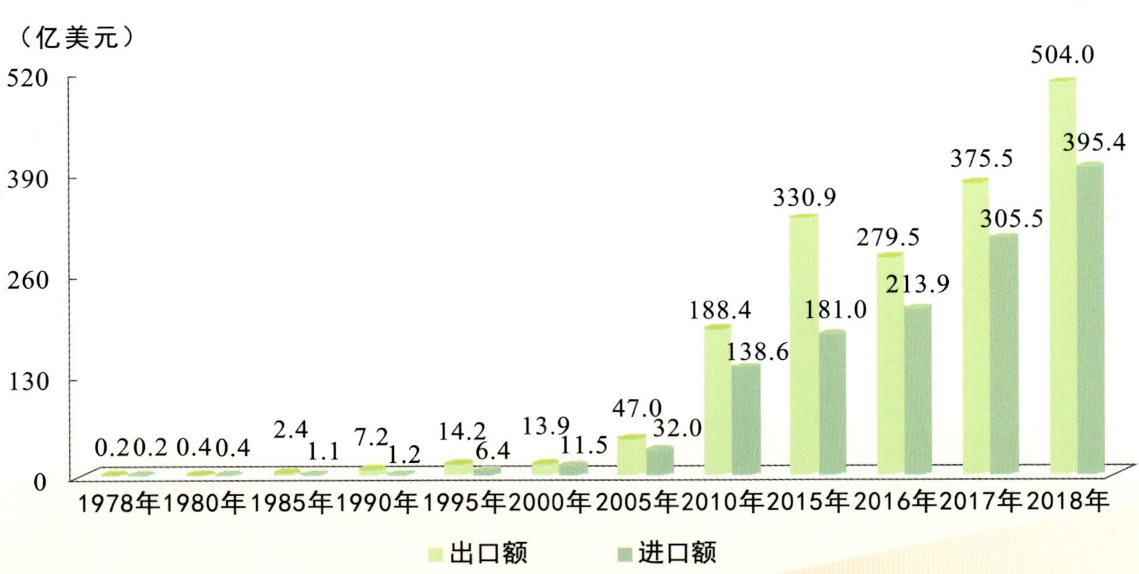

地方一般公共预算收入和支出

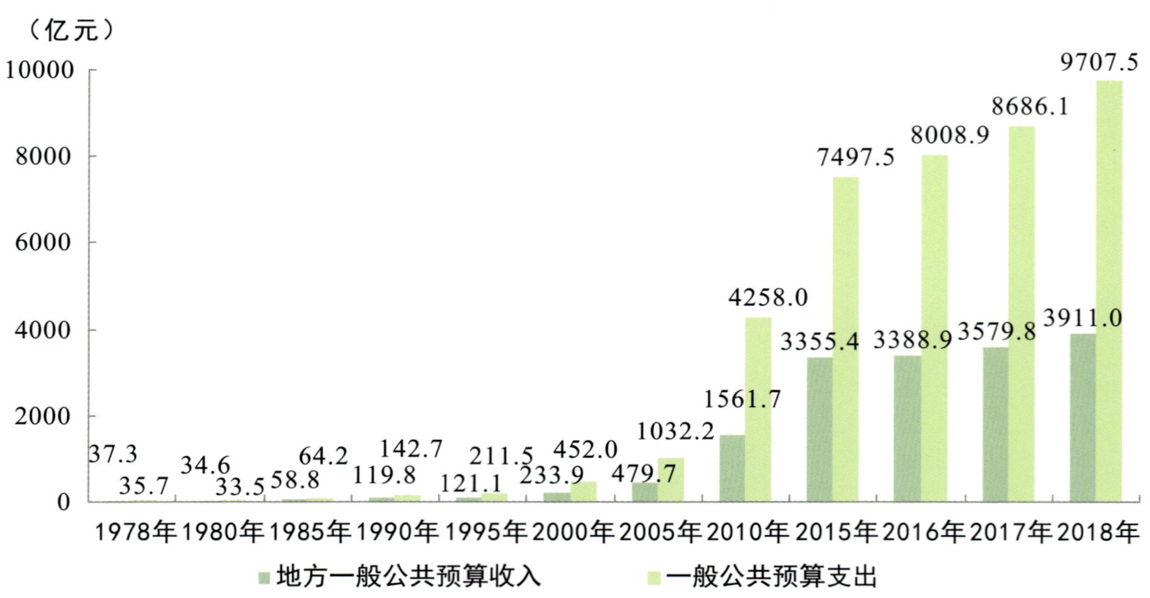

年末金融机构人民币各项存贷款余额

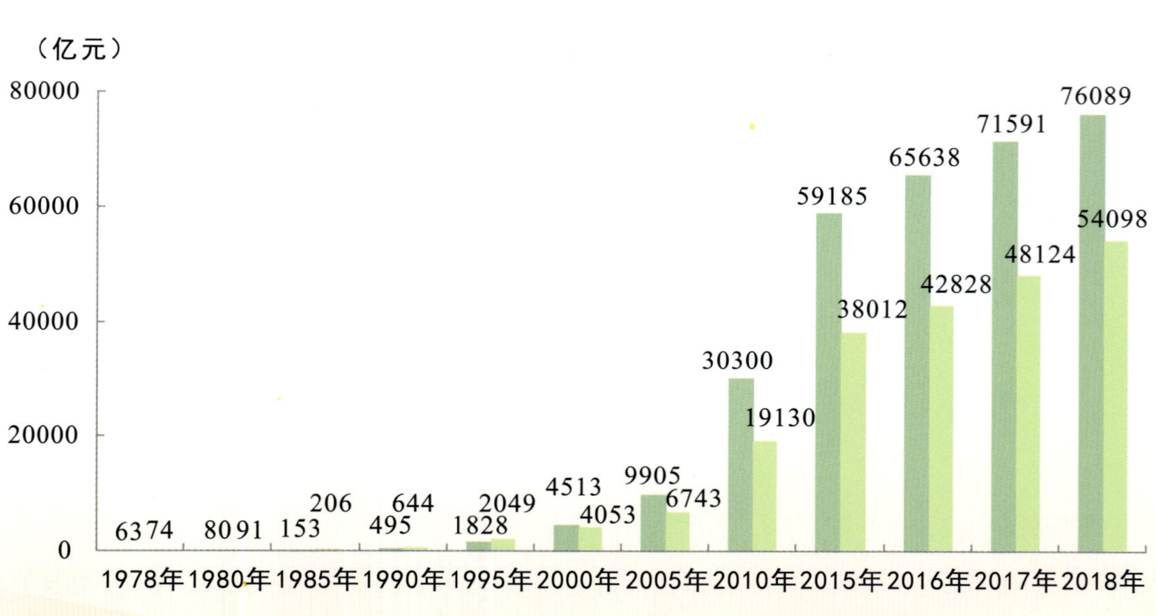

城镇居民人均可支配收入构成

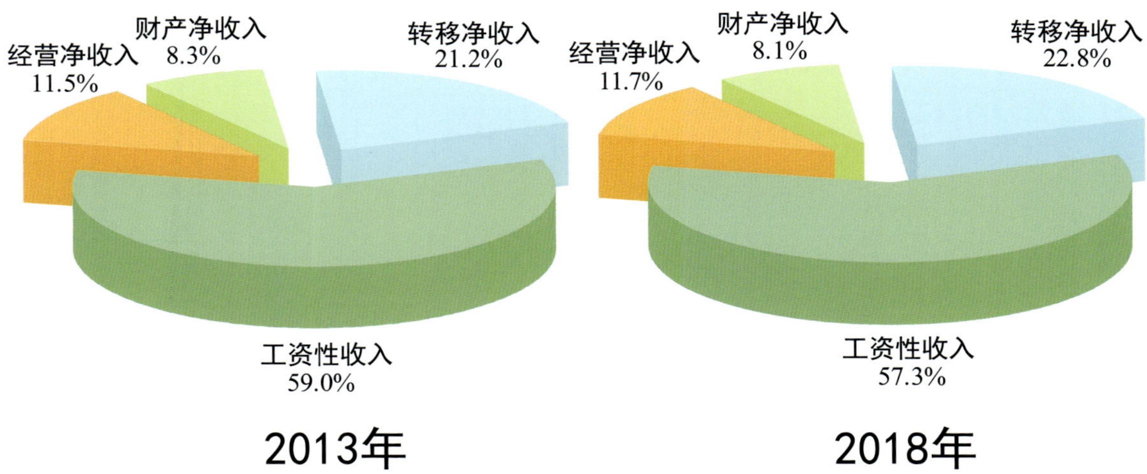

农村居民人均可支配收入构成

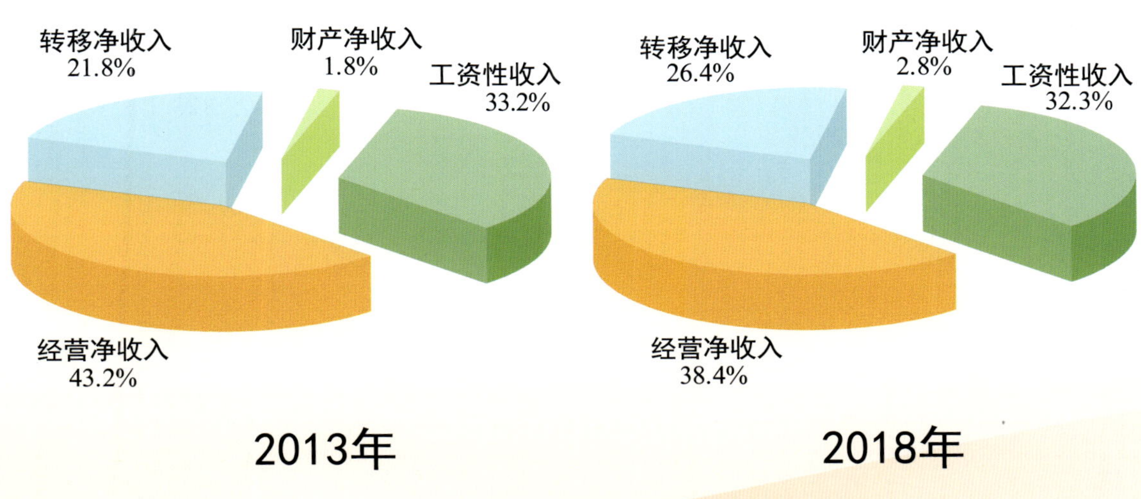

居民消费价格涨跌情况

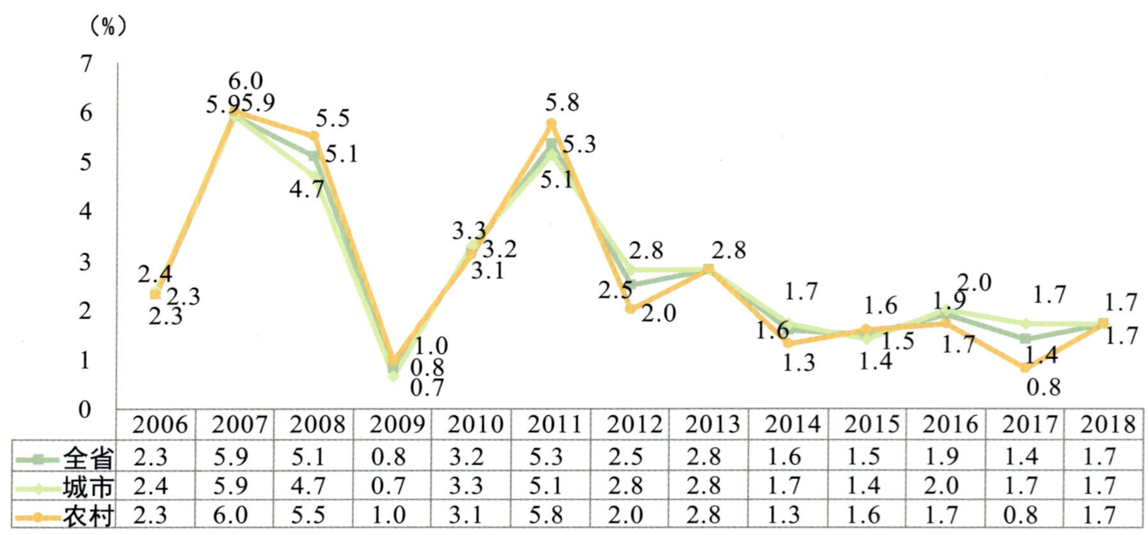

	2006	2007	2008	2009	2010	2011	2012	2013	2014	2015	2016	2017	2018
全省	2.3	5.9	5.1	0.8	3.2	5.3	2.5	2.8	1.6	1.5	1.9	1.4	1.7
城市	2.4	5.9	4.7	0.7	3.3	5.1	2.8	2.8	1.7	1.4	2.0	1.7	1.7
农村	2.3	6.0	5.5	1.0	3.1	5.8	2.0	2.8	1.3	1.6	1.7	0.8	1.7

工业生产者出厂价格涨跌情况

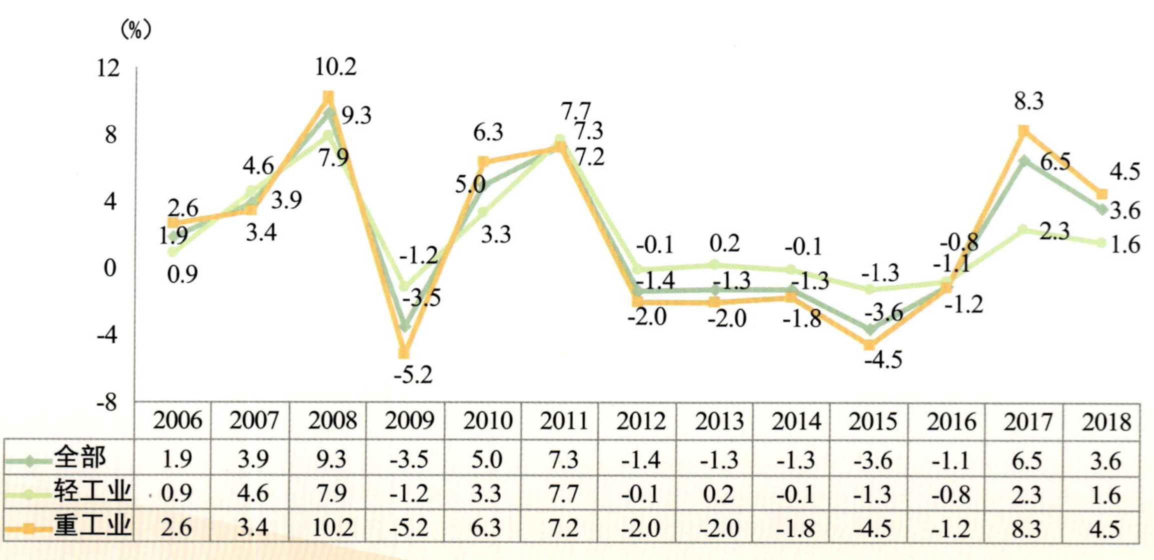

	2006	2007	2008	2009	2010	2011	2012	2013	2014	2015	2016	2017	2018
全部	1.9	3.9	9.3	-3.5	5.0	7.3	-1.4	-1.3	-1.3	-3.6	-1.1	6.5	3.6
轻工业	0.9	4.6	7.9	-1.2	3.3	7.7	-0.1	0.2	-0.1	-1.3	-0.8	2.3	1.6
重工业	2.6	3.4	10.2	-5.2	6.3	7.2	-2.0	-2.0	-1.8	-4.5	-1.2	8.3	4.5

货物周转量和旅客周转量

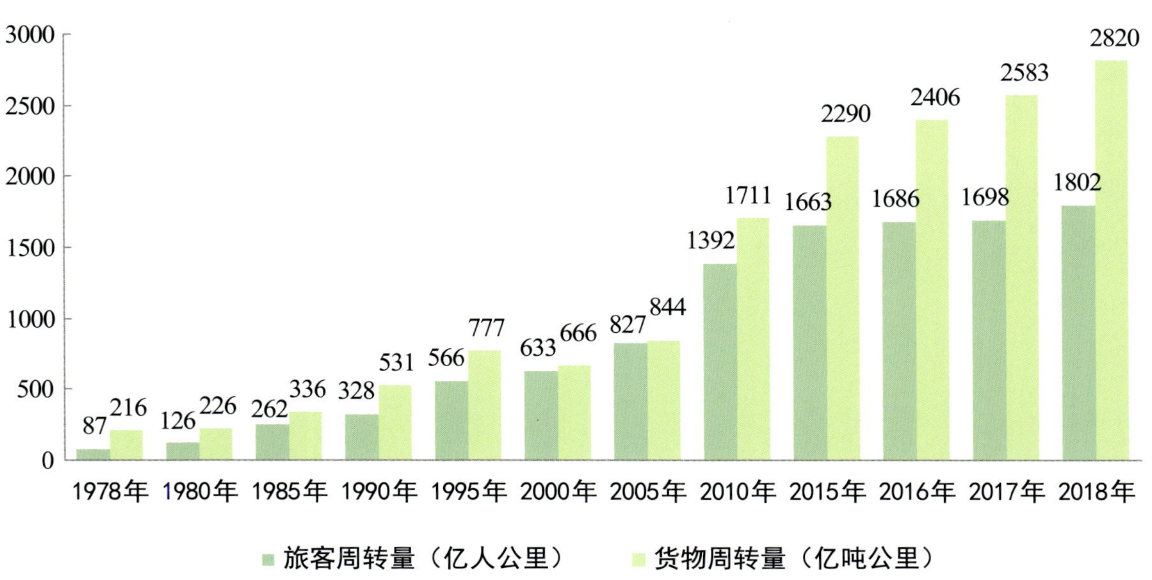

广播覆盖率和电视覆盖率

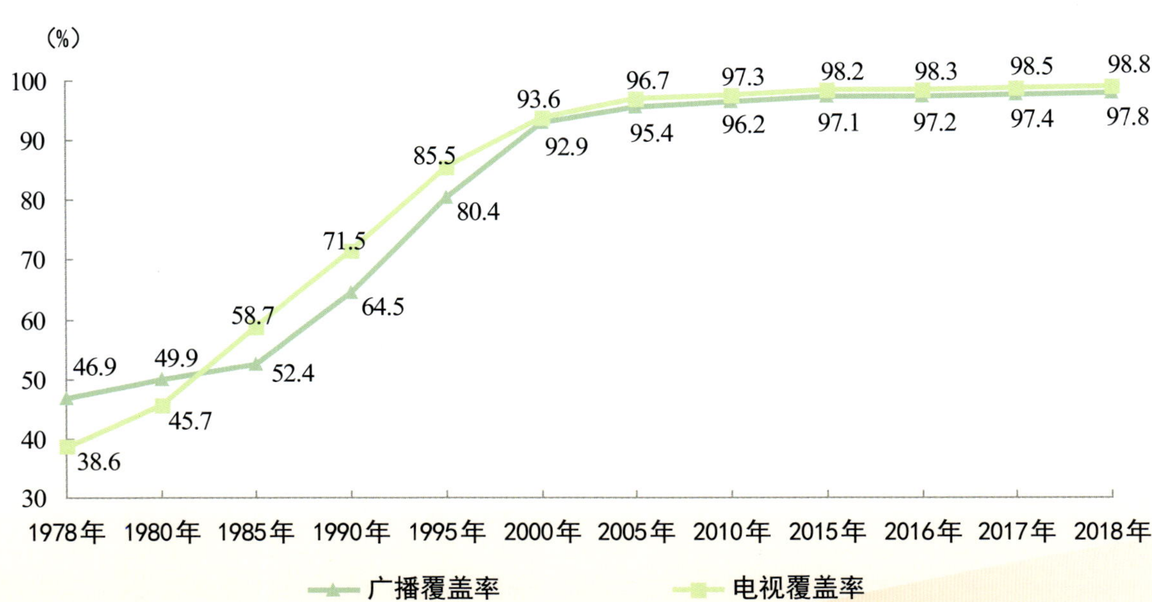

各类学校在校学生数

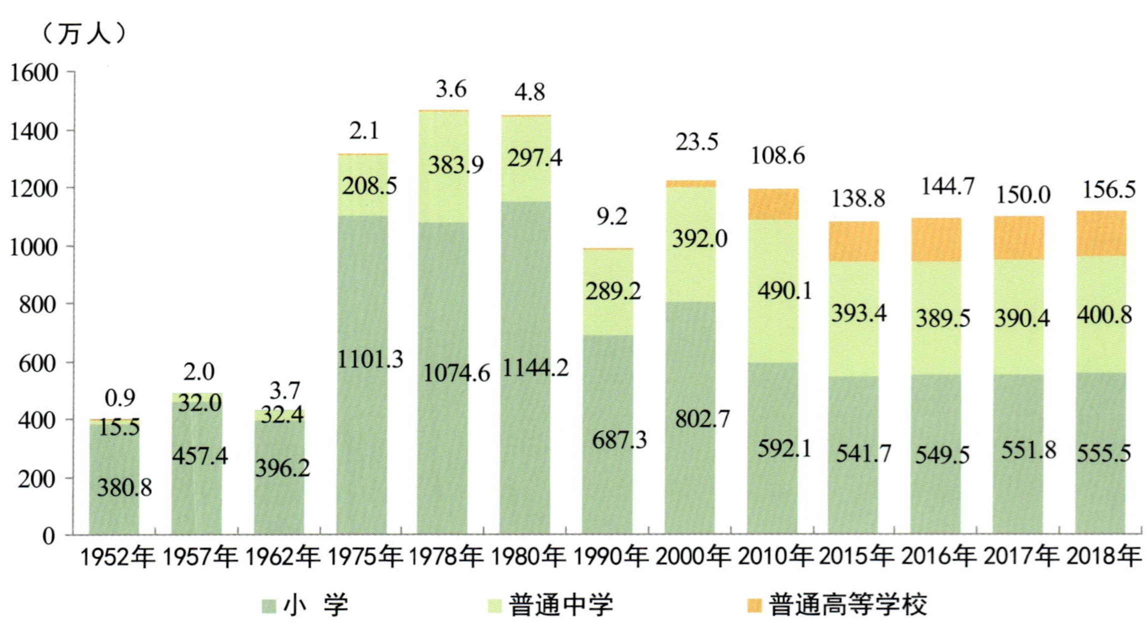

卫生机构床位数

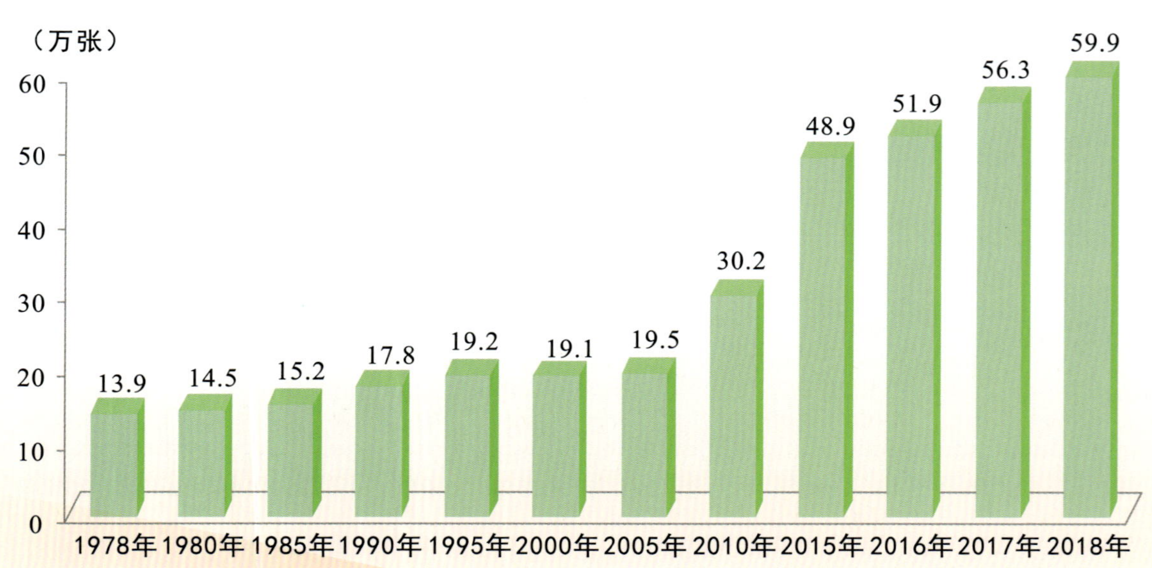

1 综　合

Chapter 1 General Survey

1-1 各市(州)行政区划及辖区面积(2018年底)
Administrative Divisions and Area by Region (End of 2018)

单位：个、平方公里 (unit, sq.km)

市(州)	Region	县(市、区) Counties,Cities at County Level and Districts under City Administration					乡、镇、街道办事处 Township,Towns and Street Communities					辖区面积 Administrative Area
		合计 Total	市辖区 Districts under City Administration	县级市 Cities at County Level	县 Coun-ties	自治县 Autono-mous Counties	合计 Total	乡 Town-ship	#民族乡 Ethnic Community Township	镇 Towns	街道办事处 Street Communities	
全　省	**Sichuan**	**183**	**54**	**17**	**108**	**4**	**4605**	**2023**	**98**	**2229**	**353**	**486052**
成都市	Chengdu	20	11	5	4		375	52		206	117	14335
自贡市	Zigong	6	4		2		108	18		78	12	4381
攀枝花市	Panzhihua	5	3		2		60	23	13	21	16	7401
泸州市	Luzhou	7	3		4		144	10	8	111	23	12236
德阳市	Deyang	6	2	3	1		129	20		99	10	5910
绵阳市	Mianyang	9	3	1	4	1	293	92	15	177	24	20248
广元市	Guangyuan	7	3		4		239	123	2	107	9	16311
遂宁市	Suining	5	2		3		124	34		71	19	5323
内江市	Neijiang	5	2	1	2		121	4		103	14	5385
乐山市	Leshan	11	4	1	4	2	218	109	2	102	7	12723
南充市	Nanchong	9	3	1	5		424	213	1	180	31	12477
眉山市	Meishan	6	2		4		131	41		85	5	7140
宜宾市	Yibin	10	3		7		185	49	13	123	13	13266
广安市	Guangan	6	2	1	3		182	79		91	12	6341
达州市	Dazhou	7	2	1	4		315	136	4	171	8	16582
雅安市	Yaan	8	2		6		143	89	18	48	6	15046
巴中市	Bazhong	5	2		3		200	71		116	13	12293
资阳市	Ziyang	3	1		2		120	47		69	4	5744
阿坝藏族羌族自治州	Aba	13		1	12		219	157	2	62		83016
甘孜藏族自治州	Ganzi	18		1	17		325	252	7	71	2	149599
凉山彝族自治州	Liangshan	17		1	15	1	550	404	13	138	8	60294

注：行政区划情况由四川省民政厅提供。
a) Data of administrative division are provided by Sichuan Provincial Civil Affairs Department.

1-2 各市(州)基层群众自治组织情况(2018年底)
Basic Statistics on Grass Roots Organizations by Region(End of 2018)

单位：个 (unit)

市(州)	Region	社区居委会 Community (Neighborhood Committee)	居民小组 Residents Unit	村民委员会 Villagers Committee	村民小组 Villagers Group
全　省	**Sichuan**	**7482**	**61903**	**45524**	**322880**
成都市	Chengdu	1647	21898	2678	32925
自贡市	Zigong	300	3470	1070	9134
攀枝花市	Panzhihua	132	1452	349	2230
泸州市	Luzhou	290	1983	1336	12970
德阳市	Deyang	367	3702	1417	16860
绵阳市	Mianyang	531	3848	3247	23661
广元市	Guangyuan	338	1508	2398	14540
遂宁市	Suining	317	1793	1894	12332
内江市	Neijiang	348	2823	1609	17448
乐山市	Leshan	265	1927	1983	14974
南充市	Nanchong	589	4130	5241	33684
眉山市	Meishan	309	1671	1055	5646
宜宾市	Yibin	351	2640	2816	20147
广安市	Guangan	285	1964	2721	22434
达州市	Dazhou	505	2170	2719	13770
雅安市	Yaan	81	539	1005	6755
巴中市	Bazhong	438	1846	2228	13143
资阳市	Ziyang	151	1283	1988	21471
阿坝藏族羌族自治州	Aba	58	139	1354	3613
甘孜藏族自治州	Ganzi	58	138	2679	5733
凉山彝族自治州	Liangshan	122	979	3737	19410

1-3 各市(州)行政区划一览表(2018年底)
Administrative Division Schedule by Region (End of 2018)

市(州) Region	县、市、区 Counties, Cities at County Level and Districts under City Administration
成都市	锦江区、青羊区、金牛区、武侯区、成华区、龙泉驿区、青白江区、新都区、温江区、双流区、郫都区、都江堰市、彭州市、邛崃市、崇州市、简阳市、金堂县、大邑县、蒲江县、新津县
Chengdu	Jinjiang, Qingyang, Jinniu, Wuhou, Chenghua, Longquanyi, Qingbaijiang, Xindu, Wenjiang, Shuangliu, Pidu, Dujiangyan, Pengzhou, Qionglai, Chongzhou, Jianyang, Jintang, Dayi, Pujiang, Xinjin
自贡市	自流井区、贡井区、大安区、沿滩区、荣县、富顺县
Zigong	Ziliujing, Gongjing, Daan, Yantan, Rongxian, Fushun
攀枝花市	东区、西区、仁和区、米易县、盐边县
Panzhihua	Dongqu, Xiqu, Renhe, Miyi, Yanbian
泸州市	江阳区、龙马潭区、纳溪区、泸县、合江县、叙永县、古蔺县
Luzhou	Jiangyang, Longmatan, Naxi, Luxian, Hejiang, Xuyong, Gulin
德阳市	旌阳区、罗江区、广汉市、什邡市、绵竹市、中江县
Deyang	Jinyang, Luojiang, Guanghan, Shifang, Mianzhu, Zhongjiang
绵阳市	涪城区、游仙区、安州区、江油市、梓潼县、平武县、北川羌族自治县、三台县、盐亭县
Mianyang	Fucheng, Youxian, Anzhou, Jiangyou, Zitong, Pingwu, Beichuan, Santai, Yanting
广元市	利州区、昭化区、朝天区、剑阁县、旺苍县、青川县、苍溪县
Guangyuan	Lizhou, zhaohua, Chaotian, Jiange, Wangcang, Qingchuan, Cangxi
遂宁市	船山区、安居区、蓬溪县、射洪县、大英县
Suining	Chuanshan, Anju, Pengxi, Shehong, Daying
内江市	市中区、东兴区、隆昌市、资中县、威远县
Neijiang	Downtown, Dongxing, Longchang, Zizhong, Weiyuan
乐山市	市中区、五通桥区、沙湾区、金口河区、峨眉山市、犍为县、井研县、夹江县、沐川县、峨边彝族自治县、马边彝族自治县
Leshan	Downtown, Wutongqiao, Shawan, Jinkouhe, Emeishan, Qianwei, Jingyan, Jiajiang, Muchuan, Ebian, Mabian
南充市	顺庆区、高坪区、嘉陵区、阆中市、南部县、西充县、营山县、仪陇县、蓬安县
Nanchong	Shunqing, Gaoping, Jialing, Langzhong, Nanbu, Xichong, Yingshan, Yilong, Pengan
眉山市	东坡区、彭山区、仁寿县、洪雅县、丹棱县、青神县
Meishan	Dongpo, Pengshan, Renshou, Hongya, Danling, Qingshen
宜宾市	翠屏区、南溪区、叙州区、江安县、长宁县、高县、筠连县、珙县、兴文县、屏山县
Yibin	Cuiping, Nanxi, Xuzhou, Jiangan, Changning, Gaoxian, Junlian, Gongxian, Xingwen, Pingshan
广安市	广安区、前锋区、华蓥市、岳池县、武胜县、邻水县
Guangan	Guanganqu, Qianfeng, Huaying, Yuechi, Wusheng, Linshui
达州市	通川区、达川区、万源市、宣汉县、开江县、大竹县、渠县
Dazhou	Tongchuan, Dachuan, Wanyuan, Xuanhan, Kaijiang, Dazhu, Quxian
雅安市	雨城区、名山区、荥经县、汉源县、石棉县、天全县、芦山县、宝兴县
Yaan	Yucheng, Mingshan, Yingjing, Hanyuan, Shimian, Tianquan, Lushan, Baoxing
巴中市	巴州区、恩阳区、平昌县、通江县、南江县
Bazhong	Bazhou, Enyang, Pingchang, Tongjiang, Nanjiang
资阳市	雁江区、安岳县、乐至县
Ziyang	Yanjiang, Anyue, Lezhi
阿坝藏族羌族自治州	马尔康市、汶川县、理县、茂县、松潘县、九寨沟县、金川县、小金县、黑水县、壤塘县、阿坝县、若尔盖县、红原县
Aba	Maerkang, Wenchuan, Lixian, Maoxian, Songpan, Jiuzhaigou, Jinchuan, Xiaojin, Heishui,Rangtang, Abaxian, Ruoergai, Hongyuan
甘孜藏族自治州	康定市、泸定县、丹巴县、九龙县、雅江县、道孚县、炉霍县、甘孜县、新龙县、德格县、白玉县、石渠县、色达县、理塘县、巴塘县、乡城县、稻城县、得荣县
Ganzi	Kangding, Luding, Danba, Jiulong, Yajiang, Daofu, Luhuo, Ganzixian, Xinlong, Dege, Baiyu, Shiqu, Seda, Litang, Batang, Xiangcheng, Daocheng, Derong
凉山彝族自治州	西昌市、木里藏族自治县、盐源县、德昌县、会理县、会东县、宁南县、普格县、布拖县、金阳县、昭觉县、喜德县、冕宁县、越西县、甘洛县、美姑县、雷波县
Liangshan	Xichang, Muli, Yanyuan, Dechang, Huili, Huidong, Ningnan, Puge, Butuo, Jinyang, Zhaojue, Xide,Mianning, Yuexi, Ganluo, Meigu, Leibo

1-4 四川经济社会发展70年总量与速度指标

指　　标		Item	
人口		**Population**	
年末户籍人口	(万人)	Total Registered Population (year-end)	(10 000 persons)
#男性	(万人)	Male	(10 000 persons)
女性	(万人)	Female	(10 000 persons)
#城镇	(万人)	Urban	(10 000 persons)
乡村	(万人)	Rural	(10 000 persons)
就业		**Employment**	
就业人员数	(万人)	Employment	(10 000 persons)
#第一产业	(万人)	Primary Industry	(10 000 persons)
第二产业	(万人)	Secondary Industry	(10 000 persons)
第三产业	(万人)	Tertiary Industry	(10 000 persons)
#非私营单位就业人员	(万人)	Staff and Workers of Non-private Units	(10 000 persons)
#国有经济单位职工	(万人)	State-owned Units	(10 000 persons)
城镇集体经济单位职工	(万人)	Urban Collective-owned Units	(10 000 persons)
国民经济核算		**National Accounting**	
地区生产总值	(亿元)	Gross Regional Product	(100 million yuan)
第一产业	(亿元)	Primary Industy	(100 million yuan)
第二产业	(亿元)	Secondary Industy	(100 million yuan)
第三产业	(亿元)	Tertiary Industy	(100 million yuan)
人均地区生产总值	(元)	Per Capita Gross Regional Product	(yuan)
支出法地区生产总值	(亿元)	Gross Regional Product by Expenditure Appı	(100 million yuan)
最终消费	(亿元)	Final Consumption Expenditure	(100 million yuan)
居民消费	(亿元)	Household Consumption Expenditure	(100 million yuan)
政府消费	(亿元)	Government Consumption Expenditure	(100 million yuan)
资本形成总额	(亿元)	Gross Capital Formation	(100 million yuan)
固定资本形成	(亿元)	Gross Fixed Capital Formation	(100 million yuan)
存货增加	(亿元)	Changes in Inventories	(100 million yuan)
人民生活		**People's Livelihood**	
居民人均消费水平	(元)	Per Capita Consumption of Residents	(yuan)
农村居民	(元)	Urban Residents	(yuan)
城镇居民	(元)	Rural Residents	(yuan)
城镇居民人均可支配收入	(元)	Per Capita Disposable Income of Urban Resi	(yuan)

Indicators of Principal Aggregate and Growth Rates on Sichuan Economy and Social Development in 70 years

总量指标 Aggregate Data					指数(%) Indices (2018年为以下各年) (2018 as Percentage of)				平均增长速度(%) Average Annual Growth Rate		
1952	1978	2000	2017	2018	1952	1978	2000	2017	1953~2018	1979~2018	2001~2018
4628.5	7071.9	8407.5	9113.4	9121.8	197.1	129.0	108.5	100.1	1.0	0.6	0.5
2357.9	3621.5	4358.9	4677.8	4678.3	198.4	129.2	107.3	100.0	1.0	0.6	0.4
2270.6	3450.4	4048.6	4435.6	4443.5	195.7	128.8	109.8	100.2	1.0	0.6	0.5
365.7	784.2	1565.0	3116.3	3271.5	894.7	417.2	209.0	105.0	3.4	3.6	4.2
4262.8	6287.7	6842.5	5997.1	5850.3	137.2	93.0	85.5	97.6	0.5	-0.2	-0.9
2027.92	3087.02	4658.40	4872.00	4881.00	240.7	158.1	104.8	100.2	1.3	1.2	0.3
1753.89	2524.21	2643.35	1792.90	1752.30	99.9	69.4	66.3	97.7	0.0	-0.9	-2.3
89.37	279.50	871.12	1315.40	1327.60	1485.5	475.0	152.4	100.9	4.2	4.0	2.4
184.66	283.31	1143.93	1763.70	1801.10	975.4	635.7	157.4	102.1	3.5	4.7	2.6
63.56	457.92	515.45	792.21	780.64	1228.2	170.5	151.4	98.5	3.9	1.3	2.3
61.82	364.80	371.68	343.29	327.60	529.9	89.8	88.1	95.4	2.6	-0.3	-0.7
1.74	93.12	69.73	23.20	20.20	1160.9	21.7	29.0	87.1	3.8	-3.7	-6.7
24.61	184.61	3928.20	36980.22	40678.13	18244.8	4838.2	676.7	108.0	8.2	10.2	11.2
14.56	82.20	945.58	4262.35	4426.66	1168.6	663.6	209.2	103.6	3.8	4.8	4.2
3.67	65.55	1433.11	14328.12	15322.72	125547.6	9909.0	1035.2	107.5	11.4	12.2	13.9
6.38	36.86	1549.51	18389.75	20928.75	45386.6	8681.4	663.8	109.0	9.7	11.8	11.1
53	261	4956	44651	48883	10289.2	4138.9	649.0	107.4	7.3	9.8	10.9
24.61	184.61	3928.20	36980.22	40678.13	18244.8	4838.2	676.7	108.0	8.2	10.2	11.2
22.80	136.56	2545.13	19365.69	21481.09	10199.2	3403.1	552.9	108.6	7.3	9.2	10.0
21.11	114.13	2021.66	14841.19	16566.20	8053.7	2981.7	519.6	109.1	6.9	8.9	9.6
1.69	22.43	523.47	4524.50	4914.89	37240.2	5244.4	668.9	106.9	9.4	10.4	11.1
1.75	47.49	1521.43	18021.18	19528.52	141208.3	9909.4	826.1	106.6	11.6	12.2	12.4
1.73	44.96	1400.69	17689.34	19212.29	140120.0	10373.9	878.7	106.8	11.6	12.3	12.8
0.02	2.53	120.74	331.84	316.23	270875.0	3416.0	191.6	94.5	12.7	9.2	3.7
46	161	2550	17920	19861		2738.8	525.1	110.8		8.6	9.7
37	135	1614	12856	14821		2392.8	607.1	115.3		8.3	10.5
147	373	5315	22983	24460		1461.9	315.2	106.4		6.9	6.6
	338	5894	30727	33216		9819.9	563.5	108.1		12.2	10.1

1-4 续表 1

指 标		Item	
城镇居民人均消费支出	(元)	Per Capita Living Expenditures for Consumption of Urban Residents	(yuan)
#食品烟酒	(元)	Food, Tobacco and Liquor	(yuan)
城镇居民恩格尔系数	(%)	Engel Coefficient of Urban Residents	(%)
农村居民人均可支配收入	(元)	Annual per Capita Disposible Income of Rural Residents	(yuan)
农村居民人均生活消费支出	(元)	Expenditure for Consumption of Rural Residents	(yuan)
#食品烟酒	(元)	Food, Tobacco and Liquor	(yuan)
农村居民恩格尔系数	(%)	Engel Coefficient of Rural Residents	(%)
全部单位就业人员工资总额	(亿元)	Total Wages of Staff and Workers in all Units	(100 million yuan)
#国有经济单位	(亿元)	State-owned Units	(100 million yuan)
城镇集体经济单位	(亿元)	Urban Collective-owned Units	(100 million yuan)
全部单位就业人员平均货币工资	(元)	Average Money Wages of Staff and Workers in all Units	(yuan)
#国有经济单位	(元)	State-owned Units	(yuan)
城镇集体经济单位	(元)	Urban Collective-owned Units	(yuan)
财政		**Government Finance**	
地方一般公共预算收入	(亿元)	Local General Public Budget Income	(100 million yuan)
一般公共预算支出	(亿元)	Local General Public Budget Expenditure	(100 million yuan)
能源		**Energy**	
一次能源生产量	(万吨标准煤)	Primary Energy Production	(10 thousand tons of standard coal)
能源消费总量	(万吨标准煤)	Total Energy Consumption	(10 thousand tons of standard coal)
房地产完成投资额	(亿元)	**Compeleted Investment Of Real Estate**	**(100 million yuan)**
农业		**Agriculture**	
农林牧渔业总产值	(亿元)	Gross Output Value of Farming, Forestry, Animal Husbandry and Fishery	(100 million yuan)
#农业	(亿元)	Farming	(100 million yuan)
牧业	(亿元)	Animal Husbandry	(100 million yuan)
粮食产量	(万吨)	Grain Yield	(10 000 tons)
油料产量	(万吨)	Oil Bearing Crops Yield	(10 000 tons)
肉猪出栏头数	(万头)	Number of Slaughtered Fatterned Hogs	(10 000 heads)
猪年末头数	(万头)	Number of Hogs (year-end)	(10 000 heads)
牛年末头数	(万头)	Number of Cattle(year-end)	(10 000 heads)
肉类总产量	(万吨)	Output of Meat	(10 000 tons)
#猪肉	(万吨)	Output of Pork	(10 000 tons)

注：2010年以前农村居民人均可支配收入为农村居民人均纯收入统计口径。

continued

总量指标 Aggregate Data					指数(%) Indices (2018年为以下各年) (2018 as Percentage of)				平均增长速度(%) Average Annual Growth Rate		
1952	1978	2000	2017	2018	1952	1978	2000	2017	1953~2018	1979~2018	2001~2018
	314	4856	21991	23484		7474.2	483.6	106.8		11.4	9.2
	186	2014	7329	7462		4013.3	370.5	101.8		9.7	7.5
	59.2	41.5	33.3	31.8		-27.4个百分点	-9.7个百分点	-1.5个百分点		-0.7个百分点	-0.5个百分点
	127	1904	12227	13331		10488.9	700.3	109.0		12.3	11.4
	120	1490	11397	12723		10576.2	854.2	111.6		12.4	12.7
	89	813	4235	4483		5065.2	551.2	105.8		10.3	9.9
	73.6	54.6	37.2	35.2		-38.4个百分点	-19.4个百分点	-2.0个百分点		-1.0个百分点	-1.1个百分点
	26.32	436.95	7186.52	7979.50		30317.7	1826.2	111.0		15.4	17.5
	21.95	338.72	2722.32	2926.94		13335.7	864.1	107.5		13.0	12.7
	4.37	40.52	122.37	119.92		2743.1	296.0	98.0		8.6	6.2
319	590	8323	58671	64717	20287.5	10969.0	777.6	110.3	8.4	12.5	12.1
325	622	8909	80321	90390	27812.3	14532.2	1014.6	112.5	8.9	13.3	13.7
289	475	5749	55115	59146	20465.7	12451.8	1028.8	107.3	8.4	12.8	13.8
	37.31	233.86	3579.78	3911.01		10482.5	1672.4	109.3		12.3	16.9
	35.72	452.00	8686.10	9707.50		27176.7	2147.7	111.8		15.0	18.6
	2552	6279	19294	19172		751.3	305.3	99.4		5.2	6.4
	2552	6518	19229	19916		780.5	305.6	103.6		5.3	6.4
		195.97	5149.89	5701.09			2909.2	110.7			20.6
21.70	95.71	1483.52	6955.55	7195.65	1402.5	680.8	220.5	103.9	4.1	4.9	4.5
18.50	73.91	785.37	4004.20	4153.71	713.7	382.1	188.2	104.6	3.0	3.4	3.6
2.80	18.23	611.76	2199.72	2246.08	4955.7	1615.8	231.1	102.4	6.1	7.2	4.8
1170.10	2381.80	3568.50	3488.90	3493.70	298.6	146.7	97.9	100.1	1.7	1.0	-0.1
25.20	52.80	193.00	357.89	362.54	1438.6	686.6	187.8	101.3	4.1	4.9	3.6
393.00	1614.00	6594.37	6579.10	6638.34	1689.1	411.3	100.7	100.9	4.4	3.6	0.0
943.00	3243.00	5229.23	4376.64	4258.47	451.6	131.3	81.4	97.3	2.3	0.7	-1.1
474.00	745.00	1046.66	853.19	824.30	173.9	110.6	78.8	96.6	0.8	0.3	-1.3
17.10	78.00	641.25	653.82	664.74	3887.4	852.2	103.7	101.7	5.7	5.5	0.2
15.60	76.00	478.59	472.23	481.20	3084.6	633.2	100.5	101.9	5.3	4.7	0.0

1)The indicator of Annual Per Capita Disposible Income of Rural Residents is the Statistical Caliber of Per Capita Net Income of Rural Residents before 2010.

1-4 续表 2

指 标		Item	
农作物总播种面积	(万公顷)	Total Sown Areas	(10 000 hectares)
#粮食	(万公顷)	Sown Areas of Grain Crops	(10 000 hectares)
农村用电量	(亿千瓦时)	Electricity Consumed in Rural Areas	(100 million kwh)
化肥施用量	(万吨)	Consumption of Chemical Fertilizers	(10 000 tons)
#氮肥	(万吨)	Nitrogen	(10 000 tons)
造林面积	(万公顷)	Afforested Hilly Area	(10 000 hectares)
规模以上工业企业		**Industrial Enterprises above Designated Size**	
主要财务指标		Principal Financial Indicators	
资产总计	(亿元)	Total Assets	(100 million yuan)
负债合计	(亿元)	Total Liability	(100 million yuan)
所有者权益合计	(亿元)	Owners' Equities	(100 million yuan)
营业收入	(亿元)	Business Revenue	(100 million yuan)
营业成本	(亿元)	Business Cost	(100 million yuan)
利润总额	(亿元)	Total Profits	(100 million yuan)
全部从业人员年平均人数	(万人)	Annual Average Employed Persons	(10 000 persons)
主要产品产量		Output of Major Products	
布	(亿米)	Cloth	(100 million m)
机制纸及纸板	(万吨)	Machine-made Paper and Paperboards	(10 000 tons)
原盐	(万吨)	Salt	(10 000 tons)
卷烟	(亿支)	Cigarettes	(100 million pieces)
白酒(商品量)	(万千升)	Liquor	(10 000 kiloliter)
天然气	(亿立方米)	Natural Gas	(100 million cu.m)
发电量	(亿千瓦小时)	Electricity	(100 million kwh)
#水电	(亿千瓦小时)	Hydropower	(100 million kwh)
生铁	(万吨)	Pig Iron	(10 000 tons)
粗钢	(万吨)	Crude Steel	(10 000 tons)
成品钢材	(万吨)	Steel Products	(10 000 tons)
水泥	(万吨)	Cement	(10 000 tons)
农用氮、磷、钾化肥(折纯)	(万吨)	Chemical Fertilizer	(10 000 tons)

注：①2017年及以前营业收入、营业成本分别为主营业务收入、主营业务成本；②2000年及以前卷烟产量的计量单位为万箱。

continued

总量指标 Aggregate Data					指数(%) Indices (2018年为以下各年) (2018 as Percentage of)				平均增长速度(%) Average Annual Growth Rate		
1952	1978	2000	2017	2018	1952	1978	2000	2017	1953~ 2018	1979~ 2018	2001~ 2018
827.66	885.91	960.91	957.51	961.54	116.2	108.5	100.1	100.4	0.2	0.2	0.0
686.30	744.10	685.40	629.20	626.56	91.3	84.2	91.4	99.6	-0.1	-0.4	-0.5
	7.70	82.80	188.44	198.62		2579.5	239.9	105.4		8.5	5.0
0.40	62.50	212.60	241.95	235.21	58801.6	376.3	110.6	97.2	10.1	3.4	0.6
0.40	46.40	123.00	117.04	112.15	28037.1	241.7	91.2	95.8	8.9	2.2	-0.5
2.13	20.05	48.91	65.84	43.68	2050.7	217.9	89.3	66.3	4.7	2.0	-0.6
		4586.11	43253.61	46015.75			1003.4	106.4			13.7
		2955.77	25120.16	26150.93			884.7	104.1			12.9
		1630.26	18033.84	19864.82			1218.5	110.2			14.9
		2073.17	41631.26	41833.78			2017.9	100.5			18.2
		1613.98	34660.03	34465.16			2135.4	99.4			18.5
		71.32	2824.26	3055.93			4284.8	108.2			23.2
		208.00	318.97	299.18			143.8	93.8			2.0
1.56	5.18	6.03	16.40	15.60	1000.0	301.2	258.7	95.1	3.55	2.79	5.4
1.61	26.40	71.52	237.10	261.50	16242.2	990.5	365.6	110.3	8.02	5.90	7.5
42.58	127.66	215.48	581.70	494.50	1161.3	387.4	229.5	85.0	3.79	3.44	4.7
2.40	50.37	128.65	734.10	755.20	31466.7	1499.3	587.0	102.9	9.11	7.00	10.3
		63.68	372.40	358.30			562.7	96.2			10.1
0.06	60.79	88.60	356.39	369.82	616366.7	608.4	417.4	103.8	14.14	4.62	8.3
2.49	139.30	500.24	3339.96	3499.39	140537.8	2512.1	699.5	104.8	11.61	8.39	11.4
0.28	54.78	315.11	2909.89	2983.03	1065367.9	5445.5	946.7	102.5	15.09	10.51	13.3
9.17	223.98	555.61	1899.70	1978.60	21576.9	883.4	356.1	104.2	8.48	5.60	7.3
4.98	238.17	602.35	2026.30	2400.70	48206.8	1008.0	398.6	118.5	9.81	5.95	8.0
11.23	174.02	541.34	2491.20	2896.70	25794.3	1664.6	535.1	116.3	8.78	7.28	9.8
4.40	454.83	766.42	13810.00	13748.70	312470.5	3022.8	1793.9	99.6	12.97	8.90	17.4
	102.50	263.51	414.90	369.50		360.5	140.2	89.1		3.26	1.9

1) The data of business revenue and business cost are revenue from principal business and cost of principal business respectively in 2017 and before;
2)The unit of measurement of cigarette output is 10,000 boxes in 2000 and before.

1-4 续表 3

指 标		Item	
贸易		**Domestic Trade**	
社会消费品零售总额	(亿元)	Total Retail Sales of Consumer Goods	(100 million yuan)
进出口总额	(万美元)	Total Import and Export	(USD 10 000)
出口总额	(万美元)	Total Export	(USD 10 000)
进口总额	(万美元)	Total Import	(USD 10 000)
实际利用外商直接投资	(万美元)	Actual Utilization of Foreign Direct Investment	(USD 10 000)
旅游		**Tourism**	
入境游客	(万人次)	Inbound Tourists	(10 thousand people)
国际旅游(外汇)收入	(亿美元)	International Tourism (Foreign Exchange) Revenue	(USD 100 million)
国内游客	(万人次)	Domestic Tourists	(10 thousand people)
国内旅游收入	(亿元)	Domestic Tourism Revenue	(100 million yuan)
交通运输		**Transportation**	
铁路营业里程	(公里)	Railways in Operation	(km)
公路里程	(公里)	Highways	(km)
#高速公路	(公里)	Expressway	(km)
民用汽车拥有量	(万辆)	Possession of Civil Motor Vehicles	(10 000 units)
旅客周转量	(亿人公里)	Total Passenger-Kilometers	(100 million passenger-km)
货物周转量	(亿吨公里)	Total Freight Ton-kilometers	(100 million ton-km)
文化、教育和卫生		**Culture,Education and Health**	
图书出版总印数	(万册)	Total Printed Copies of Published Books	(10 000 copies)
杂志出版总印数	(万册)	Total Printed Copies of Published Magazines	(10 000 copies)
报纸出版总印数	(万份)	Total Printed Copies of Published Newspapers	(10 000 copies)
专任教师数		Full-time Teachers	
普通高等学校	(万人)	Regular Institutions of Higher Education	(10 000 persons)
普通中学	(万人)	Regular Secondary Schools	(10 000 persons)
小学	(万人)	Primary Schools	(10 000 persons)
在校学生数		Number of Students Enrollment	
普通高等学校	(万人)	Regular Institutions of Higher Education	(10 000 persons)
普通中学	(万人)	Regular Secondary Schools	(10 000 persons)
小学	(万人)	Primary Schools	(10 000 persons)
医院数	(个)	Number of Hospitals	(unit)
医院床位数	(万张)	Number of Beds in Hospitals	(10 000 units)

continued

总量指标 Aggregate Data					指数(%) Indices (2018年为以下各年) (2018 as Percentage of)				平均增长速度(%) Average Annual Growth Rate		
1952	1978	2000	2017	2018	1952	1978	2000	2017	1953~2018	1979~2018	2001~2018
14.00	61.60	1671.43	17480.53	18254.54	130389.6	29634.0	1092.2	104.4	11.5	15.3	14.2
	4067	254517	6810677	8993788		221140.6	3533.7	132.1		21.2	21.9
	1905	139435	3755394	5039827		264557.8	3614.5	134.2		21.8	22.1
	2162	115082	3055283	3953961		182884.4	3435.8	129.4		20.7	21.7
		43694	810135	896375			2051.5	110.6			18.3
	0.25	46.20	336.17	369.82		147929.3	800.5	110.0		20.0	12.2
		1.22	14.47	15.12			1240.4	104.5			15.0
		5401	66924	70198			1299.7	104.9			15.3
		248.00	8825.39	10012.72			4037.4	113.5			22.8
124	2813	2333	4832	4950	3991.9	176.0	212.2	102.4	5.7	1.4	4.3
9259	82391	90875	329950	331592	3581.3	402.5	364.9	100.5	5.6	3.5	7.5
		1000	6821	7131			713.1	104.5			11.5
		76.5	991.8	1099.6			1437.4	110.9			16.0
	87	633	1698	1802		2079.1	284.5	106.2		7.9	6.0
	216	666	2583	2820		1306.8	423.2	109.1		6.6	8.3
1481	24993	27315	29195	32520	2195.8	130.1	119.1	111.4	4.8	0.7	1.0
565	562	4950	5128	4997	884.4	889.1	100.9	97.4	3.4	5.6	0.1
6799	51889	133590	141828	133057	1957.0	256.4	99.6	93.8	4.6	2.4	0.0
0.12	0.90	1.84	8.39	8.70	7084.4	961.6	472.3	103.6	6.7	5.8	9.0
0.60	16.75	21.70	29.88	30.46	5116.5	181.8	140.3	101.9	6.1	1.5	1.9
11.12	34.27	33.16	32.50	32.99	296.6	96.3	99.5	101.5	1.7	-0.1	0.0
0.91	3.57	23.55	149.97	156.47	17187.1	4381.1	664.5	104.3	8.1	9.9	11.1
15.53	383.88	391.98	390.43	400.76	2581.4	104.4	102.2	102.6	5.0	0.1	0.1
380.78	1074.59	802.65	551.84	555.46	145.9	51.7	69.2	100.7	0.6	-1.6	-2.0
	603	1128	2219	2343		388.6	207.7	105.6		3.5	4.1
	6.22	11.11	41.19	44.22		711.1	398.1	107.4		5.0	8.0

1-5 四川经济社会发展70年比例和效益指标

Indicators of Proportions and Efficiency on Sichuan Economy and Social Development in 70 years

指　　标		Item		1952	1978	2000	2017	2018
人口与就业		**Population and Employment**						
出生率	(‰)	Birth Rate	(‰)	41.0	15.1	12.1	11.3	11.1
死亡率	(‰)	Death Rate	(‰)	18.2	7.0	7.0	7.0	7.0
自然增长率	(‰)	Natural Growth Rate	(‰)	22.8	8.1	5.1	4.2	4.0
城镇登记失业率	(%)	Unemployment Rate in Urban Areas	(%)		10.9	4.0	4.0	3.5
国民经济核算		**National Accounting**						
人均地区生产总值	(元)	Per Capita GDP	(yuan)	53	261	4956	44651	48883
人民生活		**People's Living Conditions**						
城乡收入比(农村居民收入为1)		Urban and Rural Income Ratio(Rural Income as 1)			2.66	3.10	2.51	2.49
财政		**Government Finance**						
地方一般公共预算收入与地区生产总值之比	(%)	Local General Public Budget Income to GDP	(%)		20.2	6.0	9.7	9.6
一般公共预算支出与地区生产总值之比	(%)	Local general public budget expenditure to GDP	(%)		19.3	11.5	23.5	23.9
农业		**Agriculture**						
每公顷播种面积农产品产量		Output of Farm Crops per Hectare of Sown Area	(kg)					
粮食	(公斤)	Grain	(kg)	1705	3201	5206	5545	5576
油料	(公斤)	Oilseeds	(kg)	735	1278	1881	2420	2431
国内贸易		**Domestic Trade**						
人均社会消费品零售总额	(元)	Per Capita Retail Sales of Consumer Goods	(yuan)	30	87	2109	21107	21937
金融		**Financial Intermediation**						
金融机构存款与地区生产总值之比	(%)	Bank Deposits as Percentage of GDP	(%)		34.2	114.9	193.6	187.1
金融机构贷款与地区生产总值之比	(%)	Bank Loans as Percentage of GDP	(%)		39.8	103.2	130.1	133.0
教育		**Education**						
每万人口在校大学生数	(人)	Number of College Students per 10000 Population	(person)	2.0	5.1	29.7	181.1	188.0
文化		**Culture**						
每百万人有公共图书馆	(个)	Number of Public Libraries per Million Persons	(unit)	0.1	0.8	1.6	2.5	2.5
每百万人有文化馆、文化站	(个)	Number of Cultural Centers and Stations per Million Persons	(unit)	6.3	2.6	48.4	57.8	57.5
人均年出版报纸	(份)	Annual Number of Newspaper Published per Capita	(copy)	1.5	7.3	16.9	17.1	16.0
人均年出版图书、杂志	(册)	Annual Number of Books and Magazines Published per Capita	(copy)	0.4	3.6	4.1	4.1	4.5
卫生		**Public Health**						
每万人口医院数	(个)	Number of Hospitals per 10000 Population	(unit)		0.09	0.14	0.27	0.28
每万人口医院床位数	(张)	Number of Beds of Hospitals per 10000 Population	(bed)		8.79	14.01	49.74	53.14

注：人均指标均按年平均常住人口计算。

a) The per capita data is calculated by average permanent resident population.

1-6 四川经济社会发展70年结构指标
Structural Indicators on Sichuan Economy and Social Development in 70 years

单位：% (%)

指 标	Item	1952	1978	2000	2017	2018
户籍人口结构	**Structure of Resident Population**					
城镇人口	Urban Population	7.9	11.1	18.6	34.2	35.9
乡村人口	Rural Population	92.1	88.9	81.4	65.8	64.1
就业人员结构	**Employment Structure**					
第一产业	Primary Industy	86.5	81.8	56.7	36.8	35.9
第二产业	Secondary Industy	4.4	9.1	18.7	27.0	27.2
第三产业	Tertiary Industy	9.1	9.2	24.6	36.2	36.9
地区生产总值结构	**GDP Structure**					
第一产业	Primary Industry	59.2	44.5	24.1	11.6	10.9
第二产业	Secondary Industry	14.9	35.5	36.5	38.7	37.7
第三产业	Tertiary Industry	25.9	20.0	39.4	49.7	51.4
进出口总额构成	**Composition of Total Import and Export**					
出口	Export		46.8	54.8	55.1	56.0
进口	Import		53.2	45.2	44.9	44.0
农林牧渔业总产值构成	**Composition of Gross Output Value of Farming, Forestry, Animal Husbandry and Fishery**					
#农业	Farming	85.3	77.2	52.9	57.6	57.7
林业	Forestry	2.3	3.3	3.3	5.0	5.0
牧业	Animal Husbandry	12.9	19.0	41.2	31.6	31.2
渔业	Fishery		0.4	2.5	3.4	3.4
旅客周转量构成	**Composition of Passenger-Kilometers**					
铁路	Railways		56.5	21.3	18.7	21.1
公路	Highways		39.2	64.3	30.7	25.9
水运	Waterways		1.0	0.5	0.1	0.1
民用航空	Civil Aviation		2.8	13.9	50.4	53.0
货物周转量构成	**Composition of Freight Ton-kilometers**					
铁路	Railways		84.8	63.5	24.7	25.6
公路	Highways		10.7	34.4	64.9	64.4
水运	Waterways		4.5	1.8	9.9	9.6
民用航空	Civil Aviation		0.0	0.3	0.5	0.5

主要统计指标解释

行政区划 指国家对行政区域的划分。根据有关法规规定，我国的行政区域划分如下：(1)全国分为省、自治区、直辖市；(2)省、自治区分为自治州、县、自治县、市；(3)自治州分为县、自治县、市；(4)县、自治县分为乡、民族乡、镇；(5)直辖市和较大的市分为区、县；(6)国家在必要时设立的特别行政区。

平均增长速度 平均增长速度表明社会经济现象在一个较长的时期内逐期平均增长变化的程度，它不能根据各个环比增长速度直接求得，但与平均发展速度之间存在着一定的数量关系：平均增长速度=平均发展速度-1。

平均发展速度是一种根据环比发展速度计算的序时平均数，由于各时期对比的基础不同，所以计算平均发展速度不能采用一般的序时平均数的计算方法，计算方法分为水平法和累计法。水平法，又称几何平均法，即将环比发展速度按连乘法用几何平均数公式计算。累计法，也称方程法，根据一段时期内各年发展水平总和与基期水平的关系，列出方程式计算平均发展速度。水平法着重考虑最后一年所达到的发展水平；累计法着重考虑整个时期累计发展水平的总量。

本《年鉴》内所列的增长速度，均用“水平法”计算。从某年到某年平均增长速度的年份，均不包括基期年在内。如2005年以来的平均增长速度是以2005年为基期计算的，则写为2006-2016年平均增长速度，其余类推。

国民经济行业分类 自2012年定期报表开始使用新的《国民经济行业分类》(GB/T4754-2011)。该分类是由国家统计局组织修订，国家质量监督检验检疫总局和中国国家标准化管理委员会于2011年4月29日发布。这次修订是在2002年分类标准的基础上，参照联合国《全部经济活动的国际标准产业分类》(ISIC/Rev.4)进行的。修订后的《国民经济行业分类》(GB/T4754-2012)共有门类20个，大类96个，中类432个，小类1094个。

企业(单位)登记注册类型 是以在工商行政管理机关登记注册的各类企业为划分对象，以工商行政管理部门对企业登记注册的类型为依据，将企业登记注册类型分为内资企业、港澳台商投资企业和外商投资企业三大类。内资企业包括国有企业、集体企业、股份合作企业、联营企业、有限责任公司、股份有限公司、私营企业和其他企业；港澳台商投资企业和外商投资企业分别包括合资经营企业、合作经营企业、独资经营企业和股份有限公司等。对不在工商行政管理部门进行登记注册的行政机关、事业单位和社会团体，主要按其经费来源和管理方式进行划分。

国有企业 指企业全部资产归国家所有，并按《中华人民共和国企业法人登记管理条例》规定登记注册的非公司制的经济组织。不包括有限责任公司中的国有独资公司。

集体企业 指企业资产归集体所有，并按《中华人民共和国企业法人登记管理条例》规定登记注册的经济组织。

股份合作企业 指以合作制为基础，由企业职工共同出资入股，吸收一定比例的社会资产投资组建，实行自主经营，自负盈亏，共同劳动，民主管理，按劳分配与按股分红相结合的一种集体经济组织。

联营企业 指两个及两个以上相同或不同所有制性质的企业法人或事业单位法人，按自愿、平等、互利的原则，共同投资组成的经济组织。联营企业包括国有联营企业、集体联营企业、国有与集体联营企业和其他联营企业。

有限责任公司 指根据《中华人民共和国公司登记管理条例》规定登记注册，由两个以上、五十个以下的股东共同出资，每个股东以其所认缴的出资额对公司承担有限责任，公司以其全部资产对其债务承担责任的经济组织。有限责任公司包括国有独资公司以及其他有限责任公司。

股份有限公司 指根据《中华人民共和国公司登记管理条例》规定登记注册，其全部注册资本由等额股份构成并通过发行股票筹集资本，股东以其认购的股份对公司承担有限责任，公司以其全部资产对其债务承担责任的经济组织。

私营企业 指由自然人投资设立或由自然人控股，以雇佣劳动为基础的营利性经济组织。包括按照《公司法》、《合伙企业法》、《私营企业暂行条例》规定登记注册的私营有限责任公司、私营股份有限公司、私营合伙企业和私营独资企业。

其他企业 指上述企业之外的其他内资经济组织。

合资经营企业(港或澳、台资) 指港澳台地区投资者与内地企业依照《中华人民共和国中外合资经营企业法》及有关法律的规定，按合同规定的比例投资设立、分享利润和分担风险的企业。

合作经营企业(港或澳、台资) 指港澳台地区投资者与内地企业依照《中华人民共和国中外合作经营企业法》及有关法律的规定，依照合作合同的约定进行投资或提供条件设立、分配利润和分担风险的企业。

港澳台商独资经营企业 指依照《中华人民共和国外资企业法》及有关法律的规定，在内地由港澳台地区投资者全额投资设立的企业。

港澳台商投资股份有限公司 指根据国家有关规定，经原外经贸部依法批准设立，其中港、澳、台商的股本占公司注册资本的比例达25%以上的股份有限公司。凡其中港、澳、台商的股本占公司注册资本的比例小于25%的，属于内资企业中的股份有限公司。

其他港澳台商投资企业 指在中国境内参照《外国企业或个人在中国境内设立合伙企业管理办法》和《外商投资合

伙企业登记管理规定》，依法设立的港、澳、台商投资合伙企业等。

中外合资经营企业 指外国企业或外国人与中国内地企业依照《中华人民共和国中外合资经营企业法》及有关法律的规定，按合同规定的比例投资设立、分享利润和分担风险的企业。

中外合作经营企业 指外国企业或外国人与中国内地企业依照《中华人民共和国中外合作经营企业法》及有关法律的规定，依照合作合同的约定进行投资或提供条件设立、分配利润和分担风险的企业。

外资企业 指依照《中华人民共和国外资企业法》及有关法律的规定，在中国内地由外国投资者全额投资设立的企业。

外商投资股份有限公司 指根据国家有关规定，经原外经贸部依法批准设立，其中外资的股本占公司注册资本的比例达 25%以上的股份有限公司。凡其中外资股本占公司注册资本的比例小于 25%的，属于内资企业中的股份有限公司。

其他外商投资企业 指在中国境内依照《外国企业或个人在中国境内设立合伙企业管理办法》和《外商投资合伙企业登记管理规定》，依法设立的外商投资合伙企业等。

行政机关、事业单位和社会团体 参照企业登记注册类型，主要按其经费来源和管理方式划分。具体规定如下：

⑴行政机关：包括国家机关和政党机关，原则上均列为“国有”。但有特殊规定的，如供销社等，则列为“集体”。

⑵事业单位：包括经国家机构编制部门和有关业务主管部门批准成立的各类事业单位，不包括实行企业化管理的事业单位。事业单位的划分办法如下：

①由国家财政预算拨款或列入财政预算外资金管理以及经费主要来源于国有主管部门或国有上级单位的事业单位，列为“国有”。

②经费主要来源于集体单位的事业单位，列为“集体”。

③公民个人(或个人合伙)开办的事业单位，列为“私营”。

④上述以外的其他事业单位，如果其经费来源不明确，按管理方式进行归类。

⑶社会团体：包括经民政部门批准成立以及未纳入社会团体管理条例范围的工会、妇联等各类社会团体。社会团体的划分办法如下：

①未纳入民政部社会团体管理条例范围的工会、妇联、共青团、青联、工商联、科协、侨联等社会团体，国家拨款设立的基金会或基金管理组织以及经费主要来源于国有业务主管部门或国有上级单位的社会团体，列为“国有”。

②经费主要来源于集体单位的社会团体，列为“集体”。

③公民个人(或个人合伙)开办的社会团体，划为“私营”。

④上述以外的其他社会团体，如果其经费来源不明确，改按管理方式进行归类。

Explanatory Notes on Main Statistical Indicators

Divisions of Administrative Areas refers to the division of administrative areas by the State. The relative laws stipulate that 1) the whole country is divided into provinces, autonomous regions and municipalities directly under the Central Government; 2) provinces and autonomous regions are further divided into autonomous prefectures, counties, autonomous counties and cities; 3) autonomous prefectures are further divided into counties, autonomous counties and cities; 4) counties and autonomous counties are further divided into townships, ethnic townships and towns; 5) municipalities directly under the Central Government and large cities are divided into districts and counties, 6) the State shall, when necessary, establish special administrative regions.

Average Annual Growth Rate shows the average growth rate of social and economic development during a longer period. It can not be directly calculated by chain based growth rate. The relation is:

Average Annual Growth Rate = Average Speed of Development – 1

Average speed of development is the time series average of speed which calculated by chain based. Because the reference bases during the different periods are not same, average speed of development can not be calculated by the general method. Level approach and accumulative approach for calculating average speed of development rate are applied. The "level approach", or the method of calculating the geometric average, is derived by the formula of geometric average of the chain-based speeds of development, or comparing the level of the last year of the interval with that of the beginning year; the other is called the "accumulative approach" or the "algebraic average", "equation" method, which is derived by the summation of the actual figure of each year in the interval divided by the figure in the base year. The level approach focuses on the level of the last year, while the accumulative approach emphasizes the aggregate development in the duration.

The average annual growth rates listed in the Yearbook are calculated by the level approach. The base year is not listed in the duration for which average annual growth rates are computed. For instance, the average annual growth rate of the years since 2005 is shown as the average annual growth rate of 2006-2016 without showing the base year 2005.

Industrial Classification of the National Economy The new Industrial Classification of the National Economy (GB/T 4754-2011) is introduced starting from the compilation of 2012 annual statistics. The revision, based on the 2002 classification, was organized by the National Bureau of Statistics taking into consideration of the International Standards of the Industrial Classification of All Economic Activities (ISIC/Rev.4) of the United Nation. The new Classification was promulgated by the National Administration of Quality Supervision, Inspection and Quarantine and the Standardization Administration of the People's Republic of China on April 29, 2011. The revised version of the Industrial Classification of the National Economy (GB/T 4754-2012) is composed of 20 sections, 96 divisions, 432 groups and 1094 classes.

Registration Status of Enterprises Enterprises are classified into 3 categories, namely domestic-funded enterprises, enterprises with investment from Hong Kong, Macau and Taiwan, and enterprises with foreign investment, according to the registration status of an enterprise in industrial and commercial administration agencies. Domestic-funded enterprises include State-owned enterprises, collective-owned enterprises, cooperative enterprises, joint ownership enterprises, limited liability corporations, share-holding corporations Ltd., private enterprises and other enterprises. Included in the enterprises with investment from Hong Kong, Macau and Taiwan and enterprises with foreign investment are joint-venture enterprises, cooperative enterprises, sole investment enterprises and share-holding corporations Ltd, etc. For government agencies, institutions and social organizations which are not registered in industrial and commercial administration agencies, they are classified mainly by their sources of funding and manner of management.

State-owned Enterprises refers to non-corporation economic units where the entire assets are owned by the State and which have been registered in accordance with the Regulation of the People's Republic of China on the Management of Registration of Corporate Enterprises. Not included from this category are solely State-funded corporations in the limited liability corporations.

Collective-owned Enterprises refers to economic units where the assets are owned collectively and which have been registered in accordance with the Regulation of the People's Republic of China on the Management of Registration of Corporate Enterprises.

Cooperative Enterprises refers to a form of collective economic units (enterprises) where capitals come mainly from employees as their shares, with certain proportion of capital from the outside, where production is organized on the basis of independent operation, independent accounting for profits and losses, joint work, democratic management, and a distribution system that integrates remuneration according to work with dividend according to capital share.

Joint Ownership Enterprises refers to economic units established by two or more corporate enterprises or corporate institutions of the same or different ownership, through joint investment on the basis of voluntary participation, equality, and mutual benefits. They include State joint ownership enterprises; collective joint ownership enterprises; joint State-collective enterprises; and other joint ownership enterprises.

Limited Liability Corporations refers to economic units established with investment from 2-50 investors and registered in accordance with the Regulation of the People's Republic of China on the Management of Registration of Corporations, each investor bearing limited liability to the corporation depending on its share of investment, and the corporation bearing liability to its debt to the maximum of its total assets. Limited liability corporations include solely State-funded limited liability corporations and other limited liability corporations.

Share-holding Corporations Ltd. refers to economic units registered in accordance with the Regulation of the People's Republic of China on the Management of Registration of Corporations, with total registered capital divided into equal shares and raised through issuing stocks. Each investor bears limited liability to the corporation depending on the holding of shares, and the corporation bears liability to its debt to the maximum of its total assets.

Private Enterprises refers to profit-making economic units invested and established by natural persons, or controlled by natural persons using employed labour. Included in this category are private limited liability corporations, private share-holding corporations Ltd., private partnership enterprises and private-funded enterprises registered in accordance with the Company Law, the Law on Partnership Business and Interim Regulations on Private Enterprises .

Other Domestic-funded Enterprises refers to domestic-funded economic units other than those mentioned above.

Joint Venture Enterprises (Funds are from Hong Kong, Macau and Taiwan.) are enterprises established by investors from Hong Kong, Macau and Taiwan with enterprises in the mainland of China in accordance with the Law of the People's Republic of China on Sino-foreign Equity Joint Ventures and other relevant laws, where the establishment of the investment and the sharing of profits and risks are stipulated under joint venture contracts.

Cooperative Enterprises (Funds are from Hong Kong, Macau and Taiwan.) refers to enterprises established by investors from Hong Kong, Macau and Taiwan with enterprises in the mainland of China in accordance with the Law of the People's Republic of China on Sino-foreign Contractual Joint Venture and other relevant laws, where the investment or provision of facilities and the sharing of profits and risks are stipulated under cooperative contracts.

Enterprises with Sole (exclusive) Investment from Hong Kong, Macau and Taiwan refers to enterprises established in the mainland of China with exclusive investment from investors from Hong Kong, Macau and Taiwan in accordance with the Law of the People's Republic of China on Wholly Foreign-owned Enterprises and other relevant laws.

Share-holding Corporations Ltd. with Investment from Hong Kong, Macau and Taiwan refers to share-holding corporations Ltd. established with the approval from the former Ministry of Foreign Trade and Economic Relations in line with relevant State regulations, where the share of investment from Hong Kong, Macau or Taiwan businessmen exceeds 25% of the total registered capital of the corporation. In case the share of investment from Hong Kong, Macau or Taiwan is less than 25% of the total registered capital, the enterprise is to be classified as domestic-funded share-holding corporation Ltd.

Other Enterprises with Funds from Hong Kong, Macau and Taiwan refers to partnership enterprises with investment from Hong Kong, Macau and Taiwan established within the territory of China in accordance with Administrative Measures on the Establishment of Partnership Enterprises in China by Foreign Enterprises or Foreign Individuals and Regulations for the Administration of the Registration of Foreign-invested Partnership Enterprises.

Joint Venture Enterprises with Foreign Investment refers to enterprises jointly established by foreign enterprises or foreigners with enterprises in the mainland of China in accordance with the Law of the People's Republic of China on Sino-foreign Equity Joint Ventures and other relevant laws, where the sharing of investment, profits and risks is stipulated under contract.

Cooperative Enterprises with Foreign Investment refers to enterprises jointly established by foreign enterprises or foreigners with enterprises in the mainland of China in accordance with the Law of the People's Republic of China on Sino-foreign Contractual Joint Venture and other relevant laws, where the investment or provision of facilities and the sharing of profits and risks are stipulated under cooperative contracts.

Enterprises with Sole (exclusive) Foreign Investment refers to enterprises established in the mainland of China with exclusive investment from foreign investors in accordance with the Law of the People's Republic of China on Wholly Foreign-owned Enterprises and other relevant laws.

Share-holding Corporations Ltd. with Foreign Investment refers to share-holding corporations Ltd. established with the approval from the former Ministry of Foreign Trade and Economic Relations in line with relevant State regulations, where the share of investment from foreign investors exceeds 25% of the total registered capital of the corporation. In case the share of foreign investment is less than 25% of the total registered capital, the enterprise is to be classified as domestic-funded share-holding corporation Ltd.

Other Enterprises with Foreign Funds refers to partnership enterprises established within the territory of China in accordance with Administrative Measures on the Establishment of Partnership Enterprises in China by Foreign Enterprises or Foreign Individuals and Regulations for the Administration of the Registration of Foreign-invested Partnership Enterprises.

Government Agencies, Institutions and Social Organizations are classified into the following categories by source of funds and manner of management taking reference of the registration status of enterprises:

(1) Government agencies: include State and party agencies, classified in principle as State-owned. There are exceptions, such as supply and marketing cooperatives which are classified as collective-owned.

(2) Institutions: include institutions of various types established with the approval by organization and staffing departments of the government, but exclude institutions where enterprise management system is introduced. Institutions are further classified as follows:

(a) Institutions for which their main budgets are from government budget appropriations or extra-budget funds, or allocated from the budget of their competent government agencies. Such institutions are classified as state-owned.

(b) Institutions for which their budget mainly come from collective units. Such institutions are classified as collective-owned.

(c) Social institutions established by individual or a group of citizens, which are classified as private.

(d) Institutions other than those mentioned above for which their sources of budget are not clear. Such institutions are classified by the manner of management.

(3) Social organizations: include social organizations established with the approval from the Ministry of Civil Affairs, and organizations that are not covered by social organization management regulations such as trade unions, women's federations etc.. Social organizations are further classified as follows:

(a) Social organizations that are not covered by social organization management regulations of the Ministry of Civil Affairs such as trade unions, women federations, communist youth leagues, youth associations, industrial and commerce associations, scientist associations, overseas Chinese associations, etc., foundations and fund management organizations established with funds from the state, and social organizations whose funds mainly come from the budget of their competent government agencies. Such institutions are classified as State-owned.

(b) Social organizations for which their budget mainly come from collective units. Such institutions are classified as collective-owned.

(c) Social organizations established by individual or a group of citizens, which are classified as private.

(d) Social organizations other than those mentioned above for which their sources of budget are not clear. Such organizations are classified by the manner of management.

2 国民经济核算

Chapter 2 National Accounts

2-1 生产法地区生产总值
Gross Regional Product by Production Approach

单位: 亿元 (100 million yuan)

年份 Year	地区生产总值 Gross Regional Product	第一产业 Primary Industry	第二产业 Secondary Industry	第三产业 Tertiary Industry	农林牧渔业 Agriculture, Forestry, Animal Husbandry and Fishery	工业 Industry	建筑业 Construction
1978	184.61	82.20	65.55	36.86	82.20	59.40	6.15
1979	205.76	91.95	72.31	41.50	91.95	65.43	6.88
1980	229.31	101.68	81.05	46.58	101.68	73.18	7.87
1981	242.32	108.02	83.36	50.94	108.02	74.58	8.78
1982	275.23	125.36	92.84	57.03	125.36	82.49	10.35
1983	311.00	138.17	105.69	67.14	138.17	93.71	11.98
1984	358.06	156.11	121.68	80.27	156.11	105.97	15.71
1985	421.15	172.90	148.11	100.14	172.90	127.13	20.98
1986	458.23	181.20	160.62	116.41	181.20	138.12	22.50
1987	530.86	202.25	187.88	140.73	202.25	160.49	27.39
1988	659.69	241.95	238.32	179.42	241.95	206.44	31.88
1989	744.98	263.15	263.44	218.39	263.15	231.08	32.36
1990	890.95	321.41	312.64	256.90	321.41	276.08	36.56
1991	1016.31	339.00	376.48	300.83	339.00	331.37	45.11
1992	1177.27	372.04	441.57	363.66	372.04	378.67	62.90
1993	1486.08	449.38	580.38	456.32	449.38	495.24	85.14
1994	2001.41	597.37	782.77	621.27	597.37	667.85	114.92
1995	2443.21	662.46	980.91	799.84	662.46	833.17	147.74
1996	2871.65	770.02	1156.01	945.62	770.02	977.68	178.33
1997	3241.47	880.28	1265.32	1095.87	880.28	1055.21	210.11
1998	3474.09	912.24	1324.01	1237.84	912.24	1076.35	247.66
1999	3649.12	926.03	1349.63	1373.46	926.03	1099.48	250.15
2000	3928.20	945.58	1433.11	1549.51	945.58	1154.46	278.65
2001	4293.49	981.67	1572.01	1739.81	981.67	1253.19	318.82
2002	4725.01	1047.95	1733.38	1943.68	1047.95	1372.64	360.74
2003	5333.09	1128.61	2014.80	2189.68	1128.61	1604.49	410.31
2004	6379.63	1379.93	2489.40	2510.30	1379.93	2013.80	475.60
2005	7385.10	1481.14	3067.23	2836.73	1481.14	2527.08	540.15
2006	8690.24	1595.48	3775.14	3319.62	1595.48	3144.67	630.47
2007	10562.39	2032.00	4648.79	3881.60	2032.00	3921.41	727.38
2008	12601.23	2216.15	5823.39	4561.69	2216.15	4956.13	867.26
2009	14151.28	2206.53	6123.53	5821.22	2240.61	5140.31	1033.63
2010	17185.48	2443.20	7902.18	6840.10	2482.89	6727.42	1240.73
2011	21026.68	2937.70	10045.72	8043.26	2983.51	8591.90	1538.08
2012	23872.80	3245.94	11240.02	9386.84	3297.21	9551.01	1782.75
2013	26392.07	3368.66	12378.71	10644.70	3425.61	10447.52	2038.17
2014	28536.66	3531.05	12839.60	12166.01	3594.17	10729.18	2225.44
2015	30053.10	3677.30	13248.08	13127.72	3745.32	11039.08	2321.38
2016	32934.54	3929.33	13448.92	15556.29	4005.42	11058.79	2472.96
2017	36980.22	4262.35	14328.12	18389.75	4365.11	11576.16	2838.34
2018	40678.13	4426.66	15322.72	20928.75	4543.55	12190.46	3223.69

注：本表按当年价格计算。从2013年起，地区生产总值核算执行国家统计局新的《国民经济行业分类》和《三次产业划分规定》(以下有关各表同)。

a) The data in this table are calculated at current prices.The regional GDP accounting has executed the NBS new "Classification of National Economic Industries" and the "Provisions of Three Industrial Division" since 2013.(the same as the following related tables).

2-1 续表 continued

单位: 亿元 (100 million yuan)

年份 Year	批发和零售业 Wholesale and Retail Trades	交通运输、仓储和邮政业 Transport, Storage and Post	住宿和餐饮业 Hotels and Catering Services	金融业 Financial Intermediation	房地产业 Real Estate	其他 Others	人均地区生产总值(元) Per Capita Gross Regional Product (yuan)
1978	7.75	6.17	3.02	4.88	2.42	12.62	261
1979	8.71	6.74	3.39	5.77	2.63	14.26	289
1980	9.68	7.39	3.77	6.71	2.94	16.09	320
1981	10.83	7.82	4.21	7.15	3.33	17.60	337
1982	12.69	8.49	4.93	7.59	3.66	19.67	379
1983	15.39	9.75	5.98	8.36	4.14	23.52	425
1984	19.27	11.32	7.52	9.22	4.93	28.01	487
1985	24.85	14.31	9.67	11.71	5.93	33.67	570
1986	28.84	17.88	11.21	13.21	6.85	38.42	614
1987	35.09	22.64	13.65	15.98	8.11	45.26	702
1988	47.19	27.80	18.35	19.84	9.92	56.32	861
1989	56.45	33.82	22.04	23.55	11.68	70.85	960
1990	61.29	40.71	24.57	29.79	14.56	85.98	1136
1991	65.94	48.96	27.64	34.09	17.76	106.44	1283
1992	78.45	56.70	31.34	40.68	24.41	132.08	1477
1993	90.29	70.18	39.00	51.13	30.34	175.38	1854
1994	121.26	85.71	54.28	65.01	68.91	226.10	2338
1995	181.21	113.01	70.47	71.31	80.41	283.43	3043
1996	220.19	129.83	85.63	82.13	95.63	332.21	3550
1997	240.78	145.08	93.64	93.19	124.13	399.05	4032
1998	254.51	165.91	99.41	108.45	148.09	461.47	4294
1999	270.84	179.25	109.25	118.32	165.17	530.63	4540
2000	283.26	217.41	120.08	153.05	180.05	595.66	4956
2001	311.95	248.34	133.51	168.86	198.60	678.55	5376
2002	341.12	271.19	151.41	183.13	210.82	786.01	5890
2003	372.68	302.44	168.24	206.24	231.72	908.36	6623
2004	425.54	334.50	195.10	236.50	264.30	1054.36	7895
2005	475.16	380.28	221.42	262.26	286.23	1211.38	9060
2006	537.68	451.19	255.19	299.50	336.20	1439.86	10613
2007	624.74	511.50	299.75	359.11	376.84	1709.66	12963
2008	736.42	567.51	335.13	411.14	453.63	2057.86	15495
2009	980.23	574.02	433.82	561.50	629.72	2557.44	17339
2010	1158.66	639.42	517.50	708.39	648.72	3061.75	21182
2011	1367.39	719.36	615.00	949.23	728.38	3533.83	26133
2012	1537.07	791.43	675.32	1416.36	820.48	4001.17	29608
2013	1681.11	838.47	742.66	1755.22	886.85	4576.46	32617
2014	1787.12	1175.47	802.59	1953.51	1121.29	5147.89	35128
2015	1871.55	1219.77	859.49	2202.23	1252.20	5542.08	36775
2016	2138.45	1472.57	941.28	2729.45	1516.61	6599.01	40003
2017	2574.15	1595.80	1023.46	3203.27	2039.83	7764.10	44651
2018	2755.33	1833.51	1110.75	3371.03	2321.34	9328.47	48883

2-2 生产法地区生产总值指数
Indices of Gross Regional Product by Production Approach

(上年=100) (preceding year=100)

年份 Year	地区生产总值 Gross Regional Product	第一产业 Primary Industry	第二产业 Secondary Industry	第三产业 Tertiary Industry	农林牧渔业 Agriculture, Forestry, Animal Husbandry and Fishery	工业 Industry	建筑业 Construction
1978	117.4	113.8	121.2	117.4	113.8	126.0	88.4
1979	110.1	108.0	110.5	113.0	108.0	110.5	110.7
1980	109.5	104.0	109.7	118.3	104.0	109.5	111.5
1981	104.1	104.4	101.6	107.4	104.4	100.8	109.5
1982	110.9	112.7	109.3	109.4	112.7	108.6	115.3
1983	111.0	107.5	112.3	116.8	107.5	112.0	115.0
1984	112.2	109.2	113.4	116.7	109.2	111.5	128.2
1985	111.9	104.3	118.0	117.1	104.3	117.0	125.0
1986	105.5	101.0	106.5	111.9	101.0	107.0	103.3
1987	108.7	103.0	112.2	112.5	103.0	112.0	113.2
1988	107.5	101.9	113.8	106.2	101.9	116.4	97.0
1989	103.2	102.8	101.9	105.7	102.8	103.5	89.1
1990	109.1	106.9	109.5	111.3	106.9	110.0	105.7
1991	109.1	108.5	106.3	113.4	108.5	104.4	120.6
1992	112.6	104.6	120.5	113.1	104.6	118.9	131.1
1993	113.1	105.0	120.1	113.5	105.0	120.3	118.8
1994	111.3	104.4	117.3	110.7	104.4	118.5	110.1
1995	110.7	105.5	111.5	114.7	105.5	110.7	117.0
1996	110.6	107.3	109.2	115.4	107.3	108.2	115.2
1997	110.5	106.2	111.6	112.8	106.2	111.4	112.7
1998	109.7	104.6	110.8	112.2	104.6	109.8	116.6
1999	106.6	105.0	106.0	108.6	105.0	105.8	106.8
2000	108.5	102.3	108.2	113.1	102.3	108.0	109.2
2001	109.0	105.7	110.2	109.8	105.7	110.2	110.1
2002	110.3	105.6	111.9	111.5	105.6	112.2	110.9
2003	111.3	105.1	115.2	111.2	105.1	116.3	110.6
2004	112.7	106.0	118.3	110.9	106.0	119.8	111.6
2005	112.6	105.4	118.0	110.6	105.4	120.2	108.0
2006	113.5	102.6	118.2	114.2	102.6	121.5	102.8
2007	114.5	104.8	120.4	112.5	104.8	121.5	114.3
2008	111.0	101.0	113.7	112.1	101.0	115.6	102.3
2009	114.5	104.0	115.9	116.7	104.0	114.9	122.7
2010	115.1	104.3	122.4	110.3	104.4	123.4	116.3
2011	115.0	104.4	121.4	111.4	104.5	122.7	114.8
2012	112.6	104.4	115.5	111.6	104.5	115.7	114.0
2013	110.0	103.5	111.7	109.8	103.6	111.2	114.5
2014	108.5	103.8	108.7	109.6	103.9	108.7	108.6
2015	107.9	103.7	107.5	109.5	103.9	107.2	109.0
2016	107.8	103.8	107.6	109.2	104.0	107.8	106.6
2017	108.1	103.8	107.5	109.8	103.9	108.3	103.9
2018	108.0	103.6	107.5	109.4	103.8	108.1	104.6

注：本表按可比价格计算。
a) The indices in this table are calculated at comparable prices.

2-2 续表 continued

(上年=100) (preceding year=100)

年份 Year	批发和零售业 Wholesale and Retail Trades	交通运输、仓储和邮政业 Transport, Storage and Post	住宿和餐饮业 Hotels and Catering Services	金融业 Financial Intermediation	房地产业 Real Estate	其他 Others	人均地区生产总值 Per Capita Gross Regional Product
1978							116.8
1979	112.8	109.6	112.8	118.4	109.2	113.4	109.4
1980	117.2	115.6	117.2	122.9	117.6	118.8	109.0
1981	109.8	104.1	109.8	104.6	111.2	107.4	103.6
1982	114.5	104.8	114.5	105.3	107.6	109.2	109.8
1983	120.5	110.5	120.5	113.0	112.2	118.4	110.1
1984	122.4	108.0	122.8	114.1	116.5	115.7	111.8
1985	120.7	129.7	120.5	107.1	112.6	113.6	111.3
1986	111.7	120.3	111.6	108.7	111.2	108.9	104.5
1987	113.2	117.7	113.2	113.5	110.1	105.7	107.3
1988	112.1	102.4	112.0	101.8	101.9	103.8	106.1
1989	102.4	106.8	102.8	103.1	106.0	111.5	101.9
1990	104.0	112.5	106.8	120.4	113.7	108.1	107.9
1991	105.2	115.3	110.0	109.9	107.4	120.6	108.1
1992	109.9	116.2	104.7	107.6	121.2	114.0	111.9
1993	104.5	114.4	113.0	112.0	129.1	115.1	112.5
1994	107.8	100.2	111.7	109.0	169.1	100.2	110.6
1995	129.8	117.4	112.8	103.6	110.0	125.9	111.3
1996	121.5	112.0	121.5	105.3	120.0	122.2	109.8
1997	105.7	109.0	105.7	109.7	125.5	117.4	111.2
1998	109.3	110.3	109.2	113.2	116.7	112.5	109.0
1999	106.4	103.7	109.9	106.1	113.4	109.3	107.3
2000	107.0	122.7	113.1	129.5	105.5	115.7	110.0
2001	109.3	109.6	110.3	108.3	108.6	111.4	108.2
2002	110.0	109.0	114.1	108.4	105.1	116.9	109.8
2003	109.1	109.1	111.0	110.5	108.2	112.7	110.9
2004	110.1	109.2	111.8	109.2	109.6	112.7	112.3
2005	111.0	110.0	112.8	107.9	105.3	112.2	111.6
2006	110.7	111.4	113.0	111.3	112.2	116.9	113.0
2007	110.2	112.6	108.9	113.8	109.1	115.3	115.1
2008	111.9	107.0	101.5	105.5	103.4	119.6	111.2
2009	123.6	97.1	121.5	130.7	127.3	114.4	114.0
2010	111.2	108.3	111.1	108.7	98.3	112.8	115.7
2011	111.6	107.8	112.4	129.8	104.9	108.8	115.9
2012	111.3	107.6	105.7	125.9	109.5	110.0	112.3
2013	107.9	105.8	105.4	119.4	107.9	109.5	109.6
2014	107.5	108.1	106.7	113.4	110.9	109.6	108.1
2015	105.8	106.6	104.3	113.1	107.9	111.5	107.2
2016	105.4	106.1	106.6	110.6	108.7	111.0	107.0
2017	106.7	107.1	107.3	106.8	107.4	113.5	107.5
2018	105.5	107.8	107.3	101.1	107.5	114.6	107.4

2-3 生产法地区生产总值指数

Indices of Gross Regional Product by Production Approach

(1978年=100) (year of 1978=100)

年份 Year	地区生产总值 Gross Regional Product	第一产业 Primary Industry	第二产业 Secondary Industry	第三产业 Tertiary Industry	农林牧渔业 Agriculture, Forestry, Animal Husbandry and Fishery	工业 Industry	建筑业 Construction
1978	100.0	100.0	100.0	100.0	100.0	100.0	100.0
1979	110.1	108.0	110.5	113.0	108.0	110.5	110.7
1980	120.6	112.3	121.2	133.7	112.3	121.0	123.4
1981	125.5	117.3	123.2	143.6	117.3	122.0	135.2
1982	139.2	132.2	134.6	157.1	132.2	132.5	155.8
1983	154.5	142.1	151.2	183.5	142.1	148.3	179.2
1984	173.3	155.1	171.4	214.1	155.1	165.4	229.7
1985	194.0	161.8	202.3	250.7	161.8	193.5	287.2
1986	204.6	163.4	215.4	280.5	163.4	207.1	296.7
1987	222.4	168.3	241.7	315.6	168.3	231.9	335.8
1988	239.1	171.5	275.1	335.2	171.5	270.0	325.7
1989	246.8	176.3	280.3	354.3	176.3	279.4	290.2
1990	269.2	188.5	306.9	394.3	188.5	307.4	306.8
1991	293.7	204.5	326.3	447.1	204.5	320.9	370.0
1992	330.7	213.9	393.1	505.7	213.9	381.5	485.0
1993	374.1	224.6	472.2	574.0	224.6	459.0	576.2
1994	416.3	234.5	553.8	635.4	234.5	543.9	634.4
1995	460.9	247.4	617.5	728.8	247.4	602.1	742.3
1996	509.7	265.5	674.4	841.0	265.5	651.4	855.1
1997	563.3	281.9	752.6	948.7	281.9	725.7	963.7
1998	617.9	294.9	833.9	1064.4	294.9	796.8	1123.7
1999	658.7	309.6	883.9	1156.0	309.6	843.0	1200.1
2000	714.7	316.8	956.4	1307.4	316.8	910.5	1310.5
2001	779.0	334.8	1053.9	1435.5	334.8	1003.4	1442.9
2002	859.2	353.6	1179.3	1600.6	353.6	1125.8	1600.1
2003	956.3	371.6	1358.6	1779.9	371.6	1309.3	1769.8
2004	1077.8	393.9	1607.2	1973.9	393.9	1568.5	1975.1
2005	1213.6	415.2	1896.5	2183.2	415.2	1885.3	2133.1
2006	1377.4	426.0	2241.7	2493.2	426.0	2290.7	2192.8
2007	1577.1	446.4	2699.0	2804.8	446.4	2783.2	2506.4
2008	1750.6	450.9	3068.8	3144.2	450.9	3217.3	2564.0
2009	2004.4	468.9	3556.7	3669.3	468.9	3696.7	3146.0
2010	2307.1	489.1	4353.4	4047.2	489.5	4561.8	3658.8
2011	2653.2	510.6	5285.0	4508.6	511.6	5597.3	4200.3
2012	2987.5	533.0	6104.2	5031.6	534.6	6476.1	4788.4
2013	3286.2	551.7	6818.4	5524.7	553.8	7201.4	5482.7
2014	3565.6	572.7	7411.6	6055.0	575.4	7827.9	5954.2
2015	3847.2	593.9	7967.4	6630.3	597.9	8391.5	6490.1
2016	4147.3	616.4	8573.0	7240.3	621.8	9046.0	6918.4
2017	4483.3	639.8	9215.9	7949.8	646.0	9796.9	7188.3
2018	4841.9	662.9	9907.1	8697.1	670.6	10590.4	7518.9

注：本表按可比价格计算。

a) The indices in this table are calculated at comparable prices.

2-3 续表 continued

(1978年=100) (year of 1978=100)

年份 Year	批发和零售业 Wholesale and Retail Trades	交通运输、仓储和邮政业 Transport, Storage and Post	住宿和餐饮业 Hotels and Catering Services	金融业 Financial Intermediation	房地产业 Real Estate	其他 Others	人均地区生产总值 Per Capita Gross Regional Product
1978	100.0	100.0	100.0	100.0	100.0	100.0	100.0
1979	112.8	109.6	112.8	118.4	109.2	113.4	109.4
1980	132.2	126.7	132.2	145.5	128.4	134.7	119.2
1981	145.2	131.9	145.2	152.2	142.8	144.7	123.5
1982	166.2	138.2	166.2	160.3	153.7	158.0	135.6
1983	200.3	152.7	200.3	181.1	172.4	187.1	149.3
1984	245.1	165.0	245.9	206.6	200.8	216.4	167.0
1985	295.9	213.9	296.4	221.3	226.2	245.9	185.8
1986	330.5	257.4	330.7	240.6	251.5	267.8	194.2
1987	374.1	302.9	374.4	273.1	276.9	283.0	208.4
1988	419.4	310.2	419.3	278.0	282.1	293.8	221.1
1989	429.5	331.3	431.1	286.6	299.1	327.6	225.3
1990	446.6	372.7	460.4	345.0	340.0	354.1	243.1
1991	469.9	429.7	506.4	379.2	365.2	427.0	262.8
1992	516.4	499.4	530.2	408.0	442.6	486.8	294.0
1993	539.6	571.3	599.1	457.0	571.4	560.3	330.8
1994	581.7	572.4	669.2	498.1	966.3	561.5	365.9
1995	755.1	672.0	754.9	516.0	1062.9	706.9	407.2
1996	917.4	752.6	917.2	543.4	1275.5	863.8	447.1
1997	969.7	820.4	969.5	596.1	1600.8	1014.1	497.2
1998	1059.9	904.9	1058.7	674.8	1868.1	1140.9	541.9
1999	1127.7	938.4	1163.5	716.0	2118.4	1247.0	581.5
2000	1206.6	1151.4	1315.9	927.2	2234.9	1442.7	639.6
2001	1318.9	1261.9	1451.4	1004.1	2427.2	1607.2	692.1
2002	1450.7	1375.5	1656.1	1088.5	2550.9	1878.8	759.9
2003	1582.8	1500.6	1838.3	1202.8	2760.1	2117.4	842.8
2004	1742.6	1638.7	2055.2	1313.4	3025.1	2386.4	946.4
2005	1934.3	1802.6	2318.2	1417.2	3185.4	2677.5	1063.8
2006	2141.3	2008.1	2619.6	1577.3	3574.0	3130.0	1202.1
2007	2359.7	2261.1	2852.8	1795.0	3899.3	3608.9	1383.6
2008	2640.5	2419.3	2895.6	1893.7	4031.9	4316.2	1538.5
2009	3263.7	2349.2	3518.1	2475.1	5132.5	4937.7	1753.9
2010	3629.2	2544.2	3908.6	2690.4	5045.3	5569.8	2031.1
2011	4050.2	2742.6	4393.3	3492.1	5292.5	6059.9	2356.0
2012	4507.8	2951.0	4643.7	4396.6	5795.3	6665.9	2645.8
2013	4864.0	3122.2	4894.5	5249.5	6253.1	7299.2	2899.8
2014	5228.8	3375.1	5222.4	5953.0	6934.7	7999.9	3134.7
2015	5532.0	3597.9	5446.9	6732.8	7482.6	8919.9	3360.4
2016	5830.8	3817.3	5806.4	7446.5	8133.5	9901.1	3595.6
2017	6221.4	4088.4	6230.3	7952.8	8735.4	11237.7	3865.3
2018	6563.6	4407.3	6685.1	8040.3	9390.6	12878.4	4151.3

2-4 按所有制分地区生产总值
Gross Regional Product by Ownership

单位：亿元 (100 million yuan)

年份 Year	地区生产总值 Gross Regional Product	公有制经济 State-owned	非公有制经济 Non-public	民营经济 Civilian-owned	外商经济 Foreign-owned	港澳台经济 Hongkong,Macao and Taiwan owned
1978	184.61	178.25	6.36	6.36		
1980	229.31	207.09	22.22	22.22		
1985	421.15	361.82	59.33	59.12	0.10	0.11
1990	890.95	729.94	161.01	159.03	1.24	0.74
1991	1016.31	820.22	196.09	190.51	3.61	1.97
1992	1177.27	937.63	239.64	232.66	4.56	2.42
1993	1486.08	1160.91	325.17	315.22	6.62	3.33
1994	2001.41	1587.40	414.01	400.71	8.95	4.35
1995	2443.21	1901.10	542.11	522.74	13.23	6.14
1996	2871.65	2178.78	692.87	666.97	16.79	9.11
1997	3241.47	2415.07	826.40	792.97	22.04	11.39
1998	3474.09	2550.93	923.16	883.86	26.30	13.00
1999	3649.12	2618.76	1030.36	987.27	27.97	15.12
2000	3928.20	2760.35	1167.85	1113.55	34.07	20.23
2001	4293.50	2894.07	1399.43	1328.79	46.59	24.05
2002	4725.01	3079.89	1645.12	1551.54	64.51	29.07
2003	5333.10	3329.88	2003.22	1885.49	81.95	35.78
2004	6379.63	3784.22	2595.41	2451.93	101.29	42.19
2005	7385.10	4177.61	3207.49	3025.38	129.04	53.07
2006	8690.24	4618.44	4071.80	3827.60	169.29	74.91
2007	10562.39	5256.67	5305.72	4942.62	257.76	105.34
2008	12601.23	6037.95	6563.28	6097.16	332.33	133.79
2009	14151.28	6488.12	7663.16	7108.81	393.36	160.99
2010	17185.48	7570.00	9615.48	8867.83	533.75	213.90
2011	21026.68	8883.12	12143.56	11127.72	703.55	312.29
2012	23872.80	9798.03	14074.77	12845.71	821.79	407.27
2013	26392.07	10622.58	15769.49	14419.64	895.66	454.19
2014	28536.66	11337.41	17199.25	15709.84	995.94	493.47
2015	30053.10	11817.41	18235.69	16735.46	974.39	525.84
2016	32934.54	12902.34	20032.20	18410.41	1052.69	569.10
2017	36980.22	14443.67	22536.55	20738.91	1154.09	643.55
2018	40678.13	15898.52	24779.61	22868.37	1228.02	683.22

注：本表按当年价格计算。
a) The data in this table are calculated at current prices.

2-5 按所有制分地区生产总值指数
Indices of Gross Regional Product by Ownership

(上年=100) (preceding year=100)

年份 Year	地区生产总值 Gross Regional Product	公有制经济 State-owned	非公有制经济 Non-public	民营经济 Civilian-owned	外商经济 Foreign-owned	港澳台经济 Hongkong,Macao and Taiwan owned
1991	109.1	107.5	115.9	116.0	115.3	112.2
1992	112.6	110.6	119.9	119.6	132.0	125.0
1993	113.1	115.3	105.5	105.1	120.3	117.0
1994	111.3	109.5	118.4	117.7	139.4	133.1
1995	110.7	107.9	120.8	120.7	119.1	138.8
1996	110.6	108.6	117.0	116.5	131.1	124.9
1997	110.5	109.0	115.1	114.5	128.7	123.0
1998	109.7	107.3	116.4	116.3	113.3	124.5
1999	106.6	104.5	112.2	111.5	121.0	132.0
2000	108.5	103.9	119.4	118.8	136.9	117.8
2001	109.0	104.9	118.6	118.0	137.9	119.7
2002	110.3	106.1	118.8	117.9	141.4	123.0
2003	111.3	106.6	120.2	119.9	126.4	122.0
2004	112.7	107.0	122.2	122.6	118.4	112.8
2005	112.6	107.7	119.8	119.6	122.9	121.5
2006	113.5	108.0	120.7	120.1	128.1	137.5
2007	114.5	109.1	120.9	119.8	142.0	132.3
2008	111.0	106.2	116.0	115.5	122.9	119.4
2009	114.5	110.5	118.2	118.0	121.3	122.0
2010	115.1	111.0	118.8	118.5	123.2	122.2
2011	115.0	111.5	117.8	116.9	124.1	138.0
2012	112.6	109.3	115.0	114.4	116.2	130.5
2013	110.0	107.0	112.1	112.2	110.5	112.1
2014	108.5	107.0	109.5	109.5	110.4	110.2
2015	107.9	107.2	108.3	108.7	103.4	108.3
2016	107.8	107.4	108.1	108.0	108.6	108.8
2017	108.1	108.0	108.2	108.2	108.7	109.2
2018	108.0	108.2	107.8	108.1	104.2	103.4

注：本表按可比价格计算。
a) The data in this table are calculated at comparable prices.

2-6 按所有制分地区生产总值指数

Indices of Gross Regional Product by Ownership

(1978年=100) (year of 1978=100)

年份 Year	地区生产总值 Gross Regional Product	公有制经济 State-owned	非公有制经济 Non-public	民营经济 Civilian-owned	外商经济 Foreign-owned	港澳台经济 Hongkong,Macao and Taiwan owned
1978	100.0	100.0	100.0	100.0		
1980	120.6	112.5	354.5	354.5		
1985	194.0	172.8	808.5	805.5	100.0	100.0
1990	269.2	230.3	1398.7	1378.1	907.2	490.8
1991	293.7	247.6	1621.1	1598.6	1046.0	550.7
1992	330.7	273.8	1943.7	1911.9	1380.7	688.3
1993	374.1	315.7	2050.6	2009.4	1661.0	805.4
1994	416.3	345.7	2427.9	2365.1	2315.4	1071.9
1995	460.9	373.0	2932.9	2854.7	2757.7	1487.9
1996	509.7	405.1	3431.5	3325.7	3615.3	1858.3
1997	563.3	441.5	3949.7	3807.9	4652.9	2285.7
1998	617.9	473.8	4597.4	4428.6	5271.8	2845.8
1999	658.7	495.1	5158.3	4937.9	6378.9	3756.4
2000	714.7	514.4	6159.0	5866.2	8732.7	4425.0
2001	779.0	539.6	7304.6	6922.1	12042.3	5296.8
2002	859.2	572.5	8677.8	8161.2	17027.9	6515.0
2003	956.3	610.3	10430.7	9785.3	21523.2	7948.3
2004	1077.8	653.0	12746.4	11996.8	25483.5	8965.7
2005	1213.6	703.3	15270.1	14348.1	31319.2	10893.3
2006	1377.4	759.6	18431.1	17232.1	40119.9	14978.4
2007	1577.1	828.7	22283.2	20644.1	56970.3	19816.4
2008	1750.6	880.1	25848.5	23843.9	70016.5	23660.7
2009	2004.4	972.5	30552.9	28135.8	84930.0	28866.1
2010	2307.1	1079.5	36296.8	33340.9	104633.7	35274.4
2011	2653.2	1203.6	42757.7	38975.5	129850.4	48678.6
2012	2987.5	1315.6	49171.3	44588.0	150886.2	63525.6
2013	3286.2	1407.7	55121.0	50027.8	166729.3	71212.2
2014	3565.6	1506.2	60357.5	54780.4	184069.1	78475.9
2015	3847.2	1614.6	65367.2	59546.3	190327.4	84989.4
2016	4147.3	1734.1	70662.0	64310.0	206695.6	92468.4
2017	4483.3	1872.8	76456.3	69583.4	224678.1	100975.5
2018	4841.9	2026.4	82419.8	75219.7	234114.6	104408.7

注：本表按可比价格计算。

a) The data in this table are calculated at comparable prices.

2-7 地区生产总值构成
Composition of Gross Regional Product

单位: % (%)

年份 Year	地区生产总值 Gross Regional Product	第一产业 Primary Industry	第二产业 Secondary Industry	第三产业 Tertiary Industry
1978	100.0	44.5	35.5	20.0
1979	100.0	44.7	35.1	20.2
1980	100.0	44.3	35.3	20.4
1981	100.0	44.6	34.4	21.0
1982	100.0	45.5	33.8	20.7
1983	100.0	44.4	34.0	21.6
1984	100.0	43.6	34.0	22.4
1985	100.0	41.1	35.2	23.7
1986	100.0	39.5	35.0	25.5
1987	100.0	38.1	35.4	26.5
1988	100.0	36.7	36.1	27.2
1989	100.0	35.3	35.3	29.4
1990	100.0	36.1	35.1	28.8
1991	100.0	33.4	37.0	29.6
1992	100.0	31.6	37.5	30.9
1993	100.0	30.2	39.0	30.8
1994	100.0	29.8	39.1	31.1
1995	100.0	27.1	40.1	32.8
1996	100.0	26.8	40.2	33.0
1997	100.0	27.2	39.1	33.7
1998	100.0	26.3	38.1	35.6
1999	100.0	25.4	37.0	37.6
2000	100.0	24.1	36.5	39.4
2001	100.0	22.9	36.6	40.5
2002	100.0	22.2	36.7	41.1
2003	100.0	21.2	37.8	41.0
2004	100.0	21.6	39.1	39.3
2005	100.0	20.1	41.5	38.4
2006	100.0	18.4	43.4	38.2
2007	100.0	19.2	44.0	36.8
2008	100.0	17.6	46.2	36.2
2009	100.0	15.6	43.3	41.1
2010	100.0	14.2	46.0	39.8
2011	100.0	14.0	47.8	38.2
2012	100.0	13.6	47.1	39.3
2013	100.0	12.8	46.9	40.3
2014	100.0	12.4	45.0	42.6
2015	100.0	12.2	44.1	43.7
2016	100.0	11.9	40.8	47.3
2017	100.0	11.6	38.7	49.7
2018	100.0	10.9	37.7	51.4

注：本表按当年价格计算。
a) The data in this table are calculated at current prices.

2-8 各市(州)按三次产业分地区生产总值(2018年)
Gross Regional Product by Three Strata of Industry and Region (2018)

单位：亿元 (100 million yuan)

市(州)	Region	地区生产总值 Gross Regional Product	第一产业 Primary Industry	第二产业 Secondary Industry	第三产业 Tertiary Industry	人均地区生产总值(元) Per Capita Gross Regional Product (yuan)
成都市	Chengdu	15342.77	522.59	6516.19	8303.99	94782
自贡市	Zigong	1406.71	151.55	653.71	601.45	48329
攀枝花市	Panzhihua	1173.52	39.74	731.13	402.65	94938
泸州市	Luzhou	1694.97	190.58	882.97	621.42	39230
德阳市	Deyang	2213.87	243.31	1071.13	899.43	62569
绵阳市	Mianyang	2303.82	301.27	929.40	1073.15	47538
广元市	Guangyuan	801.85	118.10	358.56	325.19	30105
遂宁市	Suining	1221.39	165.64	565.22	490.53	37943
内江市	Neijiang	1411.75	219.31	610.80	581.64	37885
乐山市	Leshan	1615.09	165.92	721.78	727.39	49397
南充市	Nanchong	2006.03	381.87	824.05	800.11	31203
眉山市	Meishan	1256.02	186.50	554.46	515.06	42157
宜宾市	Yibin	2026.37	248.57	1006.73	771.07	44604
广安市	Guangan	1250.24	173.52	575.23	501.49	38520
达州市	Dazhou	1690.17	326.24	603.91	760.02	29627
雅安市	Yaan	646.10	85.83	303.00	257.27	41985
巴中市	Bazhong	645.88	98.27	316.39	231.22	19458
资阳市	Ziyang	1066.53	166.79	507.61	392.13	42112
阿坝藏族羌族自治州	Aba	306.67	49.55	139.53	117.59	32552
甘孜藏族自治州	Ganzi	291.20	65.47	121.78	103.95	24446
凉山彝族自治州	Liangshan	1533.19	307.61	613.13	612.45	31472

注：本表按当年价格计算；人均GDP系按年平均常住人口计算。

a) The data in this table are calculated at current prices and the per capita GDP are calculated based on the annual average date of resident population.

2-9 各市(州)按三次产业分地区生产总值指数(2018年)
Indices of Gross Regional Product by Three Strata of Industry and Region(2018)

上年=100 (preceding year=100)

市(州)	Region	地区生产总值 Gross Regional Product	第一产业 Primary Industry	第二产业 Secondary Industry	第三产业 Tertiary Industry	人均地区生产总值 Per Capita Gross Regional Product
成都市	Chengdu	108.0	103.6	107.0	109.0	106.6
自贡市	Zigong	108.7	103.7	108.8	110.0	106.1
攀枝花市	Panzhihua	107.5	104.0	107.2	108.5	107.5
泸州市	Luzhou	107.6	103.7	108.7	107.2	107.4
德阳市	Deyang	109.0	103.7	109.4	110.0	108.6
绵阳市	Mianyang	109.0	103.7	109.4	110.1	108.4
广元市	Guangyuan	108.4	103.8	109.0	109.3	107.7
遂宁市	Suining	108.8	103.5	109.2	110.3	110.4
内江市	Neijiang	107.8	103.8	108.4	108.7	108.5
乐山市	Leshan	108.7	103.8	108.5	110.3	108.7
南充市	Nanchong	109.0	103.8	110.1	110.5	108.6
眉山市	Meishan	107.5	103.8	107.1	109.5	107.8
宜宾市	Yibin	109.2	103.6	109.9	110.3	108.7
广安市	Guangan	108.0	103.5	107.9	109.8	108.4
达州市	Dazhou	108.3	103.6	108.6	110.2	107.1
雅安市	Yaan	108.1	103.9	108.6	108.8	108.0
巴中市	Bazhong	108.0	103.7	109.4	108.1	107.9
资阳市	Ziyang	107.8	103.7	108.8	108.1	108.4
阿坝藏族羌族自治州	Aba	104.7	103.5	104.5	105.4	104.1
甘孜藏族自治州	Ganzi	109.3	103.5	114.9	106.9	108.5
凉山彝族自治州	Liangshan	104.0	103.8	100.6	107.9	103.1

注:本表按可比价格计算。
a) The indices in this table are calculated at comparable prices.

2-10 各市(州)地区生产总值
Gross Regional Product by Region

单位：亿元 (100 million yuan)

市(州)	Region	2010	2011	2012	2013	2014	2015	2016	2017	2018
成都市	Chengdu	5551.33	6950.58	8138.94	9108.89	10056.59	10801.16	12170.23	13889.39	15342.77
自贡市	Zigong	647.73	780.36	884.80	1001.60	1073.40	1143.11	1234.56	1312.07	1406.71
攀枝花市	Panzhihua	523.99	645.66	740.03	800.88	870.85	925.18	1014.68	1144.25	1173.52
泸州市	Luzhou	714.79	900.87	1030.45	1140.48	1259.73	1353.41	1481.91	1596.21	1694.97
德阳市	Deyang	921.27	1137.45	1280.20	1395.94	1515.65	1605.06	1752.45	1960.55	2213.87
绵阳市	Mianyang	960.22	1189.11	1346.42	1455.12	1579.89	1700.33	1830.42	2074.75	2303.82
广元市	Guangyuan	321.87	403.54	468.66	518.75	566.19	605.43	660.01	732.12	801.85
遂宁市	Suining	491.50	582.47	656.00	736.61	809.55	915.81	1008.45	1138.06	1221.39
内江市	Neijiang	690.28	854.68	978.18	1069.34	1156.77	1198.58	1297.67	1332.09	1411.75
乐山市	Leshan	743.92	918.06	1037.75	1134.79	1207.59	1301.23	1406.58	1507.79	1615.09
南充市	Nanchong	827.82	1029.48	1180.36	1328.55	1432.02	1516.20	1651.40	1827.93	2006.03
眉山市	Meishan	552.25	673.34	775.22	860.04	944.89	1029.86	1117.23	1183.35	1256.02
宜宾市	Yibin	870.85	1091.18	1242.76	1342.89	1443.81	1525.90	1653.05	1847.23	2026.37
广安市	Guangan	537.22	659.90	752.22	835.14	919.61	1005.61	1078.62	1173.79	1250.24
达州市	Dazhou	819.20	1011.83	1135.46	1245.41	1347.83	1350.76	1447.08	1583.94	1690.17
雅安市	Yaan	286.54	350.13	398.05	417.97	462.41	502.58	545.33	602.77	646.10
巴中市	Bazhong	264.98	326.67	372.40	415.94	456.66	501.34	544.66	601.44	645.88
资阳市	Ziyang	657.90	836.44	984.72	1092.36	1195.60	1270.38	943.44	1022.21	1066.53
阿坝藏族羌族自治州	Aba	132.76	168.48	203.74	233.99	247.79	265.04	281.32	295.16	306.67
甘孜藏族自治州	Ganzi	122.83	152.22	175.02	201.22	206.81	213.04	229.80	261.50	291.20
凉山彝族自治州	Liangshan	784.19	1000.13	1122.67	1214.40	1314.30	1314.84	1403.92	1480.91	1533.19

注：本表按当年价格计算。
a) The data in this table are calculated at current prices.

2-11 各市(州)地区生产总值指数
Indices of Gross Regional Product by Region

上年=100 (preceding year=100)

市(州)	Region	2010	2011	2012	2013	2014	2015	2016	2017	2018
成都市	Chengdu	115.0	115.2	113.0	110.2	108.9	107.9	107.7	108.1	108.0
自贡市	Zigong	115.6	115.6	113.9	111.3	107.6	108.4	107.7	108.3	108.7
攀枝花市	Panzhihua	115.1	115.3	114.0	110.7	109.3	108.1	108.0	107.4	107.5
泸州市	Luzhou	116.5	115.9	114.8	111.2	111.0	111.0	109.5	109.1	107.6
德阳市	Deyang	114.4	115.6	113.0	110.0	109.0	108.2	108.4	109.0	109.0
绵阳市	Mianyang	115.3	115.2	113.3	110.0	109.1	108.6	108.3	109.1	109.0
广元市	Guangyuan	115.9	115.6	113.8	110.5	109.2	108.6	108.0	108.1	108.4
遂宁市	Suining	115.3	115.2	113.9	111.1	109.7	113.2	109.1	108.3	108.8
内江市	Neijiang	116.2	115.3	113.6	110.3	108.9	108.0	107.8	107.1	107.8
乐山市	Leshan	116.2	116.0	114.4	110.4	107.0	109.1	108.2	108.2	108.7
南充市	Nanchong	115.3	115.3	114.2	111.0	107.2	107.6	107.8	108.5	109.0
眉山市	Meishan	115.6	115.3	114.5	110.8	110.1	110.2	108.4	105.3	107.5
宜宾市	Yibin	115.6	115.6	114.1	108.1	108.0	108.5	108.3	108.8	109.2
广安市	Guangan	115.6	115.3	114.0	110.8	110.2	110.6	107.9	108.1	108.0
达州市	Dazhou	115.1	115.2	113.6	110.2	108.4	103.1	107.5	108.2	108.3
雅安市	Yaan	115.3	115.3	114.0	103.9	111.0	109.0	108.1	108.0	108.1
巴中市	Bazhong	114.7	115.2	113.9	110.7	109.0	108.6	107.8	108.1	108.0
资阳市	Ziyang	117.0	116.1	114.3	110.6	110.0	108.8	107.8	107.8	107.8
阿坝藏族羌族自治州	Aba	118.1	115.2	113.7	110.2	105.6	107.9	106.2	104.0	104.7
甘孜藏族自治州	Ganzi	114.1	114.2	112.6	112.1	104.2	105.1	107.0	109.1	109.3
凉山彝族自治州	Liangshan	117.5	115.2	113.8	110.2	108.5	102.8	106.0	105.3	104.0

注:本表按可比价格计算。
a) The indices in this table are calculated at comparable prices.

2-12 各市(州)第一产业增加值
Primary Industry by Region

单位：亿元 (100 million yuan)

市(州)	Region	2010	2011	2012	2013	2014	2015	2016	2017	2018
成都市	Chengdu	285.09	327.34	348.10	353.17	357.07	373.15	474.94	500.87	522.59
自贡市	Zigong	84.68	98.99	109.39	119.42	121.77	127.97	136.13	142.94	151.55
攀枝花市	Panzhihua	21.49	24.24	25.77	27.88	29.02	31.31	34.25	37.16	39.74
泸州市	Luzhou	108.81	130.83	143.60	155.60	159.85	167.84	178.07	183.19	190.58
德阳市	Deyang	152.39	177.74	186.91	188.60	199.33	208.18	219.52	228.46	243.31
绵阳市	Mianyang	166.49	199.23	219.19	238.96	247.64	260.05	280.29	291.66	301.27
广元市	Guangyuan	76.52	83.80	91.82	94.31	95.85	99.76	106.44	113.17	118.10
遂宁市	Suining	105.66	120.06	123.97	132.51	136.15	141.66	153.62	160.41	165.64
内江市	Neijiang	112.39	139.76	163.31	176.32	182.61	191.15	204.52	209.60	219.31
乐山市	Leshan	100.08	114.58	123.72	130.94	135.13	142.50	153.27	158.80	165.92
南充市	Nanchong	201.62	240.02	270.47	293.59	310.02	335.46	354.98	363.68	381.87
眉山市	Meishan	103.80	121.42	135.91	144.57	149.34	159.64	169.45	176.62	186.50
宜宾市	Yibin	133.84	163.27	181.94	198.61	206.87	216.35	231.99	238.84	248.57
广安市	Guangan	109.91	125.26	140.00	149.99	155.76	163.31	170.23	169.81	173.52
达州市	Dazhou	192.09	229.53	245.49	262.58	277.47	290.82	310.02	322.13	326.24
雅安市	Yaan	49.97	56.87	60.39	62.40	66.58	72.44	76.58	80.85	85.83
巴中市	Bazhong	65.72	69.59	75.00	79.01	80.66	83.98	89.92	93.30	98.27
资阳市	Ziyang	151.81	185.02	216.13	235.10	241.90	250.88	155.34	160.35	166.79
阿坝藏族羌族自治州	Aba	25.13	27.86	31.57	35.04	37.25	40.84	44.05	46.44	49.55
甘孜藏族自治州	Ganzi	28.50	37.42	42.75	46.92	51.02	54.41	59.27	61.29	65.47
凉山彝族自治州	Liangshan	172.06	194.56	218.80	233.89	249.39	263.58	280.71	296.52	307.61

注：本表按当年价格计算。
a) The data in this table are calculated at current prices.

2-13 各市(州)第一产业增加值指数
Primary Industry by Region

上年=100 (preceding year=100)

市(州)	Region	2010	2011	2012	2013	2014	2015	2016	2017	2018
成都市	Chengdu	104.1	103.7	103.8	103.6	103.4	103.9	104.0	103.9	103.6
自贡市	Zigong	104.6	103.8	104.8	103.8	104.1	103.8	104.0	104.1	103.7
攀枝花市	Panzhihua	103.9	104.5	104.6	104.5	104.5	104.1	104.4	104.3	104.0
泸州市	Luzhou	104.2	103.0	104.9	104.3	104.2	103.8	103.9	103.9	103.7
德阳市	Deyang	104.1	103.8	104.4	103.6	104.2	103.7	103.6	103.9	103.7
绵阳市	Mianyang	104.0	103.8	104.0	103.5	103.9	103.8	103.9	104.0	103.7
广元市	Guangyuan	104.6	104.4	104.9	103.6	104.2	103.7	103.9	103.8	103.8
遂宁市	Suining	104.5	103.3	104.5	103.3	103.7	103.6	103.7	103.6	103.5
内江市	Neijiang	104.6	104.2	104.5	104.0	103.8	103.9	104.0	102.8	103.8
乐山市	Leshan	104.1	104.0	104.1	103.3	103.8	103.9	103.8	103.9	103.8
南充市	Nanchong	104.5	104.1	104.5	103.6	104.2	103.8	103.7	103.9	103.8
眉山市	Meishan	104.4	104.0	104.7	103.6	104.0	104.0	104.0	103.9	103.8
宜宾市	Yibin	104.9	103.4	104.8	103.6	103.7	103.9	103.6	103.5	103.6
广安市	Guangan	104.5	104.0	104.7	103.5	104.1	103.8	102.9	103.4	103.5
达州市	Dazhou	104.4	103.5	104.6	103.7	103.8	103.9	104.1	103.8	103.6
雅安市	Yaan	103.1	103.4	104.0	102.1	104.6	103.9	103.7	103.9	103.9
巴中市	Bazhong	104.1	104.0	103.7	103.4	103.1	103.7	103.7	103.6	103.7
资阳市	Ziyang	104.3	103.6	104.6	103.6	104.2	103.9	103.9	103.9	103.7
阿坝藏族羌族自治州	Aba	105.5	105.1	106.1	104.9	104.7	104.2	104.5	103.2	103.5
甘孜藏族自治州	Ganzi	104.2	106.9	104.0	104.0	104.6	103.9	104.1	104.5	103.5
凉山彝族自治州	Liangshan	104.3	104.4	104.6	104.8	104.5	104.3	104.2	103.8	103.8

注:本表按可比价格计算。

a) The indices in this table are calculated at comparable prices.

2-14 各市(州)第二产业增加值
Secondary Industry by Region

单位：亿元 (100 million yuan)

市(州)	Region	2010	2011	2012	2013	2014	2015	2016	2017	2018
成都市	Chengdu	2480.90	3143.82	3765.62	4181.49	4508.53	4723.49	5201.99	5998.19	6516.19
自贡市	Zigong	370.84	458.63	529.27	598.61	636.20	664.41	695.37	638.25	653.71
攀枝花市	Panzhihua	386.63	487.75	561.41	597.19	637.41	661.03	702.72	745.02	731.13
泸州市	Luzhou	403.71	538.16	624.03	684.37	758.93	806.74	875.77	850.56	882.97
德阳市	Deyang	532.72	682.39	770.31	831.62	904.86	903.27	946.41	941.81	1071.13
绵阳市	Mianyang	468.27	616.55	706.22	747.61	805.33	858.93	876.04	838.76	929.40
广元市	Guangyuan	125.67	180.16	220.29	249.58	269.90	285.53	307.41	327.01	358.56
遂宁市	Suining	254.69	309.43	359.20	406.47	448.78	514.32	530.18	548.60	565.22
内江市	Neijiang	419.53	534.00	610.10	661.33	711.04	717.78	741.62	660.67	610.80
乐山市	Leshan	442.45	567.37	643.91	698.81	720.30	767.05	761.01	691.41	721.78
南充市	Nanchong	401.57	523.85	609.66	688.70	723.15	741.11	760.63	749.69	824.05
眉山市	Meishan	303.31	379.59	443.33	491.23	534.74	578.14	586.95	538.82	554.46
宜宾市	Yibin	519.21	675.69	773.97	814.46	858.82	889.89	907.17	918.74	1006.73
广安市	Guangan	259.25	339.07	392.68	437.42	482.85	520.19	557.01	546.05	575.23
达州市	Dazhou	374.17	491.39	555.85	599.82	636.99	581.19	601.20	558.12	603.91
雅安市	Yaan	157.83	200.38	233.56	238.53	264.16	280.92	291.26	284.64	303.00
巴中市	Bazhong	94.97	138.99	167.45	191.46	210.24	233.81	253.94	293.39	316.39
资阳市	Ziyang	348.40	460.19	548.45	607.64	669.43	702.93	511.46	503.94	507.61
阿坝藏族羌族自治州	Aba	58.53	79.67	102.12	120.84	125.31	130.02	132.90	141.34	139.53
甘孜藏族自治州	Ganzi	44.92	57.72	68.12	80.78	77.20	75.79	82.71	103.82	121.78
凉山彝族自治州	Liangshan	371.05	523.57	587.87	642.21	693.34	648.65	684.15	621.88	613.13

注：本表按当年价格计算。
a) The data in this table are calculated at current prices.

2-15 各市(州)第二产业增加值指数
Secondary Industry by Region

上年=100 (preceding year=100)

市(州)	Region	2010	2011	2012	2013	2014	2015	2016	2017	2018
成都市	Chengdu	119.8	119.8	115.6	112.2	109.8	107.2	106.7	107.5	107.0
自贡市	Zigong	121.1	120.7	116.7	112.6	107.9	108.2	108.1	108.4	108.8
攀枝花市	Panzhihua	117.5	117.5	115.5	111.7	109.6	108.5	108.1	107.2	107.2
泸州市	Luzhou	126.6	122.5	118.4	112.3	112.2	112.5	110.4	110.0	108.7
德阳市	Deyang	118.3	121.0	115.8	111.4	110.1	108.3	109.2	109.5	109.4
绵阳市	Mianyang	123.2	122.8	117.9	112.2	110.0	109.3	108.9	109.2	109.4
广元市	Guangyuan	129.3	126.2	122.2	113.8	109.5	109.6	108.9	108.2	109.0
遂宁市	Suining	124.7	122.2	118.6	113.9	111.4	116.3	109.7	108.6	109.2
内江市	Neijiang	123.8	120.5	116.8	111.4	109.6	108.2	108.6	107.2	108.4
乐山市	Leshan	120.7	120.3	117.5	111.5	106.2	109.8	108.6	108.5	108.5
南充市	Nanchong	123.5	122.5	119.6	113.8	106.7	107.9	108.5	109.2	110.1
眉山市	Meishan	123.8	120.1	118.6	112.3	111.1	111.4	109.2	102.9	107.1
宜宾市	Yibin	121.7	121.1	116.9	108.0	108.1	108.6	109.0	109.3	109.9
广安市	Guangan	124.5	122.3	118.9	113.4	111.1	111.6	108.6	107.8	107.9
达州市	Dazhou	124.8	123.5	118.6	112.4	108.8	99.8	107.6	108.1	108.6
雅安市	Yaan	122.2	121.0	118.3	103.2	112.7	110.2	109.1	108.3	108.6
巴中市	Bazhong	130.3	131.4	123.6	115.5	110.0	109.0	109.7	109.7	109.4
资阳市	Ziyang	125.4	122.7	118.8	112.8	111.6	109.7	108.7	108.5	108.8
阿坝藏族羌族自治州	Aba	131.2	122.5	119.1	113.0	105.9	107.9	106.1	106.6	104.5
甘孜藏族自治州	Ganzi	120.5	122.9	120.0	117.0	102.4	104.7	110.3	116.1	114.9
凉山彝族自治州	Liangshan	129.6	123.7	118.8	114.8	110.6	100.1	106.6	105.0	100.6

注:本表按可比价格计算。
a) The indices in this table are calculated at comparable prices.

2-16 各市(州)第三产业增加值
Tertiary Industry by Region

单位：亿元 (100 million yuan)

市(州)	Region	2010	2011	2012	2013	2014	2015	2016	2017	2018
成都市	Chengdu	2785.34	3479.42	4025.22	4574.23	5190.99	5704.52	6493.30	7390.33	8303.99
自贡市	Zigong	192.21	222.74	246.14	283.57	315.43	350.73	403.06	530.88	601.45
攀枝花市	Panzhihua	115.87	133.67	152.85	175.81	204.42	232.84	277.71	362.07	402.65
泸州市	Luzhou	202.27	231.88	262.82	300.51	340.95	378.83	428.07	562.46	621.42
德阳市	Deyang	236.16	277.32	322.98	375.72	411.46	493.61	586.52	790.28	899.43
绵阳市	Mianyang	325.46	373.33	421.01	468.55	526.92	581.35	674.09	944.33	1073.15
广元市	Guangyuan	119.68	139.58	156.55	174.86	200.44	220.14	246.16	291.94	325.19
遂宁市	Suining	131.15	152.98	172.83	197.63	224.62	259.83	324.65	429.05	490.53
内江市	Neijiang	158.36	180.92	204.77	231.69	263.12	289.65	351.53	461.82	581.64
乐山市	Leshan	201.39	236.11	270.12	305.04	352.16	391.68	492.30	657.58	727.39
南充市	Nanchong	224.63	265.61	300.23	346.26	398.85	439.63	535.79	714.56	800.11
眉山市	Meishan	145.14	172.33	195.98	224.24	260.81	292.08	360.83	467.91	515.06
宜宾市	Yibin	217.80	252.22	286.85	329.82	378.12	419.66	513.89	689.65	771.07
广安市	Guangan	168.06	195.57	219.54	247.73	281.00	322.11	351.38	457.93	501.49
达州市	Dazhou	252.94	290.91	334.12	383.01	433.37	478.75	535.86	703.69	760.02
雅安市	Yaan	78.74	92.88	104.10	117.04	131.67	149.22	177.49	237.28	257.27
巴中市	Bazhong	104.29	118.09	129.95	145.47	165.76	183.55	200.80	214.75	231.22
资阳市	Ziyang	157.69	191.23	220.14	249.62	284.27	316.57	276.64	357.92	392.13
阿坝藏族羌族自治州	Aba	49.10	60.95	70.05	78.11	85.23	94.18	104.37	107.38	117.59
甘孜藏族自治州	Ganzi	49.41	57.08	64.15	73.52	78.59	82.84	87.82	96.39	103.95
凉山彝族自治州	Liangshan	241.08	282.00	316.00	338.30	371.57	402.61	439.06	562.51	612.45

注：本表按当年价格计算。

a) The data in this table are calculated at current prices.

2-17 各市(州)第三产业增加值指数
Tertiary Industry by Region

上年=100 (preceding year=100)

市(州)	Region	2010	2011	2012	2013	2014	2015	2016	2017	2018
成都市	Chengdu	111.8	112.4	111.5	108.8	108.6	109.0	109.0	108.9	109.0
自贡市	Zigong	111.0	110.9	111.8	111.5	108.0	110.5	108.3	109.5	110.0
攀枝花市	Panzhihua	109.0	110.2	110.5	108.0	108.8	107.2	108.0	108.0	108.5
泸州市	Luzhou	107.3	109.7	111.7	112.0	110.9	110.5	110.0	109.5	107.2
德阳市	Deyang	111.3	111.1	111.4	109.9	108.7	110.0	109.0	110.0	110.0
绵阳市	Mianyang	110.2	109.9	110.4	109.1	109.7	109.4	109.5	110.8	110.1
广元市	Guangyuan	111.4	111.6	109.1	110.0	111.3	109.7	108.7	109.6	109.3
遂宁市	Suining	108.1	111.4	111.2	110.5	109.7	112.0	111.0	110.0	110.3
内江市	Neijiang	107.9	109.3	110.7	110.7	109.8	109.3	108.3	109.0	108.7
乐山市	Leshan	112.2	112.6	111.9	110.5	110.4	109.4	109.1	109.1	110.3
南充市	Nanchong	110.2	112.6	111.9	111.0	110.4	109.6	109.6	110.5	110.5
眉山市	Meishan	108.0	113.5	112.0	112.0	111.1	110.8	109.3	109.5	109.5
宜宾市	Yibin	108.9	110.1	112.0	111.0	110.0	110.3	109.1	110.2	110.3
广安市	Guangan	110.0	111.9	111.3	110.5	111.6	112.0	109.1	110.3	109.8
达州市	Dazhou	107.0	110.0	110.6	110.4	110.9	109.6	109.3	110.5	110.2
雅安市	Yaan	109.3	111.4	110.6	106.4	110.6	108.9	108.3	109.2	108.8
巴中市	Bazhong	109.4	109.2	111.0	109.0	110.9	110.5	107.3	108.1	108.1
资阳市	Ziyang	110.5	113.5	112.0	110.7	110.1	110.0	108.5	108.6	108.1
阿坝藏族羌族自治州	Aba	110.6	111.6	110.4	108.8	105.6	109.4	107.0	100.8	105.4
甘孜藏族自治州	Ganzi	112.0	110.5	110.0	110.9	106.0	106.0	105.8	105.3	106.9
凉山彝族自治州	Liangshan	110.3	110.0	111.3	105.0	106.7	107.6	106.1	106.5	107.9

注:本表按可比价格计算。
a) The indices in this table are calculated at comparable prices.

2-18 各市(州)人均地区生产总值

Per Capita Gross Regional Product by Region

单位：元 (yuan)

市(州)	Region	2010	2011	2012	2013	2014	2015	2016	2017	2018
成都市	Chengdu	41253	49438	57624	63977	70019	74273	76960	86911	94782
自贡市	Zigong	23612	29102	32787	36746	39145	41447	44481	46182	48329
攀枝花市	Panzhihua	43959	53054	60391	65001	70646	75078	82221	92584	94938
泸州市	Luzhou	16698	21339	24317	26848	29655	31714	34497	37020	39230
德阳市	Deyang	25335	31562	35945	39573	43091	45701	49835	55607	62569
绵阳市	Mianyang	20053	25755	29080	31237	33558	35754	38202	43015	47538
广元市	Guangyuan	12313	16225	18672	20443	22117	23263	25072	27653	30105
遂宁市	Suining	14389	17887	20099	22517	24691	27868	30615	34835	37943
内江市	Neijiang	18022	23062	26341	28735	31024	32080	34667	35521	37885
乐山市	Leshan	22490	28339	31942	34863	37125	39973	43110	46130	49397
南充市	Nanchong	13212	16388	18757	21059	22639	23881	25871	28516	31203
眉山市	Meishan	18586	22791	26168	28934	31664	34379	37227	39605	42157
宜宾市	Yibin	19499	24433	27865	30093	32318	34060	36735	40868	44604
广安市	Guangan	15588	20572	23410	25933	28489	31046	33130	36034	38520
达州市	Dazhou	14623	18474	20685	22632	24411	24342	25921	28066	29627
雅安市	Yaan	18881	23153	26157	27317	30052	32523	35335	39172	41985
巴中市	Bazhong	8219	9925	11278	12556	13756	15076	16405	18148	19458
资阳市	Ziyang	16644	22931	27283	30514	33592	35702	37308	40137	42112
阿坝藏族羌族自治州	Aba	14662	18672	22525	25728	27043	28647	30171	31487	32552
甘孜藏族自治州	Ganzi	11660	13882	15753	17809	18096	18423	19596	22097	24446
凉山彝族自治州	Liangshan	17560	22044	24668	26556	28556	28276	29549	30669	31472

注：本表按当年价格计算；人均GDP系按年平均常住人口计算。

a) The data in this table are calculated at current prices and the per capita GDP are calculated based on the annual average date of resident population.

2-19 各市(州)人均地区生产总值指数
Indices of Per Capita Gross Regional Product by Region

上年=100 (preceding year=100)

市(州)	Region	2010	2011	2012	2013	2014	2015	2016	2017	2018
成都市	Chengdu	109.3	110.3	112.5	109.3	108.0	106.6	106.2	107.0	106.6
自贡市	Zigong	118.4	118.3	113.2	110.2	106.9	107.8	107.0	105.8	106.1
攀枝花市	Panzhihua	112.0	113.0	113.3	110.1	109.2	108.2	107.8	107.2	107.5
泸州市	Luzhou	117.6	117.5	114.3	110.9	111.0	110.5	108.8	108.7	107.4
德阳市	Deyang	114.9	116.7	114.4	111.1	109.4	108.4	108.3	108.7	108.6
绵阳市	Mianyang	119.5	119.4	113.0	109.3	107.9	107.5	107.5	108.4	108.4
广元市	Guangyuan	121.5	121.5	112.7	109.3	108.2	106.9	106.7	107.4	107.7
遂宁市	Suining	120.6	120.8	113.7	110.8	109.4	113.0	108.9	109.2	110.4
内江市	Neijiang	120.1	119.2	113.4	110.0	108.7	107.7	107.6	106.9	108.5
乐山市	Leshan	118.3	118.4	114.1	110.1	107.1	109.1	108.0	108.1	108.7
南充市	Nanchong	115.0	115.0	114.0	110.8	107.0	107.2	107.2	108.1	108.6
眉山市	Meishan	116.7	116.0	114.2	110.5	109.7	109.8	108.2	105.8	107.8
宜宾市	Yibin	115.4	115.6	114.2	108.1	107.9	108.1	107.8	108.3	108.7
广安市	Guangan	124.5	123.9	113.8	110.6	109.9	110.2	107.3	108.0	108.4
达州市	Dazhou	115.2	117.8	113.3	109.9	108.0	102.6	106.8	107.1	107.1
雅安市	Yaan	115.9	115.7	113.3	103.3	110.4	108.5	108.2	108.4	108.0
巴中市	Bazhong	112.4	112.8	113.6	110.3	108.8	108.4	108.0	108.3	107.9
资阳市	Ziyang	125.4	125.8	115.5	111.5	110.6	108.8	107.0	107.0	108.4
阿坝藏族羌族自治州	Aba	117.3	114.8	113.5	109.6	104.9	106.8	105.4	103.5	104.1
甘孜藏族自治州	Ganzi	108.2	109.7	111.2	110.2	103.0	103.8	105.5	108.1	108.5
凉山彝族自治州	Liangshan	115.3	113.4	113.4	109.6	107.8	101.8	103.7	103.7	103.1

注:本表按可比价格计算。
a) The indices in this table are calculated at comparable prices.

2-20 支出法地区生产总值
Gross Regional Product by Expenditure Approach

单位：亿元 (100 million yuan)

年份 Year	地区支出总额 Gross Regional Product by Expenditure Approach	最终消费 Final Consumption Expenditure					资本形成总额 Gross Capital Formation		
			居民消费 Household Consumption Expenditure			政府消费 Government Consumption Expenditure		固定资本形成总额 Gross Fixed Capital Formation	存货增加 Changes in Inventories
				农村居民 Rural Household	城镇居民 Urban Household				
1978	184.61	136.56	114.13	84.88	29.25	22.43	47.49	44.96	2.53
1979	205.76	146.94	122.13	91.44	30.69	24.81	58.26	54.89	3.37
1980	229.31	164.26	137.32	105.63	31.69	26.94	64.42	60.36	4.06
1981	242.32	185.47	157.70	122.56	35.14	27.77	56.56	51.70	4.86
1982	275.23	208.05	176.87	139.62	37.25	31.18	67.01	60.34	6.67
1983	311.00	232.95	198.86	155.86	43.00	34.09	77.77	69.25	8.52
1984	358.06	258.88	220.28	169.72	50.55	38.60	98.87	86.93	11.94
1985	421.15	301.07	256.39	185.65	70.74	44.68	119.50	103.58	15.92
1986	458.23	332.31	283.92	200.31	83.61	48.39	125.70	111.56	14.14
1987	530.86	384.39	329.30	232.80	96.50	55.09	146.33	128.31	18.02
1988	659.69	476.46	407.52	287.00	120.52	68.94	182.86	147.51	35.35
1989	744.98	552.17	475.73	332.76	142.97	76.44	192.48	151.19	41.29
1990	890.95	652.05	553.97	381.02	172.96	98.08	238.68	191.31	47.37
1991	1016.31	725.83	604.40	413.68	190.72	121.43	290.22	233.22	57.00
1992	1177.27	802.66	665.99	433.16	232.83	136.67	374.14	300.06	74.08
1993	1486.08	941.63	770.40	485.28	285.12	171.23	544.03	457.17	86.86
1994	2001.41	1320.35	1103.04	686.38	416.66	217.31	680.66	580.93	99.73
1995	2443.21	1593.58	1321.95	783.70	538.25	271.63	848.81	745.56	103.25
1996	2871.65	1856.98	1520.28	867.34	652.94	336.70	1013.46	881.35	132.11
1997	3241.47	2066.71	1670.50	937.75	732.75	396.21	1173.14	1015.48	157.66
1998	3474.09	2240.54	1814.92	950.51	864.41	425.62	1264.17	1175.04	89.13
1999	3649.12	2359.95	1886.74	953.48	933.26	473.21	1336.84	1218.36	118.48
2000	3928.20	2545.13	2021.66	955.84	1065.82	523.47	1521.43	1400.69	120.74
2001	4293.49	2778.76	2161.96	954.93	1207.03	616.80	1693.10	1570.89	122.21
2002	4725.01	3014.27	2337.76	995.86	1341.90	676.51	1925.31	1801.06	124.25
2003	5333.09	3330.47	2579.30	1069.96	1509.34	751.17	2248.78	2145.07	103.71
2004	6379.63	3805.64	2954.34	1197.16	1757.18	851.30	2728.10	2587.14	140.96
2005	7385.10	4267.69	3366.47	1328.28	2038.19	901.22	3326.22	3179.92	146.30
2006	8690.24	4824.88	3686.82	1397.96	2288.86	1138.06	4203.05	4040.03	163.02
2007	10562.39	5671.56	4285.21	1563.20	2722.01	1386.35	5242.55	5060.57	181.98
2008	12601.23	6540.17	4937.87	1711.33	3226.54	1602.30	6574.63	6352.86	221.77
2009	14151.28	7212.50	5601.30	1967.10	3634.20	1611.20	7720.13	7464.20	255.93
2010	17185.48	8609.53	6638.53	2333.15	4305.38	1971.00	9219.92	8911.05	308.87
2011	21026.68	10424.40	7967.50	2791.80	5175.70	2456.90	11067.68	10691.30	376.38
2012	23872.80	11926.70	9095.30	3255.70	5839.60	2831.40	12496.00	12096.20	399.80
2013	26392.07	13289.19	10152.98	3617.55	6535.43	3136.21	13562.06	13147.11	414.95
2014	28536.66	14529.94	11174.20	4018.10	7156.10	3355.74	14426.45	13990.55	435.90
2015	30053.10	15774.96	12073.44	4348.24	7725.20	3701.52	14806.21	14415.31	390.90
2016	32934.54	17237.92	13183.40	4707.98	8475.42	4054.52	16165.27	15800.46	364.81
2017	36980.22	19365.69	14841.19	5323.09	9518.10	4524.50	18021.18	17689.34	331.84
2018	40678.13	21481.09	16566.20	5897.92	10668.28	4914.89	19528.52	19212.29	316.23

注：本表按当年价格计算。
a) Data in this table are calculated at current prices.

2-21 支出法地区生产总值指数
Indices of Gross Regional Product by Expenditure Approach

(上年=100) (preceding year=100)

年份 Year	地区支出总额 Gross Regional Product by Expenditure Approach	最终消费 Final Consumption Expenditure	居民消费 Household Consumption Expenditure	农村居民 Rural Household	城镇居民 Urban Household	政府消费 Government Consumption Expenditure	资本形成总额 Gross Capital Formation	固定资本形成总额 Gross Fixed Capital Formation	存货增加 Changes in Inventories
1979	110.1	106.7	106.1	106.9	103.9	110.1	120.7	120.1	132.0
1980	109.5	109.7	110.0	112.1	103.5	108.6	108.9	108.2	119.4
1981	104.1	113.0	113.1	114.3	108.9	101.2	86.1	84.0	117.6
1982	110.9	109.4	109.4	108.2	114.0	109.0	116.3	114.6	134.0
1983	111.0	111.4	111.8	113.7	105.3	109.3	109.6	107.7	126.9
1984	112.2	107.5	107.0	105.2	113.7	110.8	127.3	126.0	137.0
1985	111.9	109.6	109.7	102.4	134.7	108.9	117.8	116.5	127.1
1986	105.5	106.8	106.8	104.4	112.8	107.2	102.7	105.3	85.9
1987	108.7	110.0	110.2	111.3	107.6	108.6	105.5	103.4	121.8
1988	107.5	106.1	106.1	106.1	106.2	106.0	111.2	102.3	171.3
1989	103.2	104.5	104.3	104.0	105.1	105.4	99.8	98.0	106.9
1990	109.1	102.6	101.5	99.2	107.2	109.1	126.9	131.7	109.1
1991	109.1	106.9	104.8	104.3	105.8	119.3	115.0	115.2	114.3
1992	112.6	108.0	107.7	102.6	118.9	109.1	124.2	123.7	126.6
1993	113.1	103.4	100.8	97.3	107.4	116.0	134.6	143.2	100.4
1994	111.3	116.4	120.1	121.1	118.4	100.4	102.8	103.7	97.8
1995	110.7	112.1	113.6	106.2	126.3	104.7	108.0	109.4	99.6
1996	110.6	110.4	108.7	105.6	113.2	119.4	111.0	110.2	116.6
1997	110.5	111.1	108.0	103.8	113.7	126.9	109.3	108.0	117.3
1998	109.7	109.6	110.0	106.8	114.0	107.7	112.9	121.6	62.9
1999	106.6	105.4	104.4	100.3	109.1	109.7	110.6	109.4	123.8
2000	108.5	109.9	109.5	102.3	117.2	111.8	112.4	113.4	102.9
2001	109.0	109.3	107.2	101.1	112.7	117.1	110.2	111.0	100.6
2002	110.3	109.4	109.2	104.7	112.9	110.2	112.8	113.5	103.3
2003	111.3	110.0	110.2	107.2	112.5	109.2	113.8	116.1	81.8
2004	112.7	107.4	106.5	103.9	108.4	110.5	115.3	114.4	133.0
2005	112.6	110.4	111.8	109.0	113.7	105.8	117.1	118.0	102.0
2006	113.5	108.2	107.0	102.8	109.7	112.4	120.2	120.8	108.8
2007	114.5	110.8	109.6	105.7	112.1	114.6	118.0	118.5	105.5
2008	111.0	107.8	107.0	101.9	109.9	110.2	114.5	114.8	106.6
2009	114.5	113.8	112.5	113.6	112.0	117.5	121.4	121.7	110.7
2010	115.1	114.0	113.0	113.3	112.9	116.7	112.8	112.8	114.3
2011	115.0	114.5	113.5	113.2	113.6	118.0	112.7	112.7	114.5
2012	112.6	112.9	112.4	112.2	112.6	114.2	112.0	112.1	106.5
2013	110.0	109.7	109.1	109.0	109.2	111.3	109.2	109.3	104.4
2014	108.5	108.3	108.8	109.0	108.7	106.7	107.9	107.9	106.5
2015	107.9	108.1	108.6	108.8	108.5	106.6	107.3	107.6	99.3
2016	107.8	107.8	108.1	107.9	108.2	106.7	107.2	107.6	95.3
2017	108.1	108.8	109.3	108.2	109.9	107.2	106.7	107.1	88.5
2018	108.0	108.6	109.1	108.1	109.7	106.9	106.6	106.8	94.5

注：本表按可比价格计算。
a) The indices in this table are calculated at comparable prices.

2-22 支出法地区生产总值指数
Indices of Gross Regional Product by Expenditure Approach

(1978年=100) (year of 1978=100)

年份 Year	地区支出总额 Gross Regional Product by Expenditure Approach	最终消费 Final Consumption Expenditure	居民消费 Household Consumption Expenditure	农村居民 Rural Household	城镇居民 Urban Household	政府消费 Government Consumption Expenditure	资本形成总额 Gross Capital Formation	固定资本形成总额 Gross Fixed Capital Formation	存货增加 Changes in Inventories
1978	100.0	100.0	100.0	100.0	100.0	100.0	100.0	100.0	100.0
1979	110.1	106.7	106.1	106.9	103.9	110.1	120.7	120.1	132.0
1980	120.6	117.0	116.7	119.8	107.5	119.6	131.4	129.9	157.6
1981	125.5	132.3	134.6	137.0	117.1	121.0	113.2	109.2	185.3
1982	139.2	144.7	147.2	148.2	133.5	131.9	131.6	125.1	248.4
1983	154.5	161.2	164.6	168.5	140.6	144.2	144.3	134.7	315.2
1984	173.3	173.3	176.1	177.3	159.8	159.7	183.6	169.8	431.8
1985	194.0	189.9	193.2	181.5	215.3	173.9	216.3	197.8	548.8
1986	204.6	202.8	206.3	189.5	242.9	186.5	222.2	208.2	471.4
1987	222.4	223.1	227.4	210.9	261.3	202.5	234.4	215.3	574.2
1988	239.1	236.7	241.2	223.8	277.5	214.7	260.6	220.3	983.6
1989	246.8	247.4	251.6	232.7	291.7	226.2	260.1	215.9	1051.5
1990	269.2	253.8	255.4	230.9	312.7	246.8	330.1	284.3	1147.1
1991	293.7	271.3	267.6	240.8	330.8	294.5	379.6	327.5	1311.2
1992	330.7	293.0	288.3	247.1	393.3	321.3	471.5	405.1	1660.0
1993	374.1	303.0	290.6	240.4	422.4	372.7	634.6	580.2	1666.6
1994	416.3	352.7	349.0	291.1	500.2	374.2	652.3	601.6	1629.9
1995	460.9	395.4	396.4	309.2	631.7	391.8	704.5	658.2	1623.4
1996	509.7	436.5	430.9	326.5	715.1	467.8	782.0	725.3	1892.9
1997	563.3	484.9	465.4	338.9	813.1	593.6	854.8	783.3	2220.4
1998	617.9	531.5	511.9	361.9	926.9	639.3	965.0	952.5	1396.6
1999	658.7	560.2	534.5	363.0	1011.2	701.3	1067.3	1042.1	1729.0
2000	714.7	615.6	585.2	371.4	1185.2	784.0	1199.7	1181.7	1779.2
2001	779.0	672.9	627.4	375.5	1335.7	918.1	1322.0	1311.7	1789.8
2002	859.2	736.1	685.1	393.1	1508.0	1011.8	1491.3	1488.8	1848.9
2003	956.3	809.8	755.0	421.4	1696.5	1104.8	1697.1	1728.5	1512.4
2004	1077.8	869.7	804.0	437.8	1839.0	1220.9	1956.7	1977.4	2011.5
2005	1213.6	960.1	898.9	477.3	2090.9	1291.7	2291.3	2333.3	2051.7
2006	1377.4	1038.9	961.8	490.6	2293.8	1451.8	2754.1	2818.6	2232.3
2007	1577.1	1151.1	1054.2	518.6	2571.3	1663.8	3249.9	3340.1	2355.0
2008	1750.6	1240.8	1128.0	528.4	2825.9	1833.5	3721.1	3834.4	2510.5
2009	2004.4	1412.1	1269.0	600.3	3165.0	2154.4	4517.4	4666.5	2779.1
2010	2307.1	1609.8	1433.9	680.1	3573.2	2514.2	5095.7	5263.8	3176.5
2011	2653.2	1843.2	1627.5	769.9	4059.2	2966.7	5742.8	5932.3	3637.1
2012	2987.5	2081.0	1829.3	863.8	4570.7	3388.0	6432.0	6650.1	3873.5
2013	3286.2	2282.8	1995.8	941.6	4991.2	3770.8	7023.7	7268.6	4043.9
2014	3565.6	2472.3	2171.4	1026.3	5425.4	4023.5	7578.6	7842.8	4306.8
2015	3847.2	2672.5	2358.1	1116.7	5886.5	4289.0	8131.8	8438.8	4276.7
2016	4147.3	2881.0	2549.2	1204.9	6369.2	4576.4	8717.3	9080.2	4075.6
2017	4483.3	3134.5	2786.2	1303.7	6999.8	4905.9	9301.3	9724.9	3606.9
2018	4841.9	3404.1	3039.7	1409.3	7678.8	5244.4	9915.2	10386.2	3408.5

注：本表按可比价格计算。

a) The indices in this table are calculated at comparable prices.

2-23 居民消费水平
Annual Per Capita Consumption of Residents

单位:元/人 (yuan/person)

年份 Year	居民人均消费水平 Annual per Capita Consumption of Residents	农村居民消费水平 Annual per Capita Consumption of Rural Residents	城镇居民消费水平 Annual per Capita Consumption of Urban Residents	城镇与农村对比(以农村居民消费=1) Urban / Rural Consumption Ratio (Rural Residents =1)	平均人口(百人) Average Population (100 Persons)	农村居民 Rural Residents	城镇居民 Urban Residents
1978	161	135	373	1：2.76	707190	628770	78420
1979	172	145	377	1：2.60	712050	630650	81400
1980	192	167	382	1：2.29	715480	632520	82960
1981	219	193	416	1：2.15	718520	634105	84415
1982	244	219	427	1：1.95	725800	638580	87220
1983	272	243	480	1：1.98	731865	642245	89620
1984	300	264	543	1：2.05	735045	641870	93175
1985	347	290	714	1：2.46	739165	640050	99115
1986	380	311	817	1：2.63	746560	644200	102360
1987	435	357	934	1：2.62	756255	652920	103335
1988	532	434	1141	1：2.63	766480	660815	105665
1989	613	498	1326	1：2.66	775980	668170	107810
1990	706	564	1583	1：2.81	784517	675285	109232
1991	763	609	1684	1：2.76	792020	678761	113259
1992	836	642	1897	1：2.95	797000	674262	122738
1993	961	725	2156	1：2.97	801475	669232	132243
1994	1367	1027	3003	1：2.92	806805	668035	138770
1995	1646	1192	3703	1：3.11	802995	657653	145342
1996	1880	1327	4204	1：3.17	808833	653537	155296
1997	2078	1460	4534	1：3.11	804000	642396	161604
1998	2243	1512	4791	1：3.17	809000	628593	180407
1999	2348	1551	4941	1：3.19	803713	614840	188873
2000	2550	1614	5315	1：3.29	792660	592117	200543
2001	2707	1631	5661	1：3.47	798610	585381	213229
2002	2914	1729	5932	1：3.43	802145	575940	226205
2003	3203	1890	6312	1：3.34	805185	566045	239140
2004	3656	2153	6970	1：3.24	808035	555928	252107
2005	4130	2432	7577	1：3.12	815110	546124	268986
2006	4501	2572	8305	1：3.23	819050	543453	275597
2007	5259	2949	9559	1：3.24	814800	530041	284759
2008	6072	3362	10608	1：3.16	813250	509090	304160
2009	6863	3891	11701	1：3.01	816150	505550	310600
2010	8182	4748	13457	1：2.83	811341	491401	319940
2011	9903	5882	15687	1：2.67	804590	474664	329926
2012	11280	7147	16649	1：2.33	806310	455565	350745
2013	12548	8114	17988	1：2.22	809160	445847	363313
2014	13755	9092	19318	1：2.12	812360	441915	370445
2015	14774	10039	20114	1：2.00	817210	433140	384070
2016	16013	11094	21246	1：1.92	823300	424390	398910
2017	17920	12856	22983	1：1.79	828200	414065	414135
2018	19861	14821	24460	1：1.65	834100	397950	436150

注：居民消费水平按当年价格计算。

a) Annual per capita consumption of residents in this table are calculated at current prices.

2-24 居民消费水平指数

Indices of Annual Per Capita Consumption of Residents

年份 Year	上年=100 preceding year = 100			1978年=100 (year of 1978=100)		
	居民人均 消费水平 Annual Per Capita Consumption of Residents	农村居民 消费水平 Annual Per Capita Consumption of Rural Residents	城镇居民 消费水平 Annual Per Capita Consumption of Urban Residents	居民人均 消费水平 Annual Per Capita Consumption of Residents	农村居民 消费水平 Annual Per Capita Consumption of Rural Residents	城镇居民 消费水平 Annual Per Capita Consumption of Urban Residents
1978				100.0	100.0	100.0
1979	105.4	106.5	100.1	105.4	106.5	100.1
1980	109.4	111.8	101.6	115.3	119.1	101.7
1981	114.8	114.1	107.0	132.4	135.9	108.8
1982	108.3	107.4	110.3	143.4	145.9	120.0
1983	110.9	113.1	102.5	159.0	165.0	123.0
1984	106.5	105.2	109.4	169.3	173.6	134.6
1985	109.1	102.7	126.6	184.7	178.3	170.4
1986	105.7	103.7	109.2	195.3	184.9	186.1
1987	108.8	109.8	106.6	212.4	203.0	198.4
1988	104.7	104.8	103.8	222.4	212.8	205.9
1989	103.1	102.9	103.0	229.3	218.9	212.1
1990	100.4	98.1	105.8	230.2	214.8	224.4
1991	103.8	103.8	102.0	239.0	222.9	228.9
1992	107.1	103.3	109.7	256.0	230.3	251.1
1993	100.2	98.0	99.7	256.5	225.7	250.3
1994	119.3	121.3	112.9	306.0	273.7	282.6
1995	114.1	107.9	120.6	349.1	295.4	340.8
1996	107.9	106.3	106.0	376.7	314.0	361.3
1997	108.7	105.6	109.3	409.5	331.6	394.8
1998	109.3	109.2	102.1	447.5	362.1	403.1
1999	105.0	102.5	104.2	469.9	371.1	420.1
2000	111.0	106.2	110.4	521.6	394.1	463.8
2001	106.4	102.3	106.0	555.0	403.2	491.6
2002	108.7	106.4	106.4	603.3	429.0	523.0
2003	109.8	109.1	106.4	662.4	468.0	556.5
2004	106.1	105.8	102.8	702.8	495.2	572.1
2005	110.8	110.9	106.5	778.7	549.1	609.3
2006	106.5	103.3	107.1	829.3	567.3	652.6
2007	110.2	108.4	108.5	913.9	614.9	708.0
2008	107.1	106.1	102.9	978.8	652.4	728.6
2009	112.1	114.4	109.7	1097.2	746.4	799.2
2010	113.7	116.5	109.6	1247.5	869.5	875.9
2011	114.4	117.2	110.2	1427.2	1019.1	965.3
2012	112.2	116.9	105.9	1601.3	1191.3	1022.2
2013	108.7	111.4	105.4	1740.6	1327.1	1077.4
2014	108.4	110.0	106.6	1886.8	1459.8	1148.6
2015	108.0	111.0	104.7	2037.8	1620.4	1202.5
2016	108.4	110.5	105.6	2209.0	1790.6	1269.9
2017	111.9	115.9	108.2	2471.8	2075.3	1374.0
2018	110.8	115.3	106.4	2738.8	2392.8	1461.9

注：本表按可比价格计算。

a) The data in this table are calculated at comparable prices.

2-25 各市(州)民营经济增加值(2018年)
Civillian-owned Value Added by Region(2018)

单位：亿元 (100 million yuan)

市(州)	Region	民营经济增加值 Civilian-owned Value Added	第一产业 Primary Industry	第二产业 Secondary Industry	第三产业 Tertiary Industry	人均民营经济增加值(元) Per Capita Civilian-owned Value Added (yuan)
成都市	Chengdu	7464.79	108.97	3759.02	3596.80	46115
自贡市	Zigong	800.50	47.03	408.30	345.17	27502
攀枝花市	Panzhihua	584.86	14.70	366.01	204.15	47315
泸州市	Luzhou	993.25	48.63	581.42	363.20	22989
德阳市	Deyang	1243.08	73.71	643.01	526.36	35132
绵阳市	Mianyang	1352.17	85.69	674.80	591.68	27901
广元市	Guangyuan	449.26	40.45	255.75	153.06	16867
遂宁市	Suining	763.19	62.06	450.97	250.16	23709
内江市	Neijiang	836.84	81.98	405.05	349.81	22457
乐山市	Leshan	875.44	80.91	505.76	288.77	26775
南充市	Nanchong	1220.69	198.89	655.96	365.84	18987
眉山市	Meishan	692.98	77.26	358.62	257.10	23259
宜宾市	Yibin	1169.79	95.21	651.18	423.40	25749
广安市	Guangan	721.38	48.04	361.12	312.22	22226
达州市	Dazhou	1046.54	87.77	520.23	438.54	18345
雅安市	Yaan	388.18	17.39	214.01	156.78	25224
巴中市	Bazhong	385.79	38.96	201.75	145.08	11622
资阳市	Ziyang	598.29	73.70	393.38	131.21	23624
阿坝藏族羌族自治州	Aba	139.38	27.92	79.26	32.20	14795
甘孜藏族自治州	Ganzi	136.25	43.96	55.19	37.10	11438
凉山彝族自治州	Liangshan	779.12	102.19	377.25	299.68	15993

注：本表按当年价格计算；人均民营经济增加值年平均人口数按常住人口计算。
a) The data in this table are calculated at current prices. Per capita civilian value added are calculated on the annual average resident population.

2-26 各市(州)民营经济增加值指数(2018年)
Indices of Civillian-owned Value Added by Region(2018)

上年=100 (preceding year=100)

市(州)	Region	民营经济增加值 Civilian-owned Value Added	第一产业 Primary Industry	第二产业 Secondary Industry	第三产业 Tertiary Industry	人均民营经济增加值 Per Capita Civilian-owned Value Added
成都市	Chengdu	108.1	101.1	107.4	109.2	106.8
自贡市	Zigong	108.8	103.6	108.3	110.2	106.2
攀枝花市	Panzhihua	107.6	104.1	107.3	108.6	107.6
泸州市	Luzhou	107.7	101.8	108.1	107.9	107.5
德阳市	Deyang	109.2	101.9	109.7	110.2	108.8
绵阳市	Mianyang	109.1	103.6	109.2	109.9	108.6
广元市	Guangyuan	108.6	103.9	109.4	108.4	107.9
遂宁市	Suining	108.9	102.5	107.5	113.2	110.5
内江市	Neijiang	107.9	103.8	107.8	109.2	108.6
乐山市	Leshan	108.8	103.9	108.7	110.5	108.7
南充市	Nanchong	109.1	104.8	107.7	114.2	108.8
眉山市	Meishan	107.6	103.8	107.6	108.9	107.9
宜宾市	Yibin	109.5	102.5	110.4	109.8	108.9
广安市	Guangan	108.1	105.0	106.6	110.7	108.5
达州市	Dazhou	108.4	101.8	108.2	110.1	107.3
雅安市	Yaan	108.2	94.1	108.4	109.8	108.2
巴中市	Bazhong	108.1	103.6	109.1	108.1	108.0
资阳市	Ziyang	107.9	103.7	108.6	108.1	108.5
阿坝藏族羌族自治州	Aba	104.8	103.3	105.1	105.2	104.3
甘孜藏族自治州	Ganzi	109.4	103.4	117.3	106.5	108.7
凉山彝族自治州	Liangshan	106.5	103.8	105.8	108.4	105.6

注：本表按可比价格计算。
a) The data in this table are calculated at comparable prices.

主要统计指标解释

国内生产总值(GDP) 指一个国家（或地区）所有常住单位在一定时期内生产活动的最终成果。国内生产总值有三种表现形态，即价值形态、收入形态和产品形态。从价值形态看，它是所有常住单位在一定时期内生产的全部货物和服务价值与同期投入的全部非固定资产货物和服务价值的差额，即所有常住单位的增加值之和；从收入形态看，它是所有常住单位在一定时期内创造的各项收入之和，包括劳动者报酬、生产税净额、固定资产折旧和营业盈余；从产品形态看，它是所有常住单位在一定时期内最终使用的货物和服务价值与货物和服务净出口价值之和。在实际核算中，国内生产总值有三种计算方法，即生产法、收入法和支出法。三种方法分别从不同的方面反映国内生产总值及其构成。

对于一个地区来说，称为地区生产总值或地区 GDP。

三次产业 三次产业的划分是世界上较为常用的产业结构分类，但各国的划分不尽一致。根据《国民经济行业分类》（GB/T 4754—2017），我国的三次产业划分是:

第一产业是指农、林、牧、渔业（不包括农、林、牧、渔服务业）。

第二产业是指采矿业（不含开采辅助活动），制造业（不含金属制品、机械和设备修理业），电力、热力、燃气及水生产和供应业，建筑业。

第三产业即服务业，是指除第一产业、第二产业以外的其他行业。

支出法国内生产总值 是从最终使用的角度反映一个国家(或地区)一定时期内生产活动最终成果的一种方法，包括最终消费支出、资本形成总额及货物和服务净出口三部分。计算公式为:

支出法国内生产总值=最终消费支出+资本形成总额+货物和服务净出口

最终消费支出 指常住单位为满足物质、文化和精神生活的需要，从本国经济领土和国外购买的货物和服务的支出。它不包括非常住单位在本国经济领土内的消费支出。最终消费支出分为居民消费支出和政府消费支出。

居民消费支出 指常住住户在一定时期内对于货物和服务的全部最终消费支出。居民消费支出除了直接以货币形式购买的货物和服务的消费支出之外，还包括以其他方式获得的货物和服务的消费支出，后者称为虚拟消费支出。居民虚拟消费支出主要包括: 单位以实物报酬及实物转移的形式提供给劳动者的货物和服务；住户生产用于自身消费的货物（如自产自用的农产品），以及纳入生产核算范围并用于自身消费的服务（如住户的自有住房服务）；银行和保险机构提供的间接计算的金融服务。

政府消费支出 指政府部门为全社会提供的公共服务的消费支出和免费或以较低的价格向居民住户提供的货物和服务的净支出，前者等于政府服务的产出价值减去政府单位所获得的经营收入的价值，后者等于政府部门免费或以较低价格向居民住户提供的货物和服务的市场价值减去向住户收取的价值。

资本形成总额 指常住单位在一定时期内获得减去处置的固定资产和存货的净额，包括固定资本形成总额和存货变动两部分。

固定资本形成总额 指常住单位在一定时期内获得的固定资产减处置的固定资产的价值总额。固定资产是通过生产活动生产出来的，且其使用年限在一年以上、单位价值在规定标准以上的资产，不包括自然资产、耐用消费品、小型工器具。固定资本形成总额包括住宅、其他建筑和构筑物、机器和设备、培育性生物资源、知识产权产品（研发支出、矿藏的勘探、计算机软件）的价值获得减处置。

存货变动 指常住单位在一定时期内存货实物量变动的市场价值，即期末价值减期初价值的差额，再扣除当期由于价格变动而产生的持有收益。存货变动可以是正值，也可以是负值，正值表示存货上升，负值表示存货下降。存货包括生产单位购进的原材料、燃料和储备物资等存货，以及生产单位生产的产成品、在制品和半成品等存货。

公有制经济 指资产归国家或公民集体所有的经济成分，包括国有经济和集体经济。

非公有制经济 指资产归我国内地公民私人所有或归港澳台商、外商所有的经济成分，包括民营经济、港澳台经济和外商经济。

Explanatory Notes on Main Statistical Indicators

Gross Domestic Product (GDP) refers to the final products produced by all resident units in a country during a certain period of time. Gross domestic product is expressed in three different perspectives, namely value, income, and products respectively. GDP in its value perspective refers to the balance of total value of all goods and services produced by all resident units during a certain period of time, minus the total value of input of goods and services of the nature of non-fixed assets; in other words, it is the sum of the value-added of all resident units. GDP from the perspective of income refers to the sum of all kinds of revenue, including Compensation of Employees, Net Taxes on Production, Depreciation of Fixed Assets, and Operating Surplus. GDP from the perspective of products refers to the value of all goods and services for final demand by all resident units plus the net exports of goods and services during a given period of time. In the practice of national accounting, gross domestic product is calculated from three approaches, namely production approach, income approach and expenditure approach, which reflect gross domestic product and its composition from different angles.

For a region, it is called as Gross Regional Product(GRP) or regional GDP.

Three Strata of Industry Classification of economic activities into three strata of industry is a common practice in the world, although the grouping varies to some extent from country to country. In China, according to Industrial classification for National Economic Activities (GB/T 4754—2017), economic activities are categorized into the following three strata of industry:

Primary industry refers to agriculture, forestry, animal husbandry and fishery industries (not including services in support of agriculture, forestry, animal husbandry and fishery industries).

Secondary industry refers to mining and quarrying(not including support activities for mining), manufacturing(not including repair service of metal products, machinery and equipment), production and supply of electricity, heat, gas and water, and construction.

Tertiary industry refers to all other economic activities not included in the primary or secondary industries.

GDP by Expenditure Approach refers to the method of measuring the final results of production activities of a country (region) during a given period from the perspective of final uses. It includes final consumption expenditure, gross capital formation and net export of goods and services. The formula for computation is.:

GDP by expenditure approach = final consumption expenditure + gross capital formation + net export of goods and services

Final Consumption Expenditure refers to the total expenditure of resident units for purchases of goods and services from both the domestic economic territory and abroad to meet the needs of material, cultural and spiritual life. It does not include the expenditure of non-resident units on consumption in the economic territory of the country. The final consumption expenditure is broken down into household consumption expenditure and government consumption expenditure.

Household Consumption Expenditure refers to the total expenditure of resident households on the final consumption of goods and services. In addition to the consumption of goods and services bought by the households directly with money, the household consumption expenditure also includes expenditure on goods and services obtained by the households in other ways, i.e. the latter so-called imputed consumption expenditure, which mainly includes: (a) the goods and services provided to households by employers in the form of payment in kind and transfer in kind; (b) goods and services produced and consumed by the households themselves (such as self produced agricultural products); (c) financial intermediate services provided by banking and insurance institutions.

Government Consumption Expenditure refers to the consumption expenditure spent for the provision of public services provided by the government to the whole country and the net expenditure on the goods and services provided by the government to households free of charge or at reduced prices. The former equals to the output value of the government services minus the value of operating income obtained by the government departments. The latter equals to the market value of the goods and services provided by the government free of charge or at reduced prices to the households minus the value received by the government from the households.

Gross Capital Formation refers to the fixed assets acquired minus disposals and the net value of inventory, thus including gross fixed capital formation and changes in inventories.

Gross Fixed Capital Formation refers to the value of acquisitions less those disposals of fixed assets during a given period. Fixed assets are the assets produced through production activities with unit value above a specified amount and which could be used for over one year. Natural assets, consumer durables, small instruments are not included. Gross Fixed Capital Formation includes the value of housing, other buildings and structure, equipment and machinery, breeding biological resources, intellectual property right product (expenditure for R&D, the prospecting of minerals and the acquisition of computer software) minus the disposal of them.

Changes in Inventories refers to the market value of

the change in the physical volume of inventory of resident units during a given period, i.e. the difference between the values at the beginning and at the end of the period minus the gains due to the change in prices. The changes in inventories can have a positive or a negative value. A positive value indicates an increase in inventory while a negative value indicates a decrease in inventory. The inventory includes raw materials, fuels and reserve materials purchased by the production units as well as the inventory of finished products, semi-finished products and work-in-progress.

Public Economy refers to the economic components owned by the national or citizen of the collective economic components, including the state-owned economy and collective economy.

Non-public refers to the economic components owned by private citizens in the Mainland of China and naturalized by Hong Kong, Macao and Taiwan entrepreneurs, including the Self-employed Individuals, Civilian-owend, Hong Kong, Macao and Taiwan Economy and foreign economy.

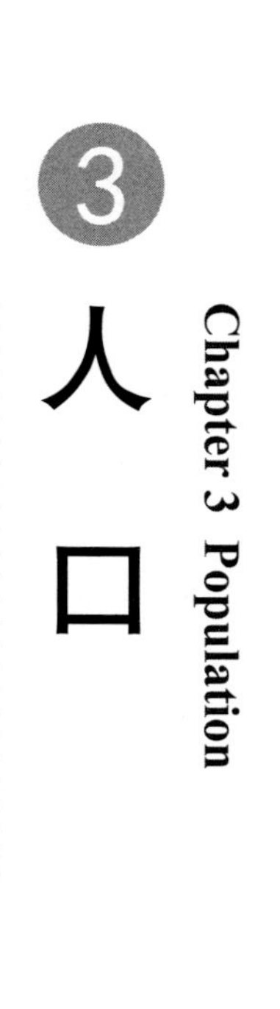

3 人口

Chapter 3 Population

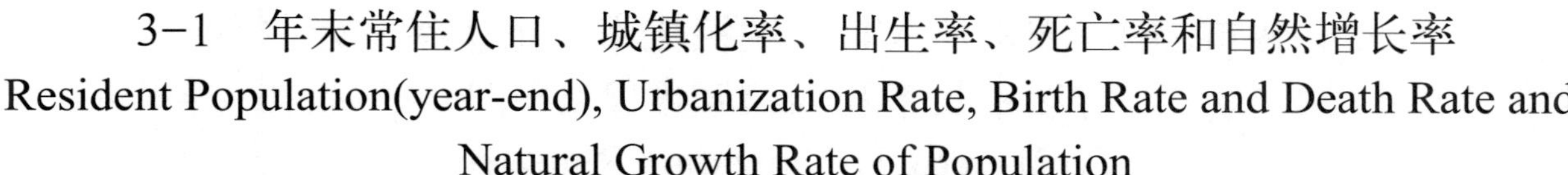

3-1 年末常住人口、城镇化率、出生率、死亡率和自然增长率
Resident Population(year-end), Urbanization Rate, Birth Rate and Death Rate and Natural Growth Rate of Population

年份 Year	年末常住人口(万人) Resident Population (year-end) (10 000 persons)	城镇化率 (%) Urbanization Rate (%)	出生率 (‰) Birth Rate (‰)	死亡率 (‰) Death Rate (‰)	自然增长率 (‰) Natural Growth Rate (‰)
1952			41.0	18.2	22.8
1957			29.2	12.1	17.1
1962			28.0	14.6	13.4
1965			42.4	11.4	31.0
1970			38.7	9.2	29.5
1975			31.2	8.9	22.3
1978			15.1	7.0	8.1
1980			13.0	6.8	6.2
1985			15.4	7.2	8.2
1990			19.1	7.7	11.4
1991			15.8	7.3	8.5
1992			16.3	7.0	9.3
1993			16.8	7.2	9.6
1994			16.9	7.0	9.9
1995			17.1	7.2	9.9
1996			16.6	7.3	9.3
1997			15.7	7.0	8.7
1998			14.6	7.1	7.5
1999			13.8	7.0	6.8
2000	8234.8	26.7	12.1	7.0	5.1
2001	8143.0	27.2	11.2	6.8	4.4
2002	8110.0	28.2	10.4	6.5	3.9
2003	8176.0	30.1	9.2	6.1	3.1
2004	8090.0	31.1	9.1	6.3	2.8
2005	8212.0	33.0	9.70	6.80	2.90
2006	8169.0	34.3	9.14	6.28	2.86
2007	8127.0	35.6	9.21	6.29	2.92
2008	8138.0	37.4	9.54	7.15	2.39
2009	8185.0	38.7	9.15	6.43	2.72
2010	8041.8	40.2	8.93	6.62	2.31
2011	8050.0	41.8	9.79	6.81	2.98
2012	8076.2	43.5	9.89	6.92	2.97
2013	8107.0	44.9	9.90	6.90	3.00
2014	8140.2	46.3	10.22	7.02	3.20
2015	8204.0	47.7	10.30	6.94	3.36
2016	8262.0	49.2	10.48	6.99	3.49
2017	8302.0	50.8	11.26	7.03	4.23
2018	8341.0	52.3	11.05	7.01	4.04

注：本表中出生率、死亡率和自然增长率在1981年及以前均根据公安年报计算，1982年以后按人口变动抽样调查计算。

a) Data of birth rate, death rate and natural growth rate in this table before 1981 were taken from the annual reports of the Bureau of Public Security. Since 1982, the data of province have been estimated on the basis of the annual National Sample Surveys on Population Changes, the data of population by county were taken from the annual reports of the Bureau of Public Security.

3-2 各市(州)年末常住人口、城镇化率、出生率、死亡率、自然增长率和人口密度(2018年)

Resident Population(year-end), Urbanization Rate, Birth rate, Death rate, Natural Growth Rate and Population Density by Region(2018)

市(州)	Region	年末常住人口(万人) Resident Population (year-end) (10 000 persons)	城镇化率(%) Urbanization Rate (%)	出生率(‰) Birth Rate (‰)	死亡率(‰) Death Rate (‰)	自然增长率(‰) Natural Growth Rate (‰)	人口密度(人/平方公里) Population Density (person/sq.km)
全 省	**Sichuan**	**8341.0**	**52.29**	**11.05**	**7.01**	**4.04**	**172**
成都市	Chengdu	1633.0	73.12	11.46	5.96	5.50	1139
自贡市	Zigong	292.0	52.61	9.78	7.23	2.55	667
攀枝花市	Panzhihua	123.6	66.59	9.72	6.00	3.72	167
泸州市	Luzhou	432.4	50.46	9.95	6.33	3.63	353
德阳市	Deyang	354.5	52.35	9.46	7.46	2.00	600
绵阳市	Mianyang	485.7	52.53	9.74	8.11	1.63	240
广元市	Guangyuan	266.7	45.63	9.31	6.27	3.03	164
遂宁市	Suining	320.2	50.02	9.78	6.34	3.44	602
内江市	Neijiang	369.9	49.10	9.66	8.92	0.73	687
乐山市	Leshan	326.7	51.83	9.92	7.47	2.45	257
南充市	Nanchong	644.0	48.14	9.11	5.30	3.81	516
眉山市	Meishan	298.4	46.32	10.14	7.72	2.41	418
宜宾市	Yibin	455.6	49.64	11.22	6.20	5.02	343
广安市	Guangan	324.1	41.86	9.41	6.03	3.38	511
达州市	Dazhou	572.0	45.52	9.52	5.22	4.30	345
雅安市	Yaan	154.0	46.85	9.89	8.01	1.88	102
巴中市	Bazhong	332.2	41.85	9.49	5.72	3.77	270
资阳市	Ziyang	251.2	42.71	9.11	8.61	0.50	437
阿坝藏族羌族自治州	Aba	94.4	40.00	9.80	4.16	5.64	11
甘孜藏族自治州	Ganzi	119.6	31.66	9.77	3.40	6.37	8
凉山彝族自治州	Liangshan	490.8	35.71	11.95	5.51	6.44	81

3-3 各市(州)年末常住人口数
Resident Population(year-end) by Region

单位：万人 (10 000 persons)

市(州)	Region	2010	2011	2012	2013	2014	2015	2016	2017	2018
全 省	**Sichuan**	**8041.8**	**8050.0**	**8076.2**	**8107.0**	**8140.2**	**8204.0**	**8262.0**	**8302.0**	**8341.0**
成都市	Chengdu	1404.8	1407.1	1417.8	1429.8	1442.8	1465.8	1591.8	1604.5	1633.0
自贡市	Zigong	267.9	268.4	271.3	273.8	274.6	277.0	278.1	290.1	292.0
攀枝花市	Panzhihua	121.4	122.0	123.1	123.3	123.2	123.3	123.6	123.6	123.6
泸州市	Luzhou	421.8	422.5	425.0	424.6	425.0	428.5	430.6	431.7	432.4
德阳市	Deyang	361.6	359.2	353.1	352.4	351.1	351.3	352.0	353.2	354.5
绵阳市	Mianyang	461.4	462.0	464.0	467.6	473.9	477.2	481.1	483.6	485.7
广元市	Guangyuan	248.4	249.0	253.0	254.5	257.5	263.0	263.5	266.0	266.7
遂宁市	Suining	325.2	326.0	326.8	327.5	328.3	329.0	329.8	323.6	320.2
内江市	Neijiang	370.3	370.9	371.8	372.5	373.3	374.0	374.7	375.4	369.9
乐山市	Leshan	323.6	324.3	325.4	325.6	325.0	326.1	326.5	327.2	326.7
南充市	Nanchong	627.9	628.5	630.0	631.7	633.4	636.4	640.2	641.8	644.0
眉山市	Meishan	295.0	295.8	296.6	297.8	299.0	300.1	300.1	297.5	298.4
宜宾市	Yibin	447.2	446.0	446.0	446.5	447.0	449.0	451.0	453.0	455.6
广安市	Guangan	320.5	321.0	321.6	322.4	323.2	324.7	326.5	325.0	324.1
达州市	Dazhou	546.8	548.6	549.3	551.3	553.0	556.8	559.8	569.0	572.0
雅安市	Yaan	150.7	151.7	152.7	153.4	154.4	154.7	154.0	153.8	154.0
巴中市	Bazhong	328.4	329.6	330.8	331.7	332.2	332.9	331.1	331.7	332.2
资阳市	Ziyang	366.5	363.0	358.9	357.1	354.7	356.9	254.1	255.3	251.2
阿坝藏族羌族自治州	Aba	89.9	90.2	90.7	91.2	92.0	93.0	93.5	94.0	94.4
甘孜藏族自治州	Ganzi	109.2	110.0	112.2	113.8	114.8	116.5	118.1	118.6	119.6
凉山彝族自治州	Liangshan	453.3	454.1	456.1	458.5	462.0	468.0	482.2	483.5	490.8

3-4 各市(州)常住人口城镇化率
Urbanization Rate of Resident Population by Region

单位：% (%)

市(州)	Region	2010	2011	2012	2013	2014	2015	2016	2017	2018
全　省	**Sichuan**	**40.18**	**41.83**	**43.53**	**44.90**	**46.30**	**47.69**	**49.21**	**50.79**	**52.29**
成都市	Chengdu	65.75	67.00	68.44	69.40	70.37	71.47	70.62	71.85	73.12
自贡市	Zigong	41.02	42.69	44.44	45.52	46.62	47.88	49.14	50.92	52.61
攀枝花市	Panzhihua	60.10	61.64	63.01	63.43	64.03	64.74	65.34	65.99	66.59
泸州市	Luzhou	38.80	39.92	41.73	43.29	44.84	46.08	47.50	48.95	50.46
德阳市	Deyang	41.32	42.99	44.79	45.86	47.27	48.47	49.58	50.98	52.35
绵阳市	Mianyang	39.85	41.84	43.64	45.09	46.51	48.00	49.50	51.01	52.53
广元市	Guangyuan	32.98	34.66	36.42	37.80	39.33	40.83	42.40	43.98	45.63
遂宁市	Suining	38.38	39.95	41.71	43.11	44.61	45.91	47.01	48.52	50.02
内江市	Neijiang	39.36	40.23	41.84	42.67	44.21	45.61	46.70	47.90	49.10
乐山市	Leshan	39.48	41.20	42.97	44.53	45.93	47.31	48.73	50.17	51.83
南充市	Nanchong	35.91	37.55	39.34	40.89	42.43	43.82	45.07	46.47	48.14
眉山市	Meishan	34.11	35.77	37.57	38.95	40.46	41.87	43.38	44.77	46.32
宜宾市	Yibin	38.00	39.35	41.08	42.45	43.85	45.10	46.63	48.12	49.64
广安市	Guangan	29.07	30.93	32.91	34.29	35.81	37.22	38.81	40.24	41.86
达州市	Dazhou	32.71	34.31	36.10	37.80	39.39	40.87	42.42	43.92	45.52
雅安市	Yaan	34.62	36.56	38.30	39.80	41.30	42.55	43.95	45.35	46.85
巴中市	Bazhong	29.31	31.26	33.22	34.77	36.12	37.52	39.10	40.54	41.85
资阳市	Ziyang	32.73	34.45	36.15	36.89	38.20	39.50	40.08	41.34	42.71
阿坝藏族羌族自治州	Aba	30.10	31.65	33.37	34.59	35.69	36.77	37.86	38.92	40.00
甘孜藏族自治州	Ganzi	20.53	22.39	24.41	25.81	26.87	28.06	29.26	30.56	31.66
凉山彝族自治州	Liangshan	27.52	28.16	29.57	30.57	31.44	32.44	33.04	34.30	35.71

3-5 年末户籍总人口数及构成
Total Registered Population and its Composition(year-end)

单位：万人 (10 000 persons)

年份 Year	年末户籍总人口 Total Registered Population (year-end)	按性别分 By Sex		按城乡分 By Residence	
		男 Male	女 Female	城镇人口 Urban Population	乡村人口 Rural Population
1952	4628.5	2357.9	2270.6	365.7	4262.8
1957	5088.8	2601.0	2487.8	568.0	4520.8
1962	4688.3	2368.9	2319.4	535.9	4152.4
1965	5162.1	2623.3	2538.8	606.4	4555.7
1970	6052.4	3089.0	2963.4	688.9	5363.5
1975	6874.7	3508.2	3366.5	736.6	6138.1
1978	7071.9	3621.5	3450.4	784.2	6287.7
1980	7154.8	3668.3	3486.5	829.6	6325.2
1985	7419.3	3828.9	3590.4	1025.9	6393.4
1990	7892.5	4088.1	3804.4	1101.7	6790.8
1991	7947.8	4119.5	3828.3	1119.3	6828.5
1992	7992.2	4144.1	3848.1	1172.6	6819.6
1993	8037.4	4171.2	3866.2	1211.9	6825.5
1994	8098.7	4205.3	3893.4	1277.1	6821.6
1995	8161.2	4238.9	3922.3	1331.8	6829.4
1996	8215.4	4266.6	3948.8	1378.1	6837.3
1997	8264.7	4291.4	3973.3	1420.1	6844.6
1998	8315.7	4317.5	3998.2	1460.3	6855.4
1999	8358.6	4337.7	4020.9	1507.7	6850.9
2000	8407.5	4358.9	4048.6	1565.0	6842.5
2001	8436.6	4375.4	4061.2	1622.1	6814.5
2002	8474.5	4395.3	4079.2	1677.6	6796.9
2003	8529.4	4424.7	4104.7	1795.2	6734.2
2004	8595.3	4460.0	4135.3	1914.3	6681.0
2005	8642.1	4483.6	4158.5	2013.8	6628.3
2006	8722.5	4520.3	4202.2	2070.8	6651.7
2007	8815.2	4566.4	4248.8	2140.0	6675.2
2008	8907.8	4607.7	4300.1	2203.4	6704.4
2009	8984.7	4639.2	4345.5	2286.3	6698.4
2010	9001.3	4640.4	4360.9	2355.2	6646.1
2011	9058.4	4665.6	4392.8	2462.7	6595.7
2012	9097.4	4685.0	4412.4	2512.0	6585.4
2013	9132.6	4700.8	4431.8	2632.4	6500.2
2014	9159.1	4710.4	4448.7	2694.0	6465.1
2015	9102.0	4680.1	4421.9	2785.2	6316.8
2016	9137.0	4696.2	4440.8	2997.5	6139.5
2017	9113.4	4677.8	4435.6	3116.3	5997.1
2018	9121.8	4678.3	4443.5	3271.5	5850.3

注：本篇章所列户籍人口资料均由四川省公安厅提供；2014年及以前的城镇人口、乡村人口为非农业人口、农业人口。

a) Data in this table were taken from the annual reports of the Bureau of Sichuan Provincial Public Security. Data of urban population and rural population before 2015 are those of non-agricultural population and agricultural population.

3-6 各市(州)年末户籍总户数及人口数(2018年)
Number of Registered Households and Population by Region(year-end)(2018)

市(州)	Region	年末户籍总户数(万户) Total Registered Households (year-end) (10 000 households)	年末户籍总人口(万人) Total Registered Population (year-end) (10 000 persons)	男性 Male	女性 Female	城镇人口 Urban Population	乡村人口 Rural Population
全　省	**Sichuan**	**3251.4**	**9121.8**	**4678.3**	**4443.5**	**3271.5**	**5850.3**
成都市	Chengdu	563.8	1478.1	733.2	744.9	901.6	576.5
自贡市	Zigong	108.7	322.4	163.9	158.5	135.7	186.7
攀枝花市	Panzhihua	37.3	108.3	55.0	53.4	56.5	51.8
泸州市	Luzhou	156.9	509.7	263.1	246.6	210.1	299.6
德阳市	Deyang	157.4	386.8	196.4	190.4	124.2	262.6
绵阳市	Mianyang	206.0	536.0	274.6	261.4	187.3	348.7
广元市	Guangyuan	114.5	300.5	154.1	146.5	72.8	227.7
遂宁市	Suining	139.0	365.4	189.0	176.4	100.6	264.8
内江市	Neijiang	154.5	411.8	212.2	199.5	113.6	298.2
乐山市	Leshan	126.9	350.5	178.3	172.2	129.0	221.5
南充市	Nanchong	264.2	728.7	380.3	348.4	211.1	517.6
眉山市	Meishan	129.0	344.4	174.8	169.5	116.7	227.7
宜宾市	Yibin	170.4	552.3	286.7	265.6	196.6	355.7
广安市	Guangan	154.5	462.2	241.8	220.4	117.3	344.9
达州市	Dazhou	241.2	665.8	349.3	316.5	218.2	447.6
雅安市	Yaan	57.4	153.3	78.3	75.1	67.4	85.9
巴中市	Bazhong	130.4	368.3	192.2	176.1	99.8	268.5
资阳市	Ziyang	128.0	346.1	180.8	165.3	56.9	289.2
阿坝藏族羌族自治州	Aba	29.2	90.3	45.9	44.4	25.5	64.8
甘孜藏族自治州	Ganzi	29.7	110.1	55.5	54.5	19.2	90.9
凉山彝族自治州	Liangshan	152.4	530.8	272.9	257.9	111.4	419.4

3-7 各市(州)年末户籍人口数
Registered Population(year-end) by Region

单位：万人 (10 000 persons)

市(州)	Region	2010	2011	2012	2013	2014	2015	2016	2017	2018
全 省	**Sichuan**	**9001.3**	**9058.4**	**9097.4**	**9132.6**	**9159.1**	**9102.0**	**9137.0**	**9113.4**	**9121.8**
成都市	Chengdu	1149.1	1163.3	1173.4	1188.0	1210.7	1228.1	1398.9	1435.3	1478.1
自贡市	Zigong	326.0	327.1	328.5	329.7	330.0	327.5	327.4	323.9	322.4
攀枝花市	Panzhihua	111.3	111.7	111.9	112.0	111.9	110.6	110.5	109.4	108.3
泸州市	Luzhou	502.3	503.0	505.2	508.4	508.9	505.7	508.3	509.6	509.7
德阳市	Deyang	389.2	390.5	391.5	392.0	392.5	390.0	391.7	387.7	386.8
绵阳市	Mianyang	541.9	543.4	545.4	547.4	548.8	545.5	545.2	536.8	536.0
广元市	Guangyuan	310.9	311.2	311.7	310.2	310.1	305.3	304.8	302.6	300.5
遂宁市	Suining	381.4	382.7	376.1	379.4	380.4	378.8	377.9	369.7	365.4
内江市	Neijiang	425.5	426.1	426.6	426.8	426.0	420.4	420.0	415.1	411.8
乐山市	Leshan	353.4	354.4	355.1	356.0	355.7	353.8	354.7	351.9	350.5
南充市	Nanchong	751.7	756.2	759.6	759.0	759.0	742.3	741.3	732.7	728.7
眉山市	Meishan	349.1	350.8	350.4	352.2	353.0	349.1	350.2	345.1	344.4
宜宾市	Yibin	539.0	542.9	546.6	550.4	554.3	552.1	555.9	555.4	552.3
广安市	Guangan	466.1	468.5	468.5	470.4	471.7	467.4	467.3	464.6	462.2
达州市	Dazhou	685.5	690.7	695.6	687.6	688.1	682.8	683.6	671.7	665.8
雅安市	Yaan	154.9	155.8	156.5	157.0	157.2	154.9	155.0	153.9	153.3
巴中市	Bazhong	388.0	389.4	390.0	390.2	383.1	379.5	375.3	376.2	368.3
资阳市	Ziyang	501.1	503.9	505.9	507.3	507.3	503.7	354.5	348.9	346.1
阿坝藏族羌族自治州	Aba	89.9	90.7	91.4	92.0	92.2	91.4	92.0	91.5	90.3
甘孜藏族自治州	Ganzi	106.1	108.8	110.3	110.2	111.3	109.2	110.1	110.1	110.1
凉山彝族自治州	Liangshan	478.9	487.3	497.2	506.4	506.9	503.9	512.4	521.3	530.8

3-8 各市(州)年末户籍城镇人口数
Registered Urban Population(year-end) by Region

单位：万人 (10 000 persons)

市(州)	Region	2010	2011	2012	2013	2014	2015	2016	2017	2018
全　省	**Sichuan**	**2355.2**	**2462.7**	**2512.0**	**2632.4**	**2694.0**	**2785.2**	**2997.5**	**3116.3**	**3271.5**
成都市	Chengdu	650.9	705.7	716.7	728.7	755.8	720.6	784.6	851.1	901.6
自贡市	Zigong	105.4	108.3	111.4	112.5	113.2	126.5	132.1	134.2	135.7
攀枝花市	Panzhihua	59.4	60.0	60.1	59.9	59.5	58.9	58.0	57.1	56.5
泸州市	Luzhou	91.8	94.5	95.8	152.3	154.0	123.0	192.5	209.1	210.1
德阳市	Deyang	103.4	107.3	110.5	117.4	120.6	136.1	121.6	120.5	124.2
绵阳市	Mianyang	145.4	150.4	152.8	158.0	163.0	176.8	178.7	179.0	187.3
广元市	Guangyuan	68.4	70.0	71.3	72.2	73.5	73.5	68.6	70.9	72.8
遂宁市	Suining	86.2	88.4	89.1	97.5	99.2	107.4	98.0	96.4	100.6
内江市	Neijiang	88.5	92.7	94.6	96.4	97.4	110.3	115.4	114.5	113.6
乐山市	Leshan	107.6	111.3	114.9	118.5	120.4	134.0	122.1	126.5	129.0
南充市	Nanchong	164.9	169.4	172.0	176.6	179.1	173.1	207.2	206.6	211.1
眉山市	Meishan	91.0	93.9	96.2	98.9	100.6	100.2	111.0	111.3	116.7
宜宾市	Yibin	100.9	103.4	104.9	106.2	108.2	118.1	132.3	147.1	196.6
广安市	Guangan	82.1	85.4	87.8	90.6	94.1	103.9	107.5	107.7	117.3
达州市	Dazhou	129.0	133.3	137.3	139.6	144.2	160.0	204.3	212.0	218.2
雅安市	Yaan	37.5	38.6	39.3	42.6	43.6	54.0	65.8	65.9	67.4
巴中市	Bazhong	68.2	69.5	73.1	78.1	79.2	89.0	93.8	99.4	99.8
资阳市	Ziyang	79.8	84.8	87.3	89.2	90.7	93.4	57.0	56.3	56.9
阿坝藏族羌族自治州	Aba	20.2	20.4	20.8	20.5	20.8	31.5	26.3	27.0	25.5
甘孜藏族自治州	Ganzi	16.2	16.3	16.4	16.2	16.2	16.3	18.1	19.3	19.2
凉山彝族自治州	Liangshan	58.4	59.1	59.7	60.5	60.7	78.6	102.6	104.4	111.4

主要统计指标解释

人口数 指一定时点、一定地区范围内有生命的个人总和。

年度统计的年末人口数指每年12月31日24时的人口数。

常住人口 指实际经常居住在某地半年以上的人口。常住人口主要包括：①调查时点居住在本乡、镇、街道，户口也在本乡、镇、街道的人；②调查时点居住在本乡、镇、街道，户口不在本乡、镇、街道，离开户口登记地半年以上的人；③调查时点居住在本乡、镇、街道，尚未办理常住户口的人；④户口在本乡、镇、街道，调查时点居住在港澳台或国外的人。

户籍人口 指不管是否外出和外出时间长短，只要在某地公安户籍管理部门登记了常住户口，则为该地区的户籍人口。户籍人口数据由公安部门统计。

城镇人口和乡村人口 城镇人口是指居住在城镇范围内的全部常住人口；乡村人口是除上述人口以外的全部人口。

城镇化率 城镇化指伴随工业化的发展，非农产业向城镇聚集，农村人口向城镇集中的自然历史过程，是世界各国工业化进程中必然经历的历史阶段。城镇化率是指一个国家（地区）城镇的常住人口占该国家（地区）总人口的比例，是衡量城镇化水平高低，反映城镇化进程的一个重要指标。

出生率（又称粗出生率） 指在一定时期内(通常为一年)一定地区的出生人数与同期内平均人数(或期中人数)之比，用千分率表示。本资料中的出生率指年出生率，其计算公式为:

$$出生率=\frac{年出生人数}{年平均人数}\times 1000‰$$

式中：出生人数指活产婴儿，即胎儿脱离母体时(不管怀孕月数)，有过呼吸或其他生命现象。年平均人数指年初、年底人口数的平均数，也可用年中人口数代替。

死亡率（又称粗死亡率） 指在一定时期内(通常为一年)一定地区的死亡人数与同期内平均人数(或期中人数)之比，用千分率表示。本资料中的死亡率指年死亡率，其计算公式为:

$$死亡率=\frac{年死亡人数}{年平均人数}\times 1000‰$$

人口自然增长率 指在一定时期内(通常为一年)人口自然增加数(出生人数减死亡人数)与该时期内平均人数(或期中人数)之比，用千分率表示。计算公式为:

$$人口自然增长率=\frac{本年出生人数-本年死亡人数}{年平均人数}\times 1000‰$$

$$=人口出生率-人口死亡率$$

Explanatory Notes on Main Statistical Indicators

Total Population refers to the total number of people alive at a certain point of time within a given area.

The annual statistics on total population is taken at midnight, the 31st of December.

Usual Resident Population refers to the population that actually reside in a place, usually longer than half a year. Usual Resident Population mainly includes 1) those who live in their own townships, towns and streets at the time of investigation, and whose household registration is also in their own townships, towns and streets;2) those who live in their own townships, towns and streets at the time of investigation, and whose household registration is not in their own townships, towns and streets, and who have left the registered place of household registration for more than half a year;3) those who live in their own townships, towns and streets at the time of investigation, but have not yet processed permanent household registration;4) Household registration in their own townships, towns and streets, and people living in Hong Kong, Macao, Taiwan or abroad at the time of investigation.

Household Registration Population refers to the population that regardless of whether or not to go out and the length of time, as long as the permanent residence registration is registered in the local public security household registration administration department, it will be the registered residence population in the area. The household registration data are collected by the public security department.

Urban Population and Rural Population Urban population refers to all people residing in cities and towns, while rural population refers to population other than urban population.

Urbanization rate Urbanization refers to the natural historical process in which non-agricultural industries gather in cities and towns and rural population concentrate in cities and towns with the development of industrialization. It is the inevitable historical stage in the process of industrialization in all countries of the world. Urbanization rate refers to the proportion of the permanent population of a country (region) to the total population of the country (region), which is an important index to measure the level of urbanization and reflect the process of urbanization.

Birth Rate or (Crude Birth Rate) refers to the ratio of the number of births to the average population (or mid-period population) during a certain period of time (usually a year), expressed in ‰. Birth rate in the chapter refers to annual birth rate. The following formula is used:

$$\text{Birth Rate} = \frac{\text{Number of Births}}{\text{Annual Average Population}} \times 1000‰$$

Number of births in the formula refers to live births, i.e. when a baby has breathed or showed any vital phenomena regardless of the length of pregnancy.

Annual average population is the average of the number of population at the beginning of the year and that at the end of the year. Sometimes it is substituted by the mid-year population.

Death Rate (or Crude Death Rate) refers to the ratio of the number of deaths to the average population (or mid-period population) during a certain period of time (usually a year), expressed in ‰. Death rate in the chapter refers to annual death rate. The following formula is used:

$$\text{Death Rate} = \frac{\text{Number of Deaths}}{\text{Annual Average Population}} \times 1000‰$$

Natural Growth Rate of Population refers to the ratio of natural increase in population (number of births minus number of deaths) in a certain period of time (usually a year) to the average population (or mid-period population) of the same period, expressed in ‰. The following formula is applied:

$$\begin{matrix}\text{Natural Growth}\\ \text{Rate of Population}\end{matrix} = \frac{\text{Number of Births - Number of Deaths}}{\text{Annual Average Population}} \times 1000‰$$

Natural Growth Rate of Population = Birth Rate-Death Rate

4

就业和工资

Chapter 4 Employment and Wages

4-1 就业基本情况
Employment

项　目	Item	2010	2011	2012	2013	2014	2015	2016	2017	2018
就业人员合计(万人)	**Total Number of Employed Persons (10000 persons)**	**4772.53**	**4785.47**	**4798.30**	**4817.31**	**4833.00**	**4847.01**	**4860.00**	**4872.00**	**4881.00**
第一产业	Primary Industry	2083.20	2043.36	1991.30	1955.79	1909.00	1870.91	1827.40	1792.90	1752.30
第二产业	Secondary Industry	1188.82	1210.78	1233.18	1254.51	1275.90	1289.31	1302.50	1315.40	1327.60
第三产业	Tertiary Industry	1500.51	1531.33	1573.83	1607.01	1648.10	1686.79	1730.10	1763.70	1801.10
就业人员构成（合计=100）	**Composition of Employed Persons (total=100)**	**100.0**	**100.0**	**100.0**	**100.0**	**100.0**	**100.0**	**100.0**	**100.0**	**100.0**
第一产业	Primary Industry	43.7	42.7	41.5	40.6	39.5	38.6	37.6	36.8	35.9
第二产业	Secondary Industry	24.9	25.3	25.7	26.0	26.4	26.6	26.8	27.0	27.2
第三产业	Tertiary Industry	31.4	32.0	32.8	33.4	34.1	34.8	35.6	36.2	36.9
按城乡分就业人员（万人）	**Number of Employed Persons by Urban and Rural Areas (10000 persons)**									
城镇非私营单位就业人员	Employed Persons of Urban Non-private Units	570.60	614.00	640.90	846.20	808.80	795.47	787.50	792.21	780.64
#国有单位	Stste-owned Units	335.80	346.50	358.80	361.30	351.10	344.08	343.40	343.29	327.60
集体单位	Collective-owned Units	33.70	33.80	33.80	31.40	29.10	26.25	26.30	23.20	20.20
其他单位	Other Units	201.10	233.70	248.30	453.50	428.60	425.14	417.80	425.72	432.80
#企业	Enterprises	342.30	378.40	349.90	590.13	551.10	533.70	523.25	519.32	507.80
事业	Institutions	154.90	160.30	169.10	169.30	174.60	174.30	175.51	179.04	177.50
机关	Organizations	73.20	74.80	76.30	78.02	80.50	85.60	87.08	91.15	93.20
私营单位就业人员	Employed Persons of Private-owned Units	285.80	299.70	329.80	342.10	287.10	307.10	347.40	377.98	423.80
个体就业人员	Self-employed Individuals	369.10	390.10	419.30	428.30	412.60	433.40	435.50	438.13	440.74
乡村就业人员	Rural Employed Persons	3390.60	3368.00	3343.30	3324.30	3302.00	3281.00	3257.00	3230.00	3201.00
城镇登记失业人数（万人）	**Number of Registered Unemployed (10000 persons) Persons in Urban Areas**	**34.56**	**36.93**	**41.67**	**42.87**	**54.36**	**54.64**	**56.26**	**55.78**	**53.31**
城镇登记失业率(%)	**Registered Unemployment Rate in Urban Areas (%)**	**4.1**	**4.1**	**4.1**	**4.1**	**4.2**	**4.1**	**4.2**	**4.0**	**3.5**

4-2 按三次产业分就业人员数

Number of Employed Persons by Three Strata of Industry

(年末数) (year-end)

年 份 Year	就业人员 (万人) Number of Employed Persons (10 000 persons)	第一产业 Primary Industry	第二产业 Secondary Industry	第三产业 Tertiary Industry	构成 Composition in Percentage (合计=100) (total = 100) 第一产业 Primary Industry	第二产业 Secondary Industry	第三产业 Tertiary Industry
1952	2027.92	1753.89	89.37	184.66	86.5	4.4	9.1
1957	2258.38	1947.49	108.57	202.32	86.2	4.8	9.0
1962	2101.58	1810.90	117.47	173.21	86.2	5.6	8.2
1965	2267.18	1925.30	163.38	178.50	84.9	7.2	7.9
1970	2737.59	2339.83	210.36	187.40	85.5	7.7	6.8
1975	2998.60	2474.11	271.48	253.01	82.5	9.1	8.4
1978	3087.02	2524.21	279.50	283.31	81.8	9.1	9.1
1980	3259.78	2638.03	309.24	312.51	80.9	9.5	9.6
1985	3742.97	2824.95	491.67	426.35	75.5	13.1	11.4
1990	4265.20	3108.89	578.08	578.23	72.9	13.5	13.6
1991	4425.10	3190.83	602.81	631.46	72.1	13.6	14.3
1992	4521.20	3200.21	636.79	684.20	70.8	14.1	15.1
1993	4556.80	3108.06	709.98	738.76	68.2	15.6	16.2
1994	4587.90	3037.47	728.46	821.97	66.2	15.9	17.9
1995	4619.10	2983.94	752.91	882.25	64.6	16.3	19.1
1996	4627.20	2875.86	772.74	978.60	62.2	16.7	21.1
1997	4641.20	2872.41	780.44	988.35	61.9	16.8	21.3
1998	4651.40	2824.40	786.09	1040.91	60.7	16.9	22.4
1999	4654.30	2747.08	800.54	1106.68	59.0	17.2	23.8
2000	4658.40	2643.35	871.12	1143.93	56.7	18.7	24.6
2001	4664.80	2595.84	867.65	1201.31	55.6	18.6	25.8
2002	4667.60	2517.48	896.18	1253.94	53.9	19.2	26.9
2003	4683.50	2482.80	906.70	1294.00	53.0	19.4	27.6
2004	4691.00	2445.70	916.00	1329.30	52.2	19.5	28.3
2005	4702.00	2421.50	926.30	1354.20	51.5	19.7	28.8
2006	4715.00	2306.90	946.00	1462.10	48.9	20.1	31.0
2007	4731.10	2266.22	1065.71	1399.15	47.9	22.5	29.6
2008	4740.00	2186.18	1108.32	1445.50	46.1	23.4	30.5
2009	4756.62	2144.13	1141.59	1470.90	45.1	24.0	30.9
2010	4772.53	2083.20	1188.82	1500.51	43.7	24.9	31.4
2011	4785.47	2043.36	1210.78	1531.33	42.7	25.3	32.0
2012	4798.30	1991.30	1233.18	1573.83	41.5	25.7	32.8
2013	4817.31	1955.79	1254.51	1607.01	40.6	26.0	33.4
2014	4833.00	1909.00	1275.90	1648.10	39.5	26.4	34.1
2015	4847.01	1870.91	1289.31	1686.79	38.6	26.6	34.8
2016	4860.00	1827.40	1302.50	1730.10	37.6	26.8	35.6
2017	4872.00	1792.90	1315.40	1763.70	36.8	27.0	36.2
2018	4881.00	1752.30	1327.60	1801.10	35.9	27.2	36.9

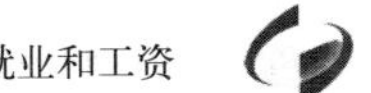

4-3 各市(州)就业人员数

Number of Employed Persons by Three Strata of Industry and Region

(年末数)单位：万人 (year-end)(10 000 persons)

市(州)	Region	2010	2011	2012	2013	2014	2015	2016	2017	2018
全　省	**Sichuan**	**4772.53**	**4785.47**	**4798.30**	**4817.31**	**4833.00**	**4847.01**	**4860.00**	**4872.00**	**4881.00**
成都市	Chengdu	766.41	784.28	791.07	820.64	824.40	827.92	879.02	892.70	894.96
自贡市	Zigong	184.25	189.96	190.75	196.34	197.20	197.95	169.46	169.67	169.98
攀枝花市	Panzhihua	65.38	70.44	66.18	72.56	72.90	59.94	61.81	62.57	62.83
泸州市	Luzhou	243.52	241.05	240.27	249.97	250.10	250.87	253.15	249.58	250.00
德阳市	Deyang	203.49	211.66	209.92	218.71	219.20	220.27	222.97	216.45	216.81
绵阳市	Mianyang	279.49	287.01	293.33	299.88	300.70	301.74	303.80	303.72	304.40
广元市	Guangyuan	164.07	168.59	160.38	163.77	164.10	164.15	164.50	164.66	165.03
遂宁市	Suining	160.42	161.02	163.91	161.00	161.70	162.68	162.72	163.55	163.87
内江市	Neijiang	202.67	173.15	174.09	173.80	174.40	176.06	176.57	177.88	178.40
乐山市	Leshan	188.47	188.09	193.67	183.43	184.20	184.30	185.13	184.40	184.78
南充市	Nanchong	249.14	270.16	275.78	293.13	294.10	294.68	297.86	303.23	303.89
眉山市	Meishan	192.45	193.64	189.52	187.38	188.30	188.65	190.08	189.32	189.60
宜宾市	Yibin	310.77	315.27	323.01	313.27	314.20	315.76	315.81	316.09	316.71
广安市	Guangan	212.65	211.12	217.07	217.21	217.60	218.16	218.26	219.21	219.71
达州市	Dazhou	303.21	308.93	330.77	328.54	328.80	329.05	332.00	330.49	331.28
雅安市	Yaan	95.28	96.54	104.77	101.97	102.40	103.50	103.73	103.77	104.06
巴中市	Bazhong	184.47	171.82	172.35	167.79	168.20	169.50	170.67	171.51	171.73
资阳市	Ziyang	205.50	204.06	207.32	222.16	222.30	224.12	189.05	187.65	187.94
阿坝藏族羌族自治州	Aba	54.41	54.35	50.25	50.80	50.80	51.42	51.79	51.86	52.02
甘孜藏族自治州	Ganzi	63.06	66.62	64.29	65.50	65.70	66.61	66.65	66.66	66.78
凉山彝族自治州	Liangshan	281.50	291.59	302.30	284.77	285.30	286.27	288.74	289.17	289.63

4-4 各市(州)按三次产业分就业人员数(2018年)
Number of Employed Persons by Three Strata of Industry and Region(2018)

(年末数) (year-end)

市(州)	Region	就业人员 (万人) Number of Employed Persons (10 000 persons)	第一产业 Primary Industry	第二产业 Secondary Industry	第三产业 Tertiary Industry	构成 Composition in Percentage (合计=100) (total = 100) 第一产业 Primary Industry	第二产业 Secondary Industry	第三产业 Tertiary Industry
全 省	**Sichuan**	**4881.00**	**1752.30**	**1327.60**	**1801.10**	**35.9**	**27.2**	**36.9**
成都市	Chengdu	894.96	102.85	323.10	469.01	11.5	36.1	52.4
自贡市	Zigong	169.98	62.81	49.82	57.35	37.0	29.3	33.7
攀枝花市	Panzhihua	62.83	18.61	17.91	26.31	29.6	28.5	41.9
泸州市	Luzhou	250.00	98.96	77.57	73.47	39.6	31.0	29.4
德阳市	Deyang	216.81	71.46	59.47	85.88	33.0	27.4	39.6
绵阳市	Mianyang	304.40	86.74	102.55	115.11	28.5	33.7	37.8
广元市	Guangyuan	165.03	67.23	38.30	59.50	40.7	23.2	36.1
遂宁市	Suining	163.87	68.42	43.49	51.96	41.8	26.5	31.7
内江市	Neijiang	178.40	50.44	50.42	77.54	28.2	28.3	43.5
乐山市	Leshan	184.78	74.72	40.98	69.08	40.4	22.2	37.4
南充市	Nanchong	303.89	113.42	92.47	98.00	37.3	30.4	32.3
眉山市	Meishan	189.60	82.37	47.94	59.29	43.4	25.3	31.3
宜宾市	Yibin	316.71	139.90	91.19	85.62	44.2	28.8	27.0
广安市	Guangan	219.71	100.37	52.60	66.74	45.7	23.9	30.4
达州市	Dazhou	331.28	160.01	65.42	105.85	48.3	19.7	32.0
雅安市	Yaan	104.06	48.54	22.02	33.50	46.6	21.2	32.2
巴中市	Bazhong	171.73	72.86	44.59	54.28	42.4	26.0	31.6
资阳市	Ziyang	187.94	92.64	42.43	52.87	49.3	22.6	28.1
阿坝藏族羌族自治州	Aba	52.02	28.43	4.38	19.21	54.7	8.4	36.9
甘孜藏族自治州	Ganzi	66.78	47.15	2.40	17.23	70.6	3.6	25.8
凉山彝族自治州	Liangshan	289.63	164.37	43.93	81.33	56.7	15.2	28.1

注：全省合计中包括省直综单位就业人员和灵活形式就业人员，市(州)数据未包括(以下有关各表同)。

a) The number of persons employed in directly affiliated units and comprehensive units, and persons employed in flexible forms was included in the Sichuan's number of employed persons, but was not included in regional number of employed persons.(the same as the following related tables).

4-5 按城乡分就业人员数

Number of Employed Persons by Residence in Urban and Rural Areas

(年末数)单位：万人 (year-end)(10 000 persons)

年份 Year	就业人员合计 Total Number of Employed Persons	#非私营单位就业人员 Staff and Workers in Non-private Units	国有经济单位职工 State-owned Units Staff	城镇集体经济单位职工 Urban Collective-owned Units Staff	其他各种经济单位职工 Other Staff	#城镇个体私营企业就业人员 Urban Private Enterprises and Self-employed Individuals	#乡村就业人员 Rural Employed Persons
1952	2027.92	63.56	61.82	1.74		132.77	1831.59
1957	2258.38	208.22	132.72	75.50		18.93	2031.23
1962	2101.58	233.16	160.16	73.00		10.21	1858.21
1965	2267.18	290.53	208.91	81.62		6.05	1970.60
1970	2737.59	338.68	255.68	83.00		2.39	2396.52
1975	2998.60	394.26	302.48	91.78		1.52	2602.82
1978	3087.02	457.92	364.80	93.12		6.50	2621.50
1980	3259.78	498.31	388.64	109.67		10.10	2748.60
1985	3742.97	576.12	429.99	145.67	0.46	46.00	3103.00
1990	4265.20	644.21	496.90	145.75	1.56	107.10	3465.10
1991	4425.10	666.02	515.05	148.95	2.02	131.10	3568.50
1992	4521.20	684.31	526.04	155.71	2.56	157.80	3607.00
1993	4556.80	693.30	523.94	149.40	19.96	182.70	3595.30
1994	4587.90	692.27	515.47	144.56	32.24	210.60	3587.10
1995	4619.10	696.03	522.39	138.43	35.21	239.20	3573.30
1996	4627.20	692.78	520.38	133.41	38.99	270.10	3552.10
1997	4641.20	681.56	506.18	131.04	44.34	299.20	3538.00
1998	4651.40	662.94	467.29	111.90	83.75	348.50	3573.50
1999	4654.30	547.15	394.31	80.67	72.17	370.20	3567.00
2000	4658.40	515.45	371.68	69.73	74.04	391.70	3564.50
2001	4664.80	486.70	350.45	58.39	77.86	429.60	3556.20
2002	4667.60	481.19	326.97	52.66	101.56	446.30	3542.00
2003	4683.50	486.70	315.90	48.70	122.10	471.50	3516.60
2004	4691.00	480.70	305.60	43.70	131.40	497.30	3481.80
2005	4702.00	492.80	303.70	40.90	148.20	505.90	3473.10
2006	4715.00	500.90	304.40	40.10	156.40	514.40	3452.30
2007	4731.10	520.37	312.70	39.23	168.44	574.80	3432.70
2008	4740.00	528.94	310.80	37.10	181.04	573.32	3430.00
2009	4756.62	536.48	312.21	36.87	187.40	634.27	3410.76
2010	4772.53	570.58	335.77	33.69	201.12	662.23	3390.63
2011	4785.47	587.49	331.63	32.12	223.74	689.75	3368.00
2012	4798.30	611.80	342.70	32.30	236.80	749.08	3343.30
2013	4817.31	685.57	349.10	30.10	306.37	770.32	3324.30
2014	4833.00	808.70	351.10	29.00	428.60	699.73	3302.00
2015	4847.01	795.47	344.08	26.25	425.14	740.53	3281.00
2016	4860.00	787.53	343.36	26.33	417.84	782.92	3257.00
2017	4872.00	792.21	343.29	23.20	425.72	816.11	3230.00
2018	4881.00	780.64	327.60	20.20	432.80	864.54	3201.00

注：就业人员合计中包括灵活形式就业人员。

a) Total Number of Employed Persons includes the flexible forms of employment.

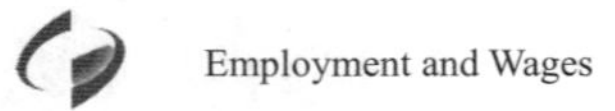

4-6 按行业分就业人员数

(年末数)单位：万人

年份 Year	合计 Total	农、林、牧、渔业 Agriculture, Forestry, Animal Husbandry and Fishery	采矿业 Mining	制造业 Manufacturing	电力、热力、燃气及水生产和供应业 Production and Supply of Electricity, Heat,Gas and Water	建筑业 Construction	批发和零售业 Wholesale and Retail Trades	交通运输、仓储和邮政业 Transport, Storage and Post	住宿和餐饮业 Hotels and Catering Services	信息传输、软件和信息技术服务业 Information Transmission, Software and Information Technology
1978	3087.02	2524.21	43.80	172.77	9.60	53.33	57.46	43.25	20.03	
1980	3259.78	2638.03	48.44	189.98	10.48	60.34	68.03	45.50	23.31	
1985	3742.97	2824.95	86.18	261.63	7.73	136.13	107.82	62.26	34.96	1.73
1986	3885.74	2885.97	93.87	265.64	8.27	171.64	116.55	64.25	40.47	2.55
1987	3967.27	2926.27	98.80	275.76	8.40	191.29	114.04	66.49	40.29	3.07
1988	4090.08	2986.06	101.58	290.53	9.82	198.26	132.05	69.57	44.99	3.61
1989	4179.57	3086.83	98.14	281.25	10.18	194.01	126.23	70.21	45.67	4.13
1990	4265.20	3108.89	98.49	273.04	13.95	192.60	166.95	71.23	60.60	4.69
1991	4425.10	3190.83	101.05	287.68	10.63	203.45	197.23	73.11	71.94	5.17
1992	4521.20	3200.21	104.56	300.82	13.42	217.99	213.05	75.95	76.69	6.11
1993	4556.80	3108.06	105.79	303.60	11.90	288.69	245.60	75.70	83.11	7.29
1994	4587.90	3037.47	111.47	312.14	12.15	292.70	248.66	82.14	91.76	7.52
1995	4619.10	2983.94	114.70	319.99	13.47	304.75	264.66	87.68	92.73	8.41
1996	4627.20	2875.86	116.56	325.82	14.31	316.05	282.10	95.40	94.17	8.65
1997	4641.20	2872.41	118.95	329.85	14.97	316.67	293.73	95.70	95.72	8.78
1998	4651.40	2824.40	114.52	331.73	14.37	325.47	211.35	92.06	189.12	9.09
1999	4654.30	2747.08	116.72	337.17	14.40	332.25	211.48	84.44	214.11	9.38
2000	4658.40	2643.35	121.36	346.95	14.64	388.17	211.66	85.84	226.42	9.86
2001	4664.80	2595.84	118.56	345.95	15.29	387.85	211.95	98.33	237.78	10.25
2002	4667.60	2517.48	122.05	358.35	15.35	400.43	212.08	108.38	243.02	11.76
2003	4683.50	2482.80	123.90	360.30	16.50	405.90	212.80	104.70	248.70	12.10
2004	4691.00	2445.70	120.70	371.40	18.50	405.40	213.14	119.00	264.25	18.00
2005	4702.00	2421.50	118.50	374.90	21.20	411.70	213.64	133.70	287.16	21.60
2006	4715.00	2306.90	116.50	422.00	20.50	387.00	214.24	137.80	323.56	20.60
2007	4731.10	2266.22	119.15	482.09	21.04	443.43	214.97	141.90	362.95	24.40
2008	4740.00	2186.18	107.32	487.39	27.48	486.13	215.37	149.66	362.17	25.55
2009	4756.62	2144.13	106.39	515.37	27.45	492.38	216.13	156.77	392.44	29.25
2010	4772.53	2083.20	108.80	540.66	25.99	513.38	216.85	154.05	405.23	33.08
2011	4785.47	2043.36	111.75	554.79	27.27	516.96	217.44	152.40	417.57	33.21
2012	4798.30	1991.30	116.99	577.78	27.26	511.15	218.02	135.22	400.10	40.17
2013	4817.31	1955.79	106.31	578.63	36.57	533.00	234.55	134.30	424.68	52.29
2014	4833.00	1908.95	111.37	584.33	41.44	538.73	244.73	141.28	402.19	50.69
2015	4847.01	1870.91	100.62	591.23	42.13	555.34	281.30	135.91	366.49	81.90
2016	4860.00	1827.40	101.15	601.17	39.50	560.68	294.86	122.74	381.04	81.78
2017	4872.00	1792.90	100.51	611.96	38.93	564.00	298.30	122.80	384.81	84.46
2018	4881.00	1752.30	98.22	599.53	39.91	589.94	302.38	122.37	393.39	85.05

Number of Employed Persons by Sector

(year-end)(10 000 persons)

金融业 Financial Interme-diation	房地产业 Real Estate	租赁和商务服务业 Leasing and Business Services	科学研究和技术服务业 Scientific Research, and Technical Services	水利、环境和公共设施管理业 Management of Water Con-servancy,En-vironment and Public Facilities	居民服务、修理和其他服务业 Services to Households, Repair and Other Services	教育 Education	卫生和社会工作 Health and Social Service	文化、体育和娱乐业 Culture, Sports and Entertain-ment	公共管理、社会保障和社会组织 Public Mana-gement,Social Security and Social Organization
4.61	0.43		6.00	3.20	35.81	57.03	18.20	1.96	35.33
5.78	1.09		8.70	4.39	36.07	58.98	19.93	2.43	38.30
7.50	1.22	4.27	12.63	6.25	37.19	71.77	25.89	3.12	49.74
7.94	1.18	5.89	12.95	6.80	48.56	72.19	26.11	3.62	51.29
8.54	1.15	6.33	13.05	7.04	51.01	73.76	26.27	3.97	51.74
9.22	1.20	8.77	13.49	7.06	55.19	71.04	26.21	4.08	57.35
9.23	1.21	10.08	13.35	7.26	57.72	74.17	27.10	4.44	58.36
10.02	1.32	12.77	13.21	6.95	63.00	76.45	27.32	4.65	59.07
10.06	1.40	16.54	13.20	7.00	63.80	78.18	28.04	4.97	60.82
11.45	1.62	18.07	13.80	7.13	80.02	81.63	30.15	5.04	63.49
13.62	1.86	21.92	13.32	8.22	83.02	83.56	31.40	5.55	64.59
14.28	1.94	22.67	16.55	8.85	133.49	91.22	31.45	5.84	65.60
14.68	2.14	23.01	15.98	9.07	164.74	90.91	32.11	6.01	70.12
15.17	2.35	23.13	15.67	9.41	215.43	98.04	34.96	6.32	77.80
14.94	2.50	25.91	15.05	9.88	218.08	100.02	35.59	6.67	65.78
15.42	2.77	26.43	14.87	10.84	258.45	100.56	36.18	6.93	66.84
16.27	2.73	27.10	13.04	10.56	331.10	86.08	28.37	7.02	65.00
16.62	3.17	27.95	12.63	9.68	349.85	88.36	28.58	7.23	66.07
16.72	2.98	28.28	10.47	9.21	382.10	90.86	28.19	7.01	67.18
16.25	3.68	29.17	10.58	9.43	387.50	93.40	33.26	6.90	88.53
16.10	5.90	30.70	11.00	7.40	389.80	95.00	41.80	7.10	111.00
16.20	14.20	26.20	12.90	9.30	395.90	90.10	43.30	22.10	84.70
17.40	18.30	35.80	11.60	10.00	365.50	91.30	47.50	22.50	78.20
16.60	28.40	45.10	11.80	13.10	386.20	98.00	57.70	22.90	86.10
17.12	27.53	52.40	12.08	13.16	274.60	106.16	44.07	23.43	84.41
18.70	28.24	47.71	13.28	13.30	294.83	104.60	59.41	23.74	88.94
21.71	29.07	49.14	16.36	14.36	277.55	97.17	52.21	25.07	93.66
23.00	29.07	53.84	17.56	16.37	285.36	98.70	56.12	21.98	89.30
23.78	29.55	52.89	18.62	19.82	265.63	100.59	60.29	33.20	106.34
25.19	33.89	53.50	20.22	20.43	316.97	104.95	62.25	33.37	109.52
26.11	38.01	61.55	24.16	21.56	276.83	107.63	65.94	37.86	101.51
28.42	46.00	73.32	26.94	26.68	290.75	108.92	70.15	31.92	106.19
30.07	45.38	64.70	30.25	27.24	293.94	109.59	68.39	45.31	106.33
32.55	48.32	65.03	30.38	22.65	341.60	105.08	64.93	33.47	105.66
33.96	51.16	68.27	31.87	22.53	345.13	107.02	68.27	34.39	110.73
34.74	54.86	73.88	31.24	21.42	356.34	107.34	68.88	34.89	114.32

4-7 各市(州)按行业分就业人员数(2018年)

(年末数)单位：万人

市(州)	Region	合计 Total	农、林、牧、渔业 Agriculture, Forestry, Animal Husbandry and Fishery	采矿业 Mining	制造业 Manufacturing	电力、热力、燃气及水生产和供应业 Production and Supply of Electricity, Heat,Gas and Water	建筑业 Construction	批发和零售业 Wholesale and Retail Trades	交通运输、仓储和邮政业 Transport, Storage and Post	住宿和餐饮业 Hotels and Catering Services
全　省	**Sichuan**	**4881.00**	**1752.30**	**98.22**	**599.53**	**39.91**	**589.94**	**302.38**	**122.37**	**393.39**
成都市	Chengdu	894.96	102.85	0.64	158.62	4.76	159.08	94.73	63.01	78.14
自贡市	Zigong	169.98	62.81	4.48	23.65	0.68	21.01	11.96	3.33	12.38
攀枝花市	Panzhihua	62.83	18.61	4.27	8.55	0.65	4.44	6.92	2.55	2.87
泸州市	Luzhou	250.00	98.96	4.89	24.61	1.32	46.75	15.11	4.73	6.20
德阳市	Deyang	216.81	71.46	1.13	35.34	0.40	22.60	13.38	2.89	19.72
绵阳市	Mianyang	304.40	86.74	2.47	51.66	4.15	44.27	17.51	5.07	25.65
广元市	Guangyuan	165.03	67.23	4.84	12.80	0.49	20.17	6.80	1.25	16.56
遂宁市	Suining	163.87	68.42	0.19	19.84	0.54	22.92	9.59	2.09	14.14
内江市	Neijiang	178.40	50.44	5.42	21.59	1.45	21.96	6.91	4.10	16.36
乐山市	Leshan	184.78	74.72	3.88	18.60	2.35	16.15	8.53	1.93	25.63
南充市	Nanchong	303.89	113.42	2.56	47.68	1.03	41.20	12.79	2.93	21.94
眉山市	Meishan	189.60	82.37	0.88	28.48	1.28	17.30	13.17	2.08	15.19
宜宾市	Yibin	316.71	139.90	19.95	41.83	2.01	27.40	11.27	2.89	25.85
广安市	Guangan	219.71	100.37	4.48	23.04	0.78	24.30	12.70	2.61	16.77
达州市	Dazhou	331.28	160.01	13.93	25.07	1.66	24.76	15.55	2.66	30.58
雅安市	Yaan	104.06	48.54	3.11	9.33	1.74	7.84	9.43	1.97	5.14
巴中市	Bazhong	171.73	72.86	5.15	13.24	1.73	24.47	8.92	2.46	12.84
资阳市	Ziyang	187.94	92.64	0.21	20.41	0.35	21.46	7.20	1.81	17.38
阿坝藏族羌族自治州	Aba	52.02	28.43	0.27	1.46	0.81	1.84	3.61	1.16	2.86
甘孜藏族自治州	Ganzi	66.78	47.15	0.11	0.31	1.03	0.95	2.51	0.95	3.69
凉山彝族自治州	Liangshan	289.63	164.37	9.29	13.37	2.33	18.94	13.74	3.48	23.43

 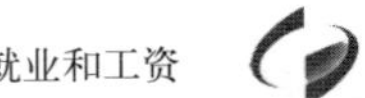

Number of Employed Persons by Sector and Region(2018)

(year-end)(10 000 persons)

信息传输、软件和信息技术服务业 Information Transmission, Software and Information Technology	金融业 Financial Intermediation	房地产业 Real Estate	租赁和商务服务业 Leasing and Business Services	科学研究和技术服务业 Scientific Research, and Technical Services	水利、环境和公共设施管理业 Management of Water Conservancy,Environment and Public Facilities	居民服务、修理和其他服务业 Services to Households, Repair and Other Services	教育 Education	卫生和社会工作 Health and Social Service	文化、体育和娱乐业 Culture, Sports and Entertainment	公共管理、社会保障和社会组织 Public Management,Social Security and Social Organization
85.05	**34.74**	**54.86**	**73.88**	**31.24**	**21.42**	**356.34**	**107.34**	**68.88**	**34.89**	**114.32**
37.20	11.43	19.84	29.24	14.46	4.48	43.71	25.19	17.54	7.58	22.46
0.88	1.06	4.81	2.72	0.66	0.47	8.15	3.48	2.79	1.32	3.34
0.41	0.89	0.63	0.77	0.52	0.28	4.58	1.48	1.63	0.80	1.98
1.12	1.03	1.73	1.79	0.33	1.80	21.85	6.95	3.83	2.40	4.60
3.29	2.17	2.16	4.87	1.85	1.60	18.47	5.24	3.06	2.09	5.09
6.81	2.82	3.11	8.09	7.54	1.25	19.72	6.53	3.84	1.53	5.64
2.37	1.08	0.77	1.20	0.18	1.31	17.35	2.52	2.00	0.45	5.66
1.07	0.66	1.01	1.05	0.25	0.18	12.99	2.76	1.91	1.57	2.69
3.30	2.04	2.75	4.38	0.52	1.01	21.08	4.10	4.15	2.83	4.01
2.15	0.88	1.67	1.97	0.49	0.69	13.66	3.22	2.19	1.48	4.59
3.06	2.05	2.81	4.73	0.83	1.13	22.85	7.74	4.85	1.63	8.66
0.71	0.31	1.29	0.38	0.21	1.57	15.35	2.84	1.75	1.09	3.35
3.57	2.09	0.81	2.58	0.57	0.59	15.98	7.01	3.69	2.28	6.44
2.94	1.11	1.33	0.68	0.13	0.39	16.09	3.88	2.21	0.77	5.13
4.77	1.27	3.73	2.20	0.58	2.20	23.51	6.54	4.28	2.82	5.16
1.21	0.51	0.38	0.83	0.13	0.27	7.03	1.88	1.30	0.46	2.96
2.72	0.61	3.02	0.77	0.18	0.21	11.08	4.27	1.94	0.70	4.56
3.03	1.21	1.59	1.57	0.41	0.30	10.75	2.78	1.93	0.58	2.33
1.01	0.25	0.20	0.67	0.13	0.47	2.28	1.58	0.61	0.32	4.06
0.28	0.21	0.05	0.29	0.22	0.17	1.70	1.84	0.75	0.42	4.15
3.13	1.06	1.17	2.70	0.89	1.05	13.34	5.50	2.62	1.76	7.46

4-8 按行业分乡村就业人员数
Number of Employed Persons in Rural Areas by Sector

(年末数)单位: 万人 (year-end)(10 000 persons)

年份 Year	合 计 Total	#农、林、牧、渔业 Agriculture, Forestry, Animal Husbandry and Fishery	#采矿业 Mining	#制造业 Manufacturing	#建筑业 Construction	#批发和零售业 Wholesale and Retail Trades	#交通运输、仓储和邮政业 Transport, Storage and Post
1978	2621.50	2508.44	12.13	18.20	7.84	5.59	4.08
1980	2748.60	2625.70	16.98	25.47	10.57	6.88	4.66
1985	3103.00	2811.56	49.10	73.65	69.06	28.10	18.49
1986	3221.80	2872.71	56.26	84.38	86.59	35.79	20.48
1987	3275.00	2913.12	60.72	91.09	99.45	40.33	22.72
1988	3359.90	2972.82	63.80	95.70	104.65	44.68	24.13
1989	3423.30	3073.65	59.47	88.39	98.38	42.69	24.51
1990	3465.10	3102.72	57.20	85.80	97.09	44.60	25.03
1991	3568.50	3177.29	59.26	88.90	102.36	48.51	25.88
1992	3607.00	3154.64	62.97	94.46	116.00	54.33	27.79
1993	3595.30	3077.54	98.75	139.19	128.05	62.96	29.88
1994	3587.10	2825.89	82.22	268.53	150.02	126.93	45.84
1995	3573.30	2835.08	98.48	256.45	164.83	132.81	49.10
1996	3552.10	2863.84	98.27	259.94	185.71	99.93	53.59
1997	3538.00	2859.62	95.75	258.92	193.80	108.45	56.34
1998	3573.50	2811.89	89.17	242.08	203.06	113.96	58.33
1999	3567.00	2735.08	45.77	123.73	193.65	101.83	51.31
2000	3564.50	2631.07	47.38	128.11	212.46	113.62	54.05
2001	3556.20	2582.64	105.71	139.86	226.94	124.98	56.71
2002	3542.00	2503.26	78.44	117.43	246.62	134.04	60.75
2003	3516.60	2469.12	103.05	184.63	270.40	145.60	65.29
2004	3481.80	2432.00	65.00	188.90	281.50	157.90	75.40
2005	3473.10	2376.30	86.40	161.30	295.60	173.10	78.50
2006	3452.30	2293.60	85.10	202.60	261.90	178.80	80.60
2007	3432.74	2252.80	84.82	265.10	303.30	144.20	82.20
2008	3430.00	2173.28	74.50	273.50	341.60	176.71	89.78
2009	3410.76	2132.06	71.76	297.39	338.07	181.97	93.41
2010	3390.63	2069.72	74.19	308.03	352.68	184.55	92.55
2011	3368.00	2029.65	74.34	296.36	338.40	183.43	91.11
2012	3343.30	1975.24	73.02	297.51	323.51	117.79	34.69
2013	3324.30	1939.71	68.25	309.88	329.54	114.72	37.32
2014	3302.00	1888.77	70.18	299.12	316.09	129.67	37.22
2015	3281.00	1853.69	65.47	313.64	332.36	116.35	31.51
2016	3257.00	1810.69	64.92	326.04	332.44	125.02	33.17
2017	3230.00	1775.77	64.28	328.32	335.78	125.60	33.65
2018	3201.00	1734.77	63.70	327.94	339.59	127.87	33.47

4-9 各市(州)按行业分乡村就业人员数(2018年)

Number of Households and Employed Persons in Rural Areas by Sector and Region(2018)

(年末数)单位：万人 (year-end)(10 000 persons)

市(州)	Region	乡村就业人员合计 Total Rural Employed Persons	农、林、牧、渔业 Agriculture, Forestry, Animal Husbandry and Fishery	工业 Industry	建筑业 Constr-uction	批发和零售业 Wholesale and Retail Trades	交通运输、仓储和邮政业 Transport, Storage and Post	住宿和餐饮业 Hotels and Catering Services	信息传输、软件和信息技术服务业 Information Transmission, Software and Information Technology	其他非农行业 Other Non-agricul-tural Industries
全 省	**Sichuan**	**3201.00**	**1734.77**	**404.37**	**339.59**	**127.87**	**33.47**	**216.46**	**22.07**	**322.40**
成都市	Chengdu	350.36	98.27	70.13	74.04	26.82	12.51	37.99	5.40	25.20
自贡市	Zigong	120.79	62.54	16.62	12.78	5.37	1.52	6.95	0.41	14.60
攀枝花市	Panzhihua	26.79	18.27	1.56	0.54	0.85	1.12	0.64	0.04	3.77
泸州市	Luzhou	177.76	98.17	19.90	26.02	7.26	1.06	2.43	0.32	22.60
德阳市	Deyang	157.28	71.16	21.19	16.87	6.77	1.32	13.30	1.52	25.15
绵阳市	Mianyang	192.64	85.86	35.20	30.12	6.91	1.45	11.51	1.54	20.05
广元市	Guangyuan	123.57	66.93	13.07	15.03	3.95	0.34	6.80	0.32	17.13
遂宁市	Suining	122.78	67.85	13.39	16.26	4.62	1.47	6.83	0.51	11.85
内江市	Neijiang	125.32	49.81	20.19	15.30	3.74	1.81	9.37	0.95	24.15
乐山市	Leshan	129.18	73.37	11.62	10.91	4.28	0.70	14.94	0.33	13.03
南充市	Nanchong	208.69	112.31	31.42	25.34	5.28	0.88	10.52	0.89	22.05
眉山市	Meishan	140.30	82.13	18.14	9.45	5.94	0.74	7.78	0.17	15.95
宜宾市	Yibin	235.32	138.59	38.49	15.67	6.01	1.42	15.60	1.27	18.27
广安市	Guangan	169.20	99.72	19.77	15.97	6.89	0.68	9.23	1.66	15.28
达州市	Dazhou	249.96	158.99	24.06	12.16	8.85	0.85	18.78	1.87	24.40
雅安市	Yaan	76.13	48.07	7.44	5.74	4.70	0.99	2.45	0.82	5.92
巴中市	Bazhong	126.81	72.62	13.90	10.58	5.31	1.01	8.77	0.80	13.82
资阳市	Ziyang	155.23	92.34	14.81	14.61	3.94	0.80	16.50	1.43	10.80
阿坝藏族羌族自治州	Aba	37.10	28.04	1.05	1.09	2.11	0.50	1.14	0.51	2.66
甘孜藏族自治州	Ganzi	51.74	46.63	0.47	0.53	0.62	0.33	1.83	0.01	1.32
凉山彝族自治州	Liangshan	224.05	163.10	11.95	10.58	7.65	1.97	13.10	1.30	14.40

4-10 按行业分国有经济单位就业人员数
Number of Staff and Workers in State-owned Units by Sector

(年末数)单位：万人

行　业	Sector	2015	2016	2017	2018
总　计	**Total**	**344.08**	**343.36**	**343.29**	**327.58**
农、林、牧、渔业	Agriculture, Forestry, Animal Husbandry and Fishery	2.59	2.53	2.34	1.97
采矿业	Mining	2.18	0.88	0.64	0.65
制造业	Manufacturing	8.21	7.51	5.22	4.71
电力、热力、燃气及水生产和供应业	Production and Supply of Electricity, Heat,Gas and Water	13.22	12.72	12.56	12.40
建筑业	Construction	26.13	25.36	21.31	12.22
批发和零售业	Wholesale and Retail Trades	3.86	3.45	3.17	2.69
交通运输、仓储和邮政业	Transport, Storage and Post	19.55	20.02	19.06	17.65
住宿和餐饮业	Hotels and Catering Services	0.93	0.85	0.67	0.53
信息传输、软件和信息技术服务业	Information Transmission,Software and Information Technology Services	1.74	1.69	1.60	1.42
金融业	Financial Intermediation	10.83	11.39	11.18	10.63
房地产业	Real Estate	0.70	0.83	0.65	0.54
租赁和商务服务业	Leasing and Business Services	4.72	3.71	4.60	2.86
科学研究和技术服务业	Scientific Research and Technical Services	15.18	15.18	14.67	13.06
水利、环境和公共设备管理业	Management of Water Conservancy,Environment and Public Facilities	10.09	10.11	9.55	7.96
居民服务、修理和其他服务业	Services to Households, Repair and Other Services	0.48	0.72	0.73	0.37
教育	Education	88.90	88.32	89.94	89.55
卫生和社会工作	Health and Social Service	39.36	40.48	42.68	42.65
文化、体育和娱乐业	Culture, Sports and Entertainment	4.66	4.54	4.59	4.14
公共管理、社会保障和社会组织	Public Management, Social Security and Social Organization	90.74	93.08	98.13	101.58

4-11 按行业分城镇集体经济单位就业人员数
Number of Staff and Workers in Urban Collective-owned Units by Sector

(年末数)单位：万人　　(year-end)(10 000 persons)

行　业	Sector	2015	2016	2017	2018
总　计	**Total**	**26.25**	**26.33**	**23.20**	**20.25**
农、林、牧、渔业	Agriculture, Forestry, Animal Husbandry and Fishery	0.18	0.20	0.06	0.04
采矿业	Mining	0.19	0.19	0.04	0.04
制造业	Manufacturing	1.11	1.03	0.93	0.66
电力、热力、燃气及水生产和供应业	Production and Supply of Electricity, Heat,Gas and Water	0.26	0.25	0.21	0.20
建筑业	Construction	12.45	12.68	11.31	10.59
批发和零售业	Wholesale and Retail Trades	0.84	0.76	0.61	0.35
交通运输、仓储和邮政业	Transport, Storage and Post	0.90	0.84	0.80	0.65
住宿和餐饮业	Hotels and Catering Services	0.11	0.10	0.08	0.08
信息传输、软件和信息技术服务业	Information Transmission,Software and Information Technology Services	0.01	0.01	0.01	0.01
金融业	Financial Intermediation	2.47	2.41	2.26	1.77
房地产业	Real Estate	0.05	0.03	0.12	0.14
租赁和商务服务业	Leasing and Business Services	1.18	1.09	0.75	0.65
科学研究和技术服务业	Scientific Research and Technical Services	0.17	0.18	0.21	0.14
水利、环境和公共设备管理业	Management of Water Conservancy,Environment and Public Facilities	0.39	0.45	0.46	0.19
居民服务、修理和其他服务业	Services to Households, Repair and Other Services	0.09	0.04	0.03	0.02
教育	Education	0.78	0.80	0.12	0.31
卫生和社会工作	Health and Social Service	4.97	5.17	5.09	4.36
文化、体育和娱乐业	Culture, Sports and Entertainment	0.08	0.08	0.10	0.05
公共管理、社会保障和社会组织	Public Management, Social Security and Social Organization		0.01		

4-12 各市(州)国有、集体和其他各种经济单位就业人员数(2018年)

Number of Employed Persons in State-owned , Collective-owned Units and Other Types of Ownership by Region(2018)

(年末数)单位：万人 (year-end)(10 000 persons)

市(州)	Region	合计 Total	国有经济单位 State-owned Units	城镇集体经济单位 Urban Collective-owned Units	其他各种经济单位 Units of Other Types of Ownership	内资 Domestic Funded	港澳台投资 Funded by Entrepreneurs from Hong Kong, Macao and Taiwan	外商投资 Foreign Funded
全　省	**Sichuan**	**780.64**	**327.58**	**20.25**	**432.81**	**394.37**	**17.17**	**21.28**
成都市	Chengdu	269.26	81.26	3.84	184.16	153.06	13.70	17.40
自贡市	Zigong	20.55	9.06	0.29	11.19	10.99	0.01	0.19
攀枝花市	Panzhihua	17.65	5.74	0.14	11.77	11.69	0.01	0.08
泸州市	Luzhou	36.92	14.79	2.48	19.65	19.45	0.08	0.13
德阳市	Deyang	30.97	11.23	0.99	18.75	17.74	0.72	0.28
绵阳市	Mianyang	50.55	19.45	1.13	29.98	28.77	0.70	0.50
广元市	Guangyuan	17.19	10.08	0.80	6.31	6.22	0.03	0.06
遂宁市	Suining	20.46	7.75	1.23	11.48	10.96	0.22	0.30
内江市	Neijiang	21.54	10.76	0.55	10.24	9.49	0.10	0.65
乐山市	Leshan	24.05	10.43	0.24	13.38	12.46	0.55	0.37
南充市	Nanchong	43.85	21.24	1.44	21.17	20.75	0.26	0.16
眉山市	Meishan	18.51	8.96	0.26	9.29	8.91	0.17	0.21
宜宾市	Yibin	38.19	15.23	0.77	22.19	21.49	0.15	0.55
广安市	Guangan	16.16	10.07	1.88	4.21	4.04	0.13	0.05
达州市	Dazhou	33.90	17.20	1.87	14.83	14.58	0.10	0.14
雅安市	Yaan	11.52	6.61	0.13	4.78	4.62	0.12	0.03
巴中市	Bazhong	24.77	10.91	1.23	12.63	12.52	0.07	0.04
资阳市	Ziyang	17.55	8.05	0.56	8.94	8.83	0.04	0.07
阿坝藏族羌族自治州	Aba	9.11	7.18	0.09	1.84	1.82	0.02	
甘孜藏族自治州	Ganzi	9.33	8.11	0.12	1.10	1.08	0.01	
凉山彝族自治州	Liangshan	26.85	17.44	0.22	9.19	9.13		0.06

注：全省合计中包括了省直综单位就业人员，市(州)数据未包括(以下有关各表同)。

a) The number of persons employed in directly affiliated units and comprehensive units was included in the Sichuan's number of employed persons, but was not included in regional number of employed persons.(the same as the following related tables)

4-13 各市(州)按行业分城镇私营单位就业人员数(2018年)

(年末数)单位：万人

市(州)	Region	私营单位就业人员 Number of Employed Persons in Private Enterprises	#农、林、牧、渔业 Agriculture, Forestry, Animal Husbandry and Fishery	#采矿业 Mining	#制造业 Manufacturing	#建筑业 Construction	#批发和零售业 Wholesale and Retail Trades
全　省	**Sichuan**	**423.80**	**8.76**	**19.63**	**115.64**	**74.42**	**39.07**
成都市	Chengdu	140.24	3.64	0.04	28.39	33.05	15.49
自贡市	Zigong	15.15	0.07	1.70	5.67	2.84	2.48
攀枝花市	Panzhihua	10.75	0.19	2.19	2.28	0.80	2.15
泸州市	Luzhou	16.24	0.25	0.41	4.81	4.23	1.77
德阳市	Deyang	15.95	0.26	0.03	4.62	1.32	0.45
绵阳市	Mianyang	37.28	0.56	0.18	9.99	3.20	3.13
广元市	Guangyuan	10.68	0.20	0.25	1.89	2.01	0.16
遂宁市	Suining	7.98	0.27	0.06	2.57	0.43	1.10
内江市	Neijiang	19.46	0.50	1.69	2.33	1.78	0.78
乐山市	Leshan	14.90	0.61	0.81	6.15	0.77	0.48
南充市	Nanchong	24.18	0.05	0.28	11.36	4.63	1.55
眉山市	Meishan	13.75	0.14	0.04	6.10	1.93	2.10
宜宾市	Yibin	21.54	0.16	4.85	7.94	3.73	0.81
广安市	Guangan	12.91	0.24	0.83	3.90	3.47	1.53
达州市	Dazhou	16.43	0.32	3.14	3.88	1.76	1.22
雅安市	Yaan	7.20	0.22	0.47	2.56	0.50	1.05
巴中市	Bazhong	8.67	0.08	0.42	2.59	2.81	0.19
资阳市	Ziyang	10.38	0.26	0.03	3.65	1.22	0.85
阿坝藏族羌族自治州	Aba	2.43	0.14	0.09	0.40	0.29	0.23
甘孜藏族自治州	Ganzi	1.85	0.11	0.08	0.15	0.11	0.29
凉山彝族自治州	Liangshan	15.83	0.49	2.04	4.41	3.54	1.26

Number of Employed Persons in Urban Private Enterprises by Sector and Region(2018)

(year-end)(10 000 persons)

#交通运输、仓储和邮政业 Transport, Storage and Post	#住宿和餐饮业 Hotels and Catering Services	#信息传输、软件和信息技术服务业 Information Transmission, Software and Information Technology	#房地产业 Real Estate	#租赁和商务服务业 Leasing and Business Services	#居民服务、修理和其他服务业 Services to Households, Repair and Other Services	#教育 Education	#卫生和社会工作 Health and Social Service	#文化、体育和娱乐业 Culture, Sports and Entertainment
12.83	**45.65**	**10.30**	**16.55**	**29.24**	**21.09**	**2.61**	**4.80**	**7.11**
2.95	15.53	4.13	6.15	13.61	8.74	1.05	1.99	1.63
0.46	0.41	0.12	0.64	0.18	0.15	0.09	0.07	0.07
0.25	0.59	0.13	0.45	0.46	0.77	0.03	0.03	0.03
1.26	0.36	0.43	0.66	0.83	0.15	0.28	0.15	0.29
0.74	2.47	0.29	0.76	2.45	0.64	0.04	0.10	0.30
2.41	5.26	0.52	1.21	4.32	2.02	0.09	0.04	0.61
0.16	3.19	0.42	0.49	0.58	1.02		0.03	0.15
0.10	1.37	0.21	0.18	0.41	0.26	0.04	0.02	0.74
1.00	1.69	1.06	0.95	1.89	3.57	0.01	0.98	1.01
0.41	2.87	0.25	0.37	0.76	0.37	0.04	0.04	0.48
0.39	1.55	0.10	1.65	0.75	0.26	0.32	0.45	0.33
0.24	1.88	0.28	0.43		0.02	0.04	0.08	
0.46	1.18	0.39	0.12	0.44	0.09	0.12	0.20	0.19
0.25	0.77	0.06	0.40	0.14	0.85	0.04	0.06	0.11
0.54	2.32	0.54	0.57	0.39	0.70	0.23	0.25	0.08
0.15	0.48	0.08	0.12	0.25	0.27	0.01	0.03	0.25
0.11	0.94	0.45	0.32	0.13	0.08	0.13	0.10	0.23
0.29	0.77	0.37	0.85	0.97	0.50	0.03	0.08	0.18
0.20	0.31	0.20	0.05	0.09	0.09		0.03	0.11
0.11	0.24	0.08	0.03	0.17	0.14			0.19
0.35	1.47	0.19	0.15	0.42	0.40	0.02	0.07	0.13

4-14 各市(州)按行业分城镇个体就业人员数(2018年)

(年末数)单位: 万人

市(州)	Region	城镇个体就业人员 Number of Employed Persons in Self-employed Individuals	#农、林、牧、渔业 Agriculture, Forestry, Animal Husbandry and Fishery	#采矿业 Mining	#制造业 Manufacturing	#建筑业 Construction	#批发和零售业 Wholesale and Retail Trades
全　省	**Sichuan**	**440.74**	**6.63**	**1.39**	**28.66**	**15.56**	**107.92**
成都市	Chengdu	135.10	0.82		6.74	3.91	37.24
自贡市	Zigong	13.49	0.14	0.01	1.49	0.10	3.67
攀枝花市	Panzhihua	7.64	0.07	0.01	0.36	0.01	3.42
泸州市	Luzhou	19.08	0.51	0.05	2.64	0.49	4.71
德阳市	Deyang	12.61	0.03		0.15	0.01	5.29
绵阳市	Mianyang	23.93	0.25		0.66	0.03	6.17
广元市	Guangyuan	13.59	0.05	0.12	0.77	0.11	2.34
遂宁市	Suining	12.65	0.30	0.03	0.53	0.05	3.18
内江市	Neijiang	12.08	0.07	0.02	0.57	0.03	2.03
乐山市	Leshan	16.68	0.62	0.02	1.04	0.04	3.03
南充市	Nanchong	27.15	0.99	0.13	1.34	1.14	4.95
眉山市	Meishan	17.04	0.04	0.02	1.71	1.79	4.69
宜宾市	Yibin	21.64	0.98	0.02	0.35	0.89	3.73
广安市	Guangan	21.44	0.35	0.16	1.70	2.22	3.99
达州市	Dazhou	30.99	0.52	0.27	3.83	2.44	4.39
雅安市	Yaan	9.21	0.17	0.03	1.05	0.09	3.48
巴中市	Bazhong	11.50	0.09	0.11	1.33	0.51	2.90
资阳市	Ziyang	4.78	0.03		0.14	0.35	2.09
阿坝藏族羌族自治州	Aba	3.38	0.03	0.02	0.13	0.02	1.08
甘孜藏族自治州	Ganzi	3.86	0.08	0.03	0.12	0.02	1.44
凉山彝族自治州	Liangshan	22.90	0.49	0.34	2.01	1.31	4.10

Number of Employed Persons in Self-employed Individuals by Sector and Region(2018)

(year-end)(10 000persons)

#交通运输、仓储和邮政业 Transport, Storage and Post	#住宿和餐饮业 Hotels and Catering Services	#信息传输、软件和信息技术服务业 Information Transmission, Software and Information Technology	#房地产业 Real Estate	#租赁和商务服务业 Leasing and Business Services	#居民服务、修理和其他服务业 Services to Households, Repair and Other Services	#教育 Education	#卫生和社会工作 Health and Social Service	#文化、体育和娱乐业 Culture, Sports and Entertain-ment
38.68	**121.72**	**33.35**	**1.68**	**10.20**	**57.82**	**1.44**	**4.29**	**11.40**
30.93	18.50	14.14	0.73	5.34	12.20	0.19	0.81	3.55
0.13	4.79	0.06	0.08	0.18	2.31	0.04	0.14	0.35
0.65	1.54	0.11	0.01	0.15	1.14	0.01	0.06	0.10
1.42	3.24	0.05	0.04	0.26	3.97	0.08	0.31	1.31
0.10	3.66	1.13	0.01	0.12	2.00	0.01	0.04	0.06
0.11	8.46	3.88	0.01	0.51	3.54	0.05	0.10	0.16
0.10	6.49	1.27	0.05	0.38	1.57	0.02	0.14	0.18
0.13	5.85	0.11	0.08	0.23	1.90	0.02	0.07	0.17
0.49	5.19	1.08	0.06	0.53	1.46	0.03	0.25	0.27
0.06	7.57	1.32		0.38	2.28	0.01	0.07	0.24
0.23	9.62	1.48	0.03	0.45	5.79	0.11	0.43	0.46
0.57	5.37	0.08	0.30	0.03	1.83	0.20	0.26	0.15
0.19	8.91	1.66	0.02	0.22	3.09	0.09	0.10	1.39
1.30	6.69	1.05	0.04	0.25	2.54	0.17	0.49	0.49
0.23	9.28	1.94	0.08	0.42	5.30	0.17	0.52	1.60
0.53	2.16	0.13		0.19	1.28	0.01	0.03	0.06
0.75	2.93	1.31	0.06	0.07	1.05	0.11	0.15	0.13
0.10	0.01	0.98	0.07	0.08	0.70	0.08	0.14	0.01
0.16	1.28	0.16		0.04	0.39	0.01	0.01	0.05
0.09	1.55	0.04		0.04	0.34	0.01	0.02	0.08
0.41	8.63	1.37	0.01	0.33	3.14	0.02	0.15	0.59

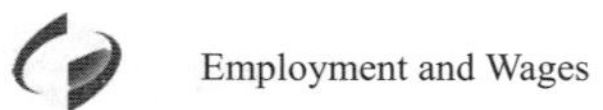

4-15 按行业分其他经济单位就业人员数
Number of Staff and Workers in Units of Other Types of Ownership by Sector

(年末数)单位：万人 (year-end)(10 000persons)

登记注册类型及行业	Registration Status and Sector	2014	2015	2016	2017	2018
总　计	**Total**	**428.65**	**425.14**	**417.84**	**425.72**	**432.81**
按登记注册类型分组	**Grouped by Registration Status**					
内资	Domestic Funded	384.58	381.94	380.79	386.31	394.37
股份合作单位	Cooperative Units	5.56	5.35	4.78	4.28	3.56
联营单位	Jiont Ownership Units	0.64	0.53	0.54	0.39	0.35
有限责任公司	Limited Liability Corporations	289.37	283.35	284.04	289.92	308.03
股份有限公司	Share-holding Corporations Ltd.	80.26	81.92	81.33	80.90	72.71
其他	Others	8.75	10.78	10.10	10.82	9.73
港澳台商投资单位	Units with Funds form Hong Kong, Macao and Taiwan	22.00	22.52	17.31	17.22	17.17
外商投资单位	Foreign Funded Units	22.06	20.68	19.74	22.19	21.28
按国民经济行业分组	**Grouped by Economic Sector**					
农、林、牧、渔业	Agriculture,Forestry, Animal Husbandry and Fishery	0.11	0.13	0.10	0.09	0.12
采矿业	Mining	18.49	17.18	17.52	16.33	12.81
制造业	Manufacturing	160.20	150.33	139.79	141.13	121.93
电力、热力、燃气及水生产和供应业	Production and Supply of Electricity, Heat, Gas and Water	11.63	12.66	10.20	9.35	9.78
建筑业	Construction	116.29	115.28	113.44	112.91	137.58
批发和零售业	Wholesale and Retail Trades	27.11	26.19	26.29	26.46	24.48
交通运输、仓储和邮政业	Transport, Storage and Post	19.42	20.26	19.58	19.06	19.09
住宿和餐饮业	Hotels and Catering Services	10.27	9.52	8.74	8.59	8.95
信息传输、软件和信息技术服务业	Information Transmission, Software and Information Technology Services	13.57	16.50	16.71	18.52	17.91
金融业	Financial Intermediation	11.21	12.57	16.59	18.25	20.00
房地产业	Real Estate	16.65	17.87	18.98	20.76	21.21
租赁和商务服务业	Leasing and Business Services	6.66	8.30	10.77	11.45	14.99
科学研究和技术服务业	Scientific Research and Technical Services	5.30	5.66	5.70	6.97	7.16
水利、环境和公共设施管理业	Management of Water Conservancy, Environment and Public Facilities	2.43	2.37	2.40	2.68	3.30
居民服务、修理和其他服务业	Services to Households, Repair and Other Services	1.15	1.37	1.46	1.90	1.44
教育	Education	4.44	5.12	5.24	5.99	6.27
卫生和社会工作	Health and Social Service	2.43	2.43	2.83	3.67	4.34
文化、体育和娱乐业	Culture, Sports and Entertainment	1.28	1.36	1.46	1.58	1.35
公共管理、社会保障和社会组织	Public Management, Social Security and Social Organization	0.01	0.04	0.05	0.04	0.10

4-16 按行业分国有、集体和其他各种经济单位女性就业人员数

Number of Female Employed Persons in State-owned , Collective-owned Units and Other Types of Ownership by Sector

(年末数)单位：万人 (year-end)(10 000 persons)

行　业	Sector	2014	2015	2016	2017	2018
总　计	**Total**	**280.82**	**278.70**	**280.80**	**293.13**	**288.89**
按经济类型分	**Grouped by Ownership**					
国有经济单位	State-owned Units	136.52	135.72	138.68	143.99	143.07
城镇集体经济单位	Urban Collective-owned Units	7.79	7.68	7.58	7.08	6.05
其他各种经济单位	Units of Other Types of Ownership	136.51	135.31	134.54	142.06	139.77
按行业分	**Grouped by Sector**					
农、林、牧、渔业	Agriculture, Forestry, Animal Husbandry and Fishery	0.95	0.85	0.84	0.71	0.63
采矿业	Mining	5.24	3.79	3.57	3.10	2.46
制造业	Manufacturing	64.37	58.84	55.10	55.34	47.12
电力、热力、燃气及水生产和供应业	Production and Supply of Electricity, Heat, Gas and Water	8.24	7.96	7.20	6.80	6.70
建筑业	Construction	19.73	18.63	18.62	20.25	23.82
批发和零售业	Wholesale and Retail Trades	16.24	15.88	15.67	15.70	14.73
交通运输、仓储和邮政业	Transport, Storage and Post	12.78	12.41	12.50	12.11	11.70
住宿和餐饮业	Hotels and Catering Services	6.93	5.75	5.01	5.69	5.83
信息传输、软件和信息技术服务业	Information Transmission, Software and Information Technology Services	6.43	7.25	7.17	7.38	7.65
金融业	Financial Intermediation	12.04	13.68	16.49	17.67	17.64
房地产业	Real Estate	6.83	7.19	7.57	8.58	9.08
租赁和商务服务业	Leasing and Business Services	3.72	3.69	4.03	4.68	4.90
科学研究和技术服务业	Scientific Research and Technical Services	6.45	6.35	6.37	6.72	5.22
水利、环境和公共设施管理业	Management of Water Conservancy, Environment and Public Facilities	6.04	6.12	6.26	6.22	5.53
居民服务、修理和其他服务业	Services to Households, Repair and Other Services	0.75	0.81	1.04	1.23	0.84
教育	Education	46.29	47.77	48.76	51.07	53.36
卫生和社会工作	Health and Social Service	27.48	28.97	30.51	32.91	33.86
文化、体育和娱乐业	Culture, Sports and Entertainment	2.88	2.78	2.75	2.92	2.56
公共管理、社会保障和社会组织	Public Management, Social Security and Social Organization	27.44	29.98	31.32	34.05	35.26

4-17 各市(州)国有、集体和其他经济单位女性就业人员数
Number of Female Employed Persons in State-owned, Collective-owned Units and Other Types of Ownership Units by Region

(年末数)单位：万人 (year-end)(10 000 persons)

市(州)	Region	2005	2010	2013	2014	2015	2016	2017	2018
全　省	**Sichuan**	**174.60**	**192.73**	**232.56**	**280.82**	**278.70**	**280.80**	**293.13**	**288.89**
成都市	Chengdu	46.50	58.81	83.27	95.75	96.13	100.40	108.28	106.08
自贡市	Zigong	6.60	5.79	6.32	7.84	7.32	7.07	7.22	7.44
攀枝花市	Panzhihua	6.90	6.14	7.48	10.89	6.73	5.79	6.03	5.98
泸州市	Luzhou	8.50	8.58	8.40	11.62	11.45	11.75	11.07	13.28
德阳市	Deyang	8.00	8.19	9.58	11.73	11.37	10.82	10.76	10.47
绵阳市	Mianyang	11.60	13.05	15.52	18.76	18.44	18.88	19.51	18.24
广元市	Guangyuan	4.60	4.71	5.18	5.82	5.92	6.36	6.44	6.55
遂宁市	Suining	5.10	4.39	5.46	7.33	7.60	7.07	7.35	7.06
内江市	Neijiang	8.00	7.39	8.14	9.92	9.49	9.39	9.18	8.28
乐山市	Leshan	10.30	9.74	8.57	10.14	10.56	10.75	10.58	9.32
南充市	Nanchong	6.70	7.67	11.00	14.19	15.17	15.24	15.93	15.35
眉山市	Meishan	4.50	5.50	6.01	7.65	7.57	7.97	7.97	6.99
宜宾市	Yibin	10.50	11.71	12.35	13.23	13.18	13.12	13.57	14.20
广安市	Guangan	3.30	3.51	4.44	5.20	5.58	5.97	6.59	6.40
达州市	Dazhou	7.80	7.65	8.32	9.93	9.84	10.21	10.59	11.07
雅安市	Yaan	3.10	3.43	3.61	4.21	4.35	4.49	4.52	4.61
巴中市	Bazhong	3.30	4.16	5.27	6.75	7.05	7.03	7.84	7.90
资阳市	Ziyang	5.20	5.77	7.17	8.48	9.43	6.29	6.43	6.45
阿坝藏族羌族自治州	Aba	2.90	2.82	3.39	3.68	3.76	3.90	4.06	4.18
甘孜藏族自治州	Ganzi	2.40	2.84	3.16	3.39	3.49	3.60	3.83	3.94
凉山彝族自治州	Liangshan	6.80	7.46	8.00	8.54	8.72	9.20	9.91	9.98

4-18 按登记注册类型分全部单位就业人员工资总额及指数
Total Wage of Employment in all Units and Related Indices by Registered Types

年份 Year	工资总额 (万元) Total Wage Bill (10 000 yuan)					指数 (上年=100) Indices (Preceding year=100)				
	全部单位 all Units	国有经济单位 State-owned Units	城镇集体经济单位 Urban Colletive-owned Units	私营经济单位 Private Units	其他各种经济单位 Units of Other Types of Ownership	全部单位 all Units	国有经济单位 State-owned Units	城镇集体经济单位 Urban Colletive-owned Units	私营经济单位 Private Units	其他各种经济单位 Units of Other Types of Ownership
1978	263196	219481	43715			114.3	119.6	93.6		
1980	364892	300829	64063			121.2	120.9	122.4		
1985	598403	478883	119128		392	120.6	121.1	119.2		80.0
1986	719269	582177	136524		568	120.2	121.6	114.6		144.9
1987	802261	650498	150931		832	111.5	111.7	110.6		146.5
1988	987813	807670	178923		1220	123.1	124.2	118.5		146.6
1989	1135724	937712	195894		2118	115.0	116.1	109.5		173.6
1990	1294823	1071715	220375		2733	114.0	114.3	112.5		129.0
1991	1450034	1197509	248487		4038	111.8	111.7	111.4		147.7
1992	1667894	1377792	283759		6343	115.3	115.1	115.6		157.1
1993	2046047	1635013	333417		77617	122.7	118.7	117.5		1223.7
1994	2776839	2227867	386038		162934	135.7	135.7	115.8		209.9
1995	3217827	2574023	437256		206548	115.9	115.9	113.3		126.8
1996	3550444	2841447	469060		239937	110.3	110.3	107.3		116.2
1997	3806429	3020053	513532		272844	107.2	106.3	109.5		113.8
1998	3927403	3010629	438565		478209	103.2	99.7	85.4		175.3
1999	3985709	3076087	398702		510920	105.3	105.8	94.0		112.5
2000	4369495	3387240	405185		577070	109.6	110.1	101.6		112.9
2001	4902582	3824669	389753		688160	112.2	112.9	96.2		119.3
2002	5391189	4069680	388119		933390	110.0	106.4	99.6		135.6
2003	6224989	4530295	436951		1257743	115.5	111.3	112.6		129.5
2004	6926273	4954541	433210		1538522	111.3	109.4	99.1		122.4
2005	7960325	5575919	457007		1927399	114.9	112.5	105.5		125.7
2006	9100898	6278120	512573		2310205	114.3	112.6	112.2		119.7
2007	11198309	7702452	597311		2898546	123.0	122.7	116.5		125.7
2008	13555288	9131401	698158		3725729	121.0	118.6	116.9		128.5
2009	21294971	10581526	791894	5511793	4409758		115.9	113.4		118.4
2010	25409121	12266436	785441	7003940	5353304	119.3	115.9	99.2	127.1	121.4
2011	31597970	14479483	951634	8908497	7258356	124.4	118.0	121.2	127.2	135.6
2012	37723598	17060258	1107287	10725843	8830210	119.4	117.8	116.4	120.4	121.7
2013	46912922	18626143	1137642	12837994	14311143	124.4	109.2	102.7	119.7	162.1
2014	56316799	20162618	1238152	13887133	21028896	120.0	108.2	108.8	108.2	146.9
2015	61686544	22612943	1254899	15251264	22567438	109.5	112.2	101.4	109.8	107.3
2016	66123764	24582334	1340078	16660512	23540840	107.2	108.7	106.8	109.2	104.3
2017	71865217	27223176	1223720	17992586	25425735	108.7	110.7	91.3	108.0	108.0
2018	79794982	29269353	1199158	20189632	29136839	111.0	107.5	98.0	112.2	114.6

4-19 各市(州)全部单位就业人员工资总额
Total Wage Bill of Employment in all Units and Related Indices by Region

单位：万元 (10 000 yuan)

市(州)	Region	2012	2013	2014	2015	2016	2017	2018
全　省	**Sichuan**	**37723598**	**46912922**	**56316799**	**61686544**	**66123764**	**71865217**	**79794982**
成都市	Chengdu	12653666	18422819	20466285	22626222	24534429	26995090	29551120
自贡市	Zigong	1157363	1373640	1639374	1725944	1844418	2085190	2272596
攀枝花市	Panzhihua	1212831	1546716	2173505	1581520	1593336	1751952	1855665
泸州市	Luzhou	1570148	1915854	2566125	2906380	3212536	3172932	4031314
德阳市	Deyang	1835928	2151248	2591398	2835979	3096978	3376194	3766400
绵阳市	Mianyang	2371720	2779487	3342347	3716393	4031238	4220725	4762933
广元市	Guangyuan	864261	879123	1036591	1180469	1277392	1394616	1442570
遂宁市	Suining	891676	1050449	1272754	1402752	1510837	1699599	1913406
内江市	Neijiang	986458	1234743	1522065	1728616	1794629	1789805	1757424
乐山市	Leshan	1465367	1518466	1843517	2029251	2199716	2336892	2462660
南充市	Nanchong	1769899	2457586	2904331	3447612	3714843	4063304	4658537
眉山市	Meishan	1058067	1167904	1431391	1594594	1728087	1869924	1975006
宜宾市	Yibin	2033710	2202832	2411899	2672713	3010537	3329666	3972375
广安市	Guangan	986788	1214477	1351317	1415294	1561262	1726856	1829391
达州市	Dazhou	1524672	1579152	1936903	2043926	2222663	2457777	3084228
雅安市	Yaan	493662	494876	613293	676563	724920	764434	775676
巴中市	Bazhong	700836	788062	1073792	1282501	1399797	1519006	1736745
资阳市	Ziyang	956116	1226217	1474160	1795941	1307512	1327911	1448500
阿坝藏族羌族自治州	Aba	388879	491962	582164	614251	707371	772226	877233
甘孜藏族自治州	Ganzi	356846	409872	474020	581288	630721	710379	778706
凉山彝族自治州	Liangshan	1405649	1418893	1514073	1712642	1883924	2066811	2307231

4-20 各市(州)按登记注册类型分全部单位就业人员工资总额及指数(2018年)

Total Wage of Employment in all Units and Related Indices by Region and Registered Types(2018)

市(州)	Region	工资总额 (万元) Total Wage Bill (10 000 yuan)					指数 (上年=100) Indices (Preceding year=100)				
		合计 Total	国有经济单位 State-owned Units	城镇集体经济单位 Urban Collective-owned Units	私营经济单位 Private Units	其他各种经济单位 Units of Other Types of Ownership	合计 Total	国有经济单位 State-owned Units	城镇集体经济单位 Urban Collective-owned Units	私营经济单位 Private Units	其他各种经济单位 Units of Other Types of Ownership
全 省	**Sichuan**	**79794982**	**29269353**	**1199158**	**20189632**	**29136839**	**111.0**	**107.5**	**98.0**	**112.2**	**114.6**
成都市	Chengdu	29551120	8130962	283254	6718594	14418310	103.0	89.6	97.8	113.4	107.6
自贡市	Zigong	2272596	816782	16476	839560	599779	109.0	108.1	87.5	107.1	113.8
攀枝花市	Panzhihua	1855665	564608	5655	436021	849380	105.9	104.9	28.7	102.5	110.5
泸州市	Luzhou	4031314	1220912	165068	1538097	1107238	127.1	111.2	116.3	119.2	172.5
德阳市	Deyang	3766400	1076713	58860	1335374	1295452	111.6	102.4	105.5	109.3	123.8
绵阳市	Mianyang	4762933	1889376	86633	943511	1843413	112.8	114.2	89.4	109.0	115.0
广元市	Guangyuan	1442570	763776	47330	297768	333696	103.4	104.5	84.4	93.0	116.0
遂宁市	Suining	1913406	709933	68081	595141	540251	112.6	116.1	100.9	111.4	111.0
内江市	Neijiang	1757424	838288	23461	375426	520249	98.2	114.8	68.0	96.4	81.8
乐山市	Leshan	2462660	890895	13417	774895	783452	105.4	106.2	58.5	111.1	100.8
南充市	Nanchong	4658537	1799910	90178	1689210	1079240	114.6	120.1	145.3	119.1	99.5
眉山市	Meishan	1975006	777659	14942	667320	515086	105.6	109.7	104.4	105.7	100.0
宜宾市	Yibin	3972375	1329533	32939	1137460	1472443	119.3	111.0	98.6	109.5	139.0
广安市	Guangan	1829391	835593	88256	656610	248933	105.9	107.4	92.3	106.6	104.9
达州市	Dazhou	3084228	1288116	98287	827006	870819	125.5	121.9	114.0	122.1	136.6
雅安市	Yaan	775676	428123	6896	112535	228123	101.5	104.6	94.4	85.1	105.9
巴中市	Bazhong	1736745	727403	47975	377412	583955	114.3	109.1	113.3	131.8	111.6
资阳市	Ziyang	1448500	626912	23210	405406	392972	109.1	114.1	59.7	117.0	99.9
阿坝藏族羌族自治州	Aba	877233	717249	7095	48768	104120	113.6	115.3	87.3	100.7	111.1
甘孜藏族自治州	Ganzi	778706	657958	6523	24269	89956	109.6	109.9	106.7	108.3	108.2
凉山彝族自治州	Liangshan	2307231	1376514	14624	389248	526845	111.6	105.1	56.9	120.2	129.5

注：全省合计中包括省直综单位就业人员工资总额，市(州)数据未包括(以下有关各表同)。

a) The number of persons employed in directly affiliated units and comprehensive units was included in the Sichuan's number of employed persons, but was not included in regional number of employed persons.(the same as the following related tables)

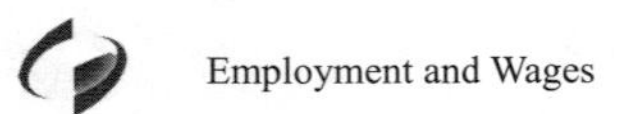

4-21 按行业分全部单位就业人员工资总额

单位：万元

年份 Year	合计 Total	农、林、牧、渔业 Agriculture, Forestry, Animal Husbandry and Fishery	采矿业 Mining	制造业 Manufacturing	电力、热力、燃气及水生产和供应业 Production and Supply of Electricity, Heat,Gas and Water	建筑业 Construction	批发和零售业 Wholesale and Retail Trades	交通运输、仓储和邮政业 Transport, Storage and Post	住宿和餐饮业 Hotels and Catering Services	信息传输、软件和信息技术服务业 Information Transmission, Software and Information Technology
1978	263196	7016	22921	91621	5233	23383	26693	25436	3685	
1980	364892	8186	28667	126922	8134	32823	37726	30802	5176	
1985	598403	12035	46417	219817	8405	48027	28322	46800	6512	1268
1986	719269	14787	57236	258144	10810	58789	65333	54971	8262	2126
1987	802261	15341	59949	297304	12852	67477	71835	60359	9066	2501
1988	987813	17477	70663	371196	16092	81136	90556	74328	11539	3164
1989	1135724	19005	76612	439876	19804	88267	101140	86963	12958	4399
1990	1294823	21185	104553	476728	29408	99025	112974	96980	14458	5711
1991	1450034	23443	112731	547026	29410	115319	123849	108156	16005	6291
1992	1667894	25979	118366	615493	35459	135228	137426	124006	17127	7489
1993	2046047	29031	116455	775305	41259	221791	175633	103846	21044	8356
1994	2776839	38639	171556	956517	55749	262082	220732	138631	28381	18195
1995	3217827	44168	188235	1121615	79256	303939	255632	171773	34916	18645
1996	3550444	50134	211692	1210693	95247	320058	273788	193317	38553	19078
1997	3806429	54280	213126	1249005	119344	349282	279658	223444	39983	19589
1998	3927403	57111	207010	1185340	129699	346700	260947	228139	36486	20084
1999	3985709	63225	171492	1071310	140643	345079	229458	249831	33056	23999
2000	4369495	72727	214016	1108247	155720	360460	217446	274101	29718	26618
2001	4902582	90629	158455	1117906	181767	411914	195433	297310	32305	34640
2002	5391189	95174	195370	1180244	205600	493233	179869	330353	32116	45931
2003	6224989	103745	207903	1357229	240706	627520	212843	299198	41968	96957
2004	6926273	97595	247519	1496103	261516	695040	236843	329732	49262	127251
2005	7960325	95400	340874	1690892	300129	815528	270334	398077	58340	144989
2006	9100898	103637	402290	1958532	328948	997151	284486	479269	61669	160441
2007	11198309	114676	522447	2294500	393339	1257432	309381	545062	74852	168658
2008	13555288	111457	653566	2784093	475273	1603208	384950	630662	85024	193001
2009	21294971	98415	1255861	5130324	576252	3167298	965673	894140	287608	309578
2010	25409121	111552	1506249	6132399	675721	3873904	1176499	1038718	356303	387007
2011	31597970	200867	1779562	8103028	844533	4672108	1480791	1199619	485624	431563
2012	37723598	243409	2254256	9447049	1003965	5603892	1170441	1482261	1148340	586057
2013	46912922	238570	1998425	11597697	2022631	6957229	2096116	2234350	871092	1400298
2014	56316799	225041	2293080	14101830	2159013	9535256	2508880	2735747	1078258	1533657
2015	61686544	235715	2083618	14532969	2267013	10056042	2732732	3013325	1031735	1907386
2016	66123764	259072	1985880	15174238	2171097	10735972	2752547	3130586	1044356	2033157
2017	71865217	263046	2119605	15912709	2159550	10925975	3004453	3345831	1045377	2424533
2018	79794982	258107	2141026	16770293	2392033	13380723	3277549	3702221	1053877	2577192

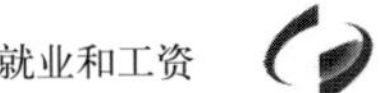

Total Wage of Staff and Workers in all Units by Sector

(10 000 yuan)

金融业 Financial Interme-diation	房地产业 Real Estate	租赁和商务服务业 Leasing and Business Services	科学研究和技术服务业 Scientific Research, and Technical Services	水利、环境和公共设施管理业 Management of Water Con-servancy,En-vironment and Public Facilities	居民服务、修理和其他服务业 Services to Households, Repair and Other Services	教育 Education	卫生和社会工作 Health and Social Service	文化、体育和娱乐业 Culture, Sports and Entertain-ment	公共管理、社会保障和社会组织 Public Mana-gement,Social Security and Social Organization
2096	197		11766	757	307	21420	6069	1042	13554
3468	778		15088	3021	417	30902	10746	2898	19138
6905	1155	1117	26872	4817	463	51174	17595	3782	36920
9307	1450	1847	29932	5937	589	61038	23114	6009	49588
10474	1510	2185	30870	6985	698	65819	25034	6917	55085
12924	1803	2760	35675	8643	761	84250	30796	8435	65615
14102	2053	3863	39444	11762	815	89940	34583	11037	79101
17470	2437	5066	46459	15061	978	99358	39529	13358	94085
19297	2795	5765	51742	16480	996	107925	43028	13774	106002
25366	4005	6998	64707	19620	783	134970	51266	12593	131013
40457	5216	7827	69586	21830	8053	157693	63269	12508	166888
69270	8886	16756	98468	46332	9316	244518	104740	29282	258789
80619	10459	17626	120187	47932	9687	242074	122049	29689	289326
92634	12751	18124	126915	48639	9804	332534	140925	30614	324991
110358	14601	19137	134609	49533	9840	368133	158473	31191	363001
136365	20341	20515	142113	50345	10137	436783	181650	31955	425980
158688	22735	24961	125873	58322	10817	518933	214225	36587	486655
183778	27647	27311	141697	63432	13251	601173	246975	40099	565261
214232	29128	30006	203335	71987	20125	771304	294859	49890	697637
231703	41850	32574	186623	76808	17648	896710	335438	53535	761243
276380	52517	40900	218656	67579	32828	996203	385244	71653	894960
315060	56713	50438	260908	72086	17409	1100797	425419	76188	1010394
379710	60560	110355	278465	81137	28546	1201121	487875	91225	1126767
415539	76292	110317	341389	100592	32356	1339277	566718	89067	1252926
503492	101872	145778	417854	124712	43016	1720414	710029	101941	1648852
676824	109496	184636	523409	135675	21894	1946943	856137	113486	2065555
791821	357901	374472	665465	180718	123001	2541547	1040967	144975	2388957
1007152	430062	468560	783046	207955	171475	2927686	1277654	177429	2699750
1315866	564549	567142	1014862	269933	230330	3366310	1713105	239082	3119096
1605422	713886	630263	1159404	344307	295883	4013182	2133160	261911	3626511
1869129	921904	857038	1582766	462475	348657	4525646	2550911	317131	4060858
2065994	1380710	1162998	1821159	531393	330096	5022372	2940353	429376	4461588
2267734	1546288	1336259	1975685	567042	355036	6075938	3507362	470626	5724040
2654525	1750841	1502037	2104478	618346	417070	6667027	4044483	509211	6568841
2974108	1978298	1680327	2407865	673142	461608	7400464	4676656	582792	7828877
3182901	2274021	1843401	2781473	693098	423722	8111213	5208228	610853	9113053

4-22 各市(州)按行业分全部单位就业人员工资总额(2018年)

单位：万元

市(州)	Region	合计 Total	农、林、牧、渔业 Agriculture, Forestry, Animal Husbandry and Fishery	采矿业 Mining	制造业 Manufacturing	电力、热力、燃气及水生产和供应业 Production and Supply of Electricity, Heat,Gas and Water	建筑业 Construction	批发和零售业 Wholesale and Retail Trades	交通运输、仓储和邮政业 Transport, Storage and Post	住宿和餐饮业 Hotels and Catering Services
全 省	**Sichuan**	**79794982**	**258107**	**2141026**	**16770293**	**2392033**	**13380723**	**3277549**	**3702221**	**1053877**
成都市	Chengdu	29551120	45893	12662	6593164	215068	4290466	1776497	1755572	510214
自贡市	Zigong	2272596	6268	68218	610605	32429	453092	50468	88647	28390
攀枝花市	Panzhihua	1855665	12801	181696	476299	99900	214820	103369	55850	20295
泸州市	Luzhou	4031314	3550	37080	517762	40462	1515381	210978	127516	19399
德阳市	Deyang	3766400	2166	22443	1701527	24675	427053	142773	61066	40549
绵阳市	Mianyang	4762933	11784	13249	1095064	120469	873532	158076	103500	55780
广元市	Guangyuan	1442570	5069	62308	146207	31779	217552	28346	50938	5198
遂宁市	Suining	1913406	3850	13421	518129	48117	344238	50287	22170	47862
内江市	Neijiang	1757424	11685	36752	246862	57484	322248	43943	69774	12513
乐山市	Leshan	2462660	11607	121241	525716	80531	377458	90975	76011	38626
南充市	Nanchong	4658537	5903	10975	1187447	73288	963922	107544	104956	49144
眉山市	Meishan	1975006	7887	7798	463503	77054	490872	40560	43260	11641
宜宾市	Yibin	3972375	20582	242579	1217774	80628	663625	83720	67460	60781
广安市	Guangan	1829391	11437	62675	252837	52236	364654	59069	47030	16285
达州市	Dazhou	3084228	25197	254508	329380	105432	629149	131329	104920	59793
雅安市	Yaan	775676	4479	17530	135610	51866	52070	13421	23221	2032
巴中市	Bazhong	1736745	10789	30590	155260	15604	578949	56047	43589	34954
资阳市	Ziyang	1448500	2885	2533	392422	10550	291528	20457	45603	9383
阿坝藏族羌族自治州	Aba	877233	18928	3339	29790	35675	30027	13346	28733	7761
甘孜藏族自治州	Ganzi	778706	15348	3339	5774	44086	15167	17443	31065	4915
凉山彝族自治州	Liangshan	2307231	20000	168941	163773	118802	252173	73542	91947	10864

Total Wage of Employment in all Units by Sector and Region(2018)

(10 000 yuan)

信息传输、软件和信息技术服务业 Information Transmission, Software and Information Technology	金融业 Financial Interme-diation	房地产业 Real Estate	租赁和商务服务业 Leasing and Business Services	科学研究和技术服务业 Scientific Research, and Technical Services	水利、环境和公共设施管理业 Management of Water Con-servancy,En-vironment and Public Facilities	居民服务、修理和其他服务业 Services to Households, Repair and Other Services	教育 Education	卫生和社会工作 Health and Social Service	文化、体育和娱乐业 Culture, Sports and Entertain-ment	公共管理、社会保障和社会组织 Public Mana-gement,Social Security and Social Organization
2577192	**3182901**	**2274021**	**1843401**	**2781473**	**693098**	**423722**	**8111213**	**5208228**	**610853**	**9113053**
1829996	1341964	1353585	1126110	1674038	265762	257666	2248590	1790663	293611	2169600
34359	90226	47916	28321	35948	20396	6650	244762	155450	14674	255779
21620	79738	26907	22093	37083	15657	21141	139513	108595	10955	207332
71483	124097	107157	86198	22480	15833	10008	409605	275908	31742	404676
46395	155742	44681	19165	73285	28766	7249	324203	230532	15050	399080
102782	199312	100806	60732	602124	43363	26642	449404	251040	27239	468035
42813	80214	29355	17175	22639	36639	7350	195507	168353	8283	286848
36258	89065	45305	11993	9377	8279	2755	243092	170905	12348	235955
25231	94648	20478	20241	16168	10651	3788	275922	177558	15606	295873
34140	88350	65659	27500	17525	44076	10207	249434	150957	20068	432580
49359	189870	115790	117697	44930	46827	7450	643185	329179	33779	577293
22877	35970	68435	30941	19098	28724	5310	185451	112829	8111	314686
37692	144997	50389	40442	45999	15405	5210	431426	230737	23445	509487
18307	82261	41839	16055	12176	6141	2565	324102	164233	10365	285124
54142	98105	64881	39863	43089	23815	30537	457088	226939	17065	388996
16003	37303	11720	13213	4127	8147	2675	112022	85487	3396	181354
30269	47262	34023	16389	8494	7521	7071	273365	123406	15976	247190
24643	75275	16090	14765	15483	13140	1097	180375	132446	8560	191265
19180	25709	1086	16056	11159	24787	324	154104	45613	15098	396208
19172	19167	1559	3208	16065	7705	1967	148986	60660	7301	355780
37040	83627	26361	45207	26567	21464	5748	419267	214985	17012	509913

4-23 按行业分国有经济单位就业人员工资总额

单位：万元

年份 Year	合计 Total	农、林、牧、渔业 Agriculture, Forestry, Animal Husbandry and Fishery	采矿业 Mining	制造业 Manufacturing	电力、热力、燃气及水生产和供应业 Production and Supply of Electricity, Heat,Gas and Water	建筑业 Construction	批发和零售业 Wholesale and Retail Trades	交通运输、仓储和邮政业 Transport, Storage and Post	住宿和餐饮业 Hotels and Catering Services	信息传输、软件和信息技术服务业 Information Transmission, Software and Information Technology
1978	219481	6349	22831	74597	4340	18879	20283	16845	3004	
1980	300829	7372	28477	99448	7386	25251	27993	22265	4146	
1985	478883	10261	46083	171148	7091	34381	30018	35210	3520	1268
1986	582177	12437	56860	202705	9315	41875	33865	43168	5016	2126
1987	650498	12771	59515	233891	11144	48446	38226	47836	5601	2501
1988	807670	14621	70124	295218	14050	58163	50429	59942	7402	3164
1989	937712	15841	76031	354269	17519	64933	57942	70353	8505	4399
1990	1071715	17282	102004	383120	25290	71988	64293	79263	9437	5711
1991	1197509	19023	109427	435869	25167	83375	71962	88995	10658	6291
1992	1377792	20726	114231	489232	30605	94239	77834	102479	11425	7489
1993	1635013	23775	111770	583654	39022	158721	95545	83740	14151	8356
1994	2227867	30480	162306	667528	50161	186311	135672	120653	19915	18195
1995	2574023	34834	177415	775878	71687	224438	155143	151492	22978	18645
1996	2841447	39432	200710	833479	84574	230079	168030	170865	24886	18902
1997	3020053	43054	197505	834145	102870	244728	171901	199996	25460	19213
1998	3010629	46216	179302	684660	101734	239295	151032	202615	22369	19585
1999	3076087	51346	143862	593000	110565	230424	139215	217647	20746	22588
2000	3387240	59933	184541	592493	120520	225360	134067	239453	16648	24570
2001	3824669	75018	125230	571708	139577	244940	121802	259421	18151	31592
2002	4069680	82734	154215	548757	146069	240261	106741	280217	15990	35021
2003	4530295	88554	140691	587018	148665	297628	131224	239658	18271	85531
2004	4954541	83699	157343	600863	169126	282400	135253	258843	20289	110752
2005	5575919	83116	239878	638221	193349	306660	144843	304666	20955	118181
2006	6278120	90978	285074	734517	199945	356909	146570	372775	23045	128043
2007	7702452	101012	352462	753978	235789	458057	162859	452216	31019	124192
2008	9131401	99407	438487	858128	280334	568157	188586	503641	32225	135208
2009	10581526	82798	474721	841874	299880	754787	217955	586030	38219	133791
2010	12266436	89000	508371	1000888	365831	945472	239082	638792	47135	142432
2011	14479483	109802	586060	1142657	424599	1066283	285194	738607	65346	157237
2012	17060258	120858	757792	1208273	488184	1253206	340260	887444	74819	188169
2013	18626143	117956	167358	624643	1118242	1345478	301876	1211920	43517	328983
2014	20162618	115713	245317	858750	1185590	1296410	335643	1337051	40707	153454
2015	22612943	126083	125432	581565	1133565	1223801	329621	1398129	36436	115376
2016	24582334	133765	61366	593236	1161217	1129758	301232	1470809	35460	117796
2017	27223176	133919	54997	481404	1228190	1003385	303439	1547206	31486	117811
2018	29269353	125889	65488	495809	1303666	548290	297263	1592407	29728	114573

Total Wage of Employment in State-owned Units by Sector

(10 000 yuan)

金融业 Financial Interme-diation	房地产业 Real Estate	租赁和商务服务业 Leasing and Business Services	科学研究和技术服务业 Scientific Research, and Technical Services	水利、环境和公共设施管理业 Management of Water Con-servancy,En-vironment and Public Facilities	居民服务、修理和其他服务业 Services to Households, Repair and Other Services	教育 Education	卫生和社会工作 Health and Social Service	文化、体育和娱乐业 Culture, Sports and Entertain-ment	公共管理、社会保障和社会组织 Public Mana-gement,Social Security and Social Organization
1291	197		11766	741	276	20683	3840	626	12933
2298	722		15045	2602	403	29999	7327	1120	18975
5001	1007	1099	26858	4226	338	50587	13232	1520	36035
6668	1319	1818	29913	5261	484	60431	17143	3226	48547
7415	1464	2138	30852	6189	569	65223	19036	3797	53884
9352	1768	2705	35664	7830	720	83713	23804	4802	64199
9954	2039	3760	39428	10884	1000	89338	27229	6676	77612
12916	2373	4882	46436	14132	1299	98724	31471	8668	92426
14264	2699	5378	51691	15568	1431	107248	34584	9548	104331
18787	3792	6402	64162	18531	1703	134291	41393	11366	129105
31212	4435	7126	69232	20627	1896	156780	51976	12651	160364
51439	8186	15555	98395	45024	4138	243744	86932	27615	255618
60204	9183	15940	120084	46137	4241	271087	100158	28297	286182
67827	11088	16159	126780	46772	4299	331478	115868	28686	321533
79359	12509	16425	134463	47543	4370	366933	131611	29159	358809
95639	16872	16744	141354	48464	4455	435622	152990	29724	421957
106978	17534	19311	125413	55895	5138	517475	181524	34281	483145
132984	20076	21006	139874	60801	5589	599029	211852	37290	561154
155476	19642	22846	201759	68539	6887	767319	255393	46786	692583
159284	22069	22234	184792	71540	7949	892619	291260	50919	757009
216061	21277	30328	212133	61359	10671	972935	324749	68870	874672
234371	22093	37714	254427	66402	12630	1075808	368214	73572	990742
254672	22539	93189	270784	74621	23906	1168545	424735	87222	1105837
267175	25028	90112	323556	93617	27640	1301738	493157	85156	1233085
306566	32309	118842	399501	115458	34630	1680347	619126	96982	1627107
400300	32123	149122	504981	127698	11951	1895316	754873	107952	2042912
441378	35731	135691	597805	158474	11079	2401045	886229	111815	2372224
516101	33100	150504	695501	184052	11869	2772615	1107000	129903	2688788
604086	38892	180883	889573	225598	16400	3245013	1434644	149821	3118788
805333	38603	154291	1001168	281403	18410	3845719	1790195	181617	3624514
916641	39955	210708	1173202	309213	19720	4263469	2150242	222751	4060270
941028	42842	238873	1169828	359516	20434	4686084	2417634	256300	4461444
1006672	42008	256513	1207960	417354	22402	5654698	2932106	280746	5722481
1065128	64722	244829	1274217	449963	43821	6193590	3381745	293120	6566561
1115731	46661	303256	1366131	476927	47349	6886975	3904657	347058	7826594
1140434	37533	232323	1537111	443005	24260	7493738	4333771	346937	9107130

4-24 各市(州)按行业分国有经济单位就业人员工资总额(2018年)

单位：万元

市(州)	Region	合计 Total	农、林、牧、渔业 Agriculture, Forestry, Animal Husbandry and Fishery	采矿业 Mining	制造业 Manufacturing	电力、热力、燃气及水生产和供应业 Production and Supply of Electricity, Heat,Gas and Water	建筑业 Construction	批发和零售业 Wholesale and Retail Trades	交通运输、仓储和邮政业 Transport, Storage and Post	住宿和餐饮业 Hotels and Catering Services
全　省	**Sichuan**	**29269353**	**125889**	**65488**	**495809**	**1303666**	**548290**	**297263**	**1592407**	**29728**
成都市	Chengdu	8130962	9647		344723	74467	242016	67256	408622	15944
自贡市	Zigong	816782	2445		2875	13598	6029	6146	37495	
攀枝花市	Panzhihua	564608	5278			22190	67	10972	27044	1071
泸州市	Luzhou	1220912	2302	4471	694	14334	65717	19598	29933	
德阳市	Deyang	1076713	687	2200	26457	7880	5371	15116	26977	945
绵阳市	Mianyang	1889376	3126		16633	41558	17992	15759	26219	321
广元市	Guangyuan	763776	3335		6702	2824	13649	8727	25336	
遂宁市	Suining	709933						11522	9479	
内江市	Neijiang	838288	3758		121	1863	6379	7590	32873	
乐山市	Leshan	890895	5941		454	1211	3470	9012	19146	112
南充市	Nanchong	1799910	2236		19149	22961	36528	13921	47221	
眉山市	Meishan	777659	3516		615	59361	7296	561	21070	
宜宾市	Yibin	1329533	11034	75	53006	15686	1970	3195	26503	176
广安市	Guangan	835593	4382			5077	9154	8931	15946	
达州市	Dazhou	1288116	12747		2715	29580	54338	18877	30348	1034
雅安市	Yaan	428123	2822			3140	563	3497	13407	43
巴中市	Bazhong	727403	4386		2951	932	36067	8794	20537	1231
资阳市	Ziyang	626912	468			2274	18898	8669	38016	243
阿坝藏族羌族自治州	Aba	717249	17366		43	1189	2967	6475	25365	437
甘孜藏族自治州	Ganzi	657958	14238	250	432	9879	1095	3365	21123	
凉山彝族自治州	Liangshan	1376514	16176	8880	12852	13349	5978	43921	30352	672

Total Wage of Employment in State-owned Units by Sector and Region(2018)

(10 000 yuan)

信息传输、软件和信息技术服务业 Information Transmission, Software and Information Technology	金融业 Financial Intermediation	房地产业 Real Estate	租赁和商务服务业 Leasing and Business Services	科学研究和技术服务业 Scientific Research, and Technical Services	水利、环境和公共设施管理业 Management of Water Conservancy,Environment and Public Facilities	居民服务、修理和其他服务业 Services to Households, Repair and Other Services	教育 Education	卫生和社会工作 Health and Social Service	文化、体育和娱乐业 Culture, Sports and Entertainment	公共管理、社会保障和社会组织 Public Management,Social Security and Social Organization
114573	**1140434**	**37533**	**232323**	**1537111**	**443005**	**24260**	**7493738**	**4333771**	**346937**	**9107130**
12731	485543	15006	91545	646676	122188	5250	1946973	1325067	150880	2166430
12727	49085	1644	2417	23484	16779	1342	235668	138163	11253	255633
159	12664		1656	13163	14072	439	136298	103292	8912	207332
3588	14829	270	2401	11888	7630	1222	365680	256887	14791	404676
580	53814	269	3741	22768	24583	1638	299594	173848	11178	399066
21809	64501	1667	1852	586965	27723	1851	379760	199507	14098	468035
1382	26280	1898	3212	10404	34027	1121	186588	145567	5878	286848
8873	36387	140	990	7531	5384	537	233870	150087	9180	235955
2369	15716	543	2340	10322	8337	1547	266556	171256	10847	295873
3555	10865	322	4497	9997	10199	2721	239994	133271	4829	431300
12329	75489	2578	8710	27011	40000	1150	612275	282555	18504	577293
908	21668	730	12522	17319	26989	1052	181909	102295	5163	314686
1912	32824	5240	2632	16869	10101	694	418636	204275	15239	509468
892	48978	1324	3432	9458	3291	222	299664	132315	7535	284993
7990	34004	2145	4748	34640	22982	998	432826	196519	12630	388996
2203	16040	231	1988	3267	6438	542	110912	79830	1846	181354
2463	29229	2419	1956	4093	5340	609	251505	102599	5105	247190
8215	23959		1018	9021	10552	657	178506	130178	5888	190349
1323	15615		5355	9177	22377		153382	45238	14732	396208
1594	13908	683	187	15358	4637	52	148815	60350	6459	355534
3538	59035	424	5088	24082	19377	617	412520	198923	10819	509913

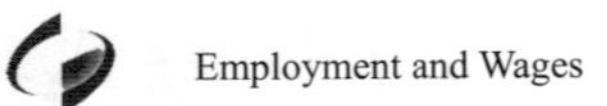

4-25 按行业分城镇集体经济单位就业人员工资总额

单位：万元

年份 Year	合计 Total	农、林、牧、渔业 Agriculture, Forestry, Animal Husbandry and Fishery	采矿业 Mining	制造业 Manufacturing	电力、热力、燃气及水生产和供应业 Production and Supply of Electricity, Heat,Gas and Water	建筑业 Construction	批发和零售业 Wholesale and Retail Trades	交通运输、仓储和邮政业 Transport, Storage and Post	住宿和餐饮业 Hotels and Catering Services	信息传输、软件和信息技术服务业 Information Transmission, Software and Information Technology
1978	43715	667	90	17024	893	4504	6410	8591	681	
1980	64063	814	190	27474	748	7572	9733	8537	1030	
1985	119128	1771	334	48288	1314	13640	28302	11590	2992	
1986	136524	2350	376	54932	1495	16911	31458	11781	3246	
1987	150931	2551	434	62764	1708	18982	33588	12496	3465	
1988	178923	2856	519	75028	2042	22836	40100	14376	4137	
1989	195894	3164	581	83936	2285	23191	43160	16570	4453	
1990	220375	3903	2336	91734	3930	26934	48654	17675	5021	
1991	248487	4412	3304	108281	4092	31737	51829	19098	5347	
1992	283759	5245	4135	122023	4622	40688	55192	21470	5694	
1993	333417	5249	1707	123261	668	62216	82368	20016	8498	
1994	386038	8136	5336	152631	908	72730	77060	15152	7950	
1995	437256	9278	6491	171307	1305	77318	89791	17904	9264	
1996	469060	10649	6641	176610	2032	86352	94694	19875	9773	
1997	513532	11088	11096	194942	4656	97367	92604	22281	9458	
1998	438565	10731	8709	147082	2159	89767	80893	16535	8346	
1999	398702	11185	5871	120091	1530	93697	63837	15619	5597	
2000	405185	11743	5868	115103	1777	104879	55143	14006	4835	
2001	389753	11871	6174	96486	2571	106128	41886	14296	4342	
2002	388119	10884	4392	86753	2772	121904	31071	12794	3746	
2003	436951	10216	5300	83384	4769	138528	24230	13661	4139	413
2004	433210	9601	4568	87663	4995	137981	22814	14537	4705	380
2005	457006	8858	5361	91342	5737	140681	20758	15562	4889	74
2006	512573	9141	6776	94908	5911	167259	22544	16935	4294	19
2007	597311	9971	7412	105164	7401	197172	22154	12905	4219	24
2008	698158	8125	6732	120797	5739	246516	23903	13482	4621	36
2009	791894	6887	10821	131300	5875	293821	22772	16791	7309	4848
2010	785441	8403	10906	66130	7405	333319	18287	17359	7434	607
2011	951634	8026	12318	74501	9556	417220	20405	22474	7358	1016
2012	1107287	5659	24591	73141	11400	489349	20919	27777	6796	322
2013	1137642	7050	13166	53171	10822	464722	25512	28882	6755	525
2014	1238152	8502	11303	48608	12940	519198	25307	36645	5438	837
2015	1254899	8241	7131	51445	11728	499008	27449	32750	3391	404
2016	1340078	10337	6724	44472	12425	521062	26195	32508	3383	441
2017	1223720	4334	1318	41608	9308	454088	23329	33391	2760	453
2018	1199158	2966	1837	34657	9483	502479	15722	32803	2712	446

Total Wage of Employment in Urban Collective-owned Units by Sector

(10 000 yuan)

金融业 Financial Interme-diation	房地产业 Real Estate	租赁和商务服务业 Leasing and Business Services	科学研究和技术服务业 Scientific Research, and Technical Services	水利、环境和公共设施管理业 Management of Water Con-servancy,En-vironment and Public Facilities	居民服务、修理和其他服务业 Services to Households, Repair and Other Services	教育 Education	卫生和社会工作 Health and Social Service	文化、体育和娱乐业 Culture, Sports and Entertain-ment	公共管理、社会保障和社会组织 Public Mana-gement,Social Security and Social Organization
805				16	92	737	2229	355	621
1170	56		43	419	1094	903	3419	698	163
1904	148	18	14	591	2172	587	4363	786	885
2639	131	29	19	676	2059	607	5971	803	1041
3059	46	47	18	796	2313	596	5998	869	1201
3572	35	55	11	813	2727	537	6992	871	1416
4148	14	63	16	858	3111	602	7354	899	1489
4754	64	84	23	889	3218	634	8058	805	1659
5033	96	87	51	852	2688	677	8444	788	1671
6579	161	96	545	989	3045	679	9873	815	1908
9239	595	101	354	1083	2575	913	11293	793	2488
17783	141	501	73	1148	3852	774	17808	909	3146
20174	344	886	103	1595	4365	987	21891	1145	3108
23561	481	967	83	1632	4977	1056	25057	1209	3411
28429	734	959	146	1677	4781	1200	26862	1218	4034
32017	744	902	138	1507	4525	1078	28660	1046	3726
35504	858	904	117	1518	4279	995	32619	1151	3330
40028	1815	893	576	1461	5761	1272	35046	1054	3925
44857	1524	831	812	1663	10642	1315	39110	832	4413
53208	1604	730	383	2628	5840	1399	43815	382	3814
61245	2028	3038	1543	3561	19931	1032	57277	569	2087
70237	2253	3504	2039	3959	2540	833	57677	606	2318
86376	2223	5507	792	4225	2831	948	59658	928	256
94929	2462	7229	1067	4648	3103	806	69250	1060	232
116767	2444	9800	1248	5929	2741	1506	88354	1874	226
133789	2580	11954	1791	7216	3482	977	103971	2261	186
132613	2855	12949	2132	8773	4633	2836	122624	1712	343
131634	3166	11744	2200	8659	4769	2914	147656	2074	775
156012	4062	15446	2551	9993	5841	3161	179377	2050	265
172321	4784	23309	5293	9415	7132	4350	216294	2500	1935
201658	3635	27543	5545	9732	3894	31457	240218	3181	172
214854	2345	35485	7957	9518	3271	32766	260681	2479	19
211423	2184	36509	6658	10592	4626	53491	284000	3640	229
226857	1344	36918	7972	14837	1743	64474	323687	4231	467
223274	5269	30940	14190	14636	1439	6729	350914	5154	589
188130	7036	29110	7059	6457	912	22921	329670	4135	626

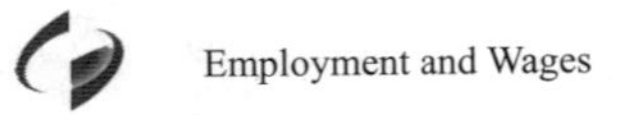

4-26 各市(州)按行业分城镇集体经济单位就业人员工资总额(2018年)

单位：万元

市(州)	Region	合计 Total	农、林、牧、渔业 Agriculture, Forestry, Animal Husbandry and Fishery	采矿业 Mining	制造业 Manufacturing	电力、热力、燃气及水生产和供应业 Production and Supply of Electricity, Heat,Gas and Water	建筑业 Construction	批发和零售业 Wholesale and Retail Trades	交通运输、仓储和邮政业 Transport, Storage and Post	住宿和餐饮业 Hotels and Catering Services
全　省	**Sichuan**	**1199158**	**2966**	**1837**	**34657**	**9483**	**502479**	**15722**	**32803**	**2712**
成都市	Chengdu	283254	638		14744	1601	69332	6724	3283	2088
自贡市	Zigong	16476	1547		2535		2645	332	3466	
攀枝花市	Panzhihua	5655			205		634	953	956	73
泸州市	Luzhou	165068	20		1918	128	131657	539	1040	
德阳市	Deyang	58860			4025		13652	338	902	
绵阳市	Mianyang	86633	555		5297		3016	312		
广元市	Guangyuan	47330			128	1574	18601	775		
遂宁市	Suining	68081			238		32917			
内江市	Neijiang	23461			28		16413	59	904	77
乐山市	Leshan	13417		780	1235	998	202	525	5297	130
南充市	Nanchong	90178	20		1132	3164	29080	515	2640	
眉山市	Meishan	14942					6199		1927	182
宜宾市	Yibin	32939			251	50	14745	335	4097	
广安市	Guangan	88256					54561	196	288	
达州市	Dazhou	98287	13			14	58841	997	4710	
雅安市	Yaan	6896					2063		23	
巴中市	Bazhong	47975			976	1237	31070	1711		
资阳市	Ziyang	23210			1056	516	13207	876	1611	36
阿坝藏族羌族自治州	Aba	7095				15	875	451		25
甘孜藏族自治州	Ganzi	6523			62		1781			
凉山彝族自治州	Liangshan	14624	174	1057	829	186	990	85	1659	102

Total Wage of Employment in Urban Collective-owned Units by Sector and Region(2018)

(10 000 yuan)

信息传输、软件和信息技术服务业 Information Transmission, Software and Information Technology	金融业 Financial Interme-diation	房地产业 Real Estate	租赁和商务服务业 Leasing and Business Services	科学研究和技术服务业 Scientific Research, and Technical Services	水利、环境和公共设施管理业 Management of Water Con-servancy,En-vironment and Public Facilities	居民服务、修理和其他服务业 Services to Households, Repair and Other Services	教育 Education	卫生和社会工作 Health and Social Service	文化、体育和娱乐业 Culture, Sports and Entertain-ment	公共管理、社会保障和社会组织 Public Mana-gement,Social Security and Social Organization
446	**188130**	**7036**	**29110**	**7059**	**6457**	**912**	**22921**	**329670**	**4135**	**626**
	16760	940	2242	457	1933	282	13137	145805	2677	612
					1074		353	4524		
			2823	13						
	19656	366	2590		2144	46	367	4542	56	
	2747			1061			901	35221		14
	34095	4416	2507	1436	12		1414	33553	21	
	9677		350	1274				14873	79	
	23130	162	115	14	464			10722	319	
			4059		488		703	252	480	
91	626		503	122		21	2238	650		
	19550	527	10017	161	343		229	22647	150	
	2528		120					3986		
			871	944		63		11583		
	20696							12515		
355	12393	611	992	354			376	18635		
	4665		145							
	7407		344				588	4642		
	4441		243	1224						
	5433		297							
	4327								354	
		13	891			501	2618	5521		

4-27 按行业分其他各种经济单位就业人员工资总额
Total Wage of Employment in Units of Other Types of Ownership by Sector

单位：万元 (10 000 yuan)

行　业	Sector	2013	2014	2015	2016	2017	2018
总　计	**Total**	**14311143**	**21028896**	**22567438**	**23540840**	**25425735**	**29136839**
农、林、牧、渔业	Agriculture, Forestry, Animal Husbandry and Fishery	3017	3612	4119	3573	3612	5633
采矿业	Mining	843912	1205438	1120534	1107847	1221170	1168403
制造业	Manufacturing	5934662	7740774	7790550	7751266	8206380	8269374
电力、热力、燃气及水生产和供应业	Production and Supply of Electricity, Heat,Gas and Water	640377	810326	946720	842848	762884	894729
建筑业	Construction	2672685	4615913	4996988	5282577	5335645	7390105
批发和零售业	Wholesale and Retail Trades	635985	1111633	1184929	1246842	1367069	1502695
交通运输、仓储和邮政业	Transport, Storage and Post	700750	1086454	1243056	1265983	1372465	1530187
住宿和餐饮业	Hotels and Catering Services	201487	340238	350534	329463	330580	355022
信息传输、软件和信息技术服务业	Information Transmission, Software and Information Technology Services	693518	1090558	1433318	1518619	1774584	2021701
金融业	Financial Intermediation	711300	838265	939601	1259500	1515532	1724653
房地产业	Real Estate	386657	820801	922732	1070944	1216545	1404742
租赁和商务服务业	Leasing and Business Services	221833	343546	449490	564132	650001	803890
科学研究和技术服务业	Scientific Research and Technical Services	292526	478117	577284	612912	788714	981482
水利、环境和公共设施管理业	Management of Water Conservancy, Environment and Public Facilities	85882	114542	90396	102949	127910	182288
居民服务、修理和其他服务业	Services to Households, Repair and Other Services	29584	44316	57541	59423	76653	63747
教育	Education	147202	198032	253129	273348	347983	411969
卫生和社会工作	Health and Social Service	77076	121242	134005	160959	231425	328382
文化、体育和娱乐业	Culture, Sports and Entertainment	32275	64964	71185	85843	94888	92540
公共管理、社会保障和社会组织	Public Management, Social Security and Social Organization	415	125	1330	1814	1694	5298

4-28 按登记注册类型分全部单位就业人员平均工资及指数

Average Wage of Employment in all Units and Related Indices by Registered Type

年份 Year	平均货币工资（元） Average Money Wage (yuan)					指数（上年为100） Indices (preceding year=100) 平均货币工资 Average Money Wage					实际工资 Average Real Wage				
	全部单位 all Units	国有经济单位 State-owned Units	城镇集体经济单位 Urban Collective Owned Units	私营经济单位 Private Units	其他各种经济单位 Units of Other Types of Ownership	全部单位 all Units	国有经济单位 State-owned Units	城镇集体经济单位 Urban Collective Owned Units	私营经济单位 Private Units	其他各种经济单位 Units of Other Types of Ownership	全部单位 all Units	国有经济单位 State-owned Units	城镇集体经济单位 Urban Collective-owned Units	私营经济单位 Private Units	其他各种经济单位 Units of Other Types of Ownership
1978	590	622	475			106.0	107.6	105.6							
1980	743	789	590			116.3	117.2	113.5			107.6	108.5	105.0		
1985	1062	1138	845		854	116.4	117.0	114.7		110.4	109.0	109.5	107.4		
1986	1237	1338	944		993	116.5	117.6	111.7		116.7	112.1	113.2	107.5		112.3
1987	1340	1441	1040		1087	108.3	107.7	123.1		109.5	100.8	100.2	102.5		101.8
1988	1598	1726	1211		1380	119.3	119.8	116.4		127.0	99.4	99.8	97.0		105.8
1989	1796	1941	1342		1587	112.4	112.5	110.8		115.0	95.0	95.1	93.7		97.2
1990	2011	2177	1490		1737	112.0	112.2	111.0		109.5	108.6	108.8	107.7		106.2
1991	2194	2351	1693		2178	109.1	108.0	113.6		125.4	106.6	105.6	111.1		122.6
1992	2458	2643	1885		2665	112.0	112.4	111.3		122.4	105.3	105.7	104.6		115.0
1993	2984	3148	2274		3890	121.2	119.1	120.6		146.0	106.6	101.9	103.2		124.9
1994	4064	4366	2726		5198	136.2	138.7	119.9		133.6	106.5	108.4	93.7		104.5
1995	4703	5002	3242		5944	115.7	114.6	118.9		114.4	97.2	96.3	99.9		96.1
1996	5218	5527	3666		6248	111.0	110.5	113.1		105.1	101.0	100.6	103.0		95.7
1997	5626	5996	3982		6206	107.8	108.5	108.6		99.3	102.6	103.2	103.3		94.5
1998	5939	6441	3966		5741	105.6	107.4	99.6		92.5	105.8	107.6	99.8		92.7
1999	7249	7771	4927		6992	110.2	110.3	106.2		110.0	112.3	112.4	108.3		112.1
2000	8323	8909	5749		7763	114.8	114.6	116.7		110.0	115.1	114.9	117.1		110.3
2001	9934	10783	6575		8650	119.4	121.0	114.4		111.4	117.2	118.9	112.3		109.5
2002	11183	12388	7395		9233	112.6	114.9	112.5		106.8	113.0	115.3	112.8		107.2
2003	12441	13923	8723		10038	110.2	111.1	116.9		108.7	109.4	110.5	116.0		106.9
2004	14063	15818	9758		11362	112.7	113.2	111.9		113.2	107.8	108.3	106.6		107.9
2005	15826	17898	11067		12812	112.6	113.2	113.4		112.8	110.7	111.3	111.5		110.9
2006	17852	20230	12726		14480	112.6	112.7	115.0		113.0	110.2	108.9	111.4		109.8
2007	21312	24365	15176		17007	119.7	120.9	119.5		117.5	113.0	114.2	112.9		110.9
2008	25038	28596	18464		20196	117.3	117.0	121.9		118.8	112.2	112.1	116.2		113.4
2009	23686	32210	21043	16085	22666		114.5	114.5		112.9		113.7	113.7		112.2
2010	26952	36729	23411	18316	27081	113.8	114.0	111.3	113.9	119.5	109.7	110.4	107.7	110.2	115.7
2011	31489	42048	28342	22175	31575	116.8	114.5	121.1	121.1	116.6	111.1	108.9	115.2	115.2	110.9
2012	35873	47721	33409	25912	35749	113.9	113.5	117.9	116.9	113.2	110.9	110.4	114.7	113.7	110.1
2013	41795	53896	39112	29830	43857	116.5	112.9	117.1	115.1	122.7	113.3	109.9	113.9	112.0	119.3
2014	45697	57018	43707	32671	49435	109.3	105.8	111.7	109.5	112.7	107.5	104.0	109.9	107.7	110.8
2015	50466	66551	48924	35127	53384	110.4	116.7	111.9	107.5	108.0	108.9	115.1	110.4	106.0	106.5
2016	54425	72980	52180	37763	57243	107.8	109.7	106.7	107.5	107.2	105.7	107.5	104.6	105.4	105.1
2017	58671	80321	55115	40087	61279	107.8	110.1	105.6	106.2	107.1	106.0	108.2	103.9	104.4	105.3
2018	64717	90390	59146	43352	68853	110.3	112.5	107.3	108.1	112.4	108.5	110.7	105.5	106.3	110.5

注：2009年及以后全部单位就业人员平均工资包括私营单位(以下有关各表同)。

a)Average wage of employment in all units includes wage in the private units from 2009.(the same as the following related tables)

4-29 各市(州)全部单位就业人员平均工资

Total Wage of Employment in all Units and Related Indices by Region

单位：元 (yuan)

市(州)	Region	2010	2011	2012	2013	2014	2015	2016	2017	2018
全　省	**Sichuan**	**26127**	**31300**	**35873**	**41795**	**45697**	**50466**	**54425**	**58671**	**64717**
成都市	Chengdu	30515	34008	38221	48358	51681	56872	61330	65098	71300
自贡市	Zigong	23223	27975	32681	37081	40162	43157	46595	52339	56040
攀枝花市	Panzhihua	30029	35997	40846	44220	50221	51999	55508	61005	65124
泸州市	Luzhou	22448	27053	31340	37648	41121	44749	47871	52455	58614
德阳市	Deyang	28355	32325	36684	41426	44169	48090	52249	56815	62612
绵阳市	Mianyang	26347	31717	35544	40989	44640	49817	53222	56966	63500
广元市	Guangyuan	25328	30548	34030	37300	41518	46888	51379	54086	58362
遂宁市	Suining	22621	27316	30641	34633	37894	42188	45840	49962	56261
内江市	Neijiang	22340	28126	31646	35479	37695	40617	45234	48790	56574
乐山市	Leshan	23865	28001	32362	37742	41181	45805	49839	53764	58881
南充市	Nanchong	22197	27409	32441	35981	39192	44033	47272	51521	58294
眉山市	Meishan	22897	27782	33034	36595	41161	45379	48293	52410	59325
宜宾市	Yibin	25265	30068	34670	38674	40978	46019	49966	54195	62126
广安市	Guangan	22913	27819	33190	36213	39213	44079	48054	52493	57111
达州市	Dazhou	22809	27507	32241	35292	38271	42446	46281	50756	57940
雅安市	Yaan	23065	28061	32837	35464	39548	42533	46458	48895	53231
巴中市	Bazhong	22996	26389	30909	36825	39205	43080	46849	49341	52317
资阳市	Ziyang	24224	27627	30434	33587	36694	44150	46827	51568	54899
阿坝藏族羌族自治州	Aba	33788	38374	42138	48011	51149	59526	68637	73432	85395
甘孜藏族自治州	Ganzi	34306	41041	43286	47771	53705	63729	69388	74415	79509
凉山彝族自治州	Liangshan	32668	35535	41463	44163	47295	54195	58980	60352	64346

4-30 各市(州)按登记注册类型分全部单位就业人员平均工资及指数(2018年)
Average Wage of Employment in all Units and Related Indices by Region and Registered Types (2018)

市(州)	Region	平均货币工资 (元) Average Money Wage (yuan)					指数 (上年=100) Indices (preceding year=100) 平均货币工资 Arerage Money Wage				
		全部单位 all Units	国有经济单位 State-owned Units	城镇集体经济单位 Urban Collective-owned Units	私营经济单位 Private Units	其他各种经济单位 Units of Other Types of Ownership	全部单位 all Units	国有经济单位 State-owned Units	城镇集体经济单位 Urban Collective-owned Units	私营经济单位 Private Units	其他各种经济单位 Units of Other Types of Ownership
全 省	**Sichuan**	**64717**	**90390**	**59146**	**43352**	**68853**	**110.3**	**112.5**	**107.3**	**108.1**	**112.4**
成都市	Chengdu	71300	102882	72425	45108	78973	109.5	115.3	107.4	108.8	110.1
自贡市	Zigong	56040	94200	57870	40228	55909	107.1	116.8	99.2	104.2	104.3
攀枝花市	Panzhihua	65124	98709	39219	39444	73373	106.8	109.0	87.8	102.7	107.5
泸州市	Luzhou	58614	83347	61377	45475	62854	111.7	109.7	120.1	109.6	118.8
德阳市	Deyang	62612	96356	60531	45197	70165	110.2	113.1	115.8	106.1	116.1
绵阳市	Mianyang	63500	97398	76796	38616	61352	111.5	113.1	103.9	108.5	111.9
广元市	Guangyuan	58362	75915	60633	37572	56073	107.9	106.5	94.8	103.5	114.0
遂宁市	Suining	56261	91737	57769	41340	50511	112.6	116.7	119.5	107.5	113.7
内江市	Neijiang	56574	78383	45066	38305	51776	116.0	116.2	66.9	103.0	121.2
乐山市	Leshan	58881	85678	57387	42240	60982	109.5	113.4	111.7	107.3	111.4
南充市	Nanchong	58294	85190	60134	45909	52666	113.1	116.7	114.3	111.0	111.0
眉山市	Meishan	59325	87439	57712	44826	55676	113.2	123.4	115.8	111.7	104.4
宜宾市	Yibin	62126	87982	46314	42510	68932	114.6	110.2	107.5	106.5	127.6
广安市	Guangan	57111	84237	47701	40848	59445	108.8	108.5	97.2	106.2	123.0
达州市	Dazhou	57940	74259	54230	43416	57959	114.2	114.5	118.1	111.5	117.0
雅安市	Yaan	53231	64924	52360	35466	48817	108.9	105.2	100.9	109.1	108.6
巴中市	Bazhong	52317	67038	40197	42058	47949	106.0	105.9	110.4	106.8	108.2
资阳市	Ziyang	54899	79620	41835	43914	45043	106.5	115.6	88.3	106.0	98.4
阿坝藏族羌族自治州	Aba	85395	100223	81646	39402	58119	116.3	116.7	107.8	104.1	116.9
甘孜藏族自治州	Ganzi	79509	82953	60066	37579	81195	106.8	106.4	104.7	105.4	110.2
凉山彝族自治州	Liangshan	64346	79383	65430	39902	61704	106.6	109.6	89.7	105.3	109.9

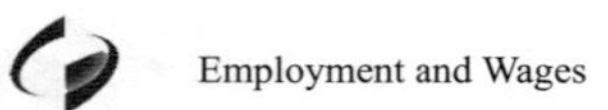

4-31 按行业分全部单位就业人员平均工资

单位：元

年份 Year	合计 Total	农、林、牧、渔业 Agriculture, Forestry, Animal Husbandry and Fishery	采矿业 Mining	制造业 Manufacturing	电力、热力、燃气及水生产和供应业 Production and Supply of Electricity, Heat,Gas and Water	建筑业 Construction	批发和零售业 Wholesale and Retail Trades	交通运输、仓储和邮政业 Transport, Storage and Post	住宿和餐饮业 Hotels and Catering Services	信息传输、软件和信息技术服务业 Information Transmission, Software and Information Technology
1978	590	575	719	577	552	658	509	655	501	
1980	743	649	914	742	795	834	645	756	637	
1985	1062	890	1264	1079	1113	1170	883	1080	870	1343
1986	1237	1119	1520	1211	1337	1364	998	1268	987	1424
1987	1340	1153	1589	1339	1461	1528	1093	1391	1081	1861
1988	1598	1320	1887	1618	1705	1732	1341	1671	1328	2105
1989	1796	1449	2247	1827	1988	1945	1477	1928	1449	2438
1990	2011	1588	2515	2033	2145	2192	1635	2122	1602	2771
1991	2194	1714	2677	2238	2574	2434	1774	2340	1748	2950
1992	2458	1981	2816	2469	2747	2705	1869	2624	1838	3857
1993	2984	2683	2955	3132	3661	3243	2335	3032	2307	5103
1994	4064	3404	4158	3941	4776	4267	2828	4221	2809	6946
1995	4703	3957	4819	4671	5961	5063	3326	4999	3314	7522
1996	5218	4310	5348	5181	6773	5485	3686	5712	3669	9019
1997	5626	4418	5631	5466	8138	5908	3850	6614	3823	10801
1998	5939	4609	5561	5539	8732	6072	4789	6873	4761	12347
1999	7249	5481	6337	6873	9760	7066	5060	8936	5043	14237
2000	8323	6140	8083	7774	10764	7693	5755	10352	5726	15819
2001	9934	7373	7753	8892	12039	8355	6895	12340	6858	18687
2002	11183	8114	9866	9853	13506	8444	8043	13952	8017	20763
2003	12320	8902	10591	11126	15099	9202	9971	12997	9202	22057
2004	13887	9264	12937	12686	16918	10090	11793	14903	10442	26305
2005	15638	10016	16907	14226	19253	11113	13999	17422	11133	30091
2006	17612	11224	18682	16404	21469	12839	15682	20776	12555	32229
2007	21081	13377	21752	18906	25518	14902	17321	23420	14493	34622
2008	24725	15231	28632	22046	30484	17746	20949	27344	16531	37462
2009	23572	17234	24348	19692	30360	18887	18253	27416	16308	29766
2010	26127	19481	25470	22722	35774	20711	20192	29518	18006	32863
2011	31300	23095	32927	27200	41321	25323	24082	36967	21401	36517
2012	35873	26700	38437	30827	46059	29629	31074	46169	24444	34204
2013	41795	29416	41540	37519	58181	35289	34976	52331	27633	54618
2014	45697	34203	46595	40486	69409	38303	39361	55458	31013	62052
2015	50466	38023	47865	43311	72902	41357	41181	59552	33349	67829
2016	54425	40087	50006	46228	79969	44151	43622	62903	34491	72527
2017	58671	42940	56446	49093	83009	45789	46287	69063	36363	76065
2018	64717	46429	62625	54366	90664	50725	50813	74481	39112	90210

Average Wage of Employment in all Units by Sector

(yuan)

金融业 Financial Intermediation	房地产业 Real Estate	租赁和商务服务业 Leasing and Business Services	科学研究和技术服务业 Scientific Research, and Technical Services	水利、环境和公共设施管理业 Management of Water Conservancy,Environment and Public Facilities	居民服务、修理和其他服务业 Services to Households, Repair and Other Services	教育 Education	卫生和社会工作 Health and Social Service	文化、体育和娱乐业 Culture, Sports and Entertainment	公共管理、社会保障和社会组织 Public Management,Social Security and Social Organization
574	493		679	590	570	520	541	513	617
720	669		872	692	592	678	698	667	773
1076	974	1005	1275	986	933	1040	998	901	1039
1356	1247	1286	1509	1178	1115	1220	1271	1213	1312
1419	1332	1359	1623	1201	1195	1246	1346	1287	1383
1624	1542	1512	1895	1289	1382	1525	1595	1501	1579
1730	1711	1983	2119	1451	1590	1662	1775	1697	1776
1970	1874	2109	2458	1698	1784	1882	1980	1884	1991
2086	2014	2507	2681	1813	1981	1962	2142	1989	2158
2513	2553	3121	3163	1994	2292	2356	2489	2276	2595
2589	3134	4003	3718	2367	2764	2716	2995	2798	3050
5483	4976	4865	6045	2944	3936	4221	4662	4573	4676
6058	5207	5405	6583	3403	4549	4580	5344	5281	5089
6703	5814	6014	7385	3863	5164	4981	6038	5834	5601
8021	6215	6682	8142	4140	5535	5363	6628	6579	6179
9540	7347	7422	8457	4564	6102	5941	7310	6918	7035
11249	8678	8242	9360	5529	7392	6860	8538	8077	8059
13274	9104	9157	11376	6111	8170	7923	9788	9193	9236
15567	10671	10174	15631	7073	9456	9998	11657	10866	11564
17603	11877	11304	17269	8693	11621	11766	13349	12376	13057
19452	12461	12412	19656	9495	13120	12647	14719	13673	14380
21969	13379	14890	21270	10567	13865	13787	16761	16758	15871
24764	14333	19186	24933	11498	15356	14952	18709	18591	17782
28282	16765	19556	29754	13014	17605	16374	21205	20204	19405
33843	19928	25101	36394	15629	22115	20937	25887	23597	24960
42055	37022	26158	42806	16901	18493	23491	30020	25859	29540
43127	20070	20672	43405	18903	14759	28819	32202	25599	32295
52258	23440	24320	48115	20304	16607	33666	38189	26998	35015
59391	27582	26754	57449	24613	21113	38621	44617	31002	39555
68840	31744	29441	60922	28635	23664	43923	51849	37105	44117
74682	40001	35789	70563	33285	28005	48695	57541	43257	48635
80704	43439	41304	73246	36497	31642	51753	61092	45614	52062
80165	47161	44881	78812	40117	33270	62412	70935	49988	63704
82847	51720	47585	82348	43431	36218	68597	78874	54297	71074
87323	53248	51083	90666	48106	37401	74604	86251	59877	79636
92631	57310	51671	108877	53604	39249	81371	94187	63057	90039

4-32 各市(州)按行业分全部单位就业人员平均工资(2018年)

单位：元

市(州)	Region	合计 Total	农、林、牧、渔业 Agriculture, Forestry, Animal Husbandry and Fishery	采矿业 Mining	制造业 Manufacturing	电力、热力、燃气及水生产和供应业 Production and Supply of Electricity, Heat,Gas and Water	建筑业 Construction	批发和零售业 Wholesale and Retail Trades	交通运输、仓储和邮政业 Transport, Storage and Post	住宿和餐饮业 Hotels and Catering Services
全　省	**Sichuan**	**64717**	**46429**	**62625**	**54366**	**90664**	**50725**	**50813**	**74481**	**39112**
成都市	Chengdu	71300	38932	44664	60946	85416	59290	53243	88462	42085
自贡市	Zigong	56040	57771	39971	44260	80569	47383	40458	54562	31041
攀枝花市	Panzhihua	65124	40447	51259	62337	163048	59458	42008	56850	32582
泸州市	Luzhou	58614	47201	49315	48661	70015	52649	48496	52684	40047
德阳市	Deyang	62612	33172	49862	58261	83163	47988	47494	57751	34678
绵阳市	Mianyang	63500	39137	36916	50531	73537	51089	50825	50027	36493
广元市	Guangyuan	58362	53638	56469	38796	76317	44082	46211	47173	31559
遂宁市	Suining	56261	43604	47458	45189	85058	42671	68839	41727	31874
内江市	Neijiang	56574	43278	41858	44450	57744	40301	43072	57018	35159
乐山市	Leshan	58881	42735	48699	45941	74249	48885	44165	60150	35278
南充市	Nanchong	58294	46963	46664	48083	63957	45736	47668	58763	42641
眉山市	Meishan	59325	57151	33298	50954	93558	45402	50454	52737	41265
宜宾市	Yibin	62126	44367	44646	63942	70056	48638	48173	53595	41146
广安市	Guangan	57111	41528	62165	39320	84854	42430	45019	52980	32253
达州市	Dazhou	57940	58789	55394	48418	71533	51733	42511	48507	38294
雅安市	Yaan	53231	49168	37789	44212	60351	29691	54337	52054	31262
巴中市	Bazhong	52317	46907	66878	41395	58312	44521	48425	53137	37723
资阳市	Ziyang	54899	25947	43596	47017	51819	40437	59744	68907	31008
阿坝藏族羌族自治州	Aba	85395	72134	41943	40970	73435	46554	54672	86442	38362
甘孜藏族自治州	Ganzi	79509	55088	37136	45501	81160	50090	68030	70377	39385
凉山彝族自治州	Liangshan	64346	52016	41605	55241	93353	46544	70979	58993	35024

Average Wage of Employment in all Units by Sector and Region(2018)

(yuan)

信息传输、软件和信息技术服务业 Information Transmission, Software and Information Technology	金融业 Financial Interme-diation	房地产业 Real Estate	租赁和商务服务业 Leasing and Business Services	科学研究和技术服务业 Scientific Research, and Technical Services	水利、环境和公共设施管理业 Management of Water Con-servancy,En-vironment and Public Facilities	居民服务、修理和其他服务业 Services to Households, Repair and Other Services	教育 Education	卫生和社会工作 Health and Social Service	文化、体育和娱乐业 Culture, Sports and Entertain-ment	公共管理、社会保障和社会组织 Public Mana-gement,Social Security and Social Organization
90210	**92631**	**57310**	**51671**	**108877**	**53604**	**39249**	**81371**	**94187**	**63057**	**90039**
97295	103405	66639	54208	120946	59794	38214	90031	108065	68508	103967
78392	109232	42794	45162	72665	68904	38219	87990	86189	65538	106327
58718	93098	37475	37193	61113	58162	31544	94836	107723	62671	105571
64087	113403	40437	47185	61352	35068	40062	75601	103975	53072	94776
68856	89978	47680	41411	57312	51878	54998	82775	98061	74212	105978
91696	79366	48001	42580	152537	55637	51039	73697	82928	61781	89022
83553	77143	46818	44831	53672	49036	36063	73787	86847	50504	74417
55339	129062	38689	33230	59723	51808	38804	80141	107766	57755	88112
85269	85153	52454	36509	55733	55562	45531	76609	87983	66978	73944
74590	98484	57274	46414	66181	72780	39018	78965	78709	39834	94265
73725	92978	50610	52370	61853	41743	45874	86489	96920	54544	85756
91179	141504	63255	56607	85105	50677	51154	75155	85483	65252	94206
78166	65161	60856	44127	57578	45563	33373	78150	84251	61826	95301
70302	77972	47249	40584	83798	55080	40643	83321	91089	55728	79015
68439	75142	46984	43217	70999	41239	43364	72566	77117	64106	75381
76681	75421	42992	40137	51721	35025	36894	59498	70656	57947	66258
67070	75691	50757	43647	51413	41120	39570	68986	69914	46374	64007
87480	66911	39542	39681	57029	45848	48987	74091	87974	70221	82399
98559	85441	34709	49848	95455	72796	43200	99763	85162	101193	105703
125390	90794	48719	37786	79649	45030	33066	83634	83612	74726	86518
104074	84660	41816	39369	70375	42841	37519	78423	87112	58162	77365

4-33 按行业分国有经济单位就业人员平均工资

单位：元

年份 Year	合计 Total	农、林、牧、渔业 Agriculture, Forestry, Animal Husbandry and Fishery	采矿业 Mining	制造业 Manufacturing	电力、热力、燃气及水生产和供应业 Production and Supply of Electricity, Heat,Gas and Water	建筑业 Construction	批发和零售业 Wholesale and Retail Trades	交通运输、仓储和邮政业 Transport, Storage and Post	住宿和餐饮业 Hotels and Catering Services	信息传输、软件和信息技术服务业 Information Transmission, Software and Information Technology
1978	622	519	722	620	603	703	539	682	518	
1980	789	674	918	803	826	890	688	836	663	
1985	1138	941	1268	1174	1334	1157	978	1178	954	1512
1986	1338	1169	1527	1319	1438	1568	1115	1414	996	1866
1987	1441	1202	1595	1459	1563	1733	1225	1536	1209	1975
1988	1726	1389	1895	1773	1814	2012	1537	1853	1506	2413
1989	1941	1527	2259	1998	2122	2268	1686	2126	1642	2858
1990	2177	1700	2560	2232	2331	2527	1865	2336	1827	3177
1991	2351	1812	2723	2432	2622	2765	2011	2557	1983	3843
1992	2643	2120	2882	2678	2945	3056	2102	2878	2085	4620
1993	3148	2916	2956	3302	3714	3660	2454	3402	2396	5431
1994	4366	3652	4220	4135	4822	4881	3219	4815	3149	7872
1995	5002	4167	4907	4838	6057	5926	3701	5648	3544	8655
1996	5527	4479	5471	5362	6833	6356	4064	6376	3971	9310
1997	5996	4585	5791	5702	8292	6903	4251	7499	4148	10044
1998	6441	4821	5849	5832	8279	6983	4312	7974	4201	12786
1999	7771	5727	6616	7314	10469	8480	5924	9889	5719	13899
2000	8909	6353	8705	8323	11508	8907	6443	11410	6222	17001
2001	10783	7735	8302	9566	12940	10064	7717	13557	7487	19123
2002	12388	8384	10884	11137	14995	10636	8883	15109	8485	21247
2003	13769	9095	11943	13136	16327	11775	11420	14151	10123	22463
2004	15592	9433	14588	15320	19016	13269	14060	15914	11879	27235
2005	17644	10206	20692	17783	22067	14466	17461	18255	12883	31395
2006	19884	11430	22602	22373	24328	15964	20068	22484	13976	32947
2007	24045	13707	25671	24778	28980	18715	22506	25031	16883	34077
2008	28131	15453	35692	29039	34560	21377	28070	29519	19452	37033
2009	32210	17920	39083	33169	37326	25284	33574	34183	21450	40649
2010	36729	19934	46629	37871	44559	28886	41334	38996	26240	44039
2011	42048	26451	52419	43179	49809	32067	48097	46270	31380	44616
2012	47721	31514	57092	47075	54557	37259	54348	55021	34732	53353
2013	53896	35211	48146	54977	71319	45202	66927	60511	34048	65885
2014	57018	39817	52019	58440	79841	44511	76326	64722	37800	56396
2015	66551	48555	54657	65789	85266	51156	84761	70884	38894	66465
2016	72980	53470	69012	78192	90858	51452	85687	74242	41792	70389
2017	80321	59437	83748	91783	97175	51898	94553	81897	46576	74081
2018	90390	66202	99678	104645	106354	52959	109489	90779	55743	81873

Average Wage of Employment in State-owned Units by Sector

(yuan)

金融业 Financial Interme-diation	房地产业 Real Estate	租赁和商务服务业 Leasing and Business Services	科学研究和技术服务业 Scientific Research, and Technical Services	水利、环境和公共设施管理业 Management of Water Con-servancy,En-vironment and Public Facilities	居民服务、修理和其他服务业 Services to Households, Repair and Other Services	教育 Education	卫生和社会工作 Health and Social Service	文化、体育和娱乐业 Culture, Sports and Entertain-ment	公共管理、社会保障和社会组织 Public Management, Social Security and Social Organization
623	493		676	618	593	540	575	622	623
751	679		725	633	624	683	754	703	775
1185	990	986	1223	1074	1058	1043	1103	1066	1037
1460	1268	1258	1482	1265	1247	1222	1358	1304	1313
1496	1353	1342	1509	1386	1328	1248	1437	1373	1382
1726	1546	1533	1783	1597	1524	1527	1699	1576	1578
1805	1712	1664	1987	1811	1724	1664	1923	1768	1773
2071	1885	1832	2146	2108	1940	1884	2152	1987	1989
2179	2030	1973	2201	2371	2121	1963	2295	2153	2156
2668	2585	2450	2889	2893	2427	2358	2679	2582	2594
3943	3060	2900	3876	3158	3027	2716	3234	3169	3052
5872	5023	4761	5751	4466	4106	4225	5144	5078	4684
6505	5254	4980	6389	4890	4749	4583	5808	5736	5091
7156	5896	5539	7098	5519	5430	4984	6549	6137	5604
8670	6374	5988	8474	5795	5712	5366	7187	6519	6182
10271	7620	7158	10193	6384	6302	5945	8012	7098	7039
11788	9076	8526	11658	7731	7583	6861	9334	8014	8062
14403	9344	8778	14064	8647	8415	7928	10721	9081	9246
17012	11334	10643	16737	9898	9751	9997	12909	11150	11568
18860	13793	12952	18009	10042	11731	11769	14656	12922	13059
21309	14740	13934	19769	9574	14516	12631	16277	13862	14382
24320	15980	17189	21357	10733	16218	13767	18335	17036	15873
26744	17285	21531	25100	11719	17133	14912	20051	18871	17783
30830	19248	22195	29911	13333	19946	16340	22688	17806	19407
35986	23745	29596	36600	16035	25766	20920	27528	23901	24963
44898	26987	28529	43119	17522	22436	23465	31920	26194	29542
47335	30409	35599	48319	19506	28979	29473	34379	28400	33204
59311	30448	41002	54707	20978	30725	34392	40552	32426	35018
65572	32826	46130	64236	25296	38606	39240	47425	37631	39555
74670	40669	62383	67431	29369	38824	44598	55064	44509	44126
83191	43221	53195	74713	32137	42343	49521	60988	48735	48638
91670	45943	50290	77454	35029	44440	52597	65341	52161	52063
94957	60356	54238	80846	41518	47211	63957	76705	60967	63718
94466	78518	66785	85280	44814	60854	70565	86057	67097	71091
101667	72999	67908	95199	49740	64773	77061	94029	76664	79651
108929	69739	80763	117814	55377	66629	84152	102805	84590	90068

4-34 各市(州)按行业分国有经济单位就业人员平均工资(2018年)

单位：元

市(州)	Region	合计 Total	农、林、牧、渔业 Agriculture, Forestry, Animal Husbandry and Fishery	采矿业 Mining	制造业 Manufac-turing	电力、热力、燃气及水生产和供应业 Production and Supply of Electricity, Heat,Gas and Water	建筑业 Construc-tion	批发和零售业 Wholesale and Retail Trades	交通运输、仓储和邮政业 Transport, Storage and Post	住宿和餐饮业 Hotels and Catering Services
全 省	**Sichuan**	**90390**	**66202**	**99678**	**104645**	**106354**	**52959**	**109489**	**90779**	**55743**
成都市	Chengdu	102882	92231		112747	78452	61166	128916	97194	53288
自贡市	Zigong	94200	87642		51701	102086	76407	98652	68222	
攀枝花市	Panzhihua	98709	65403			97839	28913	119129	65323	40866
泸州市	Luzhou	83347	57259	62011	68020	128791	32872	120456	85498	
德阳市	Deyang	96356	129642	31649	126409	109597	62096	125656	80891	53390
绵阳市	Mianyang	97398	51581		150796	91076	56559	85739	69972	49431
广元市	Guangyuan	75915	74939		66485	62338	49381	94243	70593	
遂宁市	Suining	91737						96902	44502	
内江市	Neijiang	78383	67829		109727	71111	38127	126286	84725	
乐山市	Leshan	85678	50305		60480	52442	46704	109497	82278	30270
南充市	Nanchong	85190	81912		52206	67276	49150	83257	74752	
眉山市	Meishan	87439	83518		38419	116578	43247	67578	83347	
宜宾市	Yibin	87982	62621	57846	110155	87289	98480	74125	81396	38196
广安市	Guangan	84237	76071			109181	41589	149844	85043	
达州市	Dazhou	74259	67196		61018	89043	66347	87598	63054	47000
雅安市	Yaan	64924	52751			60614	59926	107920	74402	22789
巴中市	Bazhong	67038	64687		61349	35842	47625	91034	76118	34873
资阳市	Ziyang	79620	80741			54145	51564	155636	80254	27011
阿坝藏族羌族自治州	Aba	100223	79805		28600	54541	50721	117521	107207	46989
甘孜藏族自治州	Ganzi	82953	58114	67649	36906	66483	80544	58324	72363	
凉山彝族自治州	Liangshan	79383	57423	72550	77419	91685	67390	117907	84475	30121

Average Wages of Employment in State-owned Units by Sector and Region(2018)

(yuan)

信息传输、软件和信息技术服务业 Information Transmission, Software and Information Technology	金融业 Financial Interme-diation	房地产业 Real Estate	租赁和商务服务业 Leasing and Business Services	科学研究和技术服务业 Scientific Research, and Technical Services	水利、环境和公共设施管理业 Management of Water Con-servancy,En-vironment and Public Facilities	居民服务、修理和其他服务业 Services to Households, Repair and Other Services	教育 Education	卫生和社会工作 Health and Social Service	文化、体育和娱乐业 Culture, Sports and Entertain-ment	公共管理、社会保障和社会组织 Public Mana-gement,Social Security and Social Organization
81873	**108929**	**69739**	**80763**	**117814**	**55377**	**66629**	**84152**	**102805**	**84590**	**90068**
80935	131136	76094	77864	111546	75672	59928	95301	128520	91832	104038
96710	106753	69970	91905	93300	85041	74160	91072	90061	85124	106474
66417	113276		106160	100788	62404	74475	97009	114388	78104	105571
126774	80113	26252	89940	84130	46984	82013	79629	111802	85056	94776
73443	103449	69000	49617	92967	50980	90508	85486	115063	88155	105982
114724	92316	68045	79502	158498	53789	84525	76130	88246	68975	89022
48505	104450	63050	89482	71504	49172	73268	76757	93276	60348	74417
89171	117188	87375	80520	87873	51376	71533	85887	118458	78395	88112
76660	91374	53743	39323	78612	66854	76564	77795	90804	80765	73944
70251	119662	47338	56635	80359	44753	50860	80387	82833	80488	94403
56920	139407	65603	30337	70673	41254	71881	90177	107829	72113	85756
87260	168361	90160	85124	93160	52816	79659	76829	90455	97053	94206
74695	117230	102546	42310	92888	47916	81671	79042	90628	93150	95301
73752	69296	65232	49521	89144	63781	88960	87981	105313	68126	79020
66086	73079	46939	61337	74880	41062	60461	74927	81781	82012	75381
43708	81628	50130	51642	55945	35665	62345	59862	72414	52601	66258
82381	70893	55855	60755	58722	41109	54838	71310	76310	58008	64007
78463	106722		56872	83839	44940	56120	74087	89802	93166	82843
76890	110356		47052	109778	88587		100165	85988	103963	105703
76635	97395	105077	56606	82303	38836	103400	83754	84158	84102	86528
87140	81260	37558	60423	79503	44750	49726	78850	90436	72907	77365

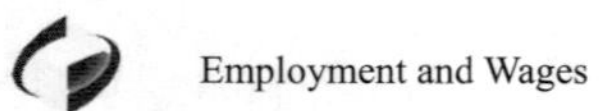

4-35 按行业分城镇集体经济单位就业人员平均工资

单位：元

年份 Year	合计 Total	农、林、牧、渔业 Agriculture, Forestry, Animal Husbandry and Fishery	采矿业 Mining	制造业 Manufacturing	电力、热力、燃气及水生产和供应业 Production and Supply of Electricity, Heat,Gas and Water	建筑业 Construction	批发和零售业 Wholesale and Retail Trades	交通运输、仓储和邮政业 Transport, Storage and Post	住宿和餐饮业 Hotels and Catering Services	信息传输、软件和信息技术服务业 Information Transmission, Software and Information Technology
1978	475	412	397	447	397	580	422	611	459	
1980	590	497	586	586	586	696	537	611	611	
1985	845	664	879	879	879	902	795	869	905	831
1986	944	901	929	940	940	1042	885	930	1015	907
1987	1040	960	1038	1038	1038	1185	966	1036	1096	1222
1988	1211	1069	1221	1221	1221	1293	1143	1201	1273	1477
1989	1342	1172	1363	1363	1363	1416	1241	1401	1371	1635
1990	1490	1254	1461	1507	1455	1639	1384	1526	1517	1920
1991	1693	1431	1772	1735	1896	1891	1527	1723	1860	2010
1992	1885	1625	1756	1903	1937	2157	1598	1874	2031	2744
1993	2274	1969	2248	2288	2552	2523	2168	2087	2601	3111
1994	2726	2712	2813	2763	3290	3194	2211	2101	2644	3515
1995	3242	3321	3169	3333	4710	3576	2694	2559	3127	3873
1996	3666	3781	3372	3735	5265	4038	3038	3078	3471	4218
1997	3982	3865	4060	4039	7328	4407	3156	3285	3589	4666
1998	3966	3875	3945	3937	6348	4657	2985	2933	3674	4924
1999	4927	4570	4016	4900	6917	5159	3748	4459	4437	5491
2000	5749	5173	4645	5549	7074	6124	4408	4651	5097	5867
2001	6575	5781	4889	6220	9685	6496	5086	5505	5775	6455
2002	7395	6568	4117	7095	13656	6641	5844	6322	6533	6943
2003	8647	7566	6624	8045	14556	7558	6579	7261	7281	7802
2004	9680	8084	6260	9396	14456	8255	7573	8829	7903	8125
2005	10974	8470	7280	10678	16523	8997	7901	9374	8754	11323
2006	12624	9302	8742	11852	15149	10886	8659	10870	9789	9895
2007	15089	10952	9204	13985	20513	12528	9819	11240	10402	13389
2008	18386	13512	19378	17938	23433	15080	12346	14069	12258	20056
2009	21043	16385	23127	20438	18055	17496	14484	16362	16627	21730
2010	23441	20181	26369	19411	24364	19418	16016	18139	18844	23076
2011	28342	28582	25802	23553	26934	24161	18258	23219	21197	22584
2012	33409	34911	33558	27778	33649	28499	21908	26371	23101	40263
2013	39112	27770	36142	35310	34474	32820	25814	28358	29485	29011
2014	43707	35979	32535	38289	42206	37427	28879	32611	31635	28469
2015	48924	44379	36969	46556	45090	41400	32608	35590	31898	30142
2016	52180	51711	35057	43134	49580	42556	34604	38508	32658	37709
2017	55115	69791	31232	44706	44092	43077	38025	41567	33696	42717
2018	59146	76628	42512	52598	48136	47130	44908	50660	36012	61889

Average Wage of Employment in Urban Collective-owned Units by Sector

(yuan)

金融业 Financial Interme-diation	房地产业 Real Estate	租赁和商务服务业 Leasing and Bussiness Services	科学研究和技术服务业 Scientific Research, and Technical Services	水利、环境和公共设施管理业 Management of Water Con-servancy,En-vironment and Public Facilities	居民服务、修理和其他服务业 Services to housholds, Repair and Other Services	教育 Education	卫生和社会工作 Health and Social Service	文化、体育和娱乐业 Culture, Sports and Entertain-ment	公共管理、社会保障和社会组织 Public Management, Social Security and Social Organization
513				488	489	261	482	472	523
669	566		488	595	566	552	596	545	576
874	883	772	568	771	736	807	768	791	1095
1156	968	921	623	1095	885	1064	1071	1036	1277
1268	915	1056	653	1178	953	1111	1117	1101	1401
1415	1350	1107	938	1313	1095	1228	1322	1203	1627
1582	1622	1289	1239	1385	1281	1449	1384	1418	1919
1752	1562	1392	1933	1531	1395	1588	1513	1545	2081
1880	1666	1598	1923	1722	1518	1758	1701	1731	2295
2171	1925	1945	2435	1969	1711	1913	1918	1902	2650
2755	3510	2277	2142	2432	1625	2621	2213	2487	2849
4600	3381	2801	3596	3177	2953	3200	3164	3149	3997
5031	4195	3247	5954	3254	3450	3832	3882	3638	4875
5604	4129	3588	4577	3895	3710	4192	4406	3963	5336
6383	4597	3693	6092	4467	4288	4450	4770	4185	5903
7202	5133	3796	7704	4792	4251	4596	4944	4276	6431
8601	5865	4589	5288	5083	5399	5340	5757	5113	7424
9743	7766	5275	9254	5957	6029	6475	6383	6255	7435
11233	8747	5894	12278	6491	7853	7214	7109	7031	10658
13813	8539	6641	13812	7107	8262	8925	8388	7842	12299
14726	9892	7172	14921	8125	12935	10773	9569	8205	13516
17439	11085	7311	20064	8810	8917	10316	10859	8897	16983
21328	13201	9449	15656	9484	8948	12519	12758	10712	12721
24183	13477	11055	17640	10217	10324	11409	14613	13362	15039
31523	13766	13148	21560	12138	10937	14574	18415	18817	15277
37801	15926	18284	20852	11927	12353	16467	21109	22457	16342
41319	18032	18666	23350	16888	13821	25461	25969	20530	20896
48800	20283	16268	33619	18279	15626	31066	31745	24082	26478
54793	25548	21066	45964	19915	18561	32124	37638	28004	43016
64181	31270	26032	45085	21080	21651	35450	44098	29762	33996
76785	31268	26131	41339	24545	21278	51909	50455	35229	29816
83950	41067	29131	51071	24753	18597	56698	53185	38258	38200
85482	48978	31986	39467	27257	49533	68525	59176	46667	67471
94135	46041	34561	43948	32979	41794	81090	64898	53018	91549
99057	42419	42936	67926	31811	44006	58614	71750	54028	125234
106589	49934	45350	49056	33808	52397	74323	76136	78770	152610

4-36 各市(州)按行业分城镇集体经济单位就业人员平均工资(2018年)

单位：元

市(州)	Region	合计 Total	农、林、牧、渔业 Agriculture, Forestry, Animal Husbandry and Fishery	采矿业 Mining	制造业 Manufacturing	电力、热力、燃气及水生产和供应业 Production and Supply of Electricity, Heat,Gas and Water	建筑业 Construction	批发和零售业 Wholesale and Retail Trades	交通运输、仓储和邮政业 Transport, Storage and Post	住宿和餐饮业 Hotels and Catering Services
全　省	**Sichuan**	**59146**	**76628**	**42512**	**52598**	**48136**	**47130**	**44908**	**50660**	**36012**
成都市	Chengdu	72425	99641		49675	128096	56793	64717	37737	36057
自贡市	Zigong	57870	92641		47470		56149	47457	60704	
攀枝花市	Panzhihua	39219			25024		48038	38720	50289	36500
泸州市	Luzhou	61377	49500		36111	32692	59055	33925	31605	
德阳市	Deyang	60531			87123		43727	39291	23613	
绵阳市	Mianyang	76796	68469		73066		48021	44557		
广元市	Guangyuan	60633			41226	50624	46724	29360		
遂宁市	Suining	57769			49500		37892			
内江市	Neijiang	45066			12636		47754	21000	61911	28407
乐山市	Leshan	57387		37311	55631	37082	91864	53061	63818	28822
南充市	Nanchong	60134	40200		30027	53002	47101	47704	60281	
眉山市	Meishan	57712					55494		64671	37917
宜宾市	Yibin	46314			34315	31375	38388	35232	37011	
广安市	Guangan	47701					37180	25737	55365	
达州市	Dazhou	54230	41667			34000	48794	33334	71901	
雅安市	Yaan	52360					30242		38500	
巴中市	Bazhong	40197			38557	36604	34496	36950		
资阳市	Ziyang	41835			74380	28683	39972	29705	38090	32636
阿坝藏族羌族自治州	Aba	81646				12417	51471	57038		35714
甘孜藏族自治州	Ganzi	60066			27000		37333			
凉山彝族自治州	Liangshan	65430	27571	47386	86354	23506	77313	34040	93191	63563

Average Wage of Employment in Urban Collective-owned Units by Sector and Region(2018)

(yuan)

信息传输、软件和信息技术服务业 Information Transmission, Software and Information Technology	金融业 Financial Intermediation	房地产业 Real Estate	租赁和商务服务业 Leasing and Business Services	科学研究和技术服务业 Scientific Research, and Technical Services	水利、环境和公共设施管理业 Management of Water Conservancy,Environment and Public Facilities	居民服务、修理和其他服务业 Services to Households, Repair and Other Services	教育 Education	卫生和社会工作 Health and Social Service	文化、体育和娱乐业 Culture, Sports and Entertainment	公共管理、社会保障和社会组织 Public Management,Social Security and Social Organization
61889	**106589**	**49934**	**45350**	**49056**	**33808**	**52397**	**74323**	**76136**	**78770**	**152610**
	108761	54046	102849	64380	30923	58688	81242	87744	86909	161000
					27259		98000	74897		
			38245	3706						
	136978	46910	38375		30712	41364	66655	79406	39929	
	58812			104049			62117	71082		46333
	118303	46532	41440	65250	24800		61996	68714	42400	
	103053		63564	101928				71231	65417	
	156708	64880	63944	71500	81351			75506	61404	
			31914		97520		67548	55978	63973	
53588	66574		35430	36909		42600	87086	69096		
	91272	70307	49736	47382	42383		44000	78718	68364	
	72438		119600					51969		
			64059	86633		32895		67502		
	127516							60285		
64455	72176	59941	88607	65463			65877	61970		
	77237		58040							
	96320		78273				48620	49378		
	89352		59293	18679						
	95981		84857							
	78812								95541	
		21000	31946			55022	63534	86401		

4-37 按行业分其他各种经济单位就业人员平均工资
Average Wage of Employment in Units of Other Types of Ownership by Sector

单位：元 (yuan)

行 业	Sector	2010	2013	2014	2015	2016	2017	2018
总 计	**Total**	**27081**	**43857**	**49435**	**53384**	**57243**	**61279**	**68853**
农、林、牧、渔业	Agriculture,Forestry, Animal Husbandry and Fishery	20653	26905	34274	34847	37765	43621	48685
采矿业	Mining	27824	52840	62391	62892	65016	75942	94060
制造业	Manufacturing	26274	43396	47972	51353	55359	59059	68536
电力、热力、燃气及水生产和供应业	Production and Supply of Electricity, Heat, Gas and Water	34908	61185	69530	74641	82958	81604	91092
建筑业	Construction	22416	35999	40718	44413	48032	49649	55951
批发和零售业	Wholesale and Retail Trades	23405	38022	41807	45585	47764	52570	62344
交通运输、仓储和邮政业	Transport, Storage and Post	32345	57757	57808	62523	65948	73054	81009
住宿和餐饮业	Hotels and Catering Services	20480	30217	32945	36657	38115	40112	43207
信息传输、软件和信息技术服务业	Information Transmission, Software and Information Technology Services	41301	71454	81626	84607	90676	97738	112806
金融业	Financial Intermediation	48132	69564	78004	78364	80725	84389	89071
房地产业	Real Estate	30246	46051	49957	53350	58286	59652	65678
租赁和商务服务业	Leasing and Business Services	26093	49588	52300	54903	54048	58610	55358
科学研究和技术服务业	Scientific Research and Technical Services	40007	86030	90609	102976	108827	115856	138741
水利、环境和公共设施管理业	Management of Water Conservancy, Environment and Public Facilities	14335	42281	46524	39209	42885	49043	55734
居民服务、修理和其他服务业	Services to Households, Repair and Other Services	23943	36046	40309	42785	41430	40945	44672
教育	Education	36355	41925	46712	50986	53696	59843	67178
卫生和社会工作	Health and Social Service	34539	47026	50450	55182	57884	64247	76496
文化、体育和娱乐业	Culture, Sports and Entertainment	30200	40449	50746	52415	58905	59036	67024
公共管理、社会保障和社会组织	Public Management, Social Security and Social Organization					37164	40245	55941

4-38 各市(州)非私营企业单位就业人员和平均工资(2018年)
Average Wage and Number of Employment in Non-private Enterprises by Region(2018)

单位：人、元 (person,yuan)

市(州)	Region	就业人员 Number of Empoyment				平均工资 Average Wage			
		合计 Total	国有单位 State-owned Units	集体单位 Urban Collective-owned Units	其他单位 Units of Other Types of Ownership	合计 Total	国有单位 State-owned Units	集体单位 Urban Collective-owned Units	其他单位 Units of Other Types of Ownership
全省	**Sichuan**	**5078384**	**647423**	**151504**	**4279457**	**71374**	**92548**	**54466**	**68822**
成都市	Chengdu	2039941	212143	19701	1808097	80645	97515	60685	79068
自贡市	Zigong	127056	14335	1627	111094	59329	89053	54968	55695
攀枝花市	Panzhihua	128143	9054	1352	117737	73849	85229	39219	73373
泸州市	Luzhou	247215	27477	23421	196317	61260	51512	61813	62703
德阳市	Deyang	202922	13669	4724	184529	71687	97700	47990	70322
绵阳市	Mianyang	322117	22743	5954	293420	63229	85039	84016	61129
广元市	Guangyuan	81699	12912	5840	62947	59751	78162	56653	56015
遂宁市	Suining	133117	7664	10729	114724	53152	87870	55215	50488
内江市	Neijiang	116672	9193	5131	102348	53307	75440	43307	51771
乐山市	Leshan	141520	6031	2002	133487	61633	77689	53026	61004
南充市	Nanchong	248517	27164	11402	209951	55553	76484	55752	52731
眉山市	Meishan	106270	11555	1818	92897	60593	100654	59801	55676
宜宾市	Yibin	240575	12999	6040	221536	69604	93292	39345	68925
广安市	Guangan	70076	11997	16602	41477	57368	67633	46067	59027
达州市	Dazhou	187616	24763	15216	147637	59214	70963	52063	57985
雅安市	Yaan	54063	5286	1294	47483	51137	70999	52250	48834
巴中市	Bazhong	153162	15866	11108	126188	48710	61213	38960	47941
资阳市	Ziyang	106321	12834	4592	88895	48987	78664	45371	45094
阿坝藏族羌族自治州	Aba	24427	5168	906	18353	66683	93039	81373	58147
甘孜藏族自治州	Ganzi	17512	5348	1206	10958	78304	76129	58815	81195
凉山彝族自治州	Liangshan	111658	18935	839	91884	65123	80627	65090	61706

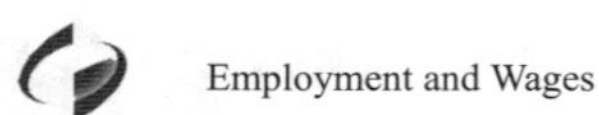

4-39 各市(州)非私营事业单位就业人员和平均工资(2018年)
Average Wage and Number of People Employed in Institutions of Non-private Enterprises by Region(2018)

单位：人、元 (person,yuan)

市(州)	Region	就业人员 Number of Employment				平均工资 Average Wage			
		合计 Total	国有单位 State-owned Units	集体单位 Urban Collective-owned Units	其他单位 Units of Other Types of Ownership	合计 Total	国有单位 State-owned Units	集体单位 Urban Collective-owned Units	其他单位 Units of Other Types of Ownership
全　省	**Sichuan**	**1774979**	**1690468**	**49600**	**34911**	**88094**	**88722**	**73586**	**78067**
成都市	Chengdu	442861	400187	17820	24854	101866	103963	86437	78814
自贡市	Zigong	55824	53882	1291	651	88485	89041	61625	95265
攀枝花市	Panzhihua	31121	31121			96591	96591		
泸州市	Luzhou	83231	81693	1343	195	87126	87420	53075	201150
德阳市	Deyang	73262	66626	5069	1567	87497	89045	71793	72886
绵阳市	Mianyang	131184	120042	5319	5823	100523	103167	68578	74043
广元市	Guangyuan	53763	51587	2176		75608	75805	70936	
遂宁市	Suining	47273	45752	1521		92892	93472	75219	
内江市	Neijiang	64243	63881	333	29	80476	80535	70475	68448
乐山市	Leshan	55818	55340	358	120	79109	79091	81746	79667
南充市	Nanchong	130196	126381	2971	844	85841	86258	77917	51701
眉山市	Meishan	48240	47467	773		76439	76828	52839	
宜宾市	Yibin	93326	91640	1664	22	83568	83806	70476	53739
广安市	Guangan	60885	58066	2149	670	86152	87113	60373	85085
达州市	Dazhou	97120	93649	3410	61	71960	72309	62812	37443
雅安市	Yaan	35548	35472	13	63	63011	63020	52714	60286
巴中市	Bazhong	63387	62149	1238		68743	69098	50955	
资阳市	Ziyang	47809	47113	696		76768	77604	21072	
阿坝藏族羌族自治州	Aba	33444	33432	12		94408	94406	101083	
甘孜藏族自治州	Ganzi	31828	31791	37		79111	79091	95541	
凉山彝族自治州	Liangshan	94616	93197	1407	12	80332	80554	65641	53750

4-40 各市(州)国有单位分隶属关系就业人员平均工资(2018年)
Average Wage of Employment in State-owned Units by Region and Affiliations(2018)

单位：元 (yuan)

市(州)	Region	合计 Total	中央单位 Enterprises Belong to Central Government	地方单位 Local Units	其他单位 Units of Other Types of Ownership
全 省	**Sichuan**	**90390**	**117084**	**86373**	**77920**
成都市	Chengdu	102882	125417	98460	101477
自贡市	Zigong	94200	103507	93606	70628
攀枝花市	Panzhihua	98709	112863	97473	71083
泸州市	Luzhou	83347	124587	80822	65798
德阳市	Deyang	96356	104673	95919	66613
绵阳市	Mianyang	97398	153020	83707	56548
广元市	Guangyuan	75915	102991	74796	35024
遂宁市	Suining	91737	108313	91228	70189
内江市	Neijiang	78383	92583	77973	86281
乐山市	Leshan	85678	101130	85182	85440
南充市	Nanchong	85190	103356	85294	55020
眉山市	Meishan	87439	126022	84055	71037
宜宾市	Yibin	87982	107801	86895	43176
广安市	Guangan	84237	121432	83591	61782
达州市	Dazhou	74259	72031	75040	62164
雅安市	Yaan	64924	81504	64145	61773
巴中市	Bazhong	67038	83343	66835	52063
资阳市	Ziyang	79620	96955	79385	36141
阿坝藏族羌族自治州	Aba	100223	117812	99248	116222
甘孜藏族自治州	Ganzi	82953	95403	82712	56746
凉山彝族自治州	Liangshan	79383	94664	78412	75930

4-41 各市(州)国有企业就业人员和平均工资(2018年)

Average Wage and Number of Employment in State-owned Enterprises by Region(2018)

单位：人、元 (person,yuan)

市(州)	Region	就业人员 Number of Employment			平均工资 Average Wage of Staff and Worker		
		合计 Total	中央单位 Enterprises Belong to Central Government	地方单位 Local Units	合计 Total	中央单位 Enterprises Belong to Central Government	地方单位 Local Units
全 省	**Sichuan**	**647423**	**366376**	**281047**	**92548**	**106755**	**72566**
成都市	Chengdu	212143	80429	131714	97515	120802	80883
自贡市	Zigong	14335	9932	4403	89053	99776	63662
攀枝花市	Panzhihua	9054	4892	4162	85229	103416	63977
泸州市	Luzhou	27477	5341	22136	51512	98472	40475
德阳市	Deyang	13669	6142	7527	97700	107716	89609
绵阳市	Mianyang	22743	5923	16820	85039	80409	86647
广元市	Guangyuan	12912	3795	9117	78162	103057	67948
遂宁市	Suining	7664	1863	5801	87870	111180	80440
内江市	Neijiang	9193	3198	5995	75440	95583	64701
乐山市	Leshan	6031	2686	3345	77689	88474	69060
南充市	Nanchong	27164	11870	15294	76484	94646	62690
眉山市	Meishan	11555	6829	4726	100654	125970	62085
宜宾市	Yibin	12999	8627	4372	93292	101510	76916
广安市	Guangan	11997	5687	6310	67633	89035	46219
达州市	Dazhou	24763	14236	10527	70963	64556	80106
雅安市	Yaan	5286	2220	3066	70999	82265	62724
巴中市	Bazhong	15866	12057	3809	61213	68068	39899
资阳市	Ziyang	12834	7663	5171	78664	79285	77718
阿坝藏族羌族自治州	Aba	5168	1904	3264	93039	133825	70106
甘孜藏族自治州	Ganzi	5348	1171	4177	76129	97401	70136
凉山彝族自治州	Liangshan	18935	9624	9311	80627	94053	67259

4-42　各市(州)国有事业单位就业人员和平均工资(2018年)
Average Wage and Number of Employment in State-owned Institutions(2018)

单位：人、元　　(person,yuan)

市(州)	Region	就业人员 Number Of Employment			平均工资 Average Wage of Staff And Worker		
		合 计 Total	中央单位 Institutions Belong to Central Government	地方单位 Local Units	合 计 Total	中央单位 Institutions Belong to Central Government	地方单位 Local Units
全 省	**Sichuan**	**1690468**	**103798**	**1586670**	**88722**	**130620**	**85977**
成都市	Chengdu	400187	44101	356086	103963	125200	101325
自贡市	Zigong	53882	134	53748	89041	84017	89052
攀枝花市	Panzhihua	31121		31121	96591		96591
泸州市	Luzhou	81693	2837	78856	87420	160005	84839
德阳市	Deyang	66626	7355	59271	89045	94959	88328
绵阳市	Mianyang	120042	35447	84595	103167	161593	78588
广元市	Guangyuan	51587	45	51542	75805	82455	75800
遂宁市	Suining	45752	189	45563	93472	112153	93395
内江市	Neijiang	63881	2788	61093	80535	107791	79310
乐山市	Leshan	55340	6260	49080	79091	74559	79672
南充市	Nanchong	126381	1196	125185	86258	56074	86548
眉山市	Meishan	47467	49	47418	76828	73653	76831
宜宾市	Yibin	91640	499	91141	83806	112159	83647
广安市	Guangan	58066	70	57996	87113	101042	87096
达州市	Dazhou	93649	304	93345	72309	70375	72315
雅安市	Yaan	35472	1671	33801	63020	69688	62687
巴中市	Bazhong	62149	78	62071	69098	58759	69111
资阳市	Ziyang	47113	38	47075	77604	76158	77605
阿坝藏族羌族自治州	Aba	33432	154	33278	94406	105314	94354
甘孜藏族自治州	Ganzi	31791	144	31647	79091	86678	79055
凉山彝族自治州	Liangshan	93197	439	92758	80554	82333	80546

4-43 各市(州)国有机关单位就业人员和平均工资(2018年)
Average Wage and Number of Employment in Government by Region(2018)

单位：人、元 (person,yuan)

市(州)	Region	就业人员 Number of Employment			平均工资 Average Wage of Staff and Worker		
		合计 Total	中央单位 Agencies Belong to Central Government	地方单位 Local Units	合计 Total	中央单位 Agencies Belong to Central Government	地方单位 Local Units
全　省	**Sichuan**	**930792**	**37363**	**893429**	**92015**	**114237**	**91077**
成都市	Chengdu	196443	12652	183791	106344	148179	103472
自贡市	Zigong	21936	254	21682	111181	82377	111497
攀枝花市	Panzhihua	17168	1282	15886	109996	129277	108405
泸州市	Luzhou	38547	1618	36929	97738	119279	96770
德阳市	Deyang	31960	206	31754	110978	118574	110929
绵阳市	Mianyang	51564	2274	49290	89620	69444	90544
广元市	Guangyuan	36150	266	35884	75281	95015	75134
遂宁市	Suining	24041	478	23563	89668	97391	89511
内江市	Neijiang	34240	937	33303	75205	60891	75602
乐山市	Leshan	42228	3384	38844	94988	102910	94285
南充市	Nanchong	58903	2722	56181	86961	119066	85387
眉山市	Meishan	30545	860	29685	98959	98646	98969
宜宾市	Yibin	46758	1216	45542	94729	111562	94269
广安市	Guangan	30570	640	29930	85036	109289	84512
达州市	Dazhou	53546	1233	52313	79230	81353	79179
雅安市	Yaan	25322	2884	22438	66315	74031	65317
巴中市	Bazhong	31114	858	30256	65905	78712	65539
资阳市	Ziyang	20548	726	19822	84753	105732	83971
阿坝藏族羌族自治州	Aba	32977	1207	31770	107331	106318	107369
甘孜藏族自治州	Ganzi	43965	384	43581	86467	86196	86469
凉山彝族自治州	Liangshan	62267	1282	60985	77255	94077	76900

4-44 城镇登记失业人数及失业率

Number of Registered Unemployed Persons and Unemployment Rate in Urban Areas

年 份 Year	城镇登记失业人数 (万人) Unemployed Persons in Urban Areas (10 000 persons)	#女性 Female	女性占失业人数的百分比(%) Percentage of Unemployed Female to Unemployed Persons (%)	登记失业率 (%) Unemployment Rate in Urban Areas (%)
1978	52.00	30.00	57.7	10.9
1979	33.00	18.51	56.1	6.7
1980	28.00	15.60	55.7	5.0
1981	25.00	13.50	54.0	4.4
1982	16.90	9.00	53.3	3.0
1983	18.10	9.61	53.1	3.0
1984	15.84	8.40	53.0	2.7
1985	14.35	7.47	52.1	2.3
1986	14.44	7.51	52.0	2.3
1987	14.53	7.56	52.0	2.2
1988	16.75	8.65	51.6	2.4
1989	25.63	14.65	57.2	3.7
1990	26.61	14.86	55.8	3.7
1991	25.17	14.04	55.8	3.4
1992	27.16	15.24	56.1	3.6
1993	26.47	14.50	54.8	3.5
1994	27.65	15.79	57.1	3.6
1995	27.94	15.44	55.3	3.6
1996	27.16	14.55	53.6	3.5
1997	26.72	14.43	54.0	3.4
1998	30.18	16.04	53.1	3.7
1999	29.59	15.11	51.1	3.7
2000	30.79	15.11	49.1	4.0
2001	31.90	15.11	47.4	4.3
2002	33.82	16.02	47.4	4.5
2003	33.10	15.70	47.4	4.4
2004	33.30	15.30	46.0	4.4
2005	34.30	15.70	45.8	4.6
2006	36.10	16.50	45.6	4.5
2007	34.80	15.40	44.3	4.3
2008	37.86	16.04	42.4	4.6
2009	36.28	13.59	37.5	4.3
2010	34.56	14.07	40.7	4.1
2011	36.93	15.24	41.3	4.1
2012	41.67	16.81	40.3	4.1
2013	42.87	19.63	45.8	4.1
2014	54.36	26.73	49.2	4.2
2015	54.64	27.45	50.2	4.1
2016	56.26	28.05	49.9	4.2
2017	55.78	27.53	49.4	4.0
2018	53.31	26.58	49.9	3.5

4-45 各市(州)城镇登记失业人数及失业率
Number of Registered Unemployed Persons and Unemployment Rate in Urban Areas by Region

市(州)	Region	城镇登记失业人数（万人）Unemployed Persons (10 000 persons)					登记失业率（%）Unemployment Rate (%)				
		2005	2010	2015	2017	2018	2005	2010	2015	2017	2018
全　省	**Sichuan**	**34.30**	**34.56**	**54.64**	**55.78**	**53.31**	**4.6**	**4.1**	**4.1**	**4.0**	**3.5**
成都市	Chengdu	5.90	5.62	17.05	18.46	20.47	3.1	2.5	3.2	3.2	3.3
自贡市	Zigong	1.70	1.66	2.61	2.51	2.10	4.0	4.1	4.2	3.9	3.6
攀枝花市	Panzhihua	1.30	1.13	1.24	1.44	1.45	4.4	3.5	3.6	4.0	4.1
泸州市	Luzhou	1.80	1.66	1.48	1.70	1.56	4.4	3.5	3.5	3.2	3.1
德阳市	Deyang	1.30	1.50	2.06	2.10	1.96	3.3	3.7	3.9	3.9	3.7
绵阳市	Mianyang	3.30	3.04	3.51	3.35	2.20	3.9	3.7	3.9	3.7	2.6
广元市	Guangyuan	1.00	1.22	1.48	1.49	1.47	4.3	3.9	3.9	3.9	3.7
遂宁市	Suining	1.40	1.38	4.37	4.22	3.14	4.9	4.5	4.0	4.0	3.6
内江市	Neijiang	1.70	1.57	1.41	1.39	1.38	4.5	4.0	4.0	3.9	3.7
乐山市	Leshan	1.90	2.16	2.41	2.46	2.27	4.2	4.1	4.1	3.9	3.8
南充市	Nanchong	2.00	2.29	3.12	2.86	2.78	4.8	4.5	4.2	3.9	3.7
眉山市	Meishan	1.10	1.15	1.54	1.60	1.35	4.4	4.3	4.1	4.1	4.0
宜宾市	Yibin	2.10	1.81	3.07	3.08	2.74	4.7	3.5	3.9	4.0	3.8
广安市	Guangan	1.60	1.25	0.86	1.11	1.16	4.0	3.7	3.2	3.6	3.5
达州市	Dazhou	1.30	2.01	1.93	1.95	1.92	4.1	4.0	4.0	4.0	4.0
雅安市	Yaan	0.60	0.64	0.52	0.51	0.52	4.0	4.0	3.8	3.9	3.9
巴中市	Bazhong	1.00	1.16	1.50	1.61	1.58	4.2	4.3	4.3	4.3	4.3
资阳市	Ziyang	1.20	1.36	2.05	1.41	1.45	4.5	3.9	4.0	4.0	4.0
阿坝藏族羌族自治州	Aba	0.40	0.35	0.39	0.45	0.34	4.1	3.7	3.7	3.7	3.6
甘孜藏族自治州	Ganzi	0.30	0.37	0.54	0.56	0.43	5.0	4.1	4.1	4.0	3.2
凉山彝族自治州	Liangshan	1.30	1.22	1.54	1.50	1.04	4.1	4.1	4.0	3.8	2.8

主要统计指标解释

就业人员　指在一定年龄以上，有劳动能力，为取得劳动报酬或经营收入而从事一定社会劳动的人员。具体指年满16周岁，为取得报酬或经营利润，在调查周内从事了1个小时（含1小时）以上的劳动的人员；或由于学习、休假等原因在调查周内暂时处于未工作状态，但有工作单位或场所的人员；或由于临时停工放假、单位不景气放假等原因在调查周内暂时处于未工作状态，但不满三个月的人员。

单位就业人员　指报告期末最后一日在本单位中工作，并取得工资或其他形式劳动报酬的人员数。该指标为时点指标，不包括最后一日当天及以前已经与单位解除劳动合同关系的人员，是在岗职工、劳务派遣人员及其他就业人员之和。

就业人员不包括：（1）离开本单位仍保留劳动关系，并定期领取生活费的人员；（2）在本单位实习的各类在校学生；（3）本单位以劳务外包形式使用的人员。

城镇私营和个体就业人员　城镇私营就业人员指在工商管理部门注册登记，其经营地址设在县城关镇（含县城关镇）以上的私营企业就业人员，包括私营企业投资者和雇工。城镇个体就业人员指在工商管理部门注册登记，并持有城镇户口或在城镇长期居住，经批准从事个体工商经营的就业人员，包括个体经营者和在个体工商户劳动的家庭帮工和雇工。

在岗职工　指在本单位工作且与本单位签订劳动合同，并由单位支付各项工资和社会保险、住房公积金的人员，以及上述人员中由于学习、病伤、产假等原因暂未工作仍由单位支付工资的人员。在岗职工还包括：

（1）应订立劳动合同而未订立劳动合同人员（如使用的农村户籍人员）；

（2）处于试用期人员；

（3）编制外招用的人员，如临时人员；

（4）派往外单位工作，但工资仍由本单位发放的人员（如挂职锻炼、外派工作等情况）。

工资总额　指根据《关于工资总额组成的规定》（1990年1月1日国家统计局发布的一号令）进行修订，本单位在报告期内（季度或年度）直接支付给本单位全部就业人员的劳动报酬总额。包括计时工资、计件工资、奖金、津贴和补贴、加班加点工资、特殊情况下支付的工资，是在岗职工工资总额、劳务派遣人员工资总额和其他就业人员工资总额之和。

工资总额是税前工资，包括单位从个人工资中直接为其代扣或代缴的房费、水费、电费、住房公积金和社会保险基金个人缴纳部分等。

工资总额不论是计入成本的还是不计入成本的，不论是以货币形式支付的还是以实物形式支付的，均应列入工资总额的计算范围。

平均工资　指单位就业人员在一定时期内平均每人所得的工资额。它表明一定时期工资收入的高低程度，是反映就业人员工资水平的主要指标。计算公式为：

$$平均工资=\frac{报告期就业人员工资总额}{报告期就业人员平均人数}$$

平均实际工资　指扣除物价变动因素后的就业人员平均工资。计算公式为：

$$平均实际工资=\frac{报告期就业人员平均工资}{报告期城镇居民消费价格指数}$$

平均工资指数　指报告期就业人员平均工资与基期就业人员平均工资的比率，是反映不同时期就业人员货币工资水平变动情况的相对数。计算公式为：

$$平均工资指数=\frac{报告期就业人员平均工资}{基期就业人员平均工资}\times 100\%$$

平均实际工资指数　是反映实际工资变动情况的相对数，表明就业人员实际工资水平提高或降低的程度。计算公式为：

$$平均实际工资指数=\frac{报告期就业人员平均工资指数}{报告期城镇居民消费价格指数}\times 100\%$$

城镇登记失业人员　指有非农业户口，在一定的劳动年龄内（16周岁至退休年龄），有劳动能力，无业而要求就业，并在当地劳动保障部门进行失业登记的人员。

城镇登记失业率　指城镇登记失业人员与城镇单位就业人员（扣除使用的农村劳动力、聘用的离退休人员、港澳台及外方人员）、城镇单位中的不在岗职工、城镇私营业主、个体户主、城镇私营企业和个体就业人员、城镇登记失业人员之和的比。

Explanatory Notes on Main Statistical Indicators

Employed Persons refers to persons above a specified age who had labor capacity and performed some social work for compensation or business gains. Specifically, it refers to persons, aged 16 and over, who performed some work for compensation or business gains for one hour or more during the reference period; or persons who do not work for the reasons of study or on holiday, but had work units or sites during the reference period; or persons temporary absence from a job for disorganization or suspension of work, recession, etc, but not exceeding three months during the reference period.

Persons Employed in Various Units refers to the total number of employees who work at various units and obtain wages or other forms of payment at the end of the reference period. This indicator is a kind of time point index and it equals to the sum of the number of employed staff and workers, labor dispatch personnel and other employed persons.

Employed persons do not include:

1) persons who have left their working units while keeping their labor contract (employment relation) unchanged and receiving regular alimony;

2)all kinds of enrolled students who do internship in various units;

3)persons employed due to labor outsourcing, for example, persons employed in the organizational system of construction industry.

Persons Employed in Private Enterprises and Self-employed Individuals in Urban Areas Persons employed in private enterprises refers to the persons employed in the private enterprises which have been registered at the departments of industrial and commercial administration and are situated at a county town (i.e. a town where the county government is located) for business operation or at urban areas with the level higher than a county town. The self-employed individuals in urban areas refers to persons who hold the certificates of residence in urban areas or have resided in the urban areas for a long time and have been registered at the departments of industrial and commercial administration and approved to be engaged in individual industrial or commercial business, including self-employed persons as well as helpers and hired laborers who work in the individual households engaged in industrial or commercial business.

Staff and Workers refers to persons who signed labor contracts with working units and working units would pay wages, social insurance and housing funds for them. Persons who have their work posts but are temporarily absent from work for reasons of study or on sick, injury or maternal leave and still receive wages from their working units are also included. Employed staff and workers also include:

1) Persons who should have signed the labor contracts but not (like people with rural household registration);

2) Employees on probation;

3) Employees beyond the staffing quota, for example, temporary employees;

4) Employees who are sent to other working units but still obtain wages from their original units (situations like on-the-job placement, expatriated assignment, etc.).

Total Wages Bill It is revised according to the "Provision of Composition of Total Wages" (Order No.1 by National Bureau of Statistics on January, 1st, 1990), total wage bill refers to the total remuneration payment to all employed persons in various units during the reporting period (by quarter or by year), including hourly-paid wages, piece-rate wages, bonuses, allowance and subsidies, overtime wages and wages paid under special circumstances. It equals to the sum of total wages of employed staff and workers, dispatch labors and other employed persons.

Total wage bill is pre-tax wages, including the room charges, utility bills, housing funds and social insurance paid or withheld by employee's units.

Total wage bill, whether or not included in cost, whether or not paid in money or in kind, shall be included in the calculation of total wage.

Average Wage refers to the average per capita wage during a certain period of time for employed persons. It shows the general level of wage income during a certain period of time, one major indicator to reflect the wage level. It is calculated as follows:

$$\text{Average Wage} = \frac{\text{Total Wage Bill of Employed Persons at Reference Time}}{\text{Average Number of Persons Employed at Reference Time}}$$

Average Real Wage refers to average wage of staff and workers after removing the effects of price changes, which is calculated as follows:

$$\text{Average Real Wage} = \frac{\text{Average Wage of Employed Persons at Reference Time}}{\text{Urban Consumer Price Indices at Reference Time}} \times 100\%$$

Average Wage Indices refers to the ratio of average wage of staff and workers in the report period to that in the base period, which reflects the change of wage of staff and workers at the different period. It is calculated as follows:

$$\text{Average Wage Indices} = \frac{\text{Average Wage Indices of Employed Persons at Reference Time}}{\text{Average Wage of Persons Employeds at Base Period}} \times 100\%$$

Average Real Wage Indices reflects the relative changing degree of average real wage, and indicates the degree of the rising or declining degree of real wage of staff and

worker, which is calculated as following:

$$\text{Average Real Wage Indices} = \frac{\text{Average Wage Indices of Employed Persons at the Reference Time}}{\text{Urban Consumer Price Indices at Reference Time}} \times 100\%$$

Registered Unemployed Persons in Urban Areas refers to the persons with non-agricultural household registration at certain working ages (16 years old to retirement age), who are capable of working, unemployed and willing to work, and have been registered at the local Department of labor and social security to apply for a job.

Registered Urban Unemployment Rate refers to the ratio of the number of the registered unemployed to the sum of the number of persons employed in various units(minus the rural labor force, retirees ,and Hong Kong, Macao, Taiwan and foreign employees they employ),laid-off workers in urban units, unban self-employed individuals and the registered unban unemployed persons.

5

固定资产投资

Chapter 5 Investment in Fixed Assets

5-1 全社会固定资产投资增长情况(2018年)
The Growth of Total Investment in Fixed Assets(2018)

指 标	Item	比上年增长(%) Growth Rate Over Preceding Year (%)	市(州)	Region	比上年增长(%) Growth Rate Over Preceding Year (%)
全社会固定资产投资	**Total Investment**	**10.2**	**全 省**	**Sichuan**	**10.2**
#国有及国有控股	State-owned and State Holding Units	11.2	成都市	Chengdu	10.0
按登记注册类型分	Grouped by Registration		自贡市	Zigong	15.6
内资	Domestic Funds	11.0	攀枝花市	Panzhihua	8.1
港澳台投资	UnitsWith Funds From Hong Kong, Macao and Taiwan	-9.9	泸州市	Luzhou	5.9
外商投资	Foreign Funded Units	9.1	德阳市	Deyang	12.4
个体经营	Indivuduals Economy	-11.9	绵阳市	Mianyang	15.8
按建设性质分	Grouped by Character		广元市	Guangyuan	14.1
新建	New Constrution	10.4	遂宁市	Suining	11.2
扩建	Expansion	21.0	内江市	Neijiang	3.1
改建	Reconstruction	6.2	乐山市	Leshan	13.8
按构成分	Grouped by Use of Funds		南充市	Nanchong	15.5
建筑安装工程	Construction and Installation	8.2	眉山市	Meishan	12.7
设备工器具购置	Purchase of Equipment And Instruments	6.0	宜宾市	Yibin	13.6
其他费用	Others	27.2	广安市	Guangan	3.2
按三次产业分	Grouped by Three Strata of Industry		达州市	Dazhou	12.3
第一产业	Primary Industry	10.1	雅安市	Yaan	12.2
第二产业	Secondary Industry	7.3	巴中市	Bazhong	9.2
第三产业	Tertiary Industry	11.2	资阳市	Ziyang	8.3
			阿坝藏族羌族自治州	Aba	11.3
			甘孜藏族自治州	Ganzi	13.7
			凉山彝族自治州	Liangshan	-4.3

注：2018年起，计划投资在500-5000万项目按财务支出法统计，增速按可比口径计算(以下有关各表同)。
a)Planned investment in 5-50 million projects is counted according to the financial expenditure method, and the growth rate is calculated by comparable caliber(the same as the related following tables).

5-2 分行业全社会固定资产投资增长情况(2018年)
The Growth of Total Investment in Fixed Assets by Sector(2018)

指　　标	Item	比上年增长(%) Growth Rate Over Preceding Year (%)
全社会固定资产投资	**Total Investment**	**10.2**
农、林、牧、渔业	Agriculture, Forestry, Animal Husbandry and Fishery	8.7
采矿业	Mining	49.9
制造业	Manufacturing	6.7
电力、热力、燃气及水生产和供应业	Production and Supply of Electricity, Heat, Gas and Water	2.1
建筑业	Construction	-28.6
批发和零售业	Wholesale and Retail Trades	-20.0
交通运输、仓储和邮政业	Transport, Storage and Post	11.7
住宿和餐饮业	Hotels and Catering Services	-12.5
信息传输、软件和信息技术服务业	Information Transmission, Software and Information Technology Services	20.6
金融业	Financial Intermediation	-0.5
房地产业	Real Estate	5.5
租赁和商务服务业	Leasing and Business Services	31.1
科学研究和技术服务业	Scientific Research and Technical Services	56.1
水利、环境和公共设施管理业	Management of Water Conservancy, Environment and Public Facilities	17.7
居民服务、修理和其他服务业	Services to Households, Repair and Other Services	-2.8
教育	Education	22.5
卫生和社会工作	Health and Social Service	11.1
文化、体育和娱乐业	Culture, Sports and Entertainment	64.1
公共管理、社会保障和社会组织	Public Management, Social Security and Social Organization	52.7
国际组织	International Organization	

5-3 项目固定资产投资增长情况(2018年)
The Growth of Item Investment in Fixed Assets(2018)

指　　标	Item	比上年增长(%) Growth Rate Over Preceding Year(%)
投资总额	**Total Investment**	**10.7**
#国有及国有控股	State-owned and State Holding Units	12.3
按产业分	Grouped By Industry	
第一产业	Primary Industry	13.3
第二产业	Secondary Industry	7.5
#工业	Industry	8.2
第三产业	Tertiary Industry	12.2
按建设性质分	Grouped By Character	
新建	New Construction	10.4
扩建	Expansion	21.0
改建	Reconstruction	6.2
按构成分	Grouped by Use of the Funds	
建筑安装工程	Construction and Installation	11.5
设备工器具购置	Purchurse of the Equipment And Instrument	7.2
其他费用	Others	8.3
新增固定资产	**Increased Investment**	**-19.0**
施工项目个数	**Number of Projects Under Construction**	**-24.1**
#新开工	Number of Projects Started This Year	-36.5
竣工项目个数	**Number of Projects Completed**	**-33.5**
房屋建筑面积	**Floor Space of Buildings**	
施工面积	Floor Space of Buildings under Construction	-18.8
#住宅	Residential Buildings	-39.8
竣工面积	Floor Space of Buildings Completed	-22.8
#住宅	Residential Buildings	-51.0

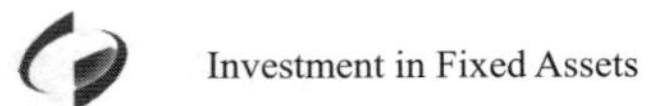

5-4 分行业按构成分项目固定资产投资增长情况(2018年)
The Growth of Item Investment in Fixed Assets by Sector and Constitution(2018)

单位: % (%)

指 标	Item	合计 Total	建筑安装工程 Construction and Installation	设备工具器具购置 Purchase of Equipment and Instruments	其他费用 Others
投资总额	**Total Investment**	**10.7**	**11.5**	**7.2**	**8.3**
农、林、牧、渔业	Agriculture, Forestry, Animal Husbandry and Fishery	13.3	11.4	60.8	6.3
采矿业	Mining	49.9	70.7	18.9	-27.2
制造业	Manufacturing	6.7	9.6	3.2	-2.3
电力、热力、燃气及水生产和供应业	Production and Supply of Electricity, Heat, Gas and Water	2.1	14.3	-30.6	
建筑业	Construction	-34.5	-34.6	-10.1	-69.1
批发和零售业	Wholesale and Retail Trades	-20.0	-16.6	-49.1	-11.8
交通运输、仓储和邮政业	Transport, Storage and Post	12.1	13.7	121.9	-13.7
住宿和餐饮业	Hotels and Catering Services	-12.5	-14.4	11.6	9.0
信息传输、软件和信息技术服务业	Information Transmission, Software and Information Technology Services	20.6	4.2	44.9	-51.7
金融业	Financial Intermediation	-0.5	-10.7	171.7	295.3
房地产业	Real Estate	-5.7	-6.9	-6.6	11.5
租赁和商务服务业	Leasing and Business Services	31.1	28.3	38.7	59.5
科学研究和技术服务业	Scientific Research and Technical Services	56.1	70.3	-21.0	88.2
水利、环境和公共设施管理业	Management of Water Conservancy, Environment and Public Facilities	17.7	14.0	37.8	40.4
居民服务、修理和其他服务业	Services to Households, Repair and Other Services	11.6	10.6	-31.3	131.3
教育	Education	22.5	20.9	6.1	61.4
卫生和社会工作	Health and Social Service	11.1	12.4	4.8	9.7
文化、体育和娱乐业	Culture, Sports and Entertainment	67.7	64.6	64.2	118.8
公共管理、社会保障和社会组织	Public Management, Social Security and Social Organization	52.7	56.3	33.8	9.6
国际组织	International Organization				

5-5 各市(州)按构成分项目固定资产投资增长情况(2018年)

The Growth of Item Investment in Fixed Assets by Region and Institution(2018)

单位：%　　　　(%)

市(州)	Region	投资额 Total Investment	建筑安装工程 Construction and Installation	设备工具器具购置 Purchase of Equipment and Instruments	其他费用 Others
全　省	**Sichuan**	**10.7**	**11.5**	**7.2**	**8.3**
成都市	Chengdu	18.9	19.1	7.9	33.7
自贡市	Zigong	2.8	5.5	-8.3	-5.1
攀枝花市	Panzhihua	2.0	2.2	11.9	-32.5
泸州市	Luzhou	3.5	2.3	6.7	20.7
德阳市	Deyang	9.7	3.9	28.9	37.0
绵阳市	Mianyang	17.4	19.1	38.7	-50.1
广元市	Guangyuan	19.0	29.0	-6.8	-42.5
遂宁市	Suining	14.2	16.5	7.0	-48.8
内江市	Neijiang	-3.3	-9.0	22.4	21.8
乐山市	Leshan	19.3	25.5	16.9	-19.4
南充市	Nanchong	10.5	10.2	0.8	56.7
眉山市	Meishan	7.4	8.3	29.2	-22.8
宜宾市	Yibin	8.9	12.3	-15.1	15.4
广安市	Guangan	5.3	3.8	37.8	-7.9
达州市	Dazhou	10.3	9.5	32.5	-41.3
雅安市	Yaan	8.9	21.5	-56.3	55.8
巴中市	Bazhong	8.2	8.7	-4.9	31.6
资阳市	Ziyang	15.7	17.1	-18.8	59.6
阿坝藏族羌族自治州	Aba	14.2	14.2	-33.6	44.6
甘孜藏族自治州	Ganzi	21.6	28.9	1.7	1.8
凉山彝族自治州	Liangshan	-20.0	-13.0	-52.7	-43.0

注：本表各市(州)数不包括跨区投资。
a)The region data in this table excludes multiregional investment.

5-6 分行业施工和投产项目个数(2018年)
Number of Projects under Construction and Production by Sector(2018)

行　业	Sector	施工项目 (个) Number of Projets Under Construction (unit)	新开工项目个数 (个) Number of Projects Started This Year (unit)	全部建成投产项目 (个) Number of Projects Completed (unit)	项目建成投产率 (%) Rate of Projects Completed (%)
总　计	**Total**	**34344**	**16855**	**18666**	**54.35**
农、林、牧、渔业	Agriculture, Forestry, Animal Husbandry and Fishery	4234	2342	2409	56.90
采矿业	Mining	848	506	507	59.79
制造业	Manufacturing	6745	3558	4093	60.68
电力、热力、燃气及水生产和供应业	Production and Supply of Electricity, Heat,Gas and Water	2165	1122	1164	53.76
建筑业	Construction	227	129	116	51.10
批发和零售业	Wholesale and Retail Trades	479	229	291	60.75
交通运输、仓储和邮政业	Transport, Storage and Post	5030	2310	2634	52.37
住宿和餐饮业	Hotels and Catering Services	563	243	280	49.73
信息传输、软件和信息技术服务业	Information Transmission, Software and Information Technology Services	360	226	277	76.94
金融业	Financial Intermediation	23	6	19	82.61
房地产业	Real Estate	2499	967	1221	48.86
租赁和商务服务业	Leasing and Business Services	477	208	221	46.33
科学研究和技术服务业	Scientific Research and Technical Services	149	76	60	40.27
水利、环境和公共设施管理业	Management of Water Conservancy, Environment and Public Facilities	6469	2965	3206	49.56
居民服务、修理和其他服务业	Services to Households, Repair and Other Services	170	78	93	54.71
教育	Education	1421	639	729	51.30
卫生和社会工作	Health and Social Service	946	388	531	56.13
文化、体育和娱乐业	Culture, Sports and Entertainment	811	499	375	46.24
公共管理、社会保障和社会组织	Public Management, Social Security and Social Organization	728	364	440	60.44
国际组织	International Organization				

5-7 各市(州)施工和投产项目个数(2018年)
Number of Projects under Construction and Production by Region(2018)

市(州)	Region	施工项目 (个) Number of Projects under Construction (unit)	新开工项目个数 (个) Number of Projects Started This Year (unit)	全部建成投产项目 (个) Number of Projects Completed and Put into Use (unit)	项目建成投产率 (%) Rate of Projects Completed (%)
全　省	**Sichuan**	**34344**	**16855**	**18666**	**54.35**
成都市	Chengdu	4358	2031	2482	56.87
自贡市	Zigong	983	434	539	54.50
攀枝花市	Panzhihua	1173	669	810	68.88
泸州市	Luzhou	1579	944	991	62.56
德阳市	Deyang	1809	1102	1134	62.38
绵阳市	Mianyang	1618	740	879	53.69
广元市	Guangyuan	1930	995	1163	60.18
遂宁市	Suining	1672	697	1103	65.93
内江市	Neijiang	1277	748	637	49.65
乐山市	Leshan	1248	563	600	47.77
南充市	Nanchong	2425	1011	1192	49.11
眉山市	Meishan	1018	496	453	43.77
宜宾市	Yibin	2432	1298	1421	58.39
广安市	Guangan	2090	1244	1377	65.85
达州市	Dazhou	3300	1374	1425	43.17
雅安市	Yaan	602	316	308	50.83
巴中市	Bazhong	1631	687	919	56.35
资阳市	Ziyang	509	299	172	33.59
阿坝藏族羌族自治州	Aba	636	330	200	31.21
甘孜藏族自治州	Ganzi	1239	564	501	40.40
凉山彝族自治州	Liangshan	777	311	360	46.21
不分地区	Others	38	2		

注：本表各市(州)数不包括跨区项目。
a)The region data in this table exclude multiregional projects.

5-8 各市(州)建设施工和竣工房屋建筑面积(2018年)

Floor Space of Buildings under Construction and Completed by Region(2018)

单位: 万平方米 (10 000 sq.m)

市(州)	Region	施工面积 Floor Space of Buildings under Construction	#住宅 Residential Buildings	竣工面积 Floor Space of Buildings Completed	#住宅 Residential Buildings	竣工率(%) Rate of Floor Space of Buildings Completed	#住宅 Residential Buildings
全　省	**Sichuan**	**9056.96**	**1746.00**	**4038.12**	**687.69**	**44.6**	**39.4**
成都市	Chengdu	1964.31	215.90	827.68	104.53	42.1	48.4
自贡市	Zigong	532.95	99.25	381.32	37.06	71.6	37.3
攀枝花市	Panzhihua	73.84	24.58	53.20	20.65	72.1	84.0
泸州市	Luzhou	589.47	57.45	402.06	26.05	68.2	45.3
德阳市	Deyang	631.24	106.69	278.46	44.70	44.1	41.9
绵阳市	Mianyang	253.24	19.59	169.11	4.15	66.8	21.2
广元市	Guangyuan	457.79	43.97	195.32	17.60	42.7	40.0
遂宁市	Suining	300.65	88.42	125.25	48.91	41.7	55.3
内江市	Neijiang	87.96	45.43	57.61	15.27	65.5	33.6
乐山市	Leshan	300.26	78.54	137.19	37.25	45.7	47.4
南充市	Nanchong	338.41	58.63	117.25	35.91	34.7	61.3
眉山市	Meishan	444.19	26.04	143.47	19.19	32.3	73.7
宜宾市	Yibin	787.34	119.51	219.20	29.49	27.8	24.7
广安市	Guangan	216.42	33.70	129.56	13.23	59.9	39.3
达州市	Dazhou	410.90	126.48	142.70	19.68	34.7	15.6
雅安市	Yaan	52.99	20.25	38.25	17.38	72.2	85.8
巴中市	Bazhong	442.79	82.38	193.32	33.40	43.7	40.5
资阳市	Ziyang	100.14	7.54	39.09	1.92	39.0	25.5
阿坝藏族羌族自治州	Aba	20.98	2.55	10.06	1.01	48.0	39.6
甘孜藏族自治州	Ganzi	253.96	89.62	83.09	31.15	32.7	34.8
凉山彝族自治州	Liangshan	789.79	399.47	294.94	129.17	37.3	32.3
不分地区	Others	7.34					

注：本表数据不包括房地产开发项目的施工和竣工房屋建筑面积。
a)Data in this table do not include the construction and completed building area of real estate development projects.

5-9 房地产开发主要指标
Major Indicators of Real Estate Development

指　　标		Item		2014	2015	2016	2017	2018
企业个数	**（个）**	**Number of Enterprises**	**(unit)**	**4061**	**4032**	**4061**	**4010**	**4166**
国有		State-owned		107	109	106	108	119
集体		Collective-owned		19	15	13	10	7
私营		Private-owned		1781	1728	1699	1730	1824
其他		Others		2154	2180	2243	2162	2216
平均从业人数	**（人）**	**Average Employed Persons**	**(person)**	**138352**	**139303**	**138887**	**145344**	**157034**
国有		State-owned		4460	4151	5451	5448	6554
集体		Collective-owned		494	443	297	296	265
私营		Private-owned		56758	55625	53081	58406	64074
其他		Others		76640	79084	80058	81194	86141
本年土地购置面积	**（万平方米）**	**Land Space Purchased This Year**	**(10 000 sq.m)**	**1535.43**	**1061.98**	**1304.72**	**800.76**	**1541.10**
本年完成投资额	**（亿元）**	**Investment Completed This Year**	**(100 million yuan)**	**4380.09**	**4813.03**	**5282.64**	**5149.89**	**5701.09**
#住宅		Residential Buildings		2847.82	3048.72	3185.64	3182.34	3764.17
本年新增固定资产	**（亿元）**	**Newly Increased Fixed Assets This Year**	**(100 million yuan)**	**1944.62**	**1686.83**	**2407.73**	**1880.60**	**2021.42**
资金来源	**（亿元）**	**Sources of Funds**	**(100 million yuan)**	**5863.11**	**6079.00**	**6635.69**	**7430.97**	**8166.20**
国内贷款		Domestic Loans		817.88	916.21	751.74	890.39	887.24
利用外资		Foreign Investment		39.34	0.97	0.88	0.55	0.17
自筹资金		Self-raising Funds		2513.68	2645.83	2679.98	2779.07	2933.66
#自有资金		Self-owned		1423.51	1385.69	1332.60		
其他资金		Others		2492.22	2515.99	3203.09	3760.96	258.05
#定金及预收款		Earnest and Money Collected in Advance		1573.28	1452.64	1826.28	2372.91	2980.13
房屋建筑面积	**（万平方米）**	**Floor Space of Buildings**	**(10 000 sq.m)**					
施工面积		Floor Space of Buildings under Construction		36499.35	38981.36	41532.14	41294.89	44052.13
#住宅		Residential Buildings		24732.35	25300.45	26425.45	26272.05	28534.21
竣工面积		Floor Space of Buildings Completed		5334.45	4545.71	7050.24	5620.73	5647.86
#住宅		Residential Buildings		3871.28	3149.25	4677.37	3675.76	3718.16
本年新开工面积		Floor Space Started This Year		11328.04	9587.21	10825.16	11521.59	14076.17
#住宅		Residential Buildings		7335.98	6026.32	6941.73	7604.00	9723.10
商品房屋销售面积	**（万平方米）**	**Floor Space of Selling House**	**(10 000 sq.m)**	**7142.44**	**7671.20**	**9300.47**	**10869.07**	**12210.38**
#住宅		Residential Buildings		6176.51	6495.43	7884.09	8786.61	9889.35
商品房销售额	**（亿元）**	**Total Sales of Commercial Houses**	**(100 million yuan)**	**3997.37**	**4199.84**	**5358.91**	**6757.11**	**8527.29**
#住宅		Residential Buildings		3145.02	3269.52	4296.27	5173.60	6612.36

注：2018年房地产开发相关指标数据为第四次全国经济普查数据(以下有关各表同)。
a)Data of the related indicators of Real Estate Development in 2018 are the data of the fouth national economic census(the following related tables).

5-10 各市(州)按经济类型分房地产开发企业个数(2018年)
Number of Enterprises of Real Estate Development by Ownership and Region(2018)

单位：个 (unit)

市(州)	Region	合计 Total	国有经济 State-owned	集体经济 Collective-owned	私营经济 Private-owned	其他经济 Others
全 省	**Sichuan**	**4166**	**119**	**7**	**1824**	**2216**
成都市	Chengdu	1453	49	3	439	962
自贡市	Zigong	94	5		64	25
攀枝花市	Panzhihua	85	4		63	18
泸州市	Luzhou	181		1	103	77
德阳市	Deyang	200	2		109	89
绵阳市	Mianyang	268	12	1	124	131
广元市	Guangyuan	145	4		88	53
遂宁市	Suining	186	2	1	76	107
内江市	Neijiang	89	6		46	37
乐山市	Leshan	159	2		54	103
南充市	Nanchong	262	5	1	137	119
眉山市	Meishan	180	4		90	86
宜宾市	Yibin	178	5		113	60
广安市	Guangan	172	4		104	64
达州市	Dazhou	169	4		89	76
雅安市	Yaan	79	4		25	50
巴中市	Bazhong	117	3		49	65
资阳市	Ziyang	90	2		32	56
阿坝藏族羌族自治州	Aba	9			4	5
甘孜藏族自治州	Ganzi	6			2	4
凉山彝族自治州	Liangshan	44	2		13	29

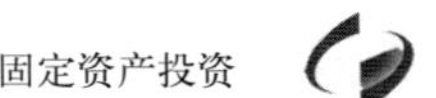

5-11 各市(州)按资质等级分房地产开发企业个数(2018年)

Number of Enterprises of Real Estate Development by Region and Qualification Criteria(2018)

单位：个 (unit)

市(州)	Region	合计 Total	一级 First Grade	二级 Second Grade	三级 Third Grade	四级 Fourth Grade	其他 Others
全　省	**Sichuan**	**4166**	**58**	**682**	**2372**	**77**	**977**
成都市	Chengdu	1453	23	203	899	22	306
自贡市	Zigong	94	5	24	35	5	25
攀枝花市	Panzhihua	85	3	10	52	3	17
泸州市	Luzhou	181	2	37	92	3	47
德阳市	Deyang	200	1	20	116	8	55
绵阳市	Mianyang	268		51	178	4	35
广元市	Guangyuan	145		17	101	4	23
遂宁市	Suining	186	2	49	90	1	44
内江市	Neijiang	89	1	27	45	2	14
乐山市	Leshan	159	3	28	91		37
南充市	Nanchong	262		32	118	4	108
眉山市	Meishan	180	3	32	83	2	60
宜宾市	Yibin	178	8	33	116	4	17
广安市	Guangan	172	1	26	96	1	48
达州市	Dazhou	169	4	53	91	4	17
雅安市	Yaan	79		4	29	6	40
巴中市	Bazhong	117	2	16	47		52
资阳市	Ziyang	90		12	52	1	25
阿坝藏族羌族自治州	Aba	9		1	3		5
甘孜藏族自治州	Ganzi	6		1	1	2	2
凉山彝族自治州	Liangshan	44		6	37	1	

5-12 各市(州)按经济类型分房地产开发企业从业人员数(2018年)
Number of Employees in Enterprises of Real Estate Devoelopment by Ownership and Region(2018)

单位：人 (person)

市(州)	Region	合计 Total	国有经济 State-owned	集体经济 Collective-owned	私营经济 Private-owned	其他经济 Others
全　省	**Sichuan**	**157034**	**6554**	**265**	**64074**	**86141**
成都市	Chengdu	48757	3798	72	10767	34120
自贡市	Zigong	4932	69		3251	1612
攀枝花市	Panzhihua	4257	228		3042	987
泸州市	Luzhou	9901		78	4207	5616
德阳市	Deyang	5428	30		2726	2672
绵阳市	Mianyang	11048	442	22	6545	4039
广元市	Guangyuan	4481	403		2364	1714
遂宁市	Suining	9227	155	26	2665	6381
内江市	Neijiang	4029	151		1827	2051
乐山市	Leshan	6862	58		2148	4656
南充市	Nanchong	10518	161	67	6306	3984
眉山市	Meishan	7744	152		3771	3821
宜宾市	Yibin	7348	178		4280	2890
广安市	Guangan	6208	161		3984	2063
达州市	Dazhou	5655	191		2701	2763
雅安市	Yaan	2112	101		712	1299
巴中市	Bazhong	4233	163		1416	2654
资阳市	Ziyang	2338	43		885	1410
阿坝藏族羌族自治州	Aba	134			58	76
甘孜藏族自治州	Ganzi	146			82	64
凉山彝族自治州	Liangshan	1676	70		337	1269

5-13 各市(州)按资质等级分房地产开发企业从业人员数(2018年)

Number of Employees in Enterprises of Real Estate Development by Region and Qualification Criteria(2018)

单位：人 (person)

市(州)	Region	合 计 Total	一级 First Grade	二级 Second Grade	三级 Third Grade	四级 Fourth Grade	其他 Others
全　省	**Sichuan**	**157034**	**6680**	**36411**	**80643**	**1378**	**31922**
成都市	Chengdu	48757	1846	10236	27989	255	8431
自贡市	Zigong	4932	912	1807	1144	107	962
攀枝花市	Panzhihua	4257	1038	506	1851	44	818
泸州市	Luzhou	9901	430	2519	4625	134	2193
德阳市	Deyang	5428	50	690	2806	121	1761
绵阳市	Mianyang	11048		3438	6651	46	913
广元市	Guangyuan	4481		666	3074	99	642
遂宁市	Suining	9227	117	4820	2984	2	1304
内江市	Neijiang	4029	90	1462	1872	130	475
乐山市	Leshan	6862	334	1625	3671		1232
南充市	Nanchong	10518		1034	5741	82	3661
眉山市	Meishan	7744	536	1625	2946	42	2595
宜宾市	Yibin	7348	737	1418	4321	52	820
广安市	Guangan	6208	17	1463	3014	75	1639
达州市	Dazhou	5655	443	1628	2901	51	632
雅安市	Yaan	2112		127	733	52	1200
巴中市	Bazhong	4233	130	737	1499		1867
资阳市	Ziyang	2338		321	1343	20	654
阿坝藏族羌族自治州	Aba	134		22	61		51
甘孜藏族自治州	Ganzi	146		18	24	32	72
凉山彝族自治州	Liangshan	1676		249	1393	34	

5-14 各市(州)房地产投资完成额
Completion of Real Estate Investment by Region

单位：亿元 (100 million yuan)

市(州)	Region	2010	2011	2012	2013	2014	2015	2016	2017	2018
全 省	**Sichuan**	**2194.63**	**2836.71**	**3266.40**	**3853.00**	**4380.09**	**4813.03**	**5282.64**	**5149.89**	**5701.09**
成都市	Chengdu	1278.34	1595.64	1890.03	2110.27	2220.80	2441.95	2638.89	2487.88	2272.98
自贡市	Zigong	54.00	76.08	62.77	77.78	101.23	125.81	123.87	122.59	209.31
攀枝花市	Panzhihua	34.20	35.73	54.69	51.16	75.20	58.94	55.03	59.96	98.50
泸州市	Luzhou	54.52	68.70	71.64	130.92	192.56	196.87	239.20	258.62	318.39
德阳市	Deyang	46.96	73.25	79.87	82.66	95.23	115.38	125.78	105.04	149.81
绵阳市	Mianyang	105.84	132.28	145.69	169.94	210.74	198.35	205.58	176.65	204.54
广元市	Guangyuan	18.72	35.13	32.89	58.67	83.32	86.80	94.63	83.58	84.89
遂宁市	Suining	67.90	73.26	76.79	85.99	86.36	111.91	144.56	173.48	172.23
内江市	Neijiang	41.01	54.35	58.03	78.64	115.43	123.88	122.81	115.05	155.56
乐山市	Leshan	58.79	67.55	75.46	110.19	126.07	152.86	212.02	194.15	194.91
南充市	Nanchong	102.23	146.18	187.07	207.91	229.14	213.22	216.64	212.39	310.03
眉山市	Meishan	47.77	64.49	78.18	130.31	151.12	195.15	194.29	193.58	257.12
宜宾市	Yibin	60.22	105.41	104.52	141.13	171.86	150.42	189.55	228.15	312.04
广安市	Guangan	29.58	38.49	51.04	65.25	122.11	184.26	258.22	244.19	238.10
达州市	Dazhou	60.68	82.62	85.10	100.53	94.98	82.58	93.28	113.64	156.70
雅安市	Yaan	11.91	28.62	30.01	27.02	25.46	27.45	53.94	58.38	85.28
巴中市	Bazhong	27.27	38.00	49.28	63.99	88.65	104.49	118.96	136.97	156.99
资阳市	Ziyang	74.65	94.57	109.60	136.98	164.77	195.14	150.18	127.89	132.41
阿坝藏族羌族自治州	Aba	0.62	0.83	0.60	4.04	4.25	7.80	12.26	4.87	3.10
甘孜藏族自治州	Ganzi	1.92	2.90	2.63	1.98	1.71	1.10	1.28	1.51	6.43
凉山彝族自治州	Liangshan	17.48	22.66	20.51	17.64	19.11	38.67	31.67	51.32	181.78

5-15 各市(州)按用途分房地产开发投资完成额(2018年)

Actually Completed Investment of Enterprises for Real Estate Development by Region and Use(2018)

单位：亿元 (100 million yuan)

市(州)	Region	本年完成投资额 Investment Completed in Current Year	住宅 Residential Buildings	办公楼 Office Buildings	商业营业用房 Houses for Business Use	其他 Others
全　省	**Sichuan**	**5701.09**	**3764.17**	**210.51**	**1002.23**	**724.19**
成都市	Chengdu	2272.98	1243.71	180.88	486.81	361.58
自贡市	Zigong	209.31	158.22	0.32	30.72	20.06
攀枝花市	Panzhihua	98.50	70.96	0.01	17.84	9.69
泸州市	Luzhou	318.39	239.21	3.15	41.14	34.89
德阳市	Deyang	149.81	106.18	0.29	20.98	22.36
绵阳市	Mianyang	204.54	153.51	1.78	30.80	18.45
广元市	Guangyuan	84.89	57.74	0.19	20.02	6.94
遂宁市	Suining	172.23	143.17	0.78	19.24	9.04
内江市	Neijiang	155.56	100.46	3.36	24.21	27.53
乐山市	Leshan	194.91	145.51	0.47	33.40	15.53
南充市	Nanchong	310.03	238.33	4.54	46.02	21.14
眉山市	Meishan	257.12	174.29	0.85	44.82	37.16
宜宾市	Yibin	312.04	229.06	3.40	44.35	35.23
广安市	Guangan	238.10	181.30	3.69	36.96	16.15
达州市	Dazhou	156.70	118.46	0.30	24.35	13.59
雅安市	Yaan	85.28	55.09	0.56	21.46	8.16
巴中市	Bazhong	156.99	106.14	0.34	32.50	18.01
资阳市	Ziyang	132.41	115.07	1.14	10.51	5.68
阿坝藏族羌族自治州	Aba	3.10	0.71		2.36	0.03
甘孜藏族自治州	Ganzi	6.43	4.21		1.72	0.51
凉山彝族自治州	Liangshan	181.78	122.84	4.46	12.03	42.46

5-16 各市(州)房地产开发建设房屋建筑面积和造价(2018年)
Floor Space of Buildings and the Cost in Real Estate Development by Region(2018)

市(州)	Region	施工房屋面积 (万平方米) Floor Space of Buildings under Construction (10 000 sq.m)	竣工房屋面积 (万平方米) Floor Space of Buildings Completed (10 000 sq.m)	房屋建筑面积竣工率 (%) Rate of Floor Space of Buildings Completed (%)	竣工房屋价值 (万元) Value of Buildings Completed (10 000 yuan)	竣工房屋造价 (元/平方米) Cost of Buildings Completed (yuan / sq.m)
全　省	**Sichuan**	**44052.13**	**5647.86**	**12.8**	**16244205**	**2876**
成都市	Chengdu	19482.96	1737.33	8.9	6060203	3488
自贡市	Zigong	1252.22	203.39	16.2	509075	2503
攀枝花市	Panzhihua	861.51	69.24	8.0	173142	2501
泸州市	Luzhou	2027.08	630.78	31.1	1425123	2259
德阳市	Deyang	1582.74	183.62	11.6	423194	2305
绵阳市	Mianyang	1741.37	155.02	8.9	411330	2653
广元市	Guangyuan	1102.33	160.49	14.6	427872	2666
遂宁市	Suining	1479.31	310.15	21.0	848696	2736
内江市	Neijiang	1142.06	176.32	15.4	415437	2356
乐山市	Leshan	1854.32	319.82	17.2	827759	2588
南充市	Nanchong	2581.17	428.94	16.6	1046598	2440
眉山市	Meishan	1676.15	186.19	11.1	710478	3816
宜宾市	Yibin	2005.52	509.66	25.4	1374679	2697
广安市	Guangan	1495.73	141.70	9.5	352890	2490
达州市	Dazhou	1206.19	202.72	16.8	588863	2905
雅安市	Yaan	479.99	44.24	9.2	127660	2886
巴中市	Bazhong	940.14	92.40	9.8	185803	2011
资阳市	Ziyang	545.04	40.42	7.4	110889	2743
阿坝藏族羌族自治州	Aba	13.75	7.73	56.2	25446	3292
甘孜藏族自治州	Ganzi	47.17				
凉山彝族自治州	Liangshan	535.38	47.69	8.9	199068	4174

5-17 各市(州)商品房销售情况(2018年)
Selling of Commercial Houses by Region(2018)

市(州)	Region	房屋销售面积(万平方米) Floor Space of Commercial Houses (10 000 sq.m)	#住宅 Residential Buildings	#办公楼 Office Buildings	#商业营业用房 Houses for Business Use	房屋销售额(亿元) Total Sale of Commercial Houses (100 million yuan)	#住宅 Residential Buildings	#办公楼 Office Buildings	#商业营业用房 Houses for Business Use
全 省	**Sichuan**	**12210.38**	**9889.35**	**323.99**	**1045.28**	**8527.29**	**6612.36**	**345.68**	**1200.43**
成都市	Chengdu	3677.27	2651.66	276.90	327.41	3626.75	2592.54	312.33	537.38
自贡市	Zigong	388.32	331.49	5.25	25.03	225.73	189.90	4.31	25.43
攀枝花市	Panzhihua	162.73	131.65	0.35	13.02	89.59	70.60	0.15	12.93
泸州市	Luzhou	843.21	680.66	4.30	92.96	472.70	352.33	2.70	86.74
德阳市	Deyang	372.10	321.00	1.44	27.99	196.16	170.48	0.91	20.28
绵阳市	Mianyang	589.03	481.16	2.46	61.15	379.28	302.03	1.75	64.54
广元市	Guangyuan	213.91	171.56	0.69	27.57	107.99	82.90	0.35	19.92
遂宁市	Suining	680.84	609.97	1.15	43.49	363.36	308.69	1.11	40.38
内江市	Neijiang	434.77	336.37	2.62	39.98	236.07	177.34	1.65	35.23
乐山市	Leshan	477.58	398.93	2.15	45.96	287.42	234.37	1.38	43.33
南充市	Nanchong	934.88	828.16	11.82	61.88	525.14	450.35	7.52	55.05
眉山市	Meishan	480.85	410.46	4.97	30.33	401.94	353.17	2.63	36.58
宜宾市	Yibin	745.74	567.47	2.89	89.14	413.27	302.95	1.90	80.42
广安市	Guangan	550.13	486.12	1.91	47.53	267.54	224.57	1.27	38.53
达州市	Dazhou	516.00	465.34	2.15	36.18	317.71	273.67	1.53	35.57
雅安市	Yaan	138.48	119.98	0.17	12.01	92.11	75.05	0.12	15.43
巴中市	Bazhong	409.83	352.30		40.60	174.44	139.06		29.94
资阳市	Ziyang	431.27	400.38		16.34	204.13	187.87		9.91
阿坝藏族羌族自治州	Aba	4.32	3.57		0.31	2.13	1.70		0.37
甘孜藏族自治州	Ganzi	3.48	1.36		2.11	4.76	0.79		3.97
凉山彝族自治州	Liangshan	155.64	139.73	2.77	4.29	139.07	122.00	4.07	8.49

5-18 各市(州)商品房期房销售情况(2018年)
Selling of Commercial Houses under Construction by Region(2018)

市(州)	Region	房屋销售面积 (万平方米) Floor Space of Commercial Houses (10 000 sq.m)	#住宅 Residential Buildings	#办公楼 Office Buildings	#商业营业用房 Houses for Business Use	房屋销售额 (亿元) Total Sale of Commercial Houses (100 million yuan)	#住宅 Residential Buildings	#办公楼 Office Buildings	#商业营业用房 Houses for Business Use
全　省	**Sichuan**	**10782.82**	**9075.51**	**281.67**	**765.49**	**7643.48**	**6174.15**	**306.23**	**888.72**
成都市	Chengdu	3328.86	2530.46	248.54	243.97	3292.96	2463.99	281.97	406.97
自贡市	Zigong	349.45	317.02	5.25	18.54	209.46	184.18	4.31	17.70
攀枝花市	Panzhihua	133.44	114.55		9.74	75.83	62.36		9.89
泸州市	Luzhou	669.99	567.20	3.87	60.05	392.12	308.91	2.56	57.94
德阳市	Deyang	330.89	302.92		20.05	180.06	162.12		15.67
绵阳市	Mianyang	493.58	430.07	0.01	32.94	316.40	274.03	0.01	35.40
广元市	Guangyuan	162.46	132.76	0.69	19.24	87.27	68.53	0.35	14.91
遂宁市	Suining	592.49	528.82	1.14	38.21	322.60	275.18	1.11	33.74
内江市	Neijiang	385.94	291.03	2.62	38.72	215.26	157.55	1.65	34.49
乐山市	Leshan	438.02	377.95	2.15	32.63	263.15	222.56	1.38	32.61
南充市	Nanchong	837.27	752.84	6.52	50.93	474.09	413.99	3.54	46.56
眉山市	Meishan	460.72	400.09	4.97	25.91	387.19	346.00	2.63	30.11
宜宾市	Yibin	607.71	519.66	1.41	54.84	345.18	283.38	1.07	48.60
广安市	Guangan	497.49	452.93	0.61	36.39	241.83	210.55	0.82	28.64
达州市	Dazhou	420.02	390.81	0.93	21.14	259.92	235.18	0.63	21.60
雅安市	Yaan	127.94	114.21	0.17	8.59	86.68	71.98	0.12	13.39
巴中市	Bazhong	360.65	311.34		33.81	150.81	123.17		22.92
资阳市	Ziyang	431.27	400.38		16.34	204.13	187.87		9.91
阿坝藏族羌族自治州	Aba	1.53	1.28		0.01	0.67	0.63		0.02
甘孜藏族自治州	Ganzi	1.29	1.18		0.10	0.91	0.70		0.21
凉山彝族自治州	Liangshan	151.80	138.01	2.77	3.33	136.98	121.30	4.07	7.47

5-19 各市(州)商品房现房销售情况(2018年)
Selling of Commercial Houses Completed by Region(2018)

市(州)	Region	房屋销售面积(万平方米) Floor Space of Commercial Houses (10 000 sq.m)	#住宅 Residential Buildings	#办公楼 Office Buildings	#商业营业用房 Houses for Business Use	房屋销售额(亿元) Total Sale of Commercial Houses (100 million yuan)	#住宅 Residential Buildings	#办公楼 Office Buildings	#商业营业用房 Houses for Business Use
全 省	**Sichuan**	**1427.56**	**813.83**	**42.32**	**279.79**	**883.81**	**438.21**	**39.45**	**311.71**
成都市	Chengdu	348.41	121.20	28.35	83.44	333.79	128.55	30.36	130.41
自贡市	Zigong	38.86	14.47		6.49	16.27	5.72		7.74
攀枝花市	Panzhihua	29.29	17.10	0.35	3.28	13.76	8.24	0.15	3.05
泸州市	Luzhou	173.22	113.46	0.43	32.91	80.59	43.42	0.13	28.81
德阳市	Deyang	41.21	18.08	1.44	7.94	16.10	8.36	0.91	4.61
绵阳市	Mianyang	95.45	51.09	2.45	28.21	62.89	28.00	1.75	29.14
广元市	Guangyuan	51.46	38.80		8.33	20.72	14.36		5.01
遂宁市	Suining	88.35	81.15		5.28	40.76	33.51	0.00	6.64
内江市	Neijiang	48.83	45.34		1.26	20.81	19.79		0.75
乐山市	Leshan	39.56	20.98		13.33	24.27	11.81		10.72
南充市	Nanchong	97.61	75.32	5.30	10.95	51.05	36.36	3.97	8.49
眉山市	Meishan	20.13	10.38		4.42	14.75	7.17		6.48
宜宾市	Yibin	138.02	47.81	1.48	34.30	68.09	19.57	0.82	31.83
广安市	Guangan	52.64	33.19	1.30	11.14	25.71	14.02	0.45	9.89
达州市	Dazhou	95.99	74.53	1.21	15.04	57.80	38.49	0.90	13.97
雅安市	Yaan	10.54	5.78		3.41	5.43	3.07		2.04
巴中市	Bazhong	49.18	40.96		6.79	23.63	15.90		7.02
资阳市	Ziyang								
阿坝藏族羌族自治州	Aba	2.79	2.28		0.29	1.46	1.07		0.35
甘孜藏族自治州	Ganzi	2.19	0.18		2.01	3.85	0.09		3.76
凉山彝族自治州	Liangshan	3.85	1.72		0.96	2.09	0.70		1.02

5-20 各市(州)商品房待售情况(2018年)
Selling of Commercial Houses on Sale by Region(2018)

市(州)	Region	商品房待售面积 (万平方米) Space of Commercial Houses on Sale (10 000 sq.m)	#住宅 Residential Buildings	#办公楼 Office Buildings	#商业营业用房 Houses for Business Use	其中：待售1-3年的面积 (万平方米) Space Empty on Sale During 3 Years (10 000 sq.m)	#住宅 Residential Buildings	#办公楼 Office Buildings	#商业营业用房 Houses for Business Use
全 省	**Sichuan**	**2428.82**	**596.11**	**92.02**	**679.86**	**1237.63**	**315.12**	**32.69**	**347.31**
成都市	Chengdu	1028.27	153.82	69.91	253.73	446.34	81.90	19.52	113.87
自贡市	Zigong	80.20	14.42	0.73	20.89	62.63	13.02	0.57	13.54
攀枝花市	Panzhihua	62.51	21.31	3.13	14.83	6.82	5.06		0.21
泸州市	Luzhou	127.64	52.64	1.67	41.06	87.53	37.85	0.94	26.29
德阳市	Deyang	143.23	21.60	2.77	48.98	63.47	3.26	2.20	27.53
绵阳市	Mianyang	114.66	13.12	1.77	55.46	56.83	5.73	1.77	25.21
广元市	Guangyuan	111.20	41.39	1.43	39.99	52.91	20.48	0.04	18.79
遂宁市	Suining	45.99	34.53	0.46	9.11	7.21	4.43		2.78
内江市	Neijiang	14.15	5.74		1.05	11.34	3.55		0.91
乐山市	Leshan	89.65	56.96		26.99	61.80	38.47		19.65
南充市	Nanchong	124.31	39.19	0.04	34.72	88.06	29.26		24.87
眉山市	Meishan	118.04	25.49	2.05	29.45	90.74	14.65	0.68	22.37
宜宾市	Yibin	159.06	27.85	5.55	33.35	76.15	9.00	4.99	11.70
广安市	Guangan	36.10	19.25	0.30	9.78	24.73	15.78	0.20	4.80
达州市	Dazhou	71.23	27.70	0.44	34.81	39.89	10.61		27.28
雅安市	Yaan	9.85	2.45		5.62	4.28	0.48		2.77
巴中市	Bazhong	47.04	28.53		6.58	30.17	15.48		2.99
资阳市	Ziyang								
阿坝藏族羌族自治州	Aba	4.94	1.70		1.19	4.64	1.70		0.89
甘孜藏族自治州	Ganzi	5.56	4.39	0.48	0.38	5.56	4.39	0.48	0.38
凉山彝族自治州	Liangshan	35.20	4.02	1.32	11.89	16.53	0.04	1.32	0.47

主要统计指标解释

全社会固定资产投资 是以货币形式表现的在一定时期内全社会建造和购置固定资产的工作量以及与此有关的费用的总称。该指标是反映固定资产投资规模、结构和发展速度的综合性指标,又是观察工程进度和考核投资效果的重要依据。全社会固定资产投资按登记注册类型可分为国有、集体、联营、股份制、私营和个体、港澳台商、外商、其他等。

固定资产投资(不含农户) 指城镇和农村各种登记注册类型的企业、事业、行政单位及城镇个体户进行的计划总投资500万元及500万元以上的建设项目投资和房地产开发投资,包含原口径的城镇固定资产投资加上农村企事业组织项目投资,该口径自2011年起开始使用。

固定资产投资的实际到位资金 根据固定资产投资的资金来源不同,分为国家预算资金、国内贷款、利用外资、自筹资金和其他资金。

(1)国家预算资金 国家预算包括一般预算、政府性基金预算、国有资本经营预算和社保基金预算。各类预算中用于固定资产投资的资金全部作为国家预算资金填报,其中一般预算中用于固定资产投资的部分包括基建投资、车购税、灾后恢复重建基金和其他财政投资。各级政府债券也应归入国家预算资金。

(2)国内贷款 指报告期固定资产项目投资单位向银行及非银行金融机构借入用于固定资产投资的各种国内借款,包括银行利用自有资金及吸收存款发放的贷款、上级主管部门拨入的国内贷款、国家专项贷款(包括煤代油贷款、劳改煤矿专项贷款等),地方财政专项资金安排的贷款、国内储备贷款、周转贷款等。

(3)利用外资 指报告期收到的境外(包括外国及港澳台地区)资金(包括设备、材料、技术在内)。包括对外借款(外国政府贷款、国际金融组织贷款、出口信贷、外国银行商业贷款、对外发行债券和股票)、外商直接投资、外商其他投资(包括利用外商投资收益在国内进行固定资产再投资活动的资金)。不包括我国自有外汇资金(国家外汇、地方外汇、留成外汇、调剂外汇和国内银行自有资金发放的外汇贷款等)。各类外资按报告期末的外汇牌价(中间价)折成人民币计算。

(4)自筹资金 指固定资产投资单位在报告期收到的,由各企、事业单位筹集用于固定资产投资的资金,包括各类企事业单位的自有资金和从其他单位筹集的用于固定资产投资的资金,但不包括各类财政性资金、从各类金融机构借入资金和国外资金。

(5)其他资金 指在报告期收到的除以上各种资金之外的用于固定资产投资的资金,包括社会集资、个人资金、无偿捐赠的资金及其他单位拨入的资金等。

固定资产投资按国民经济行业分 指根据其从事的社会经济活动性质对各类单位进行的分类。应根据建设项目建成投产后的主要产品种类或主要用途及社会经济活动种类来划分,不能根据项目单位本身的行业类别来划分。如果项目投产后有几种产品,应根据主要产品来确定行业类别。一般情况下,一个建设项目只能属于一种国民经济行业。

固定资产投资按隶属关系分 是按建设单位或企业、事业、行政单位的主管上级机关确定的。

(1)中央 是指中共中央、人大常委会和国务院各部、委、局、总公司以及直属机构直接领导的建设项目和企业、事业、行政单位。这些单位的固定资产投资计划由国务院各部门直接编制和下达,统一组织或委托下级实施。包括有中央垂直管理的部门(如国家统计局各级调查队)和中央直属企业、事业单位(如工商银行、中国电信、中国石油)等。

(2)地方 是由省(自治区、直辖市)、地(区、市、州、盟)、县(区、市、旗)三级政府及业务主管部门直接领导和管理的建设项目、企业、事业、行政单位。地方项目还包括不隶属以上各级政府及主管部门的建设项目和企业、事业单位,如外商投资企业和无主管部门的企业等。

固定资产投资按建设性质分 按整个建设项目情况来确定。建设项目的性质一般分为新建、扩建、改建和技术改造、单纯建造生活设施、迁建、恢复、单纯购置。房地产开发单位、农户投资不划分建设性质。

(1)新建 指从无到有"平地起家"开始建设的项目。现有企业、事业、行政单位投资的项目一般不属于新建。但如有的单位原有基础很小,经过建设后新增的固定资产价值超过该企业、事业、行政单位原有固定资产价值(原值)三倍以上的,也应作为新建。

(2)扩建 指在厂内或其他地点,为扩大原有产品的生产能力(或效益)或增加新的产品生产能力,而增建的生产车间(或主要工程)、分厂、独立的生产线等项目。行政、事业单位在原单位增建业务性用房(如学校增建教学用房、医院增建门诊部、病房等)也作为扩建。

现有企、事业单位为扩大原有主要产品生产能力或增加新的产品生产能力,增建一个或几个主要生产车间(或主要工程)、分厂,同时进行一些更新改造工程的,也应作为扩建。

(3)改建和技术改造 指现有企业、事业单位对原有设施进行技术改造或更新(包括相应配套的辅助性生产、生活福利设施)的建设项目。改建项目包括现有企业、事业单位为适应市场变化的需要,而改变企业的主要产品种类(如军工企业转民产品等)的建设项目,原有产品生产作业线由于各工序(车间)之间能力不平衡，为填平补齐充分发挥原有生产能力而增建不增加本企业主要产品设计能力的车间的建设项目。技术改造是指企业、事业单位在现有基础上，用先进的技术代替落后的技术，用先进的工艺和装备代替落后的工艺和装备，以改变企业落后的技术经济面貌，实现以内涵为主的扩大再生产，达到提高产品质量、促进产品更新换代、节约能源、降低消耗、扩大生产规模、全面提高社会经济效益的目的。技术改造具体包括以下内容：机器设备和工具的更新改造；生产工艺改革、节约能源和原材料的改造；厂房建筑和公共设施的改造；保护环境进行的“三废”治理改造；劳动条件和生产环境的改造等。

固定资产投资按构成分

(1)建筑工程　指各种房屋、建筑物的建造工程，又称建筑工作量。这部分投资额必须兴工动料，通过施工活动才能实现，是固定资产投资额的重要组成部分。

(2)安装工程　指各种设备、装置的安装工程，又称安装工作量。

在安装工程中，不包括被安装设备本身价值。

(3)设备工具器具购置　指报告期内购置或自制的，达到固定资产标准的设备、工具、器具的价值。新建单位及扩建单位的新建车间，按照设计或计划要求购置或自制的全部设备、工具、器具，不论是否达到固定资产标准均计入“设备工具器具购置”中。

(4)其他费用　指在固定资产建造和购置过程中发生的，除建筑安装工程和设备、工器具购置投资完成额以外的应当分摊计入固定资产投资的费用，不指经营中财务上的其他费用。

施工项目个数　是指本年正式进行过建筑或安装施工活动的建设项目个数。包括本年新开工项目，以前年度开工跨入本年继续施工项目，本年全部建成投产项目、以前年度全部停缓建在本年恢复施工的项目，本年进行过施工又在本年内全部停缓建的项目。施工项目个数可以反映一定时期固定资产投资的实际规模，与同期全部建成投产项目个数相比，可以从建设速度的角度反映固定资产投资的效果。

本年投产项目个数　指报告期内按设计文件规定建成主体工程和相应配套的辅助设施，形成生产能力或工程效益，经过验收合格，并且已正式投入生产或交付使用的建设项目。

新增生产能力(或工程效益)　指通过固定资产投资活动而增加的设计能力(或工程效益)。主要指标包括建设规模、本年施工规模、自开始建设累计新增生产能力(或工程效益)、本年新增生产能力(或工程效益)等。

新增固定资产　是指已经完成建造和购置过程，并已交付生产或使用单位的固定资产的价值，包括已经建成投入生产或交付使用的工程投资和达到固定资产标准的设备、工具、器具的投资及有关应摊入的费用。该指标是表示固定资产投资成果的价值指标，也是反映建设进度，计算固定资产投资效果的重要指标。

项目建成投产率　指一定时期内全部建成投产项目个数与同期施工项目个数的比率。该指标从建设单位建设速度的角度反映投资效果。

固定资产交付使用率　指一定时期新增固定资产与同期完成投资额的比率。该指标是反映固定资产动用速度，衡量建设过程中宏观投资效果的综合指标。由于新增固定资产是较长时期内形成的结果，而投资额则是当年完成的，因此，该指标一般适宜于反映较长时期内固定资产的动用情况。

房地产开发投资　指房地产开发企业本年完成的全部用于房屋建设工程、土地开发工程的投资额以及公益性建筑和土地购置费等的投资。

房屋施工面积　指房地产开发企业本年施工的全部房屋建筑面积。包括本年新开工的房屋建筑面积、上年跨入本年继续施工的房屋建筑面积、上年停缓建在本年恢复施工的房屋建筑面积、本年竣工的房屋建筑面积以及本年施工后又停缓建的房屋建筑面积。多层建筑应填各层建筑面积之和。

房屋竣工面积　指房地产开发企业本年按照设计要求已全部完工，达到住人和使用条件，经验收鉴定合格或达到竣工验收标准，可正式移交使用的各栋房屋建筑面积的总和。

房屋建筑面积竣工率　指一定时期内房屋竣工面积占同期房屋施工面积的比率。它是从房屋建筑施工速度的角度反映投资效果的指标。

商品房销售面积　指房地产开发企业本年出售商品房屋的合同总面积(即双方签署的正式买卖合同中所确定的建筑面积)。

商品房销售额　指房地产开发企业本年出售商品房屋的合同总价款(即双方签署的正式买卖合同中所确定的合同总价)。该指标与商品房销售面积同口径。

Explanatory Notes on Main Statistical Indicators

Total Investment in Fixed Assets in the Whole Country refers to the volume of activities in construction and purchases of fixed assets of the whole country and related fees, expressed in monetary terms during the reference period. It is a comprehensive indicator which shows the size, structure and growth of the investment in fixed assets, providing a basis for observing the progress of construction projects and evaluating results of investment. Total investment in fixed assets in the whole country includes, by type of ownership, the investment by State-owned units, collective-owned units, joint ownership units, share-holding units, private units, individuals as well as investments by entrepreneurs from Hong Kong, Macao and Taiwan, foreign investors and others.

Investment in Fixed Assets (Excluding Rural Households) refers to the investment in construction projects with a total planned investment of 5 million yuan and over by enterprises of various ownerships, institutions, administrative units and urban self-employed individuals, and the investment in real estate development in both urban and rural areas. Since 2011, it covers the urban investment in fixed assets under the previous statistical coverage plus project investments by rural enterprises and institutions.

Actual Funds in Place for Investment in Fixed Assets are categorized as funds from the State budget, domestic loans, foreign investment, self-raised funds, and others, depending on the sources of investment.

(1) Fund from the State budget: State budget consists of general budget, government fund budget, operation budget of state-owned assets and social security fund budget. Funds for investment in fixed assets from various budgets are reported as fund from the state budget, of which, the general budget utilized on fixed assets investment includes investment on infrastructure construction, vehicle purchase tax, post-disaster restoration and reconstruction funds and other financial investment. Government bonds at all levels should also be included.

(2) Domestic loans refer to loans of various forms borrowed by investing units from banks and non-bank financial institutions during the reference period for the purpose of investment in fixed assets, including loans issued by banks from their self-owned funds and deposit, loans appropriated by higher responsible authorities, special loans by government (including loan for substituting petroleum with coal, special loans for reform-through-labour coal mines), loans arranged by local government from special funds, domestic reserve loan, and revolving loan, etc.

(3) Foreign investment refers to overseas (including foreign countries, Hongkong, Macao and Taiwan) funds received during the reference period (covering equipment, materials and technology), including foreign borrowings (loans from foreign governments and international financial institutions, export credit, commercial loans from foreign banks, issue of bonds and stocks overseas), foreign direct investment and other foreign investments (including funds from foreign direct investment income that are reinvested in fixed assets domestically). Excluded from this category is capital in foreign exchanges owned by China (foreign exchanges owned by the central and local governments, foreign exchanges retained by enterprises, foreign exchanges by enterprises through the regulating mechanism, loans in foreign exchanges issued by the Bank of China with its own fund, etc.). In calculating the utilization of foreign capital, foreign currencies are converted into Chinese Renminbi applying the exchange rate (central parity rate) at the end of the reference period.

(4) Self-raised funds refer to funds for investment in fixed assets received during the reference period by investing units, including investment in fixed assets using own funds of various enterprises and institutions or funds raised from other units other than financial funds, funds borrowed from financial institutions and overseas funds.

(5) Others refer to funds for investment in fixed assets received from sources other than those listed above, including funds raised from individuals and through donations, and funds transferred from other units.

Investment in Fixed Assets by Sector refers to the classification of investment by the nature of social economic activities the investing units are engaged in. The classification of construction projects by sector is determined by the major products or the purpose of the projects when they are put into production or use, and by the nature of their social economic activities, instead of being determined by industrial classification of the project enterprises. The project will be classified according to major product if there are several kinds of products yielded. In general, one project can only be classified into one sector.

Investment in Fixed Assets by Jurisdiction of Management refers to the classification of investment by the competent authorities under which investment is made by construction units, enterprises, institutions or administrative units.

(1) Central investment refers to the investment in projects or by enterprises, institutions or administrative units which are under the direct leadership and management of the State Council and of the national commissions, ministries, agencies and State-owned large corporations. Various ministries and departments of the State Council prepare and implement plans through unified organization or lower-level commissions, which include departments direct under central government (i.e. survey offices at all level of the National Bureau of Statistics)

and enterprises and institutions directly under central government (like the Industrial and Commercial Bank of China, China Telecom and China National Petroleum Corporation)..

(2) Local investment refers to the investment in projects or by enterprises, institutions or administrative units which are under the direct leadership and management of competent departments and governments at the level of province (autonomous regions and municipalities directly under the Central Government), prefecture （prefectures, cities and leagues） and county (districts, cities and banners). Also included are projects by foreign-invested enterprises and enterprises without competent managing authorities.

Investment in Fixed Assets by Type of Construction Construction projects in general can be classified, by the type of construction, into new construction, expansion, reconstruction and technical transformation, purely construction of living facilities, moving, restoration and purely purchasing. However, investment by type of construction is not applied to investment by real-estate development units and investment by rural households.

(1) New construction in general refers to construction projects, which start from scratch. The existing projects invested by enterprises, institutions and administrative agencies cannot be classified as new construction. In case the size of the existing unit is quite small, and the value of newly added fixed assets is more than three times of the original value, the expansion will be considered as new construction.

(2) Expansion refers to projects of construction of new production workshop, branch factory or independent production line within a factory or in other locations, for the purpose of increasing the production capacity (or improving efficiency) or adding new production capacity. Newly constructed accommodation for the operation of institutions and administrative organizations (such as newly constructed buildings for teaching in schools, buildings for clinics or wards in hospitals, etc.) are also classified as expansion.

Also included in expansion are investments by existing enterprises or institutions in building major production line(s) or branch factory (ies) along with some work on innovation, for the purpose of expanding the production capacity of original products or producing new products.

(3) Reconstruction and technical transformation refers to construction projects by existing enterprises or institutions in innovation or technical transformation of the old facilities (including auxiliary production equipment and welfare facilities). Also considered as reconstruction is the construction of new workshops by the existing enterprises or institutions to change the variety of products to meet the market demand (such as the production of civil products by defence industries), or to bring the designed production capacity into full play through a more balanced production process on production lines. Technical transformation refers to replacement of old technology or equipment by new technology or equipment, in order to expand the reproduction through improvement of technology contents in production, to improve product quality, to promote new products, to save energy, to reduce consumption, to expand the production scale and to improve overall social-economic efficiency. Contents of technical transformation include: updating of machinery, equipment and tools; reforming production process by using energy or materials saving technology; construction of factory workshops and transformation of public facilities; treatment transformation of "three wastes" (waste gas, waste water and industrial residue) aiming at environmental protection; improvement of working conditions and environment, etc.

Investment in Fixed Assets by Structure

(1) Construction refers to the construction of houses and buildings, also known as work volume of construction. This part of investment can only be achieved through construction activities, it is the major component of the total investment in fixed assets.

(2) Installation refers to the installation of various kinds of equipment and instruments, also known as work volume of installation.

The value of equipment installed itself is not included in the value of installation projects.

(3) Purchase of equipment and instruments refers to the total value of equipment, tools, and instruments purchased or self-produced which come up to the cut-off point for fixed assets during the reference period. Equipment, tools and instruments purchased or self-produced for new workshops by newly established or expanded units are categorized as "purchase of equipment and instruments" no matter whether they come up to the cut-off point for fixed assets.

(4) Other expenses refer to expenses arising during the construction or purchase of fixed assets other than those expenses on construction, installation and purchase of equipment and instruments. Other financial expenses arising in operation are not included.

Number of Projects under Construction refers to number of all projects with actual construction or installation activities in current year, including newly started projects, projects started previously and extended into the current year, projects completed and put into operation in current year, projects suspended previously and resumed in current year, and projects started this year but suspended or postponed in current year. The number of projects under construction can reflect the actual size of investment in fixed assets during a given period, and when compared with the number of projects completed and put into use during the same period, it demonstrates the results of investment in fixed assets from the angle of the speed of the construction.

Number of Projects Put into Use This Year refer to projects have completed the main construction and correspondent auxiliary facilities in accordance with the design documents, resulting in forming production capacity (efficiency) and have been checked and accepted after relevant tests, and have been formally delivered for use.

Newly Increased Production Capacity (or Project Efficiency) refers to the increase in design capacity (or project efficiency) through investment in fixed assets. The main indicators include: construction scale, scale of projects under construction in current year, the accumulated newly increased production capacity (project efficiency) since the start of the projects and the newly increased production capacity (project efficiency) of current year.

Newly Increased Fixed Assets refer to the value of fixed assets that has completed the construction and purchase, and has been delivered to the production or owner units, including investment in projects that have been completed and put into operation in current year and the investment in equipment, tools and appliance that meet the standard of fixed assets and fees that should be apportioned. This is an indicator that demonstrates the results of investment in fixed assets in monetary terms, and an important indicator to reflect the speed of construction and to calculate the efficiency of investment.

Rate of Construction Projects Completed and Put into Use refers to the ratio of the number of construction projects completed and put into use in a certain period of time to the number of projects under construction in the same period. This reflects the investment efficiency from the perspective of the speed of projects construction.

Rate of Projects of Fixed Assets Completed and Put into Operation refers to the ratio of the newly increased fixed assets to the total investment made in the same period. This is a comprehensive indicator reflecting the speed of the employment of fixed assets and the investment efficiency at the macro-level. As the newly increase fixed assets is the result of a long period while the investment is completed in the current year, this indicator is expected to be used to reflect the employment of fixed assets over a long period of time.

Investment in Real Estate Development refers to the investment made by real estate development companies in the construction of housing, development of land, nonprofit buildings and value of land purchased.

Floor Space of Buildings under Construction refers to the total space area of the buildings under construction in the year by real estate development companies. It includes buildings started in the year, continued from the previous year, suspended in earlier years but restarted in the year, completed in the year, and started in the year but suspended in the year as well. The floor space of a multi-storied building should be the sum of floor space of all the stories.

Floor Space of Buildings Completed refers to the total floor space area of the buildings completed in the year by real estate development companies, which meet the requirements as designed, reach the criteria set for people to live in or use, have passed the acceptance checks, and are ready for delivery or use.

Completion Rate of Floor Space of Buildings refers to the ratio of the floor space of buildings completed in certain period of time to the floor space of buildings under construction in the same period. this indicator reflects the investment result from the perspective of the speed of construction.

Area of Commercialized Housing Sold refers to total contracted area of commercialized housing (i.e. area of floor space as designated in the formal contracts signed by both sides) sold by real estate development companies during the reference time.

Value of Commercialized Housing Sold refers to the total contracted value (i.e. value of sales/purchase for selling/purchase of commercialized housing as designated in the contract signed by both sides) received from the sales of the buildings by real estate development companies during the reference time. This indicator has the same coverage as the area of commercialized housing sold.

6

能源

Chapter 6 Energy

6-1 综合能源平衡表
Overall Energy Balance Sheet

单位：万吨标准煤 (10 000 tons SCE)

项 目	Item	2015	2016	2017	2018
可供消费的能源总量	**Total Energy Available for Consumption**	**18306.4**	**18755.8**	**19229.0**	**19916.2**
一次能源生产量	Primary Energy Output	18179.9	18941.5	19294.0	19172.0
外省(区、市)调入量	Imports from Other Provinces	7672.1	7289.9	7809.2	8493.5
进口量	Imports				
境内轮船和飞机在境外加油量	Refueling by Chinese Airplanes and Ships Abroad	7.3	11.1	14.2	19.3
本省(区、市)调出量(−)	Exports from Sichuan(-)	7490.4	7788.9	7748.3	7557.7
出口量(−)	Exports(-)				
境外轮船和飞机在境内加油量(−)	Refueling by Foreign Airplanes and Ships in China(-)	15.1	22.2	19.2	15.9
年初年末库存差额	Stock Changes in the Year	-47.5	324.4	-121.0	-195.0
年初库存量	Stock (year-beginning)	743.9	790.9	466.7	587.7
年末库存量(−)	Stock (year-end)(-)	791.4	466.5	587.7	782.7
能源消费总量	**Total Energy Consumption**	**18306.4**	**18755.8**	**19229.0**	**19916.2**
在总量中:	Consumption by Sector				
1.农、林、牧、渔业	1.Agriculture, Forestry, Animal Husbandry and Fishery	312.2	330.8	347.3	360.7
2.工业	2.Industry	11875.2	11915.4	11924.5	12053.0
3.建筑业	3.Construction	530.7	558.7	594.3	631.0
4.交通运输、仓储和邮政业	4.Transport, Storage and Post	1561.8	1640.5	1753.4	1813.4
5.批发、零售业和住宿、餐饮业	5.Wholesale and Retail Trades, Hotels and Catering Services	740.5	767.5	812.8	891.8
6.其他服务业	6.Other services	841.5	909.9	977.6	1093.5
7.生活消费	7.Residential Consumption	2444.6	2633.1	2819.1	3072.7
在总量中:	Consumption by Usage				
1.终端消费	1.Final Consumption	17237.1	17478.9	18206.1	19142.7
#工业	Industry	10852.5	10685.3	10952.0	11333.4
2.加工转换损失	2.Losses in Processing and Transformation	448.5	636.0	385.1	80.8
火力发电损失	Thermal Power Generation				
供热损失	Heating	77.2	80.8	92.7	102.3
洗选煤损失	Coal Washing and Dressing	416.0	568.9	421.2	258.6
炼焦损失	Coking	89.2	90.0	44.9	53.9
炼油损失	Petroleum Refining	350.4	341.6	366.2	270.9
制气损失	Gas Production				
煤制品加工损失	Coal Products Processing	17.8	18.7	11.7	23.5
天然气液化损失	Natural Gas Liquefying	10.3	14.7	10.2	3.4
回收能	Recovery of Energy	-512.5	-478.7	-561.7	-631.8
3.损失量	3.Other Losses	620.9	640.9	637.8	692.6
平衡差额	**Balance**				

注：本表按等价值计算。
a)Data in this table are calculated at equal value.

6-2 能源生产量和构成
Total Production of Energy and its Composition

单位：万吨标准煤，% (10 000 tons SCE , %)

项 目	Item	2015	2016	2017	2018
一次能源产量	**Primaty Energy Output**				
标准量（当量值）	Standard Volume(Heat Value Equivalent)	12441.4	12740.4	12729.2	12344.3
构成(按当量值计算)	Composition(Calculated on the Basic of Heat Value Equivalent)	100.0	100.0	100.0	100.0
标准量（电力等价值）	Standard Volume(Equal Electricity Value)	18179.9	18941.5	19294.0	19172.0
构成(按等价值计算)	Composition(Calculated on the Basic of Equal Electricity Value)	100.0	100.0	100.0	100.0
原煤	**Coal**				
实物量(万吨)	Physical Volume(10 000 tons)	6406.5	6164.8	4798.5	3736.2
标准量（当量值）	Standard Volume(Heat Value Equivalent)	5183.6	4740.6	3828.4	2944.7
构成(按当量值计算)	Composition(Calculated on the Basic of Heat Value Equivalent)	41.7	37.2	30.1	23.9
标准量（电力等价值）	Standard Volume(Equal Electricity Value)	5183.6	4740.6	3828.4	2944.7
构成(按等价值计算)	Composition(Calculated on the Basic of Equal Electricity Value)	28.5	25.0	19.8	15.4
原油	**Crude Oil**				
实物量(万吨)	Physical Volume(10 000 tons)	15.4	10.8	8.7	8.1
标准量（当量值）	Standard Volume(Heat Value Equivalent)	22.0	15.4	12.4	11.6
构成(按当量值计算)	Composition(Calculated on the Basic of Heat Value Equivalent)	0.2	0.1	0.1	0.1
标准量（电力等价值）	Standard Volume(Equal Electricity Value)	22.0	15.4	12.4	11.6
构成(按等价值计算)	Composition(Calculated on the Basic of Equal Electricity Value)	0.1	0.1	0.1	0.1
天然气	**Natural Gas**				
实物量(亿立方米)	Physical Volume(100 million cu.m)	267.2	296.9	344.5	369.8
标准量（当量值）	Standard Volume(Heat Value Equivalent)	3553.8	3948.9	4581.3	4918.7
构成(按当量值计算)	Composition(Calculated on the Basic of Heat Value Equivalent)	28.6	31.0	36.0	39.8
标准量（电力等价值）	Standard Volume(Equal Electricity Value)	3553.8	3948.9	4581.3	4918.7
构成(按等价值计算)	Composition(Calculated on the Basic of Equal Electricity Value)	19.5	20.8	23.7	25.7
一次电力	**Primary Electricity**				
实物量(亿千瓦小时)	Physical Volume(100 million kwh)	2779.2	3020.6	3215.5	3326.2
标准量（当量值）	Standard Volume(Heat Value Equivalent)	3415.7	3712.3	3951.9	4087.9
构成(按当量值计算)	Composition(Calculated on the Basic of Heat Value Equivalent)	27.5	29.1	31.0	33.1
标准量（电力等价值）	Standard Volume(Equal Electricity Value)	9154.2	9913.4	10516.8	10915.6
构成(按等价值计算)	Composition(Calculated on the Basic of Equal Electricity Value)	50.4	52.3	54.5	56.9
其他能源	**Other Energy**				
实物量(万吨标准煤)	Physical Volume(10 000 tons SCE)	266.3	323.3	355.1	381.4
标准量（当量值）	Standard Volume(Heat Value Equivalent)	266.3	323.3	355.1	381.4
构成(按当量值计算)	Composition(Calculated on the Basic of Heat Value Equivalent)	2.1	2.5	2.8	3.1
标准量（电力等价值）	Standard Volume(Equal Electricity Value)	266.3	323.3	355.1	381.4
构成(按等价值计算)	Composition(Calculated on the Basic of Equal Electricity Value)	1.5	1.7	1.8	2.0

6-3 能源消费量和构成
Total Consumption of Energy and its Composition

单位：万吨标准煤，%　　(10 000 tons SCE , %)

项　目	Item	2015	2016	2017	2018
能源消费总量	**Total Energy Consumption**				
标准量（当量值）	Standard Volume(Heat Value Equivalent)	15079.0	15159.5	15448.7	15759.8
构成(按当量值计算)	Composition(Calculated on the Basic of Heat Value Equivalent)	100.0	100.0	100.0	100.0
标准量（电力等价值）	Standard Volume(Equal Electricity Value)	18306.4	18755.8	19229.0	19916.2
构成(按等价值计算)	Composition(Calculated on the Basic of Equal Electricity Value)	100.0	100.0	100.0	100.0
煤品燃料	**Coal Products Fuel**				
标准量（当量值）	Standard Volume(Heat Value Equivalent)	6714.1	6365.4	6085.1	5865.3
构成(按当量值计算)	Composition(Calculated on the Basic of Heat Value Equivalent)	44.5	42.0	39.4	37.2
标准量（电力等价值）	Standard Volume(Equal Electricity Value)	6714.1	6365.4	6085.1	5865.3
构成(按等价值计算)	Composition(Calculated on the Basic of Equal Electricity Value)	36.7	33.9	31.6	29.5
油品燃料	**Oil Fuel**				
标准量（当量值）	Standard Volume(Heat Value Equivalent)	3470.9	3563.1	3711.6	3680.7
构成(按当量值计算)	Composition(Calculated on the Basic of Heat Value Equivalent)	23.0	23.5	24.0	23.4
标准量（电力等价值）	Standard Volume(Equal Electricity Value)	3470.9	3563.1	3711.6	3680.7
构成(按等价值计算)	Composition(Calculated on the Basic of Equal Electricity Value)	19.0	19.0	19.3	18.5
天然气	**Natual Gas**				
标准量（当量值）	Standard Volume(Heat Value Equivalent)	2619.0	2695.4	2876.3	3152.2
构成(按当量值计算)	Composition(Calculated on the Basic of Heat Value Equivalent)	17.4	17.8	18.6	20.0
标准量（电力等价值）	Standard Volume(Equal Electricity Value)	2619.0	2695.4	2876.3	3152.2
构成(按等价值计算)	Composition(Calculated on the Basic of Equal Electricity Value)	14.3	14.4	15.0	15.8
一次电力	**Primary Electricity**				
标准量（当量值）	Standard Volume(Heat Value Equivalent)	3415.7	3712.3	3951.9	4087.9
构成(按当量值计算)	Composition(Calculated on the Basic of Heat Value Equivalent)	22.7	24.5	25.6	25.9
标准量（电力等价值）	Standard Volume(Equal Electricity Value)	9154.2	9913.4	10516.8	10915.6
构成(按等价值计算)	Composition(Calculated on the Basic of Equal Electricity Value)	50.0	52.9	54.7	54.8
电力净调入(+)、调出(−)量	**Net Amount of Electricity Transferred in (+) and out(-)**				
标准量（当量值）	Standard Volume(Heat Value Equivalent)	-1494.6	-1559.4	-1676.3	-1599.4
构成(按当量值计算)	Composition(Calculated on the Basic of Heat Value Equivalent)	-9.9	-10.3	-10.9	-10.1
标准量（电力等价值）	Standard Volume(Equal Electricity Value)	-4005.7	-4164.2	-4460.9	-4270.7
构成(按等价值计算)	Composition(Calculated on the Basic of Equal Electricity Value)	-21.9	-22.2	-23.2	-21.4
其他能源	**Other Energy**				
标准量（当量值）	Standard Volume(Heat Value Equivalent)	353.9	382.8	500.2	573.1
构成(按当量值计算)	Composition(Calculated on the Basic of Heat Value Equivalent)	2.3	2.5	3.2	3.6
标准量（电力等价值）	Standard Volume(Equal Electricity Value)	353.9	382.8	500.2	573.1
构成(按等价值计算)	Composition(Calculated on the Basic of Equal Electricity Value)	1.9	2.0	2.6	2.9

6-4 主要能源库存量和周转天数
Stock and Revolving Days of Major Energy

单位：万吨，天 (10 000 tons,day)

项　目	Item	2015	2016	2017	2018
煤炭	**Coal**				
年末库存量	Stock (year-end)	664.9	402.1	515.4	608.6
消费量	Consumption	8824.3	8468.0	7815.4	7495.8
库存周转天数	Revolving Days of Stock	27.5	17.3	24.1	29.6
原煤	**Raw Coal**				
年末库存量	Stock (year-end)	496.2	278.3	347.6	426.1
消费量	Consumption	9590.9	10116.5	8419.2	8167.4
库存周转天数	Revolving Days of Stock	18.9	10.0	15.1	19.0
洗精煤	**Coal Washed and Dressed**				
年末库存量	Stock (year-end)	119.3	95.9	111.7	140.0
消费量	Consumption	2173.1	1741.9	1535.0	1580.5
库存周转天数	Revolving Days of Stock	20.0	20.1	26.6	32.3
其它洗煤	**Other Washed Coal**				
年末库存量	Stock (year-end)	46.3	25.5	48.2	37.7
消费量	Consumption	182.2	480.8	546.6	457.7
库存周转天数	Revolving Days of Stock	92.8	19.4	32.2	30.0
焦炭	**Coke**				
年末库存量	Stock (year-end)	68.8	22.9	34.6	32.4
消费量	Consumption	1152.1	1129.4	1127.1	1165.9
库存周转天数	Revolving Days of Stock	21.8	7.4	11.2	10.1
石油	**Petroleum**				
年末库存量	Stock (year-end)	140.0	94.9	111.0	192.6
消费量	Consumption	2408.7	2474.6	2579.7	2549.0
库存周转天数	Revolving Days of Stock	21.2	14.0	15.7	27.6
原油	**Crude Oil**				
年末库存量	Stock (year-end)	52.8	43.9	45.8	74.3
消费量	Consumption	989.6	902.8	956.4	719.8
库存周转天数	Revolving Days of Stock	19.5	17.8	17.5	37.7
汽油	**Gasoline**				
年末库存量	Stock (year-end)	20.8	12.9	24.6	72.9
消费量	Consumption	767.1	800.6	828.1	874.1
库存周转天数	Revolving Days of Stock	9.9	5.9	10.8	30.4
煤油	**Kerosene**				
年末库存量	Stock (year-end)	2.9	2.0	1.9	1.4
消费量	Consumption	194.8	210.0	205.9	209.5
库存周转天数	Revolving Days of Stock	5.5	3.4	3.3	2.4
柴油	**Diesel Oil**				
年末库存量	Stock (year-end)	45.5	29.9	25.1	28.4
消费量	Consumption	842.4	862.6	888.5	902.1
库存周转天数	Revolving Days of Stock	19.7	12.6	10.3	11.5
燃料油	**Fuel Oil**				
年末库存量	Stock (year-end)	3.8	1.5	1.9	2.2
消费量	Consumption	24.9	69.6	65.5	33.3
库存周转天数	Revolving Days of Stock	56.1	8.0	10.4	24.1

6-5 能源加工转换情况
Statistics of Energy Conversion

单位：万吨标准煤，%　　　(10 000 tons SCE , %)

项　目	Item	2015	2016	2017	2018
合计	**Total**				
投入量	Input	8107.6	8270.9	7167.1	6848.3
产出量	Output	6216.9	6439.2	5498.5	5243.4
转换损失量	Losses in Conversion	1890.7	1831.7	1668.6	1604.9
转换效率	Conversion Efficiency	76.7	77.9	76.7	76.6
火电	**Thermal Power Generation**				
投入量	Input	1483.3	1146.3	1156.4	1426.5
产出量	Output	553.4	429.3	434.5	534.2
转换损失量	Losses in Conversion	929.8	717.0	721.9	892.3
转换效率	Conversion Efficiency	37.3	37.4	37.6	37.4
供热	**Heating**				
投入量	Input	220.5	222.0	251.6	266.6
产出量	Output	143.3	141.2	158.9	164.2
转换损失量	Losses in Conversion	77.2	80.8	92.7	102.3
转换效率	Conversion Efficiency	65.0	63.6	63.2	61.6
洗煤	**Coal Washing and Dressing**				
投入量	Input	2939.5	3541.9	2503.9	2400.2
产出量	Output	2523.5	2973.0	2082.7	2141.7
转换损失量	Losses in Conversion	416.0	568.9	421.2	258.6
转换效率	Conversion Efficiency	85.8	83.9	83.2	89.2
炼焦	**Coking**				
投入量	Input	1687.2	1608.4	1381.5	1459.1
产出量	Output	1598.0	1518.5	1336.6	1405.2
转换损失量	Losses in Conversion	89.2	90.0	44.9	53.9
转换效率	Conversion Efficiency	94.7	94.4	96.8	96.3
炼油	**Refined Oil**				
投入量	Input	1593.7	1535.1	1663.1	1092.2
产出量	Output	1243.2	1193.5	1296.9	821.4
转换损失量	Losses in Conversion	350.4	341.6	366.2	270.9
转换效率	Conversion Efficiency	78.0	77.7	78.0	75.2

6-6 煤炭平衡表
Coal Balance Sheet

单位：万吨 (10 000 tons)

项 目	Item	2015	2016	2017	2018
可供量	**Total Energy Available for Consumption**	**8824.3**	**8468.0**	**7815.4**	**7495.8**
生产量	Output	6406.5	6164.8	4798.5	3736.2
外省(区、市)调入量	Imports from Other Provinces	5150.4	4743.4	4948.6	5504.2
进口量	Imports				
本省(区、市)调出量(-)	Exports from Sichuan(-)	2679.2	2703.0	1818.5	1651.4
出口量(-)	Exports(-)				
年初年末库存差额	Stock Changes in the Year	-53.3	262.8	-113.2	-93.3
年初库存量	Stock (year-beginning)	611.6	664.9	402.1	515.4
年末库存量(-)	Stock (year-end)(-)	664.9	402.1	515.4	608.6
消费量	**Total Energy Consumption**	**8824.3**	**8468.0**	**7815.4**	**7495.8**
在总量中:	Consumption by Sector	8824.3	8468.0	7815.4	7495.8
1.农、林、牧、渔业	1.Agriculture, Forestry, Animal Husbandry and Fishery	50.2	53.0	50.1	45.8
2.工业	2.Industry	8511.5	8216.0	7564.3	7287.9
3.建筑业	3.Construction	23.5	20.3	25.6	10.4
4.交通运输、仓储和邮政业	4.Transport, Storage and Post	4.5	3.1	4.2	4.2
5.批发、零售业和住宿、餐饮业	5.Wholesale and Retail Trades, Hotels and Catering Services	31.1	31.9	35.1	26.3
6.其他服务业	6.Other services	34.3	23.8	29.4	19.4
7.生活消费	7.Residential Consumption	169.3	119.9	106.8	101.7
在总量中:	Consumption by Usage	8824.3	8468.0	7815.4	7495.8
1.终端消费	1.Final Consumption	4420.4	4461.0	4367.8	3934.8
#工业	Industry	4107.6	4208.9	4116.7	3727.0
2.用于加工转换	2. Consumed in Transformation	4403.9	4007.0	3447.6	3560.9
火力发电	Thermal Power Generation	1547.8	1054.5	1017.4	1216.4
供 热	Heating	152.2	160.3	213.2	231.3
洗煤损耗	Coal Washing and Dressing	815.6	990.6	684.9	496.5
炼焦	Coking	1887.9	1798.9	1535.0	1619.4
炼油及煤制油	Refining and Coal Liquefaction				
制气	Gas Production				
型煤加工损耗	Coal Products Processing Losses	0.4	2.7	-3.0	-2.7
3.损失量	3.Other Losses				
平衡差额	**Balance**				

6-7 石油平衡表
Petroleum Balance Sheet

单位：万吨 (10 000 tons)

项 目	Item	2015	2016	2017	2018
可供量	**Total Energy Available for Consumption**	**2408.7**	**2474.6**	**2579.7**	**2549.0**
生产量	Output	15.4	10.8	8.7	8.1
外省(区、市)调入量	Imports from Other Provinces	2420.1	2426.2	2590.4	2620.1
进口量	Imports				
境内轮船和飞机在境外加油量	Refueling by Chinese Airplanes and Ships Abroad	5.0	7.5	9.8	13.1
本省(区、市)调出量(-)	Exports from Sichuan(-)	33.6			
出口量(-)	Exports(-)				
境外轮船和飞机在境内加油量(-)	Refueling by Foreign Airplanes and Ships in China(-)	10.2	15.1	13.1	10.8
年初年末库存差额	Stock Changes in the Year	12.0	45.1	-16.1	-81.6
年初库存量	Stock (year-beginning)	152.0	140.0	94.9	111.0
年末库存量(-)	Stock (year-end)(-)	140.0	94.9	111.0	192.6
消费量	**Total Energy Consumption**	**2408.7**	**2474.6**	**2579.7**	**2549.0**
在总量中:	Consumption by Sector	2408.7	2474.6	2579.7	2549.0
1.农、林、牧、渔业	1.Agriculture, Forestry, Animal Husbandry and Fishery	80.2	91.8	93.3	99.7
2.工业	2.Industry	526.5	514.9	540.4	441.2
3.建筑业	3.Construction	270.3	286.8	302.3	321.9
4.交通运输、仓储和邮政业	4.Transport, Storage and Post	815.0	857.5	901.6	905.8
5.批发、零售业和住宿、餐饮业	5.Wholesale and Retail Trades, Hotels and Catering Services	177.2	163.4	164.8	169.9
6.其他服务业	6.Other sevices	167.4	176.3	175.7	184.9
7.生活消费	7.Residential Consumption	372.0	383.9	401.7	425.7
在总量中:	Consumption by Usage	2408.7	2474.6	2579.7	2549.0
1.终端消费	1.Final Consumption	2125.2	2192.7	2285.5	2321.9
#工业	Industry	243.0	233.0	246.2	214.1
2.用于加工转换	2.Consumed in Transformation	283.5	281.9	294.2	227.1
火力发电	Thermal Power Generation	0.5	3.8	2.0	3.3
供热	Heating	15.4	16.1	10.4	16.6
炼油损耗	Losses in Petroleum Refining	267.6	262.0	281.7	207.2
制气	Gas Production				
3.损失量	3.Other Losses				
平衡差额	**Balance**				

6-8 天然气平衡表
Natural Gas Balance Sheet

单位：亿立方米 (100 million cu.m)

项　目	Item	2015	2016	2017	2018
可供量	**Total Energy Available for Consumption**	**196.9**	**202.7**	**216.3**	**237.0**
生产量	Output	267.2	296.9	344.5	369.8
外省(区、市)调入量	Imports from Other Provinces		0.6	0.3	
进口量	Imports				
境内轮船和飞机在境外加油量	Refueling by Chinese Airplanes and Ships Abroad				
本省(区、市)调出量(-)	Exports from Sichuan(-)	70.3	94.8	128.1	132.8
出口量(-)	Exports(-)				
境外轮船和飞机在境内加油量(-)	Refueling by Foreign Airplanes and Ships in China(-)				
年初年末库存差额	Stock Changes in the Year			-0.4	
年初库存量	Stock (year-beginning)				0.4
年末库存量(-)	Stock (year-end)(-)			0.4	0.4
消费量	**Total Energy Consumption**	**196.9**	**202.7**	**216.3**	**237.0**
在总量中:	Consumption by Sector	196.9	202.7	216.3	237.0
1.农、林、牧、渔业	1.Agriculture, Forestry, Animal Husbandry and Fishery	0.1	0.5	1.3	1.0
2.工业	2.Industry	128.8	129.8	133.3	146.3
3.建筑业	3.Construction	0.0	0.8	1.0	1.0
4.交通运输、仓储和邮政业	4.Transport, Storage and Post	16.0	16.0	19.0	19.9
5.批发、零售业和住宿、餐饮业	5.Wholesale and Retail Trades, Hotels and Catering Services	7.9	9.9	11.0	12.6
6.其他服务业	6.Other sevices	5.8	6.2	7.1	7.5
7.生活消费	7.Residential Consumption	38.2	39.5	43.7	48.8
在总量中:	Consumption by Usage	196.9	202.7	216.3	237.0
1.终端消费	1.Final Consumption	186.2	191.5	206.1	224.5
#工业	Industry	121.6	122.1	126.9	137.8
2.用于加工转换	2.Consumed in Transformation	7.2	7.7	6.3	8.5
火力发电	Thermal Power Generation	3.3	3.6	2.9	4.0
供热	Heating	3.0	3.1	3.1	3.2
制气	Gas Production				
天然气液化	Liquefied Natural Gas	0.9	1.0	0.4	1.2
3.损失量	3.Other Losses	3.5	3.5	3.8	4.0
平衡差额	**Balance**				

6-9 电力平衡表
Electricity Balance Sheet

单位：亿千瓦小时 (100 million kwh)

项 目	Item	2015	2016	2017	2018
可供量	**Total Energy Available for Consumption**	**2013.4**	**2101.0**	**2205.2**	**2459.5**
生产量	Output	3229.6	3369.8	3569.1	3760.8
火力发电	Thermal Power	450.3	349.3	353.6	434.7
水力发电、核发电、其它发电	Hydropower, Nuclear Power and Other Power	2779.2	3020.6	3215.5	3326.2
外省(区、市)调入量	Imports from Other Provinces	50.5	47.5	65.2	104.5
进口量	Imports				
本省(区、市)调出量(-)	Exports from Sichuan(-)	1266.7	1316.3	1429.2	1405.8
出口量(-)	Exports(-)				
消费量	**Total Energy Consumption**	**2013.4**	**2101.0**	**2205.2**	**2459.5**
在总量中:	Consumption by Sector	2013.4	2101.0	2205.2	2459.5
1.农、林、牧、渔业	1.Agriculture, Forestry, Animal Husbandry and Fishery	12.4	13.8	15.5	16.5
2.工业	2.Industry	1342.5	1337.7	1377.1	1527.4
3.建筑业	3.Construction	39.4	39.7	41.1	48.9
4.交通运输、仓储和邮政业	4.Transport, Storage and Post	36.6	42.6	48.2	58.3
5.批发、零售业和住宿、餐饮业	5.Wholesale and Retail Trades, Hotels and Catering Services	97.1	108.6	118.0	129.9
6.其他服务业	6.Other sevices	144.6	166.0	182.7	212.2
7.生活消费	7.Residential Consumption	340.8	392.7	422.6	466.4
在总量中:	Consumption by Usage	2013.4	2101.0	2205.2	2459.5
1.终端消费	1.Final Consumption	1839.1	1920.0	2025.6	2264.8
#工业	Industry	1168.1	1156.6	1197.5	1332.7
2. 输配电损失量	2.Power Transmission and Distribution	174.4	181.0	179.6	194.6
平衡差额	**Balance**				

6-10 各市(州)单位地区生产总值能耗指数(等价值)

Energy Consumption Index of Gross Domestic Product per Unit Area by Region (Equivalent value)

(上年=100) (preceding year=100)

市(州)	Region	2010	2011	2012	2013	2014	2015	2016	2017	2018
全　省	**Sichuan**	**95.27**	**95.77**	**92.82**	**95.08**	**95.36**	**92.75**	**95.02**	**94.82**	**95.94**
成都市	Chengdu	95.87	95.77	92.80	95.28	102.10	96.11	97.34	96.79	94.21
自贡市	Zigong	94.83	96.00	92.68	94.58	93.45	89.66	96.89	95.50	94.50
攀枝花市	Panzhihua	95.25	95.65	95.00	96.70	91.57	89.83	90.24	89.74	92.56
泸州市	Luzhou	94.63	96.40	93.76	95.75	96.00	93.02	96.06	96.39	96.37
德阳市	Deyang	92.70	95.75	92.90	94.95	97.70	92.22	93.78	91.93	95.13
绵阳市	Mianyang	94.79	96.08	92.88	94.76	94.25	90.75	91.58	94.39	96.28
广元市	Guangyuan	93.88	96.78	94.90	94.61	93.31	96.18	94.91	96.26	95.49
遂宁市	Suining	95.12	96.75	92.81	95.76	94.17	90.44	93.48	92.00	91.34
内江市	Neijiang	95.28	95.71	93.53	96.94	94.19	92.05	95.18	96.15	96.91
乐山市	Leshan	95.50	96.13	92.70	94.99	93.41	91.64	95.34	93.49	95.62
南充市	Nanchong	95.70	96.35	95.28	95.42	95.78	94.46	95.95	95.27	94.06
眉山市	Meishan	95.35	95.30	93.42	94.87	93.03	89.31	91.09	95.85	94.72
宜宾市	Yibin	96.04	100.50	97.46	95.81	94.35	90.20	95.79	94.33	96.90
广安市	Guangan	94.97	95.55	92.81	95.59	96.13	92.26	94.57	95.85	96.52
达州市	Dazhou	95.18	96.37	92.90	95.32	93.11	93.97	87.96	100.10	95.69
雅安市	Yaan	94.87	96.60	93.38	96.58	96.85	93.82	95.98	89.90	97.78
巴中市	Bazhong	94.99	97.90	97.53	97.14	94.86	98.10	100.36	94.90	97.46
资阳市	Ziyang	95.35	96.20	92.81	95.18	94.79	92.08	94.50	92.32	95.88
阿坝藏族羌族自治州	Aba	104.63	105.00	96.02	94.71	106.95	95.20	100.10	96.40	93.84
甘孜藏族自治州	Ganzi	92.30	97.88	97.58	96.07	97.45	100.51	100.65	94.67	96.31
凉山彝族自治州	Liangshan	95.68	95.62	93.33	105.52	93.27	95.62	100.53	94.73	100.18

注：地区生产总值按可比价格计算。
a)GDP is calculated at comparable prices.

6-11 各市(州)单位工业增加值能耗指数(规模以上当量值)
Energy Consumption Index of Industrial Value Added per Unit by Region (Equivalent value above designated size)

(上年=100) (preceding year=100)

市(州)	Region	2010	2011	2012	2013	2014	2015	2016	2017	2018
全 省	**Sichuan**	**88.76**	**92.22**	**87.72**	**93.22**	**91.97**	**87.95**	**91.56**	**92.85**	**92.73**
成都市	Chengdu	91.02	91.13	85.18	86.75	113.82	92.21	92.69	93.03	84.57
自贡市	Zigong	90.23	90.40	85.43	89.19	72.15	78.93	91.67	91.47	83.95
攀枝花市	Panzhihua	92.48	90.35	90.79	93.77	87.07	83.81	88.32	88.29	92.09
泸州市	Luzhou	87.55	90.45	91.07	91.10	94.00	86.01	91.41	94.89	95.01
德阳市	Deyang	88.62	88.32	86.22	89.21	88.75	86.22	86.64	89.02	90.51
绵阳市	Mianyang	87.15	92.17	86.19	88.38	92.80	80.14	83.44	93.29	95.96
广元市	Guangyuan	91.48	95.65	93.88	91.87	88.08	95.26	90.09	95.38	93.01
遂宁市	Suining	87.28	93.00	88.25	91.89	89.07	83.12	87.31	87.92	81.54
内江市	Neijiang	83.50	89.55	87.46	94.88	89.51	85.47	93.30	94.67	95.40
乐山市	Leshan	86.06	91.41	86.62	91.30	92.06	90.78	94.23	91.32	92.53
南充市	Nanchong	86.44	88.95	90.73	92.16	89.19	92.84	93.48	92.49	92.26
眉山市	Meishan	87.90	87.88	88.74	89.55	88.11	78.89	84.85	93.17	89.20
宜宾市	Yibin	91.22	109.72	98.23	91.48	90.91	79.82	93.56	88.75	94.66
广安市	Guangan	88.21	87.72	84.38	87.73	93.28	82.86	85.73	92.21	98.51
达州市	Dazhou	82.63	91.19	87.60	92.19	88.81	93.29	78.21	102.24	92.56
雅安市	Yaan	92.34	92.67	85.89	92.84	93.94	90.95	94.97	82.36	95.30
巴中市	Bazhong	90.93	96.75	93.70	92.31	76.57	98.22	104.12	76.89	94.72
资阳市	Ziyang	87.20	91.41	86.05	90.85	89.08	91.58	88.33	83.01	79.72
阿坝藏族羌族自治州	Aba	112.50	129.28	91.74	85.91	108.76	94.85	100.21	96.59	92.83
甘孜藏族自治州	Ganzi	90.00	90.66	81.00	93.45	91.91	102.06	110.37	76.58	94.30
凉山彝族自治州	Liangshan	86.80	88.77	85.90	109.79	87.19	98.51	104.14	94.11	107.22

注：规模以上工业增加值按可比价格计算。
a)Industrial Value Added above designated size is calculated at comparable prices.

6-12 能源生产和能源消费弹性系数
Elasticity Coefficient of Energy Production and Consumption

项　目		Item		2016	2017	2018
能源生产		**Energy Production**				
能源生产比上年增长	(%)	Growth Rate of Energy Production over Preceding Year	(%)	4.2	1.9	-0.6
电力生产比上年增长	(%)	Growth Rate of Electricity Production over Preceding Year	(%)	4.3	5.9	5.4
地区生产总值比上年增长	(%)	Growth Rate of Gross Regional Product over Preceding Year	(%)	7.8	8.1	8.0
能源生产弹性系数		Elasticity Ratio of Energy Production		0.5	0.2	-0.1
电力生产弹性系数		Elasticity Ratio of Electricity Production		0.6	0.7	0.7
能源消费		**Energy Consumption**				
能源消费比上年增长	(%)	Growth Rate of Energy Consumption over Preceding Year	(%)	2.5	2.5	3.6
电力消费比上年增长	(%)	Growth Rate of Electricity Consumption over Preceding Year	(%)	4.4	5.0	11.5
地区生产总值比上年增长	(%)	Growth Rate of Gross Regional Product over Preceding Year	(%)	7.8	8.1	8.0
能源消费弹性系数		Elasticity Ratio of Energy Consumption		0.3	0.3	0.4
电力消费弹性系数		Elasticity Ratio of Electricity Consumption		0.6	0.6	1.5

注：地区生产总值增长速度按可比价格计算。
a) Gross regional product growth rate is calculated at constant price.

主要统计指标解释

能源生产总量 指一定时期内，全省一次能源生产量的总和。该指标是观察全省能源生产水平、规模、构成和发展速度的总量指标。一次能源生产量包括原煤、原油、天然气、水电、核能及其他动力能(如风能、地热能等)发电量，不包括低热值燃料生产量、太阳热能等的利用和由一次能源加工转换而成的二次能源产量。

能源消费总量 指一定地域内，国民经济各行业和居民家庭在一定时期内消费的各种能源的总和。包括：原煤、原油、天然气、水能、核能、风能、太阳能、地热能、生物质能等一次能源；一次能源通过加工转换产生的洗煤、焦炭、煤气、电力、热力、成品油等二次能源和同时产生的其他产品；其他化石能源、可再生能源和新能源。其中水能、风能、太阳能、地热能、生物质能等可再生能源，是指人们通过一定技术手段获得的，并作为商品能源使用的部分。在核算过程中，一次能源、二次能源消费不能重复计算。

能源消费总量分为终端能源消费量、能源加工转换损失量和能源损失量三部分。

(1)终端能源消费量：指一定时期内，全省生产和生活消费的各种能源在扣除了用于加工转换二次能源消费量和损失量以后的数量。

(2)能源加工转换损失量：指一定时期内，全省投入加工转换的各种能源数量之和与产出各种能源产品之和的差额。该指标是观察能源在加工转换过程中损失量变化的指标。

(3)能源损失量：指一定时期内，能源在输送、分配、储存过程中发生的损失和由客观原因造成的各种损失量，不包括各种气体能源放空、放散量。

单位地区生产总值能耗 指一定时期内，一个地区每生产一个单位的地区生产总值所消费的能源。计算公式为：

$$\text{单位地区生产总值能耗}=\frac{\text{能源消费总量}}{\text{地区生产总值}}$$

能源生产弹性系数 是研究能源生产增长速度与国民经济增长速度之间关系的指标。计算公式为：

$$\text{能源生产弹性系数}=\frac{\text{能源生产量年平均增长速度}}{\text{国民经济年平均增长速度}}$$

国民经济年平均增长速度，可根据不同的目的或需要，用国民生产总值、国内生产总值等指标来计算，本年鉴是采用国内生产总值指标计算的。

电力生产弹性系数 是研究电力生产增长速度与国民经济增长速度之间关系的指标。一般来说，电力的发展应当快于国民经济的发展，也就是说电力应超前发展。计算公式为：

$$\text{电力生产弹性系数}=\frac{\text{电力生产量年平均增长速度}}{\text{国民经济年平均增长速度}}$$

能源消费弹性系数 反映能源消费增长速度与国民经济增长速度之间比例关系的指标。计算公式为：

$$\text{能源消费弹性系数}=\frac{\text{能源消费量年平均增长速度}}{\text{国民经济年平均增长速度}}$$

电力消费弹性系数 反映电力消费增长速度与国民经济增长速度之间比例关系的指标。计算公式为：

$$\text{电力消费弹性系数}=\frac{\text{电力消费量年平均增长速度}}{\text{国民经济年平均增长速度}}$$

Explanatory Notes on Main Statistical Indicators

Total Energy Production refers to the total production of primary energy by all energy producing enterprises in the province in a given period of time. It is a comprehensive indicator to show the capacity, scale, composition and development of energy production of the province. The production of primary energy includes that of coal, crude oil, natural gas, hydro-power and electricity generated by nuclear energy and other means such as wind power and geothermal power. However, it excludes the production of fuels of low calorific value, solar thermal and the secondary energy converted from the primary energy.

Total Energy Consumption refers to the total consumption of energy of various kinds by the production sectors of the economy and the households in a given period of time. It includes the primary kinds of energy such as coal, crude oil, natural gas, hydro-power, nuclear power, wind power, solar power, geothermal power and bio-energy; the secondary kinds of energy and their products which are transformed from the primary energy such as washed coal, coke, coal gas, electricity, heating, and petroleum products; and other kinds of fossil energy, renewable energy and new energy. The renewable energy, including hydro-power, wind power, solar power, geothermal power and bio-energy, refers to the part attained with some given technical means and used for commercial purposes. Total energy consumption can be divided into three parts: end-use energy consumption, loss during the process of energy conversion and energy loss.

(1) End-use Energy Consumption: It refers to the total energy consumption by material production sectors, non material production sectors and households in the province in a given period of time, but excludes the consumption in conversion of the primary energy into the secondary energy and the loss in the process of energy conversion.

(2) Loss During the Process of Energy Conversion: It refers to the total input of various kinds of energy for conversion, minus the total output of various kinds of energy in the province in a given period of time. It is an indicator to show the loss that occurs during the process of energy conversion.

(3) Energy Loss: It refers to the total of the loss of energy during the course of energy transport, distribution and storage and the loss caused by any objective reason in a given period of time. The loss of various kinds of gas due to gas discharges and stocktaking is excluded.

Energy Consumption per Unit of GDP refers to the energy consumption per unit of Gross Regional Product in a region in the same reference period. The formula is:

$$\text{Energy Consumption per Unit of GDP} = \frac{\text{Total Energy Consumption}}{\text{Gross Regional Product}}$$

Elasticity Ratio of Energy Production is an indicator to show the relationship between the growth rate of energy production and the growth rate of the national economy. The formula is:

$$\text{Elasticity Ratio of Energy Production} = \frac{\text{Average Annual Growth Rate of Energy Production}}{\text{Average Annual Growth Rate of National Economy}}$$

The average annual growth rate of the national economy can be shown by the gross national product, gross domestic product and other indicators, depending upon the purposes or needs. The gross domestic product is used in calculation of the ratio in this chapter.

Elasticity Ratio of Electricity Production is an indicator to show the relationship between the growth rate of electricity production and the growth rate of the national economy. Generally speaking, the growth rate of electricity production should be higher than that of the national economy. The formula is:

$$\text{Elasticity Ratio of Electricity Production} = \frac{\text{Average Annual Growth Rate of Electricity Production}}{\text{Average Annual Growth Rate of National Economy}}$$

Elasticity Ratio of Energy Consumption is an indicator to show the relationship between the growth rate of energy consumption and the growth rate of the national economy. The formula is:

$$\text{Elasticity Ratio of Energy Consumption} = \frac{\text{Average Annual Growth Rate of Energy Consumption}}{\text{Average Annual Growth Rate of National Economy}}$$

Elasticity Ratio of Electricity Consumption is an indicator to show the relationship between the growth rate of electricity consumption and the growth rate of the national economy. The formula is:

$$\text{Elasticity Ratio of Electricity Consumption} = \frac{\text{Average Annual Growth Rate of Electricity Consumption}}{\text{Average Annual Growth Rate of National Economy}}$$

7 资源和环境

Chapter 7 Resources and Environment

7-1 主要城市平均气温(2018年)

Monthly Average Temperature of Major Cities(2018)

单位：摄氏度 (℃)

城　市	City	1月 Jan.	2月 Feb.	3月 Mar.	4月 Apr.	5月 May	6月 June	7月 July	8月 Aug.	9月 Sept.	10月 Oct.	11月 Nov.	12月 Dec.	年平均 Annual Average
成都市	Chengdu	5.1	7.5	14.9	18.5	22.1	23.8	25.7	26.9	22.0	16.2	10.9	6.6	16.7
自贡市	Zigong	7.6	10.1	17.7	21.3	23.8	25.2	28.5	29.0	23.2	17.2	12.6	8.6	18.7
攀枝花市	Panzhihua	13.8	16.2	21.1	24.4	26.0	24.5	26.0	25.4	23.4	19.4	16.5	15.0	21.0
泸州市	Luzhou	7.2	9.3	16.9	20.5	23.0	24.7	28.7	27.9	22.5	16.6	12.3	8.5	18.2
德阳市	Deyang	5.5	7.9	15.4	19.7	22.7	24.3	26.0	27.3	21.8	16.2	10.6	6.5	17.0
绵阳市	Mianyang	6.1	8.5	16.1	20.4	23.0	24.5	26.3	28.1	22.2	16.6	11.2	6.8	17.5
广元市	Guangyuan	4.5	7.5	14.8	18.1	21.5	24.1	25.3	27.0	21.4	15.7	10.0	5.7	16.3
遂宁市	Suining	6.1	9.0	16.3	20.0	22.7	25.3	28.2	28.8	22.5	16.8	11.4	7.6	17.9
内江市	Neijiang	6.7	9.5	16.6	20.3	23.1	24.9	28.0	28.4	22.7	16.7	11.8	8.0	18.1
乐山市	Leshan	7.8	10.1	17.8	20.9	23.3	24.8	27.3	28.4	23.0	17.4	12.6	8.6	18.5
南充市	Nanchong	5.8	8.3	15.6	19.6	22.2	25.1	28.4	28.9	22.2	16.6	11.3	7.2	17.6
眉山市	Meishan	6.6	9.4	16.8	20.3	23.2	24.9	26.9	28.2	22.9	17.2	12.0	7.6	18.0
宜宾市	Yibin	6.9	9.3	16.9	20.5	22.8	24.1	27.1	27.5	21.9	16.2	12.0	7.7	17.7
广安市	Guangan	5.8	7.8	15.2	19.7	22.0	25.0	29.4	29.2	22.0	16.3	11.3	7.1	17.6
达州市	Dazhou	5.9	7.9	15.5	19.8	22.4	25.9	30.1	30.3	23.1	17.4	11.8	7.5	18.1
雅安市	Yaan	6.1	8.2	15.7	19.0	21.6	23.5	25.5	26.5	21.4	15.8	11.5	7.1	16.8
巴中市	Bazhong	5.8	7.8	15.6	19.2	22.1	25.3	28.6	29.4	22.6	16.9	11.4	6.7	17.6
资阳市	Ziyang	6.3	9.5	17.0	20.7	23.2	24.8	26.9	28.2	22.5	16.8	11.5	7.6	17.9
马尔康市	Maerkang	1.1	3.9	7.3	10.7	13.6	15.1	17.7	17.8	15.7	8.0	3.1	-0.1	9.5
康定市	Kangding	-1.6	-0.7	6.3	9.3	12.1	13.9	16.8	16.9	13.3	6.6	3.5	-0.5	8.0
西昌市	Xichang	10.8	12.1	17.2	20.3	21.9	21.7	23.9	23.4	20.6	16.3	13.8	12.4	17.9

注：气象资料由四川省气象局提供。

a) The meteorological data are provided by the Sichuan Provincial Meteorological Bureau.

7-2 主要城市降水量(2018年)
Monthly Precipitation of Major Cities(2018)

单位：毫米 (millimeters)

城 市	City	1月 Jan.	2月 Feb.	3月 Mar.	4月 Apr.	5月 May	6月 June	7月 July	8月 Aug.	9月 Sept.	10月 Oct.	11月 Nov.	12月 Dec.	全年 Annual Total
成都市	Chengdu	2.0	11.4	33.9	48.5	127.5	253.3	381.6	175.9	155.5	33.7	13.8	13.2	1250.3
自贡市	Zigong	12.7	3.3	26.0	120.5	115.9	120.5	70.7	202.6	99.3	104.3	8.6	25.4	909.8
攀枝花市	Panzhihua	2.6	1.8	16.6	8.5	151.8	162.8	153.5	167.0	107.5	49.2		0.9	822.2
泸州市	Luzhou	58.8	8.0	33.5	77.0	135.7	105.1	262.1	348.6	136.1	135.3	30.2	58.0	1388.4
德阳市	Deyang	2.9	5.3	42.4	27.9	123.7	262.1	794.6	151.8	160.1	43.9	16.7	19.2	1650.6
绵阳市	Mianyang	2.9	5.1	36.1	41.5	103.8	128.7	677.1	171.4	119.9	43.9	14.9	21.7	1367.0
广元市	Guangyuan	4.8		37.2	100.2	85.6	78.6	442.1	188.1	87.5	36.8	15.4	10.2	1086.5
遂宁市	Suining	17.6	7.2	23.6	145.5	140.4	99.3	185.3	44.8	144.2	59.9	25.7	38.3	931.8
内江市	Neijiang	15.4	1.9	34.3	139.6	116.0	95.2	300.8	117.2	92.4	99.8	9.3	22.9	1044.8
乐山市	Leshan	9.2	12.7	65.5	98.1	303.4	190.2	296.3	274.2	156.9	62.0	20.1	23.3	1511.9
南充市	Nanchong	27.3	13.0	37.7	231.8	105.8	141.6	147.7	46.3	121.2	51.2	61.0	43.2	1027.8
眉山市	Meishan	4.3	10.4	29.0	85.3	177.8	288.6	351.6	137.8	144.1	49.5	17.8	14.3	1310.5
宜宾市	Yibin	31.5	4.4	44.0	87.1	174.7	105.5	209.6	188.2	161.3	117.8	19.9	46.0	1190.0
广安市	Guangan	23.7	11.8	63.0	138.0	107.7	87.5	170.2	51.7	175.4	66.9	62.2	16.7	974.8
达州市	Dazhou	29.2	17.6	41.5	186.7	69.3	174.9	111.7	88.8	156.9	32.1	56.6	10.8	976.1
雅安市	Yaan	18.5	16.4	72.7	143.1	249.4	292.3	557.3	398.7	250.2	100.5	31.5	30.7	2161.3
巴中市	Bazhong	31.9	5.4	82.2	121.6	138.3	200.0	218.7	80.8	142.0	39.9	54.3	42.8	1157.9
资阳市	Ziyang	6.8	3.3	28.1	91.6	126.0	257.9	286.5	165.4	142.1	60.3	12.7	22.6	1203.3
马尔康市	Maerkang	0.4	6.2	33.4	74.2	122.7	173.0	200.5	45.8	166.2	113.7	40.5	5.2	981.8
康定市	Kangding	0.7	43.9	39.1	91.7	109.6	187.0	128.4	56.3	175.1	104.5	11.7	7.2	955.2
西昌市	Xichang	0.3	0.4	16.1	21.2	136.9	254.1	301.8	94.0	266.6	42.9	0.4	3.0	1137.7

7-3 主要城市平均相对湿度(2018年)
Average Relative Humidity of Major Cities(2018)

单位：% (%)

城　市	City	1月 Jan.	2月 Feb.	3月 Mar.	4月 Apr.	5月 May	6月 June	7月 July	8月 Aug.	9月 Sept.	10月 Oct.	11月 Nov.	12月 Dec.	年平均 Annual Average
成都市	Chengdu	74	72	77	74	73	82	89	81	86	87	87	84	81
自贡市	Zigong	76	67	69	67	72	82	81	77	86	91	83	87	78
攀枝花市	Panzhihua	49	38	35	34	47	73	71	72	77	73	58	55	57
泸州市	Luzhou	86	77	75	74	77	83	78	78	88	92	86	90	82
德阳市	Deyang	71	68	74	66	69	79	87	79	85	86	85	83	78
绵阳市	Mianyang	63	62	66	56	62	73	81	70	77	78	75	75	70
广元市	Guangyuan	59	54	66	64	65	71	85	74	76	76	70	66	69
遂宁市	Suining	81	71	74	72	76	81	83	75	86	91	86	88	80
内江市	Neijiang	80	71	73	73	76	82	82	80	87	92	85	90	81
乐山市	Leshan	67	63	63	61	64	73	74	67	80	82	78	78	71
南充市	Nanchong	77	72	72	67	74	76	77	69	84	90	88	90	78
眉山市	Meishan	80	72	76	75	76	85	91	83	87	88	86	86	82
宜宾市	Yibin	82	73	73	69	73	84	83	79	89	92	86	92	81
广安市	Guangan	80	77	75	69	76	77	71	68	84	88	87	87	78
达州市	Dazhou	78	78	77	72	78	77	70	64	81	85	90	84	78
雅安市	Yaan	76	73	74	72	72	79	84	77	86	84	80	82	78
巴中市	Bazhong	73	70	72	68	73	73	74	65	78	79	81	84	74
资阳市	Ziyang	74	66	68	67	72	83	87	80	88	90	85	88	79
马尔康市	Maerkang	43	50	54	53	69	81	83	73	77	78	68	52	65
康定市	Kangding	71	77	72	74	71	77	78	70	78	77	64	66	73
西昌市	Xichang	43	39	39	39	53	79	76	71	82	71	56	48	58

7-4 主要城市日照时数(2018年)
Monthly Sunshine Hours of Major Cities(2018)

单位：小时 (hours)

城市	City	1月 Jan.	2月 Feb.	3月 Mar.	4月 Apr.	5月 May	6月 June	7月 July	8月 Aug.	9月 Sept.	10月 Oct.	11月 Nov.	12月 Dec.	全年 Annual Total
成都市	Chengdu	78.3	84.5	110.3	154.8	126.8	103.7	109.4	205.5	68.7	65.4	67.0	36.5	1210.9
自贡市	Zigong	78.2	64.6	159.0	170.5	98.3	84.1	115.3	206.8	68.3	40.5	79.3	33.5	1198.4
攀枝花市	Panzhihua	209.8	204.2	278.9	275.4	261.4	134.0	192.4	237.8	137.2	190.3	275.2	232.0	2628.6
泸州市	Luzhou	45.9	74.9	139.0	185.7	137.9	120.8	227.3	246.5	62.5	23.3	65.7	27.3	1356.8
德阳市	Deyang	73.4	90.2	113.1	160.9	148.6	108.3	104.5	233.3	86.5	86.5	54.2	42.7	1302.2
绵阳市	Mianyang	88.8	88.1	120.4	181.9	162.6	119.5	141.5	262.7	97.8	92.1	64.8	47.8	1468.0
广元市	Guangyuan	105.4	108.5	148.7	178.9	146.7	138.7	91.3	247.0	80.4	112.5	59.4	46.7	1464.2
遂宁市	Suining	53.0	64.8	120.8	154.9	118.7	89.0	146.8	208.7	72.6	34.7	35.5	24.2	1123.7
内江市	Neijiang	83.9	68.8	130.1	157.5	131.6	104.2	172.5	223.9	65.5	24.5	60.8	29.1	1252.4
乐山市	Leshan	71.0	68.0	103.2	154.0	110.4	91.6	104.1	196.2	69.6	37.1	54.8	25.6	1085.6
南充市	Nanchong	75.9	64.3	124.3	181.0	132.6	153.0	210.9	283.6	73.1	41.8	37.2	24.3	1402.0
眉山市	Meishan	42.0	67.5	110.7	150.4	115.5	87.6	104.4	187.3	66.5	39.5	36.7	15.0	1023.1
宜宾市	Yibin	61.9	67.8	116.9	174.3	126.3	92.9	119.0	209.4	49.9	23.4	46.5	15.8	1104.1
广安市	Guangan	68.0	51.5	114.3	178.3	120.3	142.1	208.7	271.3	68.1	45.0	49.0	22.6	1339.2
达州市	Dazhou	69.4	33.0	121.0	166.5	77.4	124.5	174.6	272.6	77.9	53.9	37.1	2.6	1210.5
雅安市	Yaan	39.9	60.6	92.2	133.1	91.1	83.2	115.4	193.5	59.7	37.2	48.3	23.5	977.7
巴中市	Bazhong	96.5	82.5	174.8	195.2	154.1	160.7	195.2	303.0	100.6	120.0	53.8	15.8	1652.2
资阳市	Ziyang	106.3	111.7	164.1	184.1	167.0	116.2	157.4	261.8	90.7	59.3	85.2	45.9	1549.7
马尔康市	Maerkang	200.8	144.2	163.8	186.4	162.9	123.4	122.9	191.2	142.1	117.9	175.0	199.6	1930.2
康定市	Kangding	170.8	114.4	165.9	175.2	153.0	104.8	89.0	164.5	98.1	119.9	139.5	149.8	1644.9
西昌市	Xichang	202.9	199.3	262.8	254.5	207.7	129.3	139.2	210.6	107.1	168.6	259.0	256.1	2397.1

7-5 林业发展基本情况
Basic Conditions of Development of Forestry

指标		Item		2018
森林资源覆盖率	**(%)**	**Forest Coverage Rate**	**(%)**	**38.83**
森林面积	(万公顷)	Forest Area	(10 000 hectares)	1887.11
活立木总蓄积量	(亿立方米)	Total Standing Forest Stock	(100 million cu.m)	19.95
#森林蓄积量	(亿立方米)	Stock Volume of Forest	(100 million cu.m)	18.79
林业生产情况		**Basic Situation of Forestry Production**		
人工造林面积	(万公顷)	Manual Planting	(10 000 hectares)	25.80
年末实有封山育林面积	(万公顷)	Area of Mountain Sealed for Forest Breeding(year-end)	(10 000 hectares)	78.83
#本年新封	(万公顷)	Newly Sealed for Forest Breeding in the Year	(10 000 hectares)	7.07
育苗面积	(万公顷)	Area of Breeding	(10 000 hectares)	4.18
林产品产量		**Output of Forest Products**		
木材产量	(万立方米)	Timber	(10 000 cu.m)	230.70
竹材产量	(万根)	Bamboo	(10 000 sticks)	17750
锯材产量	(万立方米)	Sawed Lumber	(10 000 cu.m)	170.16
人造板产量	(万立方米)	Man-made Board	(10 000 cu.m)	565.32
松香类产品产量	(吨)	Rosin Products	(ton)	125
油桐籽产量	(吨)	Tung-oil Seeds	(ton)	5238
油茶籽产量	(吨)	Tea-oil Seeds	(ton)	23119
竹笋干产量	(吨)	Dried Bamboo Shoot	(ton)	72900
核桃产量	(吨)	Walnuts	(ton)	573685
木本药材产量	(吨)	Wood Medicinal Materials	(ton)	269696
花椒产量	(吨)	Chinese Red Pepper	(ton)	104230
食用菌产量	(吨)	Edible Fungus	(ton)	90188
山野菜产量	(吨)	Mountain Potherb	(ton)	12604
板栗产量	(吨)	Chinese Chestnut	(ton)	52385
国有森工企业苗圃林场情况		**State-owned Forestry Enterprises, Nurserys and Centres**		
国有森工企业汇编数	(个)	Number of State-owned Forestry Enterprises	(unit)	96
苗圃个数	(个)	Number of Forestry Nurserys	(unit)	52
#纳入国家天然林保护工程的苗圃	(个)	Forestry Nurserys In National Preserve of Natural Forest	(unit)	52
苗圃经营面积	(公顷)	Working Area of Forestry Nurserys	(hectare)	641
林场个数	(个)	Number of Forestry Centres	(unit)	159
#纳入国家天然林保护工程的林场	(个)	Forestry Centres In National Preserve of Natural Forest	(unit)	159
林场经营面积	(万公顷)	Working Area of Forestry Centres	(10 000 hectares)	286.57
林业系统就业人员和劳动报酬		**Employed Persons and Earnings in Forestry System**		
单位户数	(个)	Number of Units	(unit)	3024
#行政事业单位个数	(个)	Number of Administrative Institutions	(unit)	2851
在册职工人数	(万人)	Staff and Workers Listed	(10 000 persons)	5.41
#行政事业单位人数	(万人)	Number of Employees in Administrative Institutions	(10 000 persons)	2.73
在岗职工工资总额	(万元)	Total Wages of Fully Employed Staff and Workers	(10 000 yuan)	302052
在岗职工年平均工资	(元)	Average Wage of Fully Employed Staff and Workers	(yuan)	69799

注：本表数据由四川省林业和草原局提供。
a) Data in this table are provided by the bureau of Forestry and Grassland of Sichuan Province.

7-6 森林火灾情况
Forest Fires

年份 Year	森林火灾次数 (次) Forest Fires (time)	森林火警 Fire Alarm	一般火灾 Ordinary Fires	较大火灾 Major Fires	重大火灾 Severe Fires	特大火灾 Especially Severe Fires	火场总面积 (公顷) Total Area of Fires (hectare)	受害森林面积 (公顷) Destructed Forest Area (hectare)	火灾损失率 (‰) Rate of Loss (‰)
2000	125	114	11				850.0	67.0	0.01
2001	248	226	22				3209.0	385.0	0.03
2002	185	159	26				1567.0	340.0	0.03
2003	378	302	76				5919.2	826.8	0.07
2004	169	151	18				1330.2	176.5	0.02
2005	252	202	46		4		6818.1	2256.5	0.18
2006	511	463	48				3109.0	453.1	0.03
2007	458	414	44				2076.6	455.4	0.04
2008	233	202	31				4481.0	389.0	0.03
2009	310		247	56	7		5730.9	2577.2	0.02
2010	361		301	58	2		4594.7	1241.5	0.09
2011	309		245	64			3449.5	551.1	0.03
2012	486		394	92			3082.3	815.2	0.05
2013	447		370	77			2673.6	811.2	0.05
2014	442		365	77			4713.1	765.7	0.05
2015	220		183	37			1407.5	303.0	0.02
2016	263		230	33			1206.9	217.2	0.01
2017	171		152	18	1		1610.9	1014.9	0.07
2018	229		201	26	2		3589.5	1540.2	0.10

注：从2009年起，根据《森林火灾管理条例》规定，森林火灾分类为“一般森林火灾、较大森林火灾、重大森林火灾和特别重大森林火灾”，取消了原“森林火警”指标。

a) According to the "Forest Fire Regulations ",forest fires are classified as "ordinary forest fires, major forest fires, severe forest fires and especially severe fires," and the original "fire alarm" was ablished since 2009.

7-7 林业有害生物防治情况
Prevention of Forest Biological Disasters

年份 Year	发生面积 (万公顷) Area of Occurrence (10 000 hectares)	防治面积 (万公顷) Area of Prevention (10 000 hectares)	成灾面积 (公顷) Area Covered by Natural Disaster (hectare)	测报准确率 (%) Forecasting Accurate Rate (%)	无公害防治率 (%) Pollution Prevention and Control Rate (%)	种苗产地检疫率 (%) Seeding Origin Quarantine Rate (%)
2000	61.48	57.19	183	94.7	93.0	98.2
2001	62.64	58.58	199	95.2	93.5	98.3
2002	73.93	62.52	390	95.5	84.6	99.7
2003	70.93	66.87	362	95.5	94.3	98.3
2004	71.01	68.02	754	96.5	95.8	96.0
2005	69.45	57.81	1220	90.5	83.3	99.8
2006	76.17	65.62	3065	93.3	81.7	99.8
2007	79.87	58.34	9000	90.8	73.0	99.8
2008	72.81	58.89	287	94.4	68.1	99.8
2009	77.59	61.57	227	93.4	79.4	100.0
2010	71.55	57.33	340	90.7	80.1	100.0
2011	69.87	55.42	513	94.7	93.3	100.0
2012	72.76	62.47	1415	98.4	98.3	99.5
2013	76.60	52.87	728	100.0	98.5	99.9
2014	73.21	52.09	1512	98.6	89.9	96.0
2015	71.60	50.67	3867	97.7	98.5	99.4
2016	69.90	49.90	4001	97.6	97.5	100.0
2017	68.14	45.34	6067	95.5	96.0	100.0
2018	69.13	56.20	4920	98.3	97.8	100.0

注：根据国家林业局规定，从2011年起，将“森林病虫害”改为“林业有害生物”、“监测率”改为“测报准确率”、“防治率”改为“无公害防治率”、“检疫率”改为“种苗产地检疫率”。

a) In accordance with the provisions of the State Forestry Administration, since 2011,change indicator" forest insect and disease " to "forestry pest control", change indicator "monitoring rate" to "forecast accuracy", change the "prevention rate" to "pollution prevention and control rate",change the"quarantine rate" to "seeding origin quarantine rate".

7-8 主要矿产基础储量
Ensured Reserves of Major Minerals

项目		Item		2018
煤炭	(亿吨)	Coal	(100 million tons)	51.65
铁矿	(矿石，亿吨)	Iron	(Ore, 100 million tons)	23.82
锰矿	(矿石，万吨)	Manganese	(Ore, 10 000 tons)	206.24
钛矿	(钛铁矿TiO2，万吨)	Titanium	(Ilmenite, 10 000 tons)	18821.95
钒矿	(V2O5，万吨)	Vanadium	(V2O5, 10 000 tons)	521.83
铜矿	(铜，万吨)	Copper	(Metal, 10 000 tons)	61.03
铅矿	(铅，万吨)	Lead	(Metal, 10 000 tons)	95.70
锌矿	(锌，万吨)	Zinc	(Metal, 10 000 tons)	216.76
镁矿(炼镁白云岩)	(矿石，万吨)	Magnesium(Magnesium-smelting Dolomit	(Dolomite Ore, 10 000 tons)	1781.20
金矿	(金，吨)	Gold	(Metal, ton)	132.65
银矿	(银，吨)	Silver	(Metal, ton)	737.62
锂矿	(Li2O，万吨)	Lithium	(Li2O, 10 000 tons)	36.14
石墨	(晶质石墨，万吨)	Graphite Mineral (Crystal)	(Mineral, 10 000 tons)	274.40
硫铁矿	(矿石，万吨)	Pyrite Ore	(Ore, 10 000 tons)	39876.81
石棉	(石棉，万吨)	Asbestos	(Asbestos, 10 000 tons)	1192.36
石榴子石	(矿石，万吨)	Garnet	(Ore, 10 000 tons)	550.50
芒硝	(矿石，万吨)	Mirabilite	(Ore, 10 000 tons)	758961.19
石膏	(矿石，万吨)	Gypsum	(Ore, 10 000 tons)	9640.21
菱镁矿	(矿石，万吨)	Magnesite Ore	(Ore, 10 000 tons)	186.49
熔剂用灰岩	(矿石，亿吨)	Grey Rock Used as Flux	(Ore, 100 million tons)	2.07
水泥用灰岩	(矿石，万吨)	Grey Rock Used as Cement	(Ore, 10 000 tons)	325898.29
冶金用白云岩	(矿石，亿吨)	Dolomite Ore for Metallurgy Use	(Ore, 100 million tons)	0.51
冶金用石英岩	(矿石，万吨)	Quartzite for Metallurgy Use	(Ore, 10 000 tons)	1166.45
玻璃用砂岩	(矿石，万吨)	Sandstone Used as Glass	(Ore, 10 000 tons)	2531.09
水泥配料用砂岩	(矿石，万吨)	Sandstone Used as Cement Burden	(Ore, 10 000 tons)	7306.00
砖瓦用砂岩	(矿石，万立方米)	Sandstone Used as Brick	(Ore, 10 000 cu.m)	153.16
铸型用砂岩	(矿石，万吨)	Sandstone Used as Casting Mould	(Ore, 10 000 tons)	36.00
玻璃用脉石英	(矿石，万吨)	Quartzite Gangue Used as Glass	(Ore, 10 000 tons)	883.21
硅藻土	(矿石，万吨)	Diatomaceous Earth	(Ore, 10 000 tons)	387.10
高岭土	(矿石，万吨)	Kaolin Ore	(Ore, 10 000 tons)	112.15
耐火粘土	(矿石，万吨)	Refractory Clay	(Ore, 10 000 tons)	1294.09
水泥配料用粘土	(矿石，万吨)	Clay Used as Casting Mould	(Ore, 10 000 tons)	3747.29
水泥配料用泥岩	(矿石，万吨)	Mudstone Used as Casting Mould	(Ore, 10 000 tons)	2360.00
化肥用蛇纹岩	(矿石，万吨)	Serpentine Used as Chemistry Fertilizer	(Ore, 10 000 tons)	3940.90
饰面用花岗岩	(矿石，万立方米)	Granite Used for Decorations	(Ore, 10 000 cu.m)	4071.65
霞石正长岩	(矿石，万吨)	Nepheline Syenite	(Ore, 10 000 tons)	27.70
饰面用大理岩	(矿石，万立方米)	Marble Used for Decorations	(Ore, 10 000 cu.m)	3290.67
盐矿	(矿石，万吨)	Sodium Salt NaCl	(Ore, 10 000 tons)	216808.64
磷矿	(矿石，万吨)	Phosphorus Ore	(Ore, 10 000 tons)	56927.76

注：主要矿产基础储量由四川省自然资源厅提供。

a) Data of ensured reserves of major minerals are provided by the Sichuan Provincial Department of Land and Resources.

7-9 “三废”排放及处理利用情况
Discharge,Treatment and Utilization of Waste Water, Waste Gas and Solid Wastes by Industry

单位：万吨 (10 000 tons)

指　　标	Item	2015	2016	2017
废水排放总量	Total Wastewater Discharged	341607.41	352826.44	362437.56
工业废水排放量	Industrial Wastewater Discharged	71647.44	50788.61	43157.17
城镇生活污水排放量	Urban Living Wastewater Discharged	269725.36	301732.93	318957.80
集中式治理设施污水排放量	Centralized Management Facilities of Sewage Discharged	234.62	304.89	322.59
化学需氧量(COD)排放量	Total Emission of Chemical Oxygen Demand(COD)	118.64	67.68	67.51
工业废水中COD排放量	COD Emissions from Industrial Wastewater	10.15	4.99	3.44
农业COD排放量	Agricultural COD Emissions	49.30	0.21	0.60
城镇生活污水中COD排放量	COD Emissions in Urban Sewage	58.83	62.24	63.23
集中式治理设施COD排放量	COD Emissions from Centralized Management Facilities	0.37	0.25	0.24
氨氮排放量	Ammonia Nitrogen Emissions	13.14	8.01	7.94
工业废水中氨氮排放量	Ammonia Nitrogen Emissions from Industrial Wastewater	0.53	0.32	0.26
农业氨氮排放量	Agricultural Ammonia Nitrogen Emissions	5.23	0.01	0.02
生活污水中氨氮排放量	Ammonia Nitrogen Emissions from Domestic Sewage	7.35	7.66	7.63
集中式治理设施氨氮排放量	Ammonia Nitrogen Emissions from Centralized Management Facilities	0.04	0.02	0.03
二氧化硫(SO_2)排放量	Sulphur Dioxide (SO_2) Emissions	71.76	48.72	38.91
工业SO_2排放量	Industrial SO_2 Emissions	62.24	37.18	28.05
城镇生活SO_2排放量	Urban Living SO_2 Emissions	9.50	11.52	10.85
集中式治理设施SO_2排放量	SO_2 Emissions from Centralized Management Facilities	0.02	0.02	0.01
氮氧化物排放量	Nitrogen Oxide Emissions	52.59	45.10	45.76
工业氮氧化物排放量	Industrial Nitrogen Oxide Emissions	32.83	24.65	21.00
城镇生活氮氧化物排放量	Nitrogen Oxide Emissions in Urban Life	1.62	1.53	1.61
机动车氮氧化物排放量	Motor Vehicle Emissions of Nitrogen Oxides	18.11	18.87	23.12
集中式治理设施氮氧化物排放量	Nitrogen Oxide Emissions from Centralized Management Facilities	0.02	0.04	0.03
烟(粉)尘排放量	Smoke and Dust Emissions	41.32	27.27	22.40
工业烟(粉)尘排放量	Industrial Smoke and Dust Emissions	37.56	22.00	17.75
城镇生活烟尘排放量	Urban Living Smoke and Dust Emissions	2.24	3.80	2.66
机动车烟尘排放量	Motor Vehicle Emissions of Smoke and Dust	1.46	1.46	1.99
集中式治理设施烟尘排放量	Smoke and Dust Emissions from Centralized Management Facilities	0.01	0.01	0.00
一般工业固体废物产生量	Common Industrial Solid Wastes Generation	12315.73	11764.56	13756.41
一般工业固体废物综合利用量	Common Industrial Solid Wastes Comprehensively Utilized	5507.36	4612.10	5465.87
#综合利用往年贮存量	Previous Storage	111.02	226.05	186.44
一般工业固体废物综合利用率（%）	Ratio of Common Industrial Solid Wastes Comprehensively Utilized	44.32	38.46	39.20
一般工业固体废物处置量	Common Industrial Solid Wastes Disposed	4176.72	3838.10	3006.91
#处置往年贮存量	Previous Storage	2.74	44.11	1166.94
一般工业固体废物处置率（%）	Ratio of Common Industrial Solid Wastes Disposed (%)	33.91	32.50	20.15
一般工业固体废物贮存量	Ratio of Common Industrial Solid Wastes Previous Storage	2744.96	3584.47	6634.33
一般工业固体废物倾倒丢弃量	Ratio of Common Industrial Solid Wastes Dumping Discard	0.44	550.85	26751.27
危险废物产生量	Hazardous Wastes Generation	111.94	247.48	341.19
危险废物综合利用量	Hazzardous Wastes Comprehensively Utilized	59.08	148.11	176.91
#综合利用往年贮存量	Previous Storage	0.12	0.27	3.84
危险废物综合利用率（%）	Ratio of Hazzardous Wastes Comprehensively Utilized (%)	52.72	59.78	44.17
危险废物处置量	Hazzardous Wastes Disposed	51.75	81.09	152.28
#处置往年贮存量	Previous Storage Disposed	0.58	4.03	3.59
危险废物处置率（%）	Ratio of Hazzardous Wastes Disposed (%)	45.99	32.24	0.00
危险废物贮存量	Hazzardous Wastes Storage	1.81	22.59	19.44
危险废物倾倒丢弃量	Hazzardous Wastes Dumping Discard	0.00	0.00	0.00

7-10 环境污染治理投资情况
Investment in Treatment of Environmental Pollution

单位：亿元 (100 million yuan)

指　标	Item	2015	2016	2017
环境污染治理投资总额	Total Investment in the Treatment of Environmental Pollution	367.14	470.41	492.42
城市环境基础设施投资	Investment in Urban Environmental Infrastructure	133.39	210.85	220.35
#燃气	Gas Supply	15.50	11.04	11.40
集中供热	Centralized Heating	0.28	0.84	0.01
排水	Drainage Works	38.07	61.84	73.05
园林绿化	Gardening and Greening	69.54	125.40	111.95
市容环境卫生	Environmental Sanitation	10.02	11.73	23.94
工业污染源治理投资	Investment in the Treatment of Industrial Pollution	11.83	11.60	11.60
#治理废水	Waste Water Treatment	5.51	3.05	2.11
治理废气	Waste Gas Treatment	4.69	6.27	8.80
治理固体废物	Solid Wastes Treatment	0.02	0.69	0.49
治理噪声	Noise Treatment	1.01	0.01	0.06
治理其他	Others Treatment	0.60	1.59	1.24
完成环保验收项目环保投资	Environmental Investment Projects in the Completion of Environmental Acceptance	221.92	247.95	260.47
环境污染治理投资占GDP比重（%）	Total Investment in the Treatment of Environmental Pollution as Percent of GDP (%)	1.22	1.43	1.50
工业废气治理设施运行费用	Operating Costs in the Treatment Facilities of Industrial Waste Gas	45.36	66.37	51.38
工业废水治理设施运行费用	Operating Costs in the Treatment Facilities of Industrial Waste Water	21.17	20.61	32.94
排污费收入总额	Total Revenue of Sewage Charges	6.06	6.27	7.53

注：“三废”及环境污染治理资料由四川省生态环境厅提供。

a) The data of waste water, waste gas and solid wastes by industry are provided by the Sichuan Provincial Department of Environmental Protection.

主要统计指标解释

平均气温　气温指空气的温度，我国一般以摄氏度(℃)为单位表示。气象观测的温度表是放在离地面约1.5米处通风良好的百叶箱里测量的，因此，通常说的气温指的是离地面1.5米处百叶箱中的温度。计算方法：月平均气温是将全月各日的平均气温相加，除以该月的天数而得；年平均气温是将12个月的月平均气温累加后除以12而得。

平均相对湿度　指空气中实际水气压与当时气温下的饱和水气压之比。其统计方法与气温相同。

降水量　指从天空降落到地面的液态或固态(经融化后)水，未经蒸发、渗透、流失而在地面上积聚的深度。计算方法：月降水量是将全月各日的降水量累加而得；年降水量是将12个月的月降水量累加而得。

日照时数　指太阳实际照射地面的时数，通常以小时为单位表示。其统计方法与降水量相同。

森林面积　包括郁闭度0.2以上的乔木林地面积和竹林面积，国家特别规定的灌木林地面积，农田林网以及村旁、路旁、水旁、宅旁林木的覆盖面积。

森林覆盖率　以行政区域为单位的森林面积占区域土地总面积的百分比。计算公式：

$$森林覆盖率=\frac{森林面积}{土地总面积}\times 100\%$$

活立木总蓄积量　指一定范围土地上全部树木蓄积的总量，包括森林蓄积、疏林蓄积、散生木蓄积和四旁树蓄积。

森林蓄积量　指一定森林面积上存在着的林木树干部分的总材积。

人工造林　指在宜林荒山荒地、宜林沙荒地、无立木林地、疏林地和退耕地等其他宜林地上通过播种、植苗和分植来提高森林植被覆被率的技术措施。

矿产资源　指由地质作用形成的，具有利用价值的，呈固态、液态、气态的自然资源，是社会生产发展的重要物质基础。目前我国已发现矿种有170多种，按其特点和用途，可分为能源矿产(如煤炭、石油、天然气、地热)、金属矿产(如铁矿、锰矿、铜矿、铅矿、铝土矿)、非金属矿产(如金刚石、石灰岩、粘土)和水气矿产(如地下水、矿泉水、二氧化碳气)四大类。

矿产基础储量　基础储量是查明矿产资源的一部分。它能满足现行采矿和生产所需的指标要求，是控制的、探明的并通过可行性或预可行性研究认为属于经济的、边界经济的部分，用未扣除设计、采矿损失的数量表示。

一般工业固体废物产生量　指未被列入《国家危险废物名录》或者根据国家规定的危险废物鉴别标准（GB5085）、固体废物浸出毒性浸出方法（GB5086）及固体废物浸出毒性测定方法（GB／T 15555）鉴别方法判定不具有危险特性的工业固体废物。计算公式是：

一般工业固体废物产生量=（一般工业固体废物综合利用量－其中：综合利用往年贮存量）+一般工业固体废物贮存量+（一般工业固体废物处置量－其中：处置往年贮存量）+一般工业固体废物倾倒丢弃量

一般工业固体废物综合利用量　指报告期内企业通过回收、加工、循环、交换等方式，从固体废物中提取或者使其转化为可以利用的资源、能源和其他原材料的固体废物量（包括当年利用的往年工业固体废物累计贮存量）。如用作农业肥料、生产建筑材料、筑路等。综合利用量由原产生固体废物的单位统计。

一般工业固体废物处置量　指报告期内企业将工业固体废物焚烧和用其他改变工业固体废物的物理、化学、生物特性的方法，达到减少或者消除其危险成分的活动，或者将工业固体废物最终置于符合环境保护规定要求的填埋场的活动中，所消纳固体废物的量。

一般工业固体废物贮存量　指报告期内企业以综合利用或处置为目的，将固体废物暂时贮存或堆存在专设的贮存设施或专设的集中堆存场所内的量。专设的固体废物贮存场所或贮存设施必须有防扩散、防流失、防渗漏、防止污染大气、水体的措施。

一般工业固体废物倾倒丢弃量　指报告期内企业将所产生的固体废物倾倒或者丢弃到固体废物污染防治设施、场所以外的量。

危险废物产生量　指当年全年调查对象实际产生的危险废物的量。危险废物指列入国家危险废物名录或者根据国家规定的危险废物鉴别标准和鉴别方法认定的，具有爆炸性、易燃性、易氧化性、毒性、腐蚀性、易传染性疾病等危险特性之一的废物。按《国家危险废物名录》（环境保护部、国家发展和改革委员会2008部令第1号）填报。

危险废物综合利用量　指当年全年调查对象从危险废物中提取物质作为原材料或者燃料的活动中消纳危险废物的量。包括本单位利用或委托、提供给外单位利用的量。

危险废物处置量　指报告期内企业将危险废物焚烧和用其他改变工业固体废物的物理、化学、生物特性的方法，达到减少或者消除其危险成分的活动，或者将危险废物最终置于符合环境保护规定要求的填埋场的活动中，所消纳危险废物的量。处置量包括处置本单位或委托给外单位处置的量。

危险废物贮存量　指将危险废物以一定包装方式暂时存放在专设的贮存设施内的量。专设的贮存设施指对危险废物的包装、选址、设计、安全防护、监测和关闭等符合《危险废物贮存污染控制标准》（GB18597-2001）等相关环保法律法规要求，具有防扩散、防流失、防渗漏、防止污染大气和水体措施的设施。

Explanatory Notes on Main Statistical Indicators

Average Temperature refers to the air temperature. China uses centigrade as the unit. The thermometry used for weather observation is put in a breezy shutter, which is 1.5 meters high from the ground. Therefore, the commonly used temperature refers to the temperature in the breezy shutter 1.5 meters away from the ground. The calculation method is as follows:

Monthly average temperature is the summation of average daily temperature of one month divided by the actual days of that particular month.

Annual average temperature is the summation of monthly average of a year divided by 12 months.

Average relative humidity refers to the ratio of actual water vapour pressure to the saturation water vapour pressure under the current temperature. The calculation method is the same as that of temperature.

Volume of Precipitation refers to the deepness of liquid state or solid state (thawed) water falling from the sky to the ground that has not been evaporated, infiltrated or run off. The calculation method is as follows:

Monthly precipitation is the summation of daily precipitation of a month.

Annual precipitation is the summation of 12 months precipitation of a year.

Sunshine Hours refer to the actual hours of sun irradiating the earth, usually expressed in hours. The calculation method is the same as that of the precipitation.

Forest Area refers to the area of trees and bamboo grow with canopy density above 0.2, the area of shrubby tree according to regulations of the government, the area of forest land inside farm land and the area of trees planted by the side of villages, farm houses and along roads and rivers.

Forest Coverage Rate Taking the administrative jurisdiction as the unit, the percentage of area of afforested land to the area of total land. The formula for calculating forest coverage rate is as follows:

$$\text{Forestry coverage rate} = \frac{\text{Area of Afforested Land}}{\text{Area of Total Land}} \times 100\%$$

Total Standing Stock Volume refers to the total stock volume of trees growing in land, including trees in forest, trees in sparse forest, scattered trees and trees planted by the side of villages, farm houses and along roads and rivers.

Stock Volume of Forest refers to total stock volume of wood growing in forest area, which shows the total size and level of forest resources of a country or a region.

Manual Planting refers to technical measures of sowing, planting seedlings and divided transplanting on land suitable for afforestation, including barren hills, idle land, sand dunes, non-timber forest land, woodland and "grain for green" land to increase vegetation coverage rate of forests.

Mineral Resources refer to useful minerals, with solid state, liquid state, gaseity, due to the geological process. Minerals are important natural resources, and important material base for social development. At present, there are more than 170 types of minerals discovered in China. They can be categorized into four groups: energy producing minerals (including coal, petroleum, natural gas and terrestrial heat), metallic minerals (including iron, manganese, copper, lead and bauxite), non metallic minerals (including diamond, limestone and clay), and water/gas related minerals (including ground water, mineral water and carbon dioxide). Metallic minerals can be further classified as ferrous, non-ferrous, noble metal, rare metal, rare earth metal and dispersed metals.

Ensured Mineral Reserves refer to the actual mineral reserves, which equal to the proven mineral reserves (including industrial reserves and prospective reserves) minus extracted parts and underground losses.

Common Industrial Solid Wastes Produced refers to the industrial solid wastes that are not listed in the 《National Catalogue of Hazardous Wastes》, or not regarded as hazardous according to the national hazardous waste identification standards (GB5085), solid waste-Extraction procedure for leaching toxicity (GB5086) and solid waste-Extraction procedure for leaching toxicity (GB/T 15555). The calculation formula is as followed:

Common Industrial Solid Wastes Produced = (common industrial solid wastes utilized – the proportion of utilized stock of previous years) + common industrial solid waste stock + (common industrial solid wastes disposed – the proportion of disposed stock of previous years) + common industrial solid wastes discharged.

Common Industrial Solid Wastes Comprehensively Utilized refers to volume of solid wastes from which useful materials can be extracted or which can be converted into usable resources, energy or other materials by means of reclamation, processing, recycling and exchange (including utilizing in the year the stocks of industrial solid wastes of the previous year) during the report period, e.g. being used as agricultural fertilizers, building materials or as material for paving road. Examples of such utilizations include fertilizers, building materials and road materials. The information shall be collected by the producing units of the wastes.

Common Industrial Solid Wastes Disposed refers to the quantity of industrial solid wastes which are burnt or specially disposed using other methods to alter the physical, chemical and biological properties and thus to reduce or eliminate the hazard, or placed ultimately in the sites meeting the requirements for environmental protection during the report period.

Stock of Common Industrial Solid Wastes refers to the volume of solid wastes placed in special facilities or special sites by enterprises for purposes of utilization or disposal during the report period. The sites or facilities should take measures against dispersion, loss, seepage, and air and water contamination.

Common Industrial Solid Wastes Discharged refers to the volume of industrial solid wastes dumped or discharged by producing enterprises to disposal facilities or to other sites.

Hazardous Wastes Produced refers to the volume of actual hazardous wastes produced by surveyed samples throughout the year of the survey. Hazardous waste refers to those included in the national hazardous wastes catalogue or specified as any one of the following properties in light of the national hazardous wastes identification standards and methods: explosive, ignitable, oxidizable, toxic, corrosive or liable to cause infectious diseases or lead to other dangers. The report of this indicator should follow the 《National Catalogue of Hazardous Wastes》 (the NO.1 Ministry Order in 2008 by the Ministry of Environment Protection and National Development and Reform Commission).

Hazardous Wastes Utilized refers to the volume of hazardous wastes that are used to extract materials for raw materials or fuel throughout the year of the survey, including those utilized by the producing enterprise and those provided to other enterprises for utilization.

Hazardous Wastes Disposed refers to the quantity of hazardous wastes which are burnt or specially disposed using other methods to alter the physical, chemical and biological properties and thus to reduce or eliminate the hazard, or placed ultimately in the sites meeting the requirements for environmental protection during the report period.

Stock of Hazardous Wastes refers to the volume of hazardous wastes specially packaged and placed in special facilities or special sites by enterprises. The special stock facilities should meet the requirements set in relevant environment protection laws and regulations such as “Pollution Control Standards for Hazardous Waste Stock” (GB18597-2001) in regard to package of hazardous waste, location, design, safety, monitoring and shutdown, and take measures against dispersion, loss, seepage, and air and water contamination.

8 财政和物价

Chapter 8 Local Government Finance and Price

8-1 地方一般公共预算收入
Local General Public Budget Revenue

单位：万元 (10 000 yuan)

项目	Item	2015	2016	2017	2018
地方一般公共预算收入合计	**Local General Public Budget Revenue**	**33554385**	**33888519**	**35797793**	**39110092**
税收收入	**Taxes Revenue**	**23535088**	**23292344**	**24299972**	**28197650**
增值税	Value-added Tax	3244786	6383018	9988544	11209546
营业税	Business Tax	7802595	4362999	113276	55405
企业所得税	Corporate Income Tax	2953063	2994825	3590916	4157932
个人所得税	Individual Income Tax	1091428	1283981	1527409	1785881
资源税	Resource Tax	287228	261768	304129	525197
城市维护建设税	Urban Maintenance and Construction Tax	1262973	1375497	1505892	1749815
房产税	Real Estate Tax	739070	797929	886487	1067767
印花税	Stamp Tax	300344	321446	382495	464113
城镇土地使用税	Urban Land Using Tax	646449	650964	720469	816622
土地增值税	Value-added Tax on Land	1491408	1439791	1721947	2155195
车船税	Travel Tax	266255	298196	328748	382152
耕地占用税	Tax on the Occupancy of Cultivated Land	1219599	1183578	1051173	891121
契税	Tax on Contracts	2130954	1841402	2099460	2809876
烟叶税	Tobacco Tax	98724	96950	79027	78483
环境保护税	Environmental Protection Tax				48545
非税收入	**Non-Tax Revenue**	**10019297**	**10596175**	**11497821**	**10912442**
专项收入	Special Revenve	3044453	2099006	2196079	2551749
行政事业性收费收入	Income from Administrative Fees	1846871	2079823	2095670	1716961
罚没收入	Penalty and Confiscatory Income	655072	697643	790002	843950
国有资本经营收入	State-owned Capital Operating Income	449481	423725	388800	279041
国有资源(资产)有偿使用收入	Income from State-owned Assets Compensation	2696295	3622247	4228482	3994898
捐赠收入	Donation income				133357
政府住房基金收入	Government Housing Fund Income				303496
其他收入	Other Incomes	1327125	1673731	1254942	1088990

注：地方一般公共预算收入和支出情况由四川省财政厅提供。
a) Local general public budget revenue and expenditure are provided by Sichuan Provincial Department of Finance.

8-2 一般公共预算支出
Local General Public Budget Expenditure

单位：万元 (10 000 yuan)

项　目	Item	2015	2016	2017	2018
一般公共预算支出合计	**General Public Budget Expenditure**	**74975105**	**80088868**	**86861018**	**97075048**
一般公共服务支出	Expenditure for General Public Services	6222242	6827794	8160114	8970009
外交支出	Expenditure for Diplomatic			184	599
国防支出	Expenditure for National Defense	119020	168543	115127	135419
公共安全支出	Expenditure for Public Security	3697422	4293870	4764972	5283495
教育支出	Expenditure for Education	12523250	13018472	14139530	14617756
科学技术支出	Expenditure for Science and Technology	966892	1010930	1064987	1479056
文化体育与传媒支出	Expenditure for Culture, Sport and Media	1394140	1452012	1394175	1549093
社会保障和就业支出	Expenditure for Social Safety Net and Employment Effort	11117513	13201666	15286120	16441671
医疗卫生与计划生育支出	Expenditure for Health Care and Family Planning	6864163	7722403	8632721	8808866
节能环保支出	Expenditure for Environment Protection	1693145	1663561	1963525	2269045
城乡社区支出	Expenditure for Urban and Rural Community Affairs	5140783	5509253	7548491	6988681
农林水支出	Expenditure for Agriculture, Forestry and Water Conservancy	9266496	9887068	9483708	13108851
交通运输支出	Expenditure for Transportation	6011405	5691063	5017005	6239747
资源勘探信息等支出	Expenditure for Exploration and Information	2515165	2638000	3176690	2985761
商业服务业等支出	Expenditure for Commerce and Services	825191	734124	774912	775020
金融支出	Expenditure for Finance	173952	217889	135844	235768
援助其他地区支出	Expenditure for other regional assistance	53319	54886	50558	61714
国土海洋气象等支出	Expenditure for Land, Maritime Meteorology	778679	676506	789178	1083321
住房保障支出	Expenditure for Housing Security	2889038	3122815	2963589	3507164
粮油物资储备支出	Expenditure for Management of Grain & Oil Reserves	359485	334266	311802	339603
债务付息支出	Expenditure for the Principal and Interest of Debts	175131	614736	941223	1491656
债务发行费用支出	Expenditure for Debt Issuance Expenses	10690	15465	11180	12259
其他支出	Other Expenditures	2177984	1233546	135383	690494

8-3 各市(州)地方一般公共预算收入
Local General Public Budget Revenue by Region

单位：万元 (10 000 yuan)

市(州)	Region	2010	2011	2012	2013	2014	2015	2016	2017	2018
成都市	Chengdu	5269408	6806929	7808952	8985395	10251696	11576393	11754109	12755334	14241550
自贡市	Zigong	218360	291382	329898	383331	424059	448256	487574	532240	604091
攀枝花市	Panzhihua	387841	494777	571980	585450	629076	533412	567573	605930	615026
泸州市	Luzhou	475888	654047	827882	1096014	1159216	1282652	1386632	1460444	1500905
德阳市	Deyang	457976	670907	755322	804682	835153	886148	1000653	1061672	1175813
绵阳市	Mianyang	452057	656462	804009	904782	1017482	1041308	1076241	1105883	1245419
广元市	Guangyuan	167267	227658	268374	304621	347836	408176	405661	439915	476907
遂宁市	Suining	177685	240145	284546	335604	396957	493162	545580	601803	638447
内江市	Neijiang	203856	253066	309262	377491	450832	502682	536799	560961	616958
乐山市	Leshan	457695	602039	704039	751097	787878	855322	931001	992170	1099199
南充市	Nanchong	322564	432862	528700	655666	765568	850746	943388	1032555	1138963
眉山市	Meishan	246863	340541	488088	636067	751991	831491	903008	931612	1031974
宜宾市	Yibin	556465	672298	829693	1016000	1056118	1149677	1256843	1388196	1608883
广安市	Guangan	212785	277767	328017	386177	459637	567494	642179	712493	800524
达州市	Dazhou	305924	411543	520360	603088	724120	791548	846636	907078	1010246
雅安市	Yaan	156522	216521	302166	229386	273788	303082	321792	348370	400289
巴中市	Bazhong	78160	127430	200592	273501	330371	390502	442945	455280	454580
资阳市	Ziyang	244679	324738	407333	484418	554619	617733	468360	497670	528490
阿坝藏族羌族自治州	Aba	166682	210108	258231	244616	285820	316730	325955	268146	246610
甘孜藏族自治州	Ganzi	163047	202452	215666	221242	275480	314299	322592	273660	300342
凉山彝族自治州	Liangshan	626923	800437	1000571	1100148	1123019	1070683	1210336	1345528	1462031

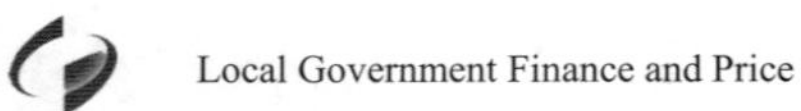

8-4 各市(州)一般公共预算支出
Local General Public Budget Revenue by Region

单位: 万元 (10 000 yuan)

市(州)	Region	2010	2011	2012	2013	2014	2015	2016	2017	2018
成都市	Chengdu	7773767	8578696	9838477	11617542	13400433	14684242	15958949	17566621	18374238
自贡市	Zigong	811614	1060433	1288014	1399376	1473005	1733530	1795524	2229037	2422700
攀枝花市	Panzhihua	750647	923018	1081729	1150583	1211774	1126499	1220322	1370352	1379392
泸州市	Luzhou	1265380	1707430	2123111	2501142	2813002	3039880	3371677	3689580	4121544
德阳市	Deyang	2244206	1532332	1666553	1899686	1970901	2196393	2271346	2401735	2719508
绵阳市	Mianyang	3453220	2135756	2505571	2906401	2946402	3042238	3350412	3650634	4081641
广元市	Guangyuan	2213188	1374163	1576394	1772708	1923836	2096211	2305016	2507023	2770144
遂宁市	Suining	888467	1100024	1333162	1441078	1560932	1828440	1999945	2305561	2522120
内江市	Neijiang	924757	1220287	1420276	1589311	1766023	1924370	2002280	2175120	2433876
乐山市	Leshan	1185123	1441546	1687162	1936946	2154123	2321550	2570351	2820171	3028632
南充市	Nanchong	1856129	2344224	2787446	3097030	3446815	3696431	4271765	4603999	4952197
眉山市	Meishan	965266	1188867	1432902	1726618	1819615	2072222	2166908	2256815	2351578
宜宾市	Yibin	1433154	1793856	2190349	2554295	2775160	3078287	3387430	3705395	4160183
广安市	Guangan	975438	1258308	1486612	1625740	1872039	2226191	2443172	2660796	2890322
达州市	Dazhou	1502741	2001711	2403530	2559609	2878203	3243334	3590680	3891551	4186791
雅安市	Yaan	774922	810256	930050	2610709	3121494	2222395	1515500	1373913	1305375
巴中市	Bazhong	1030304	1367152	1675668	1912681	2050667	2460191	2678727	2813892	3138866
资阳市	Ziyang	1011007	1300249	1540424	1648956	1886782	2160816	1883649	1803147	1917986
阿坝藏族羌族自治州	Aba	2038280	1383517	1521951	1757926	1923022	2152522	2210559	2416638	2950767
甘孜藏族自治州	Ganzi	1319779	1692042	2202819	2753253	2888630	3162038	3004766	3433265	4205713
凉山彝族自治州	Liangshan	1906966	2501155	3004763	3330204	3658972	4176198	4591525	4798725	6817064

8-5 各市(州)地方一般公共预算主要收入项目(2018年)
Major Items of Local General Public Budget Revenue by Region(2018)

单位: 万元 (10 000 yuan)

市(州)	Region	地方一般公共预算收入 Local General Public Budget Revenue	税收收入 Tax Revenue	增值税 Value-added Tax	企业所得税 Corporate Income Tax	个人所得税 Indiviual Income Tax	资源税 Resouces Tax
成都市	Chengdu	14241550	10677969	3496782	1517341	755161	20362
自贡市	Zigong	604091	399852	128371	34976	14614	1709
攀枝花市	Panzhihua	615026	433544	212476	33399	19691	24638
泸州市	Luzhou	1500905	1005440	363428	148078	32038	10311
德阳市	Deyang	1175813	764851	308490	86616	43036	10775
绵阳市	Mianyang	1245419	786208	282223	73504	46022	8820
广元市	Guangyuan	476907	302684	108990	27100	13845	15369
遂宁市	Suining	638447	433303	129731	37829	17441	31155
内江市	Neijiang	616958	406054	135749	32490	16761	7354
乐山市	Leshan	1099199	667230	266104	80117	28661	19454
南充市	Nanchong	1138963	707680	196566	64832	24913	5188
眉山市	Meishan	1031974	632060	208169	60351	20020	4822
宜宾市	Yibin	1608883	1068795	383465	165457	32100	27852
广安市	Guangan	800524	481186	130613	49346	10859	5528
达州市	Dazhou	1010246	631378	226004	51309	28724	38854
雅安市	Yaan	400289	298154	147034	30266	11406	9004
巴中市	Bazhong	454580	265456	83321	21804	12507	3979
资阳市	Ziyang	528490	304900	71928	17247	11042	6672
阿坝藏族羌族自治州	Aba	246610	187078	107557	18274	15356	5423
甘孜藏族自治州	Ganzi	300342	207881	99394	14234	12543	11781
凉山彝族自治州	Liangshan	1462031	913257	446325	110393	27109	51000

8-5 续表 continued

单位: 万元 (10 000 yuan)

市(州)	Region	城市维护建设税 Urban Maintenance and Construction Tax	房产税 Housing Property Tax	土地增值税 Increment Tax on Land Value	耕地占用税 Tax on the Occupancy of Cultivated Land	契税 Tax On Contracts	其他各项税收收入 Other Revenue	非税收入 Non-tax Revenue
成都市	Chengdu	928493	458582	1272601	148183	1357352	723112	3563581
自贡市	Zigong	27984	9661	43794	27644	81357	29742	204239
攀枝花市	Panzhihua	37882	16598	7715	4699	24712	51734	181482
泸州市	Luzhou	79252	19967	76513	75326	133353	67174	495465
德阳市	Deyang	92948	25886	37799	16443	80420	62438	410962
绵阳市	Mianyang	62185	29356	55038	54884	101854	72322	459211
广元市	Guangyuan	21505	8948	16619	28113	39108	23087	174223
遂宁市	Suining	30929	7368	45753	30344	75897	26856	205144
内江市	Neijiang	27630	10596	42954	18252	84673	29595	210904
乐山市	Leshan	54203	17497	57703	21194	72039	50258	431969
南充市	Nanchong	44488	15007	100864	59358	151306	45158	431283
眉山市	Meishan	40394	11143	63579	34139	131526	57917	399914
宜宾市	Yibin	111075	18747	55747	87750	125644	60958	540088
广安市	Guangan	26147	5791	70746	68537	82671	30948	319338
达州市	Dazhou	41166	11191	67211	33294	92981	40644	378868
雅安市	Yaan	17819	5272	21276	13009	27707	15361	102135
巴中市	Bazhong	17643	4458	24283	38204	42220	17037	189124
资阳市	Ziyang	18178	6869	66787	43611	40729	21837	223590
阿坝藏族羌族自治州	Aba	8628	5086	2179	12298	4209	8068	59532
甘孜藏族自治州	Ganzi	9618	4675	4193	35731	8481	7231	92461
凉山彝族自治州	Liangshan	50855	18574	21841	40108	51637	95415	548774

8-6 各市(州)一般公共预算主要支出项目(2018年)
Major Items of General Public Budget Expenditure by Region(2018)

单位: 万元 (10 000 yuan)

市(州)	Region	一般公共预算支出 General Public Budget Expenditure	一般公共服务 General Public Services	国防 National Denfense	公共安全 Public Safe	教育 Education	科学技术 Science Technology	文化体育与传媒 Culture, Sports and Media
成都市	Chengdu	18374238	2020784	36833	1334531	2658194	730705	376326
自贡市	Zigong	2422700	218478	2660	140466	382716	35490	27357
攀枝花市	Panzhihua	1379392	145211	991	89694	253007	12494	19219
泸州市	Luzhou	4121544	352912	8076	212810	723746	30344	55345
德阳市	Deyang	2719508	280323	1527	178244	378021	21934	33591
绵阳市	Mianyang	4081641	448986	3631	240836	618810	255424	44073
广元市	Guangyuan	2770144	207891	2483	107134	396617	8832	48572
遂宁市	Suining	2522120	248709	2132	119886	424769	13268	27126
内江市	Neijiang	2433876	241188	2305	125192	421747	16793	32149
乐山市	Leshan	3028632	295682	2978	162984	434526	10085	87008
南充市	Nanchong	4952197	441769	5492	225923	844105	19568	72326
眉山市	Meishan	2351578	316892	2349	154898	366303	9408	33118
宜宾市	Yibin	4160183	353620	3816	198777	805934	18981	46704
广安市	Guangan	2890322	238754	27877	142780	593733	6946	33582
达州市	Dazhou	4186791	301345	3421	142250	742887	15413	56057
雅安市	Yaan	1305375	221555	1600	73247	196974	15330	10317
巴中市	Bazhong	3138866	251882	3565	104972	486547	4939	34062
资阳市	Ziyang	1917986	174890	-1544	101616	308590	20008	24465
阿坝藏族羌族自治州	Aba	2950767	330408	3254	149722	343672	12148	60417
甘孜藏族自治州	Ganzi	4205713	472540	1925	194198	449125	11074	82260
凉山彝族自治州	Liangshan	6817064	545605	6005	310787	1229961	17691	78963

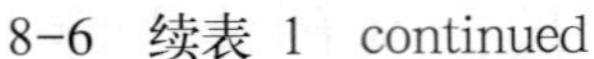

8-6 续表 1 continued

单位: 万元 (10 000 yuan)

市(州)	Region	社会保障和就业 Social Security and Employment	医疗卫生与计划生育 Health Care and Family Planning	节能环保 Energy Saving	城乡社区 Urban and Rural Community Affairs	农林水 Agriculture, Forestry and Water Affairs	交通运输 Transport	资源勘探信息等 Exploration and Information	商业服务业等 Commercial Services
成都市	Chengdu	1765819	1403813	368903	2875984	1126947	412065	1654097	276892
自贡市	Zigong	292799	282121	64875	193283	245873	193982	68002	8965
攀枝花市	Panzhihua	142385	112228	59314	92487	145863	46744	30495	6744
泸州市	Luzhou	492085	458895	130570	314330	598764	200131	123323	17298
德阳市	Deyang	401823	320459	136859	341268	263310	128192	61080	7015
绵阳市	Mianyang	524573	441036	60934	454243	503014	153141	72258	24413
广元市	Guangyuan	320193	289378	89042	83754	744754	196366	25602	24046
遂宁市	Suining	326891	291795	60159	208715	386408	91250	38528	11019
内江市	Neijiang	356196	318524	79688	123792	317124	112403	37147	10909
乐山市	Leshan	381324	337750	118453	212701	447057	188996	47232	37641
南充市	Nanchong	687517	619692	87124	154307	889876	228590	45043	21805
眉山市	Meishan	289784	289736	52562	167641	355431	77781	65572	8552
宜宾市	Yibin	479947	481501	169162	401752	629933	171760	102889	29880
广安市	Guangan	404542	365915	54117	92613	457388	96269	35648	15121
达州市	Dazhou	534108	518887	65657	93753	973240	191355	42190	19479
雅安市	Yaan	151022	167556	74184	189704	141108	9401	5392	1590
巴中市	Bazhong	336904	352807	74276	305121	613851	181477	15449	7245
资阳市	Ziyang	269384	242160	16373	312813	253587	44090	16413	8066
阿坝藏族羌族自治州	Aba	228603	231539	117306	84682	634092	303638	14404	134161
甘孜藏族自治州	Ganzi	286351	295968	92458	96587	964463	977535	14979	43237
凉山彝族自治州	Liangshan	516854	680991	134776	179807	2065896	430208	169266	39163

8-6 续表 2 continued

单位: 万元 (10 000 yuan)

市(州)	Region	金融 Financial Expenditure	援助其他地区 Other Aid Regional Expenditure	国土海洋气象等 Land, Maritime Meteorology Expenditure	住房保障 Housing Security Expenditure	粮油物资储备 Management of Grain & Oil Reserves Expenditure	债务付息 Principal and Interest of Debts Expenditure	债务发行费用支出 Debt Issuance Expenditure	其他 Other Expen-ditures
成都市	Chengdu	136185	49350	110425	506925	19908	240050	1336	268166
自贡市	Zigong	5528		33581	157863	1876	45080	320	21385
攀枝花市	Panzhihua	2337		20125	145550	881	46825	169	6629
泸州市	Luzhou	11668	11394	41446	206052	20750	73681	455	37469
德阳市	Deyang	3096	500	30168	94178	11537	37447	195	-11259
绵阳市	Mianyang	6064		39454	84841	9770	71417	341	24382
广元市	Guangyuan	3297	50	41205	104754	8730	62540	507	4397
遂宁市	Suining	4295		33013	149145	11176	52072	258	21506
内江市	Neijiang	7387		19499	103066	11068	85549	418	11732
乐山市	Leshan	3784	420	38117	113514	4376	66546	329	37129
南充市	Nanchong	3588		64504	364886	20974	101239	645	53224
眉山市	Meishan	3130		20643	64667	4778	60209	373	7751
宜宾市	Yibin	6324		67253	162372	12512	63124	560	-46618
广安市	Guangan	2960		108701	111707	11136	60606	309	29618
达州市	Dazhou	7343		53895	281897	18912	106830	657	17215
雅安市	Yaan	744		3680	15107	378	25090	115	1281
巴中市	Bazhong	2461		58045	185496	12283	100126	524	6834
资阳市	Ziyang	2423		6615	65155	2894	46347	273	3368
阿坝藏族羌族自治州	Aba	943		99400	109614	3451	13344	184	75785
甘孜藏族自治州	Ganzi	2453		47622	127866	2096	15731	340	26905
凉山彝族自治州	Liangshan	2230		121189	198661	7375	51222	1158	29256

8-7 居民消费价格指数(2018年)
General Consumer Price Index(2018)

(上年=100) (preceding year=100)

项目	Item	居民消费价格指数 General Consumer Price Index 全省 Province	城市 Urban Areas	农村 Rural Areas
居民消费价格指数	**General Consumer Price Index**	**101.7**	**101.7**	**101.7**
食品烟酒	Food, Tobacco and Liquor	101.3	101.5	100.9
粮食	Grain	100.3	100.4	100.2
鲜菜	Fresh Vegetables	109.2	110.4	106.7
畜肉	Livestock Meat	96.0	96.5	95.0
水产品	Aquatic Products	100.9	100.5	101.7
蛋	Eggs	109.6	109.7	109.6
鲜果	Fresh Fruits	104.5	104.0	105.3
衣着	Clothing	101.1	101.1	101.2
居住	Residence	102.6	102.0	103.8
生活用品及服务	Daily Necessities and Services	101.5	101.4	101.7
交通和通信	Means of Transportation and Communication	101.2	101.2	101.3
教育文化和娱乐	Education, Culture and Recreation	101.5	101.6	101.2
医疗保健	Health Care	102.8	103.6	101.7
其他用品和服务	Other Articles and Services	102.4	102.6	101.9

8-8 商品零售价格总指数(2018年)
General Retail Price Index(2018)

(上年=100) (preceding year=100)

项目	Item	商品零售价格总指数 Retail Price Index of Commodities 全省 Province	城市 Urban Areas	农村 Rural Areas
商品零售价格指数	**General Retail Price Index**	**101.4**	**101.4**	**101.3**
食品	Food	101.5	101.7	100.9
饮料、烟酒	Beverages, Tobacco and Liquor	101.6	101.6	101.7
服装、鞋帽	Garments, Shoes and Hats	100.9	100.7	101.4
纺织品	Textiles	100.6	100.9	100.0
家用电器及音像器材	Household Electrical Appliances and Audio-Visual Equipment	98.7	98.8	98.5
文化办公用品	Cultural and Office Goods	99.4	99.4	99.2
日用品	Articles for Daily Use	100.9	100.8	101.1
体育娱乐用品	Sports and Entertainment Goods	103.8	104.5	100.8
交通、通信用品	Transportation and Telecommunication Goods	96.4	96.5	96.4
家具	Furniture	103.8	103.6	104.4
化妆品	Cosmetics	99.7	99.5	100.9
金银珠宝	Precious Metal and Jewellery	98.5	98.4	99.6
中西药品及医疗保健用品	Traditional Chinese and Western Medicines, Health Care Articles	104.9	105.1	104.3
书报杂志及电子出版物	Newspapers and Magazines, Electronic Journal	102.8	103.2	101.2
燃料	Fuels	109.1	109.1	109.2
建筑材料及五金电料	Building Materials, Hardware, Electric Materials and Appliances	102.8	102.1	104.8
农业生产资料价格指数	**Agricultural Means of Production**	**101.8**		

8-9 各市(州)城市居民消费价格指数(2018年)
General Consumer Price Index by Region(2018)

(上年=100) (preceding year=100)

市(州)	Region	居民消费价格指数 Consumer Price Index	食品烟酒 Food, Tobacco and Liquor	#粮食 Grain	#鲜菜 Fresh Vegetables	#畜肉 Livestock Meat	#水产品 Aquatic Products	#蛋 Eggs	#鲜果 Fresh Fruits
成都市	Chengdu	101.4	101.9	99.5	116.2	96.3	99.9	103.9	104.6
自贡市	Zigong	102.3	101.8	98.7	107.6	98.2	100.6	126.4	97.7
攀枝花市	Panzhihua	101.8	100.3	100.5	104.9	96.4	99.0	115.9	95.4
泸州市	Luzhou	101.8	101.3	100.9	112.4	94.7	107.3	110.0	107.1
德阳市	Deyang	102.0	102.2	100.8	113.6	98.0	99.0	115.3	102.8
绵阳市	Mianyang	102.1	101.7	101.2	106.6	97.8	99.4	112.5	109.1
广元市	Guangyuan	101.6	101.8	100.5	104.8	97.6	101.3	108.1	106.1
遂宁市	Suining	101.8	101.0	100.5	109.9	95.0	98.2	108.1	100.5
内江市	Neijiang	101.6	102.3	101.0	108.6	96.7	100.7	109.7	109.6
乐山市	Leshan	102.1	101.6	100.5	108.7	95.2	96.2	107.1	106.3
南充市	Nanchong	101.8	100.9	100.0	102.9	98.3	99.2	107.1	92.8
眉山市	Meishan	101.6	101.0	104.4	107.1	96.1	101.3	106.8	100.9
宜宾市	Yibin	101.8	100.3	102.9	102.3	96.1	97.1	99.8	96.7
广安市	Guangan	101.2	100.6	99.5	108.4	93.9	98.0	106.1	109.1
达州市	Dazhou	102.3	101.5	103.1	104.3	97.2	102.2	112.6	105.0
雅安市	Yaan	101.9	102.5	100.1	107.2	95.0	100.0	106.2	104.6
巴中市	Bazhong	101.6	101.1	99.2	104.0	95.4	97.7	117.0	105.5
资阳市	Ziyang	101.6	102.2	99.1	109.7	95.8	100.9	106.0	101.1
阿坝藏族羌族自治州	Aba	101.1	101.4	100.8	104.2	96.4	99.5	107.6	106.5
甘孜藏族自治州	Ganzi	102.1	101.5	101.4	101.1	98.1	99.2	110.0	106.0
凉山彝族自治州	Liangshan	101.8	101.8	100.7	109.8	94.2	101.9	124.7	106.5

8-9 续表 continued

(上年=100) (preceding year=100)

市(州)	Region	衣着 Clothing	居住 Residence	生活用品及服务 Daily Necessities and Services	交通和通信 Means of Transportation and Communication	教育文化和娱乐 Education, Culture and Recreation	医疗保健 Health Care	其他用品和服务 Other Articles and Services
成都市	Chengdu	100.4	100.2	101.1	101.2	101.9	102.8	104.4
自贡市	Zigong	100.1	104.3	102.1	101.3	103.2	103.8	100.1
攀枝花市	Panzhihua	101.7	104.2	100.4	102.0	101.7	103.5	101.7
泸州市	Luzhou	104.7	102.6	100.8	101.0	101.5	102.1	100.6
德阳市	Deyang	102.5	102.0	100.5	102.3	102.2	102.5	99.9
绵阳市	Mianyang	100.3	104.4	103.5	99.5	100.2	105.9	101.3
广元市	Guangyuan	102.1	100.1	100.9	101.1	103.1	104.6	101.3
遂宁市	Suining	100.8	104.6	100.2	102.2	100.6	102.5	100.3
内江市	Neijiang	99.6	101.9	100.7	101.7	100.0	104.6	100.4
乐山市	Leshan	100.6	103.6	100.8	100.9	103.8	103.4	101.0
南充市	Nanchong	100.1	103.6	100.3	102.6	101.1	103.6	104.8
眉山市	Meishan	101.6	102.4	101.7	100.5	101.5	103.4	101.7
宜宾市	Yibin	101.2	104.2	102.9	101.2	99.7	107.1	100.5
广安市	Guangan	101.1	101.1	100.7	102.9	102.4	101.4	99.4
达州市	Dazhou	102.9	103.4	101.6	102.4	102.1	102.6	103.7
雅安市	Yaan	100.3	102.4	102.0	101.7	101.2	101.4	101.9
巴中市	Bazhong	102.4	102.4	100.6	101.7	101.4	100.6	103.0
资阳市	Ziyang	96.9	102.4	103.7	100.2	100.9	103.7	101.9
阿坝藏族羌族自治州	Aba	99.6	100.2	99.8	101.3	101.3	103.7	102.0
甘孜藏族自治州	Ganzi	101.2	102.0	101.9	101.3	105.5	103.0	102.0
凉山彝族自治州	Liangshan	101.4	101.1	100.1	102.9	101.5	103.8	104.3

8-10　各市(州)城市商品零售价格指数(2018年)
General Retail Price Index by Region(2018)

(上年=100)　　(preceding year=100)

市(州)	Region	商品零售价格指数 General Retail Price Index	食品 Food	饮料、烟酒 Beverages, Tobacco and Liquor	服装、鞋帽 Garments, Shoes and Hats	纺织品 Textiles	家用电器及音像器材 Household Electrical Appliances and Audio-Visual Equipment	文化办公用品 Cultural and Office Goods	日用品 Articles for Daily Use
成都市	Chengdu	100.7	102.1	101.3	100.4	100.4	98.1	99.6	100.1
自贡市	Zigong	102.0	102.3	99.9	100.0	102.1	98.7	100.6	103.5
攀枝花市	Panzhihua	102.2	100.0	102.1	101.7	99.6	99.5	101.1	100.4
泸州市	Luzhou	101.5	101.6	101.4	104.5	100.3	96.2	99.9	96.9
德阳市	Deyang	102.1	102.8	99.5	102.6	99.8	99.0	99.5	101.6
绵阳市	Mianyang	101.6	102.0	101.5	100.3	108.3	99.8	98.9	103.1
广元市	Guangyuan	101.3	101.5	103.9	101.9	100.0	99.6	100.0	102.3
遂宁市	Suining	101.4	100.7	103.0	100.6	99.8	99.9	101.1	99.9
内江市	Neijiang	102.0	102.3	102.6	99.4	102.2	98.7	99.4	103.3
乐山市	Leshan	101.9	101.3	104.0	100.6	102.1	100.8	101.0	100.6
南充市	Nanchong	101.8	100.4	103.4	99.8	101.5	97.5	96.4	101.0
眉山市	Meishan	101.8	101.5	98.7	101.3	102.1	101.5	103.2	101.3
宜宾市	Yibin	102.3	99.9	104.1	101.3	91.2	101.2	98.9	103.9
广安市	Guangan	101.4	100.4	102.3	101.1	102.2	96.3	100.3	100.9
达州市	Dazhou	101.9	101.4	100.1	102.9	101.1	100.6	99.8	101.0
雅安市	Yaan	101.3	102.2	101.5	100.3	98.9	101.9	100.7	100.5
巴中市	Bazhong	101.5	101.1	102.8	102.4	101.2	100.2	100.0	101.0
资阳市	Ziyang	101.1	102.2	102.4	96.6	99.3	100.0	102.4	103.5
阿坝藏族羌族自治州	Aba	101.4	101.1	103.3	99.3	100.6	99.2	98.9	100.3
甘孜藏族自治州	Ganzi	101.1	101.4	101.4	101.2	102.5	95.2	102.1	101.5
凉山彝族自治州	Liangshan	101.6	101.6	102.3	101.4	99.1	99.1	99.4	99.8

8-10 续表 continued

(上年=100) (preceding year=100)

市(州)	Region	交通、通信用品 Transportation and Telecom-munication Goods	家具 Furniture	化妆品 Cosmetics	金银珠宝 Precious Metal and Jewellery	中西药品及医疗保健用品 Traditional Chinese and Western Medicines,Health Care Articles	书报杂志及电子出版物 Newspapers and Magazines, Electronic Journal	燃料 Fuels	建筑材料及五金电料 Building Materials, Hardware, Electric Materials and Appliances
成都市	Chengdu	106.2	94.8	103.8	98.6	97.6	103.3	102.3	108.8
自贡市	Zigong	101.1	98.2	100.7	100.4	96.0	107.6	100.4	108.3
攀枝花市	Panzhihua	101.4	99.5	101.1	100.5	103.5	106.9	112.7	112.9
泸州市	Luzhou	100.0	98.3	106.3	99.7	98.3	106.9	107.6	107.2
德阳市	Deyang	100.5	100.2	100.0	100.3	99.2	106.3	102.9	107.8
绵阳市	Mianyang	101.1	94.3	106.2	102.0	99.0	103.1	109.7	105.6
广元市	Guangyuan	100.0	95.7	100.0	100.2	100.2	105.1	99.0	107.0
遂宁市	Suining	99.3	99.1	100.1	99.9	100.1	106.2	99.7	108.4
内江市	Neijiang	100.0	97.5	99.7	102.2	98.7	109.8	103.2	109.8
乐山市	Leshan	99.9	97.6	98.5	100.2	98.5	107.8	107.8	107.6
南充市	Nanchong	98.7	99.1	103.7	103.3	99.9	108.5	104.6	109.5
眉山市	Meishan	100.6	95.7	101.3	100.0	102.0	104.7	102.7	108.7
宜宾市	Yibin	98.4	97.8	111.1	106.8	99.2	116.1	99.1	108.0
广安市	Guangan	100.4	100.4	103.7	98.9	98.8	103.4	101.7	108.4
达州市	Dazhou	100.7	99.5	102.6	100.8	99.1	106.5	99.5	108.1
雅安市	Yaan	101.7	97.5	100.4	100.4	103.8	103.5	102.1	106.7
巴中市	Bazhong	100.2	98.9	100.9	100.1	101.4	101.5	101.1	109.6
资阳市	Ziyang	101.7	92.4	106.0	102.3	100.3	104.4	104.6	108.9
阿坝藏族羌族自治州	Aba	103.5	98.2	100.6	100.0	96.5	104.2	104.5	110.3
甘孜藏族自治州	Ganzi	101.8	95.3	106.0	101.4	96.1	105.9	106.2	109.4
凉山彝族自治州	Liangshan	100.1	96.4	99.9	101.1	99.5	108.6	102.4	111.1

8-11 农村居民消费价格指数(2018年)
Consumer Price Index in Rural Areas(2018)

(上年=100) (preceding year=100)

项 目	Item	温江区 Wenjiang	叙永县 Xuyong	梓潼县 Zitong	剑阁县 Jiange	威远县 Weiyuan	峨眉山市 Emeishan
居民消费价格指数	**Consumer Price Index**	**102.4**	**101.4**	**101.8**	**101.6**	**101.7**	**102.2**
食品烟酒	Food, Tobacco and Liquor	101.0	100.7	102.0	100.5	101.6	101.9
粮食	Grain	101.2	100.1	101.3	102.6	101.7	100.9
鲜菜	Fresh Vegetables	110.9	107.3	111.3	102.3	109.9	117.0
畜肉	Livestock Meat	95.5	96.1	96.5	93.0	99.0	95.8
水产品	Aquatic Products	99.0	96.7	105.9	105.2	96.1	98.3
蛋	Eggs	109.3	107.6	122.2	108.4	116.7	104.3
鲜果	Fresh Fruits	99.6	103.3	109.9	102.8	95.4	106.5
衣着	Clothing	99.7	101.0	103.1	102.6	100.8	100.7
居住	Residence	111.1	102.5	103.0	100.6	103.2	105.5
生活用品及服务	Daily Necessities and Services	99.0	102.4	101.5	99.8	101.7	100.2
交通和通信	Means of Transportation and Communication	99.3	101.9	101.3	101.5	100.9	99.7
教育文化和娱乐	Education, Culture and Recreation	99.6	100.9	100.1	101.1	101.0	101.5
医疗保健	Health Care	101.6	101.6	100.7	108.7	102.1	101.5
其他用品和服务	Other Articles and Services	101.2	100.9	99.9	100.6	100.3	103.9

8-11 续表 continued

(上年=100) (preceding year=100)

项 目	Item	南部县 Nanbu	仁寿县 Renshou	渠县 Quxian	汉源县 Hanyuan	平昌县 Pingchang	简阳市 Jianyang
居民消费价格指数	**Consumer Price Index**	**101.7**	**101.1**	**101.2**	**101.8**	**101.1**	**102.6**
食品烟酒	Food, Tobacco and Liquor	102.0	100.9	99.6	100.5	99.7	101.8
粮食	Grain	100.0	100.6	100.4	100.2	96.9	101.1
鲜菜	Fresh Vegetables	110.8	103.7	101.4	109.0	99.8	110.5
畜肉	Livestock Meat	96.9	94.0	94.1	93.2	91.9	96.2
水产品	Aquatic Products	102.7	103.8	97.2	98.7	106.2	106.1
蛋	Eggs	102.3	107.5	113.3	106.0	112.7	109.1
鲜果	Fresh Fruits	116.9	111.4	97.1	98.3	108.7	105.5
衣着	Clothing	101.4	98.4	105.8	101.5	105.6	99.8
居住	Residence	100.6	101.9	102.9	103.4	99.1	106.5
生活用品及服务	Daily Necessities and Services	101.6	104.0	102.7	103.8	99.9	100.2
交通和通信	Means of Transportation and Communication	102.5	100.0	100.2	102.4	103.9	101.6
教育文化和娱乐	Education, Culture and Recreation	101.3	100.9	100.0	101.2	104.4	100.3
医疗保健	Health Care	102.4	100.7	100.3	101.6	100.0	104.4
其他用品和服务	Other Articles and Services	101.8	103.7	103.3	101.3	101.3	100.2

8-12 工业生产者出厂价格指数
Producer Price Index for Industrial Products

(上年=100) (preceding year=100)

类　别	Item	2005	2010	2014	2015	2016	2017	2018
全部工业品	**Total Industrial Products**	**104.0**	**105.0**	**98.7**	**96.4**	**98.9**	**106.5**	**103.6**
按轻重工业分	**Grouped by Light & Heavy Industry**							
轻工业	Light Industry	101.3	103.3	99.9	98.7	99.2	102.3	101.6
重工业	Heavy Industry	106.2	106.3	98.2	95.5	98.8	108.3	104.5
按类别分	**Grouped by Sector**							
生产资料	Means of Production	105.5	105.7	98.1	95.3	98.7	108.7	104.6
采掘	Mining and Quarrying	114.5	112.6	96.9	90.3	95.0	116.5	102.3
原料	Raw Materials	105.9	109.0	97.8	96.4	99.1	110.2	105.3
加工	Manufacturing	104.0	103.0	98.4	95.7	99.0	107.4	104.6
生活资料	Consumer Goods	100.1	102.8	100.6	99.8	99.5	100.8	101.1
食品	Food	102.2	104.4	100.4	100.2	100.2	100.9	101.9
衣着	Clothing	101.5	101.2	109.3	103.5	104.7	101.0	103.0
一般日用品	Articles for Daily Use	102.0	102.9	99.8	98.0	98.5	101.5	101.7
耐用消费品	Durable Consumer Goods	90.1	94.2	97.3	98.1	96.6	99.6	97.3
按部门分	**Grouped by Industrial Division**							
冶金工业	Metallurgical Industry	105.7	110.6	95.1	89.3	99.9	123.0	106.7
电力工业	Power Industry	104.0	103.1	99.1	99.9	99.9	98.4	98.1
煤炭工业	Coal Industry	122.2	112.1	93.1	87.9	98.1	133.0	102.0
石油工业	Petroleum Industry	104.6	111.0	102.7	97.4	91.9	105.2	108.7
化学工业	Chemical Industry	107.5	105.5	98.0	97.5	99.1	105.8	105.5
机械工业	Machine Building Industry	99.9	100.0	99.6	99.1	98.5	102.6	101.2
建筑材料工业	Building Materials Industry	104.7	99.0	99.6	92.8	98.9	106.1	110.7
森林工业	Timber Industry	100.9	104.7	102.1	101.0	99.6	100.1	101.4
食品工业	Food Industry	102.4	104.4	100.2	99.8	99.7	100.6	101.9
纺织工业	Textile Industry	102.9	115.8	97.3	93.5	97.8	105.7	105.0
缝纫工业	Tailoring Industry	97.1	101.0	103.8	104.9	101.8	102.7	103.7
皮革工业	Leather Industry	105.6	100.7	111.8	102.8	106.8	100.4	104.9
造纸工业	Paper Industry	100.6	102.1	99.4	98.8	100.2	117.5	106.4
文教艺术用品工业	Culture, Education and Art Supply Industry	99.9	102.1	99.3	95.0	96.9	106.8	104.2

8-13 按行业分工业生产者出厂价格指数
Producer Price Index for Industrial Products by Industrial Branch

(上年=100) (preceding year=100)

类　　别	Item	2005	2010	2014	2015	2016	2017	2018
煤炭开采和洗选业	Coal Mining and Dressing	129.4	112.1	93.2	88.6	98.1	132.2	101.2
石油和天然气开采业	Petroleum and Natural Gas Extraction	103.4	110.5	102.7	96.0	77.6	99.9	102.9
黑色金属矿采选业	Ferrous Metals Mining and Dressing	123.0	120.4	97.9	80.8	94.5	106.4	98.8
有色金属矿采选业	Nonferrous Metals Mining and Dressing	118.3	132.8	91.5	91.1	100.8	131.9	105.3
非金属矿采选业	Nonmetal Minerals Mining and Dressing	110.7	104.1	99.6	97.9	100.1	102.6	102.1
食品制造业	Manufacture of Foods	102.8	103.7	103.8	101.1	99.7	101.7	101.7
饮料制造业	Manufacture of Beverage	103.1	105.5	99.0	98.4	97.7	100.0	101.8
烟草制品业	Manufacture of Tobacco	101.4	99.7	100.1	100.2	100.3	100.0	100.3
纺织业	Manufacture of Textile	102.9	115.6	97.3	93.7	97.8	105.7	105.0
皮革、羽毛(绒)及其制品业	Leather, Furs, Down and Related Products	104.5	101.8	109.9	98.2	105.5	101.2	104.0
木材加工及木、竹制品业	Timber Processing, Bamboo, Cane, Palm Fiber and Straw Products	100.9	105.4	99.6	100.0	100.4	99.8	101.4
家具制造业	Manufacture of Furniture	101.0	102.3	103.8	101.5	99.3	100.8	101.6
造纸及纸制品业	Manufacture of Paper and Paper Products	100.6	102.1	99.4	98.8	100.2	117.5	106.4
文教体育用品制造业	Cultural, Educational and Sports Goods	99.4	107.3	100.0	100.0	98.9	101.0	100.1
石油加工、炼焦及核燃料加工业	Processing of Petroleum, Coking and Processing of Nuclear Fuel	108.0	113.0	96.2	89.8	100.8	113.6	110.0
化学原料及化学制品制造业	Manufacture of Raw Chemical Materials and Chemical Products	110.5	105.1	96.8	97.0	98.5	110.8	108.3
医药制造业	Manufacture of Medicines	101.8	106.1	99.9	99.7	102.2	104.2	103.2
化学纤维制造业	Manufacture of Chemical Fibres	100.7	123.7	93.4	94.6	95.8	108.2	103.3
橡胶制品业	Rubber Products	105.2	101.8	98.4	99.4	97.4	110.8	103.1
塑料制品业	Plastic Products	107.5	100.4	100.3	96.5	97.4	101.3	100.1
非金属矿物制品业	Manufacture of Non-metallic Mineral Products	104.6	98.7	99.4	93.3	98.7	107.0	110.9
黑色金属冶炼及压延加工业	Smelting and Pressing of Ferrous Metals	105.0	106.8	93.7	86.1	101.7	130.6	110.3
有色金属冶炼及压延加工业	Smelting and Pressing of Nonferrous Metals	107.3	118.7	94.2	92.3	98.9	112.7	103.0
金属制品业	Manufacture of Metal Products	104.2	104.3	99.8	98.8	96.9	107.0	103.3
通用设备制造业	Manufacture of General Purpose Machinery	104.5	99.7	101.7	100.0	99.9	101.6	102.6
专用设备制造业	Manufacture of Special Purpose Machinery	102.3	101.2	98.7	98.9	98.8	101.8	100.5
交通运输设备制造业	Transport Equipment Manufacturing	100.1	100.8	100.6	99.9	98.4	102.1	101.9
电气机械及器材制造业	Manufacture of Electrical Machinery and Apparatus	104.6	105.3	98.4	98.4	100.2	101.3	98.8
通信设备及其他电子设备制造业	Electronic and Telecommunications Equipment	91.2	95.6	96.8	97.7	97.4	104.5	101.2
仪器仪表及文化、办公用机械制造业	Instruments, Meters, Cultural and Office Machinery	96.8	97.4	106.0	100.4	107.6	109.8	101.4
工艺品及其他制造业	Other Manufacturing	105.7	106.9	97.3	96.8	101.7	102.9	114.5
电力、热力的生产和供应业	Production and Supply of Electric and Heat Power	104.0	103.0	99.1	99.9	99.3	98.2	97.8
燃气生产和供应业	Production and Supply of Gas	102.0	108.9	106.7	106.5	86.5	102.6	105.6
水的生产和供应业	Production and Supply of Water	102.0	102.7	103.0	104.0	100.0	101.5	101.2

主要统计指标解释

一般公共预算收入 指国家财政参与社会产品分配所取得的收入，是实现国家职能的财力保证。主要包括:

(1)各项税收：包括国内增值税、国内消费税、进口货物增值税和消费税、出口货物退增值税和消费税、企业所得税、个人所得税、资源税、城市维护建设税、房产税、印花税、城镇土地使用税、土地增值税、车船税、船舶吨税、车辆购置税、关税、耕地占用税、契税、烟叶税等。

(2)非税收入：包括专项收入、行政事业性收费、罚没收入和其他收入。

财政收入按现行分税制财政体制划分为中央本级收入和地方本级收入。

一般公共预算支出 指国家财政将筹集起来的资金进行分配使用,以满足经济建设和各项事业的需要。主要包括:一般公共服务、外交、国防、公共安全、教育、科学技术、文化体育与传媒、社会保障和就业、医疗卫生与计划生育、节能环保、城乡社区、农林水、交通运输、资源勘探信息等、商业服务业等、金融、援助其他地区、国土海洋气象等、住房保障、粮油物资储备、政府债务付息等方面的支出。

财政支出根据政府在经济和社会活动中的不同职权,划分为中央财政支出和地方财政支出。

中央一般公共预算收入和地方一般公共预算收入 属于中央一般公共预算的收入包括关税,进口货物增值税和消费税，出口货物退增值税和消费税，消费税，铁道部门、各银行总行、各保险公司总公司等集中缴纳的城市维护建设税,增值税50%部分,纳入共享范围的企业所得税60%部分,未纳入共享范围的中央企业所得税、中央企业上交的利润，个人所得税60%部分，车辆购置税，船舶吨税，证券交易印花税，海洋石油资源税，中央非税收入等。属于地方一般公共预算的收入包括地方企业上交利润，城市维护建设税（不含铁道部门、各银行总行、各保险公司总公司集中缴纳的部分），房产税，城镇土地使用税，土地增值税，车船税，耕地占用税，契税，烟叶税，印花税（不含证券交易印花税），增值税50%部分，纳入共享范围的企业所得税40%部分，个人所得税40%部分，海洋石油资源税以外的其他资源税，地方非税收入等。

中央一般公共预算支出和地方一般公共预算支出 指根据政府在经济和社会活动中的不同职责,划分中央和地方政府的责权，按照政府的责权划分确定的支出。中央一般公共预算支出包括一般公共服务，外交支出，国防支出，公共安全支出,以及中央政府调整国民经济结构、协调地区发展、实施宏观调控的支出等。地方一般公共预算支出包括一般公共服务，公共安全支出，地方统筹的各项社会事业支出等。

商品零售价格指数 是反映一定时期内城乡商品零售价格变动趋势和程度的相对数。商品零售价格的变动与国家的财政收入、市场供需的平衡、消费与积累的比例关系有关。因此,该指数可以从一个侧面对上述经济活动进行观察和分析。

农业生产资料价格指数 指反映一定时期内农业生产资料价格变动趋势和程度的相对数。其编制目的是了解农业生产中投入物质资料价格的变动状况，服务于国民经济核算。1994 年以前，农业生产资料价格指数仅仅是商品零售价格指数的一个类别，此后，从商品零售价格指数中分离出来，单独编制。

居民消费价格指数 是反映一定时期内城乡居民所购买的生活消费品和服务项目价格变动趋势和程度的相对数，是对城市居民消费价格指数和农村居民消费价格指数进行综合汇总计算的结果。通过该指数可以观察和分析消费品的零售价格和服务项目价格变动对城乡居民实际生活费支出的影响程度。

城市居民消费价格指数 是反映一定时期内城市居民家庭所购买的生活消费品价格和服务项目价格变动趋势和程度的相对数。通过该指数可以观察和分析消费品的零售价格和服务项目价格变动对城镇居民收入和消费支出的影响。

农村居民消费价格指数 是反映一定时期内农村居民家庭所购买的生活消费品价格和服务项目价格变动趋势和程度的相对数。通过该指数可以观察农村消费品的零售价格和服务项目价格变动对农村居民收入和生活消费支出的影响。

工业生产者出厂价格指数 是反映一定时期内全部工业产品第一次出售时的出厂价格总水平的变动趋势和变动幅度的相对数。

工业生产者购进价格指数 是反映作为中间投入的原材料、燃料、动力购进价格总水平的变动趋势和变动幅度的相对数。

固定资产投资价格指数 是反映一定时期内固定资产投资品及取费项目的价格变动趋势和变动幅度的相对数。该指数可以准确地反映固定资产投资中涉及的各类投资品和取费项目价格变动趋势和变动幅度,消除按现价计算的固定资产投资指标中的价格变动因素,真实地反映固定资产投资的规模、速度、结构和效益。

Explanatory Notes on Main Statistical Indicators

General Public Budget Revenue refers to income for the government finance through participating in the distribution of social products. It is the financial guarantee to ensure government functioning. The contents of government revenue include the following main items:

(1) Various tax revenues, including domestic value added tax (VAT), domestic consumption tax, VAT and consumption tax from imports, VAT and consumption tax rebate for exports, corporate income tax, individual income tax, resource tax, city maintenance and construct tax, house property tax, stamp tax, urban land use tax, land appreciation tax, tax on vehicles and boat operation, ship tonnage tax, vehicle purchase tax, tariffs, farm land occupation tax, deed tax, and tobacco leaf tax, etc.

(2) Non-tax revenue, including special program receipts, charge of administrative and institutional units, penalty receipts and others non-tax receipts.

Government Revenue at the current decentralized taxation system is divided into the central level revenue and local level revenue.

General Public Budget Expenditure refers to the distribution and use of the funds which the government finance has raised, so as to meet the needs of economic construction and various undertakings. It includes the following main items: expenditure for general public services, expenditure for foreign affairs, expenditure for national defence expenditure for public security, expenditure for education, expenditure for science and technology, expenditure for culture, sport and media, expenditure for social safety net and employment effort, expenditure for medical and health care and family planning, expenditure for energy conservation and environment protection, expenditure for urban and rural community affairs, expenditure for agriculture, forestry and water conservancy, expenditure for transportation, expenditure for resource exploration and information, expenditure for commerce and services, expenditure for finance supervision, aid to other regions, expenditure for land ocean and weather, expenditure for affairs of housing security, expenditure for grain & oil reserves, interest payment for public debts. Government expenditure is divided into central government expenditure and local government expenditure according to the different functions of the governments played in economic and social activities.

General Public Budget Revenue of the Central Government and the Local Governments The general public budget revenue of the Central Government includes tariff, VAT and consumption tax from imports, VAT and consumption tax rebate for exports, consumption tax, city maintenance and construct tax from the Ministry of Railways, head offices of banks, head offices of insurance company, which are handed over to the government in a centralized way, 50% of the value added tax, 60% the share part of the corporate income tax, unshared part of corporate income tax of the central enterprises, profit handed in by the central enterprises, 60% of individual income tax, vehicle purchase tax, ship tonnage tax, stamp tax on securities transactions, resource tax on the offshore petroleum resources. The general public budget revenue of the local governments includes profit handed in by the local enterprises, city maintenance and construct tax (excluding the part of the Ministry of Railways, head offices of banks, head offices of insurance company, which are handed over to the government in a centralized way), house property tax, urban land use tax, land appreciation tax, tax on vehicles and boat operation, farm land occupation tax, deed tax, and tobacco leaf tax, stamp tax (not including stamp tax on security exchange),50% of the value added tax, 40% the share part of the corporate income tax, 40% of individual income tax, resource tax other than the tax on offshore petroleum resources, local non-tax revenue, etc.

General Public Budget Expenditure of the Central Government and the Local Governments According to the different functions of the Central Government and local governments in economic and social activities, the rights of affairs administration are demarcated between those of the Central Government and those of local governments; and the classification of the expenditure between the Central Government and local governments are made on the basis of the classification of the rights of affairs administration between them. General Public Budget Expenditure of the Central Government includes the expenditure for general public services, expenditure for foreign affairs, expenditure for public security, and the expenditure of the Central Government for adjusting the national economic structure; coordinating the development among different regions; and exercising macroeconomic regulation. General Public Budget Expenditure of the Local Governments includes mainly the expenditure for general public services, expenditure for public security, and expenditures for social development which are planed by local governments, etc.

Retail Price Index reflects the trend and degree of change in retail prices of commodities during a given period. The change in retail prices of commodities is related to government revenue, the equilibrium of market supply and demand, and the ratio of consumption to accumulation. Therefore, the retail price indices are useful from an oblique perspective for observing and analyzing the changes of the above economic activities.

Price Index for Means of Agricultural Production reflects the trend and degree of changes in the prices of the means of agricultural production during a given period. Compilation of these indices helps to understand the changes in prices of input into agricultural production and facilitate the compilation of national accounts statistics. Before 1994, price index for means of agricultural production were a sub-category in the retail price index for commodities, and it has been compiled separately since 1994.

Consumer Price Index reflects the trend and degree of changes in prices of consumer goods and services purchased by urban and rural households during a given period. They are obtained by combining Consumer Price index of Urban Household and Consumer Price index of Rural Household. The index enable the observation and analysis of the degree of impact of the changes in the prices of retailed goods and services on the actual living expenses of urban and rural residents.

Urban Consumer Price Index reflects the trend and degree of changes in prices of consumer goods and services purchased by urban households during a given period. It can be used to observe and analyze the impact of price changes in consumer goods and services on urban household income and consumption expenditure.

Rural Consumer Price Index reflects the trend and degree of changes in prices of consumer goods and services purchased by rural households during a given period. It can be used to observe the impact of change in retail prices of consumer goods and service prices on rural household income and consumption expenditure on living.

Producer Price Index for Industrial Products reflects the trend and degree of changes in general ex-factory prices of all manufactured goods for first sale during a given period.

Purchasing Price Index for Industrial Producers reflects changes in the level and degree of purchasing prices such as intermediate input such as raw materials, fuels and power.

Price Index for Investment in Fixed Assets reflects the trend and degree of changes in prices of investment goods and projects in fixed assets during a given period. Removing the factor of price change in the aggregates of investment at current prices, this indicator shows the changes in the prices of commodities and fees involved in the investment of fixed assets, and can be used to observe the actual size, growth, structure, and efficiency of investment in fixed assets.

9 人民生活和社会保障

Chapter 9 People's Living Conditions and Social Security

9-1 全体居民人均收支情况
Per Capita Income and Consumption Expenditure of all Residents

单位：元 (yuan)

项 目	Item	2014	2015	2016	2017	2018
全体居民人均收入	**Per Capita Income**					
可支配收入	Disposable Income	15749	17221	18808	20580	22461
工资性收入	Income of Wages and Salaries	7932	8610	9278	10014	11070
经营净收入	Net Business Income	3459	3698	3993	4264	4558
财产净收入	Net Income from Property	919	1074	1199	1363	1443
转移净收入	Net Income from Transfer	3439	3839	4338	4940	5389
现金可支配收入	Cash Disposable Income	14425	15859	17510	19208	21028
工资性收入	Income of Wages and Salaries	7885	8562	9229	9954	11000
经营净收入	Net Business Income	2881	3156	3568	3874	4229
财产净收入	Net Income from Property	432	547	663	746	764
转移净收入	Net Income from Transfer	3227	3594	4050	4633	5034
全体居民人均支出	**Per Capita Expenditure**					
消费支出	Consumption Expenditure	12368	13632	14839	16180	17664
食品烟酒	Food,Tobacco and Liquor	4548	5002	5321	5632	5938
衣着	Clothing	974	1071	1141	1153	1174
居住	Residence	2217	2401	2735	2947	3368
生活用品及服务	Articles for Daily Use and Services	880	918	967	1063	1182
交通通信	Transport and Communications	1437	1629	1850	2200	2399
教育文化娱乐	Education, Cultural and Recreation	1061	1208	1285	1468	1600
医疗保健	Health Care	964	1071	1173	1320	1569
其他用品及服务	Miscellaneous Goods and Services	287	332	367	397	435
现金消费支出	Cash Consumption Expenditure	10112	11123	12136	13346	14574
食品烟酒	Food,Tobacco and Liquor	3891	4277	4572	4910	5296
衣着	Clothing	974	1071	1140	1150	1173
居住	Residence	824	857	1046	1118	1252
生活用品及服务	Household Facilities, Articles and Services	869	898	958	1051	1161
交通通信	Transport and Communications	1434	1627	1850	2199	2397
教育文化娱乐	Education, Cultural and Recreation	1060	1207	1284	1467	1597
医疗保健	Health Care and Medical Services	777	857	924	1066	1271
其他商品及服务	Miscellaneous Goods and Services	283	329	361	385	427

注：从2013年开始，国家统计局开展了城乡一体化住户收支和生活状况调查，与2012年前的分城镇和农村住户调查的调查范围、调查方法、指标口径有所不同。

a) The NBS started an integrated household income and expenditure survey in 2013, including both urban and rural households. The coverage, methodology and definitions used in the survey are different from those used for the separate urban and rural household surveys prior to 2012.

9-2 全体居民人均主要食品消费量
Per Capita Consumption of Major Foods of all Residents

单位: 公斤 (kg)

项目	Item	全体居民 Whole Households		城镇居民 Urban Households		农村居民 Rural Households	
		2017	2018	2017	2018	2017	2018
粮食	Grain	160.20	146.58	130.67	108.82	184.50	178.63
谷物	Cereal	147.34	134.18	117.31	96.05	172.06	166.54
薯类	Tuber	4.25	4.24	3.57	3.48	4.81	4.90
豆类	Beans	8.61	8.16	9.80	9.29	7.64	7.19
油脂类	Oil and Fats	12.75	12.07	13.19	12.20	12.38	11.96
#植物油	Vegetable Oil	11.57	10.82	12.36	11.26	10.93	10.44
动物油	Animal Oil	1.18	1.26	0.83	0.95	1.46	1.52
蔬菜和菜制品	Vegetables and Ralated Products	132.48	120.75	139.33	129.31	126.84	113.48
#鲜菜	Fresh Vegetables	129.56	117.68	134.58	124.60	125.43	111.80
肉类	Meat	41.09	45.44	43.79	45.70	38.87	45.22
#猪肉	Pork	36.16	38.86	35.79	36.14	36.47	41.17
牛肉	Beef	1.54	1.73	2.67	2.60	0.61	1.00
羊肉	Mutton	0.53	0.48	0.69	0.63	0.40	0.35
禽类	Poultry	10.95	10.45	11.93	11.59	10.14	9.48
水产品	Aquatic Products	7.63	7.20	9.53	9.36	6.07	5.36
蛋类及蛋制品	Eggs and Related Products	8.89	8.43	8.91	8.52	8.87	8.36
奶及奶制品	Milk and Dairy Products	12.28	12.48	16.89	17.43	8.49	8.27
干鲜瓜果类	Dried and Fresh Melons and Fruits	40.68	40.56	51.20	52.17	32.01	30.70
#鲜瓜果	Fresh Melons and Fruits	35.98	35.61	44.73	46.01	28.78	26.78
坚果	Nuts and Processed Products	4.30	4.46	5.84	5.38	3.04	3.68
糖果糕点类	Confectioneries	5.66	6.09	6.09	6.80	5.31	5.48
#食糖	Sugar	2.00	1.93	1.84	1.75	2.13	2.08

9-3 全体居民平均每百户年末耐用消费品拥有量
Number of Main Durable Consumer Goods Owned per 100 Households

单位：平均每百户 (per 100 Households)

项目		Item		全体居民 Whole Households		城镇居民 Urban Households		农村居民 Rural Households	
				2017	2018	2017	2018	2017	2018
家用汽车	(辆)	Automobile	(unit)	22.62	26.92	33.61	36.31	13.39	15.45
摩托车	(辆)	Motorcycle	(unit)	35.95	34.71	19.79	23.27	49.52	48.70
电动助力车	(辆)	Electric Bicycle	(unit)	27.99	31.39	27.44	30.48	28.46	32.49
洗衣机	(台)	Washing Machine	(set)	93.98	95.69	98.80	99.98	89.93	90.46
电冰箱(柜)	(台)	Refrigerator	(set)	98.10	99.46	100.41	101.69	96.16	96.73
微波炉	(台)	Microwave Oven	(set)	30.44	29.07	51.73	43.85	12.55	11.01
彩色电视机	(台)	Color Television Set	(set)	120.84	118.41	125.32	122.11	117.08	113.89
#接入有线电视	(台)	Access to the Cable TV	(set)	68.19	72.71	98.47	91.25	42.74	50.06
空调	(台)	Air Conditioner	(set)	81.44	99.07	130.45	138.32	40.26	51.11
热水器	(台)	Water Heater	(set)	79.80	86.16	96.40	97.97	65.84	71.73
#太阳能热水器	(台)	Solar Water Heater	(set)	21.38	18.44	12.28	11.58	29.03	26.83
洗碗机	(台)	Dishwasher	(set)	0.71	0.87	1.06	1.26	0.41	0.39
排油烟机	(台)	Vacuum Cleaner	(set)	35.90	45.70	65.24	70.32	11.24	15.62
固定电话	(部)	Telephone	(unit)	26.11	22.54	43.33	34.45	11.64	7.98
移动电话	(部)	Mobile Telephone	(unit)	243.48	257.19	245.25	256.12	241.99	258.50
#接入互联网	(部)	Access to the Internet	(unit)	99.82	167.92	129.62	189.19	74.78	141.92
计算机	(台)	Private Computer	(set)	40.49	39.85	67.56	57.30	17.74	18.53
#接入互联网	(台)	Access to the Internet	(set)	31.23	31.12	55.28	47.04	11.02	11.67
照相机	(台)	Camera	(set)	11.00	7.94	20.59	12.38	2.94	2.52
中高档乐器	(架)	Medium & High Grade Musical Instrument	(unit)	2.11	2.85	3.85	4.33	0.65	1.04
健身器材	(台)	Health Equipment	(set)	2.20	3.50	3.77	5.80	0.88	0.69

9-4 城镇居民家庭基本情况
Basic Statistics of Urban Households

项 目	Item	2014	2015	2016	2017	2018
平均每户家庭常住人口(人)	**Average Resident Population per Household (person)**	**2.96**	**2.96**	**2.99**	**3.11**	**2.99**
平均每户就业人口(人)	**Average Number of Employed Persons per Household (person)**	**1.57**	**1.53**	**1.56**	**1.56**	**2.11**
平均每人总收入(元)	**Per Capita Total Income (yuan)**	**27148**	**29422**	**33016**	**36136**	**39854**
平均每人可支配收入(元)	**Per Capita Disposable Income (yuan)**	**24234**	**26205**	**28335**	**30727**	**33216**
工资性收入	Income of Wages and Salaries	14262	15242	16219	17299	19033
经营净收入	Net Business Income	2904	3054	3327	3586	3900
财产净收入	Net Income from Property	1891	2169	2363	2627	2696
转移净收入	Net Income from Transfer	5177	5740	6426	7215	7587
平均每人总支出(元)	**Per Capita Total Expenditures (yuan)**	**24914**	**27763**	**31490**	**33571**	**38626**
平均每人消费支出(元)	**Per Capita Annual Living Expenditures for Consumption (yuan)**	**17760**	**19277**	**20660**	**21991**	**23484**
食品烟酒	Food,Tobacco and Liquor	6204	6783	7118	7329	7462
衣着	Clothing	1539	1704	1768	1723	1713
居住	Residence	3186	3335	3757	3906	4470
生活用品及服务	Articles for Daily Use and Services	1211	1251	1311	1404	1562
交通通信	Transport and Communications	2169	2414	2698	3198	3366
教育文化娱乐	Education, Cultural and Recreation	1672	1963	2008	2222	2384
医疗保健	Health Care	1283	1369	1423	1596	1861
其他用品及服务	Miscellaneous Commodities and Services	495	556	577	612	666
城镇居民恩格尔系数(%)	**Engle Coefficient of Urban Households(%)**	**34.94**	**35.19**	**34.46**	**33.33**	**31.78**

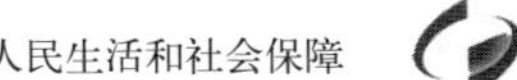

9-5 按收入五等份分组的城镇居民人均收入(2018年)
Per Capita Income of Urban Households by Income Quintile (2018)

单位：人、元 (person，yuan)

项目	Item	总平均 Average	低收入户 Low Income Households	中低收入户 Lower Middle Income Households	中等收入户 Middle Income Households	中高收入户 Upper Middle Income Households	高收入户 High Income Households
平均每户就业人口	Average Number of Employeed Persons per Household	2.11	2.19	2.30	2.18	2.02	1.87
平均每人总收入	Per Capital Total Income	39854	19180	26258	35196	48101	88015
平均每人可支配收入	Disposable Income	33216	11197	22712	30985	42667	74204
工资性收入	Income of Wages and Salaries	18530	6648	12387	16999	23617	45090
工资	Wage and Allowance	17260	6291	11791	16096	22110	40992
实物福利	Physical Welfare	94	21	38	102	157	221
其他	Other Incomes	1176	337	558	801	1350	3877
经营净收入	Net Business Income	3849	128	2900	3484	4761	10694
第一产业	Primary Industry	419	619	340	211	215	786
第二产业	Secondary Industry	99	-933	192	188	459	1008
第三产业	Tertiary Industry	3331	442	2368	3084	4087	8900
财产净收入	Net Income from Property	2820	1025	1635	2494	3168	6536
利息净收入	Net Interest Income	-192	-36	-87	-145	-312	-452
红利收入	Bonus Stock Income	477	41	104	236	388	1987
储蓄性保险净收益	Net Income of Savings Insurance	9	3	2	12	11	20
转让承包土地经营权租金净收入	Net Income of the Transfer of Contracted Land Management Rights	54	36	44	54	70	63
出租房屋财产性收入	Net Income of Rental Housing	830	259	470	912	1004	1683
转移净收入	Net Income from Transfer	8017	3395	5789	8008	11122	11884

9-6 按收入五等份分组的城镇居民人均消费支出(2018年)
Per Capita Expenditure of Urban Households by Income Quintile (2018)

单位：元 (yuan)

项目	Item	总平均 Average	低收入户 Low Income Households	中低收入户 Lower Middle Income Households	中等收入户 Middle Income Households	中高收入户 Upper Middle Income Households	高收入户 High Income Households
平均每人总支出	**Per Capita Total Expenditures**	**38626**	**25077**	**27059**	**31938**	**44196**	**78766**
平均每人全年消费支出	**Total Living Expenditures**	**23484**	**13660**	**17745**	**21579**	**28593**	**43468**
食品烟酒	Food,Tobacco and Liquor	7462	4820	6058	7566	9108	12195
食品	Food	4794	3515	4247	5107	5749	6461
谷物	Cereal	504	401	425	480	579	770
薯类	Tuber	76	72	72	81	81	82
豆类	Beans	73	64	71	75	82	81
食用油	Edible Oil	201	169	184	216	223	245
蔬菜和食用菌	Vegetable and Mushroom	718	533	640	809	863	889
肉类	Meat and Related Products	1280	1010	1170	1408	1521	1518
禽类	Poultry	347	245	313	388	425	440
水产品	Aquatic Products	218	135	176	232	266	348
蛋类	Eggs	131	102	120	140	152	170
奶类	Milk	386	236	364	403	501	525
干鲜瓜果类	Dried and Fresh Melons and Fruits	486	295	399	486	598	818
糖果糕点类	Confectioneries	171	102	140	173	210	286
其它食品	Others	205	151	174	215	248	288
烟酒	Liquor	684	411	532	627	828	1297
饮料	Beverages	130	72	108	111	153	263
饮食服务	Catering Services	1854	822	1170	1722	2378	4174
衣着	Clothing	1713	860	1221	1572	2210	3341
衣类	Garments	1371	667	956	1239	1785	2740
鞋类	Shoes	342	192	264	332	424	601
居住	Residence	4470	2478	3339	3994	5301	8322
生活用品及服务	Household Facilities, Articles and Services	1562	781	1122	1291	1928	3335
交通通信	Transportation and Communication	3366	1932	2354	2899	4166	6722
交通	Transportation	2395	1318	1577	2006	2967	5091
通信	Communication	970	614	777	894	1200	1631
教育文化娱乐	Recreation, Education and Cultural Services	2384	1331	1705	2112	2840	4819
教育	Education	1253	1026	1149	1268	1304	1672
文化娱乐	Recreation and Cultural Services	1131	304	556	844	1536	3147
医疗保健	Medicine and Medical Services	1861	1234	1483	1654	2254	3000
医疗器具及药品	Medical Equipment and Drugs	1242	369	515	533	728	1083
医疗服务	Medical Services	515	865	967	1121	1526	1917
其它商品和服务	Miscellaneous Goods and Services	666	225	464	491	787	1734

9-7 各市(州)城镇居民家庭人均收支及住房情况
Per Capita Income and Consumption Expenditure and Housing Conditions of Urban Households by Region

单位：元、平方米 (yuan、sq.m)

市(州)	Region	人均可支配收入 Per Capita Disposable Income		人均消费支出 Per Capita Expenditures for Consumption		#食品烟酒支出 Food,Tobacco and Liquor		人均住房面积 Per Capita Housing Area	
		2017	2018	2017	2018	2017	2018	2017	2018
成都市	Chengdu	38918	42128	25314	27312	8527	9012	36.6	37.1
自贡市	Zigong	31016	33597	20208	21833	7845	8483	35.6	36.7
攀枝花市	Panzhihua	35620	38510	22846	24106	7815	7811	34.9	33.6
泸州市	Luzhou	31449	34141	21121	22961	7957	8509	40.9	39.6
德阳市	Deyang	31609	34216	22735	23960	7737	7762	41.4	38.7
绵阳市	Mianyang	31822	34411	21043	22854	7307	7721	40.0	40.7
广元市	Guangyuan	28132	30592	18388	20080	7387	7767	40.0	41.5
遂宁市	Suining	29308	31830	20796	22638	6868	7881	40.2	35.6
内江市	Neijiang	30393	32982	18797	20427	6544	6662	35.2	34.8
乐山市	Leshan	31070	33663	20771	22768	7573	8003	41.4	38.9
南充市	Nanchong	28333	30810	18335	19703	6806	7080	40.8	39.5
眉山市	Meishan	31130	33697	19946	21035	6892	7466	44.3	38.2
宜宾市	Yibin	30832	33465	20490	22303	7197	7891	39.0	36.6
广安市	Guangan	30616	33079	20812	22075	7270	7656	43.8	37.9
达州市	Dazhou	28383	30882	19557	20713	7815	8075	37.3	37.4
雅安市	Yaan	29732	32198	18386	19659	6179	6643	42.9	41.4
巴中市	Bazhong	28286	30816	20497	22247	8488	9195	37.8	34.4
资阳市	Ziyang	30867	33336	20889	22437	7080	7161	42.9	33.2
阿坝藏族羌族自治州	Aba	30264	32686	20443	22047	7536	7958	41.1	39.7
甘孜藏族自治州	Ganzi	29486	31972	20566	22319	8397	9011	35.8	40.8
凉山彝族自治州	Liangshan	28170	30421	18287	19361	6244	6844	40.2	37.0

9-8 按收入五等份分组的城镇居民家庭生活设施情况(2018年)
Living Facilities of Urban Households by Income Quintile (2018)

项目		Item		总平均 Average	低收入户 Low Income Households	中低收入户 Lower Middle Income Households	中等收入户 Middle Income Households	中高收入户 Upper Middle Income Households	高收入户 High Income Households
供水情况		**Water Supply**							
管道供水入户	(%)	Piped Water Supply to Households	(%)	95.26	89.24	94.35	96.83	98.00	97.87
饮用水来源情况		**Sources of Drinking Water**							
经过净化处理的自来水	(%)	Purification Treatment of Tap Water	(%)	90.64	80.72	88.41	93.57	95.01	95.49
桶装水	(%)	Barrelled Water	(%)	1.41	0.81	1.28	1.66	1.62	1.68
厕所使用情况		**Toilet Usage**							
本住户独用	(%)	Only for the Household	(%)	98.14	98.10	97.74	97.78	98.14	98.92
几户合用	(%)	Shared by Some Households	(%)	1.36	1.36	1.72	1.37	1.61	0.74
公用厕所	(%)	Communal	(%)	0.51	0.55	0.54	0.85	0.25	0.34
洗澡设施情况		**Bathing Facilities**							
统一供热水	(%)	Unified Supply of Hot Water	(%)	1.93	1.68	2.10	1.53	2.85	1.52
家庭自装热水器	(%)	Home-self Installed Water Heaters	(%)	93.08	86.85	92.50	94.59	94.34	97.10
其他	(%)	Others	(%)	1.70	3.41	1.76	1.46	1.29	0.58
无洗澡设施	(%)	Without Bathing Facilities	(%)	3.29	8.06	3.64	2.42	1.53	0.80
取暖设备情况		**Heating Facilities**							
由市政或小区集中供暖	(%)	Central Heating by Municipal or District	(%)	0.95	0.24	0.80	0.20	0.93	2.55
自行供暖	(%)	Self-heating	(%)	61.27	58.22	58.25	62.40	61.21	66.27
无取暖设备	(%)	Without Heating Facilities	(%)	37.78	41.54	40.95	37.39	37.86	31.18
炊用能源情况		**Fuel for Cooking**							
灌装液化石油气	(%)	Liquefied Petroleum Gas filling	(%)	3.45	3.93	2.95	5.07	2.99	2.33
管道天燃气	(%)	Duct Coal Gas	(%)	75.80	60.61	76.33	78.34	81.82	81.88
电	(%)	Electricity	(%)	13.12	18.75	12.26	12.82	10.32	11.47

9-9 按收入五等份分组的城镇居民家庭住房情况(2018年)
Housing Conditions of Urban Households by Income Quintile (2018)

项目	Item	总平均 Average	低收入户 Low Income Households	中低收入户 Lower Middle Income Households	中等收入户 Middle Income Households	中高收入户 Upper Middle Income Households	高收入户 High Income Households
人均自有现住房面积 （平方米）	**Per Capita Floor Space of Buildings (sq.m)**	**34.11**	**31.24**	**31.32**	**32.64**	**35.82**	**42.56**
按居住类型划分	**Grouped by Residential Types**						
普通住宅 (%)	Average House (%)	99.50	99.65	99.68	99.17	99.54	99.47
集体宿舍和工棚 (%)	Collective Dormitory and Barrack (%)	0.35	0.35	0.32	0.57	0.15	0.36
工作地住宿 (%)	Workplace Accommodatio (%)						
按居住空间样式划分	**Grouped by House Patterns**						
单栋楼房 (%)	Independent building (%)	18.70	29.12	23.88	15.98	13.63	10.91
单栋平房 (%)	Independent bungalow (%)	5.85	13.04	5.96	4.69	2.83	2.73
四居室及以上单元房 (%)	Flats With 4 and more Bedrooms (%)	4.31	3.09	5.07	3.49	4.32	5.55
三居室单元房 (%)	Flats With 3 Bedrooms (%)	38.94	28.67	34.36	41.88	44.19	45.61
二居室单元房 (%)	Flats With 2 Bedrooms (%)	24.68	14.84	23.99	25.75	29.11	29.70
一居室单元房 (%)	Flats With 1 Bedroom (%)	5.14	5.37	4.80	6.15	4.66	4.74
筒子楼或连片平房 (%)	Tube-shaped Apartment or Continuous Bungalow (%)	1.38	2.69	1.12	1.92	0.85	0.34
其他	Others	0.99	3.19	0.82	0.14	0.41	0.40
按主要建筑材料划分	**Grouped by Main Building Materials**						
钢筋混凝土 (%)	Reinforced Concrete (%)	61.17	49.65	59.35	59.91	66.73	70.23
砖混材料 (%)	Brick Material (%)	32.72	34.21	34.41	36.10	30.72	28.14
砖瓦砖木 (%)	Brick and Tile (%)	4.96	12.29	5.55	3.38	2.45	1.11
竹草土坯 (%)	Bamboo Grass Adobe (%)	0.46	1.37	0.22	0.39		0.32
其他 (%)	Others (%)	0.69	2.49	0.47	0.22	0.11	0.19
按房屋来源划分	**Grouped by Source of Housing**						
租赁公房 (%)	Public Dwelling House Leased (%)	1.90	2.93	1.88	2.06	1.57	1.08
租赁私房 (%)	Private Dwelling House Leased (%)	6.49	5.34	6.34	5.51	6.02	9.22
自建住房 (%)	Spontaneous Housing (%)	25.26	44.55	31.03	22.10	16.38	12.23
购买商品房 (%)	Commercial Housing Purchased (%)	45.54	29.27	39.59	46.94	54.74	57.16
购买房改住房 (%)	Reformd Housing Purchased (%)	6.11	2.31	3.28	5.41	9.22	10.32
购买保障性住房 (%)	Affordable Housing Purchased (%)	1.77	1.06	1.02	1.14	2.63	2.99
拆迁安置房 (%)	Removal and Resettlement Housing (%)	10.22	11.47	14.28	13.89	6.87	4.57
继承或获赠住房 (%)	Inherited or Given Housing (%)	0.59	0.83	0.63	0.79	0.43	0.30
免费借用房 (%)	Free Housing (%)	1.47	1.36	1.40	1.79	1.42	1.37
雇主提供免费住房 (%)	Free Housing Provided by Employers (%)	0.24	0.20	0.40	0.07		0.53
其他 (%)	Others (%)	0.42	0.68	0.15	0.30	0.73	0.23

9-10 农村居民家庭基本情况
Basic Statistics of Rural Households

项　　目		Item		2014	2015	2016	2017	2018
平均每户常住人口	(人)	Average Resident Population per Household	(person)	3.03	3.03	3.05	3.07	3.04
平均每户整、半劳力	(人)	Average Number of Ablebodied and Semi-ablebodied Laborers per Household	(person)	2.07	2.09	2.14	2.12	2.09
平均每个劳动力负担人口(含本人)	(人)	Average Number of Persons Supported by a Laborer (including the laborer himself or herself)	(person)	1.46	1.45	1.45	1.45	1.43
全年人均总收入	**(元)**	**Average Annual Revenue**	**(yuan)**	**12647**	**14561**	**15907**	**17264**	**19016**
工资性收入	(元)	Wages Income	(yuan)	3157	3463	3738	4016	4311
经营性收入	(元)	Househol Business Income	(yuan)	6832	8005	8655	9167	10153
财产性收入	(元)	Property Income	(yuan)	202	243	289	340	414
转移性收入	(元)	Transfer Income	(yuan)	2456	2850	3225	3741	4138
全年人均可支配收入	**(元)**	**Per Capita Disposable Income**	**(yuan)**	**9348**	**10247**	**11203**	**12227**	**13331**
工资性收入	(元)	Income of Wages and Salaries	(yuan)	3157	3463	3738	4016	4311
经营净收入	(元)	Net Business Income	(yuan)	3878	4197	4525	4821	5117
财产净收入	(元)	Net Income from Property	(yuan)	185	224	269	323	379
转移净收入	(元)	Net Income from Transfer	(yuan)	2129	2363	2672	3067	3524
全年人均总支出	**(元)**	**Average Annual Expenditure**	**(yuan)**	**14731**	**16924**	**18706**	**20128**	**22538**
家庭经营费用支出	(元)	Expenditure for Household Business	(yuan)	2651	3522	3819	4009	4614
生活消费支出	(元)	Expenditure for Consumption	(yuan)	8301	9251	10192	11397	12723
食品烟酒	(元)	Food,Tobacco and Liquor	(yuan)	3299	3618	3887	4235	4483
#食品	(元)	Food		2580	2735	2957	3139	3225
衣着	(元)	Clothing	(yuan)	548	580	641	683	716
居住	(元)	Residence	(yuan)	1486	1675	1919	2157	2500
生活用品及服务	(元)	Household Facilities, Articles and Services	(yuan)	630	660	693	782	860
交通通信	(元)	Transportation and Communication	(yuan)	885	1020	1174	1378	1578
教育文化娱乐	(元)	Education, Recreation and Cultural Services	(yuan)	600	699	707	848	934
医疗保健	(元)	Medicine and Medical Services	(yuan)	724	840	973	1094	1414
其他商品和服务	(元)	Other Commodities and Services	(yuan)	724	840	199	220	238
恩格尔系数	(%)	Engel's Coefficient	(%)	39.75	39.12	38.14	37.16	35.24
人均经营耕地面积	(亩)	Per Capita Area of Cultivated Land under Management	(mu)	1.33	1.35	1.35	1.31	1.50
人均经营水面面积	(亩)	Per Capita Water Area under Management	(mu)	0.02	0.03	0.04	0.03	0.02
人均年内新建房屋面积	(平方米)	Per Capita Floor Space Newly Built in Current Year	(sq.m)	0.96	0.51	0.48	0.65	0.50
人均自有现住房面积	(平方米)	Per Capita Existing Housing Area	(sq.m)	44.94	47.13	47.85	48.57	47.41

9-11 按收入五等份分组的农村居民人均收入和支出情况(2018年)
Per Capita Income and Expenditure of Rural Households by Income Quintile (2018)

单位：元 (yuan)

项　　目	Item	总平均 Average	低收入户 Low Income Households	中低收入户 Lower Middle Income Households	中等收入户 Middle Income Households	中高收入户 Upper Middle Income Households	高收入户 High Income Households
平均每人全年总收入	**Per Capita Total Annual Income**	**19016**	**6725**	**10390**	**15131**	**21563**	**46533**
平均每人可支配收入	**Per Capita Disposable Income**	**13331**	**1795**	**7153**	**11260**	**16925**	**33551**
工资性收入	Income of Wages and Salaries	4311	1125	1967	3514	5969	10186
经营净收入	Net Business Income	5117	13	2536	4165	5542	15246
财产净收入	Net Income from Property	379	173	176	210	349	1123
转移净收入	Net Income from Transfer	3524	484	2475	3371	5064	6996
平均每人现金收入	**Per Capita Cash Income**	**16975**	**5414**	**8713**	**13100**	**19455**	**43209**
现金工资性收入	Cash Wages Income	4263	1103	1945	3474	5915	10075
现金经营性收入	Cash Household Business Income	8517	3113	3844	5787	7880	24921
现金财产性收入	Cash Property Income	414	214	208	235	378	1171
现金转移性收入	Cash Transfer Income	3780	984	2717	3604	5283	7042
平均每人全年总支出	**Per Capita Annual Expenditure**	**22538**	**19050**	**16737**	**18239**	**23065**	**38515**
#生产经营费用支出	Expenditure for Production	4685	3926	2493	3069	3751	11310
生活消费支出	Expenditure for Consumption	12723	10698	10549	11458	13321	18727
平均每人现金支出	**Expenditure in Cash**	**19177**	**16376**	**13757**	**14971**	**19529**	**33930**
#生产经营现金费用支出	Expenditure in Cash for Production	4200	3537	1978	2533	3235	10839
现金消费支出	Cash Consumption Expenditure	9848	8413	8085	8726	10301	14613

9-12 各市(州)农村居民家庭人均收支及住房情况
Per Capita Income and Consumption Expenditure and Housing Conditions of Rural Households by Region

单位：元、平方米 (yuan、sq.m)

市(州)	Region	人均可支配收入 Per Capita Disposable Income		人均消费支出 Per Capita Expenditures for Consumption		#食品烟酒支出 Food,Tobacco and Liquor		人均住房面积 Per Capita Housing Area	
		2017	2018	2017	2018	2017	2018	2017	2018
成都市	Chengdu	20298	22135	14616	15977	5444	5841	53.2	54.1
自贡市	Zigong	14380	15692	11790	12716	4820	5208	48.4	59.6
攀枝花市	Panzhihua	15336	16708	11807	12478	4422	4094	45.4	36.5
泸州市	Luzhou	13670	14983	10573	11399	4462	4690	47.6	45.9
德阳市	Deyang	15207	16583	11909	12944	4553	4528	45.5	43.3
绵阳市	Mianyang	14752	16101	11638	12676	4414	4735	49.0	45.9
广元市	Guangyuan	10801	11854	8958	9934	3636	3875	52.3	46.7
遂宁市	Suining	13579	14844	11342	12417	4625	4799	54.4	53.4
内江市	Neijiang	13640	14908	10681	11736	4249	4508	48.2	42.4
乐山市	Leshan	13927	15173	11241	12309	4404	4611	47.1	47.5
南充市	Nanchong	12389	13583	10296	11077	4306	4591	47.5	50.4
眉山市	Meishan	15203	16563	12407	13121	4647	4923	49.1	48.4
宜宾市	Yibin	14063	15391	11160	12066	4570	4757	46.2	48.8
广安市	Guangan	13655	14931	10593	11418	4040	4273	50.1	52.3
达州市	Dazhou	12843	14055	9261	10188	3928	4169	41.6	44.6
雅安市	Yaan	12145	13242	10202	11117	3787	3887	43.8	49.0
巴中市	Bazhong	10946	12002	9327	10155	4359	4413	47.9	47.5
资阳市	Ziyang	14670	16007	11261	12255	4022	4361	55.8	50.3
阿坝藏族羌族自治州	Aba	11751	12893	10590	11726	4520	5000	42.8	41.7
甘孜藏族自治州	Ganzi	10444	11555	7758	8537	4378	4683	32.8	30.1
凉山彝族自治州	Liangshan	11415	12548	8734	9333	3886	4042	31.1	28.8

9-13 社会保险基本情况
Social Insurance Indicators

单位：万人，亿元 (10 000 persons, 100 million yuan)

指　标	Item	2014	2015	2016	2017	2018
参加城镇职工基本养老保险人数	Persons of Urban Workers in Basic Endowment Pension Insurance	1839.69	1938.98	2157.60	2335.07	2543.71
参加养老保险职工人数	Staff and Workers in Basic Pension Insurance	1191.62	1250.06	1379.77	1519.03	1662.09
#执行企业养老保险制度职工人数	Number of Employees Under the Enterprise Endowment Insurance System	1089.27	1144.98	1196.51	1328.06	1469.57
参加养老保险离退休人数	Retired and Resigned Persons in Basic Pension Insurance	648.08	688.92	777.83	816.04	881.62
#执行企业养老保险制度人数	Number of Persons Under the Enterprise Endowment Insurance System	611.40	650.50	684.54	720.07	779.68
纳入社区管理的人数	Community Management	595.07	620.55	659.97	694.20	753.65
企业退休人员社区管理服务率(%)	Rate of Enterprise Retirees in Socialized Management (%)	97.5	95.5	96.5	96.5	96.7
城镇职工基本养老保险费征缴收入总额	Total Income of Basic Endowment Insurance for Urban Workers	1217.69	1251.90	1902.06	2569.64	2081.00
参加失业保险人数	Staff and Workers in Unemployment Insurance	635.85	660.95	701.95	776.68	875.10
城镇失业人员领取失业保险金人数	Number of Persons Drawing Unemployment Insurance	29.97	36.33	40.71	39.81	39.74
失业保险费征缴收入总额	Total Revenue of Unemployment Insurance	100.65	94.85	84.65	121.28	93.61
参加城镇职工基本医疗保险人数	Urban Workers in Medicine and Medical Insurance	1334.40	1383.53	1445.59	1531.30	1667.67
#退休人员	Retired and Resigned Persons	407.52	418.82	439.37	458.34	481.41
参加补充医疗保险人数	Persons in Supplementary Medical Insurance	1105.27	1206.72	1294.93	1362.70	1510.65
列入公务员医疗补助范围人数	Persons in Civil Servant Medical Benefits Coverage	147.61	152.52	158.40	165.70	172.62
城镇职工基本医疗保险费征缴收入总额	Total Revenue of Medical Insurance of Urban Employees	363.80	414.07	479.68	634.79	649.41
参加城乡居民基本医疗保险人数	Urban and Rural Residents in Basic Medical Insurance	1247.11	1272.13	4217.17	6642.09	6969.48
参加工伤保险人数	Persons in Work Injury Insurance	709.72	753.22	799.11	876.04	1012.59
享受工伤保险待遇人数	Persons Enjoying Work Injury Insurance Treatment	8.63	7.95	7.67	7.69	8.18
工伤保险费征缴收入总额	Total Revenue of Work Injury Insurance	28.06	29.32	26.97	31.29	40.80
参加生育保险人数	Staff and Workers in Maternity Insurance	730.36	670.29	713.07	776.34	878.18
享受生育保险待遇人(次)数	Persons(Times) Enjoying Maternity Insurance Treatment	21.68	24.84	31.78	34.34	34.12
生育保险费征缴收入总额	Total Revenue of Matenity Insurance	15.81	17.06	15.69	20.44	31.96

注：社会保险和离退休资料由四川省人力资源和社会保障厅及四川省医疗保障局提供。

a) Data of provincial social insurance and retirement are provided by Department of Human Resources and Social Security and Sichuan Medical Security Bureau .

9-14 各类社会保险参保人数
Number of Contributors to Social Insurance

(年末数)单位：万人 (year-end)(10 000 persons)

年份 Year	职工养老保险 (未包括离退休人员) Basic Pension Insurance (excluding Retired and Resigned Persons)	失业保险 Unemployment Insurance	基本医疗保险 Basic Medical Insurance	#城乡居民医疗保险 Medical Insuranc for Urban and Rural Residents	工伤保险 Work Injury Insurance	生育保险 Maternity Insurance
1995	294.5	365.0			196.5	99.8
2000	508.5	470.2			201.1	188.2
2005	556.0	358.3	649.6		285.3	215.7
2006	597.8	400.0	775.9	1.8	304.9	274.1
2007	648.0	415.2	1078.7	205	397.4	323.3
2008	711.1	434.5	1481.4	520.4	464.6	373
2009	782.7	466.3	1993.2	954.2	515.8	426.4
2010	861.9	469.8	2063.1	1011.2	583.8	484.2
2011	998.8	544.6	2254.8	1079.3	650.8	601.7
2012	1073.7	585.5	2389.1	1143	689.4	654.4
2013	1124.1	613.5	2491	1204	690.1	689.1
2014	1191.6	635.8	2581.5	1247.1	709.7	730.4
2015	1250.1	661.0	2655.7	1272.1	753.2	670.3
2016	1379.8	702.0	5662.8	4217.2	799.1	713.1
2017	1519.0	776.7	8173.4	6642.1	876.0	776.3
2018	1662.1	875.1	8637.2	6969.5	1012.6	878.2

9-15 各类社会保险基金征缴情况
Collection of Social Insurance Funds

单位：亿元，% (100 million yuan, %)

年份 Year	城镇职工基本养老保险 Basic Pension Insurance in Urban Area		失业保险 Unemployment Insurance	城镇职工基本医疗保险 Medical Insurance of Urban Workers		工伤保险 Work Injury Insurance		生育保险 Maternity Insurance	
	保险费收入 Revenue of Insurance	征缴率 Rate of Collection	保险费收入 Revenue of Insurance	保险费收入 Revenue of Insurance	征缴率 Rate of Collection	保险费收入 Revenue of Insurance	征缴率 Rate of Collection	保险费收入 Revenue of Insurance	征缴率 Rate of Collection
1995	27.3	85.3	1.1				96.2		97.2
2000	61.5	92.8	5.5			1.8	56.7	1.0	66.7
2005	189.9	96.8	11.0	49.0	98.4	4.1	93.1	1.5	94.2
2006	235.8	97.2	13.1	71.9	99.0	5.4	96.4	2.0	95.5
2007	315.8	98.0	17.5	90.5	99.1	6.7	96.5	3.4	96.8
2008	426.6	97.8	21.4	115.9	98.1	7.9	92.5	4.3	95.4
2009	606.2	96.0	24.7	127.3	98.4	9.3	95.7	4.2	97.4
2010	670.9	97.9	40.0	182.5	97.4	12.1	96.2	4.9	97.8
2011	870.3	98.0	59.2	223.4	98.6	16.6	96.0	8.5	97.0
2012	901.4	98.0	68.2	258.8	98.8	21.2	95.8	11.1	97.0
2013	1101.4	98.2	77.7	305.7	99.2	25.4	97.2	13.4	98.8
2014	1217.7	97.6	100.7	363.8	98.7	28.1	96.5	15.8	98.4
2015	1251.9	97.1	94.9	414.1	98.5	29.3	93.6	17.1	97.4
2016	1902.1	93.9	84.7	479.7	98.1	27.0	93.7	15.7	97.6
2017	2569.6	98.1	121.3	634.8		31.3	95.7	20.4	98.8
2018	2081.0	98.5	93.6	649.4	99.3	40.8	96.0	32.0	99.0

注：养老保险参保人数，2003年及以前年份未包括机关事业单位数据。

a) The contributors of basic pension insurance exclude contributors of government angencies and institutions in 2003 and before.

9-16 各市(州)社会保险参保人数(2018年)
Contributors of Social Insurance by Region(2018)

(年末数)单位：万人　　(year-end)(10 000 persons)

市(州)	Region	城镇职工基本养老保险 Basic Pension Insurance in Urban Area	失业保险 Unemployment Insurance	基本医疗保险 Basic Medical Insurance	工伤保险 Work Injury Insurance	生育保险 Maternity Insurance
全　省	**Sichuan**	**2543.71**	**875.10**	**8637.10**	**1012.59**	**878.20**
成都市	Chengdu	817.91	491.75	1682.20	528.81	511.05
自贡市	Zigong	86.45	15.08	283.10	19.43	16.04
攀枝花市	Panzhihua	51.10	17.23	113.60	16.77	17.73
泸州市	Luzhou	110.39	27.48	476.70	29.24	29.28
德阳市	Deyang	122.52	34.48	356.50	38.37	39.89
绵阳市	Mianyang	140.74	38.04	495.40	46.42	42.74
广元市	Guangyuan	60.81	16.29	272.60	16.95	14.74
遂宁市	Suining	82.61	12.03	334.50	16.02	18.83
内江市	Neijiang	92.00	16.18	366.70	23.50	19.73
乐山市	Leshan	124.16	23.27	328.00	37.75	21.66
南充市	Nanchong	126.10	19.68	626.10	27.18	15.80
眉山市	Meishan	81.32	17.67	300.70	21.77	19.14
宜宾市	Yibin	100.47	25.81	504.70	35.28	29.40
广安市	Guangan	71.16	14.90	411.90	14.47	9.86
达州市	Dazhou	105.53	13.93	613.20	22.37	13.50
雅安市	Yaan	47.97	10.30	150.90	11.60	8.92
巴中市	Bazhong	54.24	12.85	327.00	16.17	17.52
资阳市	Ziyang	51.92	10.43	290.50	14.11	10.96
阿坝藏族羌族自治州	Aba	21.82	7.42	87.70	10.26	3.71
甘孜藏族自治州	Ganzi	15.61	6.69	105.90	10.01	2.73
凉山彝族自治州	Liangshan	48.59	18.79	475.80	29.80	14.95

9-17 各市(州)社会保险基金征缴情况(2018年)
Collection of Social Insurance Funds by Region(2018)

单位：亿元 (100 million yuan)

市(州)	Region	城镇职工养老保险 Basic Pension Insurance in Urban Area		失业保险 Unemployment Insurance	城镇职工基本医疗保险 Medical Insurance of Urban Workers		工伤保险 Work Injury Insurance		生育保险 Maternity Insurance	
		保险费收入 Revenue of Insurance	征缴率(%) Rate of Collection	保险费收入 Revenue of Insurance	保险费收入 Revenue of Insurance	征缴率(%) Rate of Collection	保险费收入 Revenue of Insurance	征缴率(%) Rate of Collection	保险费收入 Revenue of Insurance	征缴率(%) Rate of Collection
全 省	**Sichuan**	**2081.00**	**98.5**	**93.61**	**649.40**	**99.3**	**40.80**	**96.0**	**31.97**	**99.0**
成都市	Chengdu	734.90	99.3	44.60	307.60	99.1	8.53	99.2	19.67	99.3
自贡市	Zigong	39.67	96.7	4.03	16.10	98.8	0.85	91.9	0.46	99.5
攀枝花市	Panzhihua	41.82	98.9	1.35	15.50	98.4	2.42	88.5	0.57	98.8
泸州市	Luzhou	60.32	96.8	5.99	21.50	100.0	1.58	99.7	1.18	99.8
德阳市	Deyang	92.50	97.5	1.88	25.40	99.0	1.74	99.3	1.06	98.8
绵阳市	Mianyang	80.77	99.3	2.16	28.60	99.8	1.72	98.8	1.15	99.3
广元市	Guangyuan	41.33	98.7	2.25	14.10	100.0	1.57	100.0	0.83	100.0
遂宁市	Suining	54.38	99.7	0.76	10.60	100.0	0.52	100.0	0.72	100.0
内江市	Neijiang	60.25	98.6	2.36	17.20	98.8	1.81	91.5		
乐山市	Leshan	66.74	96.5	1.20	17.70	96.1	2.74	87.0	0.58	91.7
南充市	Nanchong	104.77	99.8	2.02	20.50	100.0	1.10	99.3	0.68	99.1
眉山市	Meishan	58.42	99.9	0.99	12.80	100.0	1.64	98.4	0.82	99.7
宜宾市	Yibin	83.29	96.4	4.72	26.60	100.0	4.25	99.9	1.13	99.9
广安市	Guangan	58.83	99.9	6.84	12.00	100.0	1.39	100.0	0.27	100.0
达州市	Dazhou	92.24	98.3	1.44	13.90	100.0	3.05	84.2	0.39	94.3
雅安市	Yaan	37.88	98.5	0.58	8.60	100.0	1.00	92.6	0.25	94.7
巴中市	Bazhong	48.68	97.4	1.27	8.30	100.0	0.96	96.0	0.54	96.0
资阳市	Ziyang	29.19	96.6	2.43	10.70	99.1	0.61	98.5	0.63	97.5
阿坝藏族羌族自治州	Aba	21.12	99.8	0.57	8.80	100.0	0.73	99.0	0.12	99.2
甘孜藏族自治州	Ganzi	20.33	99.3	0.50	7.30	100.0	0.33	99.1	0.09	99.2
凉山彝族自治州	Liangshan	50.38	99.6	2.71	18.60	99.9	1.05	100.0	0.83	100.0

9-18 城市居民最低生活保障情况
Basic Statistics on Residents under Basic Provision Protection in Urban Area

单位：户、人、万元 (household, person, 10 000 yuan)

年份 Year	最低生活保障家庭数 Number of Households Receiving Minimum Living Allowances	最低生活保障人数 Number of Persons Receiving Minimum Living Allowances	#在职人员 Employed	#老年人 Elderly	城市低保资金 Funds for Urban Residents under Basic Provision Protection
2005	806737	1586126	11426	14744	112183
2006	848969	1652718	10110	13119	132090
2007	911724	1732899	26841	211336	179036
2008	974494	1857374	21394	186323	263932
2009	998369	1891548	28713	231127	346268
2010	1014429	1869694	25472	255385	403601
2011	1033800	1893114	13334	285339	455812
2012	1032332	1863842	15552	301762	428390
2013	1027660	1835734	17825	314598	507682
2014	989346	1734415	19440	325042	468792
2015	925095	1563548	16519	311675	490012
2016	819361	1344965	14622	301757	484439
2017	702040	1184095	13415	240296	431683
2018	568251	937070	11449	181309	387269

9-19 农村居民最低生活保障和救济情况
Basic Statistics on Residents under Basic Provision Protection and Receiving Almsgiving in Rural Area

单位：户、人、万元 (household, person, 10 000 yuan)

年份 Year	最低生活保障家庭数 Number of Households Receiving Minimum Living Allowances	最低生活保障人数 Number of Persons Receiving Minimum Living Allowances	#老年人 Elderly	#未成年人 Minors	#残疾人 Disabled	农村特困人员救助供养人数 Number of Rural Poor Personnel Relief Support	农村低保资金 Funds for Rural Residents under Basic Provision Protection
2005	296176	647007					8035
2006	717990	1580278	357390	121614	112009	420479	20929
2007	1090706	2227180	524831	188574	189501	107666	50291
2008	1662376	3480471	1066143	381232	281579	135071	131517
2009	1931727	3965356	1471447	444696	333549	175075	249586
2010	2005227	3944748	1609275	434813	339357	211323	310207
2011	2221734	4251001	1737689	464960	356790	234494	437368
2012	2360143	4344818	1825940	463760	361101	257064	411568
2013	2501780	4394553	1878508	479749	366885	510267	559692
2014	2513702	4253319	1861781	455977	361682	504771	531594
2015	2482609	4054741	1832063	410835	667113	494722	590045
2016	2243946	3566780	1646309	358976	592631	485843	705993
2017	2180895	3663099	1608418	407129	549868	459085	728896
2018	1968055	3399154	1467388	388574	489133	445371	748958

9-20 各市(州)城市居民最低生活保障和救济情况(2018年)
Basic Statistics on Residents under Basic Provision Protection and Receiving Almsgiving in Urban Area by Region(2018)

单位：户、人、万元 (household, person, 10 000 yuan)

市(州)	Region	最低生活保障家庭数 Number of Households Receiving Minimum Living Allowances	最低生活保障人数 Number of Persons Receiving Minimum Living Allowances	#在职人员 Employed	#老年人 Elderly	#登记失业 Registered Unemp-loyed	#无就业条件 Lack of Employment Conditions	城市低保资金 Funds for Urban Residents under Basic Provision Protection
全　省	**Sichuan**	**568251**	**937070**	**11449**	**181309**	**133123**	**301175**	**387269**
成都市	Chengdu	19668	24731	169	2250	3580	11290	18532
自贡市	Zigong	35349	52928	336	4492	4692	20244	19477
攀枝花市	Panzhihua	5103	7523	28	904	1800	2430	5060
泸州市	Luzhou	14749	19439	79	4134	912	8635	9165
德阳市	Deyang	19806	28802	226	3460	5380	8467	12256
绵阳市	Mianyang	33842	61735	1269	14686	4980	13455	22133
广元市	Guangyuan	50744	93195	1001	14177	22872	26851	26384
遂宁市	Suining	20041	34521	165	23704	1542	4077	13587
内江市	Neijiang	23236	34141	192	4190	9525	10614	15249
乐山市	Leshan	36532	47542	1909	10951	6071	16234	19301
南充市	Nanchong	89186	163228	593	46960	23612	41291	82359
眉山市	Meishan	34961	36962	1227	7570	3935	6466	15963
宜宾市	Yibin	18791	27496	183	5913	2950	13260	15547
广安市	Guangan	36813	67332	15	9529	8955	29337	19040
达州市	Dazhou	41358	61113	1044	8707	10370	22098	22681
雅安市	Yaan	2823	3323	20	693	277	928	1608
巴中市	Bazhong	32211	77183	1992	6956	9181	28027	30221
资阳市	Ziyang	4908	7042	70	1445	194	3249	4193
阿坝藏族羌族自治州	Aba	14642	30483	33	2988	5504	10246	12310
甘孜藏族自治州	Ganzi	8406	13181	438	3014	2323	5777	5543
凉山彝族自治州	Liangshan	25082	45170	460	4586	4468	18199	16662

注：城乡居民低保和救济资料由四川省民政厅提供；城市低保资金全省合计中含省本级数据。

a) Data of urban and rural residents under basic provision protection and relief materials are provided by Sichuan Provincial Civil Affairs Department. Data of funds for urban residents under basic provision protection include provincial data.

9-21 各市(州)农村居民最低生活保障和救济情况(2018年)

Basic Statistics on Residents under Basic Provision Protection and Receiving Almsgiving in Rural Area by Region(2018)

单位：户、人、万元 (household, person, 10 000 yuan)

市(州)	Region	最低生活保障家庭数 Number of Households Receiving Minimum Living Allowances	最低生活保障人数 Number of Persons Receiving Minimum Living Allowances	#老年人 Elderly	#未成年人 Minors	#残疾人 Disabled	农村特困人员救助供养人数 Number of Rural Poor Personnel Relief Support	农村低保资金 Funds for Rural Residents under Basic Provision Protection
全　省	**Sichuan**	**1968055**	**3399154**	**1467388**	**388574**	**489133**	**445371**	**748958**
成都市	Chengdu	55462	89268	29706	10818	24101	30254	51831
自贡市	Zigong	65754	104214	47079	3712	16557	19659	18131
攀枝花市	Panzhihua	6248	11487	4063	2003	2904	2765	3817
泸州市	Luzhou	108761	167696	69660	25372	31882	23948	37484
德阳市	Deyang	56260	78603	41298	6057	16800	19499	17121
绵阳市	Mianyang	77658	123881	66333	7304	27323	21187	28261
广元市	Guangyuan	93651	172722	66685	17246	22663	15107	25999
遂宁市	Suining	78378	106311	60606	6197	14187	22068	24125
内江市	Neijiang	55745	76285	34701	7527	19712	36625	20869
乐山市	Leshan	58661	116865	41775	19534	20309	12428	27931
南充市	Nanchong	335292	541361	304718	32977	80972	59205	86876
眉山市	Meishan	72905	85211	49145	3145	14824	20203	16350
宜宾市	Yibin	59026	122917	45000	19685	20359	23872	32068
广安市	Guangan	102257	212914	90737	22222	17404	26723	31530
达州市	Dazhou	255146	332025	196257	23623	57273	38385	79300
雅安市	Yaan	18017	24097	9439	2411	8482	4940	8536
巴中市	Bazhong	138366	257731	109181	29597	28922	13634	59954
资阳市	Ziyang	66291	94535	48747	8152	23096	22367	21430
阿坝藏族羌族自治州	Aba	42098	84874	19214	12061	6626	6796	17131
甘孜藏族自治州	Ganzi	57332	164552	33134	27148	11510	8875	40817
凉山彝族自治州	Liangshan	164747	431605	99910	101783	23227	16831	99400

注：农村低保资金全省合计中含省本级数据。

a) Funds for rural residents under basic provision protection include provicial funds.

主要统计指标解释

城乡一体化住户调查 从2012年四季度起，国家统计局对分别进行的城乡住户调查实施了一体化改革，规范了城乡划分范围，统一了城乡居民收入指标名称、分类和统计标准，建立了城乡统一的一体化住户调查，并据此采集全国居民有关数据。

居民可支配收入 指居民可用于最终消费支出和储蓄的总和，即居民可用于自由支配的收入。既包括现金收入，也包括实物收入。按照收入的来源，可支配收入包含四项，分别为：工资性收入、经营净收入、财产净收入和转移净收入。

工资性收入 指就业人员通过各种途径得到的全部劳动报酬和各种福利，包括受雇于单位或个人、从事各种自由职业、兼职和零星劳动得到的全部劳动报酬和福利。

经营净收入 指住户或住户成员从事生产经营活动所获得的净收入，是全部经营收入中扣除经营费用、生产性固定资产折旧和生产税之后得到的净收入。计算公式为：

经营净收入=经营收入-经营费用-生产性固定资产折旧-生产税

财产净收入 指住户或住户成员将其所拥有的金融资产、住房等非金融资产和自然资源交由其他机构单位、住户或个人支配而获得的回报并扣除相关的费用之后得到的净收入。财产净收入包括利息净收入、红利收入、储蓄性保险净收益、转让承包土地经营权租金净收入、出租房屋净收入、出租其他资产净收入和自有住房折算净租金等。财产净收入不包括转让资产所有权的溢价所得。

转移净收入 计算公式为：转移净收入=转移性收入-转移性支出

转移性收入 指国家、单位、社会团体对住户的各种经常性转移支付和住户之间的经常性收入转移。包括养老金或退休金、社会救济和补助、政策性生产补贴、政策性生活补贴、经常性捐赠和赔偿、报销医疗费、住户之间的赡养收入，本住户非常住成员寄回带回的收入等。转移性收入不包括住户之间的实物馈赠。

转移性支出 指调查户对国家、单位、住户或个人的经常性或义务性转移支付。包括缴纳的税款、各项社会保障支出、赡养支出、经常性捐赠和赔偿支出以及其他经常转移支出等。

居民消费支出 指居民用于满足家庭日常生活消费需要的全部支出，既包括现金消费支出，也包括实物消费支出。消费支出可划分为食品烟酒、衣着、居住、生活用品及服务、交通通信、教育文化娱乐、医疗保健以及其他用品及服务八大类。

食品烟酒支出 指用于各种食品和烟草、酒类的支出。

衣着支出 指与居民穿着有关的支出，包括服装、服装材料、鞋类、其他衣类及配件、衣着相关加工服务的支出。

居住支出 指与居住有关的支出，包括房租、水、电、燃料、物业管理等方面的支出，也包括自有住房折算租金。

生活用品及服务支出 指家庭及个人的各类生活品及家庭服务。包括家具及室内装饰品、家用器具、家用纺织品、家庭日用杂品、个人用品和家庭服务。

交通通信支出 指用于交通和通信工具及相关的各种服务费、维修费和车辆保险等支出。

教育文化娱乐支出 指用于教育、文化和娱乐方面的支出。

医疗保健支出 指用于医疗和保健的药品、用品和服务的总费用。包括医疗器具及药品，以及医疗服务。

其他用品及服务支出 指无法直接归入上述各类支出的其他用品与服务支出。

城镇家庭人口 指居住在一起，经济上合在一起共同生活的家庭成员。凡计算为家庭人口的成员其全部收支都包括在本家庭中。

农村住户 指农村常住户。农村常住户指长期(一年以上)居住在乡镇(不包括城关镇)行政管理区域内的住户，以及长期居住在城关镇所辖行政村范围内的农村住户。户口不在本地而在本地居住一年及以上的住户也包括在本地农村常住户范围内；有本地户口，但举家外出谋生一年以上的住户，无论是否保留承包耕地都不包括在本地农村住户范围内。

恩格尔系数 指食品支出金额在消费支出总额中所占的比例。

$$恩格尔系数=\frac{食品支出}{消费支出总额}\times100\%$$

城镇职工基本养老保险

1. 参保职工人数　指报告期末按照国家法律、法规和有关政策规定参加城镇职工基本养老保险并在社保经办机构已建立缴费记录档案的职工人数，包括中断缴费但未终止养老保险关系的职工人数，不包括只登记未建立缴费记录档案的人数。

2. 离退休人员人数　指报告期末参加城镇职工基本养老保险的离休、退休和退职人员的人数。

3. 基金收入　指根据国家有关规定，由纳入基本养老保险范围的缴费单位和个人按国家规定的缴费基数和缴费比例缴纳的养老保险基金，以及通过其他方式取得的形成基金来源的收入。包括单位和职工个人缴纳的基本养老保险费、基本养老保险基金利息收入、上级补助收入、下级上解收入、转移收入、财政补贴和其他收入。

基本医疗保险

1. 参保人数　指报告期末按国家有关规定参加职工基

本医疗保险和城乡居民基本医疗保险人员的合计。

2. 基金收入　指由用人单位和个人按照国家规定的缴费基数、缴费比例或缴费标准缴纳的基本医疗保险基金，财政补助资金以及通过其他方式取得的形成基金来源的款项，包括：单位缴纳收入、个人缴纳收入、财政补助收入（含医疗救助补助个人收入）、财政补贴收入、利息收入和其他收入。

失业保险

1. 参保人数　指报告期末按照国家法律、法规和有关政策规定参加了失业保险的城镇企业、事业单位的职工及地方政府规定参加失业保险的其他人员的人数。

2. 基金收入　指报告期内筹集的失业保险基金的总额，包括失业保险费收入、利息收入、财政补贴收入、其他收入、转移收入、上级补助收入、下级上解收入。

工伤保险

1. 参保人数　指报告期末依据国家有关规定参加工伤保险的职工人数和有雇工的个体工商户的雇工数。

2. 基金收入　指根据国家有关规定，由参加工伤保险的单位按国家规定的缴费基数和缴费比例缴纳的工伤保险基金，以及通过其他形式取得的形成基金来源的款项。包括：单位缴纳的社会统筹基金收入、财政补贴收入、利息收入、其他收入。

生育保险

1. 参保人数　指报告期末依据有关规定参加生育保险的人数。

2. 基金收入　指根据国家有关规定，由参加生育保险的单位按照国家规定的缴费基数和缴费比例缴纳的生育保险基金，以及通过其他方式取得的形成基金来源的款项，包括：单位缴纳的基金收入、利息收入和其他收入。

离休、退休、退职人员保险福利费用　指离休、退休、退职人员实际得到的生活费用总额，包括从社会保险经办机构和单位得到的费用。

城市居民最低生活保障人数　指在报告期末共同生活的家庭成员人均收入低于当地最低生活保障标准，且家庭财产状况符合相关规定的城镇居民，并已发放补助经费的人数。

农村居民最低生活保障人数　指报告期末共同生活的家庭成员人均收入低于当地最低生活保障标准，得到当地政府给予最低生活保障待遇的农业人口家庭人数。

Explanatory Notes on Main Statistical Indicators

Integrated Urban and Rural HouseholdS Survey In the fourth quarter of 2012, the NBS launched its reform on the household survey program, to form an integrated survey, instead of the two separate urban and rural household surveys. The reform regulates the division of urban and rural areas, integrates the concepts, classifications and standards, conducts the integrated household survey, and collects household data in the whole country thereafter.

Disposable Income of Householdsrefers to the income of households for purpose of final expenditure and savings. It includes income both in cash and in kind. By sources of income, disposable income includes four categories: income from wages and salaries, net business income, net income from properties and net income from transfer.

Income from Wages and Salaries refers to remuneration of labour and salaries from all kinds of sources, including those employed by other units or individuals, freelance work, part-time jobs, and sporadic labour.

Net Business Income refers to net income earned by households and their members engaged in production and business activities. It refers to the net income of operating revenue minus operating costs, depreciation of productive fixed assets, and production tax. The formula is:

Net Business Income=Operating Revenue-Operating Costs-Depreciation of Productive Fixed Assets-Production Tax

Net Income from Properties refers to the net income received as returns by households or members of financial assets, non-financial assets such as housing, to other institutions, households or individuals, and minus relevant costs. Net income from properties includes net income of interest, bonus income, net income of saving insurance, net income of rents of transferring management right of contract land, income of renting housing, income of renting other assets, net converted rents of self-owned housing. Net income from properties do not include premium of transferring ownership of assets.

Net Income from Transfer The formula is:

Net Income from Transfer=Income from Transfers-Expenditure from Transfer

Income from Transfer refers to the regular transfer from country, institutions, social communities to households and between households. It includes old-age and retirement pension, disaster relief funds, regular donation and compensation, applying for medical fees, supporting income between households, income from non-usual-residing members of households, etc. Income from transfer do not include presents in kinds between households.

Expenditure from Transfer refers to regular or deontic transfer from households to country, institutions, households or individuals. It includes taxes paid, expenditure of all kinds of social security, supporting expenditure, regular donation and compensation and other regular transfer expenditure, etc.

Consumption Expenditure of Households has a national coverage comparable between urban and rural households, and refers to the all the expenditures of households for consumption in daily life. It includes expenditure in cash and in kind on eight categories: food; clothing; housing; household appliances and services; transport and communications; education, cultural and recreational activities; and medical care. The expenditure on housing also includes rents, water, electricity, fuels and imputed rents of owner-occupied dwelling.

Food, Tobacco and Liquor Expenditure refers to expenditure for food, tobacco and liquor of all kinds.

Clothing Expenditure refers to expenditure related to clothing, including clothes, clothing materials, footwear, other clothing and accessories, processing services related to clothing.

Residence Expenditure refers to expenditure related to residence, including housing rents, water, electricity, fuel, property management, and including converted self-owned housing rents.

Household Facilities, Articles and Services Expenditure refers to expenditure for family and individual articles for living purpose and family services. It includes furniture and interior decoration, home appliances, home textiles, household miscellaneous daily articles, personal articles, and family services.

Transport and Communications Expenditure refers to expenditure for transport and communication and related services, maintenance and repairs, and vehicle insurance.

Education, Cultural and Recreational Activities Expenditure refers to expenditure on education, cultural and recreational activities.

Health Care and Medical Services Expenditure refers to expenditure on drugs, supplies and services of medical and health care. It includes medical appliances and drugs, and medical services.

Miscellaneous Goods and Services Expenditure refers to expenditure of all kinds of expenditure of other articles and services that can not divided into the category above.

Population of Urban Households refer to members of households living and sharing economically together in the urban areas. All the income and expenditure of all the members of such households are included in the income and expenditure of the household.

Rural Households refer to usual resident households in rural areas. Usual resident households in rural areas are households residing on a long term basis(for more than one year) in the areas under the administration of township governments (not including county towns), and in the areas under the administration of villages in county towns. Households residing in the current addresses for over one year with their household registration in other places are still considered as resident households of the locality. For households with their household registration in one place but all members of the households having moved away to make a living in another place for over one year, they will not be included in the rural households of the area where they are registered, irrespective of whether they still keep their contracted land.

EngelCoefficient refers to the percentage of expenditure on food to the total consumption, using the following formula:

$$\text{Engel Coefficient} = \frac{\text{Expenditure on Food}}{\text{Total Consumption Expenditure}} \times 100\%$$

Basic Pension Insurance of Urban Workers

1.Number of staff and workers covered refers to staff and workers participating in the basic pension insurance for urban staff and workers program according to national laws, regulations and related policies at the end of the reference period, who have already had payment records in social security management agencies, including those who have interrupt payment without terminating the insurance program. Those who have registered in the program but with no payment records are not included.

2.Number of retirees refers to the number of retirees participating in the basic pension insurance for urban staff and workers programs by the end of the reference period.

3. Revenue of insurance refers to payments made by units and individuals covered in pension insurance programs, and income from other resources according to national provision, including the premium paid by units and staff and works, interest income, subsidies from higher level agencies, income as transfer from subordinate agencies, transferred income, financial subsidies and other income.

Basic Medical Care Insurance:

1.Number of people participating in the insurance programme refers to the total number of basic medical insurance for employees and the basic medical insurance for urban and rural residents participating in the basic medical care insurance programme according to related regulations at the end of the reference period.

2.Revenue of basic medical care insurancerefers to payments made by employers and individuals participating in the medical care insurance program in accordance with the basis and proportion stipulated in State regulations, and income from other sources that become source of medical insurance fund, including income paid by units, individual paid income, financial assistance's income (including individual income from medicaid), financial subsidies' income, interest income and other income.

Unemployment Insurance

1.Number of people participated in unemployment insurance programrefers to number of staff and workers in urban enterprises or institutions and other people according to local government regulations participated in unemployment insurance program in line with national laws, regulations and related policies by the end of the reference period.

2.Revenue of insurance refers to the total unemployment insurance funds raised in the reference period, including unemployment insurance premium, interest income, financial subsidies, other income, transferred income, subsidies from higher level agencies and income as transfer from subordinate agencies.

Work Injury Insurance

1.Number of people participated in work injury insurance refers to staff and workers who have participated in the work injury insurance program and number of employees in private business according to relevant national regulations at the end of the reference period.

2. Revenue of unemployment insurance refers to payments made by units and individuals covered in unemployment insurance program, interest income, subsidies income from higher level agencies, income as transfer from subordinate agencies, transferred income, financial subsidies and other income.

Maternity Insurance

1.Number of people covered refers to people who have participated in the maternity insurance program according to relevant national regulations at the end of the reference period.

2.Revenue of maternity insurance refers to payments made by units covered in maternity insurance program according to national provisions, and income from other resources, including: income of funds paid by units, interest income and other income.

Insurance and Welfare Funds for Retired and Resigned Staff and workers refer to the total living expenses actually received by those retirees, including those from social insurance management agencies and units.

Number of Urban Residents Entitled to Minimum Living Allowancesrefers to the number of those urban residents whose average family income is below a minimum local standard, and status of family property meets the relevant regulation, and have received subsidies by the end of the reporting period.

Number of Rural Residents Entitled to Minimum Living Allowancesrefers to the number of those rural residents whose average family income is below a minimum local standard, and receiving the minimum living allowances from the local government by the end of the reporting period.

城市发展

Chapter 10 Urban Development

10-1 城市基本情况(2018年) Basic Statistics on Cities(2018)

城 市	City	年末常住人口(万人) Resident Population (year-end) (10 000 persons)	年末就业人员(万人) Number of Employed Persons (10 000 persons)	第一产业 Primary Industry	第二产业 Secondary Industry	第三产业 Tertiary Industry	城区面积(平方公里) Total Urban Area (sq.km)	#建成区面积 Area of Built Districts
全 省	**Sichuan**	**8341.00**	**4881.00**	**1752.30**	**1327.60**	**1801.10**	**8458.49**	**2982.32**
地级市	**at Prefecture Level**	**7636.20**	**4415.98**	**1512.35**	**1262.27**	**1641.36**	**6421.70**	**2530.25**
成都市	Chengdu	1633.00	894.96	102.85	323.10	469.01	1281.89	931.58
自贡市	Zigong	292.00	169.98	62.81	49.82	57.35	778.32	124.00
攀枝花市	Panzhihua	123.60	62.83	18.61	17.91	26.31	342.56	81.05
泸州市	Luzhou	432.40	250.00	98.96	77.57	73.47	411.38	169.01
德阳市	Deyang	354.50	216.81	71.46	59.47	85.88	193.59	89.24
绵阳市	Mianyang	485.70	304.40	86.74	102.55	115.11	497.00	158.62
广元市	Guangyuan	266.70	165.03	67.23	38.30	59.50	216.70	64.25
遂宁市	Suining	320.20	163.87	68.42	43.49	51.96	316.00	83.94
内江市	Neijiang	369.90	178.40	50.44	50.42	77.54	278.93	85.21
乐山市	Leshan	326.70	184.78	74.72	40.98	69.08	349.59	77.08
南充市	Nanchong	644.00	303.89	113.42	92.47	98.00	420.00	145.00
眉山市	Meishan	298.40	189.60	82.37	47.94	59.29	253.56	65.94
宜宾市	Yibin	455.60	316.71	139.90	91.19	85.62	181.20	134.31
广安市	Guangan	324.10	219.71	100.37	52.60	66.74	137.20	72.43
达州市	Dazhou	572.00	331.28	160.01	65.42	105.85	157.37	100.30
雅安市	Yaan	154.00	104.06	48.54	22.02	33.50	196.89	38.26
巴中市	Bazhong	332.20	171.73	72.86	44.59	54.28	160.29	60.03
资阳市	Ziyang	251.20	187.94	92.64	42.43	52.87	249.23	50.00
县级市	**at County Level**	**961.50**	**653.35**	**198.48**	**192.60**	**262.27**	**2036.79**	**452.07**
都江堰市	Dujiangyan	69.70	43.91	7.10	15.13	21.67	102.13	38.03
彭州市	Pengzhou	77.80	54.53	21.72	16.97	15.85	133.80	27.03
邛崃市	Qionglai	61.90	38.92	10.21	10.12	18.59	144.28	25.47
崇州市	Chongzhou	66.50	54.35	10.89	28.41	15.05	63.42	31.07
简阳市	Jianyang	106.50	74.08	27.72	15.81	30.55	112.00	36.00
广汉市	Guanghan	60.20	36.90	11.90	11.80	13.20	60.50	54.86
什邡市	Shifang	41.80	23.90	7.80	7.90	8.20	21.00	17.20
绵竹市	Mianzhu	46.00	31.00	9.40	9.50	12.10	16.50	16.50
江油市	Jiangyou	78.70	51.22	15.17	18.18	17.87	199.41	35.00
隆昌市	Longchang	62.30	48.83	7.97	19.83	21.03	57.00	25.20
峨眉山市	Emeishan	45.60	30.10	9.50	6.10	14.50	90.20	22.36
阆中市	Langzhong	73.70	48.98	14.75	10.48	23.75	150.00	35.00
华蓥市	Huaying	28.10	18.90	7.10	6.03	5.77	92.40	15.49
万源市	Wanyuan	41.50	29.05	12.03	3.51	13.51	18.27	15.36
马尔康市	Maerkang	6.00	4.98	1.66	0.51	2.81	369.16	5.26
康定市	Kangding	13.40	8.80	3.36	0.82	4.62	6.00	5.40
西昌市	Xichang	81.80	54.90	20.20	11.50	23.20	400.72	46.84

注：本篇章除“年末常住人口、年末就业人员”外，其余资料均由四川省住房和城乡建设厅提供。

a) Data of this talble are provided by Sichuan Provincial Department of Housing and Urban and Rural Construction, except indicator "Resident Population" and "Number of Employed Persons".

10-2 城市设施水平(2018年)
Level of Public Facilities in Cities(2018)

城市	City	供水普及率(%) Water Coverage Rate (%)	燃气普及率(%) Gas Coverage Rate (%)	人均城市道路面积(平方米) Per Capita Area of Roads (sq.m)	污水处理率(%) Wastewater Treatment Rate (%)	人均公园绿地面积(平方米) Per Capita Public Recreational Green Space (sq.m)	建成区绿化覆盖率(%) Green Covered Area as Percentage of Built Districts (%)	生活垃圾处理率(%) Household Garbage Treatment Rate (%)
全 省	**Sichuan**	**95.70**	**93.70**	**14.63**	**93.58**	**12.97**	**40.55**	**99.95**
地级市	**at Prefecture Level**	**96.05**	**94.18**	**14.50**	**94.07**	**13.01**	**40.57**	**99.95**
成都市区	Chengdu	98.94	95.79	14.20	94.14	13.33	41.33	100.00
自贡市区	Zigong	84.98	87.97	14.84	93.50	13.00	42.50	100.00
攀枝花市区	Panzhihua	99.98	97.03	13.28	95.13	13.16	40.47	100.00
泸州市区	Luzhou	94.07	82.92	10.52	94.21	12.50	41.27	100.00
德阳市区	Deyang	97.40	96.41	15.68	92.97	12.83	41.98	100.00
绵阳市区	Mianyang	99.95	99.91	18.15	96.12	11.98	40.11	100.00
广元市区	Guangyuan	92.00	99.10	14.06	98.79	12.77	39.30	100.00
遂宁市区	Suining	99.67	99.71	26.90	93.48	15.61	40.18	100.00
内江市区	Neijiang	98.12	95.17	9.80	90.14	11.68	36.49	100.00
乐山市区	Leshan	96.60	93.26	13.63	92.52	9.92	40.37	100.00
南充市区	Nanchong	98.54	98.54	15.15	93.01	12.81	44.28	100.00
眉山市区	Meishan	97.83	96.87	17.72	91.09	12.83	39.90	100.00
宜宾市区	Yibin	86.80	92.47	12.84	95.81	12.32	39.08	100.00
广安市区	Guangan	99.14	98.68	25.44	99.97	23.86	41.68	100.00
达州市区	Dazhou	86.78	81.36	12.71	88.49	10.66	35.73	100.00
雅安市区	Yaan	99.20	98.84	15.60	94.21	12.85	39.97	98.00
巴中市区	Bazhong	84.50	86.79	4.37	88.91	12.01	36.07	98.00
资阳市区	Ziyang	97.89	99.88	20.72	97.37	17.77	36.11	100.00
县级市	**at County Level**	**93.73**	**91.04**	**15.36**	**90.50**	**12.75**	**40.43**	**99.99**
都江堰市	Dujiangyan	98.77	94.26	15.17	89.38	11.95	43.01	100.00
彭州市	Pengzhou	98.70	98.39	12.29	88.51	11.94	38.16	100.00
邛崃市	Qionglai	99.62	98.26	22.89	94.93	26.96	42.75	100.00
崇州市	Chongzhou	99.73	99.68	23.01	92.78	12.07	42.18	100.00
简阳市	Jianyang	98.86	99.57	13.10	86.06	14.21	37.59	100.00
广汉市	Guanghan	98.20	94.74	13.60	92.02	8.41	43.97	100.00
什邡市	Shifang	86.96	91.83	16.50	90.70	14.92	39.18	100.00
绵竹市	Mianzhu	97.90	97.24	27.94	91.38	8.44	36.79	100.00
江油市	Jiangyou	98.18	94.64	18.00	92.00	12.45	41.64	100.00
隆昌市	Longchang	96.81	95.86	25.51	89.01	13.91	44.67	100.00
峨眉山市	Emeishan	92.70	76.38	16.21	95.83	16.26	46.69	100.00
阆中市	Langzhong	98.44	98.44	14.53	93.78	12.34	43.86	100.00
华蓥市	Huaying	96.10	94.77	16.34	96.84	11.70	29.71	100.00
万源市	Wanyuan	91.39	91.47	4.72	86.99	14.09	31.25	100.00
马尔康市	Maerkang	93.17	70.31	13.09	82.19	14.68	36.62	98.63
康定市	Kangding	70.59	69.85	10.22	79.92	13.10	30.77	100.00
西昌市	Xichang	75.87	70.21	8.96	87.87	10.14	36.32	100.00

10-3 城市供水情况(2018年)
Basic Statistics on Water Supply in Cities(2018)

城 市	City	供水综合生产能力(万立方米/日) Production Capacity of Tap Water Supply (10 000 cu.m / day)	供水管道长度(公里) Length of Water Supply Pipelines (km)	供水总量(万立方米) Total Volume of Water Supply (10 000 cu.m)	#居民家庭用水 Water for Residential Use	用水人口(万人) Number of Residents with Access to Tap Water (10 000 persons)	人均日生活用水量(升) Per Capita Daily Consumption of Tap Water for Residential Use (liter)
全 省	**Sichuan**	**1101.81**	**42658.76**	**258676.09**	**141911.90**	**2483.78**	**181.36**
地级市	**at Prefecture Level**	**923.55**	**36747.94**	**222260.49**	**123053.17**	**2112.84**	**183.53**
成都市区	Chengdu	388.70	15471.56	109274.78	64080.18	829.11	236.08
自贡市区	Zigong	29.20	3098.58	6783.02	3669.39	98.92	125.12
攀枝花市区	Panzhihua	57.07	1224.37	11922.25	4053.23	65.93	216.78
泸州市区	Luzhou	85.51	1967.96	11606.53	6261.00	152.37	126.50
德阳市区	Deyang	29.50	737.04	7146.53	3117.05	64.49	137.80
绵阳市区	Mianyang	57.01	3954.43	12223.71	6791.85	140.13	169.36
广元市区	Guangyuan	20.87	584.00	5204.70	3091.90	49.25	196.04
遂宁市区	Suining	27.80	1178.95	6854.62	3011.18	54.25	168.29
内江市区	Neijiang	18.10	575.81	5084.70	2900.20	64.18	136.48
乐山市区	Leshan	32.91	1860.75	5930.09	3845.18	78.44	137.86
南充市区	Nanchong	35.00	1002.00	10375.00	5310.00	135.00	153.65
眉山市区	Meishan	23.70	703.97	4862.20	2918.00	54.00	172.30
宜宾市区	Yibin	29.48	1540.75	7323.62	3892.39	112.49	120.30
广安市区	Guangan	10.00	718.82	3145.61	1579.02	36.85	142.74
达州市区	Dazhou	29.00	759.50	5978.20	3911.00	78.83	148.06
雅安市区	Yaan	16.00	522.23	2375.40	1484.00	27.40	173.90
巴中市区	Bazhong	11.50	319.22	3417.00	1743.00	38.70	129.98
资阳市区	Ziyang	22.20	528.00	2752.53	1394.60	32.50	147.57
县级市	**at County Level**	**178.26**	**5910.82**	**36415.60**	**18858.73**	**370.94**	**169.04**
都江堰市	Dujiangyan	22.95	489.99	4204.14	2242.50	32.19	242.82
彭州市	Pengzhou	18.34	1076.34	2118.41	1040.59	28.19	118.82
邛崃市	Qionglai	10.30	266.80	2165.60	760.50	18.31	134.17
崇州市	Chongzhou	6.80	285.00	2129.17	1183.16	18.59	193.23
简阳市	Jianyang	13.20	263.75	2384.86	1425.79	36.38	109.90
广汉市	Guanghan	17.06	296.90	3341.36	1814.84	33.25	168.59
什邡市	Shifang	11.20	464.49	1777.00	505.00	11.60	210.44
绵竹市	Mianzhu	8.00	122.85	1495.09	686.64	13.50	160.54
江油市	Jiangyou	15.00	686.00	2659.50	2103.50	35.00	168.88
隆昌市	Longchang	6.00	436.62	1460.00	912.00	21.27	129.71
峨眉山市	Emeishan	8.00	207.00	2305.00	1310.00	16.25	252.22
阆中市	Langzhong	11.00	253.00	2751.00	1220.00	31.50	159.69
华蓥市	Huaying	2.50	217.79	746.70	486.00	11.58	138.41
万源市	Wanyuan	2.01	76.99	793.62	382.21	12.00	94.54
马尔康市	Maerkang	1.90	41.00	417.15	287.00	2.73	298.19
康定市	Kangding	1.30	65.00	439.00	325.00	4.80	210.19
西昌市	Xichang	22.70	661.30	5228.00	2174.00	43.80	203.60

10-4 城市燃气情况(2018年)
Basic Statistics on Gas Supply in Cities(2018)

城 市	City	天然气销售量(万立方米) Total Volume of Gas Sales (10 000 cu.m)	#居民家庭 Volume of Residential Use	天然气用气人口(万人) Population with Access to Gas (10 000 persons)	液化石油气销售量(吨) Total Volume of LPG Sales (10 000 cu.m)	#居民家庭 Volume of Residential Use	液化石油气用气人口(万人) Population with Access to LPG (10 000 persons)
全 省	**Sichuan**	**828338.95**	**341840.90**	**2254.80**	**190371.25**	**93653.88**	**117.55**
地级市	**at Prefecture Level**	**741973.08**	**298417.62**	**1953.77**	**163051.04**	**76018.28**	**58.28**
成都市区	Chengdu	352852.51	160178.00	774.41	126328.79	51726.78	28.31
自贡市区	Zigong	21521.67	10995.10	102.40			
攀枝花市区	Panzhihua	1359.05	94.96	1.84	2243.00	1791.00	2.48
泸州市区	Luzhou	79300.45	13293.80	132.00	2133.30	1587.00	2.30
德阳市区	Deyang	56969.05	7112.00	61.80	3855.95	2337.00	2.03
绵阳市区	Mianyang	50451.02	17033.09	137.16	2951.00	2808.50	2.92
广元市区	Guangyuan	14085.10	7102.08	51.36	1173.00	913.00	1.69
遂宁市区	Suining	20458.73	7033.44	54.27			
内江市区	Neijiang	14902.17	5780.40	58.25	14264.00	6625.00	4.00
乐山市区	Leshan	37085.75	8827.61	75.60	140.00	15.00	0.13
南充市区	Nanchong	20850.00	9552.00	130.00	5610.00	4810.00	5.00
眉山市区	Meishan	12351.62	6679.00	53.21	541.00	138.00	0.26
宜宾市区	Yibin	23880.60	19284.43	117.97	1011.00	927.00	1.86
广安市区	Guangan	7068.71	4761.35	36.68			
达州市区	Dazhou	9443.65	5746.36	73.91			
雅安市区	Yaan	5888.00	4099.00	27.30			
巴中市区	Bazhong	8577.00	7625.00	39.75			
资阳市区	Ziyang	4928.00	3220.00	25.86	2800.00	2340.00	7.30
县级市	**at County Level**	**86365.87**	**43423.28**	**301.03**	**27320.21**	**17635.60**	**59.27**
都江堰市	Dujiangyan	8391.00	6335.00	30.31	392.73	165.06	0.41
彭州市	Pengzhou	8458.95	7048.04	25.10	935.00	854.00	3.00
邛崃市	Qionglai	5429.00	3420.00	17.32	252.00	127.00	0.74
崇州市	Chongzhou	5050.00	2850.00	14.70	3400.00	2545.00	3.88
简阳市	Jianyang	8150.00	2821.90	32.44	1678.00	1630.00	4.20
广汉市	Guanghan	11803.40	4698.00	26.10	4201.23	4088.54	5.98
什邡市	Shifang	8067.00	1773.00	11.20	740.00	350.00	1.05
绵竹市	Mianzhu	9258.00	2326.00	12.01	1343.25	1200.00	1.40
江油市	Jiangyou	7645.00	3880.00	33.74			
隆昌市	Longchang	2659.75	1953.68	21.06			
峨眉山市	Emeishan	3729.59	1344.07	13.39	1450.00		
阆中市	Langzhong	3660.00	2245.00	30.50	1335.00	790.00	1.00
华蓥市	Huaying	2160.00	1510.00	10.50	145.00	100.00	0.92
万源市	Wanyuan	789.89	572.19	10.00	670.00	670.00	2.01
马尔康市	Maerkang	69.00	32.00	0.60	227.00	227.00	1.46
康定市	Kangding	52.40	52.40	0.93	1895.00	1895.00	3.82
西昌市	Xichang	992.89	562.00	11.13	8656.00	2994.00	29.40

10-5 城市市政设施情况(2018年)
Basic Statistics on Municipal Infrastructure in Cities(2018)

城 市	City	道路长度(公里) Length of Paved Roads (km)	道路面积(万平方米) Area of Paved Roads (10 000 sq.m)	桥梁数(座) Number of Bridges (unit)	排水管道长度(公里) Length of Drain Pipes (km)	污水管道 Wastewater Pipes	雨水管道 Rainwater Pipes	雨污合流管道 Combined Pipes of Rainwater and Wastewater
全 省	**Sichuan**	**17831.84**	**37968.36**	**2845**	**33011.14**	**14342.47**	**15093.00**	**3575.67**
地级市	**at Prefecture Level**	**15177.17**	**31890.07**	**2422**	**28200.99**	**12280.75**	**13198.60**	**2721.64**
成都市区	Chengdu	4610.75	11899.46	1249	11647.03	5328.35	6093.56	225.12
自贡市区	Zigong	1452.67	1727.71	133	969.71	251.79	509.95	207.97
攀枝花市区	Panzhihua	729.17	875.78	83	662.67	478.28	183.39	1.00
泸州市区	Luzhou	881.61	1703.37	64	1429.14	606.01	583.07	240.06
德阳市区	Deyang	430.60	1038.19	48	1494.68	599.84	868.54	26.30
绵阳市区	Mianyang	1261.11	2545.18	119	2826.86	1221.45	1576.74	28.67
广元市区	Guangyuan	454.73	752.49	177	730.52	420.12	298.21	12.19
遂宁市区	Suining	621.80	1464.34	92	961.41	530.27	380.78	50.36
内江市区	Neijiang	282.80	640.88	65	542.18	198.05	174.02	170.11
乐山市区	Leshan	664.86	1106.41	55	806.17	229.61	122.30	454.26
南充市区	Nanchong	687.00	2075.00	53	1744.00	666.00	630.00	448.00
眉山市区	Meishan	486.95	978.07	60	777.28	234.88	428.40	114.00
宜宾市区	Yibin	791.31	1664.11	69	836.11	219.56	258.29	358.26
广安市区	Guangan	358.36	945.74	19	472.18	304.33	149.85	18.00
达州市区	Dazhou	456.76	1154.57	15	791.28	351.68	351.68	87.92
雅安市区	Yaan	246.90	430.77	44	389.16	140.33	79.62	169.21
巴中市区	Bazhong	380.00	200.00	35	360.00	200.00	160.00	
资阳市区	Ziyang	379.79	688.00	42	760.61	300.20	350.20	110.21
县级市	**at County Level**	**2654.67**	**6078.29**	**423**	**4810.15**	**2061.72**	**1894.40**	**854.03**
都江堰市	Dujiangyan	266.07	494.26	93	560.12	231.27	300.01	28.84
彭州市	Pengzhou	143.98	350.98	8	480.56	196.30	284.26	
邛崃市	Qionglai	124.56	420.74	2	323.16	119.23	169.93	34.00
崇州市	Chongzhou	145.60	428.95	10	488.60	240.61	217.99	30.00
简阳市	Jianyang	169.20	482.20	26	409.30	167.30	144.00	98.00
广汉市	Guanghan	234.41	460.33	19	422.69	161.19	188.50	73.00
什邡市	Shifang	124.93	220.06	37	133.00	38.00	52.00	43.00
绵竹市	Mianzhu	171.39	385.32	22	213.80	162.50	50.30	1.00
江油市	Jiangyou	222.46	641.73	28	419.60	209.80	209.80	
隆昌市	Longchang	210.43	560.35	18	170.03	78.50	16.41	75.12
峨眉山市	Emeishan	98.64	284.15	21	104.60	54.40	7.20	43.00
阆中市	Langzhong	178.00	465.00	24	386.00	153.00	133.00	100.00
华蓥市	Huaying	107.07	196.92	22	240.00	123.00	101.00	16.00
万源市	Wanyuan	48.00	62.00	59	69.35	4.55	20.00	44.80
马尔康市	Maerkang	39.30	38.36	18	12.23	12.23		
康定市	Kangding	98.60	69.50	16	42.20	30.20		12.00
西昌市	Xichang	272.03	517.44		334.91	79.64		255.27

10-6 城市绿地和园林情况(2018年)
Basic Statistics on Parks and Green Areas in Cities(2018)

城 市	City	绿化覆盖面积(公顷) Areas Covered by Green Land (hectare)	#建成区 Built Districts	绿地面积(公顷) Green Area (hectare)	#建成区 Built Districts	公园绿地面积(公顷) Public Green Area (hectare)	公园个数(个) Number of Parks (units)	公园面积(公顷) Area of Parks (hectare)
全 省	**Sichuan**	**129331**	**120929**	**113537**	**107611**	**33668**	**629**	**18238**
地级市	**at Prefecture Level**	**110645**	**102654**	**97129**	**91415**	**28621**	**512**	**14833**
成都市区	Chengdu	38499	38499	34094	34094	11173	113	3545
自贡市区	Zigong	5378	5270	4642	4534	1513	19	623
攀枝花市区	Panzhihua	3280	3280	2981	2981	868	21	611
泸州市区	Luzhou	7607	6975	6971	6339	2025	42	1592
德阳市区	Deyang	3746	3746	3182	3182	849	17	506
绵阳市区	Mianyang	6362	6362	5839	5839	1680	19	685
广元市区	Guangyuan	2525	2525	2417	2417	684	24	568
遂宁市区	Suining	7044	3372	6406	2893	850	30	690
内江市区	Neijiang	3442	3109	2848	2848	764	8	113
乐山市区	Leshan	4035	3112	3727	2900	805	40	586
南充市区	Nanchong	6732	6420	5668	5528	1755	24	1649
眉山市区	Meishan	2861	2631	2425	2201	708	12	183
宜宾市区	Yibin	5249	5249	4568	4568	1596	46	703
广安市区	Guangan	3056	3019	2594	2586	887	29	991
达州市区	Dazhou	4418	3584	3531	3308	968	19	733
雅安市区	Yaan	2370	1529	1390	1373	355	23	245
巴中市区	Bazhong	2198	2165	2126	2111	550	14	412
资阳市区	Ziyang	1841	1805	1722	1715	590	12	399
县级市	**at County Level**	**18686**	**18275**	**16408**	**16196**	**5047**	**117**	**3405**
都江堰市	Dujiangyan	1636	1636	1461	1461	389	4	126
彭州市	Pengzhou	1032	1032	861	861	341	2	18
邛崃市	Qionglai	1089	1089	968	968	495	7	495
崇州市	Chongzhou	1310	1310	1231	1231	225	1	3
简阳市	Jianyang	1353	1353	1231	1182	523	8	683
广汉市	Guanghan	2413	2412	1971	1966	285	9	116
什邡市	Shifang	674	674	538	538	199	4	49
绵竹市	Mianzhu	607	607	514	514	116	5	36
江油市	Jiangyou	1474	1457	1325	1271	444	6	191
隆昌市	Longchang	1257	1126	1041	975	306	3	39
峨眉山市	Emeishan	1044	1044	971	971	285	11	174
阆中市	Langzhong	1560	1535	1364	1330	395	8	300
华蓥市	Huaying	476	460	429	425	141	4	140
万源市	Wanyuan	480	480	446	446	185	5	312
马尔康市	Maerkang	380	193	186	186	43	2	44
康定市	Kangding	166	166	191	191	89	3	18
西昌市	Xichang	1735	1701	1680	1680	586	35	660

10-7 城市排污和市容环境卫生情况(2018年)
Basic Statistics on Sewage ,Urban Sanitation in Cities(2018)

城　市	City	污水排放量 (万立方米) Volume of Sewage Discharged (10 000 cu.m)	污水处理厂 (座) Watewater Treatment Plants (unit)	污水处理厂处理量 (万立方米) Volume of Watewater Treatment Plants (10 000 cu.m)	生活垃圾清运量 (万吨) Volume of Household Garbage Treatment (10 000 tons)
全　省	**Sichuan**	**224160**	**137**	**204036**	**1013.08**
地级市	**at Prefecture Level**	**193408**	**112**	**176205**	**867.17**
成都市区	Chengdu	104089	28	97939	446.96
自贡市区	Zigong	5270	5	4928	24.97
攀枝花市区	Panzhihua	9206	7	4090	15.85
泸州市区	Luzhou	8356	11	7109	30.91
德阳市区	Deyang	7966	5	7407	17.26
绵阳市区	Mianyang	10407	8	10003	50.68
广元市区	Guangyuan	4028	6	3979	18.28
遂宁市区	Suining	5031	7	4703	22.23
内江市区	Neijiang	3564	4	3213	24.30
乐山市区	Leshan	5388	7	4892	30.39
南充市区	Nanchong	7264	2	6756	46.02
眉山市区	Meishan	3600	4	3122	29.05
宜宾市区	Yibin	5675	6	5438	34.89
广安市区	Guangan	2963	5	2962	11.50
达州市区	Dazhou	4267	1	3776	26.65
雅安市区	Yaan	1675	2	1578	11.87
巴中市区	Bazhong	2662	1	2366	11.12
资阳市区	Ziyang	1996	3	1944	14.23
县级市	**at County Level**	**30752**	**25**	**27831**	**145.91**
都江堰市	Dujiangyan	2976	2	2660	10.55
彭州市	Pengzhou	1889	2	1672	8.87
邛崃市	Qionglai	1518	1	1441	5.74
崇州市	Chongzhou	2045	1	1897	10.22
简阳市	Jianyang	2011	1	1731	14.55
广汉市	Guanghan	2369	2	2180	14.50
什邡市	Shifang	1881	1	1706	5.54
绵竹市	Mianzhu	1961	1	1792	5.78
江油市	Jiangyou	2128	2	1957	13.68
隆昌市	Longchang	1228	1	1093	5.77
峨眉山市	Emeishan	1680	1	1610	5.52
阆中市	Langzhong	2090	2	1960	11.40
华蓥市	Huaying	759	3	735	5.35
万源市	Wanyuan	918	1	799	5.39
马尔康市	Maerkang	320	1	263	1.28
康定市	Kangding	501	1	400	2.37
西昌市	Xichang	4478	2	3935	19.39

10-7 续表 continued

城 市	City	生活垃圾无害化处理厂(场)(座) Domestic Garbage Harmless Treatment Plants (unit)	生活垃圾无害化处理量(万吨) Volume of Domestic Garbage Harmless Treatment (10 000 sq.m)	公共厕所(座) Number of Public Lavatories (unit)	市容环卫专用车辆设备总数(辆) Number of Vehicles for Environmental Sanitation (unit)
全 省	**Sichuan**	**48**	**1005.95**	**6116**	**8833**
地级市	**at Prefecture Level**	**32**	**866.71**	**4879**	**7653**
成都市区	Chengdu	6	446.96	1412	3805
自贡市区	Zigong	1	24.97	431	433
攀枝花市区	Panzhihua	4	15.85	304	200
泸州市区	Luzhou	1	30.91	222	235
德阳市区	Deyang	1	17.26	118	498
绵阳市区	Mianyang	3	50.68	333	271
广元市区	Guangyuan	4	18.28	151	205
遂宁市区	Suining	1	22.23	118	89
内江市区	Neijiang	1	24.30	257	184
乐山市区	Leshan	3	30.39	181	179
南充市区	Nanchong	2	46.02	443	150
眉山市区	Meishan	1	29.05	97	279
宜宾市区	Yibin		34.89	194	418
广安市区	Guangan		11.50	103	177
达州市区	Dazhou	1	26.65	292	182
雅安市区	Yaan	1	11.63	57	115
巴中市区	Bazhong	1	10.90	107	125
资阳市区	Ziyang	1	14.23	59	108
县级市	**at County Level**	**16**	**139.24**	**1237**	**1180**
都江堰市	Dujiangyan	1	10.55	116	113
彭州市	Pengzhou	1	8.87	127	57
邛崃市	Qionglai	1	5.74	41	219
崇州市	Chongzhou	1	10.22	79	71
简阳市	Jianyang	1	14.55	64	72
广汉市	Guanghan	1	14.50	80	67
什邡市	Shifang	1	5.54	37	85
绵竹市	Mianzhu	1	5.78	29	38
江油市	Jiangyou	1	13.68	67	57
隆昌市	Longchang	1	5.77	32	45
峨眉山市	Emeishan	2	5.52	47	46
阆中市	Langzhong	1	11.40	165	38
华蓥市	Huaying		5.35	32	51
万源市	Wanyuan	1		54	63
马尔康市	Maerkang			28	22
康定市	Kangding	1	2.37	17	6
西昌市	Xichang	1	19.39	222	130

10-8 县城市政设施水平(2018年)
Level of Municipal Infrastructure in Counties(2018)

县 城	Counties	供水普及率 (%) Water Coverage Rate (%)	燃气普及率 (%) Gas Coverage Rate (%)	建成区路网密度 (公里/平方公里) Density of Road Network of Built District (km/sq.km)	建成区道路面积率 (%) Road Area Rate of Built District (%)	污水处理厂集中处理率 (%) Centralized Treatment Rate of Watewater Treatment Plants (%)	建成区绿地率 (%) Green Space Rate of Built District (%)	生活垃圾无害化处理率 (%) Domestic Garbage Harmless Treatment Rate (%)
全 省	**Sichuan**	**90.41**	**83.32**	**4.88**	**9.52**	**74.28**	**29.28**	**90.73**
金堂县	Jintang	98.31	97.98	5.64	13.93	68.89	39.01	100.00
大邑县	Dayi	91.81	79.90	2.89	7.09	92.98	31.77	100.00
蒲江县	Pujiang	97.31	99.00	6.05	8.50	89.83	38.39	100.00
新津县	Xinjin	93.77	93.77	2.98	4.26	86.35	32.47	100.00
荣县	Rongxian	86.64	92.78	4.62	12.55	96.13	37.29	100.00
富顺县	Fushun	99.96	99.96	14.40	15.20	94.63	38.20	95.72
米易县	Miyi	64.94	60.03	6.79	9.94	82.32	35.20	100.00
盐边县	Yanbian	96.90	49.22	5.18	5.18	49.99	33.29	100.00
泸县	Luxian	80.05	61.45	4.91	13.37	83.91	34.45	100.00
合江县	Hejiang	88.76	78.93	4.08	5.62	42.16	24.37	100.00
叙永县	Xuyong	80.99	52.38	4.50	5.94	84.15	32.55	100.00
古蔺县	Gulin	96.22	62.03	3.89	11.27	88.37	32.63	100.00
中江县	Zhongjiang	93.65	85.92	4.13	11.80	65.01	32.02	100.00
三台县	Santai	97.18	94.86	5.30	13.47	85.50	36.60	100.00
盐亭县	Yanting	90.56	98.86	3.88	7.27	96.06	38.04	100.00
梓潼县	Zitong	90.38	98.49	9.35	21.00	87.11	34.50	100.00
北川羌族自治县	Beichuan	88.95	100.00	8.00	13.00	98.84	44.20	100.00
平武县	Pingwu	75.92	87.70	10.27	16.31	87.98	38.51	100.00
旺苍县	Wangcang	90.03	93.12	5.26	5.26	54.56	34.92	100.00
青川县	Qingchuan	98.21	100.00	7.59	14.79	91.45	27.08	100.00
剑阁县	Jiange	96.07	95.41	3.83	9.29	90.00	36.66	100.00
苍溪县	Cangxi	97.53	97.10	4.53	11.11	97.78	36.31	100.00
蓬溪县	Pengxi	96.28	96.28	2.77	6.64	56.67	32.48	100.00
射洪县	Shehong	93.90	91.24	6.45	12.55	97.97	35.30	100.00
大英县	Daying	99.04	97.68	5.55	11.35	85.25	30.13	100.00
威远县	Weiyuan	95.24	98.49	3.23	11.19	76.98	29.54	95.84
资中县	Zizhong	94.59	84.00	2.73	5.36	85.61	13.28	98.90
犍为县	Qianwei	99.67	98.70	5.36	11.86	80.28	25.82	100.00
井研县	Jingyan	99.85	99.71	4.31	9.04	91.67	13.09	100.00
夹江县	Jiajiang	84.76	85.77	5.58	11.27	91.74	20.74	100.00
沐川县	Muchuan	92.46	98.16	6.53	12.63	61.36	32.26	100.00
峨边彝族自治县	Ebian	95.30	4.70	3.04	3.04	86.71	8.43	100.00
马边彝族自治县	Mabian	98.82	52.94	5.16	7.91	99.44	29.24	100.00
南部县	Nanbu	97.56	96.04	8.13	15.32	93.77	35.65	100.00
营山县	Yingshan	96.85	95.50	4.19	12.52	86.41	36.33	100.00

10-8 续表 1 continued

县 城	Counties	供水普及率 (%) Water Coverage Rate (%)	燃气普及率 (%) Gas Coverage Rate (%)	建成区路网密度 (公里/平方公里) Density of Road Network of Built District (km/sq.km)	建成区道路面积率 (%) Road Area Rate of Built District (%)	污水处理厂集中处理率 (%) Centralized Treatment Rate of Watewater Treatment Plants (%)	建成区绿地率 (%) Green Space Rate of Built District (%)	生活垃圾无害化处理率 (%) Domestic Garbage Harmless Treatment Rate (%)
蓬安县	Pengan	97.55	97.29	3.83	10.84	87.14	33.02	100.00
仪陇县	Yilong	96.88	96.88	4.13	11.25	86.40	34.06	100.00
西充县	Xichong	96.93	94.48	4.06	11.72	98.65	34.06	100.00
仁寿县	Renshou	99.94	94.81	3.51	10.05	78.27	27.73	100.00
洪雅县	Hongya	96.11	98.83	5.74	11.22	93.08	33.83	100.00
丹棱县	Danling	82.81	95.16	4.27	8.38	56.73	34.57	100.00
青神县	Qingshen	90.08	89.60	5.94	5.94	73.31	25.66	100.00
江安县	Jiangan	62.54	80.74	5.41	11.19	95.10	35.40	100.00
长宁县	Changning	84.95	98.52	7.09	14.47	77.95	40.63	100.00
高县	Gaoxian	79.60	97.80	2.98	6.81	26.18	33.10	100.00
珙县	Gongxian	84.87	98.77	2.38	3.51	98.77	40.65	100.00
筠连县	Junlian	54.22	96.33	2.24	3.54	88.71	33.02	100.00
兴文县	Xingwen	71.99	91.99	3.66	4.21	95.14	30.99	100.00
屏山县	Pingshan	93.75	99.16	5.96	13.31	87.88	26.15	100.00
岳池县	Yuechi	96.35	97.17	4.52	11.28	89.49	34.76	100.00
武胜县	Wusheng	90.22	86.05	5.09	9.21	93.64	38.14	100.00
邻水县	Linshui	93.05	98.71	2.30	7.09	95.14	28.35	100.00
宣汉县	Xuanhan	95.24	98.73	6.58	12.58	90.16	15.62	100.00
开江县	Kaijiang	98.36	100.00	4.26	8.94	78.30	29.92	100.00
大竹县	Dazhu	91.99	91.72	3.47	8.90	72.29	32.70	50.28
渠县	Quxian	91.46	86.01	3.77	7.07	90.00	23.28	100.00
荥经县	Yingjing	98.82	94.35	9.13	15.77	90.22	30.29	100.00
汉源县	Hanyuan	97.91	21.16	8.76	13.62	90.60	25.17	100.00
石棉县	Shimian	95.25	22.09	8.72	12.45	71.92	34.87	100.00
天全县	Tianquan	97.67	94.19	9.55	13.57	67.96	9.34	100.00
芦山县	Lushan	99.40	93.98	7.94	9.27	80.21	42.12	99.35
宝兴县	Baoxing	79.87	98.11	8.90	7.59	98.47	32.43	100.00
通江县	Tongjiang	87.21	78.78	3.65	8.48	83.10	39.61	
南江县	Nanjiang	98.12	76.61	3.04	2.84	94.03	33.94	100.00
平昌县	Pingchang	89.98	83.18	5.61	15.32	73.76	32.46	100.00
安岳县	Anyue	78.17	91.62	3.54	6.90	96.08	14.47	100.00
乐至县	Lezhi	80.12	77.21	5.49	18.14	96.41	38.37	86.51
汶川县	Wenchuan	57.74	30.45	1.05	0.50	80.80	13.66	77.03
理县	Lixian	97.92	56.25	8.47	8.47	58.87	6.21	
茂县	Maoxian	92.73	91.98	7.64	11.42	37.30	15.03	94.59
松潘县	Songpan	96.59	56.82	14.84	18.32	14.69	17.59	
九寨沟县	Jiuzhaigou	64.10	67.31	10.90	16.18	81.35	10.12	93.99
金川县	Jinchuan	87.16	72.30	3.94	2.36		3.85	

10-8 续表 2 continued

县 城	Counties	供水普及率 (%) Water Coverage Rate (%)	燃气普及率 (%) Gas Coverage Rate (%)	建成区路网密度 (公里/平方公里) Density of Road Network of Built District (km/sq.km)	建成区道路面积率 (%) Road Area Rate of Built District (%)	污水处理厂集中处理率 (%) Centralized Treatment Rate of Watewater Treatment Plants (%)	建成区绿地率 (%) Green Space Rate of Built District (%)	生活垃圾无害化处理率 (%) Domestic Garbage Harmless Treatment Rate (%)
小金县	Xiaojin	88.69	62.50	3.65	4.07	68.76	3.81	
黑水县	Heishui	48.91	25.54	1.37	0.82		1.72	
壤塘县	Rangtang	98.31	69.49	6.38	6.38		0.64	
阿坝县	Abaxian	56.11	59.41	0.55	2.18		0.48	
若尔盖县	Ruoergai	77.31	68.07	3.09	3.47	51.17	15.75	
红原县	Hongyuan	90.97	66.45	5.00	8.38	98.83	25.72	
泸定县	Luding	86.79	69.06	10.73	15.25	19.04	6.82	
丹巴县	Danba	67.02	47.87	2.90	2.90	55.33	3.43	
九龙县	Jiulong	96.45	69.82	2.88	2.84		2.40	
雅江县	Yajiang	58.59	93.75	2.31	2.31	18.33	3.08	100.00
道孚县	Daofu	55.25	62.43	7.18	4.31		0.63	98.96
炉霍县	Luhuo	87.72	42.69	2.33	6.00		5.93	100.00
甘孜县	Ganzixian	95.35	46.51	2.01	2.09		1.64	
新龙县	Xinlong	87.76	8.16	9.12	8.53		4.71	84.00
德格县	Dege	63.73	78.43	13.33	4.67		3.40	
白玉县	Baiyu	74.34	41.59	4.67	16.83		3.00	100.00
石渠县	Shiqu	73.56	70.11	9.81	6.67		0.23	
色达县	Seda	97.56	86.59	4.31	3.05		1.46	100.00
理塘县	Litang	81.25	56.25	3.91	1.97		1.06	2.74
巴塘县	Batang	75.35	72.56	10.71	10.29		4.01	100.00
乡城县	Xiangcheng	73.17	40.65	0.79	0.86		3.67	
稻城县	Daocheng	97.09	23.30	9.63	27.00	46.15	7.93	94.59
得荣县	Derong	96.23	58.49	6.15	10.77		6.92	
木里藏族自治县	Muli	97.20	80.00	2.96	3.93	15.65	16.52	
盐源县	Yanyuan	98.37	15.04	6.40	9.13		13.29	80.55
德昌县	Dechang	97.31	51.35	12.30	18.62	44.01	33.15	100.00
会理县	Huili	97.34	78.54	7.05	13.11	90.20	34.12	100.00
会东县	Huidong	83.22	28.32	3.79	0.08	14.29	47.88	100.00
宁南县	Ningnan	70.10		1.48	0.62	33.99	3.43	34.29
普格县	Puge	94.46	44.28	2.38	3.76		14.58	100.00
布拖县	Buto	91.18	18.24	3.08	10.13	20.86	36.81	100.00
金阳县	Jinyang	76.47	48.24	4.68	4.05		13.41	87.43
昭觉县	Zhaojue	85.96	14.47	1.53	1.67	0.17	26.94	
喜德县	Xide	88.99	16.04	5.00	6.67		8.67	37.04
冕宁县	Mianning	97.08	25.00	5.08	6.68	46.43	56.11	100.00
越西县	Yuexi	90.77		5.83	5.33		42.71	40.76
甘洛县	Ganluo	73.27	18.15	5.45	6.36		17.73	
美姑县	Meigu	84.18	34.01	3.47	2.77		15.85	100.00
雷波县	Leibo	80.36	69.98	6.55	7.98	30.00	10.15	

主要统计指标解释

供水综合生产能力 指按供水设施取水、净化、送水、出厂输水干管等环节设计能力计算的综合生产能力。计算时，以四个环节中最薄弱的环节为主确定能力。

供水管道长度 指从送水泵至各类用户引入管之间所有管道的长度。不包括新安装尚未使用、水厂内以及用户建筑物内的管道。

供水总量 指报告期供水企业(单位)供出的全部水量。包括有效供水量和漏损水量。

居民家庭用水 指城市范围内所有居民家庭的日常生活用水。包括城市居民、农民家庭、公共供水站用水。

供水普及率 指报告期末城区用水人口数与总人口的比率。计算公式:

$$供水普及率=\frac{城区用水人口（含暂住人口）}{城区人口+城区暂住人口}\times100\%$$

销售气量 指报告期燃气供应企业（单位）售给本区域内各类用户的全部燃气量。

燃气普及率 指报告期末城区内使用燃气的人口与总人口的比率。计算公式为:

$$燃气普及率=\frac{城区用气人口（含暂住人口）}{城区人口+城区暂住人口}\times100\%$$

道路长度 指道路长度和与道路相通的桥梁、隧道的长度，按车行道中心线计算。

桥梁 指为跨越天然或人工障碍物而修建的构筑物。包括跨河桥、立交桥、人行天桥以及人行地下通道等。

排水管道长度 指所有排水总管、干管、支管、检查井及连接井进出口等长度之和。

绿地面积 指报告期末用作园林和绿化的各种绿地面积。包括公园绿地、生产绿地、防护绿地、附属绿地和其他绿地的面积。

公园绿地 城市中向公众开放的、以游憩为主要功能，有一定的游憩设施和服务设施，同时兼有健全生态、美化景观、防灾减灾等综合作用的绿化用地。

公园 指常年开放的供公众游览、观赏、休憩、开展科学、文化及休闲等活动，有较完善的设施和良好的绿化环境、景观优美的公园绿地。

公园面积 指报告期末综合公园、专类公园和带状公园的全部占地总面积。

市容环卫专用车辆设备 指用于环境卫生作业、监察的专用车辆和设备，包括用于道路清扫、冲洗、洒水、除雪、垃圾粪便清运、市容监察以及与其配套使用的车辆和设备。

Explanatory Notes on Main Statistical Indicators

Production Capacity of Water Supply refers to the designed overall production capacity of water facilities, covering the four segments of water collection, purification, conveyance, and outflow through trunk pipelines. The capacity is determined mainly on the weakest of the above-mentioned four segments.

Length of Water Supply Pipelines refers to the total length of all the pipelines between the water pumps and introduction pipe for various users, excluding pipelines newly installed but not used yet, pipeline in the water factory, and pipeline in the user's buildings.

Total Volume of Urban Water Supply refers to the total volume of water supplied by water-works (units) during the reference period, including both the effective water supply and loss during the water supply.

Water Use by Household Consumption refers to water of all resident families for daily use in urban areas, includes city dweller, rural household and water of public water supply station.

Coverage Rate of with Access to Water supply refers to the ratio of with access to water supply to the total population at the end of the reference period. The formula is:

$$\text{Coverage rate of urban population with access to tap water} = \frac{\text{Urbanpopulationwith access to tap water}}{\text{Urban population}} \times 100\%$$

Volume of Gas Sales refers to the total volume of gas sold to various users by gas-producing enterprises (units) during the reporting period.

Coverage Rate of Population with Access to Gas refers to the ratio of the population with access to gas to the total population at the end of the reference period.. The formula is:

$$\text{Coverage rate of urban population with access to Gas} = \frac{\text{Urbanpopulationwith access to gas}}{\text{Urban population}} \times 100\%$$

Length of Paved Roads refers to the length of roads with paved surface including bridges and tunnels connected with roads. Length of the roads is measured by the central lines.

Urban Bridges refer to bridges built to cross over natural or man-made barriers, including bridges over rivers, overpasses for traffic and for pedestrians, underpasses for pedestrians, etc.

Length of Urban Sewage Pipes refers to the total length of general drainage, trunks, branch and inspection wells, connection wells, inlets and outlets, etc.

Area of Urban Green Land refers to the total area occupied for green projects at the end of the reference period, including park green land, production green land, protection green land, green land attached to institutions, and other green areas.

Park Green Area refers to green areas open to the public for amusement and rest with the facilities of amusement, rest and services. Its function includes perfecting ecology, beautifying landscape, and preventing and reducing disaster. Park green areas.

Park refers to perennially open green spaces for public tours, ornaments, recreations, scientific, cultural and leisure activities, with perfect facilities, good greening environment and beautiful scenery.

Park area refers to the total area occupied by comprehensive parks, special parks and zonal parks at the end of the reference period.

Vehicles and Facilities Dedicated to Urban Cleanliness and Environmental Sanitation refer to vehicles and facilities dedicated for use in the operation, management and monitoring of environmental hygiene work. They include vehicles for road cleaning, washing, showering, ice removal, disposal of garbage and human wastes, cleanliness monitoring and related activities.

11

民族自治地方概况

Chapter 11 Survey of Minority Nationality Autonomous Areas

11-1 民族自治地方地区生产总值和指数
Gross Regional Product and Related Indices of Minority Nationality Autonomous Areas

年份 Year	地区生产总值 Gross Regional Product	第一产业 Primary Industry	第二产业 Secondary Industry	第三产业 Tertiary Industry	人均地区生产总值(元) Per Capita GDP (yuan)
绝对数(亿元) Value (100 million yuan)					
1978	13.17	6.48	4.19	2.50	281
1980	16.12	7.76	5.08	3.28	335
1985	28.88	13.96	8.53	6.38	564
1990	55.34	24.47	15.63	15.24	1016
1995	137.69	53.29	41.82	42.57	2414
2000	213.10	77.02	64.64	71.44	3549
2005	453.56	126.30	167.49	159.77	6962
2006	539.54	138.46	217.78	183.30	8190
2007	675.77	181.30	223.82	270.64	10045
2008	776.16	213.09	326.31	236.76	11244
2009	892.90	218.92	357.89	316.09	12556
2010	1102.59	240.33	504.08	358.18	15129
2011	1397.20	276.85	698.28	422.08	19818
2012	1587.48	311.75	800.56	475.17	22412
2013	1742.58	335.95	889.29	517.34	24432
2014	1869.25	357.84	943.72	567.68	26011
2015	1900.55	379.87	905.59	615.09	26171
2016	2031.66	406.60	949.54	675.51	27476
2017	2167.73	427.96	918.23	821.54	28927
2018	2272.04	447.44	929.17	895.43	30081
指数(1978年=100) Index (1978=100)					
1978	100.0	100.0	100.0	100.0	100.0
1980	108.8	107.0	110.8	110.6	105.9
1985	163.5	167.8	138.0	196.3	149.7
1990	209.1	187.4	192.5	309.9	179.4
1995	310.2	228.4	338.2	523.4	256.2
2000	444.3	297.3	503.5	811.7	348.8
2005	792.1	381.3	1246.8	1408.5	563.0
2006	903.8	399.6	1534.8	1577.5	619.3
2007	1034.9	425.2	1867.9	1770.0	675.0
2008	1091.8	432.4	2011.7	1863.8	693.9
2009	1276.3	452.7	2583.0	2091.2	777.2
2010	1434.6	468.1	3115.1	2250.1	831.6
2011	1651.2	490.1	3844.0	2486.4	903.1
2012	1875.8	513.1	4570.5	2759.9	1025.9
2013	2069.0	536.7	5237.8	2939.3	1123.4
2014	2226.2	560.8	5714.4	3136.2	1208.6
2015	2315.2	584.4	5828.7	3377.7	1244.9
2016	2459.3	608.9	6229.9	3595.0	1298.4
2017	2599.5	632.0	6634.8	3803.5	1354.2
2018	2729.5	655.4	6853.7	4088.8	1409.7

11-2 民族自治地方主要统计指标(2018年)

指　标		Item	
年末常住人口	(万人)	Resident Population (year-end)	(10 000 persons)
城镇人口	(万人)	Urban Population	(10 000 persons)
乡村人口	(万人)	Rural Population	(10 000 persons)
城镇化率	(%)	Urbanization Rate	(%)
就业人员	(万人)	Number of Employed Persons	(10 000 persons)
第一产业	(万人)	Primary Industy	(10 000 persons)
第二产业	(万人)	Secondary Industy	(10 000 persons)
第三产业	(万人)	Tertiary Industy	(10 000 persons)
地区生产总值(当年价)	(亿元)	Gross Regional Product (at current prices)	(100 million yuan)
第一产业增加值	(亿元)	Value-added of Primary Industy	(100 million yuan)
第二产业增加值	(亿元)	Value-added of Secondary Industy	(100 million yuan)
第三产业增加值	(亿元)	Value-added of Tertiary Industy	(100 million yuan)
人均地区生产总值(当年价)	(元)	Per Capita Gross Regional Product (at current prices)	(yuan)
耕地面积	(万公顷)	Cultivated Areas	(10 000 hectare)
耕地灌溉面积	(万公顷)	Irrigated Areas of Cultivated Land	(10 000 hectare)
农林牧渔业总产值(当年价)	(亿元)	Gross Output Value of Farming, Forestry, Animal Husbandry and Fishery (at current prices)	(100 million yuan)
规模以上工业企业营业收入	(亿元)	Revenue from Principal Business	(100 million yuan)
规模以上工业企业利润总额	(亿元)	Total Profits	(100 million yuan)
境内公路总里程	(公里)	Total Length of Highway	(km)
#等级公路	(公里)	Expressway and Class I to IV Highways	(km)
公路旅客周转量	(万人公里)	Passenger-Kilometers of Highways	(10 000 passenger-km)
公路货物周转量	(万吨公里)	Freight Ton-Kilometers of Highways	(10 000 ton-km)

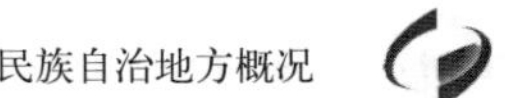

Main Statistical Indicators of Minority Nationality Autonomous Areas(2018)

合计 Total	阿坝州 Aba	甘孜州 Ganzi	凉山州 Liangshan	北川县 Beichuan	峨边县 Ebian	马边县 Mabian
759.90	94.40	119.60	490.80	22.50	13.70	18.90
272.15	37.76	37.87	175.26	9.32	5.78	6.17
487.75	56.64	81.73	315.54	13.19	7.92	12.73
35.81	40.00	31.66	35.71	41.40	42.17	32.63
441.93	52.02	66.78	289.63	12.69	9.26	11.55
254.96	28.43	47.15	164.37	4.40	4.32	6.29
57.10	4.38	2.40	43.93	3.83	1.59	0.97
129.87	19.21	17.23	81.33	4.46	3.35	4.29
2272.04	306.67	291.2	1533.19	55.94	44.86	40.18
447.44	49.55	65.47	307.61	11.14	4.83	8.84
929.17	139.53	121.78	613.13	18.67	21.26	14.80
895.43	117.59	103.95	612.45	26.14	18.77	16.53
30081	32552	24446	31472	24975	33129	21281
82.73	8.33	10.23	57.95	1.72	2.73	1.76
25.79	2.52	3.67	18.64	0.23	0.20	0.53
742.84	78.34	88.54	531.05	19.25	8.66	17.00
1264.79	177.08	104.25	891.52	30.49	38.79	22.66
132.03	10.10	4.22	113.85	2.59	1.65	-0.37
80623	13526	34879	27586	2695	1091	846
75596	13140	33630	24682	2296	1003	846
678545	166264	154386	348936		4881	4078
2189125	617663	223945	1301143		21809	24565

11-2 续表

指　　标		Item	
全社会固定资产投资增长情况	(%)	The Growth of Total Investment in Fixed Assets	(%)
#房地产开发投资	(亿元)	Real Estate Development Investment	(100 million yuan)
建筑业总产值	(亿元)	Gross Output Value of Construction	(100 million yuan)
社会消费品零售总额	(亿元)	Total Retail Sales of Consumer Goods	(100 million yuan)
出口总额	(亿元)	Total Exports	(100 million yuan)
城镇居民人均可支配收入	(元)	Per Capita Disposable Income of Urban Households	(yuan)
农村居民人均可支配收入	(元)	Per Capita Disposable Income of Rural Households	(yuan)
参加城镇职工基本养老保险人数	(万人)	Employees and Retirees Contributed to Pension Insurance	(10 000 persons)
参加基本医疗保险人数	(万人)	Contributors of Basic Medical Insurance	(10 000 persons)
地方一般公共预算收入	(亿元)	Local General Public Budget Revenue	(100 million yuan)
#税收收入	(亿元)	Taxes Revenue	(100 million yuan)
一般公共预算支出	(亿元)	General Public Budget Expenditure	(100 million yuan)
年末金融机构人民币各项存款余额	(亿元)	Deposits of Financial Instituitions	(100 million yuan)
住户存款余额	(亿元)	Balance of Household Savings	(100 million yuan)
年末金融机构人民币各项贷款余额	(亿元)	Loans of Financial Instituitions	(100 million yuan)
小学在校学生人数	(人)	Students in Primary Schools	(person)
普通中学在校学生人数	(人)	Students in Regular Secondary Schools	(person)
中等职业教育学校在校学生数	(人)	Students in Secondary Vocational Schools	(person)
卫生机构数	(个)	Number of Medical and Health Institutions	(unit)
卫生机构床位数	(张)	Beds in Medical and Health Institutions	(unit)
卫生技术人员数	(人)	Medical Technical Personnel in Medical and Health Institutions	(person)
#执业(助理)医师	(人)	Practicing Doctors (Assistants)	(person)

continued

合计 Total	阿坝州 Aba	甘孜州 Ganzi	凉山州 Liangshan	北川县 Beichuan	峨边县 Ebian	马边县 Mabian
	14.2	21.6	-20.0	8.9	17.9	17.6
196.38	3.10	6.43	181.78	2.74		2.34
324.68	37.81	23.61	248.96	10.50	2.27	1.54
889.00	79.27	100.36	649.58	20.33	18.78	20.68
6.50	1.49	1.29	3.69	0.01	0.02	
30926	32686	31972	30421	29334	30282	31060
12381	12893	11555	12548	13061	11092	11379
101.08	21.82	15.61	48.59	8.52	2.90	3.64
717.74	87.70	105.90	475.80	21.25	10.83	16.26
213.63	24.66	30.03	146.20	5.51	3.42	3.80
139.76	18.71	20.79	91.33	3.90	2.26	2.78
1470.14	295.08	420.57	681.71	26.14	21.43	25.22
3716.61	652.71	698.35	2128.87	120.18	58.69	57.81
1781.55	257.07	247.36	1116.65	79.29	41.60	39.59
1784.26	299.56	353.62	916.87	109.87	75.88	28.47
823914	63334	108303	606292	11642	11748	22595
408067	43655	53827	284586	8141	5524	12334
44326	3354	5969	31736	1856	383	1028
10396	1683	2777	5249	364	147	176
40314	4899	5207	27347	1680	590	591
40712	6723	6556	25051	1316	478	588
12282	2092	1691	7762	424	146	167

11-3 民族自治地方年末户籍总人口和就业人员
Registered Population and Employment in Minority Nationality Autonomous Areas

单位:万人 (10 000 persons)

年份 Year	年末户籍总人口 Household Population (year-end)	就业人员 Number of Employed Persons	第一产业 Primary Industry	第二产业 Secondary Industry	第三产业 Tertiary Industry
1978	471.36	216.92			
1980	484.10	229.08			
1985	514.65	261.61			
1990	549.03	296.09			
1995	573.91	346.98	258.93	33.48	54.57
1996	578.54	345.07	257.30	32.25	55.52
1997	584.60	342.22	270.79	20.91	50.52
1998	589.96	343.89	271.25	20.25	52.39
1999	594.89	345.32	273.52	19.75	52.05
2000	606.11	351.99	278.93	18.65	54.41
2001	610.93	354.43	279.69	16.49	58.25
2002	616.81	356.25	280.90	16.77	58.58
2003	639.71	373.91	284.69	22.62	66.60
2004	649.17	387.38	281.85	22.98	82.55
2005	653.76	378.56	280.80	24.96	72.80
2006	663.73	385.37	279.63	25.98	79.76
2007	681.72	397.43	283.94	30.96	82.53
2008	698.87	409.69	285.42	33.37	90.90
2009	723.42	448.49	287.57	49.53	111.39
2010	734.16	439.29	289.21	46.12	103.96
2011	746.67	444.08	280.01	47.47	116.60
2012	759.54	459.83	290.33	45.31	124.19
2013	769.56	460.11	289.26	44.81	126.04
2014	771.62	466.41	286.09	44.43	135.89
2015	764.80	442.19	276.12	45.64	120.43
2016	775.06	440.54	263.77	52.34	124.43
2017	783.22	441.08	258.69	54.62	127.77
2018	791.49	441.93	254.96	57.10	129.87

11-4 民族自治地方耕地面积和农业生产条件
Cultivated Land Areas and Production Conditions of Agriculture in Minority Nationality Autonomous Areas

年份 Year	耕地面积 (万公顷) Cultivated Areas (10 000 hectares)	耕地灌溉面积 (万公顷) Irrigated Areas of Cultivated Land (10 000 hectares)	化肥施用量 (折纯，万吨) Consumption of Chemical Fertilizers (10 000 tons)	农村用电量 (万千瓦时) Electricity Consumed in Rural Areas (10 000 kwh)	农业机械总动力 (万千瓦) Total Agricultural Machinery Power (10 000 kw)
1978	51.52	15.47	3.44	8691	27.11
1980	51.84	16.17	3.12	9001	37.21
1985	50.32	15.96	3.34	14139	53.88
1990	50.00	15.32	4.75	22770	78.58
1995	50.97	15.90	6.83	28394	109.30
1996	51.45	16.06	7.53	32542	112.00
1997	51.56	15.21	9.77	35458	119.00
1998	51.12	15.73	10.64	35448	134.00
1999	50.74	15.24	11.12	41828	135.00
2000	48.39	16.13	11.82	44996	137.00
2001	49.47	16.36	11.63	48137	142.00
2002	46.14	16.28	10.41	49790	154.00
2003	45.32	16.24	11.14	55645	162.00
2004	47.91	16.19	11.70	61174	173.00
2005	49.47	16.63	12.59	63417	201.00
2006	49.97	16.62	13.43	64103	173.00
2007	51.25	17.31	14.38	72184	250.00
2008	52.06	17.59	15.25	79387	287.00
2009	52.96	18.34	16.52	86799	333.00
2010	53.37	18.60	16.72	91006	370.00
2011	53.35	19.33	17.29	96409	415.95
2012	53.53	19.89	17.83	101566	439.04
2013	53.81	21.19	16.66	108370	480.58
2014	53.93	20.60	17.14	113355	502.76
2015	79.94	21.54	17.17	118871	529.51
2016	82.77	22.44	17.32	124037	541.75
2017	82.77	23.12	17.14	130134	556.45
2018	82.73	25.79	16.89	143520	552.54

11-5 民族自治地方邮电和卫生情况
Postal and Telecommunication, Public Health in Minority Nationality Autonomous Areas

年份 Year	邮电主营业务收入 (万元) Revenue from Principal Business of Post and Telecommunication (10 000 yuan)	医疗卫生机构床位数 (张) Beds in Medical and Health Institutions (unit)	医院、卫生院技术人员数 (人) Medical Technical Personnel (person)	#执业(助理)医师 Practicing Doctors (Assistants)
1978	1248	14225	15058	7303
1980	1290	14471	17699	9102
1985	1719	14938	19438	10203
1990	3108	15588	18481	10155
1995	8807	15688	18957	10037
1996	12028	14923	18189	9768
1997	16285	15348	19066	10414
1998	23483	15113	18441	10080
1999	29025	15313	18554	10841
2000	41608	16475	14807	7889
2001	56484	14263	22337	8867
2002	67374	13901	16180	8159
2003	90594	15097	16345	8450
2004	111646	16538	15005	7860
2005	130946	14647	19535	8686
2006	154313	15635	14384	8124
2007	176723	15898	16127	10045
2008	202155	16737	15516	8518
2009	234607	18363	17615	8807
2010	265913	19791	24848	7485
2011	302272	21448	29648	9433
2012	345136	24607	24655	7571
2013	376606	25908	22862	10069
2014	411888	31360	30263	10934
2015	416006	33443	33505	11542
2016	454941	35376	35935	11744
2017	490039	38725	38417	11768
2018	488177	40314	40712	12282

11-6 民族自治地方社会消费品零售总额、住户存款余额和各类普通学校在校学生人数

Total Retail Sales of Consumer Goods, Balance of Household Savings and Number of Student Enrollment by Type of Schools in Minority Nationality Autonomous Areas

年份 Year	社会消费品零售总额（亿元） Total Retail Sales of Consumer Goods (100 million yuan)	住户存款余额（亿元） Balance of Household Savings (100 million yuan)	普通高等院校在校学生人数（人） Number of Students in Regular Institutions of Higher Education (person)	中等职业学校在校学生人数（人） Number of Students in Specialized Secondary Schools (person)	普通中学在校学生人数（人） Number of Students in Regular Secondary Schools (person)	小学在校学生人数（人） Number of Students in Primary Schools (person)
1978	4.76	0.72	970	11756	184900	673479
1980	6.00	1.25	1231	10343	162751	605404
1985	10.70	4.39	2826	7570	126389	521659
1990	19.96	17.68	4225	10173	133208	493900
1995	39.13	51.71	6144	14497	121232	578205
1996	43.89	65.19	6467	15381	126736	605960
1997	48.52	73.15	7355	16954	129029	632731
1998	51.68	84.23	7805	18232	128916	656367
1999	55.46	95.75	9688	19573	133369	657565
2000	59.81	107.26	10725	14731	145534	640229
2001	67.92	126.98	15229	13825	164038	659357
2002	76.99	147.91	17350	11203	186065	692423
2003	90.85	175.68	20829	15942	221096	731794
2004	110.65	202.39	24488	11486	243812	756318
2005	142.96	232.37	27857	13963	283307	780372
2006	167.00	268.91	27025	19998	323742	829904
2007	197.36	299.03	25132	25977	337781	824988
2008	224.72	381.04	25092	33575	345560	811499
2009	273.67	481.67	26371	35221	360138	794927
2010	337.04	584.83	27494	39672	373524	781008
2011	396.36	712.78	28546	36839	380705	772207
2012	459.12	860.16	29673	39278	378296	766925
2013	521.83	1006.81	30728	46084	360158	740478
2014	624.82	1111.63	30953	42572	363107	744127
2015	691.78	1019.18	32013	41922	360638	759084
2016	766.81	1420.57	33530	41003	368252	783445
2017	849.26	1581.13	36580	43264	384941	803467
2018	889.00	1781.55	41394	44326	408067	823914

注：2014年及以前，“住户存款”为“城乡居民储蓄存款”。

a) Household saving was known as saving deposit of residents before 2014.

12

县（市、区）概况

Chapter 12 Survey of County(City, District)

12-1 各县(市、区)年末常住人口及城镇化率(2018年)

Resident Population and Proportion by Counties (Municipalities, Districts)(2018)

单位：万人 (10 000 persons)

县(市、区)	Counties (Municipalities, Districts)	年末常住人口 Total Resident Population (year-end)	城镇人口 Urban Population	乡村人口 Rural Population	城镇化率(%) Proportion (%)
成都市	**Chengdu**				
锦江区	Jinjiang	70.8	70.8		100.00
青羊区	Qingyang	84.7	84.7		100.00
金牛区	Jinniu	121.7	121.7		100.00
武侯区	Wuhou	186.9	186.9		100.00
成华区	Chenghua	95.4	95.4		100.00
龙泉驿区	Longquanyi	91.4	65.1	26.3	71.26
青白江区	Qingbaijiang	42.9	24.7	18.2	57.60
新都区	Xindu	90.6	64.2	26.4	70.86
温江区	Wenjiang	52.3	38.5	13.8	73.61
双流区	Shuangliu	146.5	103.7	42.8	70.79
郫都区	Pidu	85.7	62.0	23.7	72.45
金堂县	Jintang	71.4	32.0	39.4	44.80
大邑县	Dayi	51.1	23.9	27.2	46.78
蒲江县	Pujiang	26.1	11.5	14.6	44.33
新津县	Xinjin	33.1	19.5	13.6	59.03
都江堰市	Dujiangyan	69.7	42.0	27.7	60.20
彭州市	Pengzhou	77.8	36.6	41.2	47.00
邛崃市	Qionglai	61.9	30.6	31.3	49.40
崇州市	Chongzhou	66.5	30.9	35.6	46.41
简阳市	Jianyang	106.5	49.3	57.2	46.30
自贡市	**Zigong**				
自流井区	Ziliujing	50.6	46.6	4.0	92.08
贡井区	Gongjing	29.2	15.2	14.0	52.16
大安区	Daan	43.0	22.6	20.4	52.57
沿滩区	Yantan	38.8	16.4	22.4	42.16
荣县	Rongxian	54.0	21.1	32.9	39.02
富顺县	Fushun	76.4	31.7	44.7	41.56
攀枝花市	**Panzhihua**				
东区	East District	38.4	38.1	0.3	99.09
西区	West District	14.3	13.9	0.4	97.13
仁和区	Renhe	27.6	13.6	14.0	49.38
米易县	Miyi	23.3	10.4	12.9	44.70
盐边县	Yanbian	20.0	6.3	13.7	31.37
泸州市	**Luzhou**				
江阳区	Jiangyang	62.0	47.0	15.0	75.84
纳溪区	Nanxi	46.9	32.8	14.1	69.84
龙马潭区	Longmatan	38.5	30.2	8.3	78.53
泸县	Luxian	87.2	36.5	50.7	41.80
合江县	Hejiang	70.4	28.9	41.5	41.11
叙永县	Xuyong	58.2	20.3	37.9	34.90
古蔺县	Gulin	69.2	22.5	46.7	32.44

12-1 续表 1 continued

单位：万人 (10 000 persons)

县(市、区)	Counties (Municipalities, Districts)	年末常住人口 Total Resident Population (year-end)	城镇人口 Urban Population	乡村人口 Rural Population	城镇化率(%) Proportion (%)
德阳市	**Deyang**				
旌阳区	Jinyang	76.0	53.4	22.6	70.23
罗江区	Luojiang	22.8	10.4	12.4	45.77
中江县	Zhongjiang	107.7	44.1	63.6	40.91
广汉市	Guanghan	60.2	32.4	27.8	53.77
什邡市	Shifang	41.8	21.9	19.9	52.50
绵竹市	Mianzhu	46.0	23.4	22.6	50.88
绵阳市	**Mianyang**				
涪城区	Hucheng	94.7	74.6	20.1	78.75
游仙区	Youxian	52.2	28.7	23.5	55.00
安州区	Anzhou	39.3	19.9	19.4	50.52
三台县	Santai	105.8	41.1	64.7	38.90
盐亭县	Yanting	45.7	18.1	27.6	39.61
梓潼县	Zitong	30.9	12.2	18.7	39.46
北川县	Beichuan	22.5	9.3	13.2	41.40
平武县	Pingwu	15.9	5.3	10.6	33.24
江油市	Jiangyou	78.7	45.9	32.8	58.38
广元市	**Guangyuan**				
利州区	Lizhou	55.6	40.0	15.6	72.05
昭化区	Zhaohua	18.6	6.7	11.9	36.21
朝天区	Chaotian	19.0	7.2	11.8	37.75
旺苍县	Wangcang	41.5	17.6	23.9	42.41
青川县	Qingchuan	21.3	7.7	13.6	36.17
剑阁县	Jiange	49.5	19.8	29.7	40.03
苍溪县	Cangxi	61.2	22.7	38.5	37.11
遂宁市	**Suining**				
船山区	Chuanshan	68.1	56.0	12.1	82.20
安居区	Anju	64.3	20.7	43.6	32.10
蓬溪县	Pengxi	52.7	19.5	33.2	36.90
射洪县	Shehong	87.3	44.9	42.4	51.48
大英县	Daying	47.8	19.1	28.7	39.85
内江市	**Neijiang**				
内江市中区	Neijiang Downtown	53.1	31.0	22.1	58.30
东兴区	Dongxing	79.7	41.7	38.0	52.38
威远县	Weiyuan	59.1	29.8	29.3	50.40
资中县	Zizhong	115.7	45.2	70.5	39.05
隆昌市	Longchang	62.3	33.9	28.4	54.45
乐山市	**Leshan**				
乐山市中区	Leshan Downtown	69.1	50.7	18.4	73.41
沙湾区	Shawan	17.1	9.2	7.9	54.00
五通桥区	Wutongqiao	31.0	17.4	13.6	56.21

12-1 续表 2 continued

单位：万人 (10 000 persons)

县(市、区)	Counties (Municipalities, Districts)	年末常住人口 Total Resident Population (year-end)	城镇人口 Urban Population	乡村人口 Rural Population	城镇化率(%) Proportion (%)
金口河区	Jinkouhe	4.6	2.2	2.4	47.43
犍为县	Qianwei	42.7	17.3	25.4	40.63
井研县	Jingyan	30.4	12.2	18.2	40.01
夹江县	Jiajiang	33.1	14.4	18.7	43.51
沐川县	Muchuan	20.5	7.2	13.3	35.02
峨边县	Ebian	13.7	5.8	7.9	42.17
马边县	Mabian	18.9	6.2	12.7	32.63
峨眉山市	Emeishan	45.6	26.7	18.9	58.65
南充市	**Nanchong**				
顺庆区	Shunqing	72.0	59.5	12.5	82.65
高坪区	Gaoping	61.4	28.5	32.9	46.35
嘉陵区	Jialing	62.3	28.9	33.4	46.43
南部县	Nanbu	94.1	41.9	52.2	44.57
营山县	Yingshan	75.4	32.6	42.8	43.20
蓬安县	Pengan	57.6	23.9	33.7	41.53
仪陇县	Yilong	93.7	38.8	54.9	41.38
西充县	Xichong	53.8	22.0	31.8	40.86
阆中市	Langzhong	73.7	33.9	39.8	45.96
眉山市	**Meishan**				
东坡区	Dongpo	83.7	48.0	35.7	57.40
彭山区	Pengshan	32.1	17.7	14.4	55.04
仁寿县	Renshou	120.1	45.8	74.3	38.15
洪雅县	Hongya	30.9	13.5	17.4	43.52
丹棱县	Danling	14.8	6.2	8.6	41.98
青神县	Qingshen	16.8	7.0	9.8	41.71
宜宾市	**Yibin**				
翠屏区	Cuiping	89.2	69.1	20.1	77.49
南溪区	Nanxi	34.8	19.1	15.7	54.83
叙州区	Xuzhou	78.2	29.5	48.7	37.70
江安县	Jiangan	41.9	19.6	22.3	46.88
长宁县	Changning	34.7	15.8	18.9	45.57
高县	Gaoxian	41.5	17.2	24.3	41.30
珙县	Gongxian	37.5	19.4	18.1	51.79
筠连县	Junlian	33.3	13.5	19.8	40.41
兴文县	Xingwen	38.8	15.1	23.7	39.03
屏山县	Pingshan	25.7	7.9	17.8	30.59
广安市	**Guangan**				
广安区	Guanganqu	62.8	32.1	30.7	51.12
前锋区	Qianfeng	25.9	9.1	16.8	35.28
岳池县	Yuechi	78.2	30.2	48.0	38.63
武胜县	Wusheng	58.6	22.8	35.8	38.82

12-1 续表 3 continued

单位：万人 (10 000 persons)

县(市、区)	Counties (Municipalities, Districts)	年末常住人口 Total Resident Population (year-end)	城镇人口 Urban Population	乡村人口 Rural Population	城镇化率(%) Proportion (%)
邻水县	Linshui	70.5	27.5	43.0	38.94
华蓥市	Huaying	28.1	14.0	14.1	49.90
达州市	**Dazhou**				
通川区	Tongchuan	78.2	54.8	23.4	70.05
达川区	Dachuan	104.6	47.7	56.9	45.60
宣汉县	Xuanhan	102.2	41.6	60.6	40.75
开江县	Kaijiang	44.8	18.1	26.7	40.32
大竹县	Dazhu	89.1	37.7	51.4	42.28
渠县	Quxian	111.6	43.4	68.2	38.90
万源市	Wanyuan	41.5	17.1	24.4	41.36
雅安市	**Yaan**				
雨城区	Yucheng	36.5	22.6	13.9	61.92
名山区	Mingshan	26.9	11.1	15.8	41.40
荥经县	Yingjing	15.0	6.6	8.4	44.20
汉源县	Hanyuan	32.0	12.9	19.1	40.18
石棉县	Shimian	12.7	5.7	7.0	45.00
天全县	Tianquan	14.1	5.9	8.2	42.00
芦山县	Lushan	11.0	4.7	6.3	42.67
宝兴县	Baoxing	5.8	2.6	3.2	44.70
巴中市	**Bazhong**				
巴州区	Bazhou	73.8	45.6	28.2	61.73
恩阳区	Enyang	48.8	17.1	31.7	35.13
通江县	Tongjiang	69.7	24.7	45.0	35.39
南江县	Nanjiang	60.9	22.3	38.6	36.62
平昌县	Pingchang	79.0	29.3	49.7	37.12
资阳市	**Ziyang**				
雁江区	Yanjiang	91.4	48.3	43.1	52.89
安岳县	Anyue	109.5	39.8	69.7	36.33
乐至县	Lezhi	50.3	19.2	31.1	38.11
阿坝州	**Aba**				
马尔康市	Maerkang	6.0	3.1	2.9	51.42
汶川县	Wenchuan	10.3	4.9	5.4	48.26
理县	Lixian	4.9	1.9	3.0	38.15
茂县	Maoxian	11.2	5.4	5.8	48.01
松潘县	Songpan	7.5	3.0	4.5	39.71
九寨沟县	Jiuzhaigou	8.2	4.2	4.0	51.03
金川县	Jinchuan	7.5	2.6	4.9	34.17
小金县	Xiaojin	8.0	3.0	5.0	37.21
黑水县	Heishui	6.1	2.3	3.8	37.92
壤塘县	Rangtang	4.2	1.1	3.1	25.00

12-1 续表 4 continued

单位：万人 (10 000 persons)

县(市、区)	Counties (Municipalities, Districts)	年末常住人口 Total Resident Population (year-end)	城镇人口 Urban Population	乡村人口 Rural Population	城镇化率(%) Proportion (%)
阿坝县	Abaxian	7.7	2.2	5.5	29.31
若尔盖县	Ruoergai	7.8	2.4	5.4	30.70
红原县	Hongyuan	5.0	1.7	3.3	35.31
甘孜州	**Ganzi**				
康定市	Kangding	13.4	7.2	6.2	54.09
泸定县	Luding	8.8	3.9	4.9	44.45
丹巴县	Danba	6.9	2.3	4.6	32.64
九龙县	Jiulong	6.5	1.6	4.9	24.82
雅江县	Yajiang	5.8	1.5	4.3	25.71
道孚县	Daofu	6.1	2.1	4.0	33.78
炉霍县	Luhuo	5.1	1.6	3.5	30.97
甘孜县	Ganzixian	7.6	2.6	5.0	34.15
新龙县	Xinlong	5.3	1.0	4.3	18.00
德格县	Dege	9.0	2.0	7.0	22.66
白玉县	Baiyu	6.1	1.2	4.9	19.97
石渠县	Shiqu	10.1	2.0	8.1	19.37
色达县	Seda	6.4	1.5	4.9	23.88
理塘县	Litang	7.4	2.9	4.5	39.16
巴塘县	Batang	5.0	1.7	3.3	34.00
乡城县	Xiangcheng	3.6	1.0	2.6	28.29
稻城县	Daocheng	3.7	1.1	2.6	30.07
得荣县	Derong	2.8	0.7	2.1	24.74
凉山州	**Liangshan**				
西昌市	Xichang	81.8	49.5	32.3	60.51
木里县	Muli	13.6	2.3	11.3	16.91
盐源县	Yanyuan	36.1	11.4	24.7	31.58
德昌县	Dechang	22.5	8.6	13.9	38.22
会理县	Huili	42.6	19.0	23.6	44.60
会东县	Huidong	38.7	15.7	23.0	40.57
宁南县	Ningnan	18.7	6.4	12.3	34.22
普格县	Puge	16.9	4.1	12.8	24.26
布拖县	Buto	18.9	4.1	14.8	21.69
金阳县	Jinyang	18.4	3.4	15.0	18.48
昭觉县	Zhaojue	27.7	6.4	21.3	23.10
喜德县	Xide	19.7	5.2	14.5	26.40
冕宁县	Mianning	36.2	15.1	21.1	41.71
越西县	Yuexi	31.3	9.2	22.1	29.39
甘洛县	Ganluo	21.4	4.8	16.6	22.43
美姑县	Meigu	21.6	2.6	19.0	12.04
雷波县	Leibo	24.7	7.5	17.2	30.24

12-2 各县(市、区)就业人员和平均工资(2018年)

Employed Persons and Average Wage by Counties (Municipalities, Districts)(2018)

县(市、区)	Counties (Municipalities, Districts)	就业人员(万人) Number of Employed Persons (10 000 persons)	第一产业 Primary Industry	第二产业 Secondary Industry	第三产业 Tertiary Industry	非私营单位就业人员平均工资(元) Average Wage of Non-private Sector Employees (yuan)
成都市	**Chengdu**					
锦江区	Jinjiang	58.30	0.10	9.50	48.70	78555
青羊区	Qingyang	68.06	0.19	18.27	49.60	92925
金牛区	Jinniu	68.89	0.03	18.31	50.55	87280
武侯区	Wuhou	75.09	0.03	10.86	64.20	93852
成华区	Chenghua	42.90	0.40	11.10	31.40	83233
龙泉驿区	Longquanyi	44.89	4.60	15.86	24.43	90969
青白江区	Qingbaijiang	24.73	5.64	8.60	10.49	72863
新都区	Xindu	58.57	8.77	30.13	19.67	74540
温江区	Wenjiang	27.02	3.80	9.37	13.85	75066
双流区	Shuangliu	78.90	14.20	23.40	41.30	101576
郫都区	Pidu	41.07	5.96	19.36	15.75	95215
金堂县	Jintang	58.58	20.38	11.90	26.30	65001
大邑县	Dayi	35.15	7.80	13.33	14.02	68074
蒲江县	Pujiang	17.35	6.51	5.01	5.83	70797
新津县	Xinjin	18.85	3.18	8.74	6.93	78927
都江堰市	Dujiangyan	43.91	7.10	15.13	21.67	80593
彭州市	Pengzhou	54.53	21.72	16.97	15.85	83092
邛崃市	Qionglai	38.92	10.21	10.12	18.59	69064
崇州市	Chongzhou	54.35	10.89	28.41	15.05	77885
简阳市	Jianyang	74.08	27.72	15.81	30.55	69896
自贡市	**Zigong**					
自流井区	Ziliujing	28.90	2.40	11.20	15.30	73130
贡井区	Gongjing	15.44	5.32	3.88	6.24	81122
大安区	Daan	25.20	8.30	7.28	9.60	70028
沿滩区	Yantan	22.50	5.57	7.40	9.50	69109
荣县	Rongxian	29.79	11.53	8.57	9.69	75968
富顺县	Fushun	43.33	16.06	11.20	16.10	80053
攀枝花市	**Panzhihua**					
东区	East District	20.07	0.17	9.25	10.65	81049
西区	West District	5.01	0.20	2.14	2.67	60124
仁和区	Renhe	14.57	6.91	2.66	5.00	81952
米易县	Miyi	12.70	5.38	1.79	5.53	82469
盐边县	Yanbian	10.21	6.59	1.17	2.45	122984
泸州市	**Luzhou**					
江阳区	Jiangyang	39.41	9.03	15.88	14.50	88684
纳溪区	Nanxi	31.92	11.26	10.24	10.43	83358
龙马潭区	Longmatan	23.94	4.73	8.36	10.84	64777
泸县	Luxian	62.16	27.22	20.81	14.13	59043
合江县	Hejiang	50.41	19.74	19.63	11.02	55269
叙永县	Xuyong	34.91	16.45	8.72	9.73	65368

12-2 续表 1 continued

县(市、区)	Counties (Municipalities, Districts)	就业人员（万人）Number of Employed Persons (10 000 persons)	第一产业 Primary Industry	第二产业 Secondary Industry	第三产业 Tertiary Industry	非私营单位就业人员平均工资（元）Average Wage of Non-private Sector Employees (yuan)
古蔺县	Gulin	40.10	17.76	11.94	10.40	70316
德阳市	**Deyang**					
旌阳区	Jinyang	45.60	7.90	15.30	22.40	88558
罗江区	Luojiang	12.40	4.60	3.60	4.20	63949
中江县	Zhongjiang	67.10	28.20	14.80	24.10	73630
广汉市	Guanghan	36.90	11.90	11.80	13.20	86475
什邡市	Shifang	23.90	7.80	7.90	8.20	68137
绵竹市	Mianzhu	31.00	9.40	9.50	12.10	65625
绵阳市	**Mianyang**					
涪城区	Hucheng	61.08	3.81	26.50	30.77	76508
游仙区	Youxian	33.04	9.77	11.26	12.01	106413
安州区	Anzhou	24.33	7.94	7.55	8.84	77150
三台县	Santai	65.41	23.47	20.64	21.30	65672
盐亭县	Yanting	26.95	10.34	7.10	9.52	60571
梓潼县	Zitong	19.41	7.00	5.46	6.96	57809
北川县	Beichuan	12.69	4.40	3.83	4.46	68124
平武县	Pingwu	10.27	4.85	2.05	3.38	72011
江油市	Jiangyou	51.22	15.17	18.18	17.87	59848
广元市	**Guangyuan**					
利州区	Lizhou	24.59	3.48	10.18	10.93	69457
昭化区	Zhaohua	14.65	6.11	3.35	5.19	64526
朝天区	Chaotian	13.47	5.62	3.08	4.77	73217
旺苍县	Wangcang	25.16	8.25	7.69	9.22	63153
青川县	Qingchuan	12.72	7.60	1.52	3.60	70577
剑阁县	Jiange	30.92	15.52	4.93	10.47	68453
苍溪县	Cangxi	43.52	20.65	7.55	15.32	66690
遂宁市	**Suining**					
船山区	Chuanshan	37.70	6.21	11.70	19.79	83583
安居区	Anju	32.91	18.77	7.23	6.91	73190
蓬溪县	Pengxi	26.96	14.29	5.91	6.76	54144
射洪县	Shehong	41.83	16.78	10.42	14.63	67977
大英县	Daying	24.47	12.37	5.10	7.00	59661
内江市	**Neijiang**					
内江市中区	Neijiang Downtown	26.73	8.07	6.97	11.69	65997
东兴区	Dongxing	50.73	13.99	14.77	21.97	78314
威远县	Weiyuan	38.55	11.87	11.31	15.37	56963
资中县	Zizhong	54.73	17.27	18.91	18.55	72491
隆昌市	Longchang	48.83	7.97	19.83	21.03	54490
乐山市	**Leshan**					
乐山市中区	Leshan Downtown	46.08	15.23	14.00	16.85	68596
沙湾区	Shawan	12.89	4.20	4.37	4.32	74921

12-2 续表 2 continued

县(市、区)	Counties (Municipalities, Districts)	就业人员（万人） Number of Employed Persons (10 000 persons)	第一产业 Primary Industry	第二产业 Secondary Industry	第三产业 Tertiary Industry	非私营单位就业人员平均工资（元） Average Wage of Non-private Sector Employees (yuan)
五通桥区	Wutongqiao	21.00	7.10	6.00	7.90	68246
金口河区	Jinkouhe	3.10	1.30	0.70	1.10	70041
犍为县	Qianwei	32.69	10.89	9.04	12.76	80216
井研县	Jingyan	20.78	7.96	4.65	8.17	79986
夹江县	Jiajiang	21.95	7.30	7.21	7.44	73423
沐川县	Muchuan	14.86	6.90	1.82	6.14	77615
峨边县	Ebian	9.26	4.32	1.59	3.35	71639
马边县	Mabian	11.55	6.29	0.97	4.29	77919
峨眉山市	Emeishan	30.10	9.50	6.10	14.50	69665
南充市	**Nanchong**					
顺庆区	Shunqing	43.22	9.28	10.54	23.40	79513
高坪区	Gaoping	42.83	12.53	7.03	23.27	66901
嘉陵区	Jialing	42.02	15.55	9.23	17.24	66439
南部县	Nanbu	85.81	28.67	25.09	32.05	64006
营山县	Yingshan	57.03	21.21	13.40	22.42	68531
蓬安县	Pengan	33.90	11.83	5.81	16.26	67633
仪陇县	Yilong	62.55	25.90	18.62	18.03	61237
西充县	Xichong	44.37	21.87	7.14	15.36	60852
阆中市	Langzhong	48.98	14.75	10.48	23.75	67705
眉山市	**Meishan**					
东坡区	Dongpo	48.99	19.13	12.34	17.52	87986
彭山区	Pengshan	20.34	5.90	6.25	8.19	72950
仁寿县	Renshou	85.31	31.28	25.47	29.06	60436
洪雅县	Hongya	19.82	12.10	2.97	4.75	68983
丹棱县	Danling	10.62	5.07	2.88	2.67	68908
青神县	Qingshen	12.86	4.88	4.91	3.07	52564
宜宾市	**Yibin**					
翠屏区	Cuiping	59.03	15.02	20.74	23.27	88482
南溪区	Nanxi	24.52	10.00	7.83	6.69	74127
叙州区	Xuzhou	56.02	22.98	17.92	15.12	68994
江安县	Jiangan	29.23	13.25	8.95	7.03	67160
长宁县	Changning	24.87	12.01	6.06	6.80	52726
高县	Gaoxian	28.63	14.83	7.56	6.24	71364
珙县	Gongxian	26.04	12.69	7.16	6.19	67732
筠连县	Junlian	23.73	13.09	5.83	4.81	73501
兴文县	Xingwen	27.02	16.02	5.24	5.76	71089
屏山县	Pingshan	17.62	10.01	3.90	3.71	63227
广安市	**Guangan**					
广安区	Guanganqu	39.67	18.27	8.98	12.42	76640
前锋区	Qianfeng	20.58	6.38	6.82	7.38	79360
岳池县	Yuechi	50.12	23.91	8.86	17.35	62533

12-2 续表 3 continued

县(市、区)	Counties (Municipalities, Districts)	就业人员(万人) Number of Employed Persons (10 000 persons)	第一产业 Primary Industry	第二产业 Secondary Industry	第三产业 Tertiary Industry	非私营单位就业人员平均工资（元） Average Wage of Non-private Sector Employees (yuan)
武胜县	Wusheng	40.48	18.03	10.42	12.03	76634
邻水县	Linshui	47.14	20.38	11.84	14.92	78288
华蓥市	Huaying	18.90	7.10	6.03	5.77	73770
达州市	**Dazhou**					
通川区	Tongchuan	45.17	7.02	10.78	27.37	77498
达川区	Dachuan	61.87	25.22	12.18	24.47	65649
宣汉县	Xuanhan	60.54	20.12	10.04	30.38	69480
开江县	Kaijiang	32.21	12.51	4.61	15.09	53588
大竹县	Dazhu	55.59	18.96	14.63	22.00	56653
渠县	Quxian	63.74	21.71	14.53	27.50	59305
万源市	Wanyuan	29.05	12.03	3.51	13.51	70119
雅安市	**Yaan**					
雨城区	Yucheng	20.42	8.78	4.29	7.35	63339
名山区	Mingshan	17.87	8.77	4.12	4.98	66613
荥经县	Yingjing	12.81	2.82	4.71	5.28	38686
汉源县	Hanyuan	22.22	13.29	2.59	6.35	66859
石棉县	Shimian	8.69	3.11	1.95	3.63	60923
天全县	Tianquan	9.61	3.18	1.98	4.44	45742
芦山县	Lushan	8.41	2.92	2.33	3.16	52658
宝兴县	Baoxing	4.03	1.56	1.13	1.35	68600
巴中市	**Bazhong**					
巴州区	Bazhou	38.10	9.39	11.87	16.84	55815
恩阳区	Enyang	28.67	12.31	4.60	11.76	62997
通江县	Tongjiang	34.27	17.03	7.79	9.45	54939
南江县	Nanjiang	33.20	16.12	8.12	8.96	58164
平昌县	Pingchang	49.67	26.20	8.47	14.99	53074
资阳市	**Ziyang**					
雁江区	Yanjiang	49.16	13.91	15.10	20.15	64068
安岳县	Anyue	60.19	36.09	8.40	15.70	58870
乐至县	Lezhi	30.53	14.21	6.05	10.27	54151
阿坝州	**Aba**					
马尔康市	Maerkang	4.98	1.66	0.51	2.81	109927
汶川县	Wenchuan	6.08	2.48	1.11	2.49	81998
理县	Lixian	4.11	1.98	0.40	1.73	83248
茂县	Maoxian	8.35	4.49	0.94	2.92	69755
松潘县	Songpan	5.89	2.65	0.20	3.04	99862
九寨沟县	Jiuzhaigou	4.21	2.29	0.26	1.66	80770
金川县	Jinchuan	4.44	2.80	0.21	1.43	87851
小金县	Xiaojin	5.48	3.78	0.21	1.49	102251
黑水县	Heishui	4.61	1.91	0.29	2.41	105829
壤塘县	Rangtang	3.10	1.98	0.27	0.85	89830

12-2 续表 4 continued

县(市、区)	Counties (Municipalities, Districts)	就业人员（万人） Number of Employed Persons (10 000 persons)	第一产业 Primary Industry	第二产业 Secondary Industry	第三产业 Tertiary Industry	非私营单位就业人员平均工资（元） Average Wage of Non-private Sector Employees (yuan)
阿坝县	Abaxian	4.90	2.99	0.11	1.80	87280
若尔盖县	Ruoergai	5.81	3.74	0.15	1.92	99401
红原县	Hongyuan	3.18	1.91	0.13	1.14	102468
甘孜州	**Ganzi**					
康定市	Kangding	8.80	3.36	0.82	4.62	80953
泸定县	Luding	3.89	2.52	0.24	1.13	76723
丹巴县	Danba	4.20	3.22	0.13	0.86	80634
九龙县	Jiulong	4.01	2.96	0.13	0.92	83698
雅江县	Yajiang	2.97	2.39	0.05	0.52	77910
道孚县	Daofu	3.22	2.44	0.12	0.66	86092
炉霍县	Luhuo	3.13	2.38	0.12	0.62	62754
甘孜县	Ganzixian	4.12	3.04	0.07	1.01	76554
新龙县	Xinlong	2.58	1.84	0.06	0.69	76606
德格县	Dege	4.66	3.96	0.11	0.60	71779
白玉县	Baiyu	3.66	3.00	0.03	0.63	80326
石渠县	Shiqu	4.26	3.61	0.06	0.59	139312
色达县	Seda	3.48	2.80	0.06	0.62	105887
理塘县	Litang	4.29	3.33	0.03	0.93	93846
巴塘县	Batang	3.58	2.33	0.15	1.09	82172
乡城县	Xiangcheng	1.91	1.36	0.10	0.45	65616
稻城县	Daocheng	2.20	1.35	0.03	0.82	70017
得荣县	Derong	1.83	1.28	0.09	0.46	79926
凉山州	**Liangshan**					
西昌市	Xichang	54.90	20.20	11.50	23.20	70038
木里县	Muli	10.00	4.80	1.40	3.80	77932
盐源县	Yanyuan	24.00	19.90	1.10	3.00	72905
德昌县	Dechang	12.80	8.70	1.10	3.00	78218
会理县	Huili	30.10	7.00	6.60	16.50	77054
会东县	Huidong	27.80	17.40	3.00	7.40	72329
宁南县	Ningnan	13.70	10.30	0.90	2.50	75584
普格县	Puge	17.90	7.60	3.00	7.30	67027
布拖县	Buto	10.50	9.40	0.20	0.90	71609
金阳县	Jinyang	10.60	8.20	0.50	1.90	71516
昭觉县	Zhaojue	17.00	12.40	1.20	3.40	70096
喜德县	Xide	11.80	4.90	2.00	4.90	67198
冕宁县	Mianning	26.10	16.60	2.80	6.70	69447
越西县	Yuexi	19.70	9.50	2.90	7.30	73974
甘洛县	Ganluo	12.30	5.80	1.90	4.60	69408
美姑县	Meigu	14.80	11.30	0.90	2.60	87500
雷波县	Leibo	17.50	12.80	1.40	3.30	73736

12-3 各县(市、区)地区生产总值(2018年)
Gross Regional Product by Counties (Municipalities, District)(2018)

县(市、区)	Counties (Municipalities, Districts)	地区生产总值(万元) Gross Regional Product (10 000 yuan)	第一产业 Primary Industry	第二产业 Secondary Industry	第三产业 Tertiary Industry	人均地区生产总值(元) Per Capita Gross Regional Product (yuan)
成都市	**Chengdu**					
锦江区	Jinjiang	10347727	6711	1135764	9205252	146527
青羊区	Qingyang	11900924	409	1959649	9940866	140739
金牛区	Jinniu	11969366	824	2428949	9539593	98457
武侯区	Wuhou	10913678	85	2121299	8792294	100448
成华区	Chenghua	9489183	670	1717295	7771218	99855
龙泉驿区	Longquanyi	13027807	293467	9886573	2847767	145855
青白江区	Qingbaijiang	4750499	157721	3270198	1322580	113675
新都区	Xindu	7992025	298119	4628054	3065852	88446
温江区	Wenjiang	5449973	190543	2711920	2547510	105661
双流区	Shuangliu	12585432	359837	5983116	6242479	87881
郫都区	Pidu	5802179	243521	3324178	2234480	68069
金堂县	Jintang	4240703	491411	1987276	1762016	59939
大邑县	Dayi	2601247	374906	1143157	1083184	50895
蒲江县	Pujiang	1518510	198752	786030	533728	58720
新津县	Xinjin	3374149	182771	1999590	1191788	103470
都江堰市	Dujiangyan	3847951	284509	1394531	2168911	55446
彭州市	Pengzhou	4116316	539218	2189394	1387704	52909
邛崃市	Qionglai	2986779	400875	1448899	1137005	48259
崇州市	Chongzhou	3399909	377993	1671114	1350802	51134
简阳市	Jianyang	4538346	646370	2456093	1435883	55278
自贡市	**Zigong**					
自流井区	Ziliujing	3256541	49435	820839	2386267	65577
贡井区	Gongjing	1654102	163971	1022057	468074	57275
大安区	Daan	2264613	146823	1418479	699311	52434
沿滩区	Yantan	1802711	176043	1248030	378638	48920
荣县	Rongxian	2089929	505539	788600	795790	37589
富顺县	Fushun	3005805	473684	1394911	1137210	39087
攀枝花市	**Panzhihua**					
东区	Dongqu	4772338	7067	2677642	2087629	124312
西区	Xiqu	1317014	10008	985038	321968	91080
仁和区	Renhe	2556184	117636	1744099	694449	93054
米易县	Miyi	1656031	149890	935506	570635	71074
盐边县	Yanbian	1433671	112828	968967	351876	71684
泸州市	**Luzhou**					
江阳区	Jiangyang	5006279	224155	2650711	2131413	80968
纳溪区	Naxi	1527946	222917	802537	502492	32600
龙马潭区	Longmatan	2453295	110623	1609216	733456	63938
泸县	Luxian	3135461	502978	1702694	929789	35994
合江县	Hejiang	2005577	376828	756098	872651	28416
叙永县	Xuyong	1243075	241709	484680	516686	21366
古蔺县	Gulin	1578074	226540	811137	540397	22824

12-3 续表 1 continued

县(市、区)	Counties (Municipalities, Districts)	地区生产总值(万元) Gross Regional Product (10 000 yuan)	第一产业 Primary Industry	第二产业 Secondary Industry	第三产业 Tertiary Industry	人均地区生产总值(元) Per Capita Gross Regional Product (yuan)
德阳市	**Deyang**					
旌阳区	Jinyang	6308633	346308	3131692	2830633	83282
罗江区	Luojiang	1263265	217744	636894	408627	56021
中江县	Zhongjiang	3900910	874933	1496553	1529424	36234
广汉市	Guanghan	4510631	373499	2305732	1831400	74990
什邡市	Shifang	3237578	309380	1635367	1292831	77343
绵竹市	Mianzhu	2917656	311272	1505075	1101309	63607
绵阳市	**Mianyang**					
涪城区	Fucheng	8658078	242051	4062574	4353453	92313
游仙区	Youxian	2682680	304135	1131399	1247146	51511
安州区	Anzhou	1463493	306592	596367	560534	37382
三台县	Santai	2698057	810620	756540	1130897	25528
盐亭县	Yanting	1140297	383463	331082	425752	24990
梓潼县	Zitong	1126676	294063	394364	438249	36545
北川县	Beichuan	559443	111372	186705	261366	24975
平武县	Pingwu	450497	87859	201039	161599	27808
江油市	Jiangyou	4280341	472522	1647409	2160410	54264
广元市	**Guangyuan**					
利州区	Lizhou	2731166	101462	1433464	1196240	49122
昭化区	Zhaohua	546850	126907	251071	168872	29543
朝天区	Chaotian	500161	88053	260572	151536	26352
旺苍县	Wangcang	1118042	177241	593074	347727	27039
青川县	Qingchuan	391241	82126	165229	143886	18377
剑阁县	Jiange	1202054	281538	459535	460981	24284
苍溪县	Cangxi	1528986	323676	665404	539906	25012
遂宁市	**Suining**					
船山区	Chuanshan	3443059	231877	1588805	1622377	50648
安居区	Anju	1674498	400217	681678	592603	26062
蓬溪县	Pengxi	1607547	285841	684203	637503	30143
射洪县	Shehong	3773971	472156	1855847	1445968	42779
大英县	Daying	1714839	266302	847857	600680	35629
内江市	**Neijiang**					
内江市中区	Neijiang Downtown	2771093	174540	1287265	1309288	51961
东兴区	Dongxing	2287108	518807	587743	1180558	29087
威远县	Weiyuan	3509276	489895	1966469	1052912	59641
资中县	Zizhong	2699865	671862	988820	1039183	22822
隆昌市	Longchang	2849974	337959	1277525	1234490	44853
乐山市	**Leshan**					
乐山市中区	Leshan Downtown	3501676	213069	1231013	2057594	50815
沙湾区	Shawan	2121953	93413	1381191	647349	123513
五通桥区	Wutongqiao	1717047	133137	1015907	568003	54631

12-3 续表 2 continued

县(市、区)	Counties (Municipalities, Districts)	地区生产总值(万元) Gross Regional Product (10 000 yuan)	第一产业 Primary Industry	第二产业 Secondary Industry	第三产业 Tertiary Industry	人均地区生产总值(元) Per Capita Gross Regional Product (yuan)
金口河区	Jinkouhe	377305	22569	233821	120915	81845
犍为县	Qianwei	1710161	288345	677520	744296	40051
井研县	Jinyan	964851	231760	340611	392480	31864
夹江县	Jiajiang	1568711	212168	686497	670046	47350
沐川县	Muchuan	606810	144249	216783	245778	29174
峨边县	Ebian	448564	48302	212560	187702	33129
马边县	Mabian	401788	88432	148049	165307	21281
峨眉山市	Emeishan	2732083	183710	1073833	1474540	60019
南充市	**Nanchong**					
顺庆区	Shunqing	4002688	232657	1806127	1963904	55624
高坪区	Gaoping	1718149	292662	708961	716526	28061
嘉陵区	Jialing	1683397	377783	771900	533714	27095
南部县	Nanbu	3500318	627569	1714131	1158618	37226
营山县	Yingshan	1900778	421452	741149	738177	25256
蓬安县	Pengan	1724020	405609	740273	578138	30004
仪陇县	Yilong	2037690	623292	603917	810481	21768
西充县	Xichong	1350354	340979	507656	501719	25160
阆中市	Langzhong	2350840	496657	794307	1059876	31954
眉山市	**Meishan**					
东坡区	Dongpo	4307904	513214	1889759	1904931	51468
彭山区	Pengshan	1584178	149699	804183	630296	49413
仁寿县	Renshou	4083425	807547	1706930	1568948	34097
洪雅县	Hongya	1173620	178404	530756	464460	37981
丹棱县	Danling	619883	117206	273338	229339	42083
青神县	Qingshen	791204	98963	339643	352598	47067
宜宾市	**Yibin**					
翠屏区	Cuiping	7000876	257154	3660959	3082763	79106
南溪区	Nanxi	1425008	240718	682583	501707	41090
叙州区	Xuzhou	2923668	454689	1429560	1039419	37464
江安县	Jiangan	1544718	250089	792272	502357	36928
长宁县	Changning	1427440	262379	597468	567593	41220
高县	Gaoxian	1466787	225009	781438	460340	35370
珙县	Gongxian	1607782	193376	937323	477083	42897
筠连县	Junlian	1435671	213157	801375	421139	43126
兴文县	Xingwen	1072991	210508	370847	491636	27697
屏山县	Pingshan	529660	171429	181011	177220	20633
广安市	**Guangan**					
广安区	Guanganqu	2019053	250851	455320	1312882	32115
前锋区	Qianfeng	1731008	150823	1219876	360309	66475
岳池县	Yuechi	2432026	421273	1042164	968589	31096
武胜县	Wusheng	2277588	390063	1022170	865355	38847

12-3 续表 3 continued

县(市、区)	Counties (Municipalities, Districts)	地区生产总值(万元) Gross Regional Product (10 000 yuan)	第一产业 Primary Industry	第二产业 Secondary Industry	第三产业 Tertiary Industry	人均地区生产总值(元) Per Capita Gross Regional Product (yuan)
邻水县	Linshui	2495810	399619	1110317	985874	35326
华蓥市	Huaying	1546937	122534	902498	521905	54914
达州市	**Dazhou**					
通川区	Tongchuan	2393297	224559	758303	1410435	32198
达川区	Dachuan	2766345	528937	935432	1301976	26610
宣汉县	Xuanhan	3006250	616950	1222676	1166624	29181
开江县	Kaijiang	1276282	334355	374288	567639	28330
大竹县	Dazhu	3313234	594418	1393832	1324984	37086
渠县	Quxian	2747195	654810	932227	1160158	24309
万源市	Wanyuan	1413312	308324	435590	669398	33836
雅安市	**Yaan**					
雨城区	Yucheng	1777986	169921	627410	980655	48659
名山区	Mingshan	812239	210777	332768	268694	30240
荥经县	Yingjing	741120	70541	384697	285882	48822
汉源县	Hanyuan	827709	164576	383170	279963	25882
石棉县	Shimian	882198	64166	553855	264177	69355
天全县	Tianquan	641976	79624	321865	240487	45823
芦山县	Lushan	432013	60296	231312	140405	39203
宝兴县	Baoxing	342140	38422	197882	105836	61096
巴中市	**Bazhong**					
巴州区	Bazhou	1669550	169361	718588	781601	22604
恩阳区	Enyang	659550	161325	262961	235264	13920
通江县	Tongjiang	1235359	218875	494861	521623	17605
南江县	Nanjiang	1334858	192322	796932	345604	21854
平昌县	Pingchang	1559526	240810	890543	428173	19624
资阳市	**Ziyang**					
雁江区	Yanjiang	5024758	513569	2796277	1714912	54873
安岳县	Anyue	3450147	815382	1339340	1295425	31094
乐至县	Lezhi	2190375	338968	966332	885075	43177
阿坝州	**Aba**					
马尔康市	Maerkang	286896	24903	42873	219120	47816
汶川县	Wenchuan	584843	41979	369855	173009	56947
理县	Lixian	246138	21401	163861	60876	50335
茂县	Maoxian	344003	61123	207730	75150	30880
松潘县	Songpan	214304	43382	62954	107968	28536
九寨沟县	Jiuzhaigou	253697	23219	84509	145969	31052
金川县	Jinchuan	137428	31211	49729	56488	18324
小金县	Xiaojin	163201	33397	67688	62116	20400
黑水县	Heishui	224299	28147	144599	51553	36891
壤塘县	Rangtang	94032	27723	23477	42832	22389

12-3 续表 4 continued

县(市、区)	Counties (Municipalities, Districts)	地区生产总值(万元) Gross Regional Product (10 000 yuan)	第一产业 Primary Industry	第二产业 Secondary Industry	第三产业 Tertiary Industry	人均地区生产总值(元) Per Capita Gross Regional Product (yuan)
阿坝县	Abaxian	113253	35905	22512	54836	14708
若尔盖县	Ruoergai	187545	82061	36858	68626	24013
红原县	Hongyuan	130626	44176	32294	54156	26283
甘孜州	**Ganzi**					
康定市	Kangding	801100	54814	441468	304818	59385
泸定县	Luding	201700	37755	82676	81269	22843
丹巴县	Danba	166800	38257	69057	59486	24104
九龙县	Jiulong	262766	36220	169464	57082	40117
雅江县	Yajiang	129070	29027	55696	44347	22486
道孚县	Daofu	98594	27422	23305	47867	16216
炉霍县	Luhuo	73787	27791	17603	28393	14728
甘孜县	Ganzixian	108656	49779	17139	41738	14526
新龙县	Xinlong	102992	39114	21746	42132	19730
德格县	Dege	94359	39805	18633	35921	10674
白玉县	Baiyu	137485	37885	69419	30181	22539
石渠县	Shiqu	100582	49617	11966	38999	9939
色达县	Seda	85053	39451	13731	31871	13522
理塘县	Litang	129371	44320	30562	54489	17506
巴塘县	Batang	138023	34186	63923	39914	26853
乡城县	Xiangcheng	108582	25121	46495	36966	30415
稻城县	Daocheng	81537	22764	22855	35918	22904
得荣县	Derong	91583	21387	41311	28885	32476
凉山州	**Liangshan**					
西昌市	Xichang	5093777	461155	1912947	2719675	63864
木里县	Muli	316356	62592	141896	111868	23159
盐源县	Yanyuan	900096	239579	422141	238376	24606
德昌县	Dechang	750629	188689	288603	273337	33600
会理县	Huili	2000072	441212	896351	662509	46000
会东县	Huidong	1432933	429549	580960	422424	37453
宁南县	Ningnan	613297	183652	205563	224082	32381
普格县	Puge	256270	86936	60369	108965	14882
布拖县	Butuo	242190	79319	75353	87518	13056
金阳县	Jinyang	321094	74957	150691	95446	17948
昭觉县	Zhaojue	298356	111864	60728	125764	11100
喜德县	Xide	239208	75075	66839	97294	12909
冕宁县	Mianning	1249905	224528	652446	372931	34662
越西县	Yuexi	377497	126073	78986	172438	12438
甘洛县	Ganluo	326834	68910	115755	142169	14951
美姑县	Meigu	259038	98245	66039	94754	11528
雷波县	Leibo	654387	123784	355617	174986	26841

12-4 各县(市、区)地区生产总值指数(2018年)

Indices of Gross Regional Product by Counties (Municipalities, District)(2018)

上年=100 (preceding year=100)

县(市、区)	Counties (Municipalities, Districts)	地区生产总值 Gross Regional Product	第一产业 Primary Industry	第二产业 Secondary Industry	第三产业 Tertiary Industry	人均地区生产总值 Per Capita Gross Regional Product
成都市	**Chengdu**					
锦江区	Jinjiang	107.2	100.5	102.5	107.9	106.7
青羊区	Qingyang	107.2	98.6	104.0	107.9	106.8
金牛区	Jinniu	107.8	93.6	104.5	108.6	107.5
武侯区	Wuhou	107.6	117.1	105.4	108.1	107.5
成华区	Chenghua	108.5	70.9	107.2	108.8	108.0
龙泉驿区	Longquanyi	106.8	103.0	105.8	110.6	103.5
青白江区	Qingbaijiang	110.5	103.5	108.2	117.9	106.9
新都区	Xindu	108.9	103.4	107.9	111.1	107.6
温江区	Wenjiang	108.8	103.3	108.2	109.8	106.2
双流区	Shuangliu	109.6	100.3	108.6	111.3	105.6
郫都区	Pidu	107.8	103.2	107.5	108.8	106.7
金堂县	Jintang	110.5	104.3	110.4	112.5	110.6
大邑县	Dayi	110.2	104.2	111.5	111.0	110.0
蒲江县	Pujiang	110.3	104.0	111.0	111.9	108.9
新津县	Xinjin	110.3	104.1	110.6	110.8	108.0
都江堰市	Dujiangyan	107.7	104.6	106.3	109.1	106.8
彭州市	Pengzhou	98.2	103.8	91.2	109.6	98.1
邛崃市	Qionglai	110.8	103.9	113.5	109.9	110.7
崇州市	Chongzhou	110.6	104.5	110.6	112.6	110.6
简阳市	Jianyang	108.3	104.4	108.1	110.8	109.3
自贡市	**Zigong**					
自流井区	Ziliujing	106.2	103.8	97.3	110.0	96.1
贡井区	Gongjing	109.9	103.6	111.3	109.4	109.3
大安区	Daan	108.9	103.7	109.3	109.5	102.4
沿滩区	Yantan	110.8	103.7	112.1	110.6	99.8
荣县	Rongxian	108.2	103.8	110.0	109.2	113.5
富顺县	Fushun	109.4	103.8	110.3	110.7	111.6
攀枝花市	**Panzhihua**					
东区	Dongqu	107.5	104.0	106.7	108.6	107.3
西区	Xiqu	106.7	103.9	106.3	108.0	108.8
仁和区	Renhe	107.9	104.0	107.8	108.7	106.9
米易县	Miyi	107.7	104.1	107.7	108.5	107.6
盐边县	Yanbian	107.5	104.0	107.7	108.3	107.5
泸州市	**Luzhou**					
江阳区	Jiangyang	109.0	103.6	110.5	107.4	108.2
纳溪区	Naxi	107.0	103.6	108.3	106.0	106.4
龙马潭区	Longmatan	110.0	103.3	110.2	110.7	108.3
泸县	Luxian	105.8	103.9	105.7	106.9	105.6
合江县	Hejiang	105.0	103.7	105.7	105.0	105.3
叙永县	Xuyong	107.1	103.8	108.8	106.7	107.0
古蔺县	Gulin	107.9	103.7	109.0	107.8	108.5

12-4 续表 1 continued

上年=100 (preceding year=100)

县(市、区)	Counties (Municipalities, Districts)	地区生产总值 Gross Regional Product	第一产业 Primary Industry	第二产业 Secondary Industry	第三产业 Tertiary Industry	人均地区生产总值 Per Capita Gross Regional Product
德阳市	**Deyang**					
旌阳区	Jinyang	108.7	103.9	108.8	109.2	107.8
罗江区	Luojiang	109.7	103.7	112.1	109.4	108.2
中江县	Zhongjiang	109.2	103.6	110.9	111.3	109.3
广汉市	Guanghan	109.0	103.5	109.0	110.1	108.4
什邡市	Shifang	109.3	104.0	110.5	109.0	109.3
绵竹市	Mianzhu	108.5	103.8	108.5	110.0	108.1
绵阳市	**Mianyang**					
涪城区	Fucheng	109.5	103.6	109.3	110.0	107.1
游仙区	Youxian	108.8	103.7	109.8	109.2	108.3
安州区	Anzhou	109.2	103.7	110.2	111.4	108.4
三台县	Santai	108.6	103.8	109.6	111.5	108.3
盐亭县	Yanting	108.0	103.8	110.4	110.1	107.7
梓潼县	Zitong	108.1	103.8	109.6	109.7	107.6
北川县	Beichuan	109.1	103.6	109.4	111.5	108.0
平武县	Pingwu	106.4	103.5	108.4	105.3	110.3
江油市	Jiangyou	109.2	103.8	109.3	110.3	109.6
广元市	**Guangyuan**					
利州区	Lizhou	108.3	103.9	108.4	108.6	107.8
昭化区	Zhaohua	108.3	103.8	110.5	108.2	107.6
朝天区	Chaotian	108.9	104.1	110.0	110.0	109.6
旺苍县	Wangcang	108.6	103.7	110.0	108.8	107.6
青川县	Qingchuan	108.2	103.9	109.8	109.0	108.0
剑阁县	Jiange	108.5	103.8	110.0	109.9	107.1
苍溪县	Cangxi	108.3	103.9	109.1	110.3	107.9
遂宁市	**Suining**					
船山区	Chuanshan	108.8	102.4	108.0	110.4	108.0
安居区	Anju	109.0	103.6	112.2	110.5	109.2
蓬溪县	Pengxi	108.8	103.7	110.4	110.3	109.8
射洪县	Shehong	109.0	103.3	108.9	110.9	114.2
大英县	Daying	108.7	103.7	108.8	110.8	109.5
内江市	**Neijiang**					
内江市中区	Neijiang Downtown	108.6	103.9	108.2	110.0	108.5
东兴区	Dongxing	107.9	103.7	109.6	108.8	105.7
威远县	Weiyuan	108.8	104.0	109.3	109.8	109.0
资中县	Zizhong	104.6	103.7	104.8	105.0	107.0
隆昌市	Longchang	108.8	103.9	109.2	109.9	110.9
乐山市	**Leshan**					
乐山市中区	Leshan Downtown	108.2	103.9	105.7	110.7	107.5
沙湾区	Shawan	109.8	103.6	110.1	110.3	111.2
五通桥区	Wutongqiao	109.6	103.7	109.6	111.5	111.6

12-4 续表 2 continued

上年=100 (preceding year=100)

县(市、区)	Counties (Municipalities, Districts)	地区生产总值 Gross Regional Product	第一产业 Primary Industry	第二产业 Secondary Industry	第三产业 Tertiary Industry	人均地区生产总值 Per Capita Gross Regional Product
金口河区	Jinkouhe	106.5	103.6	106.2	108.5	107.5
犍为县	Qianwei	109.0	103.9	109.5	110.8	108.7
井研县	Jinyan	107.6	104.3	108.4	109.1	106.6
夹江县	Jiajiang	109.3	103.8	109.9	110.5	109.6
沐川县	Muchuan	104.2	103.6	104.8	104.0	105.9
峨边县	Ebian	107.5	103.2	109.0	106.6	107.0
马边县	Mabian	107.0	103.8	108.2	107.7	106.4
峨眉山市	Emeishan	109.1	103.7	108.3	111.0	108.5
南充市	**Nanchong**					
顺庆区	Shunqing	109.5	103.9	109.8	110.0	109.3
高坪区	Gaoping	109.4	103.8	110.8	110.5	108.9
嘉陵区	Jialing	109.4	104.0	111.0	111.4	109.0
南部县	Nanbu	109.1	103.6	110.4	110.5	108.9
营山县	Yingshan	109.2	104.0	110.6	111.2	108.9
蓬安县	Pengan	109.0	104.1	110.8	110.5	108.5
仪陇县	Yilong	108.8	103.9	109.9	112.2	108.6
西充县	Xichong	109.6	104.2	110.8	112.7	109.1
阆中市	Langzhong	109.1	104.1	109.6	111.4	108.7
眉山市	**Meishan**					
东坡区	Dongpo	108.0	103.9	107.6	109.6	108.2
彭山区	Pengshan	108.2	103.7	107.8	110.0	107.8
仁寿县	Renshou	107.0	103.7	106.6	109.4	107.8
洪雅县	Hongya	107.0	103.8	106.3	109.7	106.9
丹棱县	Danling	108.1	104.0	109.1	109.0	107.0
青神县	Qingshen	107.9	103.9	108.0	109.0	107.8
宜宾市	**Yibin**					
翠屏区	Cuiping	110.0	103.6	110.2	110.2	108.4
南溪区	Nanxi	109.3	103.8	110.1	110.9	108.4
叙州区	Xuzhou	109.4	103.6	110.2	111.1	108.9
江安县	Jiangan	108.2	103.6	108.5	110.3	107.9
长宁县	Changning	108.8	103.7	109.5	110.6	108.4
高县	Gaoxian	108.3	103.3	108.6	110.7	108.2
珙县	Gongxian	109.1	103.4	109.9	109.9	109.0
筠连县	Junlian	109.2	103.7	110.2	110.1	109.1
兴文县	Xingwen	108.5	103.8	109.8	109.6	108.3
屏山县	Pingshan	108.7	103.6	112.9	109.2	108.4
广安市	**Guangan**					
广安区	Guanganqu	107.9	103.4	105.6	109.8	107.7
前锋区	Qianfeng	108.3	103.4	108.5	109.7	108.7
岳池县	Yuechi	108.0	103.3	108.2	109.9	108.4
武胜县	Wusheng	108.0	103.6	108.1	110.0	108.4

12-4 续表 3 continued

上年=100 (preceding year=100)

县(市、区)	Counties (Municipalities, Districts)	地区生产总值 Gross Regional Product	第一产业 Primary Industry	第二产业 Secondary Industry	第三产业 Tertiary Industry	人均地区生产总值 Per Capita Gross Regional Product
邻水县	Linshui	108.1	103.7	108.2	110.0	108.8
华蓥市	Huaying	107.8	103.4	107.4	109.6	108.2
达州市	**Dazhou**					
通川区	Tongchuan	108.5	103.6	107.4	110.0	99.3
达川区	Dachuan	108.5	103.6	108.6	110.5	107.4
宣汉县	Xuanhan	108.6	103.6	109.8	110.2	109.1
开江县	Kaijiang	108.1	103.7	108.9	110.1	108.3
大竹县	Dazhu	108.6	103.7	109.1	110.3	108.5
渠县	Quxian	108.3	103.7	108.8	110.6	109.0
万源市	Wanyuan	107.6	103.7	107.4	109.6	107.8
雅安市	**Yaan**					
雨城区	Yucheng	108.0	103.9	108.0	108.8	108.2
名山区	Mingshan	108.5	103.8	110.3	109.6	108.1
荥经县	Yingjing	106.9	103.8	107.5	106.8	107.4
汉源县	Hanyuan	107.5	104.1	108.6	107.9	107.2
石棉县	Shimian	108.0	104.1	108.3	108.3	108.4
天全县	Tianquan	109.0	104.0	110.5	108.5	107.9
芦山县	Lushan	109.1	103.9	110.4	109.0	110.4
宝兴县	Baoxing	108.5	103.9	109.6	108.1	108.5
巴中市	**Bazhong**					
巴州区	Bazhou	108.1	103.6	109.1	108.2	107.9
恩阳区	Enyang	109.1	103.5	114.3	108.2	103.4
通江县	Tongjiang	108.1	103.9	109.0	109.0	109.1
南江县	Nanjiang	107.7	103.8	108.8	107.5	108.2
平昌县	Pingchang	107.9	103.7	109.3	107.6	109.2
资阳市	**Ziyang**					
雁江区	Yanjiang	108.1	103.5	109.0	108.1	107.4
安岳县	Anyue	107.1	103.8	108.1	108.0	108.6
乐至县	Lezhi	108.1	103.7	109.2	108.6	109.1
阿坝州	**Aba**					
马尔康市	Maerkang	107.5	103.3	115.9	106.5	107.3
汶川县	Wenchuan	104.9	104.7	104.6	105.5	103.4
理县	Lixian	107.0	103.3	106.6	110.0	106.4
茂县	Maoxian	100.7	103.1	99.0	104.8	100.3
松潘县	Songpan	104.2	103.7	106.2	103.1	104.3
九寨沟县	Jiuzhaigou	100.9	103.5	111.2	95.2	100.4
金川县	Jinchuan	104.0	102.7	103.2	105.5	103.8
小金县	Xiaojin	106.8	103.1	112.7	102.1	106.8
黑水县	Heishui	100.5	103.0	98.5	108.3	100.2
壤塘县	Rangtang	109.7	103.0	133.4	104.0	109.4

12-4 续表 4 continued

上年=100 (preceding year=100)

县(市、区)	Counties (Municipalities, Districts)	地区生产总值 Gross Regional Product	第一产业 Primary Industry	第二产业 Secondary Industry	第三产业 Tertiary Industry	人均地区生产总值 Per Capita Gross Regional Product
阿坝县	Abaxian	104.1	103.8	106.3	103.3	103.8
若尔盖县	Ruoergai	105.4	103.6	110.5	104.7	104.9
红原县	Hongyuan	100.6	103.7	92.7	104.1	98.8
甘孜州	**Ganzi**					
康定市	Kangding	111.2	103.5	116.9	106.1	111.8
泸定县	Luding	108.6	104.7	115.0	103.0	109.1
丹巴县	Danba	108.5	102.7	114.2	106.0	109.6
九龙县	Jiulong	109.4	103.6	112.5	103.7	110.4
雅江县	Yajiang	106.7	103.5	109.5	105.4	104.1
道孚县	Daofu	107.5	104.3	126.4	101.9	106.6
炉霍县	Luhuo	107.8	103.1	120.0	104.6	105.6
甘孜县	Ganzixian	106.7	102.8	129.2	105.0	104.1
新龙县	Xinlong	106.3	103.2	119.0	103.7	104.6
德格县	Dege	106.9	103.4	118.0	105.3	104.7
白玉县	Baiyu	107.8	103.6	110.3	107.9	107.6
石渠县	Shiqu	106.3	103.6	123.1	105.4	106.3
色达县	Seda	109.0	103.7	140.7	103.3	106.7
理塘县	Litang	108.4	103.7	123.7	104.7	107.7
巴塘县	Batang	110.0	103.4	117.2	105.1	112.8
乡城县	Xiangcheng	113.7	105.0	126.5	104.6	112.8
稻城县	Daocheng	109.5	103.5	122.3	106.0	104.0
得荣县	Derong	112.3	103.0	125.8	104.7	112.3
凉山州	**Liangshan**					
西昌市	Xichang	107.0	103.7	105.0	109.0	104.1
木里县	Muli	106.3	103.8	107.2	106.6	106.7
盐源县	Yanyuan	106.1	103.9	105.9	108.5	107.4
德昌县	Dechang	105.9	103.8	107.4	106.0	105.0
会理县	Huili	90.5	103.6	78.0	104.9	92.3
会东县	Huidong	106.9	103.8	108.7	107.5	105.5
宁南县	Ningnan	104.9	103.7	106.0	104.9	106.1
普格县	Puge	104.3	103.3	104.3	105.3	106.0
布拖县	Butuo	100.0	103.9	88.1	109.4	98.0
金阳县	Jinyang	107.3	104.0	108.1	108.5	104.1
昭觉县	Zhaojue	106.0	104.3	102.6	109.7	102.4
喜德县	Xide	105.5	103.9	111.4	102.6	98.7
冕宁县	Mianning	108.0	103.8	109.4	108.1	107.4
越西县	Yuexi	103.6	103.9	92.0	109.3	100.2
甘洛县	Ganluo	109.8	103.9	111.7	111.4	112.0
美姑县	Meigu	106.0	103.9	107.4	107.3	109.9
雷波县	Leibo	104.6	103.9	103.1	108.7	103.1

12-5 各县(市、区)民营经济增加值(2018年)
Added Value of Civillian-owned Economy by Counties (Municipalities, District)(2018)

县(市、区)	Counties (Municipalities, Districts)	民营经济增加值(万元) Added Value of Civilian-owned Economy (10 000 yuan)	第一产业 Primary Industry	第二产业 Secondary Industry	第三产业 Tertiary Industry	人均民营经济增加值(元) Per Capita Added Value of Civilian-owned Economy (yuan)
成都市	**Chengdu**					
锦江区	Jinjiang	4736917		637789	4099128	67076
青羊区	Qingyang	4845279		1094771	3750508	57300
金牛区	Jinniu	6411041		1675920	4735121	52735
武侯区	Wuhou	6287858		1848292	4439566	57873
成华区	Chenghua	4061483		844897	3216586	42739
龙泉驿区	Longquanyi	5205743	14719	3836642	1354382	58282
青白江区	Qingbaijiang	1828766	19501	996129	813136	43761
新都区	Xindu	5056309	83268	3234354	1738687	55957
温江区	Wenjiang	2675127	1692	1443513	1229922	51864
双流区	Shuangliu	7205863	40011	4261116	2904736	50317
郫都区	Pidu	3288311	433	2205803	1082075	38577
金堂县	Jintang	2590848	87557	1571641	931650	36620
大邑县	Dayi	1641163	167666	949180	524317	32110
蒲江县	Pujiang	860023	67618	544893	247512	33257
新津县	Xinjin	2389251	64252	1652746	672253	73267
都江堰市	Dujiangyan	2225015	99572	966969	1158474	32061
彭州市	Pengzhou	1397036	129857	572272	694907	17957
邛崃市	Qionglai	1994544	133066	1250455	611023	32227
崇州市	Chongzhou	2170205	77663	1572540	520002	32640
简阳市	Jianyang	2958529	238103	2101078	619348	36036
自贡市	**Zigong**					
自流井区	Ziliujing	1360525	18352	446514	895659	27397
贡井区	Gongjing	1022065	50314	717845	253906	35390
大安区	Daan	1370696	48558	947746	374392	31736
沿滩区	Yantan	1137072	59781	849557	227734	30857
荣县	Rongxian	1436997	150190	585783	701024	25845
富顺县	Fushun	1664802	165949	962636	536217	21649
攀枝花市	**Panzhihua**					
东区	Dongqu	2003009	5129	1019104	978776	52175
西区	Xiqu	680812	9757	481440	189615	47082
仁和区	Renhe	1504941	36360	1138246	330335	54785
米易县	Miyi	965553	47233	686196	232124	41440
盐边县	Yanbian	694286	46164	451983	196139	34714
泸州市	**Luzhou**					
江阳区	Jiangyang	2738555	36417	1716009	986129	44292
纳溪区	Naxi	897002	50570	564228	282204	19138
龙马潭区	Longmatan	1404852	41248	925810	437794	36613
泸县	Luxian	2033694	130396	1348398	554900	23346
合江县	Hejiang	1264934	103627	600223	561084	17922
叙永县	Xuyong	733424	60960	373511	298953	12606
古蔺县	Gulin	863072	63098	486508	313466	12483

12-5 续表 1 continued

县(市、区)	Counties (Municipalities, Districts)	民营经济增加值(万元) Added Value of Civilian-owned Economy (10 000 yuan)	第一产业 Primary Industry	第二产业 Secondary Industry	第三产业 Tertiary Industry	人均民营经济增加值(元) Per Capita Added Value of Civilian-owned Economy (yuan)
德阳市	**Deyang**					
旌阳区	Jinyang	2586717	124549	1114318	1347850	34148
罗江区	Luojiang	775427	71506	411482	292439	34387
中江县	Zhongjiang	2432223	301445	1114308	1016470	22592
广汉市	Guanghan	3251885	97751	1919662	1234472	54063
什邡市	Shifang	1480230	65168	675077	739985	35361
绵竹市	Mianzhu	1924514	76671	1177708	670135	41956
绵阳市	**Mianyang**					
涪城区	Fucheng	4933958	61169	2519003	2353786	52606
游仙区	Youxian	1525684	79303	893410	552971	29295
安州区	Anzhou	893314	77474	502525	313315	22818
三台县	Santai	1608074	259485	599905	748684	15215
盐亭县	Yanting	672233	140765	276325	255143	14732
梓潼县	Zitong	684693	84143	371773	228777	22209
北川县	Beichuan	350623	57117	157999	135507	15653
平武县	Pingwu	287175	24651	156499	106025	17727
江油市	Jiangyou	2573652	135379	1250746	1187527	32627
广元市	**Guangyuan**					
利州区	Lizhou	1539176	26850	869172	643154	27683
昭化区	Zhaohua	312798	51037	193922	67839	16899
朝天区	Chaotian	263656	23234	171458	68964	13891
旺苍县	Wangcang	657409	57482	433890	166037	15899
青川县	Qingchuan	224600	19513	148194	56893	10550
剑阁县	Jiange	695099	97079	371508	226512	14042
苍溪县	Cangxi	814231	117235	462605	234391	13320
遂宁市	**Suining**					
船山区	Chuanshan	2168974	93330	1374590	701054	31906
安居区	Anju	1023681	168155	514766	340760	15933
蓬溪县	Pengxi	997783	101485	580520	315778	18710
射洪县	Shehong	2377963	205918	1461526	710519	26955
大英县	Daying	1063491	87354	682804	293333	22096
内江市	**Neijiang**					
内江市中区	Neijiang Downtown	1560861	73564	782279	705018	29268
东兴区	Dongxing	1203015	214147	304547	684321	15300
威远县	Weiyuan	2139616	154714	1301623	683279	36363
资中县	Zizhong	1716192	234866	762537	718789	14507
隆昌市	Longchang	1740497	148885	861096	730516	27392
乐山市	**Leshan**					
乐山市中区	Leshan Downtown	1651057	117422	799279	734356	23960
沙湾区	Shawan	766647	63624	494586	208437	44624
五通桥区	Wutongqiao	1253936	70177	909354	274405	39896

12-5 续表 2 continued

县(市、区)	Counties (Municipalities, Districts)	民营经济增加值(万元) Added Value of Civilian-owned Economy (10 000 yuan)	第一产业 Primary Industry	第二产业 Secondary Industry	第三产业 Tertiary Industry	人均民营经济增加值(元) Per Capita Added Value of Civilian-owned Economy (yuan)
金口河区	Jinkouhe	226980	7608	184191	35181	49236
犍为县	Qianwei	1036458	156600	578931	300927	24273
井研县	Jinyan	637522	120075	313038	204409	21054
夹江县	Jiajiang	1039876	79159	660159	300558	31388
沐川县	Muchuan	288392	48770	163272	76350	13865
峨边县	Ebian	240931	24301	170740	45890	17794
马边县	Mabian	190246	33790	95020	61436	10077
峨眉山市	Emeishan	1422333	81218	775310	565805	31246
南充市	**Nanchong**					
顺庆区	Shunqing	2410246	121175	1432512	856559	33494
高坪区	Gaoping	1005117	152426	568431	284260	16415
嘉陵区	Jialing	949436	196760	593524	159152	15281
南部县	Nanbu	2226202	326855	1362219	537128	23675
营山县	Yingshan	1125261	219504	595655	310102	14952
蓬安县	Pengan	1041308	211252	588714	241342	18122
仪陇县	Yilong	1240953	324627	486399	429927	13257
西充县	Xichong	785906	177591	407799	200516	14643
阆中市	Langzhong	1539800	258672	641592	639536	20930
眉山市	**Meishan**					
东坡区	Dongpo	2263418	177930	1221510	863978	27042
彭山区	Pengshan	859915	87903	476896	295116	26822
仁寿县	Renshou	2288847	303670	1240829	744348	19112
洪雅县	Hongya	732210	108653	408959	214598	23696
丹棱县	Danling	341769	53551	173677	114541	23202
青神县	Qingshen	443679	87241	178918	177520	26394
宜宾市	**Yibin**					
翠屏区	Cuiping	3164396	63052	1511416	1589928	35756
南溪区	Nanxi	916280	62867	573203	280210	23789
叙州区	Xuzhou	1856529	179232	1113366	563931	26421
江安县	Jiangan	971628	99340	558921	313367	23228
长宁县	Changning	929263	103318	463104	362841	26834
高县	Gaoxian	947544	74274	621902	251368	22849
珙县	Gongxian	905181	80483	624257	200441	24151
筠连县	Junlian	947543	79714	645292	222537	28463
兴文县	Xingwen	732853	84587	352333	295933	18917
屏山县	Pingshan	326271	84000	122042	120229	12710
广安市	**Guangan**					
广安区	Guanganqu	1162704	90313	334486	737905	18494
前锋区	Qianfeng	995748	16598	753063	226087	38239
岳池县	Yuechi	1423106	99134	710726	613246	18196
武胜县	Wusheng	1318322	99730	683468	535124	22485

12-5 续表 3 continued

县(市、区)	Counties (Municipalities, Districts)	民营经济增加值(万元) Added Value of Civilian-owned Economy (10 000 yuan)	第一产业 Primary Industry	第二产业 Secondary Industry	第三产业 Tertiary Industry	人均民营经济增加值(元) Per Capita Added Value of Civilian-owned Economy (yuan)
邻水县	Linshui	1460140	97469	743296	619375	20667
华蓥市	Huaying	889456	26696	527768	334992	31575
达州市	**Dazhou**					
通川区	Tongchuan	1533634	60361	698526	774747	20633
达川区	Dachuan	1761349	135905	878847	746597	16943
宣汉县	Xuanhan	1670598	155560	848973	666065	16216
开江县	Kaijiang	808260	95851	363653	348756	17941
大竹县	Dazhu	2099128	168374	1155127	775627	23496
渠县	Quxian	1724081	176711	877450	669920	15256
万源市	Wanyuan	869226	85173	380910	403143	20810
雅安市	**Yaan**					
雨城区	Yucheng	941758	30889	383642	527227	25773
名山区	Mingshan	500861	34330	295366	171165	18647
荥经县	Yingjing	561198	14355	360720	186123	36970
汉源县	Hanyuan	470283	26047	263345	180891	14706
石棉县	Shimian	455908	13195	275267	167446	35842
天全县	Tianquan	445124	25361	259159	160604	31772
芦山县	Lushan	285925	18833	176295	90797	25946
宝兴县	Baoxing	218000	10917	139513	67570	38929
巴中市	**Bazhong**					
巴州区	Bazhou	1009625	76927	492033	440665	13669
恩阳区	Enyang	385621	67803	174736	143082	8139
通江县	Tongjiang	740863	76711	367420	296732	10558
南江县	Nanjiang	781793	67204	455928	258661	12799
平昌县	Pingchang	939964	101000	527375	311589	11828
资阳市	**Ziyang**					
雁江区	Yanjiang	2939927	233286	2156980	549661	32106
安岳县	Anyue	1693657	288580	943629	461448	15264
乐至县	Lezhi	1363152	215183	831862	316107	26871
阿坝州	**Aba**					
马尔康市	Maerkang	76433	14855	21283	40295	12739
汶川县	Wenchuan	281990	12794	220161	49035	27458
理县	Lixian	104738	5923	84060	14755	21419
茂县	Maoxian	123603	17767	78319	27517	11095
松潘县	Songpan	81297	19868	32617	28812	10825
九寨沟县	Jiuzhaigou	124719	10112	58864	55743	15265
金川县	Jinchuan	61875	15400	29599	16876	8250
小金县	Xiaojin	83602	14184	43941	25477	10450
黑水县	Heishui	122198	13268	94354	14576	20098
壤塘县	Rangtang	36665	19553	9991	7121	8730

12-5 续表 4 continued

县(市、区)	Counties (Municipalities, Districts)	民营经济增加值（万元）Added Value of Civilian-owned Economy (10 000 yuan)	第一产业 Primary Industry	第二产业 Secondary Industry	第三产业 Tertiary Industry	人均民营经济增加值（元）Per Capita Added Value of Civilian-owned Economy (yuan)
阿坝县	Abaxian	57678	27927	15388	14363	7491
若尔盖县	Ruoergai	103672	71356	15549	16767	13274
红原县	Hongyuan	70597	36361	17760	16476	14205
甘孜州	**Ganzi**					
康定市	Kangding	345578	34533	191885	119160	25617
泸定县	Luding	77038	15480	27782	33776	8725
丹巴县	Danba	67402	21806	25293	20303	9740
九龙县	Jiulong	105012	23905	66643	14464	16032
雅江县	Yajiang	59307	20319	24173	14815	10332
道孚县	Daofu	42499	21115	7820	13564	6990
炉霍县	Luhuo	27987	16119	5741	6127	5586
甘孜县	Ganzixian	58389	37334	8416	12639	7806
新龙县	Xinlong	52651	34811	7936	9904	10086
德格县	Dege	51912	37019	6697	8196	5872
白玉县	Baiyu	50415	32581	10876	6958	8265
石渠县	Shiqu	56428	42174	4212	10042	5576
色达县	Seda	48061	34007	5505	8549	7641
理塘县	Litang	71671	43434	16412	11825	9698
巴塘县	Batang	59117	20272	25883	12962	11501
乡城县	Xiangcheng	36301	13817	12705	9779	10168
稻城县	Daocheng	37216	15593	7292	14331	10454
得荣县	Derong	31199	10800	13879	6520	11063
凉山州	**Liangshan**					
西昌市	Xichang	2529083	158554	1174419	1196110	31709
木里县	Muli	144173	18649	81365	44159	10554
盐源县	Yanyuan	371912	62279	200373	109260	10167
德昌县	Dechang	482483	60598	234035	187850	21597
会理县	Huili	848083	139377	342463	366243	19505
会东县	Huidong	889424	118579	478308	292537	23247
宁南县	Ningnan	349696	65249	165380	119067	18463
普格县	Puge	84469	25258	16297	42914	4905
布拖县	Butuo	111612	25655	53547	32410	6017
金阳县	Jinyang	136615	25735	69906	40974	7636
昭觉县	Zhaojue	142998	53345	42731	46922	5320
喜德县	Xide	121651	27822	43903	49926	6565
冕宁县	Mianning	723354	82993	430921	209440	20060
越西县	Yuexi	192241	47779	60638	83824	6334
甘洛县	Ganluo	175388	27241	91253	56894	8023
美姑县	Meigu	132424	44007	48270	40147	5893
雷波县	Leibo	355567	38749	238674	78144	14584

12-6 各县(市、区)民营经济增加值指数(2018年)
Indices of Civillian-owned Economy Added Value by Counties (Municipalities, District)(2018)

上年=100 (preceding year=100)

县(市、区)	Counties (Municipalities, Districts)	民营经济增加值 Added Value of Civilian-owned Economy	第一产业 Primary Industry	第二产业 Secondary Industry	第三产业 Tertiary Industry	人均民营经济增加值 Per Capita Added Value of Civilian-owned Economy
成都市	**Chengdu**					
锦江区	Jinjiang	107.3		103.3	108.0	106.8
青羊区	Qingyang	107.3		105.0	107.9	106.9
金牛区	Jinniu	107.9		105.0	108.9	107.6
武侯区	Wuhou	107.8		105.5	108.7	107.7
成华区	Chenghua	108.5		101.8	110.0	108.0
龙泉驿区	Longquanyi	107.0	81.1	106.4	109.5	103.8
青白江区	Qingbaijiang	110.6	104.2	108.2	114.2	107.0
新都区	Xindu	109.0	98.5	108.2	110.7	107.6
温江区	Wenjiang	109.0	38.2	108.3	110.1	106.4
双流区	Shuangliu	109.6	93.0	109.0	110.6	105.6
郫都区	Pidu	107.9	20.8	107.2	110.0	106.8
金堂县	Jintang	110.6	108.1	110.9	110.2	110.7
大邑县	Dayi	110.3	114.2	112.7	104.2	110.1
蒲江县	Pujiang	110.4	90.3	111.3	116.1	108.9
新津县	Xinjin	110.5	100.1	111.8	108.1	108.1
都江堰市	Dujiangyan	107.9	102.5	106.6	109.4	107.0
彭州市	Pengzhou	107.0	91.9	108.1	108.6	106.9
邛崃市	Qionglai	110.9	99.4	113.2	109.5	110.8
崇州市	Chongzhou	110.7	104.7	111.5	110.4	110.7
简阳市	Jianyang	108.4	94.0	108.8	114.0	109.4
自贡市	**Zigong**					
自流井区	Ziliujing	106.3	104.0	98.7	111.2	96.1
贡井区	Gongjing	110.0	103.5	110.8	109.3	109.4
大安区	Daan	109.0	104.8	108.9	110.1	102.5
沿滩区	Yantan	110.9	102.0	110.4	115.8	99.9
荣县	Rongxian	108.3	103.3	109.1	108.8	113.5
富顺县	Fushun	109.5	103.8	110.2	110.1	111.7
攀枝花市	**Panzhihua**					
东区	Dongqu	107.6	104.3	106.6	108.8	107.5
西区	Xiqu	106.8	104.0	106.5	108.1	108.9
仁和区	Renhe	108.0	104.3	107.8	109.1	107.0
米易县	Miyi	107.8	104.1	107.8	108.6	107.7
盐边县	Yanbian	107.6	104.0	107.7	108.3	107.6
泸州市	**Luzhou**					
江阳区	Jiangyang	109.1	101.0	109.7	108.3	108.4
纳溪区	Naxi	107.1	101.7	107.7	106.8	106.5
龙马潭区	Longmatan	110.1	101.5	110.4	110.1	108.4
泸县	Luxian	105.9	101.8	105.7	107.7	105.7
合江县	Hejiang	105.1	102.8	104.8	105.9	105.4
叙永县	Xuyong	107.2	101.1	108.2	107.1	107.1
古蔺县	Gulin	108.0	101.8	108.6	108.4	108.7

12-6 续表 1 continued

上年=100 (preceding year=100)

县(市、区)	Counties (Municipalities, Districts)	民营经济增加值 Added Value of Civilian-owned Economy	第一产业 Primary Industry	第二产业 Secondary Industry	第三产业 Tertiary Industry	人均民营经济增加值 Per Capita Added Value of Civilian-owned Economy
德阳市	**Deyang**					
旌阳区	Jinyang	108.9	102.4	109.3	109.1	108.0
罗江区	Luojiang	109.9	102.2	110.3	111.4	108.4
中江县	Zhongjiang	109.3	103.8	110.7	110.4	109.4
广汉市	Guanghan	109.1	101.0	111.8	105.8	108.6
什邡市	Shifang	109.4	101.9	111.1	109.0	109.5
绵竹市	Mianzhu	108.7	101.2	108.6	110.5	108.4
绵阳市	**Mianyang**					
涪城区	Fucheng	109.6	103.4	109.3	110.1	107.3
游仙区	Youxian	108.9	103.5	109.6	108.6	108.4
安州区	Anzhou	109.3	102.8	109.3	111.3	108.5
三台县	Santai	108.7	103.6	109.5	109.9	108.4
盐亭县	Yanting	108.2	103.6	109.8	109.1	107.8
梓潼县	Zitong	108.3	103.6	109.4	108.2	107.9
北川县	Beichuan	109.2	103.4	109.1	112.3	108.2
平武县	Pingwu	106.6	103.4	107.9	105.4	110.5
江油市	Jiangyou	109.3	103.6	109.3	109.9	109.8
广元市	**Guangyuan**					
利州区	Lizhou	108.6	104.0	109.3	107.9	108.2
昭化区	Zhaohua	108.4	103.8	109.9	107.9	107.7
朝天区	Chaotian	108.9	103.8	109.2	110.0	109.6
旺苍县	Wangcang	108.7	103.6	109.7	107.7	107.7
青川县	Qingchuan	108.3	104.2	109.6	106.1	108.0
剑阁县	Jiange	108.6	104.0	109.5	109.2	107.3
苍溪县	Cangxi	108.5	104.1	108.5	111.0	108.0
遂宁市	**Suining**					
船山区	Chuanshan	108.8	102.4	108.4	111.0	108.1
安居区	Anju	109.1	101.6	110.4	111.7	109.3
蓬溪县	Pengxi	108.8	105.0	109.0	109.6	109.8
射洪县	Shehong	109.1	102.9	108.0	113.8	114.3
大英县	Daying	108.7	103.8	108.4	111.5	109.5
内江市	**Neijiang**					
内江市中区	Neijiang Downtown	108.8	103.8	108.7	109.6	108.6
东兴区	Dongxing	108.0	103.7	108.4	109.2	105.8
威远县	Weiyuan	108.8	104.0	108.9	109.8	109.0
资中县	Zizhong	104.6	103.7	104.8	104.6	107.0
隆昌市	Longchang	109.0	103.9	109.4	109.6	111.2
乐山市	**Leshan**					
乐山市中区	Leshan Downtown	108.4	103.9	108.3	109.3	107.7
沙湾区	Shawan	110.0	103.6	110.5	110.6	111.3
五通桥区	Wutongqiao	109.6	103.7	110.0	110.3	111.6

12-6 续表 2 continued

上年=100 (preceding year=100)

县(市、区)	Counties (Municipalities, Districts)	民营经济增加值 Added Value of Civilian-owned Economy	第一产业 Primary Industry	第二产业 Secondary Industry	第三产业 Tertiary Industry	人均民营经济增加值 Per Capita Added Value of Civilian-owned Economy
金口河区	Jinkouhe	106.6	103.6	106.4	109.0	107.6
犍为县	Qianwei	109.0	104.3	110.3	108.6	108.7
井研县	Jinyan	107.7	104.5	108.2	109.2	106.7
夹江县	Jiajiang	109.4	104.1	109.8	109.9	109.7
沐川县	Muchuan	104.2	103.9	104.4	103.9	105.8
峨边县	Ebian	107.5	103.4	108.0	107.6	107.0
马边县	Mabian	106.6	103.8	106.5	108.6	105.9
峨眉山市	Emeishan	108.7	103.7	108.1	110.6	108.1
南充市	**Nanchong**					
顺庆区	Shunqing	109.5	104.9	105.0	114.2	109.3
高坪区	Gaoping	109.4	104.8	109.6	111.7	108.9
嘉陵区	Jialing	109.6	105.0	110.0	112.3	109.2
南部县	Nanbu	109.2	104.6	108.9	113.4	109.1
营山县	Yingshan	109.3	105.0	109.9	112.3	109.0
蓬安县	Pengan	109.2	105.1	109.8	111.5	108.7
仪陇县	Yilong	109.0	104.9	106.2	117.9	108.8
西充县	Xichong	109.9	105.2	110.2	114.0	109.4
阆中市	Langzhong	109.1	105.1	107.0	114.0	108.7
眉山市	**Meishan**					
东坡区	Dongpo	108.1	103.9	108.1	109.2	108.4
彭山区	Pengshan	108.3	103.7	108.0	110.1	107.9
仁寿县	Renshou	107.1	103.7	106.7	109.2	107.9
洪雅县	Hongya	107.2	103.8	106.7	110.1	107.1
丹棱县	Danling	108.2	104.0	110.4	106.1	107.1
青神县	Qingshen	108.0	103.9	110.1	107.5	107.9
宜宾市	**Yibin**					
翠屏区	Cuiping	110.0	103.8	110.2	110.1	108.5
南溪区	Nanxi	109.7	102.5	110.0	111.3	109.3
叙州区	Xuzhou	109.7	102.4	108.9	114.1	108.9
江安县	Jiangan	108.7	101.4	110.6	106.8	108.5
长宁县	Changning	109.6	102.3	110.0	111.0	109.2
高县	Gaoxian	108.8	104.3	108.3	112.0	108.6
珙县	Gongxian	109.5	103.2	110.3	109.4	109.4
筠连县	Junlian	109.5	103.3	109.5	112.2	109.4
兴文县	Xingwen	109.0	102.7	110.1	109.1	108.8
屏山县	Pingshan	109.6	112.8	106.2	113.5	109.4
广安市	**Guangan**					
广安区	Guanganqu	108.0	101.8	105.6	110.2	107.8
前锋区	Qianfeng	108.4	101.8	108.0	110.6	108.8
岳池县	Yuechi	108.1	106.5	106.4	110.6	108.6
武胜县	Wusheng	108.2	101.9	107.9	110.2	108.7

12-6 续表 3 continued

上年=100 (preceding year=100)

县(市、区)	Counties (Municipalities, Districts)	民营经济增加值 Added Value of Civilian-owned Economy	第一产业 Primary Industry	第二产业 Secondary Industry	第三产业 Tertiary Industry	人均民营经济增加值 Per Capita Added Value of Civilian-owned Economy
邻水县	Linshui	108.2	103.0	107.6	110.1	109.0
华蓥市	Huaying	107.8	101.4	107.4	109.1	108.3
达州市	**Dazhou**					
通川区	Tongchuan	108.7	102.5	107.8	109.9	99.4
达川区	Dachuan	108.5	101.4	108.4	109.8	107.3
宣汉县	Xuanhan	108.6	101.8	108.4	110.5	109.1
开江县	Kaijiang	108.2	101.7	107.8	110.5	108.4
大竹县	Dazhu	108.8	101.8	108.7	110.4	108.7
渠县	Quxian	108.4	101.8	108.2	110.3	109.0
万源市	Wanyuan	107.8	102.5	107.4	109.2	107.9
雅安市	**Yaan**					
雨城区	Yucheng	108.0	95.1	107.6	109.2	108.2
名山区	Mingshan	108.5	95.7	109.6	109.4	108.2
荥经县	Yingjing	106.9	96.8	107.1	107.2	107.4
汉源县	Hanyuan	107.4	92.3	108.5	108.3	107.1
石棉县	Shimian	108.0	91.8	108.1	109.8	108.4
天全县	Tianquan	109.0	91.3	110.6	109.5	107.9
芦山县	Lushan	109.1	97.3	109.9	110.1	110.4
宝兴县	Baoxing	109.0	92.8	110.5	108.7	109.0
巴中市	**Bazhong**					
巴州区	Bazhou	108.2	103.3	108.7	108.5	108.0
恩阳区	Enyang	109.3	103.5	112.0	108.8	103.6
通江县	Tongjiang	108.2	103.8	108.8	108.5	109.2
南江县	Nanjiang	107.8	103.7	108.8	107.0	108.3
平昌县	Pingchang	108.0	103.6	109.1	107.5	109.3
资阳市	**Ziyang**					
雁江区	Yanjiang	108.2	103.5	108.7	108.0	107.5
安岳县	Anyue	107.2	103.8	108.0	107.8	108.7
乐至县	Lezhi	108.2	103.7	109.1	108.6	109.2
阿坝州	**Aba**					
马尔康市	Maerkang	107.3	101.5	115.2	106.0	107.1
汶川县	Wenchuan	105.0	100.8	105.7	102.7	103.6
理县	Lixian	107.1	107.3	106.7	109.8	106.4
茂县	Maoxian	100.4	101.5	97.8	108.6	100.0
松潘县	Songpan	104.0	103.8	107.2	100.6	104.1
九寨沟县	Jiuzhaigou	101.3	105.4	106.5	95.5	100.8
金川县	Jinchuan	103.2	99.2	104.3	105.3	102.9
小金县	Xiaojin	107.0	103.1	111.9	100.4	107.0
黑水县	Heishui	100.1	102.7	99.2	104.7	99.8
壤塘县	Rangtang	109.9	103.5	128.0	106.9	109.6

12-6 续表 4 continued

上年=100 (preceding year=100)

县(市、区)	Counties (Municipalities, Districts)	民营经济增加值 Added Value of Civilian-owned Economy	第一产业 Primary Industry	第二产业 Secondary Industry	第三产业 Tertiary Industry	人均民营经济增加值 Per Capita Added Value of Civilian-owned Economy
阿坝县	Abaxian	103.7	102.3	106.9	103.5	103.4
若尔盖县	Ruoergai	105.5	104.5	109.6	106.3	105.1
红原县	Hongyuan	101.2	106.9	90.7	103.1	99.4
甘孜州	**Ganzi**					
康定市	Kangding	113.1	102.7	123.9	102.4	113.7
泸定县	Luding	109.4	104.7	119.7	102.6	109.9
丹巴县	Danba	112.6	104.5	128.2	105.2	113.7
九龙县	Jiulong	110.4	103.6	114.0	104.9	111.4
雅江县	Yajiang	107.7	102.1	112.1	108.6	105.1
道孚县	Daofu	109.3	107.0	132.8	101.9	108.4
炉霍县	Luhuo	109.9	105.6	126.8	105.8	107.7
甘孜县	Ganzixian	107.7	104.4	136.1	104.8	105.1
新龙县	Xinlong	109.2	105.3	137.9	106.3	107.6
德格县	Dege	107.8	105.9	124.8	103.8	105.6
白玉县	Baiyu	113.5	108.4	144.2	106.6	113.3
石渠县	Shiqu	108.8	106.6	136.5	108.9	108.8
色达县	Seda	110.2	105.7	147.4	107.2	108.0
理塘县	Litang	111.0	105.0	136.8	104.3	110.2
巴塘县	Batang	112.6	105.8	123.2	104.6	115.4
乡城县	Xiangcheng	115.5	106.8	133.7	105.2	114.5
稻城县	Daocheng	112.5	107.9	136.1	107.5	106.8
得荣县	Derong	116.3	109.9	129.2	105.4	116.2
凉山州	**Liangshan**					
西昌市	Xichang	110.2	103.7	111.1	110.2	107.3
木里县	Muli	109.4	103.8	111.4	108.0	109.8
盐源县	Yanyuan	107.8	103.8	108.3	109.5	109.1
德昌县	Dechang	105.9	103.7	105.9	106.5	104.9
会理县	Huili	87.2	103.7	72.1	105.2	88.8
会东县	Huidong	107.0	103.7	107.5	107.4	105.6
宁南县	Ningnan	108.8	103.7	113.1	107.0	110.0
普格县	Puge	104.3	103.4	103.6	105.4	106.0
布拖县	Butuo	94.9	103.8	84.6	110.0	93.0
金阳县	Jinyang	107.3	103.8	108.0	108.1	104.1
昭觉县	Zhaojue	103.4	103.8	98.5	108.0	99.9
喜德县	Xide	105.5	103.8	110.2	102.2	98.7
冕宁县	Mianning	111.9	103.7	115.6	108.1	111.3
越西县	Yuexi	102.8	103.8	92.7	109.8	99.4
甘洛县	Ganluo	112.2	103.8	116.3	110.8	114.5
美姑县	Meigu	106.0	103.8	108.6	105.5	110.0
雷波县	Leibo	108.9	103.8	109.2	110.5	107.3

12-7 各县(市、区)固定资产投资和建筑业情况(2018年)
Investment in Fixed Assets and Construction by Counties (Municipalities, Districts)(2018)

县(市、区)	Counties (Municipalities, Districts)	全社会固定资产投资比上年增长 (%) Growth Rate of Total Investment Over Preceding Year(%)	房地产开发投资额 (万元) Real Estate Investment (10 000 yuan)	建筑企业单位数 (个) Number of Construction Enterprises (unit)	建筑业总产值 (万元) Gross Output Value of Construction Enterprises (10 000 yuan)
成都市	**Chengdu**				
锦江区	Jinjiang	4.1	1998173	95	6031473
青羊区	Qingyang	4.1	641821	215	9122167
金牛区	Jinniu	9.7	1630785	291	12413289
武侯区	Wuhou	3.0	1479613	338	5308180
成华区	Chenghua	5.0	2243973	113	2196249
龙泉驿区	Longquanyi	0.0	1345379	60	2006502
青白江区	Qingbaijiang	13.2	820674	27	1064817
新都区	Xindu	8.2	1422784	47	2150902
温江区	Wenjiang	6.3	1281163	30	702170
双流区	Shuangliu	-24.4	3965554	95	3722573
郫都区	Pidu	7.7	1424453	31	1893450
金堂县	Jintang	13.3	447552	41	1046198
大邑县	Dayi	9.0	191830	36	839147
蒲江县	Pujiang	11.6	91582	20	252282
新津县	Xinjin	11.4	416252	43	401997
都江堰市	Dujiangyan	13.5	509125	39	1598900
彭州市	Pengzhou	10.4	223348	21	161061
邛崃市	Qionglai	9.2	140209	37	887494
崇州市	Chongzhou	14.3	269841	48	1050781
简阳市	Jianyang	22.6	393396	48	832281
自贡市	**Zigong**				
自流井区	Ziliujing	4.9	676304	30	1753108
贡井区	Gongjing	24.5	195630	7	50798
大安区	Daan	18.4	101302	16	306551
沿滩区	Yantan	13.8	322355	15	475247
荣县	Rongxian	15.4	153192	21	482503
富顺县	Fushun	23.8	644309	39	1045010
攀枝花市	**Panzhihua**				
东区	East District	10.4	339420	55	2171483
西区	West District	10.0	98805	8	90050
仁和区	Renhe	4.1	313100	12	157441
米易县	Miyi	6.5	185518	3	109311
盐边县	Yanbian	10.6	67256	5	26927
泸州市	**Luzhou**				
江阳区	Jiangyang	17.9	1260995	72	2998892
纳溪区	Nanxi	12.5	166425	16	605086
龙马潭区	Longmatan	20.1	932867	53	2468443
泸县	Luxian	-22.8	186457	71	4266249
合江县	Hejiang	-14.7	317691	65	1781903
叙永县	Xuyong	9.2	136191	18	3483460

12-7 续表 1 continued

县(市、区)	Counties (Municipalities, Districts)	全社会固定资产投资比上年增长(%) Growth Rate of Total Investment Over Preceding Year(%)	房地产开发投资额(万元) Real Estate Investment (10 000 yuan)	建筑企业单位数(个) Number of Construction Enterprises (unit)	建筑业总产值(万元) Gross Output Value of Construction Enterprises (10 000 yuan)
古蔺县	Gulin	11.5	183246	13	140081
德阳市	**Deyang**				
旌阳区	Jinyang	10.1	757397	111	2020335
罗江区	Luojiang	16.6	34129	10	120004
中江县	Zhongjiang	20.0	152807	26	261460
广汉市	Guanghan	3.8	237954	48	1222406
什邡市	Shifang	20.1	141968	23	324809
绵竹市	Mianzhu	12.8	173859	25	265098
绵阳市	**Mianyang**				
涪城区	Hucheng	22.2	1079337	236	2953287
游仙区	Youxian	11.4	213120	46	1380582
安州区	Anzhou	13.5	97651	24	319535
三台县	Santai	15.0	211054	24	1176864
盐亭县	Yanting	9.1	145404	14	276584
梓潼县	Zitong	2.8	2635	16	267322
北川县	Beichuan	8.9	27351	12	105000
平武县	Pingwu	17.9	8853	3	71091
江油市	Jiangyou	14.6	260001	48	935307
广元市	**Guangyuan**				
利州区	Lizhou	11.2	625669	133	1252641
昭化区	Zhaohua	19.8	11873	8	103568
朝天区	Chaotian	19.7	11691	7	125537
旺苍县	Wangcang	19.1	29077	11	216938
青川县	Qingchuan	19.4	12077	2	15949
剑阁县	Jiange	19.4	51212	12	136898
苍溪县	Cangxi	19.6	107334	24	335823
遂宁市	**Suining**				
船山区	Chuanshan	11.7	782926	116	1669277
安居区	Anju	11.9	108141	9	259617
蓬溪县	Pengxi	12.1	266923	15	821557
射洪县	Shehong	10.0	427497	18	780882
大英县	Daying	9.6	136857	19	837156
内江市	**Neijiang**				
内江市中区	Neijiang Downtown	14.3	234520	32	521517
东兴区	Dongxing	-5.9	588815	26	758966
威远县	Weiyuan	20.5	207985	18	567484
资中县	Zizhong	-44.2	189839	18	331625
隆昌市	Longchang	19.0	334463	18	763319
乐山市	**Leshan**				
乐山市中区	Leshan Downtown	8.7	897515	116	1510199
沙湾区	Shawan	8.5	5317	4	83134

12-7 续表 2 continued

县(市、区)	Counties (Municipalities, Districts)	全社会固定资产投资比上年增长(%) Growth Rate of Total Investment Over Preceding Year(%)	房地产开发投资额(万元) Real Estate Investment (10 000 yuan)	建筑企业单位数(个) Number of Construction Enterprises (unit)	建筑业总产值(万元) Gross Output Value of Construction Enterprises (10 000 yuan)
五通桥区	Wutongqiao	18.1	32762	10	229006
金口河区	Jinkouhe	17.8		1	2360
犍为县	Qianwei	18.0	174398	14	297661
井研县	Jingyan	18.3	40852	12	140827
夹江县	Jiajiang	15.6	258323	8	126088
沐川县	Muchuan	15.0	41983	6	41945
峨边县	Ebian	17.9		6	22705
马边县	Mabian	17.6	23355	3	15378
峨眉山市	Emeishan	14.9	474591	21	343979
南充市	**Nanchong**				
顺庆区	Shunqing	16.1	401882	99	1637209
高坪区	Gaoping	15.3	322795	29	521861
嘉陵区	Jialing	14.7	453238	29	488821
南部县	Nanbu	15.2	252209	38	2379589
营山县	Yingshan	17.0	563809	15	706123
蓬安县	Pengan	15.1	276337	18	611585
仪陇县	Yilong	15.2	376809	33	2113065
西充县	Xichong	16.1	69343	9	671620
阆中市	Langzhong	15.0	383881	36	1390408
眉山市	**Meishan**				
东坡区	Dongpo	10.7	622954	41	1596042
彭山区	Pengshan	12.8	374774	17	555182
仁寿县	Renshou	16.0	1186592	32	1349423
洪雅县	Hongya	12.0	260407	13	154268
丹棱县	Danling	12.0	85392	6	174824
青神县	Qingshen	9.2	41032	7	245500
宜宾市	**Yibin**				
翠屏区	Cuiping	19.3	1304046	180	1551888
南溪区	Nanxi	12.0	150049	32	419591
叙州区	Xuzhou	11.2	409693	63	1016157
江安县	Jiangan	11.2	244195	28	505025
长宁县	Changning	12.2	291710	19	402819
高县	Gaoxian	12.1	278955	29	369535
珙县	Gongxian	10.1	102747	25	223326
筠连县	Junlian	12.5	142451	18	169905
兴文县	Xingwen	10.0	131714	21	99309
屏山县	Pingshan	13.7	64833	29	71127
广安市	**Guangan**				
广安区	Guanganqu	5.0	1255627	78	1236912
前锋区	Qianfeng	10.8	205266	4	72981
岳池县	Yuechi	10.7	167404	34	1203134

12-7 续表 3 continued

县(市、区)	Counties (Municipalities, Districts)	全社会固定资产投资比上年增长(%) Growth Rate of Total Investment Over Preceding Year(%)	房地产开发投资额(万元) Real Estate Investment (10 000 yuan)	建筑企业单位数(个) Number of Construction Enterprises (unit)	建筑业总产值(万元) Gross Output Value of Construction Enterprises (10 000 yuan)
武胜县	Wusheng	7.1	391647	23	919382
邻水县	Linshui	0.3	247403	18	571796
华蓥市	Huaying	-17.4	113617	24	1459830
达州市	**Dazhou**				
通川区	Tongchuan	13.6	599215	50	1126703
达川区	Dachuan	12.4	146094	25	961636
宣汉县	Xuanhan	12.3	219706	13	918058
开江县	Kaijiang	11.8	20671	13	515699
大竹县	Dazhu	12.2	320636	18	717731
渠县	Quxian	12.6	242342	19	895153
万源市	Wanyuan	10.0	18339	5	20581
雅安市	**Yaan**				
雨城区	Yucheng	33.0	518919	30	229018
名山区	Mingshan	30.1	153327	4	50858
荥经县	Yingjing	6.6	26405	3	135882
汉源县	Hanyuan	9.7	72775	5	51203
石棉县	Shimian	-21.6	5840	5	19336
天全县	Tianquan	8.2	75497	2	33163
芦山县	Lushan	15.2		6	49746
宝兴县	Baoxing	-13.4		1	3515
巴中市	**Bazhong**				
巴州区	Bazhou	5.1	812333	84	36284941
恩阳区	Enyang	14.1	288959	23	641774
通江县	Tongjiang	10.2	79729	49	1237977
南江县	Nanjiang	10.3	145974	24	1389753
平昌县	Pingchang	10.3	242938	31	118888
资阳市	**Ziyang**				
雁江区	Yanjiang	11.2	752062	30	1217765
安岳县	Anyue	-3.6	387899	19	571764
乐至县	Lezhi	19.5	184112	11	486341
阿坝州	**Aba**				
马尔康市	Maerkang	43.4	4653	11	14948
汶川县	Wenchuan	2.3		29	157157
理县	Lixian	13.6		17	29239
茂县	Maoxian	37.7		15	48476
松潘县	Songpan	21.7	26305	9	9167
九寨沟县	Jiuzhaigou	50.5		17	42689
金川县	Jinchuan	9.2		5	11210
小金县	Xiaojin	17.5		6	16494
黑水县	Heishui	53.7		7	21961
壤塘县	Rangtang	6.4		3	11893

12-7 续表 4 continued

县(市、区)	Counties (Municipalities, Districts)	全社会固定资产投资比上年增长(%) Growth Rate of Total Investment Over Preceding Year(%)	房地产开发投资额(万元) Real Estate Investment (10 000 yuan)	建筑企业单位数(个) Number of Construction Enterprises (unit)	建筑业总产值(万元) Gross Output Value of Construction Enterprises (10 000 yuan)
阿坝县	Abaxian	5.7		1	2550
若尔盖县	Ruoergai	3.5		7	12298
红原县	Hongyuan	2.1			
甘孜州	**Ganzi**				
康定市	Kangding	4.4	50451	29	127942
泸定县	Luding	-21.4		6	18859
丹巴县	Danba	42.8		1	5400
九龙县	Jiulong	54.4		3	4097
雅江县	Yajiang	11.5		1	2169
道孚县	Daofu	-2.0	13880	1	587
炉霍县	Luhuo	37.1		2	3956
甘孜县	Ganzixian	24.4			
新龙县	Xinlong	74.8		1	89
德格县	Dege	24.2			
白玉县	Baiyu	54.6		2	2004
石渠县	Shiqu	121.9		3	3675
色达县	Seda	-1.1		2	1982
理塘县	Litang	-22.9		1	3120
巴塘县	Batang	13.5		1	43400
乡城县	Xiangcheng	48.0		1	800
稻城县	Daocheng	12.8			
得荣县	Derong	22.4			
凉山州	**Liangshan**				
西昌市	Xichang	-5.1	1639882	108	1831541
木里县	Muli	-47.7		4	8336
盐源县	Yanyuan	-16.7	12416	15	35329
德昌县	Dechang	32.2	8013	12	18394
会理县	Huili	-37.9	47157	13	98651
会东县	Huidong	9.4	57645	20	95106
宁南县	Ningnan	92.2	3692	7	28914
普格县	Puge	-29.3		8	11266
布拖县	Buto	7.9		5	23219
金阳县	Jinyang	10.2		13	22743
昭觉县	Zhaojue	86.3		5	1971
喜德县	Xide	34.0		21	82508
冕宁县	Mianning	-33.7	48964	14	131816
越西县	Yuexi	34.3		7	16149
甘洛县	Ganluo	93.7		4	7423
美姑县	Meigu	7.3		14	30500
雷波县	Leibo	21.1		11	40562

12-8 各县(市、区)农村经济情况(2018年)

Basic Statistics on Agriculture of Counties(Municipalities,Districts)(2018)

县(市、区)	Counties (Municipalities, Districts)	年末实有耕地面积(公顷) Cultivated Land Area (year-end) (hectare)	耕地灌溉面积(公顷) Irrigated Area of Cultivated Land (hectare)	农林牧渔业增加值(万元) Gross Output Value of Farming, Forestry, Animal Husbandry and Fishery (10 000 yuan)	化肥施用量(折纯量)(吨) Consumption of Chemical Fertilizers (ton)	农村用电量(万千瓦小时) Electricity Consumed in Rural Areas (10 000 kwh)
成都市	**Chengdu**					
锦江区	Jinjiang	855	840	6711	33	7456
青羊区	Qingyang	469	430	409	17	2169
金牛区	Jinniu	752	350	824	20	6358
武侯区	Wuhou	251	80	85		1862
成华区	Chenghua	1291	1280	670	49	2635
龙泉驿区	Longquanyi	7886	7910	321547	3334	13934
青白江区	Qingbaijiang	18884	11800	166804	5441	14973
新都区	Xindu	25632	20550	309687	10492	40414
温江区	Wenjiang	13165	13410	193265	2885	5543
双流区	Shuangliu	39806	33360	369244	6369	61706
郫都区	Pidu	20485	18700	254357	15226	26634
金堂县	Jintang	56500	37250	529067	23191	10946
大邑县	Dayi	29638	19440	381668	6924	15634
蒲江县	Pujiang	23909	12320	202740	5606	7598
新津县	Xinjin	15226	13520	187194	6175	10258
都江堰市	Dujiangyan	26712	20070	305069	10764	25359
彭州市	Pengzhou	50703	38840	545535	19108	31651
邛崃市	Qionglai	44310	30620	412498	17158	14016
崇州市	Chongzhou	39124	29950	389937	16496	31832
简阳市	Jianyang	107554	58190	839330	31838	40532
自贡市	**Zigong**					
自流井区	Ziliujing	6351	2690	51138	3002	2162
贡井区	Gongjing	22366	9510	166756	11444	6128
大安区	Daan	22838	6810	148176	9889	11399
沿滩区	Yantan	26285	10320	177641	16837	8166
荣县	Rongxian	66400	39000	509559	22104	12695
富顺县	Fushun	72067	31850	482152	26867	14246
攀枝花市	**Panzhihua**					
东区	East District	486	330	7509	210	2722
西区	West District	1060	600	10355	225	494
仁和区	Renhe	19099	10810	119128	8802	5158
米易县	Miyi	26515	14090	151199	7726	8292
盐边县	Yanbian	27868	14150	114299	11055	6894
泸州市	**Luzhou**					
江阳区	Jiangyang	30064	11160	231432	13850	9803
纳溪区	Naxi	41454	15790	225864	9565	8097
龙马潭区	Longmatan	15344	8440	113020	6363	5610
泸县	Luxian	84660	40540	509534	33939	25265
合江县	Hejiang	71728	29950	383853	12720	20747
叙永县	Xuyong	78505	24020	245012	16919	11540
古蔺县	Gulin	89010	24920	231516	13803	7926

注：年末实有耕地面积由四川省自然资源厅提供，耕地灌溉面积由四川省水利厅提供，因两部门统计口径不同，部分县耕地灌溉面积大于年末实有耕地面积。

a) The year-end cultivated land area is provided by Bureau of Land and Resources of Sichuan Province and the irrigated land area is provided by Sichuan Provincial Water Resources Department. Due to the two sector statistics caliber is different, the irrigated land area of some counties is greater than the year-end cultivated land area.

12-8 续表 1 continued

县(市、区)	Counties (Municipalities, Districts)	年末实有耕地面积(公顷) Cultivated Land Area (year-end) (hectare)	耕地灌溉面积(公顷) Irrigated Area of Cultivated Land (hectare)	农林牧渔业增加值(万元) Gross Output Value of Farming, Forestry, Animal Husbandry and Fishery (10 000 yuan)	化肥施用量(折纯量)(吨) Consumption of Chemical Fertilizers (ton)	农村用电量(万千瓦小时) Electricity Consumed in Rural Areas (10 000 kwh)
德阳市	**Deyang**					
旌阳区	Jinyang	31858	21020	364696	16265	54301
罗江区	Luojiang	24767	13340	225564	19748	13958
中江县	Zhongjiang	101601	55340	895166	69763	61118
广汉市	Guanghan	32052	25170	389300	25673	57869
什邡市	Shifang	23483	18900	320264	24715	23108
绵竹市	Mianzhu	34372	23430	330091	23155	33401
绵阳市	**Mianyang**					
涪城区	Fucheng	16780	10540	249131	15427	20858
游仙区	Youxian	39432	24630	313107	24148	10883
安州区	Anzhou	37641	24490	314502	16410	9192
三台县	Santai	117901	72930	831046	48770	23661
盐亭县	Yanting	61132	23420	394013	39628	13249
梓潼县	Zitong	51503	22790	301862	17502	10397
北川县	Beichuan	17180	2290	114113	7958	3475
平武县	Pingwu	31837	2770	89919	6621	6448
江油市	Jiangyou	70695	37290	485041	29928	22021
广元市	**Guangyuan**					
利州区	Lizhou	21562	5330	118065	10012	4911
昭化区	Zhaohua	40258	9390	131554	14754	4247
朝天区	Chaotian	32652	3796	89981	7113	3475
旺苍县	Wangcang	46340	9090	181361	11858	3981
青川县	Qingchuan	33525	5180	83450	4274	4245
剑阁县	Jiange	91687	34700	288571	30719	19779
苍溪县	Cangxi	87458	24470	330192	24368	14885
遂宁市	**Suining**					
船山区	Chuanshan	27709	12670	239239	10530	4050
安居区	Anju	76175	38280	412862	37433	5015
蓬溪县	Pengxi	59544	24070	295941	37227	8370
射洪县	Shehong	70599	33280	482649	27140	15203
大英县	Daying	36155	22220	273150	20783	5289
内江市	**Neijiang**					
内江市市中区	Neijiang Downtown	22064	11690	184219	8121	14436
东兴区	Dongxing	65757	21150	524019	35736	10574
威远县	Weiyuan	55382	32620	494959	19230	29723
资中县	Zizhong	84494	40430	679830	43440	30001
隆昌市	Longchang	46089	28800	350378	11436	19440
乐山市	**Leshan**					
乐山市市中区	Leshan Downtown	25439	15490	215116	8205	15383
沙湾区	Shawan	13264	5190	95036	4286	6525
五通桥区	Wutongqiao	15764	9990	136866	4793	8692

12-8 续表 2 continued

县(市、区)	Counties (Municipalities, Districts)	年末实有耕地面积(公顷) Cultivated Land Area (year-end) (hectare)	耕地灌溉面积(公顷) Irrigated Area of Cultivated Land (hectare)	农林牧渔业增加值(万元) Gross Output Value of Farming, Forestry, Animal Husbandry and Fishery (10 000 yuan)	化肥施用量(折纯量)(吨) Consumption of Chemical Fertilizers (ton)	农村用电量(万千瓦小时) Electricity Consumed in Rural Areas (10 000 kwh)
金口河区	Jinkouhe	3632	750	22761	444	968
犍为县	Qianwei	54500	23080	290583	11621	12507
井研县	Jinyan	43108	32650	232865	14410	13550
夹江县	Jiajiang	21200	18800	215569	15503	15801
沐川县	Muchuan	26532	9040	146675	6639	7043
峨边县	Ebian	17597	1950	50774	2195	4000
马边县	Mabian	27246	5340	91836	7792	3893
峨眉山市	Emeishan	23328	18860	185360	6182	24961
南充市	**Nanchong**					
顺庆区	Shunqing	23988	11250	234223	13023	4952
高坪区	Gaoping	35396	14040	294265	14625	3703
嘉陵区	Jialing	58787	26810	381988	26886	8272
南部县	Nanbu	94779	43590	648262	21460	23954
营山县	Yingshan	70910	18660	424160	34044	10352
蓬安县	Pengan	54288	21570	413144	32000	6180
仪陇县	Yilong	69577	39260	631057	27740	5946
西充县	Xichong	49719	27870	343961	14673	10598
阆中市	Langzhong	76707	24760	503032	32843	12700
眉山市	**Meishan**					
东坡区	Dongpo	55865	46980	521275	37695	33534
彭山区	Pengshan	19800	18990	153645	10896	4080
仁寿县	Renshou	116478	73410	826576	57586	26918
洪雅县	Hongya	25048	15080	180495	8007	7916
丹棱县	Danling	10999	9520	118585	4792	5986
青神县	Qingshen	12855	7480	100036	4933	5470
宜宾市	**Yibin**					
翠屏区	Cuiping	46244	17330	261988	10293	19536
南溪区	Nanxi	32739	12670	245669	7530	7792
叙州区	Xuzhou	124666	35360	464398	19106	37998
江安县	Jiangan	38784	17530	252511	5481	7657
长宁县	Changning	34648	20280	268153	4952	14660
高县	Gaoxian	56490	25640	230332	11365	12581
珙县	Gongxian	34608	13803	197315	6900	7904
筠连县	Junlian	36895	13310	214053	4212	12292
兴文县	Xingwen	44423	16850	211858	5270	9159
屏山县	Pingshan	38112	15950	174326	6078	6123
广安市	**Guangan**					
广安区	Guanganqu	54625	24170	257818	21690	10175
前锋区	Qianfeng	21527	7300	154416	11095	7631
岳池县	Yuechi	84086	27520	430758	18771	15671
武胜县	Wusheng	58353	26280	399163	16084	10834

12-8 续表 3 continued

县(市、区)	Counties (Municipalities, Districts)	年末实有耕地面积(公顷) Cultivated Land Area (year-end) (hectare)	耕地灌溉面积(公顷) Irrigated Area of Cultivated Land (hectare)	农林牧渔业增加值(万元) Gross Output Value of Farming, Forestry, Animal Husbandry and Fishery (10 000 yuan)	化肥施用量(折纯量)(吨) Consumption of Chemical Fertilizers (ton)	农村用电量(万千瓦小时) Electricity Consumed in Rural Areas (10 000 kwh)
邻水县	Linshui	74726	15362	409167	27860	6956
华蓥市	Huaying	14361	5620	125375	8883	5016
达州市	**Dazhou**					
通川区	Tongchuan	31319	7910	229272	12806	9096
达川区	Dachuan	104029	25070	542992	28705	26671
宣汉县	Xuanhan	117318	46360	631776	41682	11498
开江县	Kaijiang	41043	19160	342987	17635	13523
大竹县	Dazhu	96029	30850	608990	48971	9386
渠县	Quxian	103825	35770	667703	42351	10827
万源市	Wanyuan	57458	16340	315722	24122	7616
雅安市	**Yaan**					
雨城区	Yucheng	14590	6640	171656	3920	18271
名山区	Mingshan	17126	12450	214152	11929	3976
荥经县	Yingjing	9427	4500	78111	4269	4403
汉源县	Hanyuan	28546	14100	165237	13792	6155
石棉县	Shimian	6333	3740	64437	2320	4115
天全县	Tianquan	12663	7520	79852	5320	5520
芦山县	Lushan	8373	4220	60656	5594	3203
宝兴县	Baoxing	4205	550	39209	2523	4956
巴中市	**Bazhong**					
巴州区	Bazhou	52943	14380	174012	30475	14610
恩阳区	Enyang	50143	15510	166298	16753	14912
通江县	Tongjiang	79525	18640	224936	23896	7056
南江县	Nanjiang	65676	13710	197548	27758	6958
平昌县	Pingchang	79299	30310	247058	29878	36237
资阳市	**Ziyang**					
雁江区	Yanjiang	86643	49503	548636	20870	13000
安岳县	Anyue	155329	46020	872935	14821	31350
乐至县	Lezhi	78749	26180	364093	15500	11786
阿坝州	**Aba**					
马尔康市	Maerkang	6372	740	26300	146	1846
汶川县	Wenchuan	6189	1520	43539	2112	4643
理县	Lixian	3188	2250	22271	669	1172
茂县	Maoxian	8662	4460	61984	2677	4188
松潘县	Songpan	13352	690	45135	989	1828
九寨沟县	Jiuzhaigou	6786	1150	25249	1150	1865
金川县	Jinchuan	6282	4070	32535	1639	1713
小金县	Xiaojin	8488	4540	34900	856	2098
黑水县	Heishui	7555	1370	30752	479	3165
壤塘县	Rangtang	3462	490	29215	136	560

12-8 续表 4 continued

县(市、区)	Counties (Municipalities, Districts)	年末实有耕地面积(公顷) Cultivated Land Area (year-end) (hectare)	耕地灌溉面积(公顷) Irrigated Area of Cultivated Land (hectare)	农林牧渔业增加值(万元) Gross Output Value of Farming, Forestry, Animal Husbandry and Fishery (10 000 yuan)	化肥施用量(折纯量)(吨) Consumption of Chemical Fertilizers (ton)	农村用电量(万千瓦小时) Electricity Consumed in Rural Areas (10 000 kwh)
阿坝县	Abaxian	8634	2530	37284	60	260
若尔盖县	Ruoergai	4170	1210	83904	35	1064
红原县	Hongyuan	129	130	45211	105	850
甘孜州	**Ganzi**					
康定市	Kangding	7557	1440	55814	138	1145
泸定县	Luding	5293	4470	38125	812	2394
丹巴县	Danba	7593	3670	39143	331	1664
九龙县	Jiulong	4419	2300	36402	413	1148
雅江县	Yajiang	4158	980	29580	39	66
道孚县	Daofu	7611	3810	27528	195	1860
炉霍县	Luhuo	6541	900	27994	54	447
甘孜县	Ganzixian	11859	3110	50425	32	74
新龙县	Xinlong	6346	10	39316	50	418
德格县	Dege	4678	910	40252	100	225
白玉县	Baiyu	7294	610	38081	33	
石渠县	Shiqu	3935	2410	49751	54	79
色达县	Seda	1100	900	39670	33	29
理塘县	Litang	4846	890	44897	43	489
巴塘县	Batang	6580	4090	34441	225	268
乡城县	Xiangcheng	3465	2380	25222	198	1116
稻城县	Daocheng	4861	2500	22878	86	240
得荣县	Derong	4200	1360	21594	248	1011
凉山州	**Liangshan**					
西昌市	Xichang	48079	44610	474240	16116	10395
木里县	Muli	16517	4150	65793	1170	480
盐源县	Yanyuan	59648	18210	242149	7950	10931
德昌县	Dechang	18814	12460	192087	8303	10746
会理县	Huili	70541	24320	449785	21840	6910
会东县	Huidong	55432	14420	435910	22358	7449
宁南县	Ningnan	24230	13850	186013	7266	14668
普格县	Puge	27517	5210	89804	4031	1756
布拖县	Butuo	22967	2120	80488	1850	680
金阳县	Jinyang	18020	2390	76429	2408	1506
昭觉县	Zhaojue	42592	4110	112703	3810	3220
喜德县	Xide	31151	3200	75441	3500	2324
冕宁县	Mianning	32693	18880	231584	9400	6550
越西县	Yuexi	32061	7330	127659	8195	4373
甘洛县	Ganluo	23153	5090	69289	10810	2298
美姑县	Meigu	31147	1950	99708	5209	2521
雷波县	Leibo	24988	4130	124013	2648	10034

12-8 续表 5 continued

县(市、区)	Counties (Municipalities, Districts)	粮食		油料			中草药材	蔬菜及食用菌
		播种面积 (公顷) Total Sown Area (hectares)	产量 (吨) Output of Grain (ton)	产量 (吨) Yield of Oil Bearing Crops (ton)	#花生 Peanut	#油菜籽 Rapeseeds	产量 (吨) Yield of Oil Medicinal Herbs (ton)	产量 (吨) Output of Vegetables and Edible Fungus (ton)
成都市	**Chengdu**							
锦江区	Jinjiang							481
青羊区	Qingyang	7	51	35		35		1316
金牛区	Jinniu	8	64	51		51		3697
武侯区	Wuhou							397
成华区	Chenghua	21	163					1507
龙泉驿区	Longquanyi	3087	15167	3394	432	2962		144031
青白江区	Qingbaijiang	11239	66982	14810	2466	12284	2622	200929
新都区	Xindu	19989	142804	18792	468	18079	752	288747
温江区	Wenjiang	1009	7627	474		467		53014
双流区	Shuangliu	17951	120790	28070	4534	23536	624	385748
郫都区	Pidu	5621	43300	9588		9451	22	779647
金堂县	Jintang	48934	262408	63855	19891	43958	7633	887799
大邑县	Dayi	24905	156876	9406	116	9290	2308	214181
蒲江县	Pujiang	8794	48550	14374	147	14227	76	202466
新津县	Xinjin	8916	62660	10432	624	9808	372	192360
都江堰市	Dujiangyan	14002	103162	25633		25605	15510	224499
彭州市	Pengzhou	37063	255842	19076	1342	17734	15209	1074584
邛崃市	Qionglai	37522	236604	26918	535	26383	6862	283454
崇州市	Chongzhou	31268	217849	26833	14	26689	6990	308113
简阳市	Jianyang	112715	561903	101201	11865	88896	1412	511571
自贡市	**Zigong**							
自流井区	Ziliujing	5694	29906	5967	636	5331	17	85223
贡井区	Gongjing	22673	115714	24067	5420	18647		313141
大安区	Daan	21466	110640	23342	7300	15979	2	251635
沿滩区	Yantan	26639	163953	20624	5369	15255	27	266495
荣县	Rongxian	67238	422407	32330	8973	23357	4011	657741
富顺县	Fushun	85579	540879	47687	6499	40773	1008	520281
攀枝花市	**Panzhihua**							
东区	East District	129	781	44	44			6865
西区	West District	346	2041	31	31			11056
仁和区	Renhe	7844	42610	983	812	156	15	272547
米易县	Miyi	17460	111206	1349	107	1242	675	393203
盐边县	Yanbian	19088	97373	1793	146	1647	246	141346
泸州市	**Luzhou**							
江阳区	Jiangyang	31812	204180	8323	821	7493	142	477513
纳溪区	Naxi	45564	282209	8965	625	8218	797	247818
龙马潭区	Longmatan	10901	68246	2736	212	2515		128153
泸县	Luxian	82090	536729	35426	4356	30802	21485	637605
合江县	Hejiang	77994	503639	7333	1912	5421	979	431612
叙永县	Xuyong	73039	355852	10336	2235	8072	26	359371
古蔺县	Gulin	73561	346146	27477	1251	25912	1419	446152

12-8 续表 6 continued

县(市、区)	Counties (Municipalities, Districts)	粮食 播种面积(公顷) Total Sown Area (hectares)	粮食 产量(吨) Output of Grain (ton)	油料 产量(吨) Yield of Oil Bearing Crops (ton)	#花生 Peanut	#油菜籽 Rapeseeds	中草药材 产量(吨) Yield of Oil Medicinal Herbs (ton)	蔬菜及食用菌 产量(吨) Output of Vegetables and Edible Fungus (ton)
德阳市	**Deyang**							
旌阳区	Jinyang	34666	232281	36337	6043	30294	224	396419
罗江区	Luojiang	17947	129922	47585	2402	45183	24	153833
中江县	Zhongjiang	143756	812471	96165	25791	70374	15799	456578
广汉市	Guanghan	43733	307751	39467	2012	37455	540	445488
什邡市	Shifang	26267	190132	13450	1117	12333	8006	490068
绵竹市	Mianzhu	44928	275945	15087	1588	13423	1717	356600
绵阳市	**Mianyang**							
涪城区	Fucheng	13543	84053	22990	3526	19464		385625
游仙区	Youxian	38676	238713	46364	6225	40132	1856	183213
安州区	Anzhou	38301	259053	40130	1555	38575	2795	191421
三台县	Santai	117060	658830	148906	33338	115568	15524	354551
盐亭县	Yanting	52128	292496	50728	13615	37095	6773	138931
梓潼县	Zitong	50881	289910	54716	11462	43122	2839	219266
北川县	Beichuan	18641	86554	8846	561	8245	2916	77093
平武县	Pingwu	25248	100235	4959	433	4514	1004	36612
江油市	Jiangyou	45721	286702	58846	5591	53209	7633	393992
广元市	**Guangyuan**							
利州区	Lizhou	17414	78568	4242	1305	2937	187	413694
昭化区	Zhaohua	24069	122219	26402	1591	24805	13753	389841
朝天区	Chaotian	28246	119259	9911	3340	6513	2970	821016
旺苍县	Wangcang	43286	232434	19090	3650	15311	11852	221893
青川县	Qingchuan	29700	124547	15782	2721	13029	5834	105514
剑阁县	Jiange	88847	453851	116580	26553	78934	4149	343072
苍溪县	Cangxi	79744	433234	61591	18751	42693	16925	351660
遂宁市	**Suining**							
船山区	Chuanshan	23147	121747	31184	3297	27751	1660	247711
安居区	Anju	76893	396719	43327	8566	34664	1879	296508
蓬溪县	Pengxi	58452	320455	47716	8692	38724	1333	215100
射洪县	Shehong	71799	378646	44956	11054	33902	1062	199351
大英县	Daying	38509	205849	29087	2379	26571	3808	112596
内江市	**Neijiang**							
内江市市中区	Neijiang Downtown	23047	118034	17005	4721	12284	191	211670
东兴区	Dongxing	67047	368502	42370	11765	30605	1479	800132
威远县	Weiyuan	61794	336365	36864	6517	30347	1953	926038
资中县	Zizhong	106581	560663	49981	14647	35334	73	656292
隆昌市	Longchang	50144	324766	23688	3726	19838	140	416381
乐山市	**Leshan**							
乐山市市中区	Leshan Downtown	15746	106634	11281	2185	9096		274500
沙湾区	Shawan	9517	50906	2770	371	2399	2264	79587
五通桥区	Wutongqiao	12608	79893	3526	649	2877	477	130273

12-8 续表 7 continued

县(市、区)	Counties (Municipalities, Districts)	粮食 播种面积(公顷) Total Sown Area (hectares)	粮食 产量(吨) Output of Grain (ton)	油料 产量(吨) Yield of Oil Bearing Crops (ton)	#花生 Peanut	#油菜籽 Rapeseeds	中草药材 产量(吨) Yield of Oil Medicinal Herbs (ton)	蔬菜及食用菌 产量(吨) Output of Vegetables and Edible Fungus (ton)
金口河区	Jinkouhe	5070	19765	228	125	103	3023	10021
犍为县	Qianwei	43114	271890	12627	3199	9428	10267	221696
井研县	Jinyan	42022	238416	14127	447	13680	1959	103697
夹江县	Jiajiang	16800	112172	13627	630	12997	2080	116238
沐川县	Muchuan	20029	99174	6412	851	5561	23307	93371
峨边县	Ebian	12551	51279	1689	365	1209	652	30754
马边县	Mabian	22567	93077	2774	610	2099	839	22099
峨眉山市	Emeishan	17665	98039	13090	231	12859	2025	172009
南充市	**Nanchong**							
顺庆区	Shunqing	25811	143721	15755	6295	9460	185	305436
高坪区	Gaoping	35893	207090	22263	5916	16346	6	449081
嘉陵区	Jialing	66373	349703	39060	12291	26559	1540	200182
南部县	Nanbu	95060	508633	73199	24312	48459	622	667041
营山县	Yingshan	68599	392778	50274	14328	35751	501	349268
蓬安县	Pengan	53614	301255	46846	14912	31847	993	331836
仪陇县	Yilong	75500	426174	66559	15371	51176	649	375371
西充县	Xichong	55062	309572	40945	8346	32342	259	445697
阆中市	Langzhong	83334	432507	44952	10379	34497	16263	467985
眉山市	**Meishan**							
东坡区	Dongpo	37575	294508	45530	1767	42527	494	675016
彭山区	Pengshan	12301	91681	10457	516	9922	6247	41404
仁寿县	Renshou	113823	645082	42055	5454	36544	643	456405
洪雅县	Hongya	13784	94102	10933	76	10837	431	68485
丹棱县	Danling	7834	52545	7492	239	7241		26617
青神县	Qingshen	9112	60088	7377	845	6532		71732
宜宾市	**Yibin**							
翠屏区	Cuiping	51751	339948	18144	8918	8857	437	296185
南溪区	Nanxi	27267	188781	10552	3084	6942	2560	567740
叙州区	Xuzhou	99123	564709	50561	27267	22338	2269	312882
江安县	Jiangan	38011	255928	11073	1545	8983	169	257679
长宁县	Changning	34749	223076	18030	3308	14695	401	157849
高县	Gaoxian	45739	262554	15160	7041	8119	139	174476
珙县	Gongxian	35191	189642	12851	6141	6710	783	271439
筠连县	Junlian	33924	175969	3993	1354	2545	387	136021
兴文县	Xingwen	39513	239826	6820	2579	4205	145	393164
屏山县	Pingshan	16273	92495	8774	934	7781	791	88935
广安市	**Guangan**							
广安区	Guanganqu	53952	328974	25376	4976	20395	462	404159
前锋区	Qianfeng	15948	107142	10213	2091	7828	433	235455
岳池县	Yuechi	71639	482277	23766	4075	19599	382	701516
武胜县	Wusheng	49874	323045	16892	3555	13054	38	337318

12-8 续表 8 continued

县(市、区)	Counties (Municipalities, Districts)	粮食 播种面积(公顷) Total Sown Area (hectares)	粮食 产量(吨) Output of Grain (ton)	油料产量(吨) Yield of Oil Bearing Crops (ton)	#花生 Peanut	#油菜籽 Rapeseeds	中草药材产量(吨) Yield of Oil Medicinal Herbs (ton)	蔬菜及食用菌产量(吨) Output of Vegetables and Edible Fungus (ton)
邻水县	Linshui	76033	453977	27728	9670	17690	2692	547207
华蓥市	Huaying	17307	103509	1825	512	1229	790	135624
达州市	**Dazhou**							
通川区	Tongchuan	31660	182691	18872	2364	16240	930	295863
达川区	Dachuan	88113	533695	60963	4113	56847	1488	464517
宣汉县	Xuanhan	94362	577028	91929	5870	83824	1026	486498
开江县	Kaijiang	51551	301444	40146	7108	33038	723	376637
大竹县	Dazhu	111320	607784	45708	5754	39954	1447	504068
渠县	Quxian	117538	648137	63337	22941	40380	5387	561722
万源市	Wanyuan	60540	320478	29776	6912	22161	10418	157075
雅安市	**Yaan**							
雨城区	Yucheng	9806	48474	1722		1722	470	208004
名山区	Mingshan	10834	67682	4052		4052	2	57306
荥经县	Yingjing	6211	35686	2892	88	2804	1427	41789
汉源县	Hanyuan	19012	91588	727	217	488	3839	198238
石棉县	Shimian	4567	20531	1199	273	926	1830	70103
天全县	Tianquan	8112	44231	2205		2205	2499	58197
芦山县	Lushan	4960	26238	1606	83	1523	6104	50047
宝兴县	Baoxing	5540	23360	267		267	7560	20007
巴中市	**Bazhong**							
巴州区	Bazhou	59931	334000	23181	3449	19725	11076	307583
恩阳区	Enyang	60306	337631	22513	3183	19292	9603	385721
通江县	Tongjiang	81668	457557	41234	2766	38006	1934	264436
南江县	Nanjiang	68912	386778	28298	2175	25761	7238	298417
平昌县	Pingchang	67501	389467	48485	5114	43185	16980	259866
资阳市	**Ziyang**							
雁江区	Yanjiang	110526	518318	73563	17545	56018	2157	536256
安岳县	Anyue	143856	736133	96453	15092	81361	2880	821880
乐至县	Lezhi	81706	406222	72056	11663	60393	2192	207041
阿坝州	**Aba**							
马尔康市	Maerkang	3073	9103	13		13	483	33341
汶川县	Wenchuan	3227	12725	602		602	195	43121
理县	Lixian	1567	7071	11		11	20	95030
茂县	Maoxian	6787	25151	626		626	623	252932
松潘县	Songpan	4073	13091	128		128	1250	89150
九寨沟县	Jiuzhaigou	2806	9988	488		488	1472	15526
金川县	Jinchuan	5859	22641	178		178	160	43033
小金县	Xiaojin	6306	21062	889		889	165	76325
黑水县	Heishui	6208	17309				253	26770
壤塘县	Rangtang	1780	4310	144		144	26	2647

12-8 续表 9 continued

县(市、区)	Counties (Municipalities, Districts)	粮食		油料			中草药材	蔬菜及食用菌
		播种面积(公顷) Total Sown Area (hectares)	产量(吨) Output of Grain (ton)	产量(吨) Yield of Oil Bearing Crops (ton)	#花生 Peanut	#油菜籽 Rapeseeds	产量(吨) Yield of Oil Medicinal Herbs (ton)	产量(吨) Output of Vegetables and Edible Fungus (ton)
阿坝县	Abaxian	3880	7193	1344		1344	17	12444
若尔盖县	Ruoergai	2166	5778	789		789	804	9380
红原县	Hongyuan							13763
甘孜州	**Ganzi**							
康定市	Kangding	6607	19749	79		71	659	28527
泸定县	Luding	3885	11938	1214	59	1132	925	98017
丹巴县	Danba	2715	9986	1012		996	127	21822
九龙县	Jiulong	4137	20698	191		191	181	44866
雅江县	Yajiang	2779	9467	46		46		17793
道孚县	Daofu	5007	13853	1887		1887	8	14401
炉霍县	Luhuo	3488	9546	2800		2800		6000
甘孜县	Ganzixian	11062	33070	1127		1127		17320
新龙县	Xinlong	3270	9762	1121		1121		8220
德格县	Dege	3560	9900				260	8100
白玉县	Baiyu	3380	10006	439		439	283	4893
石渠县	Shiqu	2354	6104	214		214		2016
色达县	Seda	901	2602	18		18		2258
理塘县	Litang	3885	13727	1300		1300	916	12815
巴塘县	Batang	4049	15454	436		436	134	9607
乡城县	Xiangcheng	2502	9192	344		344		13195
稻城县	Daocheng	2580	8822	739	9	730	2052	5059
得荣县	Derong	2649	11701	434	116	318		5815
凉山州	**Liangshan**							
西昌市	Xichang	41461	242594	2277	282	1984		599378
木里县	Muli	17571	70346	121		121	206	43766
盐源县	Yanyuan	48229	215234	574	65	122	9466	158554
德昌县	Dechang	17957	99729	755	78	677		238253
会理县	Huili	67484	338389	2615	653	1944		447652
会东县	Huidong	55362	254702	12753	1471	10988	5660	527549
宁南县	Ningnan	24882	108340	1064	979	85		385306
普格县	Puge	18235	79010	217	16	201	93	45731
布拖县	Butuo	23899	99975	107	107		2494	24473
金阳县	Jinyang	14560	63812	200	200			41823
昭觉县	Zhaojue	28068	120185					47446
喜德县	Xide	20415	83215	171		171		23061
冕宁县	Mianning	43631	217028	3007	122	2821	137	282503
越西县	Yuexi	31613	133893	5318		5253	881	91129
甘洛县	Ganluo	24869	109606	1143	45	1080	1975	60617
美姑县	Meigu	22792	92721	23	9	14	1	14944
雷波县	Leibo	19498	91339	1518	322	1195	403	64670

12-8 续表 10 continued

县(市、区)	Counties (Municipalities, Districts)	茶叶产量 (吨) Yield of Tea (ton)	水果产量 (吨) Output of Fruits (ton)	肉猪出栏头数 (头) Slaughtered Fattened Hogs (head)	猪年末存栏头数 (头) Hogs at the Year-end (head)	肉牛出栏头数 (头) Slaughtered Fattened Cattle and Buffaloes (head)	羊出栏只数 (只) Slaughtered Fattened Sheep and Goats (head)	家禽出栏只数 (只) Slaughtered Poultry (head)
成都市	**Chengdu**							
锦江区	Jinjiang		11					
青羊区	Qingyang							
金牛区	Jinniu							
武侯区	Wuhou							
成华区	Chenghua		144					
龙泉驿区	Longquanyi		183920	5518	5473	16	1428	146714
青白江区	Qingbaijiang		33188	80125	49289	1442	8562	1396089
新都区	Xindu		24525	70900	68932	998	827	4306791
温江区	Wenjiang		359	9813	6356		7	250461
双流区	Shuangliu		231855	182069	94415	304	21417	2263338
郫都区	Pidu		9841	6617	3980	8	17	123301
金堂县	Jintang		261074	616000	380700	14462	168552	7253251
大邑县	Dayi	166	44725	618000	379000	1780	21825	8201003
蒲江县	Pujiang	8673	357213	575900	385900	313	5594	3539505
新津县	Xinjin		49257	267556	147274	333	4047	9989604
都江堰市	Dujiangyan	2332	42506	288620	154062	1585	8662	7157001
彭州市	Pengzhou	48	28909	415100	270300	4621	8129	7511665
邛崃市	Qionglai	9386	156222	1117000	715000	4569	23862	7312516
崇州市	Chongzhou	402	30121	584500	370083	3968	15561	8413083
简阳市	Jianyang		218870	1021000	645400	3339	633876	8838835
自贡市	**Zigong**							
自流井区	Ziliujing		9281	55793	33739	568	8596	1213881
贡井区	Gongjing	48	23305	179423	107210	732	52038	3597791
大安区	Daan		11170	146344	86527	7494	69149	4197512
沿滩区	Yantan		38411	159738	92368	686	45185	2843118
荣县	Rongxian	12188	164105	634000	381000	6263	302535	6471809
富顺县	Fushun	66	99557	591800	355800	9361	416847	8685435
攀枝花市	**Panzhihua**							
东区	East District	24	18008	17771	9259	134	2375	729343
西区	West District		4890	13801	8710	232	4239	590770
仁和区	Renhe	2	147521	146899	103010	8190	125018	1427643
米易县	Miyi		116214	162304	133214	14817	127608	540856
盐边县	Yanbian	94	124829	222380	157003	10127	205773	866861
泸州市	**Luzhou**							
江阳区	Jiangyang	2	25000	382130	215300	985	34771	2634665
纳溪区	Naxi	9143	26195	531700	332925	1324	26570	4258292
龙马潭区	Longmatan	2	9587	103712	56552	443	15475	4285725
泸县	Luxian	1241	81785	1078000	712600	2431	78773	13643294
合江县	Hejiang	889	54562	786500	490300	3875	173395	8580848
叙永县	Xuyong	1387	28902	577100	350300	28809	33044	1460224
古蔺县	Gulin	1445	17654	554128	331774	30170	141927	1050647

12-8 续表 11 continued

县(市、区)	Counties (Municipalities, Districts)	茶叶产量(吨) Yield of Tea (ton)	水果产量(吨) Output of Fruits (ton)	肉猪出栏头数(头) Slaughtered Fattened Hogs (head)	猪年末存栏头数(头) Hogs at the Year-end (head)	肉牛出栏头数(头) Slaughtered Fattened Cattle and Buffaloes (head)	羊出栏只数(只) Slaughtered Fattened Sheep and Goats (head)	家禽出栏只数(只) Slaughtered Poultry (head)
德阳市	**Deyang**							
旌阳区	Jinyang		29595	417000	270100	7248	10039	17710290
罗江区	Luojiang		59896	400000	232000	3209	7023	5148764
中江县	Zhongjiang		63369	1051159	650260	34941	170062	18901542
广汉市	Guanghan		37167	317004	206000	10961	6821	11640786
什邡市	Shifang	92	19751	335256	209450	2936	18682	4810716
绵竹市	Mianzhu	306	46556	507000	310200	4066	6256	5130760
绵阳市	**Mianyang**							
涪城区	Fucheng		20210	211851	146464	3090	3373	7403692
游仙区	Youxian		22046	253303	169646	5713	27989	6766760
安州区	Anzhou	470	24016	249004	178655	6334	13994	8605567
三台县	Santai		78103	1105000	656700	39050	150033	13843932
盐亭县	Yanting		50845	436565	261500	16972	225808	7574720
梓潼县	Zitong		82254	500600	335000	12943	222140	6044531
北川县	Beichuan	759	4898	199803	140659	6603	222521	1458218
平武县	Pingwu	1892	2146	124961	86740	8482	41688	568742
江油市	Jiangyou	45	87762	481200	341736	12467	62614	10425916
广元市	**Guangyuan**							
利州区	Lizhou	5	27052	214397	150322	7573	30629	1377570
昭化区	Zhaohua		18801	595400	386600	6726	54606	1967845
朝天区	Chaotian		7059	199056	143212	7564	65750	1851043
旺苍县	Wangcang	5201	31572	580000	353513	12262	97188	2086956
青川县	Qingchuan	6439	18040	194321	137268	10265	67609	1869791
剑阁县	Jiange	10	64120	948000	593500	14313	155765	6923558
苍溪县	Cangxi		212353	946000	621000	20372	86824	4420992
遂宁市	**Suining**							
船山区	Chuanshan	6	26097	588000	333000	3616	45055	2364568
安居区	Anju		32232	945532	571569	3176	43389	4809850
蓬溪县	Pengxi	101	36016	695200	461900	7865	131954	3724926
射洪县	Shehong		18291	951500	566500	14658	109113	6236013
大英县	Daying		13467	572000	353800	3168	36839	3736885
内江市	**Neijiang**							
内江市市中区	Neijiang Downtown		11008	261354	154993	1721	16934	1855603
东兴区	Dongxing		47121	633482	386400	6265	113625	6209958
威远县	Weiyuan	2151	81426	501800	311000	2254	188713	4514839
资中县	Zizhong	144	257057	774000	465400	4322	158552	6176166
隆昌市	Longchang	372	36807	429580	258500	1322	30100	8208975
乐山市	**Leshan**							
乐山市市中区	Leshan Downtown	492	22036	452300	302900	1454	6805	6782193
沙湾区	Shawan	276	6028	137843	87829	1319	7587	2516214
五通桥区	Wutongqiao	1616	28908	210154	138445	909	6437	3810004

12-8 续表 12 continued

县(市、区)	Counties (Municipalities, Districts)	茶叶产量(吨) Yield of Tea (ton)	水果产量(吨) Output of Fruits (ton)	肉猪出栏头数(头) Slaughtered Fattened Hogs (head)	猪年末存栏头数(头) Hogs at the Year-end (head)	肉牛出栏头数(头) Slaughtered Fattened Cattle and Buffaloes (head)	羊出栏只数(只) Slaughtered Fattened Sheep and Goats (head)	家禽出栏只数(只) Slaughtered Poultry (head)
金口河区	Jinkouhe	135	1315	31766	23283	1353	4982	108138
犍为县	Qianwei	3453	41716	633699	395400	6259	53545	7344160
井研县	Jinyan	670	24424	725000	433800	933	55744	4233619
夹江县	Jiajiang	8136	9564	251353	166681	1617	3599	5747637
沐川县	Muchuan	7304	12326	209692	128982	1045	34035	974870
峨边县	Ebian	294	437	87164	61536	5206	38229	381549
马边县	Mabian	10950	4365	123945	89155	6489	99936	543136
峨眉山市	Emeishan	8570	26930	204217	101231	2985	9989	3277800
南充市	**Nanchong**							
顺庆区	Shunqing		17680	252828	160510	6205	155420	5021426
高坪区	Gaoping		142994	528000	321300	3550	122403	6132361
嘉陵区	Jialing		47967	576200	356200	6219	313507	5944931
南部县	Nanbu		92032	878000	536100	12759	282972	8446374
营山县	Yingshan	14	44307	758000	501000	20065	350550	7230043
蓬安县	Pengan		109469	528900	356500	11681	173247	5733293
仪陇县	Yilong	7	29400	831000	579000	31547	215497	7867943
西充县	Xichong		64822	731400	500700	5597	98363	4963439
阆中市	Langzhong	16	95780	757000	490100	19222	179174	6814957
眉山市	**Meishan**							
东坡区	Dongpo	583	180266	600000	371300	3526	46962	9428509
彭山区	Pengshan	25	66633	168694	105505	443	20464	3341268
仁寿县	Renshou		623769	1162000	730600	5400	325314	10895435
洪雅县	Hongya	16711	7372	215288	140274	9437	41313	2748248
丹棱县	Danling	2991	178048	186535	125494	468	18271	1776713
青神县	Qingshen	683	72781	197750	140065	1397	7766	2395716
宜宾市	**Yibin**							
翠屏区	Cuiping	3103	77681	445276	325200	5304	19965	3663729
南溪区	Nanxi	166	85251	407000	252100	2558	49174	5830044
叙州区	Xuzhou	7634	88170	871799	531500	6390	65599	7924000
江安县	Jiangan	2337	178142	507101	361000	3129	52100	5241853
长宁县	Changning	2278	82736	492000	331600	3967	9936	5817730
高县	Gaoxian	13631	13848	453600	301800	9941	25772	4097491
珙县	Gongxian	8808	8332	445301	310500	10959	10199	2053709
筠连县	Junlian	12430	19153	463800	315800	49419	7727	2356106
兴文县	Xingwen	1200	8978	505100	355000	22570	13961	3985637
屏山县	Pingshan	13420	109158	229884	133313	4427	156449	1285708
广安市	**Guangan**							
广安区	Guanganqu		14626	855900	526500	4489	14818	4893748
前锋区	Qianfeng	51	7793	117966	72588	1283	38581	1476398
岳池县	Yuechi		70487	862000	530300	5598	25411	6790458
武胜县	Wusheng	16	31719	985000	603700	3143	46679	7085328

12-8 续表 13 continued

县(市、区)	Counties (Municipalities, Districts)	茶叶产量（吨）Yield of Tea (ton)	水果产量（吨）Output of Fruits (ton)	肉猪出栏头数（头）Slaughtered Fattened Hogs (head)	猪年末存栏头数（头）Hogs at the Year-end (head)	肉牛出栏头数（头）Slaughtered Fattened Cattle and Buffaloes (head)	羊出栏只数（只）Slaughtered Fattened Sheep and Goats (head)	家禽出栏只数（只）Slaughtered Poultry (head)
邻水县	Linshui	368	129559	784100	502800	6760	56252	7189441
华蓥市	Huaying	120	16747	189144	119082	1464	22246	2068720
达州市	**Dazhou**							
通川区	Tongchuan	80	63625	308364	202576	16825	57845	2899416
达川区	Dachuan	197	58733	752200	488245	53171	163784	8705096
宣汉县	Xuanhan	3866	92729	782000	523700	89526	265123	8100908
开江县	Kaijiang	339	23677	349824	227558	12023	120647	10612903
大竹县	Dazhu	478	46048	775000	511100	39880	257292	16001166
渠县	Quxian	281	164138	950440	629300	48340	171880	11806751
万源市	Wanyuan	5728	11734	346000	230400	42488	146327	3963050
雅安市	**Yaan**							
雨城区	Yucheng	26110	12179	180198	126539	5537	41886	1935808
名山区	Mingshan	49962	6603	530000	368000	1511	24337	2029257
荥经县	Yingjing	3316	4338	66351	38903	5256	14698	289274
汉源县	Hanyuan	24	299274	178136	127505	14272	56884	470196
石棉县	Shimian	59	74681	53028	37523	6829	39519	416969
天全县	Tianquan	3211	4330	91628	58200	3409	16105	1772244
芦山县	Lushan	731	2018	80757	50163	2416	5998	642835
宝兴县	Baoxing	662	1091	48843	32261	12675	20246	65331
巴中市	**Bazhong**							
巴州区	Bazhou	85	31619	597700	366500	22753	86426	1810792
恩阳区	Enyang	59	19317	518000	331600	21398	56320	1706616
通江县	Tongjiang	1569	15950	834000	529000	50633	197614	2278187
南江县	Nanjiang	2478	26369	703348	476500	41843	549912	2693943
平昌县	Pingchang	6504	11946	841600	485000	51419	63641	3024118
资阳市	**Ziyang**							
雁江区	Yanjiang		254838	925000	625500	2622	308270	7076225
安岳县	Anyue		530582	1259000	840800	11554	350151	9926515
乐至县	Lezhi		20596	788000	472600	1755	591595	4867432
阿坝州	**Aba**							
马尔康市	Maerkang		772	35520	28649	39147	2871	29391
汶川县	Wenchuan	34	27747	47310	32741	4040	12664	144613
理县	Lixian		6433	16850	11236	8345	7398	58430
茂县	Maoxian		82351	66558	22588	9229	16280	43170
松潘县	Songpan		2320	26454	24315	40839	31076	25236
九寨沟县	Jiuzhaigou		5644	21061	15239	16012	6244	53088
金川县	Jinchuan		20302	68533	48546	14219	15238	121088
小金县	Xiaojin		50202	34730	29397	19491	25102	19913
黑水县	Heishui		3268	52115	50079	14177	5480	156840
壤塘县	Rangtang			330	105	43828	31142	

12-8 续表 14 continued

县(市、区)	Counties (Municipalities, Districts)	茶叶产量(吨) Yield of Tea (ton)	水果产量(吨) Output of Fruits (ton)	肉猪出栏头数(头) Slaughtered Fattened Hogs (head)	猪年末存栏头数(头) Hogs at the Year-end (head)	肉牛出栏头数(头) Slaughtered Fattened Cattle and Buffaloes (head)	羊出栏只数(只) Slaughtered Fattened Sheep and Goats (head)	家禽出栏只数(只) Slaughtered Poultry (head)
阿坝县	Abaxian				319	95243	23358	
若尔盖县	Ruoergai			13504	11538	115706	278018	
红原县	Hongyuan					111149	10218	
甘孜州	**Ganzi**							
康定市	Kangding		1815	14266	9465	34069	3156	11840
泸定县	Luding	2	3673	61791	40625	3081	17530	69691
丹巴县	Danba		1360	34898	27913	9669	12763	10084
九龙县	Jiulong	101	1900	34278	26560	15599	41548	50663
雅江县	Yajiang		352	9708	7644	15442	26059	778
道孚县	Daofu		572	4723	3049	22187	5397	
炉霍县	Luhuo		90	2226	852	31512	38707	
甘孜县	Ganzixian			998	552	42975	9725	
新龙县	Xinlong		235	1735	1226	28762	15481	
德格县	Dege		2	1225	859	61809	50884	
白玉县	Baiyu		36	763	536	31308	49544	
石渠县	Shiqu		17	1875	1371	57397	26502	
色达县	Seda					76955	63605	
理塘县	Litang			4185	3666	50830	20768	
巴塘县	Batang		1575	12829	9340	27213	23016	5180
乡城县	Xiangcheng		3656	14545	12915	10002	1734	8619
稻城县	Daocheng		350	13964	10425	15143	3237	12866
得荣县	Derong		2520	28905	21723	7358	4135	34722
凉山州	**Liangshan**							
西昌市	Xichang		92386	542000	312500	20123	169415	4580193
木里县	Muli		10000	137519	102477	43280	219700	357476
盐源县	Yanyuan		507502	341000	251200	33799	413569	3075095
德昌县	Dechang		143794	258684	165991	12238	133117	1072412
会理县	Huili		625169	802000	540200	30501	500786	2775319
会东县	Huidong	12	160377	463000	304700	44147	675768	1214973
宁南县	Ningnan	28	18828	254291	196402	18482	153125	574324
普格县	Puge		3466	128007	93571	9552	145537	323916
布拖县	Butuo		358	159545	125029	17567	214165	300215
金阳县	Jinyang		4286	129939	101944	10049	156739	459973
昭觉县	Zhaojue		6200	261580	194655	26784	394627	413133
喜德县	Xide		13697	140664	98182	8600	143609	729527
冕宁县	Mianning	3	52225	421680	260175	25508	196612	887267
越西县	Yuexi		13067	256166	174124	13432	178141	406760
甘洛县	Ganluo	7	4225	195120	144980	18973	153334	538267
美姑县	Meigu		6980	259382	188903	23776	256878	938793
雷波县	Leibo	770	15963	172289	110247	6901	134489	407029

12-9 各县(市、区)规模以上工业经济情况(2018年)

Basic Statistics on Industrial Enterprises above Designated Size by Counties (Municipalities, Districts)(2018)

单位：万元 (10 000 yuan)

县(市、区)	Counties (Municipalities, Districts)	工业企业单位数(个) Number of Industrial Enterprises (unit)	工业总产值 Gross Industrial Output Value	营业收入 Business Revenue	利润总额 Total Profits
成都市	**Chengdu**				
锦江区	Jinjiang	10	234917	216966	36543
青羊区	Qingyang	26	847404	790743	130680
金牛区	Jinniu	48	1002144	994058	115569
武侯区	Wuhou	61	1379542	1361073	174312
成华区	Chenghua	28	993259	1021443	70107
龙泉驿区	Longquanyi	254	22713325	21910927	1920363
青白江区	Qingbaijiang	283	6735776	6185214	-118579
新都区	Xindu	341	4750521	5062056	225772
温江区	Wenjiang	201	4172535	3911222	285907
双流区	Shuangliu	328	10496821	10029350	421158
郫都区	Pidu	224	2597745	2603042	161848
金堂县	Jintang	194	1975785	1813629	43127
大邑县	Dayi	143	2470598	2304689	75616
蒲江县	Pujiang	104	1436846	1148811	47808
新津县	Xinjin	184	3614359	3432209	147042
都江堰市	Dujiangyan	98	1518335	1563582	154188
彭州市	Pengzhou	163	6571524	6721503	396156
邛崃市	Qionglai	148	2257075	2109196	148922
崇州市	Chongzhou	166	3668722	3563872	207008
简阳市	Jianyang	166	4084482	4229499	254259
自贡市	**Zigong**				
自流井区	Ziliujing	40	1380549	1275378	30967
贡井区	Gongjing	75	2459623	2507638	45382
大安区	Daan	85	2556169	2495973	95401
沿滩区	Yantan	132	2867726	2550252	128631
荣县	Rongxian	92	1474748	1416968	59640
富顺县	Fushun	120	3198511	2952234	171288
攀枝花市	**Panzhihua**				
东区	East District	63	6513439	7991784	397522
西区	West District	54	2248116	2105547	57312
仁和区	Renhe	120	4204991	3785169	505197
米易县	Miyi	48	1488252	1406519	193733
盐边县	Yanbian	40	1544309	1416943	363048
泸州市	**Luzhou**				
江阳区	Jiangyang	140	3504252	3113089	573630
纳溪区	Nanxi	98	2280709	2269383	247747
龙马潭区	Longmatan	127	5380321	5329835	327322
泸县	Luxian	128	3594188	3546508	188744
合江县	Hejiang	83	1449876	1439908	113225
叙永县	Xuyong	55	468100	459580	35407

12-9 续表 1 continued

单位：万元 (10 000 yuan)

县(市、区)	Counties (Municipalities, Districts)	工业企业单位数(个) Number of Industrial Enterprises (unit)	工业总产值 Gross Industrial Output Value	营业收入 Business Revenue	利润总额 Total Profits
古蔺县	Gulin	40	1474005	1246131	52694
德阳市	**Deyang**				
旌阳区	Jinyang	366		9390578	508619
罗江区	Luojiang	125		3728965	64437
中江县	Zhongjiang	163		4009995	384643
广汉市	Guanghan	318		9474925	1419937
什邡市	Shifang	240		3808128	-26568
绵竹市	Mianzhu	128		4983082	687785
绵阳市	**Mianyang**				
涪城区	Hucheng	239	8937938	13245338	377078
游仙区	Youxian	147	3910230	3467178	197949
安州区	Anzhou	123	2471959	2231191	113972
三台县	Santai	102	1185827	1163344	116209
盐亭县	Yanting	25	149900	148559	7620
梓潼县	Zitong	50	809535	771491	13165
北川县	Beichuan	41	347714	304915	25894
平武县	Pingwu	33	302168	263989	9639
江油市	Jiangyou	240	4672221	4576721	243465
广元市	**Guangyuan**				
利州区	Lizhou	177	4926836	4900255	337627
昭化区	Zhaohua	42	1124824	1095318	41225
朝天区	Chaotian	35	735474	733681	100005
旺苍县	Wangcang	79	1135381	1117297	66756
青川县	Qingchuan	42	442956	423054	27054
剑阁县	Jiange	61	915651	865437	26086
苍溪县	Cangxi	50	882973	865090	134427
遂宁市	**Suining**				
船山区	Chuanshan	219	5804993	5781847	422769
安居区	Anju	49	854016	784456	141621
蓬溪县	Pengxi	82	1382553	1352486	100063
射洪县	Shehong	116	4307418	4140010	520031
大英县	Daying	91	1438130	1389791	127908
内江市	**Neijiang**				
内江市中区	Neijiang Downtown	84	1435776	1430572	42647
东兴区	Dongxing	34	508066	503930	37046
威远县	Weiyuan	77	5817394	5769303	324757
资中县	Zizhong	45	639505	663837	84778
隆昌市	Longchang	90	1873554	1718774	147178
乐山市	**Leshan**				
乐山市中区	Leshan Downtown	104	2634888	2490260	74194
沙湾区	Shawan	56	1391969	1364424	338412

12-9 续表 2 continued

单位：万元 (10 000 yuan)

县(市、区)	Counties (Municipalities, Districts)	工业企业单位数(个) Number of Industrial Enterprises (unit)	工业总产值 Gross Industrial Output Value	营业收入 Business Revenue	利润总额 Total Profits
五通桥区	Wutongqiao	66	1830302	1801606	194258
金口河区	Jinkouhe	9	464548	434743	4713
犍为县	Qianwei	66	896099	878736	51512
井研县	Jingyan	55	741536	730124	27444
夹江县	Jiajiang	123	2302646	2139090	44837
沐川县	Muchuan	25	361545	334678	11778
峨边县	Ebian	29	389850	387924	16470
马边县	Mabian	21	217988	226574	-3736
峨眉山市	Emeishan	71	3289899	3288514	426395
南充市	**Nanchong**				
顺庆区	Shunqing	96	4998426	4864436	435185
高坪区	Gaoping	90	3335633	3365556	146380
嘉陵区	Jialing	94	4504236	4480970	319753
南部县	Nanbu	117	4048479	4041141	415610
营山县	Yingshan	54	2046508	2023888	105265
蓬安县	Pengan	80	2887358	2872225	211375
仪陇县	Yilong	52	1238050	1164282	88841
西充县	Xichong	89	1977455	1935473	135586
阆中市	Langzhong	76	1744296	1742356	101388
眉山市	**Meishan**				
东坡区	Dongpo	185	5745972	5283729	342847
彭山区	Pengshan	112	3234177	3711642	110917
仁寿县	Renshou	156	3192840	3061656	203211
洪雅县	Hongya	31	405320	399291	18918
丹棱县	Danling	38	384793	382009	18634
青神县	Qingshen	47	947083	939673	61711
宜宾市	**Yibin**				
翠屏区	Cuiping	126	9318235	13208131	2344918
南溪区	Nanxi	88	2154404	2024457	151391
叙州区	Xuzhou	116	4752412	4649658	653734
江安县	Jiangan	65	1252985	1202705	108657
长宁县	Changning	79	1587126	1505341	120854
高县	Gaoxian	63	1557089	1535090	72422
珙县	Gongxian	57	1103450	1016108	202952
筠连县	Junlian	51	541688	514530	79264
兴文县	Xingwen	71	543503	518786	55411
屏山县	Pingshan	50	530289	415090	21230
广安市	**Guangan**				
广安区	Guanganqu	24	252648	260593	35351
前锋区	Qianfeng	132	3969326	3666184	126486
岳池县	Yuechi	84	2275397	2275831	90853

12-9 续表 3 continued

单位：万元 (10 000 yuan)

县(市、区)	Counties (Municipalities, Districts)	工业企业单位数(个) Number of Industrial Enterprises (unit)	工业总产值 Gross Industrial Output Value	营业收入 Business Revenue	利润总额 Total Profits
武胜县	Wusheng	95	3350944	3392908	134082
邻水县	Linshui	110	2802332	2692784	85809
华蓥市	Huaying	107	3420479	3335140	213317
达州市	**Dazhou**				
通川区	Tongchuan	67	2540333	2607742	125053
达川区	Dachuan	102	2487718	2296344	139040
宣汉县	Xuanhan	60	1488595	1331590	313096
开江县	Kaijiang	65	814495	770354	36657
大竹县	Dazhu	121	2620066	2521831	172530
渠县	Quxian	109	2325523	2298336	135219
万源市	Wanyuan	45	567203	508558	41580
雅安市	**Yaan**				
雨城区	Yucheng	40	779037	611245	38660
名山区	Mingshan	48	1043243	916414	30354
荥经县	Yingjing	45	501696	453995	4446
汉源县	Hanyuan	28	1035555	1023344	59843
石棉县	Shimian	45	980765	1042615	137029
天全县	Tianquan	34	392585	269329	12495
芦山县	Lushan	50	550565	458785	17183
宝兴县	Baoxing	40	520612	363252	29256
巴中市	**Bazhong**				
巴州区	Bazhou	90	1847135	1703446	97596
恩阳区	Enyang	43	836034	813752	56124
通江县	Tongjiang	50	890118	776620	31189
南江县	Nanjiang	61	1219393	1127952	81354
平昌县	Pingchang	60	2004318	1828281	32567
资阳市	**Ziyang**				
雁江区	Yanjiang	144	4176490	4226962	99312
安岳县	Anyue	114	1382868	1342996	130367
乐至县	Lezhi	67	1963938	1870572	158750
阿坝州	**Aba**				
马尔康市	Maerkang	5	8887	8955	-2093
汶川县	Wenchuan	32	812048	731716	82108
理县	Lixian	12	156895	154708	-5761
茂县	Maoxian	17	565114	556994	26695
松潘县	Songpan	4	19763	16967	1827
九寨沟县	Jiuzhaigou	4	54556	53258	-1599
金川县	Jinchuan	1	2726	2564	36
小金县	Xiaojin	8	77538	75652	1088
黑水县	Heishui	10	105969	105969	-5100
壤塘县	Rangtang				

12-9 续表 4 continued

单位：万元 (10 000 yuan)

县(市、区)	Counties (Municipalities, Districts)	工业企业单位数(个) Number of Industrial Enterprises (unit)	工业总产值 Gross Industrial Output Value	营业收入 Business Revenue	利润总额 Total Profits
阿坝县	Abaxian	1	2691	2478	-1255
若尔盖县	Ruoergai	4	55548	21985	1102
红原县	Hongyuan	9	65718	43375	2690
甘孜州	**Ganzi**				
康定市	Kangding	15	522916	523450	41634
泸定县	Luding	7	81544	82379	-7410
丹巴县	Danba	5	52848	49805	-8128
九龙县	Jiulong	13	179884	178356	19664
雅江县	Yajiang	1	9003	9003	-2082
道孚县	Daofu				
炉霍县	Luhuo	1	6671	6472	1468
甘孜县	Ganzixian	1	2749	2836	707
新龙县	Xinlong				
德格县	Dege				
白玉县	Baiyu	1	65345	30525	6204
石渠县	Shiqu				
色达县	Seda				
理塘县	Litang	1	17674	17674	-1151
巴塘县	Batang	1	6385	5678	-3458
乡城县	Xiangcheng	5	40799	38741	-9425
稻城县	Daocheng				
得荣县	Derong	2	26421	26421	-3273
凉山州	**Liangshan**				
西昌市	Xichang	67	3463000	3193000	305000
木里县	Muli	5	203000	207000	5000
盐源县	Yanyuan	24	169000	191000	12000
德昌县	Dechang	33	312000	337000	37000
会理县	Huili	52	904000	970000	-16000
会东县	Huidong	21	419000	404000	71000
宁南县	Ningnan	9	129000	122000	13000
普格县	Puge	3	79000	66000	6000
布拖县	Butuo	5	21000	27000	6000
金阳县	Jinyang	2	7000	7000	-1000
昭觉县	Zhaojue	9	70000	73000	9000
喜德县	Xide	7	29000	29000	3000
冕宁县	Mianning	31	336000	374000	41000
越西县	Yuexi	10	67000	69000	9000
甘洛县	Ganluo	16	137000	132000	4000
美姑县	Meigu	3	33000	34000	2000
雷波县	Leibo	10	287000	291000	10000

12-10 各县(市、区)财政、金融和贸易情况(2018年)
Basic Statistics on Finance, Banking and Trade by Counties (Municipalities, Districts)(2018)

单位：万元 (10 000 yuan)

县(市、区)	Counties (Municipalities, Districts)	地方一般公共预算收入 Local Government Public-budgetary Revenue	一般公共预算支出 General Public Budget Expenditure	年末金融机构各项存款余额 Total Deposits Balances of Financial Institutions	年末金融机构各项贷款余额 Total Loans Balances of Financial Institutions	社会消费品零售总额 Total Retail Sales of Consumer Goods	出口总额 Total Exports
成都市	**Chengdu**						
锦江区	Jinjiang	901279	603555			10433037	
青羊区	Qingyang	925345	564338			9097396	
金牛区	Jinniu	871870	724294			8635481	580000
武侯区	Wuhou	1036327	716692			9813093	
成华区	Chenghua	825526	794209			5202756	676178
龙泉驿区	Longquanyi	858326	1074665	10024680	6649691	1491180	143411
青白江区	Qingbaijiang	287748	529316	3679152	2037923	880772	666373
新都区	Xindu	609901	843938	9313859	4452419	1934885	238571
温江区	Wenjiang	406236	568198	7109415	4671473	1214196	242321
双流区	Shuangliu	1226004	1711858	15896931	10257538	2957919	
郫都区	Pidu	460117	560560	7882925	5011131	1228414	175000
金堂县	Jintang	343231	579672	4182737	2881195	884034	
大邑县	Dayi	142623	298303	3218792	1679784	665633	52821
蒲江县	Pujiang	87533	201683	1803042	944845	351144	59153
新津县	Xinjin	245290	324179	3129762	2414996	841577	
都江堰市	Dujiangyan	288029	440596	5318523	2856156	1269104	17441
彭州市	Pengzhou	355612	467172	6126414	2959555	974165	65344
邛崃市	Qionglai	214343	456154	4402405	2162709	910729	9131
崇州市	Chongzhou	236731	399831	4947192	1782182	974648	105470
简阳市	Jianyang	237438	589478	7437801	3403864	2859822	81640
自贡市	**Zigong**						
自流井区	Ziliujing	73464	170943			1986949	20809
贡井区	Gongjing	22932	182775			549532	17309
大安区	Daan	42819	194044			817756	117862
沿滩区	Yantan	39303	196993			755735	7055
荣县	Rongxian	58530	337931	2509575	1320993	902032	1651
富顺县	Fushun	106011	524192	3471642	1747763	1250549	17895
攀枝花市	**Panzhihua**						
东区	East District	89920	170879	6114805	6239632	2201120	38802
西区	West District	16419	94300	1133847	379110	412346	1730
仁和区	Renhe	90762	159953	1512922	339302	387315	36021
米易县	Miyi	100017	181540	963162	555320	408282	49417
盐边县	Yanbian	60019	158181	693190	533599	203580	18
泸州市	**Luzhou**						
江阳区	Jiangyang	239596	510424	9221937	7275976	2380568	47037
纳溪区	Nanxi	107555	287024	1895945	980747	796325	5930
龙马潭区	Longmatan	159768	319927	4759074	2597128	791732	204963
泸县	Luxian	151169	537610	3522561	1591369	1321448	30758
合江县	Hejiang	88053	421023	3014355	1297222	1066309	5541
叙永县	Xuyong	76160	450178	1592146	961773	790640	29692

12-10 续表 1 continued

单位：万元 (10 000 yuan)

县(市、区)	Counties (Municipalities, Districts)	地方一般公共预算收入 Local Government Public-budgetary Revenue	一般公共预算支出 General Public Budget Expenditure	年末金融机构各项存款余额 Total Deposits Balances of Financial Institutions	年末金融机构各项贷款余额 Total Loans Balances of Financial Institutions	社会消费品零售总额 Total Retail Sales of Consumer Goods	出口总额 Total Exports
古蔺县	Gulin	160544	550156	1738389	1408424	492588	701
德阳市	**Deyang**						
旌阳区	Jinyang	137514	265257	10376304	6420574	2330606	158200
罗江区	Luojiang	40223	134350	1043421	560301	332493	28600
中江县	Zhongjiang	106113	498142	4358001	1675276	1847572	66300
广汉市	Guanghan	200882	385130	5069763	2982635	1757010	240900
什邡市	Shifang	187813	318920	2754777	1510300	995649	152500
绵竹市	Mianzhu	190019	340495	3341480	1274029	942647	281200
绵阳市	**Mianyang**						
涪城区	Hucheng	208449	290911	19987555	11680052	4726515	85672
游仙区	Youxian	96067	265817	2147057	1254668	1041489	2376
安州区	Anzhou	66103	234335	1999440	1149803	765391	2413
三台县	Santai	101963	582548	4100828	1724437	1774444	3360
盐亭县	Yanting	37026	341409	1742289	806257	655665	1611
梓潼县	Zitong	26237	193425	1241033	697177	477515	687
北川县	Beichuan	55062	261360	1201763	1098667	203292	112
平武县	Pingwu	27398	189460	852946	628850	174462	
江油市	Jiangyou	207990	508933	5214933	2632557	1675994	2785
广元市	**Guangyuan**						
利州区	Lizhou	70385	273768	5948274	3607763	1655322	23401
昭化区	Zhaohua	21867	232040	862110	511319	244733	172
朝天区	Chaotian	24177	238353	568083	440959	203960	2654
旺苍县	Wangcang	48745	298778	1522706	710536	468214	746
青川县	Qingchuan	19820	223294	906063	594473	218037	213
剑阁县	Jiange	45515	473331	1963025	876808	559352	57
苍溪县	Cangxi	54916	450634	3030299	1403498	703698	6077
遂宁市	**Suining**						
船山区	Chuanshan	175003	618216	6551088	5354961	1942147	117113
安居区	Anju	71039	350172	1728543	895279	699370	1932
蓬溪县	Pengxi	51822	420917	1953094	987389	712425	1416
射洪县	Shehong	116904	476085	3686192	1982935	1668508	18209
大英县	Daying	63521	259784	1800846	1186137	684812	292
内江市	**Neijiang**						
内江市中区	Neijiang Downtown	52300	261606			1519896	25289
东兴区	Dongxing	90914	358064			766708	16304
威远县	Weiyuan	90616	308704	2531013	1610596	1040900	26978
资中县	Zizhong	91129	488416	3688719	1624396	969045	3129
隆昌市	Longchang	92086	346364	2783729	1387297	1088609	44043
乐山市	**Leshan**						
乐山市中区	Leshan Downtown	125369	235482	8987768	7115784	1722866	171600
沙湾区	Shawan	76015	126578	825183	954501	392495	200

12-10 续表 2 continued

单位：万元 (10 000 yuan)

县(市、区)	Counties (Municipalities, Districts)	地方一般公共预算收入 Local Government Public-budgetary Revenue	一般公共预算支出 General Public Budget Expenditure	年末金融机构各项存款余额 Total Deposits Balances of Financial Institutions	年末金融机构各项贷款余额 Total Loans Balances of Financial Institutions	社会消费品零售总额 Total Retail Sales of Consumer Goods	出口总额 Total Exports
五通桥区	Wutongqiao	50525	141962	1430707	760839	655090	300400
金口河区	Jinkouhe	21746	87877	73363	44478	107057	
犍为县	Qianwei	66892	254821	1998523	1301250	667659	5500
井研县	Jingyan	36379	178444	1452319	698328	466315	23700
夹江县	Jiajiang	82030	236738	2205668	1138958	680519	
沐川县	Muchuan	32119	184071	729079	456071	300784	14700
峨边县	Ebian	34233	214330	586875	758783	187801	200
马边县	Mabian	38014	252175	578087	284678	206813	
峨眉山市	Emeishan	161027	277428	3366962	2095607	1285270	63100
南充市	**Nanchong**						
顺庆区	Shunqing	177996	448578	10851122	8091089	2448032	1904
高坪区	Gaoping	74730	421256	2121572	1444035	976702	39342
嘉陵区	Jialing	88465	445281	2033044	1513556	685348	13379
南部县	Nanbu	100789	495882	3483829	1647601	1149572	3727
营山县	Yingshan	78853	581738	3537788	1411275	986370	327
蓬安县	Pengan	60908	364768	2290256	828483	646032	82
仪陇县	Yilong	79091	544887	3257447	1606079	978222	7325
西充县	Xichong	70340	373765	2110913	1099135	675902	1264
阆中市	Langzhong	117312	481899	3240591	1970463	1053646	187
眉山市	**Meishan**						
东坡区	Dongpo	205966	389028	8552500	4425800	1537625	88813
彭山区	Pengshan	151301	282525	2314239	1075128	586244	37750
仁寿县	Renshou	283109	740702	6376063	3098642	1841445	242
洪雅县	Hongya	91091	230523	1860869	1034381	460116	29247
丹棱县	Danling	38956	112566	893831	325344	258659	17053
青神县	Qingshen	50318	146018	946990	471540	280161	13317
宜宾市	**Yibin**						
翠屏区	Cuiping	258968	428652	16414624	7775601	3201610	543123
南溪区	Nanxi	100613	331881	1428021	1078524	711814	14221
叙州区	Xuzhou	132603	482287	3028888	2449907	1123195	17471
江安县	Jiangan	98598	263009	1558787	855300	808359	8903
长宁县	Changning	69903	241291	1175980	841472	885695	15663
高县	Gaoxian	61666	287637	1376035	640244	617263	3222
珙县	Gongxian	89309	264378	1271651	740571	657312	477
筠连县	Junlian	71819	276524	996265	565028	476382	1708
兴文县	Xingwen	80167	313178	1238779	741194	565058	92
屏山县	Pingshan	74492	238764	1272153	681283	260045	2618
广安市	**Guangan**						
广安区	Guanganqu	80819	411777	7419105	3342271	1225944	14256
前锋区	Qianfeng	53596	224302			337826	98072
岳池县	Yuechi	132832	543888	3648089	1367996	1089368	26562

12-10 续表 3 continued

单位：万元 (10 000 yuan)

县(市、区)	Counties (Municipalities, Districts)	地方一般公共预算收入 Local Government Public-budgetary Revenue	一般公共预算支出 General Public Budget Expenditure	年末金融机构各项存款余额 Total Deposits Balances of Financial Institutions	年末金融机构各项贷款余额 Total Loans Balances of Financial Institutions	社会消费品零售总额 Total Retail Sales of Consumer Goods	出口总额 Total Exports
武胜县	Wusheng	131203	387682	2896782	1309754	828717	28316
邻水县	Linshui	116757	531566	2896674	1157460	1089055	39966
华蓥市	Huaying	80047	264875	1822293	918439	429181	48028
达州市	**Dazhou**						
通川区	Tongchuan	86043	283095	10484970	5419474	1696382	3481
达川区	Dachuan	146559	662776	3411420	2368569	1435559	26051
宣汉县	Xuanhan	187517	692967	3710543	1675729	1339197	4639
开江县	Kaijiang	50013	310342	2043189	778288	721136	4797
大竹县	Dazhu	142888	486666	4010302	1853680	1430126	6081
渠县	Quxian	115654	644811	3884080	1834474	1631758	6154
万源市	Wanyuan	44961	409286	1726355	1098881	642834	3487
雅安市	**Yaan**						
雨城区	Yucheng	28416	148344	5054924	3007641	692847	4822
名山区	Mingshan	20111	117471	1393423	654183	348695	17
荥经县	Yingjing	27131	91706	859372	394084	290938	12
汉源县	Hanyuan	52069	159151	1469226	712347	381321	532
石棉县	Shimian	56202	119528	723613	654612	227220	147
天全县	Tianquan	20117	95748	829637	625426	244383	1153
芦山县	Lushan	16542	86915	558472	289004	139472	803
宝兴县	Baoxing	21430	80486	368658	240862	104197	4761
巴中市	**Bazhong**						
巴州区	Bazhou	78715	435546	4273586	2912414	1061065	4450
恩阳区	Enyang	61560	440303	1443568	802984	253871	1081
通江县	Tongjiang	46180	578176	2064356	982613	652679	939
南江县	Nanjiang	76011	495132	2328851	1156513	519654	909
平昌县	Pingchang	81808	643490	2319676	1309791	727202	3516
资阳市	**Ziyang**						
雁江区	Yanjiang	154416	423748	7644069	4193512	1399552	60099
安岳县	Anyue	131584	517292	4024352	1724495	1535957	12537
乐至县	Lezhi	89633	348315	2519090	1150907	854292	9107
阿坝州	**Aba**						
马尔康市	Maerkang	22129	134378	2546259	807337	100529	
汶川县	Wenchuan	34198	167767	689926	384060	102083	1947
理县	Lixian	12815	109286	320633	232436	49533	
茂县	Maoxian	18671	196309	468102	268524	91673	262
松潘县	Songpan	8367	205550	327061	139192	42513	
九寨沟县	Jiuzhaigou	9606	275680	447642	401788	100523	4
金川县	Jinchuan	7878	165320	340389	93468	53219	
小金县	Xiaojin	7548	168569	368157	213362	46301	35
黑水县	Heishui	8677	148043	255024	139558	42020	
壤塘县	Rangtang	2037	179298	168731	39889	22838	

12-10 续表 4 continued

单位：万元 (10 000 yuan)

县(市、区)	Counties (Municipalities, Districts)	地方一般公共预算收入 Local Government Public-budgetary Revenue	一般公共预算支出 General Public Budget Expenditure	年末金融机构各项存款余额 Total Deposits Balances of Financial Institutions	年末金融机构各项贷款余额 Total Loans Balances of Financial Institutions	社会消费品零售总额 Total Retail Sales of Consumer Goods	出口总额 Total Exports
阿坝县	Abaxian	5336	202505	245121	64282	49263	
若尔盖县	Ruoergai	6542	182078	222958	120279	56087	
红原县	Hongyuan	4559	145981	127137	91379	36107	
甘孜州	**Ganzi**						
康定市	Kangding	38301	217710	2628939	1911590	227364	
泸定县	Luding	17305	123714	556774	256907	138183	
丹巴县	Danba	10807	154568	365109	364910	61870	
九龙县	Jiulong	19840	133539	218679	231985	34633	
雅江县	Yajiang	21347	183315	244828	75502	41333	
道孚县	Daofu	7689	170456	223261	29972	28670	
炉霍县	Luhuo	5467	165331	204603	30189	38259	
甘孜县	Ganzixian	7082	204218	249531	43648	74949	
新龙县	Xinlong	5352	202124	163467	34161	19364	
德格县	Dege	6006	240466	214974	33045	28484	
白玉县	Baiyu	13589	199393	244436	53641	34167	
石渠县	Shiqu	5054	396361	236447	37693	45442	
色达县	Seda	7196	242223	346998	39482	27858	
理塘县	Litang	10692	229599	260275	56904	68360	
巴塘县	Batang	8891	203861	308274	76201	56931	
乡城县	Xiangcheng	6080	123938	178449	103200	29995	
稻城县	Daocheng	12925	149183	189328	83715	31410	
得荣县	Derong	4737	112211	149749	73453	16366	
凉山州	**Liangshan**						
西昌市	Xichang	439303	993395	7644327	4740890	2836633	874
木里县	Muli	62905	317767	488632	322691	87488	
盐源县	Yanyuan	78187	421553	836945	259982	261279	
德昌县	Dechang	55568	193098	841791	232080	321768	1595
会理县	Huili	87703	256589	1590326	710304	689840	869
会东县	Huidong	100906	292680	1078007	272014	562329	1027
宁南县	Ningnan	42452	158389	587611	157242	252537	6630
普格县	Puge	10078	293165	338741	91427	110438	24765
布拖县	Buto	11534	304159	338995	71528	56740	
金阳县	Jinyang	24627	369663	409741	65402	83762	
昭觉县	Zhaojue	14056	399108	591842	90646	89813	
喜德县	Xide	8884	308832	415302	89641	91035	369
冕宁县	Mianning	80080	279670	1063250	418977	504421	527
越西县	Yuexi	16188	401235	741605	204553	205329	64
甘洛县	Ganluo	22075	308287	499603	86301	120120	
美姑县	Meigu	8834	364464	476178	86235	70553	
雷波县	Leibo	87581	442665	692091	173611	151691	131

12-11 各县(市、区)公路里程、电话用户和利用外资情况(2018年)

Basic Statistics on Highway, Telephone Subscribers and Utilization of Foreign Capital by Counties (Municipalities, Districts)(2018)

县(市、区)	Counties (Municipalities, Districts)	公路里程 (公里) Length of Highway (km)	#等级公路 Express-way and Class I to IV Highways	固定电话用户 (户) Local Telephone Subscribers (year-end) (subscribers)	移动电话用户 (户) Number of Mobile Telephones Subscribers (year-end) (subscribers)	实际利用外资金额 (万元) Foreign Capital Actually Used (10 000 yuan)
成都市	**Chengdu**					
锦江区	Jinjiang					
青羊区	Qingyang	217	214			122401
金牛区	Jinniu					91752
武侯区	Wuhou					108039
成华区	Chenghua	69	61			114704
龙泉驿区	Longquanyi	1455	1409	274328	1068235	96489
青白江区	Qingbaijiang	1021	1021	127574	713334	25534
新都区	Xindu	1099	1009	359964	1782824	23578
温江区	Wenjiang	833	806	224407	1125192	18101
双流区	Shuangliu			672080	1575250	63746
郫都区	Pidu	1320	1262	206067	680289	18100
金堂县	Jintang	4279	4513	132517	812000	11691
大邑县	Dayi	1856	1819	132059	615790	5491
蒲江县	Pujiang	1583	1583	92965	284202	7888
新津县	Xinjin	844	844	89997	455298	28176
都江堰市	Dujiangyan	1584	1584	194387	907077	5471
彭州市	Pengzhou	2746	2718	157864	1008223	11801
邛崃市	Qionglai	3340	3207	107921	677102	5498
崇州市	Chongzhou	1873	1733	167894	341252	11730
简阳市	Jianyang	2299	2142			1429
自贡市	**Zigong**					
自流井区	Ziliujing	340	308	321773	974247	498
贡井区	Gongjing	572	530	50541	154781	6865
大安区	Daan	816	768	49979	202364	3
沿滩区	Yantan	762	719	45441	183110	
荣县	Rongxian	1738	1648	151603	462307	
富顺县	Fushun	2326	2174	83511	670804	
攀枝花市	**Panzhihua**					
东区	East District	206	194	130421	912854	668
西区	West District	149	144	60019	176813	1010
仁和区	Renhe	1024	899	90593	177427	1009
米易县	Miyi	1395	999	43246	160573	402
盐边县	Yanbian	1842	1499	27322	146173	308
泸州市	**Luzhou**					
江阳区	Jiangyang	1025	920			5062
纳溪区	Nanxi	1249	1119	53852	179021	378
龙马潭区	Longmatan	719	305	98962	734178	9679
泸县	Luxian	4827	3870	85492	869381	9796
合江县	Hejiang	4162	1941	51000	673884	378
叙永县	Xuyong	3170	2830	67590	508956	405

12-11 续表 1 continued

县(市、区)	Counties (Municipalities, Districts)	公路里程 (公里) Length of Highway (km)	#等级公路 Express-way and Class I to IV Highways	固定电话用户 (户) Local Telephone Subscribers (year-end) (subscribers)	移动电话用户 (户) Number of Mobile Telephones Subscribers (year-end) (subscribers)	实际利用外资金额 (万元) Foreign Capital Actually Used (10 000 yuan)
古蔺县	Gulin	3174	2830	81967	602134	1829
德阳市	**Deyang**					
旌阳区	Jinyang	863	863	227614	1279162	32043
罗江区	Luojiang	628	578	39671	225213	2500
中江县	Zhongjiang	2846	2603	123466	832261	5500
广汉市	Guanghan	1228	1205	146853	696432	11560
什邡市	Shifang	1260	1139	73249	470755	3386
绵竹市	Mianzhu	1522	1473	90130	493970	5857
绵阳市	**Mianyang**					
涪城区	Hucheng	1268	1155	246578	1606603	
游仙区	Youxian	1950	1946	250476	1021538	
安州区	Anzhou	2144	2144	73166	423234	
三台县	Santai	3274	2881	137099	919153	
盐亭县	Yanting	2453	1659	49527	337713	
梓潼县	Zitong	2138	1774	44577	292624	
北川县	Beichuan	2695	2296	31303	208909	
平武县	Pingwu	1569	1449	17632	154448	
江油市	Jiangyou	2656	1945	184343	992627	
广元市	**Guangyuan**					
利州区	Lizhou	2221	1991	177804	832415	7590
昭化区	Zhaohua	2437	1712	20539	121875	
朝天区	Chaotian	2206	1329	24381	136070	6633
旺苍县	Wangcang	3018	2249	56449	313676	
青川县	Qingchuan	2473	2117	27076	168540	
剑阁县	Jiange	3711	3077	66521	370528	
苍溪县	Cangxi	3906	3435	111863	490761	990
遂宁市	**Suining**					
船山区	Chuanshan	1190	1104	143649	1030633	21486
安居区	Anju	1688	1535	27108	330418	1203
蓬溪县	Pengxi	1922	1775	39386	369635	1400
射洪县	Shehong	2704	1969	97652	678579	2460
大英县	Daying	1479	1418	36021	336034	1250
内江市	**Neijiang**					
内江市中区	Neijiang Downtown					
东兴区	Dongxing					
威远县	Weiyuan					
资中县	Zizhong					
隆昌市	Longchang					
乐山市	**Leshan**					
乐山市中区	Leshan Downtown	849	780	221591	1176632	3305
沙湾区	Shawan	594	594	28107	188322	

12-11 续表 2 continued

县(市、区)	Counties (Municipalities, Districts)	公路里程 (公里) Length of Highway (km)	#等级公路 Express-way and Class I to IV Highways	固定电话用户 (户) Local Telephone Subscribers (year-end) (subscribers)	移动电话用户 (户) Number of Mobile Telephones Subscribers (year-end) (subscribers)	实际利用外资金额 (万元) Foreign Capital Actually Used (10 000 yuan)
五通桥区	Wutongqiao	696	630	54825	305235	
金口河区	Jinkouhe	326	319	6715	54762	
犍为县	Qianwei	1497	1418	67052	438448	1778
井研县	Jingyan	1127	992	41612	297100	
夹江县	Jiajiang	1126	1089	73143	388828	
沐川县	Muchuan	3174	3174	31777	244051	
峨边县	Ebian	1091	1003	13221	123245	
马边县	Mabian	846	846	25100	171377	682
峨眉山市	Emeishan	833	819	106654	523977	
南充市	**Nanchong**					
顺庆区	Shunqing	941	941	223429	1267162	2768
高坪区	Gaoping	1351	1351	113312	554582	1830
嘉陵区	Jialing	2512	2439	104806	489739	2157
南部县	Nanbu	4244	4076	154055	769851	266
营山县	Yingshan	2593	2593	94803	533778	245
蓬安县	Pengan	2131	2131	81617	411659	292
仪陇县	Yilong	3055	3055	114205	661771	782
西充县	Xichong	2328	2260	66177	379721	250
阆中市	Langzhong	3536	2816	138199	638075	277
眉山市	**Meishan**					
东坡区	Dongpo	1462	1369	180553	1081497	
彭山区	Pengshan	658	593	58167	386470	3803
仁寿县	Renshou	3215	2163	183456	1108604	4135
洪雅县	Hongya	1460	1214			385
丹棱县	Danling	503	492	36200	170000	200
青神县	Qingshen	539	539	37000	182400	204
宜宾市	**Yibin**					
翠屏区	Cuiping	1452	1376	239232	1278279	3300
南溪区	Nanxi	1374	1357	45980	315216	355
叙州区	Xuzhou	3769	3463	100862	705755	
江安县	Jiangan	2305	2305	50665	376808	
长宁县	Changning	1923	1857	53026	331812	
高县	Gaoxian	1681	1556	51122	384427	
珙县	Gongxian	2012	1900	49883	349533	
筠连县	Junlian	1521	1320	41557	308309	
兴文县	Xingwen	1383	1383	54957	338338	
屏山县	Pingshan	1657	1532	31565	240964	
广安市	**Guangan**					
广安区	Guanganqu	2321	1927	151026	872588	3032
前锋区	Qianfeng	1157	972	28430	205653	9508
岳池县	Yuechi	4400	4400	113011	696191	4354

12-11 续表 3 continued

县(市、区)	Counties (Municipalities, Districts)	公路里程 (公里) Length of Highway (km)	#等级公路 Express-way and Class I to IV Highways	固定电话用户 (户) Local Telephone Subscribers (year-end) (subscribers)	移动电话用户 (户) Number of Mobile Telephones Subscribers (year-end) (subscribers)	实际利用外资金额 (万元) Foreign Capital Actually Used (10 000 yuan)
武胜县	Wusheng	2756	2721	80630	514663	3914
邻水县	Linshui	3811	3789	110707	632002	3934
华蓥市	Huaying	1250	1247	58603	319626	8268
达州市	**Dazhou**					
通川区	Tongchuan	1531	1354	144671	941153	
达川区	Dachuan	2871	2818	120255	819522	
宣汉县	Xuanhan	4172	3833	111920	728119	
开江县	Kaijiang	1735	1529	42791	302759	2944
大竹县	Dazhu	3025	2662	94231	650288	152
渠县	Quxian	3004	2729	98954	608198	
万源市	Wanyuan	3229	2869	58304	369646	
雅安市	**Yaan**					
雨城区	Yucheng	966	888	256625	1513852	1000
名山区	Mingshan	797	797	40152	265553	100
荥经县	Yingjing	588	552	17940	159209	100
汉源县	Hanyuan	1510	1494	37392	307473	100
石棉县	Shimian	877	850	29702	250842	4500
天全县	Tianquan	772	712	18700	134892	100
芦山县	Lushan	522	512	17904	114607	100
宝兴县	Baoxing	670	544	10300	63477	100
巴中市	**Bazhong**					
巴州区	Bazhou	3152	2942	129700	928600	127
恩阳区	Enyang	2629	2582	35194	248353	130
通江县	Tongjiang	5075	4677	46793	783206	130
南江县	Nanjiang	5359	5359	70698	520040	127
平昌县	Pingchang	6582	5388	53984	501652	271
资阳市	**Ziyang**					
雁江区	Yanjiang	3972	3576	167477	955256	8000
安岳县	Anyue	6110	5873	142170	855863	100
乐至县	Lezhi	2265	1979	56997	427729	100
阿坝州	**Aba**					
马尔康市	Maerkang	1159	1159	23376	83908	
汶川县	Wenchuan	873	866	21707	111930	300
理县	Lixian	679	679	13066	54768	
茂县	Maoxian	1292	1292	22704	112608	
松潘县	Songpan	791	791	20826	73681	
九寨沟县	Jiuzhaigou	879	879	25726	83809	
金川县	Jinchuan	1303	1303	10818	57247	
小金县	Xiaojin	1185	1185	15518	71607	
黑水县	Heishui	1429	1429	8850	35007	
壤塘县	Rangtang	717	717	4336	24184	100

12-11 续表 4 continued

县(市、区)	Counties (Municipalities, Districts)	公路里程 (公里) Length of Highway (km)	#等级公路 Express-way and Class I to IV Highways	固定电话用户 (户) Local Telephone Subscribers (year-end) (subscribers)	移动电话用户 (户) Number of Mobile Telephones Subscribers (year-end) (subscribers)	实际利用外资金额 (万元) Foreign Capital Actually Used (10 000 yuan)
阿坝县	Abaxian	998	998	10541	63081	
若尔盖县	Ruoergai	1212	1212	10613	57364	
红原县	Hongyuan	962	962	8091	40423	
甘孜州	**Ganzi**					
康定市	Kangding	2645	2619	41646	211675	
泸定县	Luding	1660	1640	20022	90294	
丹巴县	Danba	1526	1521	8964	49869	
九龙县	Jiulong	1341	1268	8348	50662	
雅江县	Yajiang	1953	1674	7126	34886	
道孚县	Daofu	1512	1419	5738	34369	
炉霍县	Luhuo	1866	1768	6270	36665	
甘孜县	Ganzixian	1983	1983	6935	68258	
新龙县	Xinlong	1875	1875	2719	24039	
德格县	Dege	2392	2352	4109	40408	
白玉县	Baiyu	1990	1990	5062	34795	
石渠县	Shiqu	3945	3945	3242	45338	
色达县	Seda	1863	1823	4562	44142	
理塘县	Litang	1901	1864	7257	46278	
巴塘县	Batang	2168	2051	5986	39040	
乡城县	Xiangcheng	1652	1230	3989	27539	
稻城县	Daocheng	1405	1405	8743	29000	
得荣县	Derong	1155	1155	2824	21562	
凉山州	**Liangshan**					
西昌市	Xichang	1536	1148	185419	1277000	7
木里县	Muli	2774	2356	7722	79685	
盐源县	Yanyuan	2777	2511	28968	260723	
德昌县	Dechang	911	866	26954	210675	15
会理县	Huili	2721	2100	66052	434174	
会东县	Huidong	2294	2174	35829	316618	
宁南县	Ningnan	1097	1024	22261	169813	
普格县	Puge	938	857	12415	103961	
布拖县	Buto	1051	1010	5759	79871	
金阳县	Jinyang	1423	1322	7762	83059	
昭觉县	Zhaojue	1352	1277	12512	121418	1690
喜德县	Xide	1242	1212	8187	75832	
冕宁县	Mianning	1440	1394	41447	311514	
越西县	Yuexi	1073	1040	20834	188372	109
甘洛县	Ganluo	1101	984	15433	138508	
美姑县	Meigu	1737	1415	9533	121773	
雷波县	Leibo	2119	1995	22182	173636	

12-12 各县(市、区)教育情况(2018年)
Basic Statistics on Education of Counties (Municipalities, Districts)(2018)

县(市、区)	Counties (Municipalities, Districts)	小学学校数(个) Number of Primary Schools (unit)	小学在校学生(人) Students Enrollment of Primary Schools (person)	小学专任教师(人) Full-time Teachers in Primary Schools (person)	普通中学学校数(个) Number of Regular Secondary Schools (unit)	普通中学在校学生(人) Students Enrollment of Regular Secondary Schools (person)	普通中学专任教师(人) Full-time Teachers in Regular Secondary Schools (person)
成都市	**Chengdu**						
锦江区	Jinjiang	35	43321	2125	14	24956	2207
青羊区	Qingyang	32	53923	2973	15	21949	1778
金牛区	Jinniu	47	70291	3739	27	33166	2643
武侯区	Wuhou	41	50246	2704	34	39790	3399
成华区	Chenghua	28	56038	2961	20	24682	1962
龙泉驿区	Longquanyi	35	54606	3347	21	31805	2819
青白江区	Qingbaijiang	11	22487	1214	14	16914	1435
新都区	Xindu	33	78387	3233	40	39414	3928
温江区	Wenjiang	16	39600	2287	17	20247	1713
双流区	Shuangliu	44	89066	5194	52	56120	5499
郫都区	Pidu	13	55374	2256	39	29704	2419
金堂县	Jintang	49	46433	2726	27	34341	2609
大邑县	Dayi	17	24706	876	20	16599	2010
蒲江县	Pujiang	18	10003	1021	13	9975	865
新津县	Xinjin	15	15967	890	16	11402	1174
都江堰市	Dujiangyan	27	35389	2348	26	23882	2262
彭州市	Pengzhou	22	39683	2180	33	23175	2468
邛崃市	Qionglai	32	27378	1556	30	22270	1780
崇州市	Chongzhou	37	31330	1827	11	13242	1257
简阳市	Jianyang	26	63434	1668	7	15252	5104
自贡市	**Zigong**						
自流井区	Ziliujing	19	29028	1633	15	24714	1715
贡井区	Gongjing	15	14339	748	12	8614	589
大安区	Daan	16	19278	1041	13	11567	733
沿滩区	Yantan	12	19882	1046	13	10782	638
荣县	Rongxian	25	29964	1753	28	22697	1749
富顺县	Fushun	34	60516	3414	58	50358	3356
攀枝花市	**Panzhihua**						
东区	East District	10	20571	1227	20	23325	1835
西区	West District	7	6590	557	6	5185	484
仁和区	Renhe	14	13127	984	13	15201	1196
米易县	Miyi	13	14028	1079	6	9862	892
盐边县	Yanbian	16	13606	1044	7	8462	744
泸州市	**Luzhou**						
江阳区	Jiangyang	23	46352	2629	30	46650	3070
纳溪区	Nanxi	16	29324	1606	14	24555	1485
龙马潭区	Longmatan	24	28327	2000	18	39476	2673
泸县	Luxian	37	64210	3458	56	69577	4103
合江县	Hejiang	75	64551		25	52670	
叙永县	Xuyong	30	53570	2756	35	41614	2455

12-12 续表 1 continued

县(市、区)	Counties (Municipalities, Districts)	小学学校数(个) Number of Primary Schools (unit)	小学在校学生(人) Students Enrollment of Primary Schools (person)	小学专任教师(人) Full-time Teachers in Primary Schools (person)	普通中学学校数(个) Number of Regular Secondary Schools (unit)	普通中学在校学生(人) Students Enrollment of Regular Secondary Schools (person)	普通中学专任教师(人) Full-time Teachers in Regular Secondary Schools (person)
古蔺县	Gulin	31	70947	3619	41	44963	2950
德阳市	**Deyang**						
旌阳区	Jinyang	37	41539	2505	27	34207	2661
罗江区	Luojiang	22	10974	606	8	7751	690
中江县	Zhongjiang	182	68246	3630	55	45380	3280
广汉市	Guanghan	39	26640	1640	27	17309	1834
什邡市	Shifang	29	18095	1326	16	12751	1381
绵竹市	Mianzhu	30	19574	1430	13	12308	1116
绵阳市	**Mianyang**						
涪城区	Hucheng	44	74234	2322	40	93199	7054
游仙区	Youxian	31	30920	1268	19	27608	2229
安州区	Anzhou	20	22529	1061	18	15114	1413
三台县	Santai	108	63501	3114	72	42736	4209
盐亭县	Yanting	47	19592	1473	21	13764	1629
梓潼县	Zitong	34	14668	976	9	9382	844
北川县	Beichuan	25	11642	688	11	8141	764
平武县	Pingwu	39	6671	704	8	4681	536
江油市	Jiangyou	61	36713	2007	21	26952	2436
广元市	**Guangyuan**						
利州区	Lizhou	37	39703	2414	28	35537	2920
昭化区	Zhaohua	25	6308	808	13	4357	594
朝天区	Chaotian	22	7403	761	9	6011	538
旺苍县	Wangcang	37	21657	1815	20	17717	1445
青川县	Qingchuan	27	9371	1073	21	6192	946
剑阁县	Jiange	61	29981	2083	22	19669	1844
苍溪县	Cangxi	55	39720	2601	41	27463	2155
遂宁市	**Suining**						
船山区	Chuanshan	36	52624	3049	31	39498	3061
安居区	Anju	42	28997	1994	27	21932	1976
蓬溪县	Pengxi	28	26156	1956	30	17392	1687
射洪县	Shehong	60	42297	2955	44	32883	3215
大英县	Daying	30	27847	1583	26	16698	1375
内江市	**Neijiang**						
内江市中区	Neijiang Downtown	31	31902	1680	26	35221	1889
东兴区	Dongxing	52	43822	2039	31	29226	2978
威远县	Weiyuan	53	35909	2136	36	28048	2687
资中县	Zizhong	81	57947	2369	53	51888	4366
隆昌市	Longchang	56	43892	2270	30	35189	2250
乐山市	**Leshan**						
乐山市中区	Leshan Downtown	30	37607	1789	42	27974	2497
沙湾区	Shawan	7	6757	394	17	5694	600

12-12 续表 2 continued

县(市、区)	Counties (Municipalities, Districts)	小学学校数(个) Number of Primary Schools (unit)	小学在校学生(人) Students Enrollment of Primary Schools (person)	小学专任教师(人) Full-time Teachers in Primary Schools (person)	普通中学学校数(个) Number of Regular Secondary Schools (unit)	普通中学在校学生(人) Students Enrollment of Regular Secondary Schools (person)	普通中学专任教师(人) Full-time Teachers in Regular Secondary Schools (person)
五通桥区	Wutongqiao	17	10041	657	16	6687	718
金口河区	Jinkouhe	8	2544	186	4	1404	158
犍为县	Qianwei	28	25041	1423	29	19062	1678
井研县	Jingyan	28	16814	1114	24	12220	1087
夹江县	Jiajiang	24	13485	886	19	8755	985
沐川县	Muchuan	17	15237	541	17	10201	731
峨边县	Ebian	16	11748	587	14	5524	473
马边县	Mabian	31	22595	1096	11	12334	686
峨眉山市	Emeishan	21	19231	1143	18	14615	1404
南充市	**Nanchong**						
顺庆区	Shunqing	33	44534	1811	33	42803	3339
高坪区	Gaoping	34	35722	1792	36	33903	2797
嘉陵区	Jialing	30	31168	1540	44	24312	2980
南部县	Nanbu	26	57270	2064	84	47402	5268
营山县	Yingshan	25	48363	1667	68	34981	3916
蓬安县	Pengan	36	31455	1658	39	23791	2377
仪陇县	Yilong	49	54126	2382	65	45247	4590
西充县	Xichong	11	22965	949	43	17761	2684
阆中市	Langzhong	21	35049	1319	76	28731	3869
眉山市	**Meishan**						
东坡区	Dongpo	53	45020	2480	47	29955	3037
彭山区	Pengshan	15	14456	857	15	8625	805
仁寿县	Renshou	58	69711	4562	80	33204	6264
洪雅县	Hongya	22	15839	688	16	9843	1100
丹棱县	Danling	12	7446	385	7	4119	416
青神县	Qingshen	17	7271	574	7	4797	456
宜宾市	**Yibin**						
翠屏区	Cuiping	30	68925	3517	41	53508	4267
南溪区	Nanxi	18	27045	1617	17	22187	1492
叙州区	Xuzhou	57	61810	4035	53	48529	3681
江安县	Jiangan	48	32569	1882	28	22732	1533
长宁县	Changning	27	29912	1561	21	19153	1196
高县	Gaoxian	58	34866	1806	20	22855	1503
珙县	Gongxian	13	31029	1652	21	17061	1265
筠连县	Junlian	10	34896	1856	34	22971	1561
兴文县	Xingwen	32	35034	2121	27	29107	1943
屏山县	Pingshan	13	21315	1302	18	13257	1038
广安市	**Guangan**						
广安区	Guanganqu	25	47372	2781	54	50717	3909
前锋区	Qianfeng	14	16904	1117	22	12570	1040
岳池县	Yuechi	55	57040	3921	67	42568	3635

12-12 续表 3 continued

县(市、区)	Counties (Municipalities, Districts)	小学学校数(个) Number of Primary Schools (unit)	小学在校学生(人) Students Enrollment of Primary Schools (person)	小学专任教师(人) Full-time Teachers in Primary Schools (person)	普通中学学校数(个) Number of Regular Secondary Schools (unit)	普通中学在校学生(人) Students Enrollment of Regular Secondary Schools (person)	普通中学专任教师(人) Full-time Teachers in Regular Secondary Schools (person)
武胜县	Wusheng	51	38601	2766	51	32220	2884
邻水县	Linshui	33	56521	2902	60	48075	3654
华蓥市	Huaying	14	22868	1361	22	15445	1303
达州市	**Dazhou**						
通川区	Tongchuan	171	48448	2581	34	35823	2281
达川区	Dachuan	188	64478	4261	76	65201	4068
宣汉县	Xuanhan	455	91951	4961	69	66018	4002
开江县	Kaijiang	146	33729	2177	28	26911	1793
大竹县	Dazhu	154	65952	4144	51	54965	3601
渠县	Quxian	155	55798	5397	99	51414	4544
万源市	Wanyuan	211	36687	2167	36	28026	1835
雅安市	**Yaan**						
雨城区	Yucheng	20	18895	1182	22	16012	1303
名山区	Mingshan	17	15512	830	16	10776	846
荥经县	Yingjing	25	7729	599	6	7520	484
汉源县	Hanyuan	32	17711	1186	12	13593	994
石棉县	Shimian	18	10207	628	6	6010	418
天全县	Tianquan	24	9319	745	8	7386	556
芦山县	Lushan	10	6019	537	13	4912	487
宝兴县	Baoxing	12	2696	352	5	1811	217
巴中市	**Bazhong**						
巴州区	Bazhou	24	45536	3259	44	32149	2683
恩阳区	Enyang	22	20840	1626	18	20411	1635
通江县	Tongjiang	73	39659	3219	30	34797	2998
南江县	Nanjiang	55	34057	2694	38	31690	2467
平昌县	Pingchang	25	51386	4461	60	43877	3828
资阳市	**Ziyang**						
雁江区	Yanjiang	81	61183	2684	63	48826	4144
安岳县	Anyue	43	81384	2812	91	68849	5402
乐至县	Lezhi	56	33658	1905	41	24696	2263
阿坝州	**Aba**						
马尔康市	Maerkang	18	3480	406	5	3714	354
汶川县	Wenchuan	14	5214	661	5	6194	651
理县	Lixian	12	2063	463	3	1356	211
茂县	Maoxian	23	6854	669	4	5219	540
松潘县	Songpan	22	4263	507	8	2281	282
九寨沟县	Jiuzhaigou	18	4563	508	3	3414	355
金川县	Jinchuan	23	3584	435	5	2099	313
小金县	Xiaojin	23	4080	550	5	3507	370
黑水县	Heishui	12	2762	356	2	1709	166
壤塘县	Rangtang	12	5228	363	4	1564	126

12-12 续表 4 continued

县(市、区)	Counties (Municipalities, Districts)	小学学校数(个) Number of Primary Schools (unit)	小学在校学生(人) Students Enrollment of Primary Schools (person)	小学专任教师(人) Full-time Teachers in Primary Schools (person)	普通中学学校数(个) Number of Regular Secondary Schools (unit)	普通中学在校学生(人) Students Enrollment of Regular Secondary Schools (person)	普通中学专任教师(人) Full-time Teachers in Regular Secondary Schools (person)
阿坝县	Abaxian	29	8363	644	2	3589	177
若尔盖县	Ruoergai	23	7592	548	7	5799	392
红原县	Hongyuan	14	5288	421	2	3210	200
甘孜州	**Ganzi**						
康定市	Kangding	25	9029	618	7	8478	627
泸定县	Luding	15	5926	575	8	7298	615
丹巴县	Danba	15	3323	439	5	2822	269
九龙县	Jiulong	33	6385	452	4	4991	304
雅江县	Yajiang	16	4870	339	2	2487	166
道孚县	Daofu	25	4989	358	2	2090	136
炉霍县	Luhuo	13	5790	367	3	2904	188
甘孜县	Ganzixian	25	7564	469	3	3765	292
新龙县	Xinlong	22	4874	387	1	1471	113
德格县	Dege	37	10289	491	2	1702	122
白玉县	Baiyu	17	6703	350	2	1093	91
石渠县	Shiqu	24	10516	588	2	2558	194
色达县	Seda	18	6661	324	1	1471	104
理塘县	Litang	28	8684	567	3	2962	176
巴塘县	Batang	20	5584	469	2	4194	245
乡城县	Xiangcheng	15	2405	277	1	1362	99
稻城县	Daocheng	15	2801	286	2	1221	91
得荣县	Derong	13	1910	259	1	958	97
凉山州	**Liangshan**						
西昌市	Xichang	114	84971	3733	36	56323	3728
木里县	Muli	26	12225	909	9	7391	435
盐源县	Yanyuan	47	38945	1878	14	22366	1419
德昌县	Dechang	23	21282	1083	5	13372	872
会理县	Huili	49	29367	1721	15	21120	1473
会东县	Huidong	49	36309	1822	16	25383	1540
宁南县	Ningnan	35	17534	945	4	10921	718
普格县	Puge	34	31536	1429	5	11883	759
布拖县	Buto	28	35328	1240	5	6516	219
金阳县	Jinyang	38	29152	1207	8	9142	412
昭觉县	Zhaojue	63	47207	1726	12	14886	561
喜德县	Xide	46	28493	1393	7	11179	634
冕宁县	Mianning	43	43002	1998	13	19149	1187
越西县	Yuexi	53	49174	2139	9	17789	952
甘洛县	Ganluo	33	27073	1288	9	11059	651
美姑县	Meigu	54	41528	1544	6	10195	537
雷波县	Leibo	50	33166	1491	11	15912	991

13 农 业

Chapter 13 Agriculture

13-1 农林牧渔业总产值
Gross Output Value of Farming, Forestry, Animal Husbandry and Fishery

单位：亿元 (100 million yuan)

年 份 Year	农林牧渔业总产值 Total	#第一产业 Primary Industry	农 业 Farming	林 业 Forestry	牧 业 Animal Husbandry	渔 业 Fishery
1980	136.92	136.92	98.07	4.21	34.07	0.57
1981	147.02	147.02	105.41	5.34	35.63	0.64
1982	177.53	177.53	133.84	5.81	37.07	0.81
1983	193.77	193.77	142.76	7.02	42.83	1.16
1984	211.93	211.93	151.50	12.21	46.79	1.39
1985	234.82	234.82	161.14	13.09	58.74	1.85
1986	254.33	254.33	168.46	13.18	69.74	2.95
1987	294.59	294.59	187.84	13.66	89.18	3.91
1988	361.11	361.11	213.69	15.99	126.02	5.41
1989	400.40	400.40	238.04	16.75	139.24	6.37
1990	484.31	484.31	301.46	18.51	157.04	7.30
1991	513.43	513.43	317.43	19.43	168.41	8.16
1992	565.62	565.62	344.52	22.23	189.41	9.46
1993	660.69	660.69	389.21	24.90	234.30	12.28
1994	930.80	930.80	521.00	28.48	365.33	15.99
1995	1113.96	1113.96	645.17	34.32	413.84	20.63
1996	1274.32	1274.32	750.07	38.58	461.32	24.35
1997	1395.43	1395.43	798.22	41.31	527.60	28.30
1998	1455.19	1455.19	823.72	45.87	554.15	31.45
1999	1444.86	1444.86	792.80	45.34	572.63	34.09
2000	1483.52	1483.52	785.37	49.13	611.76	37.26
2001	1534.89	1534.90	769.95	50.85	673.10	41.00
2002	1651.53	1651.53	807.43	54.60	743.91	45.59
2003	1784.49	1749.64	804.70	59.26	832.34	53.34
2004	2252.30	2213.72	987.70	62.70	1097.60	65.80
2005	2457.46	2415.81	1037.20	69.94	1230.18	78.49
2006	2602.10	2556.40	1075.08	76.75	1317.41	87.16
2007	3377.00	3317.00	1317.00	106.42	1807.58	86.00
2008	3903.00	3846.00	1608.00	153.21	1980.79	104.00
2009	3689.81	3634.35	1815.98	102.60	1596.72	119.05
2010	4081.81	4007.21	2059.33	160.06	1658.00	129.83
2011	4932.73	4850.72	2454.26	203.29	2046.00	147.16
2012	5433.12	5340.03	2764.90	234.34	2177.02	163.77
2013	5620.27	5510.97	2886.48	249.02	2197.97	177.49
2014	5888.09	5765.79	3068.61	268.54	2236.29	192.35
2015	6377.84	6237.43	3315.51	297.26	2414.15	210.52
2016	6816.92	6656.50	3701.64	329.31	2405.54	220.01
2017	6955.55	6785.64	4004.20	346.80	2199.72	234.92
2018	7195.65	7006.47	4153.71	358.74	2246.08	247.94

注：①本表按当年价格计算；②从2013年起，农业核算执行国家统计局新的《国民经济行业分类》和《三次产业划分规定》；③根据第三次全国农业普查结果对2007年至2017年农林牧渔业总产值及增加值省级数据进行了修订，市(州)级数据待第四次全国经济普查后统一修订(以下有关各表同)。

a) Data of this year are calculated at current prices. b) Since 2013, agricultural accounting has been based on the "Industrial Calssification for National Economic Activities" and "Rules of Clarification of Three Industries" which were newly promulgated by National Statistical Bureau. c) The data of the total output value and added value of agriculture, forestry, animal husbandry and fishery since 2007 to 2017 have been revised according to the results of the third national agricultural census in Sichuan Province, city datas will be revised by uniform according to the results of the fourth national economic census (the same as the following related tables).

13-2 农林牧渔业总产值指数

Indices of Gross Output Value of Farming, Forestry, Animal Husbandry and Fishery

(1952年=100) (1952=100)

年 份 Year	农林牧渔业总产值 Total	农 业 Farming	林 业 Forestry	牧 业 Animal Husbandry	渔 业 Fishery	农林牧渔业服务业 Services
1980	242.2	201.9	373.4	482.6	400.0	
1985	332.7	251.1	933.0	756.5	1272.4	
1990	409.4	290.8	742.2	1104.3	2386.2	
1991	427.6	300.5	742.9	1179.3	2589.7	
1992	445.7	308.2	800.4	1255.7	2831.0	
1993	450.2	299.4	812.4	1341.1	3210.3	
1994	465.3	297.1	859.6	1461.1	3586.2	
1995	504.9	321.2	932.6	1584.8	4369.0	
1996	533.3	338.0	1004.6	1674.3	4893.1	
1997	559.4	351.8	1031.2	1772.2	5481.2	
1998	584.5	361.4	1061.6	1889.9	6126.0	
1999	605.8	368.7	1048.3	1997.8	6855.0	
2000	636.0	379.2	1080.7	2144.1	7717.7	
2001	651.3	369.0	1083.2	2318.2	8521.1	
2002	695.3	387.3	1145.4	2512.5	9551.7	100.0
2003	738.5	394.6	1257.0	2744.7	11309.2	108.0
2004	790.9	410.8	1303.5	3019.2	12756.8	113.9
2005	842.4	421.6	1422.0	3304.8	14382.0	122.1
2006	873.7	416.7	1525.5	3540.1	15689.3	132.2
2007	904.1	436.3	1604.8	3610.9	16944.4	141.7
2008	933.9	447.6	1652.9	3744.5	17961.1	147.7
2009	973.5	468.3	1743.8	3886.8	18889.8	149.7
2010	1017.3	492.2	1841.5	4022.8	19807.8	167.6
2011	1064.1	520.7	2020.1	4127.4	21134.9	183.7
2012	1112.0	545.2	2187.8	4284.2	22572.1	201.2
2013	1149.8	564.8	2378.1	4395.6	23926.4	219.1
2014	1195.8	586.8	2501.8	4567.0	25218.4	239.7
2015	1250.8	618.5	2772.2	4684.6	27502.1	257.9
2016	1300.4	648.6	2911.6	4782.4	28857.6	285.1
2017	1349.9	682.3	3067.9	4839.6	30371.1	315.7
2018	1402.5	713.7	3120.1	4955.7	31859.3	345.7

注：本表按可比价格计算；2003年起按新口径计算；2004年起指数按可比价格缩减法计算。

a) Data in this table are calculated at comparable prices. Since 2003, calculation has been based on the new range. Data have been calculated at comparable prices by deflation approach since 2004.

13-3 各市(州)按产业分农林牧渔业总产值(2018年)
Gross Output Value of Farming, Forestry, Animal Husbandry and Fishery by Industry and Region(2018)

单位：亿元 (100 million yuan)

市(州)	Region	农林牧渔业总产值 Total	#第一产业 Primary Industry	农 业 Farming	林 业 Forestry	牧 业 Animal Husbandry	渔 业 Fishery
全 省	**Sichuan**	**7195.65**	**7006.47**	**4153.71**	**358.74**	**2246.08**	**247.94**
成都市	Chengdu	909.34	883.75	576.99	20.57	254.20	32.00
自贡市	Zigong	245.26	241.76	129.91	17.87	81.83	12.16
攀枝花市	Panzhihua	70.27	69.31	44.34	1.08	19.59	4.30
泸州市	Luzhou	317.80	312.16	174.33	14.40	111.07	12.37
德阳市	Deyang	417.81	402.79	232.04	8.96	151.47	10.32
绵阳市	Mianyang	525.73	510.86	287.09	21.52	181.29	20.95
广元市	Guangyuan	218.08	212.32	110.22	8.49	84.64	8.97
遂宁市	Suining	289.59	282.87	138.14	10.76	122.62	11.35
内江市	Neijiang	376.86	369.94	190.50	14.52	136.81	28.11
乐山市	Leshan	290.07	285.75	145.63	20.79	103.09	16.25
南充市	Nanchong	638.92	632.17	353.67	19.02	238.86	20.62
眉山市	Meishan	320.28	313.82	150.11	9.37	133.69	20.66
宜宾市	Yibin	417.45	409.76	207.40	25.18	158.93	18.26
广安市	Guangan	300.68	293.70	166.23	9.65	108.59	9.23
达州市	Dazhou	535.69	523.45	304.48	17.97	186.33	14.68
雅安市	Yaan	148.37	145.83	88.10	10.46	45.23	2.04
巴中市	Bazhong	185.90	181.29	89.69	6.98	73.90	10.72
资阳市	Ziyang	295.27	276.79	138.98	11.70	117.09	9.03
阿坝藏族羌族自治州	Aba	78.34	74.33	22.94	5.15	46.20	0.04
甘孜藏族自治州	Ganzi	88.54	87.49	36.25	4.27	46.90	0.07
凉山彝族自治州	Liangshan	531.05	521.69	294.19	24.82	196.00	6.68

注：本表按当年价格计算。
a) Data in this table are calculated at current prices and based on new the range.

13-4 各市(州)按产业分农林牧渔业总产值指数(2018年)
Indices of Gross Output Value of Farming, Forestry, Animal Husbandry and Fishery by Industry and Region(2018)

(上年=100) (preceding year=100)

市(州)	Region	农林牧渔业总产值 Total	#第一产业 Primary Industry	农业 Farming	林业 Forestry	牧业 Animal Husbandry	渔业 Fishery
全 省	**Sichuan**	**103.9**	**103.8**	**104.6**	**101.7**	**102.4**	**104.9**
成都市	Chengdu	103.4	103.4	104.8	106.5	101.0	106.0
自贡市	Zigong	103.7	103.7	104.8	102.6	102.0	105.2
攀枝花市	Panzhihua	104.2	104.1	105.2	103.9	102.6	100.9
泸州市	Luzhou	103.6	103.5	104.4	105.4	101.9	105.9
德阳市	Deyang	103.7	103.5	104.7	103.5	101.8	104.6
绵阳市	Mianyang	103.8	103.6	104.6	103.6	102.2	104.8
广元市	Guangyuan	103.7	103.6	104.7	105.6	102.0	105.4
遂宁市	Suining	103.6	103.5	104.5	103.6	102.1	106.6
内江市	Neijiang	103.6	103.5	104.2	103.6	102.1	106.0
乐山市	Leshan	103.9	103.9	104.9	104.6	102.1	106.8
南充市	Nanchong	103.8	103.8	104.9	105.3	102.1	104.0
眉山市	Meishan	103.7	103.7	104.4	105.9	102.3	106.8
宜宾市	Yibin	103.6	103.4	103.9	105.6	102.4	105.1
广安市	Guangan	103.6	103.5	104.5	104.2	101.8	105.8
达州市	Dazhou	103.7	103.5	104.2	103.6	102.2	104.6
雅安市	Yaan	103.8	103.7	104.8	103.8	101.8	105.6
巴中市	Bazhong	103.8	103.7	104.6	104.3	102.5	105.2
资阳市	Ziyang	103.8	103.5	104.4	104.4	102.3	106.3
阿坝藏族羌族自治州	Aba	103.9	103.8	105.0	103.2	103.3	78.4
甘孜藏族自治州	Ganzi	103.6	103.5	104.6	104.2	102.6	106.0
凉山彝族自治州	Liangshan	103.7	103.6	104.4	104.5	102.4	102.2

13-5 各市(州)农林牧渔业总产值
Gross Output Value of Farming, Forestry, Animal Husbandry and Fishery by Region

单位：亿元 (100 million yuan)

市(州)	Region	2010	2011	2012	2013	2014	2015	2016	2017	2018
全 省	**Sichuan**	**4081.81**	**4932.73**	**5433.12**	**5620.27**	**5888.09**	**6377.84**	**6816.92**	**6955.55**	**7195.65**
成都市	Chengdu	470.19	547.00	577.84	584.60	613.00	663.06	841.25	878.87	909.34
自贡市	Zigong	134.44	157.17	173.12	188.79	194.63	207.81	222.19	231.94	245.26
攀枝花市	Panzhihua	36.52	41.75	44.49	48.08	50.82	54.94	60.96	65.88	70.27
泸州市	Luzhou	178.72	208.79	232.42	251.96	263.02	280.77	298.62	305.22	317.80
德阳市	Deyang	244.74	285.52	307.89	323.66	340.14	377.83	388.35	402.07	417.81
绵阳市	Mianyang	273.22	328.94	362.01	394.97	416.83	446.01	483.02	509.16	525.73
广元市	Guangyuan	127.78	142.99	159.84	166.83	177.96	186.16	196.69	208.95	218.08
遂宁市	Suining	176.58	200.66	207.30	222.69	234.75	252.84	270.54	281.23	289.59
内江市	Neijiang	164.49	206.98	241.71	293.85	308.82	332.27	357.42	361.53	376.86
乐山市	Leshan	167.76	195.25	212.11	223.74	234.69	249.07	267.79	276.25	290.07
南充市	Nanchong	337.29	401.60	453.10	499.69	528.04	567.51	598.80	608.96	638.92
眉山市	Meishan	169.03	198.79	228.32	243.16	256.08	276.51	293.55	304.13	320.28
宜宾市	Yibin	222.85	274.71	305.15	328.65	347.02	373.99	399.01	402.82	417.45
广安市	Guangan	183.89	211.18	237.90	255.99	265.29	285.17	294.78	293.91	300.68
达州市	Dazhou	308.85	368.93	394.38	421.50	444.72	478.46	513.30	531.33	535.69
雅安市	Yaan	82.57	94.64	100.40	104.96	111.74	125.29	134.76	140.46	148.37
巴中市	Bazhong	115.77	122.98	132.40	139.56	146.54	158.70	170.66	176.29	185.90
资阳市	Ziyang	149.27	182.35	212.15	228.11	238.25	257.71	277.43	284.53	295.27
阿坝藏族羌族自治州	Aba	36.47	40.44	45.87	50.89	56.56	62.49	67.36	72.48	78.34
甘孜藏族自治州	Ganzi	37.25	48.42	55.62	61.80	67.39	71.95	79.09	82.84	88.54
凉山彝族自治州	Liangshan	282.79	323.74	362.80	387.82	416.82	447.48	482.94	513.02	531.05

注：本表按当年价格计算。

a) Data in this table are calculated at current prices and based on new the range.

13-6 各市(州)农林牧渔业总产值指数
Indices of Gross Output Value of Farming, Forestry, Animal Husbandry and Fishery by Region

(上年=100) (preceding year=100)

市(州)	Region	2010	2011	2012	2013	2014	2015	2016	2017	2018
全 省	**Sichuan**	**104.5**	**104.6**	**104.5**	**103.4**	**104.0**	**104.6**	**104.0**	**103.8**	**103.9**
成都市	Chengdu	104.4	103.8	103.5	103.5	103.7	104.3	103.9	103.8	103.4
自贡市	Zigong	104.8	103.8	104.8	103.9	104.2	104.4	104.0	104.2	103.7
攀枝花市	Panzhihua	104.5	104.5	104.7	104.6	104.7	104.4	104.7	104.4	104.2
泸州市	Luzhou	104.4	103.4	105.0	104.4	104.2	104.4	103.8	103.8	103.6
德阳市	Deyang	103.1	103.9	104.7	103.7	104.2	104.4	103.9	103.6	103.7
绵阳市	Mianyang	104.1	103.9	104.0	103.6	105.5	104.5	104.0	104.0	103.8
广元市	Guangyuan	106.3	106.7	107.1	103.8	104.5	104.5	103.0	104.2	103.7
遂宁市	Suining	104.6	103.4	104.6	103.1	104.1	104.2	103.8	103.5	103.6
内江市	Neijiang	104.7	104.2	104.5	104.1	103.9	104.4	103.8	102.9	103.6
乐山市	Leshan	104.4	104.0	104.2	103.6	104.1	104.4	104.0	103.7	103.9
南充市	Nanchong	103.8	103.8	103.8	103.7	104.4	104.4	104.1	103.8	103.8
眉山市	Meishan	104.6	103.7	105.4	103.7	104.0	104.5	103.9	103.9	103.7
宜宾市	Yibin	105.0	103.5	104.8	103.7	103.8	104.4	103.5	103.3	103.6
广安市	Guangan	105.0	104.4	105.5	103.5	104.2	104.1	102.5	103.4	103.6
达州市	Dazhou	104.6	103.5	104.6	103.8	103.9	104.4	103.9	103.9	103.7
雅安市	Yaan	103.2	103.4	104.0	102.1	104.6	104.4	103.7	104.0	103.8
巴中市	Bazhong	104.4	104.0	103.7	103.4	103.8	104.2	103.7	103.7	103.8
资阳市	Ziyang	104.6	103.7	104.6	103.6	104.0	104.5	104.2	103.8	103.8
阿坝藏族羌族自治州	Aba	106.0	105.1	106.1	105.0	104.9	105.3	103.9	103.3	103.9
甘孜藏族自治州	Ganzi	104.1	106.2	104.6	104.1	104.8	104.6	105.1	104.6	103.6
凉山彝族自治州	Liangshan	104.5	104.4	104.6	104.9	104.7	104.6	103.7	103.9	103.7

13-7 各市(州)农林牧渔业增加值(2018年)
Value-added of Farming, Forestry, Animal Husbandry and Fishery by Region(2018)

单位：亿元 (100 million yuan)

市(州)	Region	农林牧渔业增加值 Total	#第一产业 Primary Industry	农业 Farming	林业 Forestry	牧业 Animal Husbandry	渔业 Fishery
全省	**Sichuan**	**4543.55**	**4426.66**	**2923.76**	**226.99**	**1126.54**	**149.38**
成都市	Chengdu	541.66	522.59	368.25	16.02	121.07	17.25
自贡市	Zigong	153.54	151.55	89.77	12.67	40.65	8.46
攀枝花市	Panzhihua	40.25	39.74	27.64	0.52	9.17	2.40
泸州市	Luzhou	194.02	190.57	119.41	9.51	54.04	7.62
德阳市	Deyang	252.51	243.31	156.03	5.87	75.21	6.20
绵阳市	Mianyang	309.27	301.27	188.39	12.28	87.90	12.70
广元市	Guangyuan	122.32	118.10	62.91	5.43	44.45	5.31
遂宁市	Suining	170.38	165.64	94.69	7.80	55.45	7.70
内江市	Neijiang	223.34	219.31	127.32	9.35	64.82	17.81
乐山市	Leshan	168.34	165.92	89.34	13.35	53.35	9.87
南充市	Nanchong	387.41	381.87	227.32	12.58	128.42	13.54
眉山市	Meishan	190.06	186.50	102.29	6.26	64.59	13.37
宜宾市	Yibin	252.77	248.57	140.12	18.43	76.77	13.25
广安市	Guangan	177.67	173.52	104.10	5.92	57.88	5.61
达州市	Dazhou	333.94	326.24	215.68	11.61	89.67	9.27
雅安市	Yaan	87.33	85.83	58.47	6.78	19.33	1.26
巴中市	Bazhong	100.99	98.27	53.90	4.11	33.80	6.46
资阳市	Ziyang	178.57	166.79	98.53	7.91	54.68	5.67
阿坝藏族羌族自治州	Aba	51.53	49.55	15.06	3.44	31.03	0.02
甘孜藏族自治州	Ganzi	66.11	65.47	27.77	3.04	34.61	0.06
凉山彝族自治州	Liangshan	313.31	307.61	188.01	17.63	97.67	4.30

注：本表按当年价格计算。
a) Data in this table are calculated at current prices.

13-8 各市(州)农林牧渔业增加值指数(2018年)
Indices of Value-added of Farming, Forestry, Animal Husbandry and Fishery by Region(2018)

(上年=100) (preceding year=100)

市(州)	Region	农林牧渔业增加值 Total	#第一产业 Primary Industry	农业 Farming	林业 Forestry	牧业 Animal Husbandry	渔业 Fishery
全省	**Sichuan**	**103.8**	**103.6**	**104.4**	**101.8**	**102.0**	**104.5**
成都市	Chengdu	103.6	103.6	104.5	106.5	101.1	106.3
自贡市	Zigong	103.8	103.7	104.6	102.8	101.9	105.5
攀枝花市	Panzhihua	104.0	104.0	104.8	103.4	102.2	101.9
泸州市	Luzhou	103.8	103.7	104.4	105.4	101.8	105.9
德阳市	Deyang	103.8	103.7	104.6	103.5	101.9	104.9
绵阳市	Mianyang	103.8	103.7	104.5	103.0	102.1	105.0
广元市	Guangyuan	104.0	103.8	104.6	105.6	102.5	104.8
遂宁市	Suining	103.7	103.5	104.3	103.7	102.0	105.9
内江市	Neijiang	103.8	103.8	104.4	103.5	102.1	105.8
乐山市	Leshan	103.9	103.8	104.6	104.2	102.1	107.9
南充市	Nanchong	103.9	103.8	104.8	104.9	102.0	104.2
眉山市	Meishan	103.7	103.8	104.4	105.9	102.1	106.6
宜宾市	Yibin	103.7	103.6	103.9	105.1	102.4	105.1
广安市	Guangan	103.6	103.5	104.3	104.2	101.8	106.5
达州市	Dazhou	103.9	103.6	104.3	103.4	102.1	104.6
雅安市	Yaan	104.0	103.9	104.7	103.8	101.8	105.6
巴中市	Bazhong	103.8	103.7	104.5	104.1	102.3	105.0
资阳市	Ziyang	103.9	103.7	104.4	104.4	102.2	106.0
阿坝藏族羌族自治州	Aba	103.6	103.5	104.0	103.5	103.3	80.3
甘孜藏族自治州	Ganzi	103.6	103.5	104.5	104.0	102.7	106.6
凉山彝族自治州	Liangshan	103.8	103.8	104.3	104.5	102.7	104.2

13-9 主要农业机械拥有量
Number of Main Agricultural Machinery

(年底数) (year-end)

年 份 Year	农业机械总动力(万千瓦) Total Power of Agricultural Machinery (10 000 kw)	农用大中型拖拉机 Large and Medium Agricultural Tractors		农用小型拖拉机 Mini Agricultural Tractors		机动脱粒机(万台) Power-driven Thresher (10 000 units)	谷物联合收割机(台) grain combine harvester (unit)
		数量(台) Number (unit)	动力(万千瓦) Capacity (10 000 kw)	数量(万台) Number (10 000 units)	动力(万千瓦) Capacity (10 000 kw)		
1978	350.21	14571	42.52	5.22	45.91		
1979	434.74	17790	48.18	6.99	61.47		
1980	500.34	19233	52.59	8.37	74.19	9.04	51
1981	548.37	20076	55.29	9.00	80.70	9.77	50
1982	575.65	20034	55.24	9.35	84.66	8.14	51
1983	609.82	19932	55.15	9.97	91.78	6.80	49
1984	649.40	19099	53.34	10.70	100.31	5.37	46
1985	700.42	18496	51.67	11.53	109.74	4.47	32
1986	772.77	18469	51.55	13.10	127.54	4.04	36
1987	828.98	17939	50.57	14.56	145.39	3.80	31
1988	887.72	16900	48.36	15.69	160.88	3.78	38
1989	918.92	15064	43.51	15.90	163.74	4.09	52
1990	956.00	12788	37.64	15.51	161.06	5.05	127
1991	1007.23	10553	31.62	15.17	159.81	5.86	147
1992	1035.60	8662	25.81	14.75	156.59	6.72	210
1993	1066.35	7545	23.28	14.47	154.38	7.76	321
1994	1165.11	6625	21.17	14.16	152.45	11.80	368
1995	1209.73	5632	18.05	13.78	149.09	12.81	428
1996	1263.26	4997	16.13	13.81	149.98	13.67	738
1997	1348.21	6644	18.16	13.84	151.56	19.19	1450
1998	1468.33	10144	23.48	13.98	155.43	27.62	2150
1999	1606.90	14833	37.58	14.26	159.14	33.31	2681
2000	1680.11	29645	74.59	13.29	149.22	38.25	3258
2001	1735.10	33606	86.87	13.06	148.74	40.44	3587
2002	1803.68	42156	108.21	13.09	150.99	45.82	4100
2003	1891.06	46882	128.02	12.25	141.09	45.60	4719
2004	2006.78	51585	143.82	12.59	151.29	55.70	5400
2005	2181.70	12728	35.18	12.48	155.94	69.87	5830
2006	2344.87	15936	40.74	12.83	161.15	72.61	6831
2007	2523.05	20151	49.81	13.35	171.61	80.00	7621
2008	2687.55	55488	122.75	11.43	143.11	96.14	8501
2009	2952.66	77809	179.10	11.84	147.96	103.28	9958
2010	3155.14	91112	206.02	12.03	147.37	107.62	12005
2011	3426.10	107484	246.51	12.47	147.99	115.90	14086
2012	3694.03	115036	267.45	12.55	141.66	126.60	18499
2013	3953.09	121753	291.65	11.91	134.40	135.20	22498
2014	4160.12	126104	307.48	11.36	127.07	160.60	26115
2015	4404.55	132242	331.40	10.45	115.52	172.80	29433
2016	4267.32	134754	339.74	10.06	109.29	173.12	34731
2017	4420.30	134088	348.24	9.69	104.40	169.65	36021
2018	4603.88	74614	247.22	15.34	220.01	168.82	37278

注：①农业机械数据由四川省农业农村厅提供；②自2016年起农业机械总动力不包括农用运输车数据；③自2018年大中小型拖拉机统计口径调整；④2017年及以前谷物联合收割机为联合收割机数据。

a) Data of agricultural machinery are provided by Bureau of Sichuan Agricultural and Rural of Sichuan Province; b)Since 2016, total power of agricultural machinery does not include power of agricultural transporters; c)The statistical caliber of large, medium and small tractors has been adjusted since 2018; d)Data of grain combine harvesters ware data of combine harvesters in 2017 and before.

13-10 各市(州)主要农业机械拥有量(2018年)
Number of Agricultural Machinery by Region(2018)

(年底数) (year-end)

市(州)	Region	农业机械总动力(万千瓦) Total Power of Agricultural Machinery (10 000 kw)	农用大中型拖拉机 Large and Medium Agricultural Tractors		农用小型拖拉机 Mini Agricultural Tractors		机动脱粒机(万台) Power-driven Thresher (10 000 units)	谷物联合收割机(台) grain combine harvester (unit)
			数量(台) Number (unit)	动力(万千瓦) Capacity (10 000 kw)	数量(台) Number (unit)	动力(万千瓦) Capacity (10 000 kw)		
全 省	**Sichuan**	**4603.88**	**74614**	**247.22**	**153420**	**220.01**	**168.82**	**37278**
成都市	Chengdu	412.94	9769	44.07	22515	27.49	10.07	2787
自贡市	Zigong	112.46	49	0.19	74	0.13	10.82	290
攀枝花市	Panzhihua	70.14	1275	3.54	3173	4.00	0.79	80
泸州市	Luzhou	231.26	83	0.30	10	0.01	6.47	567
德阳市	Deyang	192.03	7769	28.66	13917	23.33	3.07	5286
绵阳市	Mianyang	338.26	9497	28.72	13744	17.25	8.32	6689
广元市	Guangyuan	285.11	4090	11.50	3395	2.80	13.30	8254
遂宁市	Suining	124.10	1951	7.50	670	1.83	7.32	818
内江市	Neijiang	226.38	892	5.03	219	0.28	3.24	811
乐山市	Leshan	264.42	2005	8.81	1980	2.55	5.53	562
南充市	Nanchong	298.00	1370	4.20	1477	2.04	12.41	2636
眉山市	Meishan	215.95	2630	10.41	3259	4.51	12.43	962
宜宾市	Yibin	250.80	139	0.39	615	0.75	14.25	609
广安市	Guangan	244.91	434	1.72	571	0.72	16.49	704
达州市	Dazhou	273.48	1062	4.17	984	1.67	14.51	1430
雅安市	Yaan	164.31	918	1.79	2343	3.31	1.60	88
巴中市	Bazhong	190.24	3612	13.69	1106	1.37	6.37	1014
资阳市	Ziyang	183.73	554	1.81	1532	1.75	16.25	1375
阿坝藏族羌族自治州	Aba	73.90	4323	9.58	22694	29.79	0.69	26
甘孜藏族自治州	Ganzi	98.10	6904	17.02	27713	45.71	1.06	595
凉山彝族自治州	Liangshan	353.35	15288	44.14	31429	48.73	3.83	1695

13-11 化肥施用量和农村用电量
Consumption of Chemical Fertilizers and Electrification of Agriculture

年份 Year	化肥施用量 (万吨) Consumption of Chemical Fertilizers (10 000 tons)	氮肥 Nitrogenous Fertilizer	磷肥 Phosphate Fertilizer	钾肥 Potash Fertilizer	复合肥 Compound Fertilizer	农村用电量 (亿千瓦时) Electricity Consumed in Rural Area (100 million kwh)
1952	0.4	0.4				
1957	1.0	0.7	0.3			
1962	4.0	3.0	1.0			
1965	11.3	8.4	2.8	0.1		
1970	11.5	8.5	2.8	0.2		
1975	23.0	17.1	5.6	0.3		
1978	62.5	46.4	15.7	0.4		7.7
1980	80.4	52.6	24.0	1.0	1.1	9.4
1985	103.1	82.6	16.4	1.7	2.1	19.3
1990	143.9	101.4	28.2	2.6	11.7	33.0
1991	154.3	103.0	32.0	3.5	15.7	37.4
1992	154.0	100.2	32.2	4.3	17.2	40.6
1993	158.1	99.5	33.2	5.4	20.0	46.2
1994	170.0	104.9	35.1	6.2	23.7	53.8
1995	182.9	111.0	37.4	7.0	27.3	61.2
1996	192.8	117.8	38.4	7.4	29.2	64.1
1997	201.3	121.3	40.0	8.4	31.6	68.4
1998	205.3	123.7	40.3	8.8	32.5	73.5
1999	210.3	124.2	40.4	9.3	36.4	78.8
2000	212.6	123.0	42.0	10.0	37.5	82.8
2001	212.0	121.8	41.9	10.4	37.9	89.5
2002	209.6	118.5	42.3	11.0	37.8	93.0
2003	208.4	117.5	41.9	11.6	37.4	99.9
2004	214.7	120.2	42.9	12.2	39.3	107.8
2005	220.9	121.8	45.1	12.9	40.6	112.9
2006	228.2	124.7	46.6	13.7	43.0	117.7
2007	238.2	127.9	48.0	14.8	46.6	123.3
2008	242.8	128.6	48.9	15.8	48.0	128.2
2009	248.0	130.7	49.7	16.4	50.3	133.8
2010	248.0	129.6	49.2	16.4	51.1	141.7
2011	251.2	128.8	50.6	17.3	53.2	148.6
2012	252.8	127.9	50.7	17.5	55.0	156.0
2013	251.1	126.1	50.3	17.7	55.0	163.5
2014	252.1	125.7	49.9	17.7	56.9	169.6
2015	252.1	124.7	49.6	17.8	57.7	174.8
2016	249.0	121.9	48.9	17.9	60.2	183.1
2017	242.0	117.0	47.1	17.6	60.2	188.4
2018	235.2	112.1	45.4	17.4	60.3	198.6

13-12 各市(州)化肥施用量和农村用电量(2018年)
Consumption of Chemical Fertilizers and Electrification of Agriculture by Region(2018)

市(州)	Region	化肥施用量 (万吨) Consumption of Chemical Fertilizers (100 million tons)	氮肥 Nitrogenous Fertilizer	磷肥 Phosphate Fertilizer	钾肥 Potash Fertilizer	复合肥 Compound Fertilizer	农村用电量 (亿千瓦时) Electricity Consumed in Rural Area (100 million kwh)
全　省	**Sichuan**	**235.21**	**112.15**	**45.39**	**17.40**	**60.26**	**198.62**
成都市	Chengdu	18.11	6.91	3.53	1.95	5.71	37.15
自贡市	Zigong	9.01	3.85	2.36	1.05	1.75	5.48
攀枝花市	Panzhihua	2.80	1.00	0.31	0.32	1.18	2.36
泸州市	Luzhou	10.72	5.18	2.08	0.68	2.78	8.90
德阳市	Deyang	17.93	8.70	2.77	0.93	5.53	24.38
绵阳市	Mianyang	20.64	9.55	5.17	1.10	4.82	12.02
广元市	Guangyuan	10.31	4.56	2.07	0.95	2.74	5.55
遂宁市	Suining	13.31	6.64	2.66	0.99	3.02	3.79
内江市	Neijiang	11.80	6.95	2.65	0.44	1.76	10.42
乐山市	Leshan	8.21	4.02	1.18	0.47	2.54	11.33
南充市	Nanchong	21.73	10.87	5.13	1.04	4.68	8.67
眉山市	Meishan	12.39	4.02	1.59	1.55	5.23	8.39
宜宾市	Yibin	8.12	3.09	1.42	0.72	2.89	13.57
广安市	Guangan	10.44	6.43	2.24	0.72	1.05	5.63
达州市	Dazhou	21.63	12.42	3.63	1.60	3.97	8.86
雅安市	Yaan	4.97	2.35	0.62	0.56	1.43	5.06
巴中市	Bazhong	12.88	5.41	2.23	1.22	4.02	7.98
资阳市	Ziyang	5.12	3.57	1.03	0.04	0.49	5.61
阿坝藏族羌族自治州	Aba	1.11	0.47	0.24	0.09	0.30	2.53
甘孜藏族自治州	Ganzi	0.31	0.21	0.03	0.01	0.07	1.27
凉山彝族自治州	Liangshan	13.69	5.95	2.46	0.99	4.29	9.68

13-13 耕地面积、机耕面积、耕地灌溉面积和农作物总播种面积
Cultivated Area, Area Ploughed by Tractors, Irrigated Area of Cultivated Land and Total Sown Area of Farm Crops

单位：万公顷 (10 000 hectares)

年 份 Year	年末实有耕地面积 Cultivated Area (year-end)	机耕面积 Area Ploughed by Tractors	耕地灌溉面积 Irrigated Area of Cultivated Land	农作物总播种面积 Total Sown Area	#粮食 Grain Crops
1952	547.85		53.70	827.66	686.30
1957	569.13	0.40	86.40	968.20	784.90
1962	510.07	2.60	106.90	805.65	676.70
1965	518.96	2.60	120.90	789.59	622.50
1970	510.66	4.60	139.30	819.65	674.80
1975	497.21	45.30	175.00	903.94	728.90
1978	490.91	86.50	198.90	885.91	744.10
1980	487.16	67.90	211.40	861.90	746.10
1985	474.12	51.70	215.40	855.80	663.60
1990	464.71	59.20	222.60	905.00	698.50
1991	463.23	64.30	224.10	920.70	704.80
1992	461.19	66.30	225.30	921.90	702.90
1993	459.38	65.40	226.50	915.20	705.00
1994	457.96	70.80	227.90	916.40	701.50
1995	456.04	71.60	230.10	930.24	705.50
1996	454.31	70.10	232.50	940.08	713.80
1997	451.99	84.40	235.62	949.75	721.10
1998	449.49	85.60	239.06	971.44	733.80
1999	445.47	98.30	242.79	971.77	729.70
2000	434.61	93.70	246.90	960.91	685.40
2001	428.44	95.05	248.70	949.17	662.69
2002	405.99	95.40	250.10	934.41	642.50
2003	390.37	98.10	250.30	908.50	608.80
2004	390.44	98.80	250.30	924.44	633.33
2005	390.60	107.50	249.50	941.69	650.16
2006	391.66	115.04	248.70	953.08	644.90
2007	394.59	121.10	250.00	925.24	643.46
2008	395.95	182.20	250.70	929.47	640.88
2009	397.61	196.53	252.40	915.78	621.30
2010	401.07	219.02	255.30	915.87	619.51
2011	398.34	275.50	260.10	921.54	619.67
2012	399.15	330.28	256.60	931.96	625.56
2013	399.38	409.47	261.65	937.17	626.99
2014	673.42	459.79	266.63	937.77	624.96
2015	673.61	485.51	273.51	945.11	628.61
2016	673.54	508.10	281.50	949.38	629.13
2017	672.59	531.93	287.31	957.51	629.20
2018	672.28	514.23	293.25	961.54	626.56

注：①自2014年起耕地面积数据由四川省自然资源厅提供；②机耕面积由四川省农业农村厅提供；③耕地灌溉面积由四川省水利厅提供；④根据第三次全国农业普查结果对2007年至2017年农作物播种(种植)面积和产量数据进行了修订(以下有关各表同)。

a) Since 2014, data of cultivated area have been provided by Bureau of Natural Resources of Sichuan Province; b) Data of area ploughed by tractors are provided by Bureau of Sichuan Agricultural and Rural of Sichuan Province; c)Data of Irrigated area of cultivated land are provided by Bureau of Water Conservancy of Sichuan Province;d) Data of total sown area and yield since 2007 to 2017 were revised according to the results of the Third National Agricultural Census(the same as the following related tables).

13-14 各市(州)耕地面积、耕地灌溉面积和农作物总播种面积(2018年)
Cultivated Area, Irrigated Area of Cultivated Land and Total Sown of Farm Crops by Region(2018)

单位：千公顷 (1 000 hectares)

市(州)	Region	年末实有耕地面积 Cultivated Area (year-end)	耕地灌溉面积 Irrigated Area of Cultivated Land	农作物总播种面积 Total Sown Area	#粮食 Grain Crops
全　省	**Sichuan**	**6722.77**	**2932.54**	**9615.39**	**6265.64**
成都市	Chengdu	523.15	368.91	739.32	383.05
自贡市	Zigong	216.31	100.18	366.41	229.29
攀枝花市	Panzhihua	75.03	39.98	71.41	44.87
泸州市	Luzhou	410.76	154.82	540.67	394.96
德阳市	Deyang	248.13	157.20	476.72	311.30
绵阳市	Mianyang	444.10	221.15	661.96	400.20
广元市	Guangyuan	353.48	91.96	498.60	311.31
遂宁市	Suining	270.18	130.52	387.00	268.80
内江市	Neijiang	273.79	134.69	478.15	308.61
乐山市	Leshan	271.61	141.14	340.79	217.69
南充市	Nanchong	534.15	227.81	888.87	559.25
眉山市	Meishan	241.05	171.46	314.55	194.43
宜宾市	Yibin	487.61	188.72	591.97	421.54
广安市	Guangan	307.68	106.25	406.27	284.75
达州市	Dazhou	551.02	181.46	810.29	555.08
雅安市	Yaan	101.26	53.72	115.97	69.04
巴中市	Bazhong	327.59	92.55	508.33	338.32
资阳市	Ziyang	320.72	121.70	517.27	336.09
阿坝藏族羌族自治州	Aba	83.27	25.15	74.09	47.73
甘孜藏族自治州	Ganzi	102.34	36.74	88.90	68.81
凉山彝族自治州	Liangshan	579.55	186.43	737.86	520.53

13-15 各市(州)农作物总播种面积
Sown Areas of Farm Crops by Region

单位：千公顷　　(1 000 hectares)

市(州)	Region	2010	2011	2012	2013	2014	2015	2016	2017	2018
全 省	**Sichuan**	**9158.73**	**9215.41**	**9319.58**	**9371.69**	**9377.69**	**9451.06**	**9493.82**	**9575.05**	**9615.39**
成都市	Chengdu	823.97	806.83	792.89	778.72	753.26	740.23	728.48	730.99	739.32
自贡市	Zigong	303.57	309.49	316.81	323.93	332.52	342.53	352.49	362.65	366.41
攀枝花市	Panzhihua	63.37	65.10	66.34	67.51	67.97	69.17	70.81	70.21	71.41
泸州市	Luzhou	499.15	515.45	524.37	525.98	524.46	527.03	528.62	541.29	540.67
德阳市	Deyang	475.95	477.09	478.75	480.07	479.35	478.52	476.48	477.25	476.72
绵阳市	Mianyang	653.37	656.76	660.81	662.10	660.19	662.20	659.14	660.18	661.96
广元市	Guangyuan	433.95	444.94	457.28	469.32	477.02	486.49	493.08	495.44	498.60
遂宁市	Suining	404.82	402.49	402.26	398.75	396.66	395.03	387.62	387.71	387.00
内江市	Neijiang	413.79	416.98	429.47	438.82	444.06	455.93	464.66	476.73	478.15
乐山市	Leshan	317.28	321.49	325.11	327.13	328.80	331.75	335.87	338.55	340.79
南充市	Nanchong	872.59	878.49	886.86	886.29	883.35	883.86	882.12	885.32	888.87
眉山市	Meishan	340.45	331.81	325.25	320.88	316.82	314.31	310.51	313.40	314.55
宜宾市	Yibin	485.89	496.01	513.47	529.10	545.34	566.72	585.37	589.39	591.97
广安市	Guangan	397.19	396.99	399.36	400.44	400.29	402.54	405.29	406.71	406.27
达州市	Dazhou	773.36	776.89	787.57	794.62	795.59	802.54	807.23	809.52	810.29
雅安市	Yaan	121.13	117.40	118.40	118.32	117.46	115.90	115.74	115.61	115.97
巴中市	Bazhong	457.50	463.62	472.62	477.44	480.73	485.96	489.17	500.52	508.33
资阳市	Ziyang	519.38	520.52	523.91	522.21	518.18	516.99	513.65	516.39	517.27
阿坝藏族羌族自治州	Aba	66.32	67.00	67.13	68.28	66.89	68.35	69.76	69.77	74.09
甘孜藏族自治州	Ganzi	76.87	77.97	79.20	80.26	79.22	80.61	81.95	85.69	88.90
凉山彝族自治州	Liangshan	658.81	672.09	691.69	701.50	709.52	724.41	735.81	741.76	737.86

13-16 农作物播种面积和产量
Sown Areas of Farm Crops and Output of Major Farm Products

单位：万公顷、万吨 (10 000 hectares, 10 000 tons)

年份 Year	粮食 Grain Crops		#谷物 Cereal		#稻谷 Rice		#小麦 Wheat		#玉米 Corn	
	播种面积 Sown Area	产量 Yield	播种面积 Sown Area	产量 Yield	播种面积 Sown Area	产量 Yield	播种面积 Sown Area	产量 Yield	播种面积 Sown Area	产量 Yield
1952	686.3	1170.1			253.1	769.2	79.4	65.3	93.4	91.8
1957	784.9	1531.0			280.6	939.6	104.6	123.5	103.9	157.5
1962	676.7	1054.7			203.1	572.8	114.5	94.7	81.3	95.1
1965	622.5	1489.4			241.0	869.2	93.5	113.1	84.4	150.7
1970	674.8	1756.1			233.7	937.7	107.3	187.6	95.4	196.4
1975	728.9	1976.8			264.8	1035.4	139.8	248.8	104.2	248.6
1978	744.1	2381.8			226.9	1086.4	165.4	368.6	117.1	360.6
1980	746.1	2599.7			225.5	1207.4	182.6	410.2	124.5	457.3
1985	663.6	2875.1			230.8	1463.3	151.6	506.7	107.2	418.7
1990	698.5	3269.2			230.0	1700.8	168.0	570.9	119.9	486.1
1991	704.8	3315.2			229.3	1663.6	171.6	619.2	122.8	487.1
1992	702.9	3371.3			229.8	1720.4	173.4	634.3	121.1	476.2
1993	705.0	3174.8			223.7	1586.8	177.9	569.3	120.0	456.8
1994	701.5	3098.1			218.4	1525.0	176.8	641.9	119.8	399.8
1995	705.5	3395.3	544.1	2887.8	220.3	1657.8	178.0	682.4	120.2	471.6
1996	713.8	3483.1	552.4	2986.2	221.8	1705.7	181.0	656.9	124.7	548.6
1997	721.1	3554.4	557.9	3076.1	219.6	1700.2	182.4	687.3	129.0	605.7
1998	733.8	3626.3	566.4	3096.7	216.8	1685.3	186.5	673.2	136.5	659.4
1999	729.7	3668.4	561.3	3115.7	217.6	1724.4	181.8	620.9	135.9	693.7
2000	685.4	3568.5	520.2	2996.7	212.4	1692.5	160.5	614.3	123.5	616.6
2001	662.7	3056.5	496.4	2530.0	203.7	1452.4	150.3	517.8	120.1	493.1
2002	642.5	3275.2	481.0	2714.3	202.0	1540.0	142.5	526.5	114.5	578.2
2003	608.8	3183.3	452.3	2625.3	193.0	1498.2	128.6	488.3	110.1	572.7
2004	633.3	3326.5	461.0	2709.8	197.1	1525.4	128.3	501.5	115.6	620.4
2005	650.2	3409.2	473.0	2769.5	199.5	1526.9	136.0	543.1	118.5	641.8
2006	644.9	2859.8	475.8	2371.1	204.9	1337.2	123.5	426.7	129.0	551.7
2007	643.5	3032.7	481.3	2541.4	202.4	1411.6	125.7	432.5	136.9	651.2
2008	640.9	3111.0	474.0	2597.7	201.2	1480.1	117.2	398.7	140.2	674.8
2009	621.3	3120.4	470.6	2604.3	199.1	1493.3	111.1	366.2	145.5	701.0
2010	619.5	3182.8	468.1	2633.0	196.7	1484.1	105.1	355.9	152.1	750.7
2011	619.7	3249.5	465.3	2675.6	194.3	1478.1	99.8	346.4	157.4	810.3
2012	625.6	3271.3	462.5	2689.4	193.0	1484.0	93.4	331.5	163.0	833.6
2013	627.0	3336.1	459.6	2754.3	190.5	1483.4	87.9	311.0	168.6	920.1
2014	625.0	3324.6	456.8	2734.7	189.2	1450.5	81.4	298.0	173.9	946.7
2015	628.6	3394.6	456.0	2779.6	187.9	1465.2	74.7	284.5	181.7	992.3
2016	629.1	3469.9	453.8	2822.1	187.4	1467.3	68.4	259.6	186.6	1058.0
2017	629.2	3488.9	450.8	2831.8	187.5	1473.7	65.3	251.6	186.4	1068.0
2018	626.6	3493.7	448.0	2830.9	187.4	1478.6	63.5	247.3	185.6	1066.3

注：2007年至2017年所有农作物的播种面积和产量均依据第三次全国农业普查结果进行了修订（以下有关各表同）。

a) Data of sown area and yield of all crops in 2007 and before were approved according to the results of the third national agricultural census(the sanme as the following related tables).

13-16 续表 1 continued

单位：万公顷、万吨 (10 000 hectares, 10 000 tons)

年份 Year	#豆类 Soybeans 播种面积 Sown Area	#豆类 Soybeans 产量 Yield	#薯类 Tubers 播种面积 Sown Area	#薯类 Tubers 产量 Yield	油料 Oil-bearing Crops 播种面积 Sown Area	油料 Oil-bearing Crops 产量 Yield	#花生 Peanut 播种面积 Sown Area	#花生 Peanut 产量 Yield	#油菜籽 Rapeseeds 播种面积 Sown Area	#油菜籽 Rapeseeds 产量 Yield
1952	105.9	76.1	108.9	138.8	34.3	25.2	7.6	8.4	25.8	16.5
1957	114.9	96.5	125.3	220.5	40.3	35.1	9.8	11.4	29.5	23.4
1962	90.7	64.1	121.9	217.4	27.5	14.8	7.3	6.2	19.0	8.3
1965	92.7	93.3	102.5	214.1	38.8	35.4	10.2	10.7	27.1	24.3
1970	83.9	107.6	103.9	260.2	32.0	34.5	6.9	9.1	23.9	24.5
1975	70.8	86.9	105.3	289.8	36.2	39.9	7.3	10.8	28.2	28.7
1978	60.0	79.9	134.3	412.1	41.3	52.8	7.4	12.4	30.3	38.1
1980	55.0	77.3	117.1	349.4	47.0	68.4	8.4	11.8	39.5	56.4
1985	39.9	71.0	99.4	325.2	84.2	133.1	13.5	23.6	70.1	109.0
1990	34.3	63.4	113.6	279.6	79.7	133.5	12.6	23.7	66.9	109.5
1991	33.3	63.3	114.4	306.3	83.9	148.7	12.5	24.6	71.0	123.7
1992	37.7	70.8	113.3	388.4	81.9	136.6	12.8	25.1	68.6	111.1
1993	37.3	66.2	117.5	416.6	70.8	112.0	13.9	26.4	56.4	84.9
1994	39.1	69.4	121.7	390.2	75.2	119.6	15.2	20.8	59.8	98.4
1995	38.4	74.0	122.9	433.4	84.6	145.1	15.3	25.9	68.8	118.7
1996	37.9	74.8	123.5	422.1	82.2	133.2	15.2	28.1	66.4	104.6
1997	38.6	77.8	124.6	400.6	79.9	134.2	15.4	28.8	64.0	104.8
1998	38.9	76.9	128.5	452.7	83.6	146.4	16.6	33.3	66.4	112.6
1999	40.2	78.9	128.2	473.8	89.1	151.6	19.3	41.2	69.0	109.5
2000	44.5	98.0	120.7	473.8	102.6	193.0	24.0	54.3	77.7	137.5
2001	47.9	97.1	118.3	429.5	104.9	181.0	25.8	45.8	78.0	133.7
2002	48.1	107.1	113.4	453.8	104.9	201.5	26.4	55.4	77.3	144.8
2003	49.0	111.9	107.5	446.2	108.7	217.1	27.0	59.9	80.6	155.9
2004	50.7	119.2	121.7	497.5	108.9	226.3	26.3	59.8	81.4	165.0
2005	52.0	122.9	125.2	516.8	109.4	232.3	26.4	62.0	81.7	168.7
2006	45.2	91.6	123.9	397.1	107.0	217.3	26.1	47.1	79.7	169.0
2007	45.8	103.4	116.4	388.0	118.2	253.6	26.1	54.5	89.9	195.1
2008	45.4	101.8	121.5	411.5	126.7	276.2	25.9	58.0	98.9	213.9
2009	43.0	99.0	107.7	417.1	132.0	288.5	25.9	58.8	104.4	225.5
2010	43.0	98.0	108.4	451.9	133.7	296.1	26.1	59.9	106.0	232.0
2011	43.8	101.7	110.6	472.3	135.2	306.7	25.8	60.6	107.8	242.0
2012	44.4	103.9	118.6	478.0	136.9	315.9	25.6	60.7	109.8	251.1
2013	45.4	103.5	122.1	478.2	139.0	320.2	25.6	62.2	112.0	253.7
2014	45.8	106.1	122.3	483.8	141.4	332.0	25.7	63.1	114.4	264.8
2015	46.6	107.0	126.0	507.9	143.0	339.6	25.8	64.1	116.0	271.7
2016	49.6	113.0	125.7	534.8	144.0	346.2	26.0	64.8	116.7	277.0
2017	51.8	119.2	126.6	537.9	147.9	357.9	26.1	66.0	120.6	288.0
2018	52.5	121.5	126.1	541.4	149.1	362.5	26.3	67.7	121.8	292.2

13-16 续表 2 continued

单位：万公顷、万吨 (10 000 hectares, 10 000 tons)

年份 Year	棉花 Cotton		甘蔗 Sugarcane		生麻 Bast Fiber		烟叶(未加工) Tobacco		#烤烟 Fluecured Tobacco	
	播种面积 Sown Area	产量 Yield	播种面积 Sown Area	产量 Yield	播种面积 Sown Area	产量 Yield	播种面积 Sown Area	产量 Yield	播种面积 Sown Area	产量 Yield
1952	22.50	4.00	3.00	115.30	0.10	…	4.17	4.25	2.08	2.04
1957	30.70	6.60	3.84	164.40	…	0.10	4.00	4.38	1.97	2.12
1962	21.00	2.60	1.41	28.30	…	…	1.63	1.14	0.38	0.41
1965	26.50	10.60	3.61	133.25	0.20	0.10	3.25	3.45	0.75	1.29
1970	25.70	12.70	3.35	107.61	0.60	0.20	2.13	2.32	0.47	0.48
1975	25.70	12.30	4.50	139.63	0.80	0.80	3.65	3.98	1.07	1.49
1978	25.60	14.40	4.65	154.11	1.90	5.90	5.20	6.94	1.83	2.58
1980	24.60	9.40	3.70	141.77	2.40	10.30	4.19	5.73	1.35	1.81
1985	12.60	11.30	4.62	233.98	6.80	12.40	6.83	10.68	2.90	3.87
1990	12.30	11.50	4.24	218.15	4.20	8.20	8.35	13.26	4.91	4.32
1991	14.60	14.60	4.60	244.96	4.10	8.30	8.04	12.68	5.16	6.08
1992	15.90	15.00	4.11	211.67	3.70	7.70	9.52	15.83	5.19	8.00
1993	13.10	8.20	3.21	167.80	3.70	7.30	9.88	15.33	5.46	7.24
1994	13.00	6.70	3.19	155.55	3.20	4.30	6.31	8.67	3.15	3.57
1995	13.97	11.18	3.25	170.73	4.53	6.57	5.87	7.77	3.11	3.50
1996	15.31	12.29	3.11	164.16	4.38	6.49	6.97	12.93	3.90	7.48
1997	13.92	10.73	3.09	155.66	3.97	5.39	10.02	18.56	6.88	12.33
1998	13.96	10.16	2.96	161.48	3.11	4.28	7.24	10.67	4.62	5.89
1999	9.41	7.59	2.92	161.04	2.71	3.94	7.38	11.86	4.89	6.94
2000	7.01	5.89	3.06	166.68	2.56	4.02	8.22	15.61	5.46	9.37
2001	6.64	2.98	3.06	155.67	2.48	3.94	7.03	12.17	4.23	6.55
2002	3.30	2.36	3.19	171.21	2.99	4.47	7.01	14.09	4.68	8.85
2003	3.12	2.54	3.19	170.53	3.18	5.02	6.66	13.42	4.43	8.23
2004	3.58	3.31	2.88	146.10	3.50	6.09	6.64	14.41	4.59	9.38
2005	2.78	2.47	2.67	132.89	3.70	6.85	7.95	18.17	5.88	13.23
2006	2.45	1.57	2.64	124.61	4.00	6.58	8.88	20.01	6.86	15.39
2007	1.08	0.85	2.08	109.29	2.34	4.06	7.86	16.35	6.95	14.44
2008	0.94	0.80	1.87	98.53	2.28	3.97	9.34	18.84	8.50	17.07
2009	0.83	0.75	1.58	78.60	2.21	3.85	10.43	21.63	9.58	19.52
2010	0.82	0.72	1.56	78.13	2.08	3.75	9.12	20.24	8.17	18.01
2011	0.78	0.71	1.30	62.72	1.98	3.57	10.00	20.90	9.08	18.79
2012	0.71	0.64	1.13	48.77	1.85	3.35	10.48	23.11	9.62	21.28
2013	0.66	0.62	1.06	44.69	1.82	3.29	10.33	22.15	9.63	20.02
2014	0.64	0.60	1.02	43.29	1.76	3.20	8.94	19.97	8.31	17.94
2015	0.49	0.48	0.99	41.79	1.72	3.13	8.78	19.79	8.05	18.03
2016	0.45	0.50	0.91	35.56	1.69	3.05	8.87	19.52	8.34	18.02
2017	0.44	0.40	0.91	34.74	1.68	3.03	8.63	18.05	8.13	16.56
2018	0.40	0.40	0.93	36.18	1.70	3.10	7.65	16.25	6.77	13.97

注：1994年及以前年份“生麻”统计口径为“黄红麻”。

a) Bast fiber includes only jute and ambary hemp before 1995.

13-16 续表 3 continued

单位：万公顷、万吨 (10 000 hectares, 10 000 tons)

年份 Year	蔬菜及食用菌 Vegetables and Edible Fungus 播种面积 Sown Area	蔬菜及食用菌 Vegetables and Edible Fungus 产量 Yield	蚕茧产量 Yield of Silkworm Cocoons	茶叶产量 Yield of Tea	水果产量 Total Fruits Yield	#园林水果 Garden Fruits	#苹果 Yield of Apples	#柑桔 Yield of Citrus	#梨 Yield of Pears	水产品产量 Output of Aquatic Products
1952			0.98	0.79	10.30	10.30		0.40		0.81
1957			0.94	1.21	10.80	10.80		3.60		1.11
1962			0.77	0.70	8.60	8.60		1.80		1.10
1965			0.97	0.90	11.70	11.70		3.40		1.56
1970			1.84	1.01	7.90	7.90		2.40		1.66
1975			2.55	1.31	15.20	15.20		4.50		3.01
1978			3.66	1.90	17.80	17.80		5.90		3.06
1980			6.60	1.98	27.50	27.50	4.00	9.90	5.10	3.69
1985			7.39	3.71	57.00	57.00	4.60	37.70	6.30	9.27
1990			10.00	4.00	92.00	92.00	6.10	62.40	9.10	16.83
1991			11.70	4.20	106.50	106.50	6.50	71.90	10.20	18.31
1992			13.50	4.30	109.20	109.20	7.60	73.64	10.60	20.02
1993			15.00	4.40	131.90	131.90	7.80	89.00	11.40	22.40
1994			15.66	4.35	132.94	132.94	8.45	83.50	13.16	25.78
1995			15.16	4.35	155.76	155.76	12.26	93.33	17.26	29.86
1996			9.46	4.39	168.48	168.48	13.47	101.01	18.17	33.26
1997			8.53	4.52	185.13	185.13	16.12	106.89	20.04	37.20
1998	68.34	1888.41	9.28	5.09	273.95	212.92	17.74	117.84	24.97	42.29
1999	71.74	1942.15	8.10	5.29	297.25	234.53	18.68	116.22	27.27	46.57
2000	85.86	2312.56	8.73	5.45	321.63	252.57	20.23	132.75	34.45	51.31
2001	96.90	2440.79	9.22	5.84	361.93	272.90	19.40	149.77	39.48	57.13
2002	103.52	2684.94	9.30	6.28	425.93	306.69	20.69	166.18	46.97	64.84
2003	100.62	2639.60	9.29	7.21	464.93	348.21	22.54	186.16	54.77	76.40
2004	97.06	2623.87	9.74	8.65	494.83	385.45	24.05	198.78	62.03	86.15
2005	99.15	2714.29	9.80	9.79	527.16	415.76	24.29	213.74	68.46	98.25
2006	118.19	2971.23	9.83	11.29	535.32	423.81	24.80	205.78	74.60	81.30
2007	105.16	2863.99	10.68	13.73	580.05	469.18	29.54	229.79	76.89	91.05
2008	105.68	2927.13	10.19	14.22	625.17	513.59	38.62	255.43	78.00	95.20
2009	107.96	3087.00	10.15	15.74	679.12	564.81	40.61	275.23	80.11	100.13
2010	110.52	3206.45	10.33	17.20	707.74	594.08	42.61	289.97	82.44	105.06
2011	114.81	3403.84	10.27	18.97	752.94	637.13	44.45	315.36	85.36	112.15
2012	118.23	3569.18	10.26	21.03	791.42	676.84	47.50	334.53	88.42	116.83
2013	121.09	3705.10	9.99	21.97	822.03	709.84	51.11	340.85	90.36	123.64
2014	124.20	3838.35	9.82	23.47	862.87	747.06	57.53	357.60	90.26	130.00
2015	127.05	3988.38	9.55	24.61	912.14	793.65	60.68	375.82	90.97	135.97
2016	129.57	4118.12	8.95	26.51	960.05	838.67	61.85	397.91	92.84	142.16
2017	132.43	4252.27	9.08	27.78	1007.88	883.23	65.22	415.68	91.72	150.74
2018	136.92	4438.02	9.22	30.07	1080.67	948.39	72.55	432.98	94.75	153.48

注：①1997年及以前年份的水果产量为园林水果产量；②水产品产量数据由四川省水产局提供。

a) Total fruits yield in 1997 and before was known as garden fruits yeild. b) Data of aquatic products output were provided by Sichuan Fisheries Bureau.

13-17 各市(州)粮食作物播种面积和产量(2018年)
Sown Areas of Farm Crops and Output of Major Farm Products by Region(2018)

单位：千公顷、万吨 (1 000 hectares, 10 000 tons)

市(州)	Region	粮食 Grain Crops		谷物 Cereal		#稻谷 Rice		豆类 Soybeans		薯类 Tubers	
		播种面积 Sown Area	产量 Yield	播种面积 Sown Area	产量 Yield	播种面积 Sown Area	产量 Yield	播种面积 Sown Area	产量 Yield	播种面积 Sown Area	产量 Yield
全省	**Sichuan**	**6265.6**	**3493.7**	**4479.5**	**2830.9**	**1874.0**	**1478.6**	**524.9**	**121.5**	**1261.2**	**541.4**
成都市	Chengdu	383.1	230.3	289.0	197.1	154.0	123.1	38.2	8.7	55.8	24.5
自贡市	Zigong	229.3	138.3	136.6	105.3	80.7	73.1	48.3	13.2	44.4	19.9
攀枝花市	Panzhihua	44.9	25.4	36.8	23.0	9.3	7.5	4.6	0.9	3.5	1.5
泸州市	Luzhou	395.0	229.7	275.0	183.9	134.2	109.3	22.9	5.2	97.0	40.6
德阳市	Deyang	311.3	194.9	263.6	177.8	119.6	99.6	21.2	5.2	26.5	11.8
绵阳市	Mianyang	400.2	229.7	352.7	212.4	118.3	93.4	17.5	4.5	30.0	12.8
广元市	Guangyuan	311.3	156.4	247.4	135.5	65.5	49.9	28.7	5.9	35.3	14.9
遂宁市	Suining	268.8	142.3	206.0	118.8	56.5	44.9	19.9	4.5	42.9	19.1
内江市	Neijiang	308.6	170.8	184.1	124.3	81.8	65.6	44.9	11.9	79.6	34.7
乐山市	Leshan	217.7	122.1	158.1	102.0	85.0	65.3	19.3	3.7	40.2	16.4
南充市	Nanchong	559.2	307.1	422.0	253.7	151.7	119.8	33.9	9.0	103.4	44.5
眉山市	Meishan	194.4	123.8	157.3	111.4	98.3	78.1	17.0	3.7	20.1	8.6
宜宾市	Yibin	421.5	253.3	296.7	204.7	153.8	123.7	29.9	8.0	94.9	40.6
广安市	Guangan	284.8	179.9	208.1	152.0	130.6	105.1	19.3	3.8	57.4	24.1
达州市	Dazhou	555.1	317.1	344.2	239.0	191.1	140.0	48.2	10.1	162.7	68.0
雅安市	Yaan	69.0	35.8	51.8	30.4	17.0	12.3	3.8	0.6	13.5	4.8
巴中市	Bazhong	338.3	190.5	239.6	150.7	96.0	70.3	16.0	3.7	82.8	36.1
资阳市	Ziyang	336.1	166.1	197.6	120.1	70.0	52.5	61.7	13.0	76.8	32.9
阿坝藏族羌族自治州	Aba	47.7	15.5	27.5	9.4			5.2	1.0	15.1	5.1
甘孜藏族自治州	Ganzi	68.8	22.6	49.5	16.0	0.2	0.1	2.9	0.6	16.3	5.9
凉山彝族自治州	Liangshan	520.5	242.0	336.1	163.3	60.3	44.7	21.5	4.3	163.0	74.5

13-18 各市(州)粮食总产量
Total Grain Output by Region

单位：万吨 (10 000 tons)

市(州)	Region	2010	2011	2012	2013	2014	2015	2016	2017	2018
全 省	**Sichuan**	**3182.8**	**3249.5**	**3271.3**	**3336.1**	**3324.6**	**3394.6**	**3469.9**	**3488.9**	**3493.7**
成都市	Chengdu	265.2	259.0	251.7	247.8	237.1	232.9	230.7	231.9	230.3
自贡市	Zigong	118.2	120.9	123.4	126.9	127.6	132.0	136.4	137.8	138.3
攀枝花市	Panzhihua	20.5	20.8	21.1	22.3	22.6	23.8	25.4	25.4	25.4
泸州市	Luzhou	203.2	213.9	216.9	221.9	222.2	224.6	229.4	229.2	229.7
德阳市	Deyang	181.5	184.2	185.7	188.2	187.4	189.6	193.9	195.2	194.9
绵阳市	Mianyang	212.1	216.4	217.0	221.1	221.7	225.7	229.0	230.6	229.7
广元市	Guangyuan	131.5	137.5	139.9	146.1	148.6	153.7	156.9	157.1	156.4
遂宁市	Suining	142.5	143.1	141.8	142.4	140.4	140.9	141.0	142.0	142.3
内江市	Neijiang	144.8	149.6	150.7	155.4	155.8	162.2	168.7	170.4	170.8
乐山市	Leshan	109.2	110.5	112.2	114.8	114.3	116.9	120.4	121.6	122.1
南充市	Nanchong	289.0	296.3	297.7	300.9	298.6	302.3	304.6	306.4	307.1
眉山市	Meishan	131.7	129.6	127.3	126.9	122.9	122.8	122.3	123.4	123.8
宜宾市	Yibin	198.3	205.7	211.2	220.9	227.5	239.7	252.2	252.8	253.3
广安市	Guangan	163.2	164.5	166.0	170.0	169.2	173.4	178.2	179.3	179.9
达州市	Dazhou	282.8	291.8	295.9	304.4	302.5	310.7	316.1	316.6	317.1
雅安市	Yaan	37.3	36.1	35.4	35.4	34.6	34.5	35.5	35.8	35.8
巴中市	Bazhong	169.3	173.8	176.5	180.5	179.8	184.2	188.1	189.4	190.5
资阳市	Ziyang	157.9	160.3	159.8	161.9	160.3	163.2	164.7	165.4	166.1
阿坝藏族羌族自治州	Aba	13.8	14.2	14.1	14.3	14.4	14.6	15.3	15.5	15.5
甘孜藏族自治州	Ganzi	20.5	21.4	21.6	21.8	21.6	22.1	22.4	22.5	22.6
凉山彝族自治州	Liangshan	190.4	199.9	205.4	212.1	215.7	224.7	238.5	240.6	242.0

13-19　各市(州)经济作物播种面积和产量(2018年)
Economic Crops Sown Areas and Output by Region(2018)

单位：公顷、吨　　(hectare, ton)

市(州)	Region	棉花 Cotton		油料 Oil bearing Crops		#花生 Peanut		#油菜籽 Rapeseeds		生麻 Bast Fiber	
		播种面积 Sown Area	产量 Yield	播种面积 Sown Area	产量 Yield	播种面积 Sown Area	产量 Yield	播种面积 Sown Area	产量 Yield	播种面积 Sown Area	产量 Yield
全　省	**Sichuan**	**4029**	**3994**	**1491199**	**3625373**	**263493**	**676720**	**1218485**	**2922031**	**17010**	**30957**
成都市	Chengdu	165	225	150062	372942	15306	42434	134170	329455		1
自贡市	Zigong			70232	154017	13716	34197	56285	119342		
攀枝花市	Panzhihua			2731	4200	743	1140	1982	3045		
泸州市	Luzhou			49910	100596	5761	11412	42793	88433		
德阳市	Deyang	131	110	86238	248091	12525	38953	73577	209062		
绵阳市	Mianyang	47	42	167942	436485	23033	76306	144825	359924		
广元市	Guangyuan			97124	253598	15186	57911	81784	184222	1	1
遂宁市	Suining	3294	3296	71567	196270	13215	33988	58095	161612	7	5
内江市	Neijiang			79537	169908	20069	41376	59431	128408	47	52
乐山市	Leshan			46229	82151	4601	9663	41574	72308		
南充市	Nanchong	237	145	149423	399853	48422	112150	99939	286437	126	239
眉山市	Meishan	38	43	57136	123844	3459	8897	53541	113603	1	3
宜宾市	Yibin			74134	155958	24814	62171	48109	91175	53	92
广安市	Guangan			48207	105800	10237	24879	37695	79795	31	77
达州市	Dazhou			134271	350731	24764	55062	108086	292444	16702	30371
雅安市	Yaan			7827	14670	225	661	7589	13987		
巴中市	Bazhong			79351	163711	7486	16687	70841	145969	7	10
资阳市	Ziyang	117	133	94383	242072	17848	44300	76535	197772		
阿坝藏族羌族自治州	Aba			3117	5212			3116	5212		
甘孜藏族自治州	Ganzi			5938	13401	91	184	5820	13170	4	4
凉山彝族自治州	Liangshan			15840	31863	1992	4349	12698	26656	31	102

13-19 续表 1 continued

单位：公顷、吨 (hectare, ton)

市(州)	Region	糖料 Sugar Crops 播种面积 Sown Area	糖料 Sugar Crops 产量 Yield	#甘蔗 Sugarcane 播种面积 Sown Area	#甘蔗 Sugarcane 产量 Yield	烟叶(未加工烟草) Tobacco (unmanufactured) 播种面积 Sown Area	烟叶(未加工烟草) Tobacco (unmanufactured) 产量 Yield	中草药材 Medicinal Herbs 播种面积 Sown Area	中草药材 Medicinal Herbs 产量 Yield	蔬菜及食用菌 Vegetables and Edible Fungus 播种面积 Sown Area	蔬菜及食用菌 Vegetables and Edible Fungus 产量 Yield
全 省	**Sichuan**	**9449**	**363699**	**9341**	**361825**	**76537**	**162460**	**124114**	**448282**	**1369173**	**44380219**
成都市	Chengdu	261	9859	261	9859	166	525	13811	60392	168336	5758541
自贡市	Zigong	1145	35257	1145	35257			971	5065	59473	2094516
攀枝花市	Panzhihua	231	26423	231	26423	5310	10932	534	936	15569	825017
泸州市	Luzhou	1269	72591	1269	72591	6435	7699	3103	24848	75152	2728224
德阳市	Deyang	130	5662	130	5662	1038	4192	7360	26310	63553	2298986
绵阳市	Mianyang	146	4910	146	4910			10460	41340	70275	1980704
广元市	Guangyuan	80	1078	77	961	2734	5194	10177	55670	70965	2646690
遂宁市	Suining	166	6446	164	6390			1728	9742	34866	1071266
内江市	Neijiang	510	19368	510	19368	1	3	1203	3836	76353	3010513
乐山市	Leshan	457	16700	457	16700	761	1325	11438	46893	51266	1254245
南充市	Nanchong	984	25402	890	23893	73	305	8244	21018	148256	3591897
眉山市	Meishan	313	12524	313	12524	66	138	1907	7815	46408	1339659
宜宾市	Yibin	878	23743	878	23743	5680	12260	4085	8081	77008	2656370
广安市	Guangan	235	6234	235	6234	13	34	1612	4797	64101	2361279
达州市	Dazhou	923	23561	923	23561	1106	2939	8118	21419	85728	2846380
雅安市	Yaan	2	51	2	51			7049	23731	30301	703691
巴中市	Bazhong	781	18813	781	18813	95	281	20077	46831	63060	1516023
资阳市	Ziyang	484	16146	484	16146	4	4	1529	7229	60827	1565177
阿坝藏族羌族自治州	Aba	9	192					2974	5468	19299	713462
甘孜藏族自治州	Ganzi							1860	5545	12004	320724
凉山彝族自治州	Liangshan	445	38739	445	38739	53055	116629	5874	21316	76373	3096855

13-19 续表 2 continued

单位：吨 (ton)

市(州)	Region	蚕茧产量 Yield of Silkworm Cocoons	茶叶产量 Yield of Tea	水果产量 Yield of Fruits	#园林水果 Yield of Graden Fruits	苹果 Yield of Apples	柑桔 Yield of Citrus	梨 Yield of Pears	其他 Yield of Other Fruits	水产品产量 Output of Aquatic Products
全 省	**Sichuan**	**92154**	**300715**	**10806728**	**9483940**	**725520**	**4329755**	**947462**	**3481203**	**1534754**
成都市	Chengdu	757	21007	1672740	1437725	3884	635481	102871	695489	142518
自贡市	Zigong	2497	12302	345829	297395		259320	14542	23533	77556
攀枝花市	Panzhihua	3608	120	411462	381089	29	2943	18515	359602	13600
泸州市	Luzhou	1349	14109	243685	224602	1235	98397	12521	112449	87866
德阳市	Deyang	2500	398	256334	161611	2011	60268	42859	56473	61446
绵阳市	Mianyang	7947	3166	372280	232479	2909	72084	36606	120880	116806
广元市	Guangyuan	1586	11655	378997	366210	18823	76148	145046	126193	53420
遂宁市	Suining	530	107	126103	93822	797	52165	14614	26246	54100
内江市	Neijiang	2297	2667	433419	405319	145	322854	28073	54247	117361
乐山市	Leshan	757	41896	178049	161379	11	93591	8211	59566	119010
南充市	Nanchong	13267	37	644451	525489	1088	416341	47076	60984	112500
眉山市	Meishan	582	20993	1128869	1095204	20	776968	65341	252875	128610
宜宾市	Yibin	21289	65007	671449	598776	15	330610	91308	176843	107229
广安市	Guangan	1588	555	270931	179529	70	144513	13807	21139	66011
达州市	Dazhou	389	10969	460684	341589	3195	222966	25399	90029	97509
雅安市	Yaan	107	84075	404514	395496	87378	69444	118943	119731	10220
巴中市	Bazhong	425	10695	105201	73296	3327	27294	12451	30224	70777
资阳市	Ziyang	3959		806016	669219		629839	16016	23364	68489
阿坝藏族羌族自治州	Aba		34	199039	198984	66390		14934	117660	150
甘孜藏族自治州	Ganzi		103	18153	17154	9107	853	1874	5320	140
凉山彝族自治州	Liangshan	26719	820	1678523	1627573	525086	37676	116455	948356	29436

13-20 各市(州)油料产量
Output of Oil-bearing Crops by Region

单位：万吨 (10 000 tons)

市(州)	Region	2010	2011	2012	2013	2014	2015	2016	2017	2018
全 省	**Sichuan**	**296.1**	**306.7**	**315.9**	**320.2**	**332.0**	**339.6**	**346.2**	**357.9**	**362.5**
成都市	Chengdu	33.3	33.8	34.3	34.2	35.3	35.1	35.5	36.9	37.3
自贡市	Zigong	9.8	10.2	10.7	10.9	11.9	12.6	13.4	15.0	15.4
攀枝花市	Panzhihua	0.4	0.4	0.4	0.4	0.4	0.4	0.4	0.4	0.4
泸州市	Luzhou	6.0	6.4	6.6	6.7	7.1	7.4	7.7	10.2	10.1
德阳市	Deyang	22.1	22.6	23.4	24.2	24.5	24.7	24.7	24.7	24.8
绵阳市	Mianyang	37.0	38.5	39.3	39.6	40.9	42.2	42.5	43.0	43.6
广元市	Guangyuan	20.6	21.5	22.2	22.6	23.3	24.1	24.5	25.0	25.4
遂宁市	Suining	16.3	17.3	18.0	18.0	18.8	19.2	19.4	19.5	19.6
内江市	Neijiang	12.1	12.9	13.5	13.8	14.5	14.9	15.5	16.9	17.0
乐山市	Leshan	6.3	6.9	7.3	7.1	7.8	8.0	8.2	8.2	8.2
南充市	Nanchong	34.9	35.1	35.8	36.4	37.5	38.0	38.6	39.3	40.0
眉山市	Meishan	10.4	10.6	10.6	10.7	11.1	11.6	12.0	12.1	12.4
宜宾市	Yibin	10.6	10.9	12.0	12.5	13.3	14.0	14.8	15.4	15.6
广安市	Guangan	9.2	9.4	9.6	9.7	9.9	10.1	10.3	10.4	10.6
达州市	Dazhou	29.7	30.4	31.0	31.5	32.3	32.9	33.8	34.5	35.1
雅安市	Yaan	1.5	1.5	1.6	1.5	1.6	1.5	1.5	1.5	1.5
巴中市	Bazhong	13.6	14.2	14.5	14.7	14.9	15.4	15.8	16.1	16.4
资阳市	Ziyang	18.2	19.7	20.4	21.0	22.3	22.9	23.6	24.5	24.2
阿坝藏族羌族自治州	Aba	0.2	0.3	0.3	0.3	0.3	0.3	0.4	0.4	0.5
甘孜藏族自治州	Ganzi	0.5	0.6	0.6	0.7	0.7	0.7	0.8	0.9	1.3
凉山彝族自治州	Liangshan	3.5	3.7	3.7	3.8	3.6	3.7	2.9	3.1	3.2

13-21 牲畜饲养情况
Number of Livestock

单位：万头、万只　　(10 000 heads)

年份 Year	肉猪出栏头数 Slaughtered Fattened Hogs	猪年末头数 Hogs (year-end)	肉牛出栏头数 Slaughtered Beef Cattle	大牲畜年末头数 Large Animals (year-end)	#牛 Cattle and Buffaloes	#马 Horses	肉羊出栏只数 Slaughtered Sheep	羊年末只数 Sheep and Goats (year-end)	家禽出栏只数 Slaughtered Poultry (year-end)	家禽年末只数 Poultry (year-end)
1952	393.00	943.00		500.00	474.00	23.00		262.00		
1957	733.00	1754.00		556.00	527.00	25.00		438.00		
1962	276.00	982.00		508.00	488.00	17.00		482.00		
1965	1130.00	1804.00		615.00	591.00	20.00		578.00		
1970	1195.00	2244.00		726.00	698.00	23.00		682.00		
1975	1314.00	2988.00		769.00	737.00	27.00		800.00		
1978	1614.00	3243.00		781.00	745.00	30.00		861.00		
1980	2264.00	3823.00	48.70	809.00	773.00	32.00	372.00	923.00		
1985	3223.00	4370.00	45.10	855.00	808.00	41.00	283.90	786.00		
1990	4507.00	4842.00	70.20	936.00	876.00	51.00	247.80	833.00		
1991	4699.00	4887.00	81.59	953.00	888.00	53.00	322.85	836.00		
1992	4887.00	4933.00	93.30	947.00	883.00	54.00	343.50	828.00		
1993	5010.00	4948.00	113.10	999.00	905.00	57.00	382.30	852.00	34212.50	
1994	5363.00	5107.00	139.40	1000.00	931.00	58.00	463.15	913.00	39552.35	
1995	5844.00	5284.00	143.15	1035.00	963.00	60.00	424.74	1000.00	46318.62	
1996	6068.00	5277.00	159.05	1049.00	976.00	61.00	552.39	1095.00	43202.82	
1997	6234.00	5280.00	179.34	1073.00	996.00	64.00	687.07	1178.00	49744.21	
1998	6402.00	5271.00	194.88	1092.00	1012.00	67.00	843.72	1282.00	55430.69	
1999	6439.00	5204.00	194.86	1113.00	1030.00	69.00	1012.42	1383.00	63782.96	28891.80
2000	6594.37	5229.23	220.92	1132.90	1046.66	71.29	1249.43	1516.93	72291.88	32724.80
2001	6778.21	5222.78	244.99	1151.99	1062.27	74.59	1459.61	1633.31	79915.99	34113.57
2002	7090.89	5339.69	276.01	1176.87	1082.81	78.09	1704.59	1745.54	89018.51	37987.85
2003	7490.28	5484.17	310.05	1208.73	1110.88	81.47	1984.24	1898.97	97886.23	41537.17
2004	8103.34	5717.31	337.87	1234.09	1131.51	84.79	2314.33	2040.89	107208.79	44949.57
2005	8817.32	5970.69	366.80	1253.75	1146.92	88.45	2546.22	2140.25	119283.77	47810.85
2006	6905.58	5100.24	248.91	1096.15	985.67	91.10	1477.57	1629.32	47508.00	41309.25
2007	6014.61	5127.39	246.98	1098.40	981.31	95.18	1543.02	1659.05	51370.10	43215.29
2008	6429.19	5143.91	249.42	1044.86	930.06	94.07	1558.69	1617.71	53933.92	39804.47
2009	6914.93	4906.95	240.98	1050.93	933.46	96.45	1576.80	1572.10	54565.33	39897.82
2010	7174.95	4917.49	242.47	1054.06	934.70	97.54	1609.48	1467.39	56423.74	39745.36
2011	7000.41	4705.02	235.32	1051.34	935.37	94.58	1550.84	1424.63	57942.73	37714.54
2012	7170.70	4718.45	238.25	965.31	857.24	87.19	1562.70	1390.85	61999.60	36245.82
2013	7314.10	4507.69	242.04	958.80	858.67	80.38	1583.60	1362.79	63774.70	36052.58
2014	7445.00	4510.22	251.61	966.88	869.88	77.29	1632.70	1369.74	64667.60	37353.45
2015	7236.54	4288.39	263.34	953.72	857.80	76.22	1698.00	1352.31	66154.91	39869.79
2016	6907.82	4078.80	268.58	922.38	831.18	74.75	1739.19	1296.03	68489.75	38754.07
2017	6579.10	4376.64	267.26	947.18	853.19	75.46	1780.38	1599.26	65259.81	36619.20
2018	6638.34	4258.47	276.19	925.15	824.30	74.31	1740.89	1462.90	66070.96	38440.70

注：2007年至2017年牲畜饲养及畜禽产品产量数据根据第三次全国农业普查结果进行了修订(以下有关各表同)。

a) Data of livestock raising and livestock production in 2007 to 2017 were revised according to the results of the Third National Agricultural Census (the same as the following related tables).

13-22 各市(州)牲畜饲养情况(2018年)
Number of Livestock by Region(2018)

单位：万头、万只 (10 000 heads)

市(州)	Region	肉猪出栏头数 Slaughtered Fattened Hogs	猪年末头数 Hogs (year-end)	肉牛出栏头数 Slaughtered Beef Cattle	大牲畜年末头数 Large Animals (year-end)	#牛 Cattle and Buffaloes	#马 Horses	肉羊出栏只数 Slaughtered Sheep	羊年末只数 Sheep and Goats (year-end)	家禽出栏只数 Slaughtered Poultry (year-end)	家禽年末只数 Poultry (year-end)
全 省	**Sichuan**	**6638.34**	**4258.47**	**276.19**	**925.15**	**824.30**	**74.31**	**1740.89**	**1462.90**	**66070.96**	**38440.70**
成都市	Chengdu	585.87	367.62	3.77	7.33	7.31	0.02	92.24	49.74	7670.32	3160.00
自贡市	Zigong	176.71	105.66	2.51	4.66	4.63	0.03	89.44	46.91	2700.95	1181.16
攀枝花市	Panzhihua	56.32	41.12	3.35	9.22	8.51	0.29	46.50	42.25	415.55	310.43
泸州市	Luzhou	401.33	248.98	6.80	18.82	18.14	0.39	50.40	38.01	3591.37	2220.27
德阳市	Deyang	302.74	187.80	6.34	11.09	11.09		21.89	17.98	6334.29	2921.45
绵阳市	Mianyang	356.23	231.71	11.17	23.10	22.61	0.48	97.02	74.40	6269.21	3154.27
广元市	Guangyuan	367.72	238.54	7.91	20.51	20.51	0.01	55.84	35.20	2049.78	1825.92
遂宁市	Suining	375.22	228.68	3.25	6.47	6.47		36.64	23.04	2087.22	1429.97
内江市	Neijiang	260.02	157.63	1.59	3.26	3.11	0.15	50.79	32.63	2696.55	1719.25
乐山市	Leshan	306.71	192.92	2.96	6.19	5.76	0.43	32.09	22.31	3571.93	1708.88
南充市	Nanchong	584.13	380.14	11.68	25.71	25.12	0.48	189.11	122.93	5815.48	4215.01
眉山市	Meishan	253.03	161.32	2.07	4.80	4.80		46.01	31.93	3058.59	1459.97
宜宾市	Yibin	482.09	321.78	11.87	24.89	24.40	0.49	41.09	28.33	4225.60	2283.39
广安市	Guangan	379.41	235.50	2.27	4.85	4.83	0.02	20.40	14.20	2950.41	2118.33
达州市	Dazhou	426.38	281.29	30.23	56.34	55.75	0.38	118.29	82.33	6208.93	2968.55
雅安市	Yaan	122.89	83.91	5.19	13.55	12.60	0.89	21.97	17.10	762.19	707.32
巴中市	Bazhong	349.46	218.86	18.80	36.96	36.95	0.01	95.39	70.51	1151.37	810.66
资阳市	Ziyang	297.20	193.89	1.59	3.45	3.31	0.14	125.00	69.85	2187.02	1524.72
阿坝藏羌族自治州	Aba	38.30	27.48	53.14	226.36	216.53	9.47	46.51	89.33	65.18	50.42
甘孜藏族自治州	Ganzi	24.29	17.87	54.13	253.92	219.64	31.37	41.38	72.85	20.44	27.19
凉山彝族自治州	Liangshan	492.29	336.53	36.37	154.80	112.48	29.26	423.96	481.04	1905.47	1366.69

注：全省总量为国家统计局核定的抽样调查数据，各市州为各地上报的全面统计数据，故部分指标市州汇总数与全省总量存在一定差异(以下有关各表同)。

a) The total amount of the province is the sample survey data approved by the State Statistical Bureau, and the data of cities and states are comprehensive statistical data reported by various regions. Therefore, there are some differences between the sum-up data of cities and states with some indicators and the total amount of the province(the same as the related following tables).

13-23 各市(州)猪年末头数
Number of Hogs by Region at Year-end

单位：万头 (10 000 heads)

市(州)	Region	2010	2011	2012	2013	2014	2015	2016	2017	2018
全　省	**Sichuan**	**4917.49**	**4705.02**	**4718.45**	**4507.69**	**4510.22**	**4288.39**	**4078.80**	**4376.64**	**4258.47**
成都市	Chengdu	557.38	524.41	536.39	488.81	482.23	442.37	377.67	402.32	367.62
自贡市	Zigong	145.55	138.31	142.74	139.17	136.01	121.95	101.67	108.11	105.66
攀枝花市	Panzhihua	43.08	41.44	44.36	41.30	41.97	41.31	40.64	41.48	41.12
泸州市	Luzhou	268.27	250.40	249.34	243.31	250.21	240.98	234.21	261.39	248.98
德阳市	Deyang	215.02	206.87	205.30	214.90	214.52	192.97	177.05	194.11	187.80
绵阳市	Mianyang	250.50	236.50	238.21	243.00	240.43	222.51	218.63	232.68	231.71
广元市	Guangyuan	242.37	222.58	223.49	230.64	229.09	222.01	219.56	241.62	238.54
遂宁市	Suining	232.64	224.19	222.79	230.85	237.21	224.88	209.19	239.39	228.68
内江市	Neijiang	231.43	220.32	213.60	187.11	188.21	171.45	149.88	160.94	157.63
乐山市	Leshan	209.03	202.91	204.75	220.63	204.79	202.73	184.84	197.91	192.92
南充市	Nanchong	411.11	405.04	399.88	369.35	375.20	355.00	365.17	386.66	380.14
眉山市	Meishan	207.84	198.80	196.18	176.09	179.74	173.22	154.94	165.23	161.32
宜宾市	Yibin	321.48	309.51	307.27	291.12	311.47	302.16	280.42	315.92	321.78
广安市	Guangan	315.42	297.99	295.81	269.12	266.61	254.98	221.40	242.20	235.50
达州市	Dazhou	354.83	342.49	339.76	292.29	287.13	278.66	276.75	286.05	281.29
雅安市	Yaan	86.91	82.98	82.63	80.36	87.23	86.03	83.92	87.15	83.91
巴中市	Bazhong	231.06	217.27	222.43	218.38	210.53	202.81	217.68	227.12	218.86
资阳市	Ziyang	203.66	197.76	205.89	201.97	196.90	192.17	180.74	200.30	193.89
阿坝藏羌族自治州	Aba	22.07	22.27	25.45	26.06	27.50	27.42	27.04	26.88	27.48
甘孜藏族自治州	Ganzi	14.92	14.64	16.52	16.70	16.91	16.86	17.46	17.45	17.87
凉山彝族自治州	Liangshan	352.92	347.34	345.65	326.52	326.32	315.90	339.95	341.71	336.53

13-24 各市(州)大牲畜年末头数
Number of Large Animals by Region at Year-end

单位：万头 (10 000 heads)

市(州)	Region	2010	2011	2012	2013	2014	2015	2016	2017	2018
全　省	**Sichuan**	**1054.06**	**1051.34**	**965.31**	**958.80**	**966.88**	**953.72**	**922.38**	**947.18**	**925.15**
成都市	Chengdu	12.66	11.59	10.87	11.23	11.65	11.68	7.98	7.87	7.33
自贡市	Zigong	5.78	5.60	5.43	5.95	6.40	5.80	3.85	4.75	4.66
攀枝花市	Panzhihua	9.92	10.47	10.00	9.64	9.60	9.67	9.41	10.23	9.22
泸州市	Luzhou	27.40	27.11	25.88	24.71	22.79	19.36	17.16	18.59	18.82
德阳市	Deyang	14.58	14.84	13.36	14.15	13.92	13.72	10.72	11.31	11.09
绵阳市	Mianyang	38.42	37.77	30.73	28.11	29.04	22.99	21.22	23.48	23.10
广元市	Guangyuan	22.98	23.07	20.67	20.36	20.04	20.06	20.07	20.44	20.51
遂宁市	Suining	9.42	8.89	8.47	8.41	7.92	7.07	6.30	6.43	6.47
内江市	Neijiang	6.77	6.18	5.53	5.02	5.10	3.65	2.94	3.20	3.26
乐山市	Leshan	10.01	9.63	8.84	8.79	7.98	6.55	5.63	6.05	6.19
南充市	Nanchong	31.84	32.09	29.80	28.29	29.18	26.12	25.10	25.42	25.71
眉山市	Meishan	11.15	10.70	9.23	8.06	7.50	5.63	4.50	4.77	4.80
宜宾市	Yibin	22.49	24.29	23.01	23.87	23.95	22.81	22.02	24.72	24.89
广安市	Guangan	12.10	12.12	9.52	8.23	8.01	5.61	4.75	4.92	4.85
达州市	Dazhou	65.78	66.98	62.01	61.68	62.26	58.25	53.73	55.73	56.34
雅安市	Yaan	14.52	14.63	13.67	14.07	14.05	13.98	13.03	13.66	13.55
巴中市	Bazhong	43.63	43.31	37.48	37.85	40.43	37.73	36.87	35.98	36.96
资阳市	Ziyang	5.36	5.03	4.71	4.19	3.81	3.45	3.16	3.34	3.45
阿坝藏羌族自治州	Aba	216.35	221.80	216.19	226.73	234.42	236.15	244.24	248.22	226.36
甘孜藏族自治州	Ganzi	310.25	300.40	263.31	252.96	254.31	258.23	259.61	263.35	253.92
凉山彝族自治州	Liangshan	162.63	164.83	156.60	156.48	154.51	155.22	150.10	154.72	154.80

13-25 畜产品产量
Output of Livestock Products

年份 Year	肉类总产量 (万吨) Output of Meat (10 000 tons)	#猪肉 Pork	#牛肉 Beef	#羊肉 Mutton	#禽肉 Poultry	#兔肉 Rabbit	禽蛋产量 (万吨) Output of Poultry Eggs (10 000 tons)	奶类产量 (万吨) Output of Milk (10 000 tons)	蜂蜜产量 (吨) Output of Honey (ton)	绵羊毛产量 (吨) Output of Sheep Wool (ton)
1952	17.10	15.60								
1957	35.20	33.40								
1962	8.00	6.90								
1965	52.20	49.80								
1970	52.80	51.50								
1975	59.60	57.30								
1978	78.00	76.00						5.77		
1980	125.40	119.80	3.56	3.69				11.00		2602
1985	208.40	202.50	4.09	3.15				19.00	11584	2392
1990	301.00	292.30	6.86	3.74			35.00	22.00	14763	2729
1991	319.00	300.10	8.35	3.92			38.00	23.00	16044	2779
1992	333.00	321.90	9.50	4.30			43.00	23.00	15514	2866
1993	347.00	333.40	11.60	5.20			48.00	23.00	14702	3021
1994	373.00	355.60	14.87	6.33	64.55		54.00	23.00	15535	3008
1995	472.96	391.87	15.51	6.29	67.90		60.00	24.00	17922	3265
1996	501.64	408.71	17.07	8.09	63.35		67.00	24.00	18541	3269
1997	531.57	424.39	19.30	10.04	72.75		74.00	26.00	19403	3434
1998	568.11	447.10	21.33	12.74	81.35		80.00	27.00	21414	3760
1999	605.40	464.03	22.87	15.74	95.92		89.00	27.00	22829	3963
2000	641.25	478.59	25.27	19.19	109.68		99.70	28.92	22681	4108
2001	680.41	495.42	28.37	22.85	121.95	10.09	108.76	33.34	26567	4288
2002	735.84	522.19	33.01	27.88	139.02	11.98	121.11	39.32	29396	4800
2003	795.26	554.39	37.32	32.59	154.57	14.30	133.61	45.84	32944	5059
2004	870.62	601.37	41.55	38.53	170.44	16.77	145.21	53.00	32613	5375
2005	955.87	657.07	45.19	42.74	189.77	19.13	157.17	59.03	34704	5801
2006	622.67	481.42	28.34	21.36	68.07	21.39	140.69	62.71	38863	6047
2007	565.47	407.70	27.58	23.88	78.82	25.26	145.20	65.60	42753	6513
2008	587.53	434.46	27.69	24.06	80.76	18.92	142.96	68.93	43354	6548
2009	627.36	472.38	27.82	24.31	81.49	19.81	143.97	68.88	47370	6824
2010	651.53	492.25	27.94	24.80	84.11	20.74	144.81	71.25	46037	6892
2011	644.99	484.73	27.11	23.90	86.73	20.83	145.02	72.36	49890	6940
2012	663.16	496.40	27.24	24.00	93.00	20.81	146.40	72.12	52683	7098
2013	682.31	510.80	28.44	24.50	95.60	21.22	145.20	71.09	51107	5854
2014	704.10	527.20	30.15	25.30	97.40	22.30	145.30	71.30	53933	5939
2015	694.33	512.42	31.53	26.32	99.69	22.61	146.65	67.49	55862	6038
2016	680.36	492.32	32.44	26.78	103.10	23.98	149.68	62.77	55815	6046
2017	653.82	472.23	33.31	27.24	99.05	20.23	144.50	63.79	57668	5840
2018	664.74	481.20	34.47	26.31	100.59	20.43	148.80	64.27	54287	5475

13-26 各市(州)畜产品产量(2018年)
Output of Livestock Products by Region(2018)

市(州)	Region	肉类总产量(万吨) Output of Meat (10 000 tons)	#猪肉 Pork	#牛肉 Beef	#羊肉 Mutton	#禽肉 Poultry	#兔肉 Rabbit
全 省	**Sichuan**	**664.74**	**481.20**	**34.47**	**26.31**	**100.59**	**20.43**
成都市	Chengdu	59.36	42.73	0.46	1.42	12.69	1.92
自贡市	Zigong	22.30	12.73	0.32	1.33	4.12	3.58
攀枝花市	Panzhihua	5.86	4.05	0.43	0.72	0.63	0.02
泸州市	Luzhou	37.21	28.97	0.84	0.77	5.42	1.19
德阳市	Deyang	34.56	21.77	0.70	0.32	9.68	2.04
绵阳市	Mianyang	38.97	25.59	1.29	1.48	9.45	1.12
广元市	Guangyuan	32.56	26.50	1.00	0.85	2.81	1.37
遂宁市	Suining	32.34	27.31	0.36	0.54	3.39	0.69
内江市	Neijiang	24.84	18.77	0.19	0.74	3.96	1.18
乐山市	Leshan	28.85	21.97	0.35	0.50	5.46	0.57
南充市	Nanchong	58.38	42.52	1.42	2.81	8.32	2.84
眉山市	Meishan	24.70	18.39	0.25	0.67	4.81	0.44
宜宾市	Yibin	46.05	36.72	1.46	0.53	6.00	1.33
广安市	Guangan	33.09	27.65	0.26	0.29	4.19	0.63
达州市	Dazhou	46.01	30.66	3.53	1.81	9.52	0.41
雅安市	Yaan	11.69	8.71	0.63	0.33	1.59	0.44
巴中市	Bazhong	30.89	25.35	2.21	1.43	1.74	0.15
资阳市	Ziyang	27.10	21.51	0.18	1.70	3.29	0.32
阿坝藏族羌族自治州	Aba	10.80	2.71	7.20	0.69	0.11	0.08
甘孜藏族自治州	Ganzi	9.21	1.66	6.82	0.70	0.03	0.00
凉山彝族自治州	Liangshan	49.37	34.73	4.57	6.86	2.84	0.11

13-26 续表 continued

市(州)	Region	奶类 (万吨) Milk (10 000 tons)	出栏家禽 (万只) Slaughtered Poultry (10 000 heads)	出栏肉兔 (万只) Slaughtered Rabbit (10 000 heads)	禽蛋 (吨) Poultry Eggs (ton)	蜂蜜 (吨) Honey (ton)	蚕茧 (吨) Silkworm Cocoons (ton)
全　省	**Sichuan**	**64.27**	**66070.96**	**16415.49**	**1488026**	**54287**	**92154**
成都市	Chengdu	8.55	7670.32	1317.42	176409	2740	757
自贡市	Zigong	1.64	2700.95	3206.32	48983	780	2497
攀枝花市	Panzhihua	0.02	415.55	13.71	10077	102	3608
泸州市	Luzhou	0.13	3591.37	965.83	42289	2810	1349
德阳市	Deyang	1.05	6334.29	1636.35	115862	5163	2500
绵阳市	Mianyang	1.76	6269.21	842.81	140691	6934	7947
广元市	Guangyuan		2049.78	1071.76	37586	1273	1586
遂宁市	Suining	0.14	2087.22	598.96	90898	2055	530
内江市	Neijiang	0.80	2696.55	990.84	46199	899	2297
乐山市	Leshan	0.10	3571.93	486.34	119218	469	757
南充市	Nanchong	2.57	5815.48	2115.86	196530	1500	13267
眉山市	Meishan	11.61	3058.59	347.73	53603	11938	582
宜宾市	Yibin	0.33	4225.60	1039.69	41011	1508	21289
广安市	Guangan	0.27	2950.41	492.67	69216	599	1588
达州市	Dazhou	1.74	6208.93	325.40	98488	8882	389
雅安市	Yaan	2.99	762.19	395.38	24222	592	107
巴中市	Bazhong		1151.37	116.03	64197	1273	425
资阳市	Ziyang	1.30	2187.02	312.67	74419	1037	3959
阿坝藏族羌族自治州	Aba	12.95	65.18	57.77	1671	952	
甘孜藏族自治州	Ganzi	10.37	20.44	1.18	385	91	
凉山彝族自治州	Liangshan	4.55	1905.47	80.79	27511	2690	26719

13-27 各市(州)肉类总产量
Output of Meat by Region

单位：万吨 (10 000 tons)

市(州)	Region	2010	2011	2012	2013	2014	2015	2016	2017	2018
全 省	**Sichuan**	**651.53**	**644.99**	**663.16**	**682.31**	**704.10**	**694.33**	**680.36**	**653.82**	**664.74**
成都市	Chengdu	79.69	78.59	80.83	78.23	78.68	75.00	68.15	62.03	59.36
自贡市	Zigong	23.52	23.48	23.86	24.37	24.99	24.30	23.37	21.61	22.30
攀枝花市	Panzhihua	4.92	4.90	5.10	5.27	5.55	5.80	5.61	5.68	5.86
泸州市	Luzhou	31.46	30.95	31.89	34.79	36.62	36.55	37.06	36.40	37.21
德阳市	Deyang	34.71	34.48	35.69	37.18	36.95	36.45	35.59	34.14	34.56
绵阳市	Mianyang	38.36	37.96	39.04	41.40	41.55	40.68	38.95	37.79	38.97
广元市	Guangyuan	27.91	27.76	28.83	30.90	32.13	32.22	32.50	31.54	32.56
遂宁市	Suining	30.64	30.26	31.07	32.36	33.54	33.00	33.38	31.68	32.34
内江市	Neijiang	26.68	26.26	27.03	27.62	28.37	27.28	26.26	24.22	24.84
乐山市	Leshan	28.88	28.35	29.18	30.62	30.55	30.83	30.24	28.39	28.85
南充市	Nanchong	55.66	55.32	56.57	58.34	60.91	59.96	60.34	57.25	58.38
眉山市	Meishan	25.23	24.87	25.61	26.01	27.31	27.05	25.43	24.18	24.70
宜宾市	Yibin	39.02	38.48	39.51	42.11	45.25	44.37	44.17	44.95	46.05
广安市	Guangan	34.10	33.47	33.46	36.09	37.41	36.88	35.02	32.51	33.09
达州市	Dazhou	44.06	45.43	47.43	47.25	47.74	46.86	46.41	44.73	46.01
雅安市	Yaan	11.78	11.64	11.87	11.66	13.16	13.08	11.61	11.45	11.69
巴中市	Bazhong	30.53	29.71	30.36	30.12	30.85	30.52	30.24	30.13	30.89
资阳市	Ziyang	29.44	28.86	29.62	29.27	29.77	29.00	28.63	27.29	27.10
阿坝藏羌族自治州	Aba	6.45	6.58	7.22	8.04	9.18	9.96	10.35	10.32	10.80
甘孜藏族自治州	Ganzi	6.05	6.13	6.26	6.64	7.40	7.99	8.98	9.00	9.21
凉山彝族自治州	Liangshan	42.43	41.54	42.73	44.02	46.18	46.53	48.18	48.53	49.37

13-28 林产品产量及造林面积
Output of Major Forest Products and Areas under Afforestation

年 份 Year	林产品产量 (吨) Output of Major Forest Products (ton)					造林面积 (万公顷) Area under Afforestation (10 000 hectares)
	生 漆 Lacquer	油桐籽 Tung-oil Seeds	油茶籽 Tea-oil Seeds	核桃(干重) Walnut (dry weight)	竹笋干 Bamboo Shoots	
1952	85	94011	5643	2933	279	2.13
1957	128	80337	15276	8703	604	10.18
1962	43	36729	2793	3075	2046	12.72
1965	114	47777	2223	1750	604	11.57
1970	175	57101	1141	4162	976	15.41
1975	132	63946	3288	5474	1022	21.59
1978	160	114035	8439	9060	906	20.05
1980	313	61994	5282	9468	1119	20.29
1985	127	53921	2242	7222	1437	47.44
1990	507	49580	1878	15655	2946	26.50
1991	301	53539	1800	12736	3574	27.00
1992	300	61264	1960	13740	3236	27.40
1993	327	67628	1854	16284	3591	26.30
1994	565	70442	3049	21928	4563	25.10
1995	302	60726	4047	22928	5378	25.00
1996	377	54743	2922	24819	6146	25.60
1997	472	41498	3903	22059	5593	28.15
1998	549	40544	6479	28711	6100	38.51
1999	1274	39626	4273	23842	7886	40.46
2000	826	46534	4372	32095	8914	48.91
2001	611	37149	4278	32744	9925	51.66
2002	1091	53152	10228	70534	23722	69.46
2003	1319	50299	11854	77004	28250	72.32
2004	1091	39276	4037	56731	40696	37.01
2005	725	30314	2464	59272	62190	24.19
2006	1335	36748	3578	61112	48895	10.49
2007	909	31352	10272	76721	40434	33.23
2008	841	28277	3358	91170	62826	57.46
2009	819	24236	3426	123683	51349	48.78
2010	675	22041	4360	126109	78952	38.22
2011	663	23923	4649	176710	128841	25.19
2012	546	17281	4180	211944	42292	11.22
2013	583	15276	5361	245876	87855	12.62
2014	477	16363	13718	293750	109554	9.82
2015	489	17934	20708	458435	138195	31.82
2016	431	14490	17254	451486	135266	56.85
2017	458	6972	20852	537474	122376	65.84
2018	293	5238	23119	573685	72900	43.68

注：本表数据由四川省林业和草原局提供。
a) Data in this table are provided by the bureau of Forestry and Grassland of Sichuan Province.

13-29 受灾面积和绝收面积
Areas Covered by Natural Disaster and Total Crop Failure

单位:万公顷 (10 000 hectares)

年 份 Year	受灾面积 Area Covered by Natural Disaster	绝收面积 Area of Total Crop Failure	水 灾 Flood		旱 灾 Drought	
			受灾面积 Area Covered	绝收面积 Total Crop Failure	受灾面积 Area Covered	绝收面积 Total Crop Failure
1952	53.8	30.1	7.6	4.2	46.2	25.9
1957	28.8	16.3	2.6	1.5	25.0	14.2
1962	193.6	109.9	22.0	10.2	157.1	94.2
1965	80.6	45.5	11.1	6.3	55.9	37.9
1975	110.0	62.1	13.8	7.5	92.7	51.4
1978	302.7	273.5	7.0	4.0	273.4	185.8
1980	201.5	112.9	51.8	26.9	83.0	42.3
1985	299.3	168.2	30.5	18.4	137.5	83.3
1990	322.8	169.4	63.7	33.0	181.5	93.2
1991	320.2	166.5	90.1	50.3	124.8	65.7
1992	343.2	185.5	73.3	39.9	131.8	84.4
1993	412.6	247.2	82.0	42.7	224.3	142.9
1994	437.4	302.6	19.2	11.8	336.7	243.5
1995	288.1	185.7	89.3	51.7	163.0	92.8
1996	393.2	221.9	56.3	31.8	174.3	103.5
1997	311.5	174.9	47.2	22.3	194.9	117.5
1998	316.3	172.7	141.6	81.9	141.6	71.2
1999	297.3	163.3	81.6	45.3	117.2	63.7
2000	432.0	251.3	82.3	42.2	309.3	186.0
2001	444.9	299.9	93.5	59.0	325.4	224.5
2002	241.9	135.3	92.8	59.8	90.3	44.7
2003	259.2	203.2	94.2	78.6	124.1	95.8
2004	149.0	22.9	70.1	70.0	30.4	4.0
2005	294.3	119.8	87.6	46.4	31.7	15.7
2006	156.6	21.6	79.2	10.1	40.2	2.6
2007	260.1	22.0	89.8	11.0	138.1	8.2
2008	141.2	6.7	20.6	1.6	10.7	0.3
2009	245.9	46.9	110.5	20.3	128.8	26.4
2010	232.4	85.1	150.8	42.3	62.8	38.4
2011	206.3	112.1	72.4	37.8	98.7	56.3
2012	201.2	119.3	113.4	58.9	97.5	63.2
2013	244.2	125.8	88.2	51.2	135.4	63.1
2014	92.8	48.4	29.2	17.1	58.3	28.2
2015	40.9	22.2	25.6	12.7	9.6	5.4
2016	41.0	25.2	17.8	10.9	8.7	5.9
2017	18.6	11.9	13.7	8.7	3.2	2.2
2018	49.3	6.5	35.7	5.6	9.9	0.8

注：本表由四川省民政厅提供。2004年及以前绝收面积为成灾面积。

a) Data in this table are provided by Civil Affairs Department of Sichuan Province.Data of total crop failure were area affected in 2004 and before.

13-30 农垦系统国营农场基本情况
Basic Statistics on State Farms of Land Reclamation

指　　标	Item	2010	2015	2016	2017	2018
农垦企业个数　(个)	Number of State Farms of Land Reclamation　(unit)	48	40	39	37	33
#农场	Number of Agricultural Farms	40	35	34	33	30
年末职工人数　(人)	Number of Staff and Workers (year-end)　(person)	3496	6258	6184	5854	6207
年末耕地面积　(亩)	Cultivated Area(year-end)　(mu)	12735	13091	13091	11559	12745
#当年开荒面积　(亩)	Newly Reclaimed Wasteland in the Year　(mu)					
工农业总产值(当年价)　(万元)	Gross Industrial and Agricultural Output Value (current price)　(10 000 yuan)	43561	34627	28563	27384	20909
粮食产量　(吨)	Yield of Grain　(ton)	7640	4243	3804	3068	12672
猪出栏头数　(头)	Number of Slaughtered Fattened Hogs　(head)	7300	3136	2127	2692	1629
猪年末头数　(头)	Number of Hogs (year-end)　(head)	5700	3411	2835	3206	2010
猪肉产量　(吨)	Output of Pork　(ton)	605	264	182	244	151
牛年末头数　(万头)	Number of Cattle and Buffalos (year-end)　(10 000 heads)	7	7	7	7	7
羊年末只数　(万只)	Number of Sheep and Goats (year-end)　(10 000 heads)	2	3	3	3	2
牛奶产量　(吨)	Output of Milk　(ton)	8425	5232	4939	5248	5105
羊毛产量　(吨)	Output of Wool　(ton)	14	1	1		
茶叶产量　(吨)	Output of Tea　(ton)	785	1028	1100	1074	1242
水果产量　(吨)	Output of Fruits　(ton)	3094	1690	1397	1184	954
大中型拖拉机拥有量　(台)	Large and Medium Agricultural Tractors　(set)					
手扶拖拉机拥有量　(台)	Mini and Walking Agricultural Tractors　(set)	6	3	10	10	4

注：本表数据由四川省农业农村厅提供。

a)The data of this table are provided by the department of Agricultural and Rural of Sichuan Province.

主要统计指标解释

农林牧渔业总产值 指以货币表现的农、林、牧、渔业全部产品和对农林牧渔业生产活动进行的各种支持性服务活动的价值总量，它反映一定时期内农林牧渔业生产总规模和总成果。农林牧渔业总产值的计算方法通常是按农、林、牧、渔业产品及其副产品的产量分别乘以各自单位产品价格求得；少数生产周期较长，当年没有产品或产品产量不易统计的，则采用间接方法匡算其产值；然后将四业产品产值及农林牧渔服务业产值相加即为农林牧渔业总产值。

粮食产量 指农业生产经营者日历年度内生产的全部粮食数量。按收获季节包括夏收粮食、早稻和秋收粮食，按作物品种包括谷物、薯类和豆类。其产量计算方法：谷物按脱粒后的原粮计算，豆类按去豆荚后的干豆计算；薯类(包括甘薯和马铃薯，不包括芋头和木薯)1963 年以前按每 4 公斤鲜薯折 1 公斤粮食计算，从 1964 年开始改为按每 5 公斤鲜薯折 1 公斤粮食计算，2014 年开始按鲜薯计算；城市郊区作为蔬菜的薯类(如马铃薯等)按鲜品计算，并且不作粮食统计。

棉花产量 指全社会的产量。包括春播棉和夏播棉。产量按皮棉计算。不包括木棉。

油料产量 指全部油料作物的生产量。包括花生、油菜籽、芝麻、向日葵籽、胡麻籽(亚麻籽)和其他油料。不包括大豆、木本油料和野生油料。花生以带壳干花生计算。

水产品产量 指渔业（捕捞和养殖）生产活动的最终有效成果，包括全部海水和淡水鱼类、甲壳类（虾、蟹）、贝类、头足类、藻类和其他类渔业产品的最终产量。

猪、牛、羊肉产量 指当年出栏并已屠宰、除去头蹄下水后带骨肉(即胴体重)的重量。包括全社会范围内的产量。

期初(末)畜禽存栏头(只)数 指报告期初(末)农村各种合作经济组织和国营农场、农民个人、机关、团体、学校、工矿企业、部队等单位以及城镇居民饲养的大牲畜、猪、羊、家禽等畜禽的数量。

耕地 指种植农作物的土地，包括熟地，新开发、复垦、整理地，休闲地（含轮歇地、轮作地）；以种植农作物（含蔬菜）为主，间有零星果树、桑树或其他树木的土地；平均每年能保证收获一季的已垦滩地和海涂。耕地中包括南方宽度＜1.0 米，北方宽度＜2.0 米固定的沟、渠、路和地坎（埂）；临时种植药材、草皮、花卉、苗木等的耕地，以及其他临时改变用途的耕地。

农作物播种面积 指农业生产经营者应在日历年度内收获农作物在全部土地（耕地或非耕地）上的播种或移植面积。凡是本年内收获的农作物，无论是本年还是上年播种，都算为播种面积，但不包括本年播种，下年收获的农作物面积。

耕地灌溉面积 指具有一定的水源，地块比较平整，灌溉工程或设备已经配套，在一般年景下能够进行正常灌溉的耕地面积。

农用化肥施用量 指本年内实际用于农业生产的化肥数量，包括氮肥、磷肥、钾肥和复合肥。化肥施用量要求按折纯量计算数量。折纯量是指把氮肥、磷肥、钾肥分别按含氮、含五氧化二磷、含氧化钾的百分之百成份进行折算后的数量。复合肥按其所含主要成分折算。

农业机械总动力 指全部农业机械动力的额定功率之和。农业机械是指用于种植业、畜牧业、渔业、农产品初加工、农用运输和农田基本建设等活动的机械及设备。农机总动力按使用能源不同分为以下四部分：

柴油发动机动力：指全部柴油发动机额定功率之和；

汽油发动机动力：指全部汽油发动机额定功率之和；

电动机动力：指全部电动机（含潜水电泵的电动机）额定功率之和；

其他机械动力：指采用柴油、汽油、电力之外的其他能源，如水力、风力、煤炭、太阳能等动力机械功率之和。

Explanatory Notes on Main Statistical Indicators

Gross Output Value of Farming, Forestry, Animal Husbandry and Fishery refers to the total value of products of agriculture, forestry, animal husbandry and fishery, and total value of services in support of agriculture, forestry, animal husbandry and fishery activities. It reflects the total scale and total result of agricultural production during a given period. Gross output value of agriculture is obtained by first multiplying the output of each product or by product by its price, resulting in the output value of each single item. For a small number of products, annual output of which is not available or difficult to get due to the long production or growing process involved, the output value is estimated through an indirect approach. The sum of output values of all products of agriculture, forestry, animal husbandry and fishery and services in support to those industries is then equal to the gross output value of agriculture.

Grain Output refers to the total output of grains produced by agricultural producers within a calendar year. It includes summer grain, early rice and autumn grain if classified by harvest seasons; it covers cereal, tubers and beans if classified by type of crops. Output of cereal should be limited to husked grain only. Output of beans refers to dry beans without pods. The output of tubers (sweet potatoes and potatoes, not including taros and cassava) are converted into that of grain at the ratio 4:1, i.e. 4 kilograms of fresh tubers were equivalent to 1 kilogram of grain up to 1963. Since 1964 the ratio for conversion has been 5:1, and starting from 2014, the ratio for conversion has been 1:1. Tubers supplied as vegetables (such as potatoes) in cities and suburbs are calculated as fresh vegetables and their output is not included in the output of grain.

Cotton Output refers to the cotton production in the whole country including cotton sown in spring and in autumn. Output is measured as the weight of ginned cotton, excluding ceiba.

Yield of Oil-bearing Crops refers to the total yield of oil bearing crops of various kinds, including peanuts, (dry, in shell) rape seeds, sesame, sunflower seeds, flax seeds, and other oil bearing crops. Soybeans, oil-bearing woody plants, and wild oil-bearing crops are not included.

Output of Aquatic Products refers to final output actually yielded from fishing production (fishery and breeding), including all output of marine and freshwater fish, crustaceans (shrimps, crabs), shellfish, cephalopod, seaweed and other fishery products.

Output of Pork, Beef, and Mutton refers to the meat of slaughtered hogs, cattle, sheep and goats with head, feet, and offal taken away. Data refers to the production of the whole country.

Number of Livestock or Poultry in Stock at Beginning (or End) of Period refers to the total number of large animals, pigs, sheep, fowls, etc. raised by rural cooperative organizations, state farms, rural individuals, government agencies, schools, industrial and mining enterprises, army, and urban residents at the beginning (or end) of the reference period.

Arable Land refers to the area of land mainly for the regular cultivation of farm crops (including vegetables), with some fruit trees, mulberry trees and others, covers cultivated land, newly-developed land, reclaimed land, consolidated land, fallow, beach land that can guarantee one harvest per year on average. It also covers fixed ditch, canal, road and sill (ridge) with width less than 1 meter in the South and 2 meters in the North, lands planted temporarily with herbs, grass, flowers and nursery stocks, and other cultivated land with temporary change of use.

Sown Area of Crops refers to area of all land (cultivated or non-cultivated area) sown or transplanted with crops that are harvested within the calendar year by agricultural producers. All crops harvested within the year are counted as sown area, regardless of being sown in this year or the previous year. Crops sown this year but will be harvested in the coming year are excluded.

Irrigated Area of Cultivated Land refers to area of land that are effectively irrigated, i.e. relatively level land, where there are water sources or complete sets of irrigation facilities to lift and move adequate water for irrigation purpose under normal conditions.

Consumption of Chemical Fertilizers in Agriculture refers to the quantity of chemical fertilizers applied in agriculture in the year, including nitrogenous fertilizer, phosphate fertilizer, potash fertilizer, and compound fertilizer. The consumption of chemical fertilizers is required in calculation to convert the gross weight into weight containing 100% effective component (e.g. 100% nitrogen content in nitrogenous fertilizer, 100% phosphorous pent oxide contents in phosphate fertilizer, 100% potassium oxide contents in potash fertilizer). Compound fertilizer is converted with its major component.

Total Power of Farm Machinery refers to the total rated capacity of all agricultural machinery. Agricultural machinery refers to the machineries and equipment which are used for activities of planting, animal husbandry, fishery, primary processing of agricultural products, agricultural transport and infrastructure construction of farmland. Total power of agricultural machinery is grouped into four parts according to the energy used:

Diesel engine power refers to the total rated capacity of all diesel engines.

Gasoline engine power refers to the total rated capacity of all gasoline engines.

Motor power refers to the total rated capacity of all motors (include submersible pump motors).

Other mechanical powers refer to the total mechanical capacity of the sources of energy besides diesel, gasoline and motor power, such as hydro power, wind power, coal and solar energy.

工业

Chapter 14 Industry

14-1 规模以上工业企业主要指标(2018年)
Main Indicators of Industrial Enterprises above Designated Size(2018)

分 类	Item	企业单位数(个) Number of Enter-prises (unit)	资产总计(亿元) Total Assets (100 million yuan)	营业收入(亿元) Business Revenue (100 million yuan)	利润总额(亿元) Total Profits (100 million yuan)	全部从业人员年平均人数(万人) Annual Average Number of Employed Persons (10 000 persons)
总 计	**Total**	**13915**	**46015.75**	**41833.78**	**3055.93**	**299.18**
按轻重工业分	**Grouped by Light &Heavy Industries**					
轻工业	Light Industry	5447	9395.64	12974.84	1087.60	103.93
重工业	Heavy Industry	8468	36620.11	28858.94	1968.33	195.25
按企业规模分	**Grouped by Size of Enterprises**					
大型企业	Large-sized Enterprises	274	21197.51	14569.60	1101.27	101.27
中型企业	Medium-sized Enterprises	1623	9324.17	9860.59	792.51	84.22
小型企业	Small-sized Enterprises	12018	15494.08	17403.59	1162.16	113.69
按登记注册类型分	**Grouped by Status of Registration**					
内资企业	Domestic Funded Enterprises	13390	40919.71	37019.43	2763.22	270.91
国有企业	State-owned Enterprises	54	2193.47	1185.85	-46.46	10.59
集体企业	Collective-owned Enterprises	40	19.06	49.95	2.90	0.58
股份合作企业	Cooperative Share-holding Enterprises	43	27.24	57.06	2.66	0.61
联营企业	Joint-owned Enterprises	5	2.74	2.79	0.18	0.02
有限责任公司	Limited Liability Corporations	3979	24000.59	16585.11	1250.42	114.79
国有独资企业	Exclusively State-owned Enterprises	247	5372.05	2943.13	155.96	20.89
其他有限责任公司	Others	3732	18628.54	13641.98	1094.46	93.90
股份有限公司	Share-holding Corporations Limited	529	5559.12	3060.68	436.10	25.47
私营企业	Private Enterprises	8737	9116.14	16073.90	1117.08	118.83
私营独资企业	Exclusively Private Enterprises	604	279.12	840.96	52.70	6.02
私营合伙企业	Private Partnership Enterprises	99	67.75	149.67	12.21	1.25
私营有限责任公司	Private Limited Liability Corporations	7711	7848.14	14166.93	982.64	104.16
私营股份有限公司	Private Share-holding Corporations Ltd.	323	921.13	916.34	69.52	7.40
其他企业	Others	3	1.35	4.09	0.34	0.02
港、澳、台商投资企业	Enterprises with Funds from Hongkong, Macao and Taiwan	195	2653.05	1880.53	69.66	13.45
合资经营企业(港或澳、台资)	Joint-venture Enterprises	78	1790.37	1215.94	31.33	8.65
合作经营企业(港或澳、台资)	Cooperative Enterprises	3	1.37	0.98	-0.02	0.02
港、澳、台商独资企业	Enterprises with Sole Investment	105	818.94	616.43	30.60	4.41
港、澳、台商股份有限公司	Share-holding Corporations Ltd.	5	30.17	26.51	3.35	0.12
外商投资企业	Foreign-funded Enterprises	330	2443.00	2933.82	223.05	14.83
中外合资经营企业	Joint-venture Enterprises	173	1313.26	1562.80	137.20	6.12
中外合作经营企业	Cooperative Enterprises	4	11.13	1.99	0.49	0.01
外资企业	Enterprises with Sole Funds	143	1076.82	1338.07	82.84	8.29
外商投资股份有限公司	Share-holding Corporations Ltd.	6	37.35	23.74	1.16	0.36

注：2018年数据均为年报初步数据(以下有关各表同)。
a)The data in 2018 are preliminary data of the annual report(the same as the following related tables).

14-2 按行业分规模以上工业企业主要指标(2018年)

单位：亿元

行　业	Sector	企业单位数 (个) Number of Enterprises (unit)
总　计	**Total**	**13915**
煤炭开采和洗选业	Mining and Washing of Coal	348
石油和天然气开采业	Extraction of Petroleum and Natural Gas	11
黑色金属矿采选业	Mining and Processing of Ferrous Metal Ores	101
有色金属矿采选业	Mining and Processing of Non-Ferrous Metal Ores	61
非金属矿采选业	Mining and Processing of Non-metal Ores	211
开采辅助活动	Support Activities for Mining	4
其他采矿业	Mining of Other Ores	1
农副食品加工业	Processing of Food from Agricultural Products	1208
食品制造业	Manufacture of Foods	497
酒、饮料和精制茶制造业	Manufacture of Liquor, Beverages and Refined Tea	668
烟草制品业	Manufacture of Tobacco	3
纺织业	Manufacture of Textile	306
纺织服装、服饰业	Manufacture of Textile, Wearing Apparel and Accessories	162
皮革、毛皮、羽毛及其制品和制鞋业	Manufacture of Leather, Fur, Feather and Related Products and Footwear	134
木材加工和木、竹、藤、棕、草制品业	Processing of Timber, Manufacture of Wood, Bamboo, Rattan, Palm and Straw Products	245
家具制造业	Manufacture of Furniture	314
造纸和纸制品业	Manufacture of Paper and Paper Products	276
印刷和记录媒介复制业	Printing and Reproduction of Recording Media	265
文教、工美、体育和娱乐用品制造业	Manufacture of Articles for Culture, Education, Arts and Crafts, Sport and Entertainment Activities	62
石油加工、炼焦和核燃料加工业	Processing of Petroleum, Coking and Processing of Nuclear Fuel	57
化学原料和化学制品制造业	Manufacture of Raw Chemical Materials and Chemical Products	861
医药制造业	Manufacture of Medicines	471
化学纤维制造业	Manufacture of Chemical Fibres	22
橡胶和塑料制品业	Manufacture of Rubber and Plastics Products	539
非金属矿物制品业	Manufacture of Non-metallic Mineral Products	1829
黑色金属冶炼和压延加工业	Smelting and Pressing of Ferrous Metals	210
有色金属冶炼和压延加工业	Smelting and Pressing of Non-ferrous Metals	198
金属制品业	Manufacture of Metal Products	719
通用设备制造业	Manufacture of General Purpose Machinery	785
专用设备制造业	Manufacture of Special Purpose Machinery	557
汽车制造业	Manufacture of Automobiles	530
铁路、船舶、航空航天和其他运输设备制造业	Manufacture of Railway, Ship, Aerospace and Other Transport Equipments	171
电气机械和器材制造业	Manufacture of Electrical Machinery and Apparatus	600
计算机、通信和其他电子设备制造业	Manufacture of Computers, Communication and Other Electronic Equipments	555
仪器仪表制造业	Manufacture of Measuring Instruments and Machinery	99
其他制造业	Other Manufactures	24
废弃资源综合利用业	Utilization of Waste Resources	51
金属制品、机械和设备修理业	Repair Service of Metal Products, Machinery and Equipment	9
电力、热力生产和供应业	Production and Supply of Electric Power and Heat Power	399
燃气生产和供应业	Production and Supply of Gas	220
水的生产和供应业	Production and Supply of Water	132

Main Indicators of Industrial Enterprises above Designated Size by Industrial Sector(2018)

(100 million yuan)

资产总计 Total Assets	流动资产合计 Total Current Assets	固定资产原价 Original Value of Fixed Assets	负债合计 Total Liabilities	流动负债合计 Total Current Liabilities	所有者权益 Owners' Equities
46015.75	**19818.22**	**28047.89**	**26150.93**	**18315.72**	**19864.82**
794.03	272.66	559.53	554.96	383.81	239.06
1693.72	173.91	1027.83	487.60	240.96	1206.12
404.51	164.65	186.70	247.73	209.98	156.78
262.18	95.06	96.04	135.17	87.18	127.02
239.37	96.56	136.84	134.11	87.36	105.26
406.80	237.37	206.81	156.21	148.08	250.59
1.49	0.28	0.05	1.14	0.90	0.35
1055.04	560.20	621.15	521.83	437.44	533.22
618.05	275.11	377.39	246.07	209.77	371.98
2951.04	1933.51	1055.60	1066.40	923.29	1884.64
267.13	222.26	87.01	121.61	121.36	145.51
392.55	166.77	241.59	179.90	122.17	212.65
115.29	57.95	73.22	46.36	34.69	68.93
112.71	66.59	66.27	57.59	52.19	55.12
231.15	107.72	126.13	112.64	95.74	118.52
261.86	128.89	154.94	138.00	122.23	123.86
374.57	162.43	246.84	222.82	181.09	151.75
262.09	139.46	173.50	112.70	101.08	149.39
58.45	35.35	27.02	31.61	26.84	26.83
638.36	249.31	482.46	319.22	274.35	319.14
2300.81	984.61	1324.31	1109.23	861.27	1191.58
1422.31	840.59	464.33	619.68	466.36	802.63
237.74	103.09	146.34	189.63	152.22	48.12
582.18	331.34	286.03	273.95	234.93	308.23
2445.95	1155.24	1653.73	1205.95	1018.52	1240.00
2152.34	786.94	1867.56	1571.64	1111.62	580.71
694.06	371.24	247.80	345.06	306.71	349.00
971.15	536.15	455.25	598.91	509.58	372.25
1560.46	1066.55	541.69	921.39	809.06	639.07
1339.01	834.83	462.82	710.16	582.82	628.85
2318.35	1392.98	950.96	1423.03	1265.50	895.33
1031.53	679.52	342.07	649.96	574.38	381.57
1227.35	788.85	529.42	634.29	545.00	593.06
5706.65	3346.05	2015.68	3652.35	3202.52	2054.30
187.00	131.50	49.99	103.16	97.81	83.84
210.69	75.51	128.98	165.19	54.30	45.50
76.33	43.08	28.37	46.16	38.14	30.17
144.30	74.22	55.97	62.61	46.52	81.68
8690.69	618.74	9887.45	6082.80	1995.24	2607.89
591.80	189.95	288.79	330.69	240.23	261.11
984.63	321.18	373.43	561.43	342.47	423.20

14-2 续表

单位：亿元

行　　业	Sector	营业收入 Business Revenue
总　计	**Total**	**41833.78**
煤炭开采和洗选业	Mining and Washing of Coal	567.13
石油和天然气开采业	Extraction of Petroleum and Natural Gas	704.45
黑色金属矿采选业	Mining and Processing of Ferrous Metal Ores	243.43
有色金属矿采选业	Mining and Processing of Non-Ferrous Metal Ores	128.27
非金属矿采选业	Mining and Processing of Non-metal Ores	258.13
开采辅助活动	Support Activities for Mining	301.90
其他采矿业	Mining of Other Ores	0.23
农副食品加工业	Processing of Food from Agricultural Products	2371.24
食品制造业	Manufacture of Foods	1107.00
酒、饮料和精制茶制造业	Manufacture of Liquor, Beverages and Refined Tea	3042.59
烟草制品业	Manufacture of Tobacco	224.98
纺织业	Manufacture of Textile	672.26
纺织服装、服饰业	Manufacture of Textile, Wearing Apparel and Accessories	256.87
皮革、毛皮、羽毛及其制品和制鞋业	Manufacture of Leather, Fur, Feather and Related Products and Footwear	226.86
木材加工和木、竹、藤、棕、草制品业	Processing of Timber, Manufacture of Wood, Bamboo, Rattan, Palm and Straw Products	337.18
家具制造业	Manufacture of Furniture	409.64
造纸和纸制品业	Manufacture of Paper and Paper Products	544.88
印刷和记录媒介复制业	Printing and Reproduction of Recording Media	419.99
文教、工美、体育和娱乐用品制造业	Manufacture of Articles for Culture, Education, Arts and Crafts, Sport and Entertainment Activities	128.39
石油加工、炼焦和核燃料加工业	Processing of Petroleum, Coking and Processing of Nuclear Fuel	795.05
化学原料和化学制品制造业	Manufacture of Raw Chemical Materials and Chemical Products	2352.66
医药制造业	Manufacture of Medicines	1331.91
化学纤维制造业	Manufacture of Chemical Fibres	289.61
橡胶和塑料制品业	Manufacture of Rubber and Plastics Products	1009.61
非金属矿物制品业	Manufacture of Non-metallic Mineral Products	3480.31
黑色金属冶炼和压延加工业	Smelting and Pressing of Ferrous Metals	2272.61
有色金属冶炼和压延加工业	Smelting and Pressing of Non-ferrous Metals	869.92
金属制品业	Manufacture of Metal Products	1611.03
通用设备制造业	Manufacture of General Purpose Machinery	1658.00
专用设备制造业	Manufacture of Special Purpose Machinery	1136.75
汽车制造业	Manufacture of Automobiles	2896.19
铁路、船舶、航空航天和其他运输设备制造业	Manufacture of Railway, Ship, Aerospace and Other Transport Equipments	816.45
电气机械和器材制造业	Manufacture of Electrical Machinery and Apparatus	1409.94
计算机、通信和其他电子设备制造业	Manufacture of Computers, Communication and Other Electronic Equipments	4782.69
仪器仪表制造业	Manufacture of Measuring Instruments and Machinery	178.19
其他制造业	Other Manufactures	62.39
废弃资源综合利用业	Utilization of Waste Resources	87.48
金属制品、机械和设备修理业	Repair Service of Metal Products, Machinery and Equipment	63.46
电力、热力生产和供应业	Production and Supply of Electric Power and Heat Power	2143.77
燃气生产和供应业	Production and Supply of Gas	453.21
水的生产和供应业	Production and Supply of Water	187.14

continued

(100 million yuan)

营业成本 Business Cost	利润总额 Total Profits	销售费用 Selling Expenses	管理费用 Administrative Expenses	财务费用 Finacial Expenses	全部从业人员年平均人数(万人) Annual Average Employed Persons (10 000 persons)
34465.16	**3055.93**	**1368.80**	**1736.90**	**558.25**	**299.18**
468.77	33.91	12.33	34.34	14.80	13.04
505.01	106.26	2.32	71.04	11.50	3.40
194.23	24.32	10.87	13.79	4.67	2.00
90.71	21.60	2.22	9.48	2.51	1.45
199.72	22.00	10.82	14.62	3.87	2.27
294.36	-1.73	0.04	3.93	-2.55	2.61
0.14	0.01	0.02	0.02	0.03	0.01
2065.39	133.30	72.90	67.93	15.42	15.30
902.40	92.26	63.74	41.30	7.04	9.45
2088.49	414.10	229.84	125.04	5.41	18.03
80.59	6.76	4.96	15.83	-0.72	0.52
600.94	38.88	9.82	14.76	5.97	6.71
216.71	12.26	12.09	11.97	1.85	3.12
196.82	12.40	6.09	8.08	1.76	4.26
290.26	17.80	9.40	11.85	3.89	2.90
331.79	24.81	23.07	23.13	3.12	7.58
476.16	30.11	12.87	18.05	7.02	4.50
351.29	30.76	11.89	20.65	2.59	3.86
107.07	6.26	9.44	3.42	0.85	1.00
666.46	25.95	5.82	20.73	3.16	1.57
1908.37	226.35	78.23	118.50	26.40	15.80
852.17	153.37	212.65	95.22	13.65	11.39
268.34	10.34	5.68	6.61	7.44	1.60
856.50	63.41	36.12	38.97	9.34	7.54
2825.33	337.93	110.43	131.31	40.40	23.89
1979.67	101.02	30.67	76.95	41.01	9.16
768.51	34.22	7.97	18.96	6.99	3.79
1383.37	92.89	39.60	59.92	19.99	11.30
1368.21	91.86	60.47	96.93	15.83	12.44
921.07	93.21	41.98	61.57	10.21	9.46
2456.61	201.66	45.09	93.52	17.76	14.90
702.36	41.92	16.07	47.58	3.90	6.73
1194.71	84.05	39.32	74.54	5.85	10.92
4360.88	169.99	95.30	178.10	23.42	32.44
137.21	17.48	6.80	14.74	1.46	1.71
53.49	5.82	1.12	5.68	1.12	0.85
73.54	5.31	1.03	3.64	1.62	0.72
54.13	4.41	0.55	5.07	0.69	0.44
1689.74	187.36	4.36	36.62	209.63	15.39
350.83	54.71	19.21	25.96	3.18	2.70
132.82	26.59	5.63	16.57	6.15	2.44

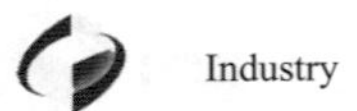

14-3 按行业分国有控股工业企业主要指标(2018年)

单位：亿元

行　业	Sector	企业单位数（个）Number of Enterprises (unit)
总　计	**Total**	**1004**
煤炭开采和洗选业	Mining and Washing of Coal	15
石油和天然气开采业	Extraction of Petroleum and Natural Gas	11
黑色金属矿采选业	Mining and Processing of Ferrous Metal Ores	6
有色金属矿采选业	Mining and Processing of Non-Ferrous Metal Ores	10
非金属矿采选业	Mining and Processing of Non-metal Ores	17
开采辅助活动	Support Activities for Mining	1
其他采矿业	Mining of Other Ores	
农副食品加工业	Processing of Food from Agricultural Products	32
食品制造业	Manufacture of Foods	8
酒、饮料和精制茶制造业	Manufacture of Liquor, Beverages and Refined Tea	18
烟草制品业	Manufacture of Tobacco	2
纺织业	Manufacture of Textile	10
纺织服装、服饰业	Manufacture of Textile, Wearing Apparel and Accessories	10
皮革、毛皮、羽毛及其制品和制鞋业	Manufacture of Leather, Fur, Feather and Related Products and Footwear	
木材加工和木、竹、藤、棕、草制品业	Processing of Timber, Manufacture of Wood, Bamboo, Rattan, Palm and Straw Products	3
家具制造业	Manufacture of Furniture	
造纸和纸制品业	Manufacture of Paper and Paper Products	2
印刷和记录媒介复制业	Printing and Reproduction of Recording Media	6
文教、工美、体育和娱乐用品制造业	Manufacture of Articles for Culture, Education, Arts and Crafts, Sport and Entertainment Activities	1
石油加工、炼焦和核燃料加工业	Processing of Petroleum, Coking and Processing of Nuclear Fuel	8
化学原料和化学制品制造业	Manufacture of Raw Chemical Materials and Chemical Products	53
医药制造业	Manufacture of Medicines	23
化学纤维制造业	Manufacture of Chemical Fibres	4
橡胶和塑料制品业	Manufacture of Rubber and Plastics Products	7
非金属矿物制品业	Manufacture of Non-metallic Mineral Products	99
黑色金属冶炼和压延加工业	Smelting and Pressing of Ferrous Metals	10
有色金属冶炼和压延加工业	Smelting and Pressing of Non-ferrous Metals	18
金属制品业	Manufacture of Metal Products	19
通用设备制造业	Manufacture of General Purpose Machinery	27
专用设备制造业	Manufacture of Special Purpose Machinery	28
汽车制造业	Manufacture of Automobiles	40
铁路、船舶、航空航天和其他运输设备制造业	Manufacture of Railway, Ship, Aerospace and Other Transport Equipments	26
电气机械和器材制造业	Manufacture of Electrical Machinery and Apparatus	35
计算机、通信和其他电子设备制造业	Manufacture of Computers, Communication and Other Electronic Equipments	60
仪器仪表制造业	Manufacture of Measuring Instruments and Machinery	10
其他制造业	Other Manufactures	5
废弃资源综合利用业	Utilization of Waste Resources	4
金属制品、机械和设备修理业	Repair Service of Metal Products, Machinery and Equipment	4
电力、热力生产和供应业	Production and Supply of Electric Power and Heat Power	223
燃气生产和供应业	Production and Supply of Gas	68
水的生产和供应业	Production and Supply of Water	81

Main Indicators of State-holding Industrial Enterprises by Industrial Sector(2018)

(100 million yuan)

资产总计 Total Assets	流动资产合计 Total Current Assets	固定资产原价 Original Value of Fixed Assets	负债合计 Total Liabilities	流动负债合计 Total Current Liabilities	所有者权益 Owners' Equities
22278.06	**7504.19**	**15718.23**	**13336.17**	**7724.40**	**8941.89**
422.46	134.37	260.34	348.57	222.63	73.89
1693.72	173.91	1027.83	487.60	240.96	1206.12
89.47	21.69	49.41	31.84	25.29	57.62
109.38	21.42	44.11	42.36	23.42	67.02
48.92	19.54	24.61	28.48	13.21	20.43
403.59	236.51	202.21	154.61	146.97	248.97
33.26	16.45	16.37	22.62	21.80	10.64
14.67	9.41	9.99	7.58	7.29	7.08
1571.77	1222.02	360.63	475.20	446.51	1096.57
267.11	222.25	86.93	121.39	121.13	145.72
38.54	18.19	11.55	18.07	10.13	20.47
17.84	10.66	9.45	10.63	8.29	7.21
8.80	7.21	6.05	8.20	7.90	0.60
36.52	12.39	21.87	32.78	26.37	3.75
45.88	28.93	43.09	7.40	6.79	38.48
1.27	0.74	0.79	0.84	0.74	0.44
482.75	188.13	379.10	205.74	186.77	277.01
616.95	264.66	394.39	301.02	220.86	315.93
138.50	71.06	56.29	49.01	36.81	89.49
205.08	87.81	120.90	173.70	138.70	31.39
33.04	14.61	21.61	17.05	14.62	15.99
440.98	165.28	318.82	255.28	227.64	185.70
1278.19	372.34	975.45	900.11	599.44	378.07
90.16	40.13	76.37	50.47	39.25	39.69
99.73	52.48	50.40	53.30	49.46	46.43
558.49	444.97	136.05	394.81	368.74	163.68
426.42	281.49	140.42	263.26	186.68	163.16
822.08	517.57	348.51	541.97	477.73	280.12
717.21	494.77	225.23	496.48	442.59	220.73
364.06	280.53	79.72	227.94	194.37	136.12
2191.40	1136.17	589.56	1376.06	1017.22	815.33
45.38	37.25	5.60	28.91	28.54	16.47
198.32	68.81	124.00	161.10	50.64	37.22
10.23	6.60	3.20	6.47	5.03	3.76
65.64	45.04	20.84	34.99	32.19	30.65
7846.31	470.40	9030.08	5551.25	1807.35	2295.06
224.91	99.49	132.75	119.99	89.63	104.93
619.05	208.92	313.67	329.10	180.71	289.95

14-3 续表

单位：亿元

行　业	Sector	营业收入 Business Revenue
总　计	**Total**	**11264.73**
煤炭开采和洗选业	Mining and Washing of Coal	100.79
石油和天然气开采业	Extraction of Petroleum and Natural Gas	704.45
黑色金属矿采选业	Mining and Processing of Ferrous Metal Ores	37.09
有色金属矿采选业	Mining and Processing of Non-Ferrous Metal Ores	41.34
非金属矿采选业	Mining and Processing of Non-metal Ores	18.25
开采辅助活动	Support Activities for Mining	298.41
其他采矿业	Mining of Other Ores	
农副食品加工业	Processing of Food from Agricultural Products	113.77
食品制造业	Manufacture of Foods	23.64
酒、饮料和精制茶制造业	Manufacture of Liquor, Beverages and Refined Tea	1140.57
烟草制品业	Manufacture of Tobacco	224.53
纺织业	Manufacture of Textile	31.03
纺织服装、服饰业	Manufacture of Textile, Wearing Apparel and Accessories	11.73
皮革、毛皮、羽毛及其制品和制鞋业	Manufacture of Leather, Fur, Feather and Related Products and Footwear	
木材加工和木、竹、藤、棕、草制品业	Processing of Timber, Manufacture of Wood, Bamboo, Rattan, Palm and Straw Products	12.35
家具制造业	Manufacture of Furniture	
造纸和纸制品业	Manufacture of Paper and Paper Products	17.35
印刷和记录媒介复制业	Printing and Reproduction of Recording Media	30.58
文教、工美、体育和娱乐用品制造业	Manufacture of Articles for Culture, Education, Arts and Crafts, Sport and Entertainment Activities	3.82
石油加工、炼焦和核燃料加工业	Processing of Petroleum, Coking and Processing of Nuclear Fuel	634.15
化学原料和化学制品制造业	Manufacture of Raw Chemical Materials and Chemical Products	429.42
医药制造业	Manufacture of Medicines	95.54
化学纤维制造业	Manufacture of Chemical Fibres	230.07
橡胶和塑料制品业	Manufacture of Rubber and Plastics Products	49.21
非金属矿物制品业	Manufacture of Non-metallic Mineral Products	368.37
黑色金属冶炼和压延加工业	Smelting and Pressing of Ferrous Metals	932.52
有色金属冶炼和压延加工业	Smelting and Pressing of Non-ferrous Metals	119.65
金属制品业	Manufacture of Metal Products	81.80
通用设备制造业	Manufacture of General Purpose Machinery	254.25
专用设备制造业	Manufacture of Special Purpose Machinery	159.65
汽车制造业	Manufacture of Automobiles	810.86
铁路、船舶、航空航天和其他运输设备制造业	Manufacture of Railway, Ship, Aerospace and Other Transport Equipments	459.31
电气机械和器材制造业	Manufacture of Electrical Machinery and Apparatus	189.97
计算机、通信和其他电子设备制造业	Manufacture of Computers, Communication and Other Electronic Equipments	1219.31
仪器仪表制造业	Manufacture of Measuring Instruments and Machinery	23.96
其他制造业	Other Manufactures	35.64
废弃资源综合利用业	Utilization of Waste Resources	6.83
金属制品、机械和设备修理业	Repair Service of Metal Products, Machinery and Equipment	53.63
电力、热力生产和供应业	Production and Supply of Electric Power and Heat Power	1972.91
燃气生产和供应业	Production and Supply of Gas	206.44
水的生产和供应业	Production and Supply of Water	121.58

continued

(100 million yuan)

营业成本 Business Cost	利润总额 Total Profits	销售费用 Selling Expenses	管理费用 Administrative Expenses	财务费用 Finacial Expenses	全部从业人员 年平均人数(万人) Annual Average Employed Persons (10 000 persons)
8933.78	**880.23**	**297.10**	**559.24**	**264.73**	**73.01**
72.21	5.78	2.19	14.39	9.96	4.09
505.01	106.26	2.32	71.04	11.50	3.40
24.42	3.26	2.74	4.40	1.03	0.49
24.47	9.03	0.70	4.77	1.27	0.47
14.39	-0.93	0.65	1.90	0.72	0.33
291.45	-2.01	0.02	3.66	-2.54	2.60
104.14	5.41	1.41	2.15	0.39	0.33
18.41	1.81	1.82	1.46	0.09	0.28
689.33	252.13	94.77	40.11	-14.15	5.64
80.19	6.95	4.96	15.61	-0.72	0.51
27.32	1.41	0.51	1.28	0.31	0.53
8.34	-0.05	0.24	3.23	0.01	0.39
11.38	0.25	0.12	0.19	0.29	0.10
15.15	2.08	0.43	0.64	0.94	0.13
20.99	5.61	0.31	4.75	-0.41	0.34
3.62	-0.04	0.14	0.07	0.02	0.06
527.72	18.76	3.68	17.13	0.88	0.96
339.88	35.58	14.68	34.76	5.61	3.65
53.47	16.07	17.38	7.23	0.45	0.69
217.24	6.52	3.91	4.33	6.92	1.20
43.21	1.00	2.29	2.64	0.42	0.37
275.84	51.23	12.17	19.11	8.60	2.37
787.98	18.89	17.55	49.34	22.78	4.92
110.25	-2.96	1.44	3.59	0.89	0.62
74.58	0.64	1.85	5.06	0.56	0.73
204.25	6.76	10.86	25.03	-1.99	1.79
133.28	6.47	4.72	11.51	2.17	1.58
700.31	59.12	8.46	21.76	3.04	3.07
413.50	10.89	4.61	29.40	0.81	3.68
155.86	10.62	6.31	20.04	-1.65	1.55
1058.30	26.71	56.22	78.49	16.61	7.54
18.47	-0.06	0.99	4.02	0.12	0.31
31.28	4.10	0.08	4.35	0.94	0.61
4.68	1.41	0.07	0.48	0.19	0.07
48.12	3.05	0.20	2.38	-0.16	0.28
1577.00	166.52	3.10	26.61	184.26	14.18
161.76	24.85	8.96	11.33	0.66	1.31
86.01	17.12	4.22	11.02	3.90	1.83

14-4 按行业分大中型工业企业主要指标(2018年)

单位：亿元

行 业	Sector	企业单位数 (个) Number of Enterprises (unit)
总 计	**Total**	**1897**
煤炭开采和洗选业	Mining and Washing of Coal	127
石油和天然气开采业	Extraction of Petroleum and Natural Gas	6
黑色金属矿采选业	Mining and Processing of Ferrous Metal Ores	14
有色金属矿采选业	Mining and Processing of Non-Ferrous Metal Ores	15
非金属矿采选业	Mining and Processing of Non-metal Ores	15
开采辅助活动	Support Activities for Mining	1
其他采矿业	Mining of Other Ores	
农副食品加工业	Processing of Food from Agricultural Products	92
食品制造业	Manufacture of Foods	86
酒、饮料和精制茶制造业	Manufacture of Liquor, Beverages and Refined Tea	81
烟草制品业	Manufacture of Tobacco	1
纺织业	Manufacture of Textile	71
纺织服装、服饰业	Manufacture of Textile, Wearing Apparel and Accessories	28
皮革、毛皮、羽毛及其制品和制鞋业	Manufacture of Leather, Fur, Feather and Related Products and Footwear	40
木材加工和木、竹、藤、棕、草制品业	Processing of Timber, Manufacture of Wood, Bamboo, Rattan, Palm and Straw Products	18
家具制造业	Manufacture of Furniture	38
造纸和纸制品业	Manufacture of Paper and Paper Products	43
印刷和记录媒介复制业	Printing and Reproduction of Recording Media	24
文教、工美、体育和娱乐用品制造业	Manufacture of Articles for Culture, Education, Arts and Crafts, Sport and Entertainment Activities	8
石油加工、炼焦和核燃料加工业	Processing of Petroleum, Coking and Processing of Nuclear Fuel	13
化学原料和化学制品制造业	Manufacture of Raw Chemical Materials and Chemical Products	103
医药制造业	Manufacture of Medicines	99
化学纤维制造业	Manufacture of Chemical Fibres	7
橡胶和塑料制品业	Manufacture of Rubber and Plastics Products	47
非金属矿物制品业	Manufacture of Non-metallic Mineral Products	161
黑色金属冶炼和压延加工业	Smelting and Pressing of Ferrous Metals	34
有色金属冶炼和压延加工业	Smelting and Pressing of Non-ferrous Metals	24
金属制品业	Manufacture of Metal Products	72
通用设备制造业	Manufacture of General Purpose Machinery	75
专用设备制造业	Manufacture of Special Purpose Machinery	65
汽车制造业	Manufacture of Automobiles	117
铁路、船舶、航空航天和其他运输设备制造业	Manufacture of Railway, Ship, Aerospace and Other Transport Equipments	38
电气机械和器材制造业	Manufacture of Electrical Machinery and Apparatus	78
计算机、通信和其他电子设备制造业	Manufacture of Computers, Communication and Other Electronic Equipments	143
仪器仪表制造业	Manufacture of Measuring Instruments and Machinery	15
其他制造业	Other Manufactures	5
废弃资源综合利用业	Utilization of Waste Resources	4
金属制品、机械和设备修理业	Repair Service of Metal Products, Machinery and Equipment	3
电力、热力生产和供应业	Production and Supply of Electric Power and Heat Power	50
燃气生产和供应业	Production and Supply of Gas	16
水的生产和供应业	Production and Supply of Water	20

Main Indicators of Large and Medium-sized Industrial Enterprises by Industrial Sector(2018)

(100 million yuan)

资产总计 Total Assets	流动资产合计 Total Current Assets	固定资产原价 Original Value of Fixed Assets	负债合计 Total Liabilities	流动负债合计 Total Current Liabilities	所有者权益 Owners' Equities
30521.68	**13762.87**	**17968.88**	**17055.01**	**12771.35**	**13466.67**
610.10	194.50	433.06	446.56	296.81	163.54
1441.44	162.66	804.49	433.59	217.38	1007.85
202.21	64.38	116.37	99.69	90.88	102.52
149.91	31.78	61.46	58.96	37.60	90.94
67.59	29.55	47.15	43.63	30.43	23.96
403.59	236.51	202.21	154.61	146.97	248.97
320.87	180.02	189.85	156.89	124.12	163.99
339.89	146.73	213.02	114.00	97.66	225.90
2395.83	1692.25	741.11	845.93	757.46	1549.90
241.59	198.95	84.15	101.75	101.49	139.85
248.18	96.46	174.40	103.19	62.84	145.00
61.96	31.81	41.80	27.17	20.20	34.79
68.58	44.08	34.49	38.40	34.99	30.19
87.88	35.76	39.86	43.34	36.65	44.54
106.56	52.49	60.65	63.17	61.14	43.39
234.06	92.28	161.05	141.28	109.83	92.78
106.17	61.69	85.49	35.68	32.83	70.50
28.25	19.86	10.91	17.71	16.15	10.53
570.45	224.08	442.13	282.65	245.95	287.80
1460.13	572.73	894.57	657.62	504.18	802.50
989.23	593.04	261.00	408.52	283.05	580.72
222.82	96.60	135.29	182.94	147.77	39.88
267.56	161.36	127.74	127.68	107.65	139.88
1069.87	456.12	780.64	448.94	371.05	620.93
1880.02	624.05	1758.48	1378.63	987.86	501.40
463.64	224.23	169.01	185.80	162.52	277.83
484.74	282.78	248.05	331.16	288.67	153.58
1022.37	740.58	290.55	641.90	565.43	380.47
775.93	500.39	253.08	426.01	333.63	349.92
1905.57	1185.47	766.45	1182.71	1055.54	722.85
780.77	532.22	260.32	520.77	478.83	260.00
734.69	468.88	333.01	392.27	332.20	342.42
5134.34	2995.33	1846.61	3348.40	2942.21	1785.95
98.72	71.98	25.64	52.10	50.44	46.61
201.16	70.60	124.10	161.78	51.32	39.38
37.36	25.09	9.67	26.89	22.00	10.47
125.00	61.19	49.79	55.17	41.69	69.84
4355.74	229.30	5401.48	2857.67	1214.66	1498.07
120.23	45.46	81.91	66.05	50.19	54.17
706.68	229.62	207.90	393.80	259.07	312.88

14-4 续表

单位: 亿元

行　　业	Sector	营业收入 Business Revenue
总　计	**Total**	**24430.19**
煤炭开采和洗选业	Mining and Washing of Coal	327.48
石油和天然气开采业	Extraction of Petroleum and Natural Gas	635.35
黑色金属矿采选业	Mining and Processing of Ferrous Metal Ores	121.90
有色金属矿采选业	Mining and Processing of Non-Ferrous Metal Ores	78.79
非金属矿采选业	Mining and Processing of Non-metal Ores	46.85
开采辅助活动	Support Activities for Mining	298.41
其他采矿业	Mining of Other Ores	
农副食品加工业	Processing of Food from Agricultural Products	656.71
食品制造业	Manufacture of Foods	586.75
酒、饮料和精制茶制造业	Manufacture of Liquor, Beverages and Refined Tea	2010.20
烟草制品业	Manufacture of Tobacco	216.30
纺织业	Manufacture of Textile	395.98
纺织服装、服饰业	Manufacture of Textile, Wearing Apparel and Accessories	110.08
皮革、毛皮、羽毛及其制品和制鞋业	Manufacture of Leather, Fur, Feather and Related Products and Footwear	98.65
木材加工和木、竹、藤、棕、草制品业	Processing of Timber, Manufacture of Wood, Bamboo, Rattan, Palm and Straw Products	66.29
家具制造业	Manufacture of Furniture	152.90
造纸和纸制品业	Manufacture of Paper and Paper Products	276.75
印刷和记录媒介复制业	Printing and Reproduction of Recording Media	115.94
文教、工美、体育和娱乐用品制造业	Manufacture of Articles for Culture, Education, Arts and Crafts, Sport and Entertainment Activities	72.44
石油加工、炼焦和核燃料加工业	Processing of Petroleum, Coking and Processing of Nuclear Fuel	709.89
化学原料和化学制品制造业	Manufacture of Raw Chemical Materials and Chemical Products	1173.72
医药制造业	Manufacture of Medicines	742.42
化学纤维制造业	Manufacture of Chemical Fibres	257.83
橡胶和塑料制品业	Manufacture of Rubber and Plastics Products	371.02
非金属矿物制品业	Manufacture of Non-metallic Mineral Products	1072.26
黑色金属冶炼和压延加工业	Smelting and Pressing of Ferrous Metals	1942.94
有色金属冶炼和压延加工业	Smelting and Pressing of Non-ferrous Metals	438.87
金属制品业	Manufacture of Metal Products	710.48
通用设备制造业	Manufacture of General Purpose Machinery	665.20
专用设备制造业	Manufacture of Special Purpose Machinery	437.65
汽车制造业	Manufacture of Automobiles	2216.05
铁路、船舶、航空航天和其他运输设备制造业	Manufacture of Railway, Ship, Aerospace and Other Transport Equipments	519.80
电气机械和器材制造业	Manufacture of Electrical Machinery and Apparatus	639.87
计算机、通信和其他电子设备制造业	Manufacture of Computers, Communication and Other Electronic Equipments	4177.44
仪器仪表制造业	Manufacture of Measuring Instruments and Machinery	95.47
其他制造业	Other Manufactures	41.58
废弃资源综合利用业	Utilization of Waste Resources	36.58
金属制品、机械和设备修理业	Repair Service of Metal Products, Machinery and Equipment	57.05
电力、热力生产和供应业	Production and Supply of Electric Power and Heat Power	1635.51
燃气生产和供应业	Production and Supply of Gas	116.70
水的生产和供应业	Production and Supply of Water	104.07

continued

(100 million yuan)

营业成本 Business Cost	利润总额 Total Profits	销售费用 Selling Expenses	管理费用 Administrative Expenses	财务费用 Finacial Expenses	全部从业人员年平均人数(万人) Annual Average Employed Persons (10 000 persons)
19898.82	**1893.77**	**824.37**	**1054.46**	**283.28**	**185.49**
264.38	17.36	7.22	26.12	12.15	9.99
456.22	83.33	2.17	69.41	11.42	3.36
89.19	20.77	5.89	8.51	2.64	1.11
52.49	15.55	1.84	6.15	1.85	0.87
34.58	3.60	1.52	4.09	1.04	0.91
291.45	-2.01	0.02	3.66	-2.54	2.60
567.60	36.82	22.42	21.82	4.68	5.85
472.16	59.06	38.03	19.17	2.11	5.52
1261.62	332.63	191.17	90.79	-2.45	12.74
74.09	5.13	4.88	15.00	-0.32	0.49
351.61	25.79	5.45	8.30	3.83	4.20
90.38	5.35	7.81	5.13	0.87	1.63
87.02	4.62	2.24	3.80	0.71	3.01
56.38	2.96	2.09	3.16	1.47	0.77
121.97	8.87	10.23	10.29	0.87	4.50
237.42	19.52	6.46	9.00	4.82	2.18
90.25	13.42	3.39	8.69	0.52	1.50
58.05	3.83	7.58	1.75	0.47	0.50
591.44	22.12	4.51	18.47	2.28	1.26
907.54	148.90	43.94	69.81	14.14	9.01
400.10	109.08	161.86	65.04	9.83	7.38
241.00	8.62	4.98	4.79	7.13	1.44
309.07	24.86	16.81	16.21	4.05	3.13
819.24	154.90	31.29	45.83	13.22	9.37
1679.62	91.89	24.76	67.85	38.24	7.71
369.70	16.64	4.58	10.98	3.96	2.17
608.01	42.12	17.37	28.53	10.22	5.47
542.87	36.64	23.85	47.36	2.29	5.51
352.25	34.24	18.17	26.91	4.08	4.50
1860.05	170.58	30.39	67.08	11.74	10.20
449.37	22.05	9.17	34.00	2.43	5.11
524.18	48.59	19.14	42.37	0.16	6.09
3858.69	118.91	77.06	137.54	19.77	27.84
72.60	12.49	2.47	7.28	0.32	0.91
36.57	4.36	0.24	4.50	1.02	0.69
31.72	1.67	0.20	1.33	0.89	0.40
49.92	3.18	0.35	4.28	0.53	0.38
1377.91	133.75	2.39	22.32	90.12	12.93
88.63	12.50	7.81	7.78	0.54	1.02
71.49	19.08	2.63	9.36	2.16	1.26

14-5 按行业分规模以上工业企业主要经济效益指标(2018年)
Main Indicators on Economic Benefits of Industrial Enterprises above Designated Size by Industrial Sector(2018)

单位：% (%)

行业	Sector	总资产贡献率 Ratio of Profits, Taxes and Interests to Average Assets	资产负债率 Ratio of Debts to Assets	工业成本费用利润率 Ratio of Profits to Industrial Costs	产品销售率 Products Sales Rate
总计	**Total**	**12.03**	**56.83**	**8.01**	**98.22**
煤炭开采和洗选业	Mining and Washing of Coal	10.96	69.89	6.40	98.47
石油和天然气开采业	Extraction of Petroleum and Natural Gas	10.46	28.79	18.01	98.99
黑色金属矿采选业	Mining and Processing of Ferrous Metal Ores	10.14	61.24	10.88	98.07
有色金属矿采选业	Mining and Processing of Non-Ferrous Metal Ores	13.29	51.55	20.58	97.05
非金属矿采选业	Mining and Processing of Non-metal Ores	16.97	56.03	9.61	99.04
开采辅助活动	Support Activities for Mining	-0.53	38.40	-0.59	99.38
其他采矿业	Mining of Other Ores	4.18	76.33	5.94	100.00
农副食品加工业	Processing of Food from Agricultural Products	18.92	49.46	6.00	98.81
食品制造业	Manufacture of Foods	22.10	39.81	9.09	99.18
酒、饮料和精制茶制造业	Manufacture of Liquor, Beverages and Refined Tea	25.58	36.14	16.91	95.50
烟草制品业	Manufacture of Tobacco	55.28	45.53	6.72	107.67
纺织业	Manufacture of Textile	15.44	45.83	6.16	97.36
纺织服装、服饰业	Manufacture of Textile, Wearing Apparel and Accessories	17.54	40.21	5.05	99.02
皮革、毛皮、羽毛及其制品和制鞋业	Manufacture of Leather, Fur, Feather and Related Products and Footwear	16.31	51.10	5.83	98.13
木材加工和木、竹、藤、棕、草制品业	Processing of Timber, Manufacture of Wood, Bamboo, Rattan, Palm and Straw Products	13.38	48.73	5.64	98.43
家具制造业	Manufacture of Furniture	15.65	52.70	6.51	97.82
造纸和纸制品业	Manufacture of Paper and Paper Products	13.98	59.49	5.86	97.45
印刷和记录媒介复制业	Printing and Reproduction of Recording Media	18.69	43.00	7.96	98.01
文教、工美、体育和娱乐用品制造业	Manufacture of Articles for Culture, Education, Arts and Crafts,Sport and Entertainment Activities	18.34	54.09	5.19	97.93
石油加工、炼焦和核燃料加工业	Processing of Petroleum, Coking and Processing of Nuclear Fuel	19.30	50.01	3.73	99.35
化学原料和化学制品制造业	Manufacture of Raw Chemical Materials and Chemical Products	14.50	48.21	10.62	97.42
医药制造业	Manufacture of Medicines	16.97	43.57	13.07	96.13
化学纤维制造业	Manufacture of Chemical Fibres	9.67	79.76	3.59	95.41
橡胶和塑料制品业	Manufacture of Rubber and Plastics Products	16.82	47.06	6.74	98.16
非金属矿物制品业	Manufacture of Non-metallic Mineral Products	20.68	49.30	10.87	97.87
黑色金属冶炼和压延加工业	Smelting and Pressing of Ferrous Metals	9.83	73.02	4.75	99.01
有色金属冶炼和压延加工业	Smelting and Pressing of Non-ferrous Metals	8.47	49.72	4.26	97.68
金属制品业	Manufacture of Metal Products	16.10	61.67	6.18	98.42
通用设备制造业	Manufacture of General Purpose Machinery	10.60	59.05	5.96	96.71
专用设备制造业	Manufacture of Special Purpose Machinery	10.46	53.04	9.01	96.06
汽车制造业	Manufacture of Automobiles	16.64	61.38	7.72	98.64
铁路、船舶、航空航天和其他运输设备制造业	Manufacture of Railway, Ship, Aerospace and Other Transport Equipments	6.07	63.01	5.44	97.04
电气机械和器材制造业	Manufacture of Electrical Machinery and Apparatus	10.96	51.68	6.39	98.51
计算机、通信和其他电子设备制造业	Manufacture of Computers, Communication and Other Electronic Equipments	4.53	64.00	3.65	99.71
仪器仪表制造业	Manufacture of Measuring Instruments and Machinery	12.48	55.17	10.91	97.44
其他制造业	Other Manufactures	3.82	78.41	9.48	92.09
废弃资源综合利用业	Utilization of Waste Resources	15.52	60.48	6.65	95.62
金属制品、机械和设备修理业	Repair Service of Metal Products, Machinery and Equipment	4.39	43.39	7.29	100.13
电力、热力生产和供应业	Production and Supply of Electric Power and Heat Power	6.62	69.99	9.66	100.33
燃气生产和供应业	Production and Supply of Gas	12.07	55.88	13.70	98.77
水的生产和供应业	Production and Supply of Water	4.25	57.02	16.5	98.35

14-6 按行业分国有控股工业企业主要经济效益指标(2018年)
Main Indicators on Economic Benefits of State-holding Industrial Enterprises by Industrial Sector(2018)

单位：% (%)

行 业	Sector	总资产贡献率 Ratio of Profits, Taxes and Interests to Average Assets	资产负债率 Ratio of Debts to Assets	工业成本费用利润率 Ratio of Profits to Industrial Cost	产品销售率 Products Sales Rate
总 计	**Total**	**8.98**	**59.86**	**8.75**	**99.08**
煤炭开采和洗选业	Mining and Washing of Coal	6.41	82.51	5.86	99.48
石油和天然气开采业	Extraction of Petroleum and Natural Gas	10.46	28.79	18.01	98.99
黑色金属矿采选业	Mining and Processing of Ferrous Metal Ores	8.43	35.59	10.02	99.94
有色金属矿采选业	Mining and Processing of Non-Ferrous Metal Ores	13.78	38.72	28.92	99.48
非金属矿采选业	Mining and Processing of Non-metal Ores	1.14	58.23	-5.27	100.36
开采辅助活动	Support Activities for Mining	-0.61	38.31	-0.69	99.39
其他采矿业	Mining of Other Ores				
农副食品加工业	Processing of Food from Agricultural Products	20.82	68.01	5.00	102.33
食品制造业	Manufacture of Foods	20.65	51.70	8.31	98.15
酒、饮料和精制茶制造业	Manufacture of Liquor, Beverages and Refined Tea	25.28	30.23	31.12	95.77
烟草制品业	Manufacture of Tobacco	55.34	45.44	6.95	107.67
纺织业	Manufacture of Textile	7.18	46.88	4.80	92.33
纺织服装、服饰业	Manufacture of Textile, Wearing Apparel and Accessories	6.36	59.60	-0.46	97.70
皮革、毛皮、羽毛及其制品和制鞋业	Manufacture of Leather, Fur, Feather and Related Products and Footwear				
木材加工和木、竹、藤、棕、草制品业	Processing of Timber, Manufacture of Wood, Bamboo, Rattan, Palm and Straw Products	9.70	93.20	2.05	98.73
家具制造业	Manufacture of Furniture				
造纸和纸制品业	Manufacture of Paper and Paper Products	9.12	89.74	12.15	96.78
印刷和记录媒介复制业	Printing and Reproduction of Recording Media	19.04	16.14	21.90	98.49
文教、工美、体育和娱乐用品制造业	Manufacture of Articles for Culture, Education, Arts and Crafts, Sport and Entertainment Activities	2.31	65.75	-1.15	100.00
石油加工、炼焦和核燃料加工业	Processing of Petroleum, Coking and Processing of Nuclear Fuel	21.72	42.62	3.41	99.45
化学原料和化学制品制造业	Manufacture of Raw Chemical Materials and Chemical Products	9.55	48.79	9.01	98.63
医药制造业	Manufacture of Medicines	16.51	35.38	20.46	99.14
化学纤维制造业	Manufacture of Chemical Fibres	8.38	84.70	2.80	94.44
橡胶和塑料制品业	Manufacture of Rubber and Plastics Products	6.01	51.61	2.06	98.63
非金属矿物制品业	Manufacture of Non-metallic Mineral Products	17.96	57.89	16.22	98.62
黑色金属冶炼和压延加工业	Smelting and Pressing of Ferrous Metals	5.94	70.42	2.15	100.08
有色金属冶炼和压延加工业	Smelting and Pressing of Non-ferrous Metals	-0.32	55.98	-2.55	98.35
金属制品业	Manufacture of Metal Products	2.39	53.45	0.79	102.16
通用设备制造业	Manufacture of General Purpose Machinery	3.11	70.69	2.84	98.56
专用设备制造业	Manufacture of Special Purpose Machinery	3.30	61.74	4.27	94.25
汽车制造业	Manufacture of Automobiles	13.91	65.93	8.06	100.48
铁路、船舶、航空航天和其他运输设备制造业	Manufacture of Railway, Ship, Aerospace and Other Transport Equipments	2.60	69.22	2.43	97.10
电气机械和器材制造业	Manufacture of Electrical Machinery and Apparatus	5.35	62.61	5.88	103.80
计算机、通信和其他电子设备制造业	Manufacture of Computers, Communication and Other Electronic Equipments	3.11	62.79	2.21	96.97
仪器仪表制造业	Manufacture of Measuring Instruments and Machinery	2.37	63.71	-0.25	93.69
其他制造业	Other Manufactures	2.86	81.23	11.18	86.78
废弃资源综合利用业	Utilization of Waste Resources	19.93	63.28	25.98	98.29
金属制品、机械和设备修理业	Repair Service of Metal Products, Machinery and Equipment	6.15	53.31	6.03	100.03
电力、热力生产和供应业	Production and Supply of Electric Power and Heat Power	6.59	70.75	9.30	100.38
燃气生产和供应业	Production and Supply of Gas	13.85	53.35	13.60	99.33
水的生产和供应业	Production and Supply of Water	4.47	53.16	16.28	98.06

14-7 按行业分大中型工业企业主要经济效益指标(2018年)
Main Indicators on Economic Benefits of Large and Medium-sized Industrial Enterprises by Industrial Sector(2018)

单位：%　　　　(%)

行　业	Sector	总资产贡献率 Ratio of Profits, Taxes and Interests to Average Assets	资产负债率 Ratio of Debts to Assets	工业成本费用利润率 Ratio of Profits to Industrial Cost	产品销售率 Products Sales Rate
总　计	**Total**	**11.55**	**55.88**	**8.58**	**98.49**
煤炭开采和洗选业	Mining and Washing of Coal	8.95	73.19	5.60	98.93
石油和天然气开采业	Extraction of Petroleum and Natural Gas	10.38	30.08	15.45	99.15
黑色金属矿采选业	Mining and Processing of Ferrous Metal Ores	15.24	49.30	19.55	98.71
有色金属矿采选业	Mining and Processing of Non-Ferrous Metal Ores	16.31	39.33	24.94	99.61
非金属矿采选业	Mining and Processing of Non-metal Ores	10.42	64.55	8.74	99.14
开采辅助活动	Support Activities for Mining	-0.61	38.31	-0.69	99.39
其他采矿业	Mining of Other Ores				
农副食品加工业	Processing of Food from Agricultural Products	18.24	48.89	5.97	98.78
食品制造业	Manufacture of Foods	25.29	33.54	11.11	99.85
酒、饮料和精制茶制造业	Manufacture of Liquor, Beverages and Refined Tea	24.90	35.31	21.58	94.40
烟草制品业	Manufacture of Tobacco	60.15	42.11	5.48	107.88
纺织业	Manufacture of Textile	15.66	41.58	6.99	97.42
纺织服装、服饰业	Manufacture of Textile, Wearing Apparel and Accessories	14.36	43.85	5.14	98.66
皮革、毛皮、羽毛及其制品和制鞋业	Manufacture of Leather, Fur, Feather and Related Products and Footwear	10.35	55.98	4.92	97.45
木材加工和木、竹、藤、棕、草制品业	Processing of Timber, Manufacture of Wood, Bamboo, Rattan, Palm and Straw Products	6.91	49.32	4.69	99.46
家具制造业	Manufacture of Furniture	14.70	59.28	6.19	97.40
造纸和纸制品业	Manufacture of Paper and Paper Products	14.16	60.36	7.58	96.61
印刷和记录媒介复制业	Printing and Reproduction of Recording Media	19.65	33.60	13.05	97.70
文教、工美、体育和娱乐用品制造业	Manufacture of Articles for Culture, Education, Arts and Crafts, Sport and Entertainment Activities	22.72	62.71	5.64	98.15
石油加工、炼焦和核燃料加工业	Processing of Petroleum, Coking and Processing of Nuclear Fuel	20.39	49.55	3.59	99.48
化学原料和化学制品制造业	Manufacture of Raw Chemical Materials and Chemical Products	14.22	45.04	14.38	96.64
医药制造业	Manufacture of Medicines	17.40	41.30	17.13	94.74
化学纤维制造业	Manufacture of Chemical Fibres	9.02	82.10	3.34	95.14
橡胶和塑料制品业	Manufacture of Rubber and Plastics Products	13.80	47.72	7.18	97.55
非金属矿物制品业	Manufacture of Non-metallic Mineral Products	20.42	41.96	17.03	98.34
黑色金属冶炼和压延加工业	Smelting and Pressing of Ferrous Metals	10.22	73.33	5.08	99.50
有色金属冶炼和压延加工业	Smelting and Pressing of Non-ferrous Metals	6.23	40.07	4.27	97.60
金属制品业	Manufacture of Metal Products	15.13	68.32	6.34	99.49
通用设备制造业	Manufacture of General Purpose Machinery	6.13	62.79	5.94	97.21
专用设备制造业	Manufacture of Special Purpose Machinery	6.89	54.90	8.53	93.77
汽车制造业	Manufacture of Automobiles	17.31	62.07	8.66	98.95
铁路、船舶、航空航天和其他运输设备制造业	Manufacture of Railway, Ship, Aerospace and Other Transport Equipments	4.40	66.70	4.46	96.31
电气机械和器材制造业	Manufacture of Electrical Machinery and Apparatus	10.25	53.39	8.29	99.57
计算机、通信和其他电子设备制造业	Manufacture of Computers, Communication and Other Electronic Equipments	3.67	65.22	2.91	100.05
仪器仪表制造业	Manufacture of Measuring Instruments and Machinery	15.09	52.78	15.10	98.31
其他制造业	Other Manufactures	3.02	80.42	10.29	89.52
废弃资源综合利用业	Utilization of Waste Resources	14.45	71.97	4.90	95.72
金属制品、机械和设备修理业	Repair Service of Metal Products, Machinery and Equipment	3.58	44.13	5.77	100.01
电力、热力生产和供应业	Production and Supply of Electric Power and Heat Power	8.07	65.61	8.96	100.52
燃气生产和供应业	Production and Supply of Gas	13.24	54.94	11.94	99.73
水的生产和供应业	Production and Supply of Water	3.93	55.73	22.27	99.8

14-8 各市(州)规模以上工业企业主要指标

Main Indicators of Industrial Enterprises above Designated Size by Region

单位：亿元 (100 million yuan)

年 份 市(州)	Year Region	企业单位数(个) Number of Enterprises (unit)	资产总计 Total Assets	流动资产合计 Total Current Assets	固定资产原价 Original Value of Fixed Assets	负债合计 Total Liabilities	流动负债合计 Total Current Liabilities	所有者权益合计 Owners' Equities
1998		4980	3901.41	1697.45	2333.82	2533.99	1674.19	1367.42
1999		4538	4468.41	1753.12	2915.58	2845.91	1701.77	1622.50
2000		4394	4586.11	1845.51	2917.04	2955.77	1773.71	1630.26
2001		4572	4862.54	1980.49	3115.87	3054.15	1919.52	1808.39
2002		4908	5245.63	2130.16	3204.04	3239.96	2054.99	2005.67
2003		5448	6024.49	2476.34	3658.81	3696.53	2418.37	2326.96
2004		7413	6817.78	2874.36	4346.45	4306.81	2970.85	2510.36
2005		7959	7908.62	3309.89	4845.07	4934.81	3354.28	2966.06
2006		8995	9182.08	3890.88	5289.43	5588.76	3766.54	3589.27
2007		10709	11690.21	4971.06	6769.68	6956.94	4792.47	4733.27
2008		13725	15589.47	6458.42	8042.60	9241.79	6228.80	6347.68
2009		13267	17986.99	7447.84	10073.14	10832.20	7126.69	7077.73
2010		13706	22564.76	9321.70	13695.10	13889.83	9502.58	8571.93
2011		12085	26113.61	11248.78	15442.86	15991.15	11119.10	10049.11
2012		12719	30362.89	13344.68	17035.75	18721.46	12768.70	11471.16
2013		12998	36239.56	14841.33	20574.50	22204.87	13935.65	13491.64
2014		13267	38359.92	15900.10	23620.98	23413.64	15559.93	14703.51
2015		13525	40401.38	16015.98	24412.86	24238.90	15127.72	16075.60
2016		13819	41514.58	17075.54	28317.19	24234.79	15879.88	17167.51
2017		13904	43253.61	18472.38	27148.14	25120.16	16893.84	18033.84
2018		13915	46015.75	19818.22	28047.89	26150.93	18315.72	19864.82
成都市	Chengdu	3435	13667.82	7933.41	5422.01	7646.26	6585.79	6021.56
自贡市	Zigong	535	925.92	566.79	344.46	504.34	423.66	421.58
攀枝花市	Panzhihua	325	2254.88	706.89	1268.15	1454.82	1079.74	800.05
泸州市	Luzhou	651	1371.83	699.59	708.74	630.27	519.58	741.56
德阳市	Deyang	1341	2743.65	1733.36	1123.30	1538.15	1348.75	1205.50
绵阳市	Mianyang	1005	2981.22	1542.12	1096.17	1893.30	1487.29	1087.92
广元市	Guangyuan	487	834.79	256.97	790.97	490.79	290.11	344.00
遂宁市	Suining	539	983.49	396.72	527.12	343.44	245.87	640.05
内江市	Neijiang	330	809.90	390.11	941.91	563.13	480.06	246.77
乐山市	Leshan	610	2043.26	700.15	1626.19	1201.80	639.17	841.46
南充市	Nanchong	748	1470.59	544.08	1149.95	583.31	346.34	887.28
眉山市	Meishan	569	884.35	419.76	555.68	441.94	366.74	442.42
宜宾市	Yibin	769	3154.26	1787.06	1431.61	1469.64	1150.99	1684.61
广安市	Guangan	547	750.47	278.39	556.78	420.41	288.37	330.06
达州市	Dazhou	634	1253.36	406.15	1087.23	699.12	449.69	554.25
雅安市	Yaan	341	1246.73	266.45	1157.75	872.45	329.98	374.28
巴中市	Bazhong	307	280.13	89.33	196.18	126.02	82.30	154.11
资阳市	Ziyang	293	439.97	210.68	232.30	260.09	218.70	179.88
阿坝藏族羌族自治州	Aba	105	583.51	106.66	578.82	421.23	180.26	162.28
甘孜藏族自治州	Ganzi	54	1113.35	91.40	1042.68	863.36	163.91	249.99
凉山彝族自治州	Liangshan	285	2506.49	410.96	2223.02	1760.81	527.90	745.68

14-8 续表 continued

单位：亿元 (100 million yuan)

年 份 市(州)	Year Region	营业收入 Business Revenue	营业成本 Business Cost	利润总额 Total Profits	销售费用 Selling Expenses	管理费用 Administrative Expenses	财务费用 Finacial Expenses	全部从业人员年平均人数(万人) Annual Average Employed Persons (10 000 persons)
1998				39.70				252.79
1999				26.42				230.03
2000				71.32	108.44	176.02	83.66	208.00
2001				84.77	122.97	186.07	85.31	195.97
2002				122.60	142.26	201.11	87.73	191.62
2003				153.08	171.10	248.74	89.92	201.62
2004		4633.36	3766.65	188.51	193.15	331.01	94.23	209.77
2005		6008.12	4900.53	326.65	232.70	339.09	99.44	219.00
2006		7711.35	6296.60	448.07	273.72	403.63	125.36	233.53
2007		10611.52	8572.00	700.05	351.30	539.95	162.84	257.46
2008		14286.43	11748.93	844.56	454.09	720.06	237.69	297.54
2009		17486.41	14400.22	1123.48	535.53	845.01	216.60	311.38
2010		23062.82	19003.96	1661.85	699.15	1215.96	292.99	351.67
2011		29887.91	24721.71	2197.84	823.18	1334.58	403.76	380.48
2012		31427.16	25755.76	2333.76	906.74	1385.65	506.12	391.44
2013		35686.14	29660.84	2328.99	1006.62	1498.64	569.61	385.05
2014		38063.87	31963.29	2237.00	1102.91	1494.21	696.40	374.10
2015		38645.91	32514.83	2171.26	1157.77	1592.69	690.41	354.47
2016		41529.25	34935.31	2339.82	1296.99	1674.17	616.15	335.48
2017		41631.26	34660.03	2824.26	1313.40	1718.32	565.54	318.97
2018		41833.78	34465.16	3055.93	1368.80	1736.90	558.25	299.18
成都市	Chengdu	11468.00	9466.24	675.83	440.26	542.74	67.85	87.20
自贡市	Zigong	1326.01	1101.25	65.50	54.38	67.19	20.15	8.82
攀枝花市	Panzhihua	1758.57	1463.62	151.03	30.57	68.90	29.47	9.98
泸州市	Luzhou	1788.32	1378.46	171.72	98.93	67.21	14.97	11.42
德阳市	Deyang	3543.72	2881.54	304.40	116.63	134.50	16.89	22.82
绵阳市	Mianyang	2731.11	2347.97	120.67	101.99	123.71	37.67	19.28
广元市	Guangyuan	1003.78	842.37	82.13	24.60	30.17	15.27	6.07
遂宁市	Suining	1361.68	1125.90	138.31	32.80	39.63	10.60	9.89
内江市	Neijiang	1014.60	879.35	63.75	19.69	32.11	16.15	7.60
乐山市	Leshan	1492.49	1188.99	174.36	41.01	58.63	27.03	11.95
南充市	Nanchong	2659.38	2159.60	195.70	108.73	122.29	40.56	18.47
眉山市	Meishan	1389.71	1210.75	73.53	41.06	47.28	10.83	9.59
宜宾市	Yibin	2692.85	2058.48	372.78	91.84	102.82	18.51	18.10
广安市	Guangan	1605.99	1430.06	70.91	32.50	44.32	10.95	8.14
达州市	Dazhou	1271.29	1044.15	105.70	35.80	54.52	16.74	12.44
雅安市	Yaan	536.12	429.83	32.84	19.16	19.69	31.27	4.58
巴中市	Bazhong	585.09	477.14	31.54	33.39	31.67	3.97	4.46
资阳市	Ziyang	562.96	457.94	29.94	20.08	43.70	8.92	6.93
阿坝藏族羌族自治州	Aba	177.08	142.34	10.10	3.02	6.18	15.23	1.32
甘孜藏族自治州	Ganzi	104.25	62.43	4.22	0.59	3.28	31.08	0.73
凉山彝族自治州	Liangshan	891.52	643.58	113.85	20.56	34.26	65.93	5.33

注：2017年及以前营业收入、营业成本分别为主营业务收入、主营业务成本(以下有关各表同)。

a) Business revenue and business cost before 2017 are revenue of principal business and cost of principal business respectively(the same as the related tables).

14-9 各市(州)规模以上工业企业资产总计
Total Assets of Industrial Enterprises above Designated Size by Region

单位：亿元 (100 million yuan)

市(州)	Region	2010	2011	2012	2013	2014	2015	2016	2017	2018
全 省	**Sichuan**	**22564.76**	**26113.61**	**30362.89**	**36239.56**	**38359.92**	**40401.38**	**41514.58**	**43253.61**	**46015.75**
成都市	Chengdu	5531.83	6597.29	10255.39	12606.49	10627.48	10952.40	11382.46	12110.16	13667.82
自贡市	Zigong	675.84	786.14	910.50	1067.68	1099.62	1040.01	1051.47	975.54	925.92
攀枝花市	Panzhihua	1773.22	2206.33	2594.04	2099.09	2129.96	2273.42	2200.59	2331.22	2254.88
泸州市	Luzhou	589.12	706.87	917.75	1117.77	1056.03	1059.23	1130.09	1222.20	1371.83
德阳市	Deyang	2222.87	2103.38	2220.11	2356.22	2424.44	2330.88	2534.85	2527.93	2743.65
绵阳市	Mianyang	1335.78	1659.14	1863.31	2163.59	2313.05	2364.58	2540.05	2738.11	2981.22
广元市	Guangyuan	263.17	301.21	366.28	496.47	604.53	692.97	696.75	752.25	834.79
遂宁市	Suining	300.06	460.07	509.24	585.87	697.87	724.94	821.21	936.07	983.49
内江市	Neijiang	570.38	660.35	830.92	974.72	933.72	911.94	889.86	754.99	809.90
乐山市	Leshan	1277.76	1397.40	1592.99	1706.68	1785.78	1871.47	1999.56	2003.05	2043.26
南充市	Nanchong	815.41	905.07	1028.00	1159.52	1225.44	1337.25	1502.81	1392.33	1470.59
眉山市	Meishan	504.43	576.04	685.34	818.45	828.49	869.67	908.61	896.13	884.35
宜宾市	Yibin	1253.48	1552.22	1828.50	2759.05	2149.60	2678.36	2531.87	2797.60	3154.26
广安市	Guangan	299.75	385.60	451.61	512.28	614.99	644.00	669.21	678.88	750.47
达州市	Dazhou	765.39	780.81	853.28	960.79	925.43	1445.50	1031.77	1038.74	1253.36
雅安市	Yaan	771.62	773.22	881.52	948.93	952.92	1179.27	1207.52	1264.89	1246.73
巴中市	Bazhong	63.78	87.74	94.95	120.81	173.64	201.35	219.96	239.51	280.13
资阳市	Ziyang	466.08	604.96	704.17	817.91	887.33	598.63	501.57	511.65	439.97
阿坝藏羌族自治州	Aba	351.30	389.67	517.15	503.39	534.05	568.78	592.66	606.66	583.51
甘孜藏族自治州	Ganzi	197.76	278.35	303.68	354.88	372.28	764.21	826.89	1081.35	1113.35
凉山彝族自治州	Liangshan	661.97	778.15	954.15	2108.97	2376.50	2924.62	2464.44	2517.03	2506.49

14-10 各市(州)规模以上工业企业营业收入
Business Revenue of Industrial Enterprises above Designated Size by Region

单位：亿元 (100 million yuan)

市(州)	Region	2010	2011	2012	2013	2014	2015	2016	2017	2018
全　省	**Sichuan**	**23062.82**	**29887.91**	**31427.16**	**35686.14**	**38063.87**	**38645.91**	**41529.25**	**41631.26**	**41833.78**
成都市	Chengdu	5626.12	7214.33	9341.43	10783.98	10234.61	10726.37	11864.26	12488.88	11468.00
自贡市	Zigong	1085.33	1288.07	1323.18	1513.11	1605.30	1664.04	1735.65	1521.51	1326.01
攀枝花市	Panzhihua	1060.96	1228.72	1356.70	1627.64	1581.22	1495.90	1554.08	1737.10	1758.57
泸州市	Luzhou	1020.49	1306.18	1140.27	1404.23	1365.02	1447.72	1604.04	1610.82	1788.32
德阳市	Deyang	1488.66	1970.55	2128.80	2406.47	2658.70	2826.05	3267.50	3321.28	3543.72
绵阳市	Mianyang	1275.97	1705.12	1811.13	1979.56	2115.45	2307.29	2450.81	2737.43	2731.11
广元市	Guangyuan	320.47	458.95	566.69	618.27	688.20	732.28	815.11	885.28	1003.78
遂宁市	Suining	640.75	1045.47	1040.53	1176.50	1297.66	1179.87	1305.63	1487.89	1361.68
内江市	Neijiang	1286.38	1637.68	1434.36	1652.69	1632.91	1618.27	1733.46	1050.46	1014.60
乐山市	Leshan	1168.93	1362.28	1346.71	1512.64	1576.94	1525.24	1702.21	1355.22	1492.49
南充市	Nanchong	1129.95	1331.08	1551.26	1834.82	1940.42	2181.35	2460.74	2320.04	2659.38
眉山市	Meishan	743.40	1022.45	833.87	1010.21	1183.61	1318.39	1480.72	1210.35	1389.71
宜宾市	Yibin	1272.74	1789.29	1846.21	1860.20	1927.34	2078.77	2253.25	2562.54	2692.85
广安市	Guangan	605.56	886.50	972.47	1136.35	1244.59	1383.33	1561.45	1566.76	1605.99
达州市	Dazhou	882.08	1062.59	1005.78	1077.39	1129.35	1365.55	945.07	1079.05	1271.29
雅安市	Yaan	288.81	381.35	375.27	378.16	409.16	417.10	462.93	481.82	536.12
巴中市	Bazhong	170.93	285.35	306.31	363.08	452.11	512.12	568.32	587.79	585.09
资阳市	Ziyang	1161.85	1563.82	1740.55	1911.51	1980.42	1169.82	997.99	840.78	562.96
阿坝藏羌族自治州	Aba	78.89	104.54	135.44	138.87	169.20	186.26	201.42	172.96	177.08
甘孜藏族自治州	Ganzi	43.55	49.94	59.53	68.80	55.79	54.63	59.88	87.26	104.25
凉山彝族自治州	Liangshan	615.98	934.29	1110.66	1231.64	1222.13	1074.56	1062.30	866.93	891.52

14-11 各市(州)规模以上工业企业利润总额
Total Profits of Industrial Enterprises above Designated Size by Region

单位：亿元 (100 million yuan)

市(州)	Region	2010	2011	2012	2013	2014	2015	2016	2017	2018
全 省	**Sichuan**	**1661.85**	**2197.84**	**2333.76**	**2328.99**	**2237.00**	**2171.26**	**2339.82**	**2824.26**	**3055.93**
成都市	Chengdu	391.64	501.64	643.67	672.15	718.76	510.98	845.01	994.19	675.83
自贡市	Zigong	65.00	86.54	81.37	77.93	75.61	76.08	71.50	76.21	65.50
攀枝花市	Panzhihua	49.89	74.58	38.59	60.29	45.57	19.44	-111.60	89.04	151.03
泸州市	Luzhou	92.11	135.05	140.15	122.36	87.65	103.42	119.93	118.17	171.72
德阳市	Deyang	120.84	154.79	154.85	152.77	84.67	180.57	235.64	250.10	304.40
绵阳市	Mianyang	93.93	122.22	106.51	99.15	102.60	101.00	125.16	141.94	120.67
广元市	Guangyuan	14.50	25.01	33.92	31.71	31.81	35.67	43.00	59.23	82.13
遂宁市	Suining	48.31	84.81	81.81	86.60	76.99	69.01	78.72	115.81	138.31
内江市	Neijiang	73.25	106.97	78.29	95.61	75.22	71.98	67.01	33.64	63.75
乐山市	Leshan	99.31	96.35	88.17	78.79	44.70	63.59	81.11	84.09	174.36
南充市	Nanchong	80.18	102.32	132.37	123.22	133.49	156.58	176.71	165.75	195.70
眉山市	Meishan	45.64	91.48	67.49	67.99	70.81	80.76	92.73	73.46	73.53
宜宾市	Yibin	148.41	209.36	240.62	221.60	177.25	207.92	198.08	247.48	372.78
广安市	Guangan	30.19	42.56	52.39	60.83	54.64	52.24	65.56	67.11	70.91
达州市	Dazhou	41.49	63.01	77.29	89.47	95.78	120.99	13.99	51.10	105.70
雅安市	Yaan	29.15	34.38	36.36	31.03	30.67	32.24	30.36	29.63	32.84
巴中市	Bazhong	3.00	10.76	7.32	9.58	13.84	16.95	20.19	22.53	31.54
资阳市	Ziyang	92.54	120.24	159.02	161.28	141.95	83.47	56.85	45.70	29.94
阿坝藏羌族自治州	Aba	13.71	14.90	12.25	-0.28	7.55	7.88	9.66	6.54	10.10
甘孜藏族自治州	Ganzi	13.62	16.68	12.53	12.95	6.74	6.60	2.16	7.47	4.22
凉山彝族自治州	Liangshan	70.34	100.23	88.81	73.95	96.86	97.39	77.46	94.64	113.85

14-12 各市(州)国有控股工业企业主要指标
Main Indicators of State-holding Industrial Enterprises by Region

单位：亿元 (100 million yuan)

年 份 市(州)	Year Region	企业单位数(个) Number of Enterprises (unit)	资产总计 Total Assets	流动资产合计 Total Current Assets	固定资产原价 Original Value of Fixed Assets	负债合计 Total Liabilities	流动负债合计 Total Current Liabilities	所有者权益合计 Owners' Equities
1998		2372	3080.34	1314.34	1923.21	1994.47	1252.47	1085.87
1999		2065	3548.38	1328.96	2442.68	2258.93	1244.29	1289.45
2000		1699	3522.23	1347.30	2383.24	2299.29	1260.77	1222.86
2001		1485	3616.84	1392.49	2506.88	2315.25	1348.07	1301.58
2002		1324	3709.04	1409.16	2442.48	2347.13	1358.96	1361.91
2003		1065	3846.39	1455.26	2627.61	2450.16	1470.03	1396.23
2004		1057	3801.84	1405.99	2896.33	2529.36	1566.75	1271.88
2005		928	4473.03	1683.30	3260.59	2877.77	1795.29	1587.51
2006		933	5109.55	1943.60	3428.41	3232.76	1952.59	1872.75
2007		878	6325.71	2448.14	4366.82	4019.44	2453.22	2306.27
2008		1006	8515.93	3098.43	4606.00	5401.06	3214.03	3114.87
2009		971	9499.46	3572.94	5401.57	6137.14	3674.12	3347.13
2010		921	11429.22	4134.86	6655.41	7641.93	4772.31	3777.87
2011		851	13189.13	4918.31	7338.88	8752.85	5711.90	4414.98
2012		888	14797.73	5412.38	8398.72	9864.31	5976.14	4906.05
2013		914	17343.43	5635.05	9389.16	11568.57	6094.28	5486.79
2014		929	19021.19	6100.45	12137.96	12496.96	7169.81	6520.19
2015		978	20092.37	5901.10	13221.06	13318.05	6951.52	6762.66
2016		977	20086.48	6469.21	15716.10	13128.84	7461.16	6958.39
2017		970	20947.40	6869.82	15983.97	13195.98	7615.47	7738.08
2018		1004	22278.06	7504.19	15718.23	13336.17	7724.40	8941.89
成都市	Chengdu	253	4309.00	2174.81	2061.53	2413.90	1833.00	1895.10
自贡市	Zigong	22	324.63	213.35	88.60	180.32	164.43	144.31
攀枝花市	Panzhihua	32	1604.22	384.89	968.54	969.09	680.52	635.13
泸州市	Luzhou	40	555.88	286.58	267.63	251.32	192.07	304.56
德阳市	Deyang	47	1030.39	728.66	404.78	677.43	569.01	352.95
绵阳市	Mianyang	75	1561.40	879.96	554.43	1080.41	843.42	481.00
广元市	Guangyuan	41	500.91	113.26	424.06	342.54	176.72	158.38
遂宁市	Suining	15	146.95	55.72	129.69	62.11	38.49	84.84
内江市	Neijiang	19	127.35	56.45	104.52	78.54	56.91	48.81
乐山市	Leshan	41	581.57	107.04	533.09	448.17	137.26	133.40
南充市	Nanchong	43	214.29	67.09	153.91	117.81	58.47	96.48
眉山市	Meishan	30	155.27	61.72	128.99	90.69	63.22	64.57
宜宾市	Yibin	73	2304.26	1397.14	874.40	1006.50	810.76	1297.76
广安市	Guangan	26	251.39	53.14	286.08	147.90	72.22	103.48
达州市	Dazhou	37	582.76	199.58	450.49	300.76	155.06	282.00
雅安市	Yaan	36	814.05	91.61	925.92	610.61	150.35	203.44
巴中市	Bazhong	27	52.76	16.28	44.39	30.55	20.05	22.21
资阳市	Ziyang	11	69.28	39.72	31.20	48.77	42.55	20.50
阿坝藏族羌族自治州	Aba	22	354.60	37.04	391.65	273.31	92.11	81.29
甘孜藏族自治州	Ganzi	29	995.44	53.83	962.69	775.55	135.58	219.89
凉山彝族自治州	Liangshan	80	2025.88	205.16	1944.80	1463.64	321.67	562.24

14-12 续表 continued

单位：亿元 (100 million yuan)

年 份 市(州)	Year Region	营业收入 Business Revenue	营业成本 Business Cost	利润总额 Total Profits	销售费用 Selling Expenses	管理费用 Administrative Expenses	财务费用 Finacial Expenses	全部从业人员年平均人数(万人) Annual Average Employed Persons (10 000 persons)
1998				23.27				179.70
1999				6.76				159.84
2000				37.79	59.06	127.13	59.91	132.09
2001				45.04	63.59	127.69	62.90	117.57
2002				63.32	66.96	130.07	62.50	101.76
2003				67.58	70.76	149.22	58.32	93.67
2004		1925.02	1507.99	97.70	56.97	158.71	49.84	79.11
2005		2506.44	1969.58	166.71	87.39	176.68	47.14	80.00
2006		3135.60	2471.32	216.68	100.48	201.13	66.56	82.44
2007		3926.09	3096.90	305.85	115.92	252.67	83.51	83.86
2008		4765.38	3874.58	198.13	130.93	317.73	117.20	87.08
2009		5296.72	4221.47	295.09	160.93	332.65	94.77	88.01
2010		6424.93	5132.85	478.18	180.37	385.65	116.79	90.16
2011		7895.50	6308.18	538.74	210.08	436.12	162.69	93.40
2012		8689.36	6962.15	589.29	227.66	470.30	210.67	97.05
2013		9545.34	7714.20	506.85	250.77	535.89	245.77	98.20
2014		9989.33	8099.70	484.94	257.91	495.14	339.84	97.64
2015		9746.25	7882.09	565.95	234.73	475.71	342.38	89.41
2016		9757.21	7872.16	460.69	276.22	494.39	294.98	81.97
2017		10299.10	8263.04	713.81	282.30	515.03	267.65	76.11
2018		11264.73	8933.78	880.23	297.10	559.24	264.73	73.01
成都市	Chengdu	2618.04	2064.87	115.52	54.31	152.48	16.46	14.48
自贡市	Zigong	182.06	151.02	6.94	6.37	14.30	-0.31	1.29
攀枝花市	Panzhihua	775.98	636.26	57.11	9.80	40.80	16.32	5.45
泸州市	Luzhou	290.97	159.21	53.45	38.63	22.72	2.43	2.27
德阳市	Deyang	454.52	364.75	24.24	14.87	38.78	-0.26	3.37
绵阳市	Mianyang	1245.21	1084.33	27.35	56.17	62.86	22.17	7.25
广元市	Guangyuan	194.17	143.83	25.52	4.05	8.28	11.07	1.42
遂宁市	Suining	108.17	78.16	19.10	2.50	5.58	1.32	0.92
内江市	Neijiang	51.25	41.46	1.79	1.98	4.43	1.59	0.61
乐山市	Leshan	181.24	142.24	24.26	3.61	8.78	7.92	1.46
南充市	Nanchong	120.66	93.39	10.27	3.84	7.24	3.84	1.18
眉山市	Meishan	128.63	111.33	6.12	2.11	6.10	1.66	0.96
宜宾市	Yibin	1539.88	1129.21	259.59	59.06	55.32	0.09	8.97
广安市	Guangan	115.94	90.34	13.14	2.65	8.13	3.30	1.22
达州市	Dazhou	231.94	158.84	39.37	4.75	19.09	6.37	1.84
雅安市	Yaan	172.91	115.94	17.31	9.11	4.50	23.62	1.16
巴中市	Bazhong	89.01	65.24	5.05	9.25	5.98	0.56	0.81
资阳市	Ziyang	77.81	67.83	0.04	2.02	7.04	1.07	0.81
阿坝藏族羌族自治州	Aba	72.08	52.43	7.08	0.22	1.80	10.64	0.39
甘孜藏族自治州	Ganzi	85.13	48.50	2.33	0.37	2.17	28.97	0.57
凉山彝族自治州	Liangshan	659.90	461.42	97.53	10.21	20.74	57.67	2.52

14-13 各市(州)大中型工业企业主要指标
Main Indicators of Large and Medium-Sized Industrial Enterprises by Region

单位：亿元 (100 million yuan)

年 份 市(州)	Year Region	企业单位数(个) Number of Enterprises (unit)	资产总计 Total Assets	流动资产合计 Total Current Assets	固定资产原价 Original Value of Fixed Assets	负债合计 Total Liabilities	流动负债合计 Total Current Liabilities	所有者权益合计 Owners' Equities
1998		870	2938.50	1300.17	1778.60	1854.56	1179.64	1083.94
1999		836	3574.60	1379.53	2398.73	2225.70	1241.21	1348.91
2000		783	3607.02	1421.73	2374.75	2305.85	1285.79	1301.09
2001		884	3918.90	1572.97	2574.24	2438.89	1466.63	1480.01
2002		972	4231.06	1690.32	2641.97	2593.73	1585.30	1637.34
2003		843	4707.48	1943.03	2910.60	2886.08	1874.30	1821.40
2004		909	4879.50	2088.53	3314.60	3112.58	958.57	1766.31
2005		984	5689.02	2452.25	3700.42	3565.22	2464.06	2116.05
2006		1050	6557.26	2823.62	3821.43	3986.70	2762.09	2566.51
2007		1228	8427.97	3666.10	4949.00	5031.63	3496.33	3396.35
2008		1423	10881.79	4556.76	5376.74	6566.77	4462.80	4315.03
2009		1603	12490.71	5346.84	6630.78	7638.68	5156.30	4812.08
2010		1989	15940.79	6874.81	9124.91	9956.92	6872.76	5935.53
2011		2790	19695.11	8621.32	11471.96	12187.05	8752.14	7446.71
2012		2769	21074.33	9714.15	11876.04	13376.19	9429.04	7651.59
2013		2635	26044.06	10838.81	14662.95	15808.26	10227.38	9811.84
2014		2521	26729.05	11240.43	16652.47	16336.70	11425.02	10347.35
2015		2386	26696.01	10992.73	15942.04	16178.16	10825.60	10516.84
2016		2260	27213.60	11722.69	19123.53	15622.92	10906.63	11590.68
2017		2100	28652.69	12821.14	18183.64	16348.27	11891.39	12304.42
2018		1897	30521.68	13762.87	17968.88	17055.01	12771.35	13466.67
成都市	Chengdu	528	9956.68	5762.67	4144.77	5582.31	4833.60	4374.37
自贡市	Zigong	59	596.82	374.68	193.15	343.33	278.32	253.49
攀枝花市	Panzhihua	38	1799.49	504.66	1039.02	1150.14	888.63	649.35
泸州市	Luzhou	72	914.35	462.87	451.67	414.44	332.26	499.91
德阳市	Deyang	138	1863.42	1255.07	635.44	1068.44	938.22	794.99
绵阳市	Mianyang	100	2161.29	1177.17	616.76	1447.06	1162.96	714.23
广元市	Guangyuan	38	293.31	120.35	256.26	215.38	162.24	77.93
遂宁市	Suining	75	638.41	239.94	349.08	194.66	122.55	443.75
内江市	Neijiang	57	532.52	265.05	717.83	418.30	356.98	114.22
乐山市	Leshan	93	1130.15	428.90	809.72	587.09	378.74	543.06
南充市	Nanchong	207	813.34	319.70	667.77	285.15	179.83	528.19
眉山市	Meishan	69	366.38	173.07	248.05	173.69	152.08	192.68
宜宾市	Yibin	111	2415.01	1554.81	1023.72	1137.92	913.03	1277.09
广安市	Guangan	48	352.77	101.00	339.97	209.61	125.99	143.16
达州市	Dazhou	115	813.72	263.19	689.89	461.89	304.37	351.83
雅安市	Yaan	26	213.96	105.39	83.37	121.60	94.83	92.35
巴中市	Bazhong	24	52.87	21.59	39.24	22.23	16.80	30.64
资阳市	Ziyang	49	257.97	117.16	147.00	162.61	137.71	95.35
阿坝藏族羌族自治州	Aba	6	70.35	32.65	51.10	34.46	25.80	35.89
甘孜藏族自治州	Ganzi	4	41.20	9.47	34.71	12.60	9.21	28.60
凉山彝族自治州	Liangshan	35	1521.89	192.32	1443.52	1045.84	246.68	476.05

14-13 续表 continued

单位：亿元 (100 million yuan)

年 份 市(州)	Year Region	营业收入 Business Revenue	营业成本 Business Cost	利润总额 Total Profits	销售费用 Selling Expenses	管理费用 Administrative Expenses	财务费用 Finacial Expenses	全部从业人员年平均人数(万人) Annual Average Employed Persons (10 000 persons)
1998				46.47				160.77
1999				26.68				149.23
2000				57.64	74.82	127.11	62.28	126.57
2001				71.57	88.78	139.58	67.83	119.39
2002				99.72	107.39	150.95	70.37	115.18
2003				122.44	126.20	189.75	69.50	125.64
2004		3068.51	2437.99	154.96	131.77	242.95	65.04	119.10
2005		3934.89	3138.94	245.57	161.13	243.65	67.43	128.00
2006		4941.02	3962.09	332.77	184.95	276.91	84.80	134.79
2007		6511.90	5171.48	496.14	231.11	366.06	106.81	146.44
2008		8262.77	6761.45	483.25	279.92	466.74	145.15	159.86
2009		9964.93	8093.80	668.87	333.12	533.54	126.03	175.95
2010		13854.97	11240.86	1069.06	452.96	792.20	181.28	211.98
2011		19862.11	16271.38	1510.47	573.44	950.07	266.26	271.53
2012		19928.38	16161.68	1585.57	609.47	934.30	313.17	276.54
2013		23506.70	19418.54	1567.71	680.47	1040.34	359.40	267.16
2014		24438.81	20434.41	1447.05	723.44	989.94	423.11	255.76
2015		22900.94	19188.78	1208.28	718.71	1019.95	398.78	237.07
2016		24920.35	20798.76	1406.09	821.51	1059.12	334.84	218.68
2017		24613.39	20169.60	1888.99	803.30	1059.00	304.29	203.70
2018		24430.19	19898.82	1893.77	824.37	1054.46	283.28	185.49
成都市	Chengdu	8094.81	6668.27	492.14	294.48	345.95	32.86	57.69
自贡市	Zigong	549.44	465.87	31.41	15.73	25.98	3.78	3.96
攀枝花市	Panzhihua	1187.46	978.38	103.15	18.21	55.10	21.89	7.79
泸州市	Luzhou	769.54	524.29	92.50	73.03	41.72	9.29	6.14
德阳市	Deyang	1461.45	1125.60	126.53	78.50	83.06	5.76	12.76
绵阳市	Mianyang	1643.82	1416.92	58.29	68.65	82.42	23.85	12.36
广元市	Guangyuan	315.28	253.53	36.27	6.62	9.51	6.03	2.36
遂宁市	Suining	709.05	563.55	91.85	16.01	20.31	5.68	5.31
内江市	Neijiang	731.35	644.32	46.48	7.96	18.99	11.82	4.96
乐山市	Leshan	771.63	594.58	107.85	23.98	35.21	11.19	6.91
南充市	Nanchong	1427.34	1146.39	109.97	62.12	70.36	21.73	11.53
眉山市	Meishan	438.90	376.08	25.21	15.19	16.69	3.88	4.30
宜宾市	Yibin	1974.78	1473.02	293.75	70.30	71.86	10.97	12.75
广安市	Guangan	443.22	388.41	25.04	8.06	13.76	4.98	3.29
达州市	Dazhou	664.68	544.92	63.17	13.15	28.36	9.64	6.85
雅安市	Yaan	178.83	155.01	5.56	10.05	7.13	2.06	2.03
巴中市	Bazhong	149.63	114.63	8.39	11.87	9.56	0.67	1.97
资阳市	Ziyang	319.16	259.47	9.84	11.56	30.44	6.94	4.69
阿坝藏族羌族自治州	Aba	69.53	65.37	1.79	0.71	1.59	0.82	0.45
甘孜藏族自治州	Ganzi	15.51	11.91	1.29	0.34	1.29	0.13	0.39
凉山彝族自治州	Liangshan	645.52	455.11	96.16	16.63	23.05	41.09	2.95

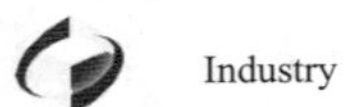

14-14 各市(州)规模以上工业企业主要经济效益指标(2018年)
Main Indicators on Economic Benefits of Industrial Enterprises above Designated Size by Region(2018)

市(州)	Region	总资产贡献率(%) Ratio of Profits,Taxes and Interests to Average Assets (%)	资产负债率(%) Ratio of Debts to Assets (%)	工业成本费用利润率(%) Ratio of Profits to Industrial Costs (%)	产品销售率(%) Products Sales Rate (%)
全 省	**Sichuan**	**12.03**	**56.83**	**8.01**	**98.22**
成都市	Chengdu	9.94	55.94	6.43	99.10
自贡市	Zigong	14.08	54.47	5.27	98.25
攀枝花市	Panzhihua	11.44	64.52	9.48	98.36
泸州市	Luzhou	23.16	45.94	11.01	96.30
德阳市	Deyang	16.64	56.06	9.66	95.89
绵阳市	Mianyang	8.45	63.51	4.62	97.46
广元市	Guangyuan	15.60	58.79	9.00	98.47
遂宁市	Suining	20.92	34.92	11.44	98.17
内江市	Neijiang	13.02	69.53	6.73	98.61
乐山市	Leshan	12.76	58.82	13.25	97.46
南充市	Nanchong	19.61	39.66	8.05	98.83
眉山市	Meishan	13.80	49.97	5.61	97.85
宜宾市	Yibin	19.25	46.59	16.41	98.11
广安市	Guangan	14.28	56.02	4.67	99.23
达州市	Dazhou	15.52	55.78	9.18	98.53
雅安市	Yaan	7.40	69.98	6.57	95.73
巴中市	Bazhong	20.39	44.99	5.77	95.56
资阳市	Ziyang	11.00	59.11	5.64	98.82
阿坝藏族羌族自治州	Aba	6.04	72.19	6.06	94.10
甘孜藏族自治州	Ganzi	4.24	77.55	4.34	97.64
凉山彝族自治州	Liangshan	9.53	70.25	14.90	99.87

14-15 各市(州)国有控股工业企业主要经济效益指标(2018年)
Main Indicators on Economic Benefits of State-holding Industrial Enterprises by Region(2018)

市(州)	Region	总资产贡献率 (%) Ratio of Profits,Taxes and Interests to Average Assets (%)	资产负债率 (%) Ratio of Debts to Assets (%)	工业成本费用利润率 (%) Ratio of Profits to Industrial Cost (%)	产品销售率 (%) Products Sales Rate (%)
全 省	**Sichuan**	**8.98**	**59.86**	**8.75**	**99.08**
成都市	Chengdu	10.27	56.02	5.05	100.18
自贡市	Zigong	4.15	55.55	4.05	98.71
攀枝花市	Panzhihua	6.81	60.41	8.12	99.92
泸州市	Luzhou	16.72	45.21	23.97	89.53
德阳市	Deyang	4.64	65.75	5.80	96.72
绵阳市	Mianyang	4.97	69.19	2.23	98.24
广元市	Guangyuan	9.67	68.38	15.26	99.33
遂宁市	Suining	18.54	42.27	21.82	110.51
内江市	Neijiang	4.41	61.67	3.63	98.53
乐山市	Leshan	7.25	77.06	14.93	96.83
南充市	Nanchong	8.31	54.98	9.48	98.16
眉山市	Meishan	8.79	58.41	5.05	99.34
宜宾市	Yibin	17.51	43.68	20.87	98.51
广安市	Guangan	8.91	58.84	12.58	99.58
达州市	Dazhou	11.85	51.61	20.82	97.53
雅安市	Yaan	7.44	75.01	11.30	98.82
巴中市	Bazhong	21.11	57.90	6.23	96.99
资阳市	Ziyang	4.24	70.40	0.05	100.06
阿坝藏族羌族自治州	Aba	6.99	77.08	10.87	100.14
甘孜藏族自治州	Ganzi	4.28	77.91	2.91	98.03
凉山彝族自治州	Liangshan	9.96	72.25	17.73	100.14

14-16 各市(州)大中型工业企业主要经济效益指标(2018年)
Main Indicators on Economic Benefits of Large and Medium-sized Industrial Enterprises by Region(2018)

市(州)	Region	总资产贡献率 (%) Ratio of Profits,Taxes and Interests to Average Assets (%)	资产负债率 (%) Ratio of Debts to Assets (%)	工业成本费用利润率 (%) Ratio of Profits to Industrial Cost (%)	产品销售率 (%) Products Sales Rate (%)
全　省	**Sichuan**	**11.55**	**55.88**	**8.58**	**98.49**
成都市	Chengdu	10.51	56.07	6.70	99.46
自贡市	Zigong	8.91	57.53	6.14	98.20
攀枝花市	Panzhihua	9.83	63.91	9.61	99.35
泸州市	Luzhou	19.27	45.33	14.27	92.81
德阳市	Deyang	11.10	57.34	9.79	95.31
绵阳市	Mianyang	6.22	66.95	3.66	96.89
广元市	Guangyuan	18.90	73.43	13.16	99.08
遂宁市	Suining	21.01	30.49	15.17	97.80
内江市	Neijiang	13.76	78.55	6.80	98.85
乐山市	Leshan	13.62	51.95	16.22	97.72
南充市	Nanchong	19.42	35.06	8.46	98.89
眉山市	Meishan	11.71	47.41	6.12	97.59
宜宾市	Yibin	20.32	47.12	18.06	98.33
广安市	Guangan	11.62	59.42	6.03	99.35
达州市	Dazhou	13.81	56.76	10.60	98.74
雅安市	Yaan	6.62	56.83	3.19	97.17
巴中市	Bazhong	33.67	42.04	6.14	96.74
资阳市	Ziyang	8.26	63.04	3.19	98.46
阿坝藏族羌族自治州	Aba	6.44	48.98	2.61	91.37
甘孜藏族自治州	Ganzi	7.52	30.58	9.44	90.48
凉山彝族自治州	Liangshan	12.11	68.72	17.94	100.04

14-17 规模以上工业企业主要产品产量
Output of Major Products of Industrial Enterprises above Designated Size

产品名称		Item		2005	2010	2014	2015	2016	2017	2018
化学纤维	(万吨)	Chemical Fiber	(10 000 tons)	26.56	51.22	110.30	118.10	118.06	126.50	86.20
纱	(万吨)	Yarn	(10 000 tons)	25.48	70.81	112.70	118.00	121.61	103.60	73.00
布	(亿米)	Cloth	(100 million m)	7.07	14.90	18.91	18.50	18.91	16.40	15.60
蚕丝及交织机织物	(万米)	Silk and Woven Fabric	(10 000 m)	11330	23042	24793	17247	20761	19864	19642
服装	(万件)	Garments	(10 000 pcs)	2764	9933	18559	18780	20310	18775	16608
机制纸及纸板	(万吨)	Machine-made Paper and Paperboard	(10 000 tons)	110.59	342.86	224.24	189.80	210.58	237.10	261.50
合成洗涤剂	(万吨)	Synthetic Detergents	(10 000 tons)	52.51	76.66	140.06	151.40	131.88	129.20	91.30
原电池	(万只)	Battery	(10 000 pcs)	5754	37980	71415	75000	107700	128000	121000
原盐	(万吨)	Salt	(10 000 tons)	412.11	763.18	388.08	325.00	337.45	581.70	494.50
卷烟	(亿支)	Cigarettes	(100 million pieces)	685.05	914.24	1003.69	945.80	668.16	734.10	755.20
乳制品	(万吨)	Dairy Products	(10 000 tons)	15.04	58.00	102.71	104.90	123.42	146.00	110.40
白酒(商品量)	(万千升)	Liquor	(10 000 kiloliter)	57.83	229.80	349.97	370.90	402.67	372.40	358.30
啤酒	(万千升)	Beer	(10 000 kiloliter)	126.22	158.30	227.75	221.00	232.11	240.70	221.40
软饮料	(万千升)	Soft Drink	(10 000 kiloliter)	120.41	495.91	1275.36	1311.90	1372.06	1408.60	1625.80
食用植物油	(万吨)	Vegetable Oil	(10 000 tons)	40.83	117.73	142.25	205.10	184.36	206.80	200.20
配、混合饲料	(万吨)	Mingled Feedstuff	(10 000 tons)	449.94	701.16	1247.84	1201.40	1568.45	1582.40	1492.00
中成药	(万吨)	Traditional Chinese Medicir	(10 000 tons)	9.83	29.81	51.71	53.60	59.53	49.50	28.20
化学原料药	(万吨)	Chemical Medicine	(10 000 tons)	5.40	2.67	19.70	22.50	19.10	29.20	13.00
塑料制品	(万吨)	Plastics Goods	(10 000 tons)	47.17	254.29	384.13	415.50	486.30	492.10	398.80
家用电冰箱	(万台)	Household Refrigerators	(10 000 units)	23.00	81.22	80.22	73.60	85.59	83.20	85.30
房间空气调节器	(万台)	Air Conditioner	(10 000 units)	145.23	119.49	172.70	142.80	203.36	316.10	263.20
电视机	(万台)	Television Sets	(10 000 units)	781.61	1208.90	1027.72	1055.70	1111.01	1051.30	1001.50
#彩色电视机	(万台)	Color Television Sets	(10 000 units)	781.61	1208.90	1027.72	1055.70	1111.01	1051.30	1001.50
原油	(万吨)	Crude Oil	(10 000 tons)	13.92	15.12	19.20	15.43	10.78	8.67	8.13
柴油	(万吨)	Diesel Oil	(10 000 tons)	49.23	83.30	313.63	340.91	289.16	291.88	179.27

14-17 续表 continued

产品名称		Item		2005	2010	2014	2015	2016	2017	2018
汽油	(万吨)	Gasoline	(10 000 tons)	28.16	57.76	194.80	217.44	256.58	280.34	181.21
天然气	(亿立方米)	Natural Gas	(100 million cu.m)	135.24	234.16	252.46	266.21	296.91	356.39	369.82
发电量	(亿千瓦小时)	Electricity	(100 million kwh)	958.03	1683.82	2930.74	2969.54	3141.62	3339.96	3499.39
#水电	(亿千瓦小时)	Hydropower	(100 million kwh)	616.99	1103.37	2341.30	2508.44	2721.83	2909.89	2983.03
焦炭	(万吨)	Coke	(10 000 tons)	827.94	1157.09	1353.98	1304.37	1275.38	1072.16	1126.87
生铁	(万吨)	Pig Iron	(10 000 tons)	1060.50	1593.81	1931.40	1747.40	1733.20	1899.70	1978.60
粗钢	(万吨)	Crude Steel	(10 000 tons)	1094.45	1580.99	2243.03	2110.40	2007.74	2026.30	2400.70
成品钢材	(万吨)	Rolled Steel Products	(10 000 tons)	1172.72	1976.55	2935.21	2702.50	2837.21	2491.20	2896.70
铁合金	(万吨)	Ferroalloy	(10 000 tons)	106.62	238.89	226.33	211.60	192.44	148.50	139.10
水泥	(万吨)	Cement	(10 000 tons)	4194.74	13227.55	14580.97	14040.60	14584.18	13810.00	13748.70
平板玻璃	(万重量箱)	Plate Glass	(10 000 wt.cases)	1304.94	4275.94	3422.65	4073.60	5363.26	5568.50	5384.10
硫酸	(万吨)	Sulfuric Acid	(10 000 tons)	324.85	388.22	695.33	642.50	645.52	631.90	495.20
浓硝酸	(万吨)	Concentrated Nitric Acid	(10 000 tons)	5.43	8.43	7.26	5.40	5.83	7.70	6.80
碳酸钠(纯碱)	(万吨)	Soda Ash	(10 000 tons)	106.51	169.78	129.60	106.90	120.56	124.20	140.50
氢氧化钠(烧碱)	(万吨)	Caustic Soda	(10 000 tons)	75.49	106.93	114.96	97.30	99.07	92.70	104.60
合成氨	(万吨)	Synthetic Ammonia	(10 000 tons)	374.47	403.34	373.24	388.40	329.17	293.90	247.80
农用氮、磷、钾化学肥料总计	(折纯)(万吨)	Chemical Fertilizers	(10 000 tons)	428.82	510.12	433.20	497.10	508.55	414.90	369.50
#氮肥	(万吨)	Nitrogen Fertilizers	(10 000 tons)	337.60	414.76	294.88	307.90	285.70	248.70	229.30
化学农药	(万吨)	Chemical Pesticide	(10 000 tons)	3.88	12.81	16.86	17.80	17.81	14.30	21.10
电石(折合量)	(万吨)	Calcium carbide	(10 000 tons)	65.76	75.98	80.74	68.30	72.34	61.80	98.00
初级形态塑料	(万吨)	Primary Form of Plastics	(10 000 tons)	61.52	104.37	190.86	208.40	231.01	228.30	236.30
轮胎外胎	(万条)	Tyres	(10 000 pcs)	615.33	1558.12	3411.84	3449.80	3836.10	4198.60	4488.20
发电设备(500千瓦及以上)	(万千瓦)	Power Generating Equipment (each above 500kw)	(10000 kw)	2327.64	3781.54	3610.27	2905.90	3038.40	3074.90	2312.30
变压器	(万千伏安)	Transformer	(10 000 kva)	846.77	1151.61	2132.73	1896.80	2014.14	2016.80	1215.30
金属切削机床	(万台)	Metal-cutting Machine Tools	(10 000 units)	0.79	0.73	1.91	0.60	0.54	0.60	0.60
汽车	(万辆)	Motor Vehicles	(10 000 units)	5.66	10.29	96.28	105.10	131.06	150.80	137.80

主要统计指标解释

工业 指从事自然资源的开采，对采掘品和农产品进行加工和再加工的物质生产部门。具体包括：(1)对自然资源的开采，如采矿、晒盐等(但不包括禽兽捕猎和水产捕捞)；(2)对农副产品的加工、再加工，如粮油加工、食品加工、缫丝、纺织、制革等；(3)对采掘品的加工、再加工，如炼铁、炼钢、化工生产、石油加工、机器制造、木材加工等，以及电力、燃气及水的生产和供应等；(4)对工业品的修理、翻新，如机器设备的修理等。

工业统计调查单位为工业法人单位。

工业法人单位 指从事工业生产经营活动的法人单位。工业法人单位应同时具备以下条件：①依法成立，有自己的名称、组织机构和场所，能够独立承担民事责任；②独立拥有（或授权）使用资产，承担负债，有权与其他单位签订合同；③具有包括资产负债表在内的帐户，或者能够根据需要编制帐户。

本篇资料中规模以上工业企业的统计范围：1998 年至 2006 年为全部国有和年主营业务收入 500 万元及以上的非国有工业法人单位；2007 至 2010 年为年主营业务收入 500 万元及以上工业法人单位；从 2011 年开始，为年主营业务收入 2000 万元及以上的工业法人单位。

国有控股企业 即原来的国有及国有控股企业，根据企业实收资本中国有经济成分的出资人的实际投资情况，或国有经济成分的出资人对企业资产的实际控制、支配程度进行分类。以下情况为国有控股：（1）在企业的全部实收资本中，国有经济成分的出资人拥有的实收资本（股本）所占企业全部实收资本（股本）的比例大于 50%的国有绝对控股。（2）在企业的全部实收资本中，国有经济成分的出资人拥有的实收资本（股本）所占比例虽未大于 50%，但相对大于其他任何一方经济成分的出资人所占比例的国有相对控股；或者虽不大于其他经济成分，但根据协议规定拥有企业实际控制权的国有协议控股。（3）投资双方各占 50%，且未明确由谁绝对控股的企业，若其中一方为国有经济成分的，一律按国有控股处理。

本篇涉及的其他企业登记注册类型的解释详见综合篇

轻工业 指主要提供生活消费品和制作手工工具的工业。按其所使用的原料不同，可分为两大类：(1)以农产品为原料的轻工业，是指直接或间接以农产品为基本原料的轻工业。主要包括食品制造、饮料制造、烟草加工、纺织、缝纫、皮革和毛皮制作、造纸以及印刷等工业；(2)以非农产品为原料的轻工业，是指以工业品为原料的轻工业。主要包括文教体育用品、化学药品制造、合成纤维制造、日用化学制品、日用玻璃制品、日用金属制品、手工工具制造、医疗器械制造、文化和办公用机械制造等工业。

重工业 指为国民经济各部门提供物质技术基础的主要生产资料的工业。按其生产性质和产品用途，可以分为下列三类：(1)采掘(伐)工业，是指对自然资源的开采，包括石油开采、煤炭开采、金属矿开采、非金属矿开采等工业；(2)原材料工业，指向国民经济各部门提供基本材料、动力和燃料的工业。包括金属冶炼及加工、炼焦及焦炭、化学、化工原料、水泥、人造板以及电力、石油和煤炭加工等工业；(3)加工工业，是指对工业原材料进行再加工制造的工业。包括装备国民经济各部门的机械设备制造工业、金属结构、水泥制品等工业，以及为农业提供的生产资料如化肥、农药等工业。

根据上述划分原则，修理业中以重工业产品为修理作业对象的划为重工业，反之划为轻工业。

资产总计 指企业过去的交易或者事项形成的、由企业拥有或者控制的、预期会给企业带来经济利益的资源。资产一般按流动性分为流动资产和非流动资产。其中流动资产可分为货币资金、交易性金融资产、应收票据、应收账款、预付款项、其他应收款、存货等；非流动资产可分为长期股权投资、固定资产、无形资产及其他非流动资产等。来源于会计“资产负债表”中“资产总计”项目的期末余额数。

流动资产合计 资产满足以下条件之一应归为流动资产：（1）预计在一个正常营业周期中变现、出售或耗用，主要包括存货、应收账款等；（2）主要为交易目的而持有；（3）预计在资产负债表日起一年内（含一年）变现；（4）自资产负债日起一年内，交换其他资产或清偿负债的能力不受限制的现金或现金等价物。包括货币资金、应收票据、应收账款、存货等项目。来源于会计“资产负债表”中“流动资产合计”项目的期末余额数。

固定资产原价 指固定资产的成本，包括企业在购置、自行建造、安装、改建、扩建、技术改造某项固定资产时所发生的全部支出总额。根据会计“固定资产”科目的期末借方余额填报。

负债合计 指企业过去的交易或者事项形成的，预期会导致经济利益流出企业的现时义务。负债一般按偿还期长短分为流动负债和非流动负债。来源于会计“资产负债表”中“负债合计”项目的期末余额数。

所有者权益 指企业资产扣除负债后由所有者享有的剩余权益。公司的所有者权益又称股东权益。包括实收资本、资本公积、盈余公积、未分配利润等。来源于会计“资产负债表”中“所有者权益合计”项目的期末余额数。

主营业务收入 指企业确认的销售商品、提供劳务等主营业务的收入。来源于会计“主营业务收入”科目的期末贷方余额（结转前）。

主营业务成本　指企业经营主要业务所发生的成本总额。来源于会计“主营业务成本”科目的期末借方余额（结转前）。

销售费用　指企业在销售商品和材料、提供劳务的过程中发生的各种费用，包括保险费、包装费、展览费和广告费、商品维修费、预计产品质量保证损失、运输费、装卸费等以及为销售本企业商品而专设的销售机构（含销售网点、售后服务网点等）的职工薪酬、业务费、折旧费等经营费用。

管理费用　指企业为组织和管理企业生产经营所发生的费用，包括企业在筹建期间内发生的开办费、董事会和行政管理部门在企业经营管理中发生的，或者应当由企业统一负担的公司经费等。来源于会计“利润表”中“管理费用”项目的本期金额数。

财务费用　指企业为筹集生产经营所需资金等而发生的筹资费用，包括企业生产经营期间发生的利息支出（减利息收入）、汇兑损失（减汇兑收益）以及相关的手续费等。来源于会计“利润表”中“财务费用”项目的本期金额数。

利润总额　指企业在一定会计期间的经营成果，是生产经营过程中各种收入扣除各种耗费后的盈余，反映企业在报告期内实现的盈亏总额。来源于会计“利润表”中“利润总额”项目的本期金额数。

总资产贡献率　反映企业全部资产的获利能力，是企业经营业绩和管理水平的集中体现，是评价和考核企业盈利能力的核心指标。计算公式为:

$$总资产贡献率=\frac{利润总额+税金总额+利息净支出}{平均资产总额}\times 100\%$$

公式中: 税金总额为主营业务税金及附加与应交增值税之和；平均资产总额为期初期末资产之和的算术平均值。

资产负债率　该指标既反映企业经营风险的大小，也反映企业利用债权人提供的资金从事经营活动的能力。计算公式为:

$$资产负债率=\frac{负债总额}{资产总额}\times 100\%$$

成本费用利润率　反映企业投入的生产成本及费用的经济效益，同时也反映企业降低成本所取得的经济效益。计算公式为:

$$成本费用利润率=\frac{利润总额}{成本费用总额}\times 100\%$$

公式中: 成本费用总额为主营业务成本、销售费用、管理费用、财务费用之和。

产品销售率　该指标反映工业产品已实现销售的程度，是分析工业产销衔接情况，研究工业产品满足社会需求程度的指标。计算公式为:

$$产品销售率=\frac{工业销售产值}{工业总产值}\times 100\%$$

Explanatory Notes on Main Statistical Indicators

Industry refers to the material production sector which is engaged in the extraction of natural resources and processing and reprocessing of minerals and agricultural products, including (1) extraction of natural resources, such as mining, salt production (but not including hunting and fishing); (2) processing and reprocessing of farm and sideline produces, such as grain and oil processing, food processing, silk reeling, spinning and weaving and leather making; (3) processing and reprocessing of mineral products, such as steel making, iron smelting, chemicals manufacturing, petroleum processing, machine building, timber processing, and production and supply of electricity, gas and water; (4) repairing and renovating of industrial products such as the machinery.

In industrial surveys, the units of enquiry are industrial corporate units.

Industrial corporate units refer to corporate units engaging in industrial production and operation activities, which meet the following requirements: (1) They are established legally, having their own names, organizations, location, and are able to take civil liability independently; (2) They possess (or are authorized to use) assets independently, assume liabilities and are entitled to sign contracts with other units; (3) They have accounts including the balance sheets or can compile the accounts according to the need.

The scopes of industrial enterprises above designated size were: all State-owned industrial enterprises and the non-State-owned industrial enterprises with revenue from principal business over 5 million yuan from 1998 to 2006; all industrial enterprises with revenue from principal business over 5 million yuan from 2007 to 2010; and all industrial enterprises with revenue from principal business above 20 million yuan since 2011.

State-holding Enterprises cover the original state-owned enterprises and state-holding enterprises. They are classified according to the actual investment made by the contributor of state-owned part in the paid-in capital of the enterprises, or the degree of control or dominance of the contributor on the assets of the enterprises. The following cases are regarded as state-holding: (1) Absolute state-holding in which the contributor of state-owned parts possess more than 50% of all the paid-in capital (stocks) of the enterprises; (2) Relative state-holding in which the contributor of state-owned parts possess no more than 50% of the paid-in capital (stocks) of the enterprises, but more than that of any other contributors; or Agreed state-holding in which the contributor of state-owned parts possess no more than other contributors but have actual control over the enterprises according to agreements; (3) In the case both contributors possess 50% and it is not clear which one is in absolute holding position, the enterprise is regarded as state-holding enterprise if one of the contributor has state-owned elements.

For explanation of types of registration covered in this chapter, please refer to General Survey.

Light Industry refers to the industry that produces consumer goods and hand tools. It consists of two categories, depending on the materials used:

(1) Industries using farm products as raw materials. These are branches of light industry which directly or indirectly use farm products as basic raw materials, including the manufacture of food and beverages, tobacco processing, textile, clothing, fur and leather manufacturing, paper making, printing, etc.

(2) Industries using non farm products as raw materials. These are branches of light industry which use manufactured goods as raw materials, including the manufacture of cultural, educational articles and sports goods, chemicals, synthetic fiber, chemical products for daily use, glass products for daily use, metal products for daily use, hand tools, medical apparatus and instruments, and the manufacture of cultural and clerical machinery.

Heavy Industry refers to the industry, which produces capital goods, and provides various sectors of the national economy with necessary material and technical basis. It consists of the following three branches according to the purpose of production or the use of products:

(1)Mining, quarrying and logging industry refers to the industry that extracts natural resources, including extraction of petroleum, coal, metal and non-metal ores and logging.

(2) Raw materials industry refers to the industry that provides various sectors of the national economy with raw materials, fuels and power. It includes smelting and processing of metals, coking and coke chemistry, chemical materials and building materials such as cement, plywood, and power, petroleum refining and coal dressing.

(3) Manufacturing industry refers to the industry that processes raw materials. It includes machine-building industry, which equips sectors of the national economy, industries of metal structure and cement products, industries producing means of agricultural production, such as chemical fertilizers and pesticides.

According to the above principle of classification, the repairing trades which are engaged primarily in repairing products of heavy industry are classified into heavy industry while these engaged in repairing products of light industry are classified into light industry.

Total Assets refer to all resources that are owned or controlled by enterprises through previous trades or transactions with expectation of making economic profits. Classified by the degree of liquidity, total assets include current assets and non-current assets. Current assets can be classified into monetary capital, trading financial assets, notes receivable, accounts receivable, advanced payments, other receivables and inventories. Non-current assets can be divided into long-term equity investment, fixed assets, intangible assets and other non-current assets. Data on this indicator can be obtained from the year-end figures of total assets in the *Balance Sheet* of accounting records.

Total Current Assets refer to the assets that meet one of the following requirements: (1) expected to be cashed, sold or used in a normal operation cycle, mainly including inventory and accounts receivable; (2) be owned for trading purpose mainly; (3) expected to be cashed in one year (including one year) from the day of the Balance Sheet; (4) unlimited cash or cash equivalents that can be exchanged with other assets or being capable of settling debts during one year since the day of the Balance Sheet. Included are monetary capital, notes receivable, accounts receivable and inventories. Data on this indicator can be obtained from the year-end figures of total current assets in the *Balance Sheet* of accounting records.

Original Value of Fixed Assets refers to the cost of fixed assets, or the total expenditure of an enterprise spent on certain fixed assets, through purchase, construction, installation, transformation, expansion or technical upgrading. It is reported according to the year-end debit balance of fixed assets of accounting records.

Total Liabilities refer to payable liabilities of enterprises that accumulated from previous trades or transactions with expectation of economic profits leaking out. In terms of payment, it can be divided into liquid liabilities and long-term liabilities. Data on this indicator can be obtained from the year-end figures of total liabilities in the *Balance Sheet* of accounting records.

Total Owner's Equity refers to the residual ownership of enterprise investors by deducting total liabilities from the total assets, including the paid-in capital, accumulation of capital, operating surplus and non-distributed profits. Data can be obtained from the year-end figures of total equity in the *Balance Sheet* of accounting records.

Revenue from Principal Business refers to the income confirmed of an enterprise from the principal business of selling products and providing labor services. Data on this indicator can be obtained from the year-end credit balance of "revenue from principal business" in the accounting record of enterprise (before carryover).

Cost of Principal Business refers to the total cost occurred from the principal business of the enterprise. Data can be obtained from the year-end debit balance of "cost of principal business" in the accounting record of enterprise (before carryover).

Selling Expense refers to the cost during the sale of goods and materials, providing labour services, including insurance, packing, exhibition fees and advertising fees, merchandise maintenance costs, expected product quality guarantee loss, transportation fees, handling fees, and operating expenses for the sales of the company's products such as employee compensation, business expenses, depreciation costs for dedicated sales offices (including sales outlets, after-sales service outlets, etc.).

Administrative Expense refers to the expenses for the organization and management of enterprise operating, including the start-up costs during the construction of enterprises, funds occurred during enterprises operating by board of directors and executive management in the enterprise management, or burden by enterprises. It comes from current amount of management cost in income statement.

Financial Expenses refers to cost of raising fund for enterprises to raise funds for production and operation, including interest payments (a reduction in interest income), exchange loss (less exchange gains) and related fees during the period of production. It comes from current amount of financial expenses in income statement.

Total Profits refers to the operation results in a certain accounting period, and it is the balance of various incomes minus various spendings in the course of operation, reflecting the total profits and losses of enterprises in reference period. Data are obtained from the amount of total profits in the profit statement of the accounting record of enterprise.

Ratio of Profits, Taxes and Interests to Average Assets reflects the profit-making capability of all assets of the enterprise and is a key indicator manifesting the performance and management and evaluating the profit-making potential of the enterprise. It is calculated as follows:

$$\text{Ratio of profits, taxes and interests to average as sets} = \frac{\text{total profits+total taxes+net interest payment}}{\text{average assets}} \times 100\%$$

In the above formula, total taxes is the sum of tax and extra charges from principal business and value-added tax payable; and average assets is the arithmetic mean of the sum of beginning assets and ending assets.

Ratio of Debts to Assets reflects both the operation risk and the capability of the enterprise in making use of the capital from the creditors. It is calculated as follows:

$$\text{Ratio of debts to assets} = \frac{\text{total debts}}{\text{total assets}} \times 100\%$$

Ratio of Profits to Total Industrial Costs refers to the ratio of profits realized in a given period to the total costs in the same period, which reflects the economic efficiency of input cost and is calculated as follows:

$$\text{Ratio of profits to total industrial cost} = \frac{\text{total profits}}{\text{total costs}} \times 100\%$$

Total costs in the above formula are the sum of cost of principal business, marketing cost, management cost and financial cost.

Ratio of Sales to Gross Output Value reflects the degree at which industrial products are sold. It helps to analyze the linkage between production and sales and the extent of the needs of the society that has been met by the supply of industrial products. It is calculated as follows:

$$\text{Ratio of sales to gross output value} = \frac{\text{Industrial sales}}{\text{gross industrial output value}} \times 100\%$$

建筑业

Chapter 15 Construction

15-1 建筑业企业个数、产值、人数及竣工面积
Number of Enterprises, Gross Output Value, Number of Persons Engaged and Floor Space of Buildings Completed of Construction

年 份 Year	企业个数 (个) Number of Enterprises (unit)	总产值 (亿元) Gross Output Value (100 million yuan)	就业人员数 (万人) Annual Average Persons Engaged (10 000 persons)	竣工房屋建筑面积 (万平方米) Floor Space of Buildings Completed (10 000 sq.m)
1952	41	0.63	3.54	20.21
1957	87	2.82	14.61	136.38
1962	133	1.58	12.14	48.01
1965	187	7.82	28.93	218.01
1970	222	9.16	43.12	238.60
1975	252	10.36	43.05	272.03
1978	276	13.17	42.38	556.56
1980	325	13.36	39.03	501.02
1985	555	31.85	49.45	835.24
1990	756	67.11	60.21	1060.60
1991	829	77.09	62.97	581.90
1992	871	93.37	70.66	705.20
1993	1090	181.79	80.10	1734.00
1994	1144	230.34	102.50	2068.00
1995	1144	279.10	89.70	2081.00
1996	2725	468.66	160.50	4537.00
1997	2779	520.64	154.24	5638.48
1998	3028	597.76	159.20	5017.25
1999	3050	649.52	160.13	5429.28
2000	3305	713.81	158.10	5839.32
2001	3125	822.87	171.85	7029.93
2002	3475	1078.25	200.42	8491.14
2003	3498	1235.04	212.68	8784.56
2004	4183	1321.22	173.84	8837.99
2005	4073	1480.88	181.80	8692.18
2006	3924	1768.87	188.50	9177.55
2007	3887	2130.17	204.71	9630.60
2008	4559	2624.96	235.78	9797.98
2009	4386	3374.06	265.24	11393.53
2010	4334	4200.86	335.53	12086.29
2011	4318	5305.89	249.46	13663.11
2012	4283	6292.67	230.23	15768.08
2013	4271	7277.41	262.65	18211.86
2014	3965	8148.52	241.79	19544.25
2015	3952	8847.59	244.23	20666.78
2016	4333	10044.16	291.82	20977.99
2017	5191	11996.22	377.99	22598.10
2018	5860	13752.24	382.56	24876.82

注：2003年建筑业统计数据仅包括当年有工作量的建筑业企业，2004年建筑业统计数据是普查数据。

a) The figure of construction enterprises of 2003 only include the enterprises which had taken in 2003.The figure of 2004 was obtained from surveys.

15-2 按登记注册类型分建筑业企业主要指标

指标		Item		合计 Total Enterprises		#国有企业 State-owned	
				2017	2018	2017	2018
建筑业企业个数	(个)	Number of Construction Enterprises		5191	5860	194	192
从业人员平均人数	(万人)	Average Number of Persons Employed	(10 000 persons)	420.44	382.49	45.96	34.75
自有固定资产原价	(万元)	Fixed Assets Owned (original value)	(10 000 yuan)	8721670	10173998	1463556	1370976
自有固定资产净价	(万元)	Fixed Assets Owned (net value)	(10 000 yuan)	4956387	5800816	753063	726184
自有机械设备净值	(万元)	Machinery Equipment Owned (net value)	(10 000 yuan)	2932201	2482224	249824	184220
自有机械设备台数	(台)	Number of Machinery and Equipment Owned	(set)	539658	561814	40509	35968
自有机械设备总功率	(万千瓦)	Total Power of Machinery and Equipment Owned	(10 000 kw)	1085.86	1180.12	138.32	132.921
建筑业总产值	(万元)	Gross Output Value of Construction	(10 000 yuan)	119962154	137522652	17431985	16369676
竣工产值	(万元)	Output Value of Completed Projects	(10 000 yuan)	59038133	61574376	7250120	4126294
房屋建筑施工面积	(万平方米)	Floor Space of Buildings under Construction	(10 000 sq.m)	60593	63481	11237	7732
房屋建筑竣工面积	(万平方米)	Floor Space of Buildings Completed	(10 000 sq.m)	22598	24877	2580	1762
利润总额	(万元)	Total Profits	(10 000 yuan)	3193749	4869972	384322	533791
税金总额	(万元)	Total Tax	(10 000 yuan)	3562820	4738243	308936	443140
利税总额	(万元)	Total Pre-Tax Profits	(10 000 yuan)	6756569	9608215	693258	976931
按总产值计算的劳动生产率	(元/人)	Overall Labor Productivity	(yuan/person)	285324	317145	379307	379670
技术装备率	(元/人)	Value of Machinery per Labourer	(yuan/person)	6974	5724	5436	4273
动力装备率	(千瓦/人)	Power of Machinery per Labourer	(kw/person)	2.58	2.72	3.01	3.08
房屋建筑面积竣工率	(%)	Rate of Floor Space of Buildings Completed	(%)	37.27	39.19	22.96	22.79
产值利润率	(%)	Ratio of Profit to Gross Output Value	(%)	2.66	3.54	2.2	3.26
产值利税率	(%)	Ratio of Pre-tax Profit to Gross Output Value	(%)	5.63	6.99	3.98	5.97

Main Indicators on Construction Enterprises by Registered Types

#集体企业 Collective-owned		#股份有限公司 Share-holding Corporations		#其他有限责任公司 Other Ltd.Company		#港澳台商投资 Funded by Entrepreneurs from Hong Kong, Macao and Taiwan		#外商投资 Foreign Funded	
2017	2018	2017	2018	2017	2018	2017	2018	2017	2018
135	113	203	183	1729	1901	7	1	3	2
14.68	12.41	21.72	19.19	163.19	147.14	0.76	0.01	0.03	0.04
174399	154611	412732	405356	4269964	5245886	22076	697	1945	5606
90103	81888	273861	228829	2468744	3024692	12071	145	1466	3445
56478	46055	255663	111890	1422604	1136797	1854	6	202	129
14663	13388	27140	26301	306300	322259	450	5	52	129
28.92	21.61	80.68	34.47	375.27	525.57	1.18	0.00	0.02	0.1876
3908396	3372489	9350512	6634288	46696166	60324498	198350	1270	28482	12136
2403687	2044807	4067017	3424006	20969465	25439728	30858	348	450	4189
1600	1355	5713	4405	21055	27617	7			
1090	939	1780	1736	7269	8974	3			
95771	140243	134031	159104	1295475	2025886	7765	12	514	1529
154871	166607	196197	233077	1426949	1875257	2091	5	35	267
250642	306850	330228	392181	2722424	3901143	9856	17	549	1796
266200	259340	430413	311756	286150	354415	261675	139560	1035709	243695
3847	3542	11768	5258	8718	6679	2446	659	7345	2590
1.97	1.66	3.71	1.62	2.30	3.09	1.56	0.16	0.76	3.77
68.09	69.26	30.64	39.42	34.53	32.49	46.30			
2.45	4.16	1.43	2.40	2.77	3.36	3.91	0.94	1.80	12.60
6.41	9.10	3.53	5.91	5.83	6.47	4.97	1.34	1.93	14.80

15-3 各市(州)建筑业企业个数
Number of Construction Enterprises by Region

单位：个 (unit)

市(州)	Region	2010	2011	2012	2013	2014	2015	2016	2017	2018
全　省	**Sichuan**	**4334**	**4318**	**4283**	**4271**	**3965**	**3952**	**4333**	**5191**	**5860**
成都市	Chengdu	1524	1582	1551	1478	1200	1206	1408	1733	1801
自贡市	Zigong	168	150	146	133	129	121	116	136	135
攀枝花市	Panzhihua	80	89	84	91	78	80	80	90	93
泸州市	Luzhou	188	187	186	164	159	175	199	257	310
德阳市	Deyang	243	245	244	255	242	240	235	256	271
绵阳市	Mianyang	272	273	268	386	411	402	404	426	448
广元市	Guangyuan	199	194	184	172	165	168	179	190	216
遂宁市	Suining	173	171	156	148	143	139	169	176	177
内江市	Neijiang	130	128	126	119	111	103	107	113	115
乐山市	Leshan	197	162	156	147	152	160	169	191	201
南充市	Nanchong	249	223	250	249	243	241	249	280	330
眉山市	Meishan	126	124	126	134	135	126	119	126	117
宜宾市	Yibin	231	216	218	213	197	188	211	300	464
广安市	Guangan	103	111	113	99	110	109	123	140	187
达州市	Dazhou	99	113	124	124	118	119	125	140	161
雅安市	Yaan	51	50	49	52	44	44	51	53	58
巴中市	Bazhong	101	99	98	97	133	139	139	181	243
资阳市	Ziyang	120	122	118	122	110	98	60	61	69
阿坝藏族羌族自治州	Aba	28	27	28	27	28	29	31	82	127
甘孜藏族自治州	Ganzi	22	22	22	26	22	24	26	32	55
凉山彝族自治州	Liangshan	30	30	36	35	35	41	133	228	282

15-4 各市(州)按登记注册类型分建筑业企业个数(2018年)
Number of Construction Enterprises by Region and Registered Types(2018)

市(州)及分组	Region and Group	企业个数(个) Number of Enterprises	国有企业 State-owned	中央企业 Central	地方企业 Local	集体企业 Collective-owned	其他企业 Others	#股份有限公司 Share-holding Corporations	#其他有限责任公司 Other Ltd. Company
全 省	**Sichuan**	**5860**	**192**	**10**	**182**	**113**	**5555**	**183**	**1901**
按市(州)分	**Grouped by Region**								
成都市	Chengdu	1801	54	3	51	24	1723	31	593
自贡市	Zigong	135	5		5	3	127	8	34
攀枝花市	Panzhihua	93	4	2	2	1	88		25
泸州市	Luzhou	310	6		6	13	291	7	86
德阳市	Deyang	271	7	3	4	8	256	4	80
绵阳市	Mianyang	448	20	1	19	1	427	13	157
广元市	Guangyuan	216	5		5	8	203	5	51
遂宁市	Suining	177	3		3	4	170	16	52
内江市	Neijiang	115	6		6	6	103	13	39
乐山市	Leshan	201	6		6		195	8	95
南充市	Nanchong	330	12		12	6	312	16	100
眉山市	Meishan	117	8		8	2	107		35
宜宾市	Yibin	464	9		9	4	451	15	86
广安市	Guangan	187	7		7	6	174	2	53
达州市	Dazhou	161	5		5	7	149	8	59
雅安市	Yaan	58	6		6	2	50	5	24
巴中市	Bazhong	243	19	1	18	7	217	8	93
资阳市	Ziyang	69	2		2	4	63	2	47
阿坝藏族羌族自治州	Aba	127	1		1	2	124	3	43
甘孜藏族自治州	Ganzi	55	1		1	3	51	4	20
凉山彝族自治州	Liangshan	282	6		6	2	274	15	129
按资质等级分	**Grouped by Qualification Grade**								
总承包企业	The General Contractor	4476	162	8	154	93	4221	154	1457
特级企业	The Special Grade	31	4	1	3		27	1	17
一级企业	The First Grade	450	29	4	25	2	419	24	190
二级企业	The Second Grade	1809	50		50	44	1715	62	595
三级企业	The Third Grade	2186	79	3	76	47	2060	67	655
专业承包企业	The Specialized Contractor	1139	28	2	26	18	1093	20	369
一级企业	The First Grade	138	2		2	1	135	5	54
二级企业	The Second Grade	557	12	2	10	10	535	7	170
三级企业及其他	The Third Grade & Others	444	14		14	7	423	8	145
劳务分包企业	The Subcontractor of Labour Services	245	2		2	2	241	9	75
一级企业	The First Grade								
二级企业	The Second Grade								
不分等级	Not Classified by Grade	245	2		2	2	241	9	75

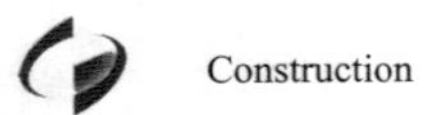

15-5 各市(州)建筑业企业就业人员
Number of Staff and Workers in Construction Enterprises by Region

单位：万人 (10 000 persons)

市(州)	Region	2010	2011	2012	2013	2014	2015	2016	2017	2018
全　省	**Sichuan**	**292.15**	**249.46**	**230.23**	**262.65**	**241.79**	**244.23**	**291.82**	**377.99**	**382.56**
成都市	Chengdu	130.05	93.42	84.45	90.10	72.91	69.93	94.29	112.91	118.22
自贡市	Zigong	6.72	8.24	8.49	9.44	8.98	9.59	8.56	10.44	12.91
攀枝花市	Panzhihua	7.00	5.22	3.41	7.65	4.26	4.22	3.97	7.30	5.19
泸州市	Luzhou	17.27	16.11	16.31	21.99	23.05	24.33	31.53	41.03	40.76
德阳市	Deyang	16.49	13.54	10.47	12.87	10.00	8.35	8.65	9.40	11.25
绵阳市	Mianyang	12.63	11.94	11.82	15.00	15.83	18.28	20.02	23.77	22.79
广元市	Guangyuan	4.24	5.40	4.53	5.09	4.83	5.24	6.08	7.82	9.63
遂宁市	Suining	8.35	8.52	7.47	8.90	8.74	8.51	10.45	11.29	10.26
内江市	Neijiang	11.68	9.91	8.03	8.48	8.47	9.40	9.24	10.90	10.26
乐山市	Leshan	5.80	6.01	5.36	5.42	5.79	6.05	6.39	8.10	9.78
南充市	Nanchong	17.31	18.41	15.03	15.44	15.02	14.28	18.73	23.14	28.30
眉山市	Meishan	6.98	6.36	7.28	8.31	8.39	8.59	10.55	11.93	11.50
宜宾市	Yibin	8.54	8.45	8.73	10.57	10.42	10.61	11.62	15.56	19.82
广安市	Guangan	11.59	11.03	10.97	11.54	12.20	11.79	12.81	13.79	15.08
达州市	Dazhou	12.51	9.44	9.73	10.94	10.72	10.32	10.56	12.20	13.58
雅安市	Yaan	1.13	1.14	1.19	1.22	1.54	1.68	1.82	2.98	3.06
巴中市	Bazhong	6.10	7.27	7.24	9.08	10.20	12.82	16.04	21.91	22.82
资阳市	Ziyang	5.82	7.43	7.19	7.68	7.74	7.45	6.21	6.84	7.79
阿坝藏族羌族自治州	Aba			0.78	0.67			0.67	0.79	1.32
甘孜藏族自治州	Ganzi					0.50	0.57	0.53	0.60	1.02
凉山彝族自治州	Liangshan	1.14	0.86	1.47	1.84	1.71	1.78	3.11	25.28	7.22

15-6 各市(州)按登记注册类型分建筑业企业就业人员(2018年)

Number of Persons Employed in Construction Enterprises by Region and Registered Types(2018)

单位：万人 (10 000 persons)

市(州)及分组	Region and Group	合计 Total	国有企业 State -owned	中央企业 Central	地方企业 Local	集体企业 Collective-owned	其他企业 Others	#股份有限公司 Share-holding Corporations	#其他股份有限公司 Other Ltd. Company
全　省	**Sichuan**	**382.56**	**34.75**	**3.63**	**31.11**	**12.41**	**335.40**	**19.27**	**147.11**
按市(州)分	**Grouped by Region**								
成都市	Chengdu	118.22	19.82	2.17	17.65	1.47	96.93	6.22	52.98
自贡市	Zigong	12.91	1.72		1.72	0.05	11.14	0.58	3.81
攀枝花市	Panzhihua	5.19	0.11	0.03	0.08	0.01	5.07		3.13
泸州市	Luzhou	40.76	2.18		2.18	2.80	35.78	0.21	12.88
德阳市	Deyang	11.25	0.48	0.35	0.12	0.37	10.40	0.06	4.42
绵阳市	Mianyang	22.79	1.90	1.05	0.85	0.06	20.83	0.58	9.04
广元市	Guangyuan	9.63	1.15		1.15	0.49	7.99	0.24	2.32
遂宁市	Suining	10.26	0.05		0.05	0.91	9.30	1.61	3.64
内江市	Neijiang	10.26	0.22		0.22	0.37	9.67	2.38	2.62
乐山市	Leshan	9.78	0.16		0.16		9.62	0.78	4.11
南充市	Nanchong	28.30	1.60		1.60	0.55	26.16	1.72	9.75
眉山市	Meishan	11.50	0.84		0.84	0.11	10.54		4.25
宜宾市	Yibin	19.82	0.41		0.41	0.47	18.94	1.74	5.16
广安市	Guangan	15.08	0.43		0.43	2.00	12.65	0.06	1.62
达州市	Dazhou	13.58	0.85		0.85	0.84	11.90	0.43	5.17
雅安市	Yaan	3.06	0.09		0.09	0.14	2.82	0.11	1.69
巴中市	Bazhong	22.82	1.75	0.03	1.72	1.29	19.78	2.04	9.85
资阳市	Ziyang	7.79	0.65		0.65	0.38	6.76	0.23	5.41
阿坝藏族羌族自治州	Aba	1.32	0.05		0.05	0.02	1.26	0.01	0.46
甘孜藏族自治州	Ganzi	1.02	0.01		0.01	0.08	0.94	0.02	0.38
凉山彝族自治州	Liangshan	7.22	0.30		0.30	0.01	6.91	0.23	4.42
按资质等级分	**Grouped by Qualification Grade**								
总承包企业	The General Contractor	351.07	33.25	3.56	29.69	11.44	306.38	16.43	134.86
特级企业	The Special Grade	14.43	1.64	0.05	1.59		12.79	0.83	9.13
一级企业	The First Grade	108.19	22.36	3.45	18.91	1.09	84.75	4.91	47.02
二级企业	The Second Grade	148.47	5.48		5.48	6.83	136.16	7.02	52.26
三级企业	The Third Grade	79.98	3.78	0.06	3.72	3.52	72.68	3.67	26.45
专业承包企业	The Specialized Contractor	25.11	1.50	0.07	1.42	0.90	22.71	2.64	10.20
一级企业	The First Grade	7.86	0.62		0.62	0.14	7.09	2.35	3.15
二级企业	The Second Grade	10.12	0.37	0.07	0.30	0.71	9.04	0.11	4.49
三级企业及其他	The Third Grade & Others	7.13	0.50		0.50	0.04	6.59	0.17	2.56
劳务分包企业	The Subcontractor of Labour Services	6.38				0.07	6.31	0.20	2.05
一级企业	The First Grade								
二级企业	The Second Grade								
不分等级	Not Classified by Grade	6.38				0.07	6.31	0.20	2.05

15-7 各市(州)建筑业企业施工、竣工房屋面积(2018年)

Floor Space of Buildings under Construction and Completed of Construction Enterprises by Region(2018)

市(州)及分组	Region and Group	房屋建筑施工面积(万平方米) Floor Space of Buildings under Construction (10 000 sq.m)	#本年新开工 Newly-started Buildings	房屋建筑竣工面积(万平方米) Floor Space of Buildings Completed (10 000 sq.m)	#住宅 Residential Housing	房屋面积竣工率(%) Rate of Floor Space Completed (%)
全　省	**Sichuan**	**63481.47**	**30096.28**	**24876.82**	**18360.56**	**39.19**
按市(州)分	**Grouped by Region**					
成都市	Chengdu	26083.82	10289.28	6813.06	4846.16	26.12
自贡市	Zigong	2562.71	1060.51	747.26	640.97	29.16
攀枝花市	Panzhihua	599.40	171.81	146.61	108.31	24.46
泸州市	Luzhou	5062.74	2375.40	2646.46	1788.13	52.27
德阳市	Deyang	2179.28	1053.55	513.15	319.41	23.55
绵阳市	Mianyang	3728.64	1725.32	1770.05	1129.93	47.47
广元市	Guangyuan	1180.89	509.88	340.35	232.68	28.82
遂宁市	Suining	1795.05	1286.46	1339.96	966.30	74.65
内江市	Neijiang	1352.94	693.21	802.04	609.67	59.28
乐山市	Leshan	1664.44	930.80	520.96	421.69	31.30
南充市	Nanchong	4430.21	2816.58	2710.07	2375.83	61.17
眉山市	Meishan	1597.53	970.79	1025.82	840.54	64.21
宜宾市	Yibin	2343.11	1426.30	905.97	593.74	38.67
广安市	Guangan	1511.37	760.79	884.42	713.40	58.52
达州市	Dazhou	2485.36	1244.32	1248.45	1009.25	50.23
雅安市	Yaan	424.96	289.64	197.51	137.96	46.48
巴中市	Bazhong	2827.20	1636.93	1629.38	1234.42	57.63
资阳市	Ziyang	772.02	375.07	274.15	244.46	35.51
阿坝藏族羌族自治州	Aba	83.24	38.77	51.77	19.11	62.20
甘孜藏族自治州	Ganzi	90.54	56.44	36.49	12.90	40.30
凉山彝族自治州	Liangshan	706.03	384.43	272.87	115.70	38.65
按资质等级分	**Grouped by Qualification Grade**					
总承包企业	The General Contractor	62199.87	29367.53	23908.05	17647.84	38.44
特级企业	The Special Grade	7583.54	2434.85	1582.70	1282.52	20.87
一级企业	The First Grade	23872.73	9225.85	6734.55	5113.44	28.21
二级企业	The Second Grade	21010.30	11757.49	10199.61	7726.38	48.55
三级企业	The Third Grade	9733.30	5949.33	5391.19	3525.49	55.39
专业承包企业	The Specialized Contractor	1281.60	728.76	968.77	712.72	75.59
一级企业	The First Grade	157.61	82.51	335.79	283.00	213.05
二级企业	The Second Grade	670.13	390.16	373.15	232.93	55.68
三级企业及其他	The Third Grade & Others	453.86	256.09	259.84	196.79	57.25

15-8 各市(州)建筑业企业房屋施工面积
Floor Space under Construction by Regional Construction Enterprises

单位：万平方米 (10 000 sq.m)

市(州)	Region	2010	2011	2012	2013	2014	2015	2016	2017	2018
全　省	**Sichuan**	**29440.82**	**34738.35**	**38550.93**	**47377.67**	**53362.63**	**52795.35**	**54048.32**	**60593.38**	**63481.47**
成都市	Chengdu	12668.80	15945.53	17266.36	22115.29	22463.04	23852.51	23327.39	25294.66	26083.82
自贡市	Zigong	859.29	1048.78	1033.49	1337.10	1689.31	1807.44	2030.35	2462.64	2562.71
攀枝花市	Panzhihua	240.36	403.17	466.34	543.93	546.12	443.54	504.24	543.15	599.40
泸州市	Luzhou	1887.51	1953.20	2544.39	3652.50	4250.37	4063.63	4493.66	4923.93	5062.74
德阳市	Deyang	1539.85	1923.51	1885.98	2124.82	2440.91	1979.12	1969.73	1970.44	2179.28
绵阳市	Mianyang	1663.43	1758.37	1947.93	2149.56	2675.96	2788.66	2696.52	3123.88	3728.64
广元市	Guangyuan	439.24	565.64	513.82	591.40	740.49	860.18	1085.02	1106.73	1180.89
遂宁市	Suining	1017.56	1035.91	1025.61	1115.87	1293.20	1470.14	1608.21	2022.84	1795.05
内江市	Neijiang	876.29	898.06	933.27	1041.99	1336.58	1372.57	1507.44	1446.66	1352.94
乐山市	Leshan	781.46	779.86	751.20	897.37	829.18	1000.99	1128.86	1513.57	1664.44
南充市	Nanchong	1971.89	2101.09	2538.98	2936.77	3123.15	3026.20	3110.31	3730.38	4430.21
眉山市	Meishan	715.49	877.23	945.04	1154.33	1334.19	1447.88	1639.34	1891.08	1597.53
宜宾市	Yibin	856.13	954.53	1075.23	1281.63	3255.42	1420.49	1524.87	1849.88	2343.11
广安市	Guangan	939.08	844.44	1054.28	1373.97	1640.87	1467.11	1505.44	1615.21	1511.37
达州市	Dazhou	1284.70	1434.92	1855.04	1925.55	2183.50	2158.90	2258.85	2337.79	2485.36
雅安市	Yaan	111.51	111.44	138.80	133.09	179.48	211.84	269.22	478.77	424.96
巴中市	Bazhong	675.57	1072.34	1318.72	1693.16	1851.24	1798.07	2038.10	2602.17	2827.20
资阳市	Ziyang	620.60	783.83	955.58	983.24	1100.23	1235.57	694.24	860.17	772.02
阿坝藏族羌族自治州	Aba	37.76	43.34	52.17	47.42	56.58	46.64	50.43	95.24	83.24
甘孜藏族自治州	Ganzi	27.34	26.58	28.64	37.99	34.95	28.50	36.73	37.82	90.54
凉山彝族自治州	Liangshan	226.97	176.58	220.09	240.71	337.88	135.36	569.37	686.35	706.03

15-9 各市(州)建筑业企业房屋竣工面积
Floor Space Completed by Regional Construction Enterprises

单位：万平方米 (10 000 sq.m)

市(州)	Region	2010	2011	2012	2013	2014	2015	2016	2017	2018
全　省	**Sichuan**	**12086.29**	**13663.11**	**15768.08**	**18211.86**	**19544.25**	**20666.78**	**20977.99**	**22598.13**	**24876.82**
成都市	Chengdu	3726.60	4864.35	5192.89	5787.99	5870.98	5985.54	6242.71	5837.73	6813.06
自贡市	Zigong	393.53	450.27	466.31	460.45	563.04	608.37	609.66	870.07	747.26
攀枝花市	Panzhihua	90.85	71.46	95.85	277.10	175.66	94.59	185.45	161.63	146.61
泸州市	Luzhou	1086.28	1056.86	1337.94	1704.97	1964.55	2177.22	2262.69	2372.83	2646.46
德阳市	Deyang	636.40	676.46	644.28	843.84	765.54	864.30	706.88	737.00	513.15
绵阳市	Mianyang	642.68	680.53	691.93	703.27	825.47	943.77	1018.21	1300.32	1770.05
广元市	Guangyuan	175.70	211.32	224.05	203.92	247.81	225.87	283.04	292.84	340.35
遂宁市	Suining	572.45	560.36	592.61	707.89	793.49	889.56	906.57	1201.15	1339.96
内江市	Neijiang	405.82	406.52	416.12	500.13	658.18	792.71	837.86	865.03	802.04
乐山市	Leshan	412.58	372.16	393.39	387.70	342.87	568.18	482.82	595.52	520.96
南充市	Nanchong	1028.98	1101.61	1651.03	1897.44	1925.93	2035.27	2030.84	2278.22	2710.07
眉山市	Meishan	428.43	479.26	529.49	670.15	641.74	729.00	808.22	866.09	1025.82
宜宾市	Yibin	441.97	523.40	619.89	675.72	776.92	805.03	818.39	949.52	905.97
广安市	Guangan	506.85	390.24	553.21	737.57	848.59	845.74	842.39	872.56	884.42
达州市	Dazhou	785.32	679.44	831.41	807.62	1106.82	1022.08	1039.44	1131.75	1248.45
雅安市	Yaan	68.06	71.92	81.61	75.33	104.85	118.05	169.13	181.95	197.51
巴中市	Bazhong	274.21	469.82	745.97	1034.10	1233.37	1147.90	1153.05	1504.32	1629.38
资阳市	Ziyang	296.09	457.93	522.69	545.93	528.08	581.06	279.48	215.99	274.15
阿坝藏族羌族自治州	Aba	27.29	30.58	31.50	31.21	41.76	38.24	34.71	58.30	51.77
甘孜藏族自治州	Ganzi	12.81	12.71	9.49	15.63	14.22	15.54	19.99	22.37	36.49
凉山彝族自治州	Liangshan	73.40	95.91	136.42	143.90	114.40	178.75	246.45	282.94	272.87

15-10 各市(州)建筑业企业动力装备情况(2018年)

Power of Machinery and Equipment Owned of Construction Enterprises by Region(2018)

市(州)及分组	Region and Group	自有机械设备总台数(台) Number of Machinery and Equipment Owned (unit)	自有机械设备总功率(万千瓦) Total Power of Machinery and Equipment Owned (10 000 kw)	自有机械设备净值(万元) Net Value of Machinery and Equipment Owned (10 000 yuan)	技术装备率(元/人) Value of Machinery per Laborer (yuan/person)	动力装备率(千瓦/人) Power of Machinery per Laborer (kw/person)
全　省	**Sichuan**	**561814**	**1180.12**	**2482224**	**6490**	**3.09**
按市(州)分	**Grouped by Region**					
成都市	Chengdu	131069	498.62	884047	7477	4.22
自贡市	Zigong	10433	17.23	42727	3312	1.34
攀枝花市	Panzhihua	7794	27.69	51260	9848	5.32
泸州市	Luzhou	28758	72.82	182915	4486	1.79
德阳市	Deyang	8943	18.56	46766	4143	1.64
绵阳市	Mianyang	15440	34.72	122670	5404	1.53
广元市	Guangyuan	18016	25.97	68824	7140	2.69
遂宁市	Suining	11581	24.67	269575	26278	2.40
内江市	Neijiang	13248	20.99	47785	4642	2.04
乐山市	Leshan	11763	21.13	69402	7100	2.16
南充市	Nanchong	190968	76.40	152628	5414	2.71
眉山市	Meishan	11078	35.01	46962	4086	3.05
宜宾市	Yibin	20006	23.73	72635	3666	1.20
广安市	Guangan	25984	114.12	96639	6413	7.57
达州市	Dazhou	20358	30.10	77671	5717	2.22
雅安市	Yaan	3782	8.59	15658	5120	2.81
巴中市	Bazhong	19862	26.00	141121	6186	1.14
资阳市	Ziyang	3540	13.62	24871	3172	1.74
阿坝藏族羌族自治州	Aba	3012	53.11	10784	8147	40.13
甘孜藏族自治州	Ganzi	1222	27.42	13563	13231	26.75
凉山彝族自治州	Liangshan	4957	9.61	43722	6059	1.33
按资质等级分	**Grouped by Qualification Grade**					
总承包企业	The General Contractor	532839	1107.92	2106767	6001	3.16
特级企业	The Special Grade	40061	157.66	318376	22066	10.93
一级企业	The first Grade	294213	423.43	565721	5229	3.91
二级企业	The Second Grade	122993	289.13	699869	4714	1.95
三级企业及其他	The Third Grade & Other	75572	237.70	522801	6536	2.97
专业承包企业	The Specialized Contractor	28920	72.16	375435	14951	2.87
一级企业	The first Grade	11162	30.21	265360	33781	3.85
二级企业	The Second Grade	10035	27.89	53968	5330	2.75
三级企业及其他	The Third Grade & Other	7723	14.06	56107	7867	1.97

15-11 各市(州)按登记注册类型和构成分建筑业企业总产值(2018年)

单位：万元

市(州)及分组	Region and Group	建筑业总产值 Total Output Value	国有企业 State-owned	中央企业 Central	地方企业 Local	集体企业 Collective-owned
全　省	**Sichuan**	**137522652**	**16369676**	**2437814**	**13931862**	**3372489**
按市(州)分	**Grouped by Region**					
成都市	Chengdu	56958394	11257451	1716077	9541373	354095
自贡市	Zigong	4088151	525612		525612	20574
攀枝花市	Panzhihua	2450241	79950	17565	62385	2109
泸州市	Luzhou	10447970	531784		531784	868934
德阳市	Deyang	4350052	332334	167697	164637	65618
绵阳市	Mianyang	7212475	828181	529162	299019	11694
广元市	Guangyuan	2242770	113450		113450	140916
遂宁市	Suining	3025877	19815		19815	180754
内江市	Neijiang	2962726	79460		79460	77165
乐山市	Leshan	2811028	38253		38253	
南充市	Nanchong	10596612	764051		764051	232999
眉山市	Meishan	3434996	215566		215566	31999
宜宾市	Yibin	4882438	112029		112029	140078
广安市	Guangan	5487875	290164		290164	541326
达州市	Dazhou	4616833	279793		279793	197539
雅安市	Yaan	543237	70487		70487	36926
巴中市	Bazhong	6401113	599178	7313	591865	369738
资阳市	Ziyang	1906140	99248		99248	80816
阿坝藏族羌族自治州	Aba	378084	20081		20081	2620
甘孜藏族自治州	Ganzi	236058	2169		2169	14244
凉山彝族自治州	Liangshan	2489581	110621		110621	2345
按新资质等级分	**Grouped by Qualification Grade**					
总承包企业	The General Contractor	127977618	16007218	2418659	13588559	3092823
特级企业	The Special Grade	15571546	2559919	116807	2443112	
一级企业	The First Grade	44364475	9368126	2276975	7091152	382199
二级企业	The Second Grade	44021443	1992893		1992893	1785367
三级企业	The Third Grade	24020153	2086280	24878	2061403	925257
专业承包企业	The Specialized Contractor	8673436	361955	19155	342800	275174
一级企业	The First Grade	3517481	142022		142022	27061
二级企业	The Second Grade	3015874	98900	19155	79745	223676
三级企业及其他	The Third Grade & Others	2140081	121033		121033	24437
劳务分包企业	The Subcontractor of Labour Services	871598	503		503	4491
一级企业	The First Grade					
二级企业	The Second Grade					
不分等级	Not Classified by Grade	871598	503		503	4491

Gross Output Value of Construction Enterprises by Region, Registered Types and Composition(2018)

(10 000 yuan)

其他企业 Others	#股份有限公司 Share-holding Corporations	#其他有限责任公司 Other Ltd. Company	建筑工程产值 Output Value of Construction	安装工程产值 Output Value of Installation	其它产值 Other Output Value	房屋工程和土木工程 Output Value of Building & Civil Engineering
117780487	**6634288**	**60324498**	**117608361**	**12291551**	**7622740**	**130133652**
45346849	3029704	29400585	49152951	4203808	3601635	53673360
3541966	179531	1404154	3694268	237672	156211	3965983
2368182		1792903	1996801	347812	105628	2327404
9047252	76532	3562374	8699586	1013860	734524	10253381
3952100	37796	2321136	3516748	642828	190476	3433882
6372600	195689	3046294	6469968	494723	247784	6774830
1988404	69328	626907	1949944	155771	137054	2131311
2825308	449792	971608	2636503	223192	166183	2912510
2806101	653415	671902	2592889	260155	109682	2828864
2772775	111782	1511219	2436336	283050	91641	2669861
9599562	682894	3594430	9032584	981783	582246	10038157
3187430		1339818	3182411	181198	71388	3319086
4630332	296593	1338402	4458041	239570	184826	4642285
4656384	16252	640795	3854773	1415742	217360	5304340
4139501	169249	1971525	3810703	357404	448725	4508164
435824	20747	279021	452261	61996	28981	500884
5432198	510056	2684167	5314418	848796	237900	6130893
1726076	69586	1350911	1667655	151124	87361	1780038
355383	2224	122245	322863	36950	18271	361689
219645	1786	79993	195395	11761	28901	236047
2376616	61334	1614108	2171264	142356	175962	2340688
108877576	5789959	55732871	111333970	9803135	6840512	124549824
13011627	1119576	11291452	14394126	590184	587237	15567682
34614151	1887196	19965540	38063730	3146796	3153950	42812704
40243183	1829926	16427404	38040121	4057949	1923373	42798358
21008615	953261	8048474	20835993	2008207	1175952	23371080
8036307	812845	4304455	5674441	2418884	580112	5033553
3348398	703897	2048164	2452712	859855	204914	2031252
2693298	72289	1281886	1882672	913315	219887	1712553
1994611	36659	974405	1339057	645714	155311	1289749
866603	31484	287172	599950	69532	202116	550275
866603	31484	287172	599950	69532	202116	550275

15-11 续表 continued

单位：万元 (10 000 yuan)

市(州)及分组	Region and Group	#房屋工程建筑业 Building	#土木工程建筑业 Civil Engineering	建筑安装业 Output Value of Installation	建筑装饰和其他建筑业 Output Value of Decoration and Other Construction	竣工产值 Output Value of Completed Construction
全　省	**Sichuan**	**93438869**	**36694783**	**4455130**	**2933870**	**61580576**
按市(州)分	**Grouped by Region**					
成都市	Chengdu	28202146	25471214	2125024	1160010	18689233
自贡市	Zigong	3774623	191360	118919	3250	1820704
攀枝花市	Panzhihua	693147	1634257	73992	48845	864151
泸州市	Luzhou	9612484	640897	141036	53553	5291031
德阳市	Deyang	2674962	758920	671213	244957	1705465
绵阳市	Mianyang	5492411	1282419	212955	224690	3870707
广元市	Guangyuan	1889350	241961	11791	99668	1127717
遂宁市	Suining	2675344	237166	33219	80149	2199434
内江市	Neijiang	2545829	283035	85555	48308	2051374
乐山市	Leshan	2485155	184706	115561	25606	1487924
南充市	Nanchong	8409872	1628285	297311	261145	5514796
眉山市	Meishan	3038126	280960	105975	9935	2107536
宜宾市	Yibin	3881360	760925	55765	184389	2331624
广安市	Guangan	3889364	1414976	161039	22495	3114282
达州市	Dazhou	4221253	286911	34314	74356	2787477
雅安市	Yaan	434351	66533	26189	16165	330676
巴中市	Bazhong	5570138	560755	68435	201786	3874131
资阳市	Ziyang	1585705	194333	24511	101591	877342
阿坝藏族羌族自治州	Aba	264414	97275	3605	12790	175095
甘孜藏族自治州	Ganzi	180726	55321		11	157811
凉山彝族自治州	Liangshan	1918110	422578	88721	60173	1202068
按新资质等级分	**Grouped by Qualification Grade**					
总承包企业	The General Contractor	91161408	33388416	2574048	853745	56815524
特级企业	The Special Grade	7001940	8565742	3864		3371125
一级企业	The First Grade	29304799	13507905	1164052	387719	16880119
二级企业	The Second Grade	36500325	6298033	946754	276332	24321172
三级企业	The Third Grade	18354344	5016736	459378	189694	12243109
专业承包企业	The Specialized Contractor	1795834	3237719	1818587	1821296	4758852
一级企业	The First Grade	94114	1937138	738875	747354	1700576
二级企业	The Second Grade	1029558	682995	599274	704047	1828057
三级企业及其他	The Third Grade & Others	672162	617587	480438	369895	1230220
劳务分包企业	The Subcontractor of Labour Services	481627	68648	62495	258829	6200
一级企业	The First Grade					
二级企业	The Second Grade					
不分等级	Not Classified by Grade	481627	68648	62495	258829	6200

15-12 各市(州)建筑业企业总产值
Gross Output Value of Construction Enterprises by Region

单位：万元 (10 000 yuan)

市(州)	Region	2010	2011	2012	2013	2014	2015	2016	2017	2018
全 省	**Sichuan**	**42008601**	**53058948**	**62926651**	**72774103**	**81485208**	**88475906**	**100441634**	**119962154**	**137522652**
成都市	Chengdu	20974379	27698033	33282864	36570771	38792821	40953808	44314587	49595545	56958394
自贡市	Zigong	851323	1061188	1242434	1604078	1782088	2033489	2432486	3112290	4088151
攀枝花市	Panzhihua	1257162	1680916	1644819	1821553	1632167	1752843	2001219	2193364	2450241
泸州市	Luzhou	1760209	2044170	2938168	4108709	5220235	5786230	7615767	10261744	10447970
德阳市	Deyang	2537597	2750077	2136726	2363317	2566878	2644426	3034254	3617901	4350052
绵阳市	Mianyang	1861597	2119381	2275935	2807690	3521134	3975714	4407795	5686736	7212475
广元市	Guangyuan	516101	703599	765481	911569	1074803	1255189	1458403	1783979	2242770
遂宁市	Suining	1051181	1175968	1305440	1556025	1825481	2105375	2481006	3308825	3025877
内江市	Neijiang	1053573	1192814	1255579	1440762	1878608	2074803	2559424	2641133	2962726
乐山市	Leshan	775628	941508	1065775	1152511	1259091	1510509	1795349	2360367	2811028
南充市	Nanchong	2150544	2777366	3557634	4339852	4965352	5312236	6028991	7663298	10596612
眉山市	Meishan	1087767	895088	1232023	1552882	1996535	2407274	3037935	3436698	3434996
宜宾市	Yibin	964233	1202530	1458229	1829460	1948325	2231710	2673171	3605742	4882438
广安市	Guangan	1559555	1890294	2253959	2687220	3322882	3705093	4439155	5251317	5487875
达州市	Dazhou	1349893	1754006	2000019	2457807	2760362	2895431	3466774	4027765	4616833
雅安市	Yaan	114596	132618	158650	168340	244349	281120	337592	454729	543237
巴中市	Bazhong	1131555	1698644	2384845	2921030	3791359	4194525	4815169	6441841	6401113
资阳市	Ziyang	687698	925593	1300978	1580879	1891727	2173625	1875901	2219734	1906140
阿坝藏族羌族自治州	Aba	74796	61822	76018	86027	93986	111016	122475	193296	378084
甘孜藏族自治州	Ganzi	35605	41067	40029	74473	96289	89581	94817	141019	236058
凉山彝族自治州	Liangshan	210607	312266	551046	739148	820736	981910	1449368	1964831	2489581

15-13 各市(州)建筑业企业主要财务指标(2018年)
Major Financial Indicators of Construction Enterprises by Region(2018)

单位：万元 (10 000 yuan)

市(州)及分组	Region and Group	资产合计 Total Assets	负债合计 Total Liabilities	所有者权益合计 Total Owners' Equities	利润总额 Total Profits	税金总额 Total Tax	利税总额 Total Pre-tax Profits
全　省	**Sichuan**	**123833608**	**85165569**	**38577865**	**4869972**	**4738243**	**9608215**
按市(州)分	**Grouped by Region**						
成都市	Chengdu	76397238	56165259	20141804	1443951	1571491	3015442
自贡市	Zigong	2396697	1728646	668051	137048	118937	255985
攀枝花市	Panzhihua	3029898	2440212	589686	44389	52009	96398
泸州市	Luzhou	4417626	2731837	1685789	313114	335300	648415
德阳市	Deyang	3063922	2235765	828157	61253	91387	152640
绵阳市	Mianyang	5675245	3644981	2030264	264710	233797	498507
广元市	Guangyuan	1632599	977874	654725	94557	130521	225078
遂宁市	Suining	2377801	1377775	1000025	121553	144975	266528
内江市	Neijiang	1375495	748087	627408	66049	119891	185939
乐山市	Leshan	2447714	1519754	927960	208408	107416	315824
南充市	Nanchong	3407148	1718344	1688804	468831	438078	906908
眉山市	Meishan	2261524	1300623	960901	149627	155806	305433
宜宾市	Yibin	3622196	2012826	1609370	250839	196986	447825
广安市	Guangan	2800116	1424093	1376024	322106	205468	527574
达州市	Dazhou	1919746	970003	949743	292159	306478	598637
雅安市	Yaan	732879	397980	334900	24666	19788	44454
巴中市	Bazhong	3079650	1907227	1172423	222664	298413	521077
资阳市	Ziyang	898832	527497	371335	60380	86208	146588
阿坝藏族羌族自治州	Aba	495295	237309	257986	5867	19931	25798
甘孜藏族自治州	Ganzi	271816	170593	101222	23884	20014	43898
凉山彝族自治州	Liangshan	1530173	928885	601288	293917	85352	379269
按资质等级分	**Grouped by Qualification Grade**						
总承包企业	The General Contractor	114732521	79063753	35578594	4514782	4437766	8952548
特级企业	The Special Grade	31354997	24354499	7000498	488220	239182	727402
一级企业	The First Grade	39310906	28592286	10696121	1152344	1407584	2559929
二级企业	The Second Grade	29054645	17462058	11524911	1739620	1840430	3580050
三级企业	The Third Grade	15011973	8654909	6357064	1134598	950570	2085167
专业承包企业	The Specialized Contractor	8682565	5861033	2821532	333347	258218	591565
一级企业	The First Grade	3809192	3025039	784154	93057	67686	160744
二级企业	The Second Grade	2931340	1787055	1144284	135773	109199	244972
三级企业及其他	The Third Grade & Others	1942033	1048939	893094	104517	81332	185850
劳务分包企业	The Subcontractor of Labour Services	418523	240783	177740	21843	42259	64102
一级企业	The First Grade						
二级企业	The Second Grade						
不分等级	Not Classified by Grade	418523	240783	177740	21843	42259	64102

15-14 各市(州)总承包和专业承包建筑业企业资产和负债(2018年)
Assets and Liabilities of General and Professional Contractor Construction Enterprises by Region(2018)

单位：万元 (10 000 yuan)

市(州)及分组	Region and Group	年末资产合计 Total Assets (year-end)	#流动资产 Current Assets	#固定资产 Fixed Assets	年末负债合计 Total Liabilities (year-end)	#流动负债 Current Liabilities	#长期负债 Long-term Liabilities
全　省	**Sichuan**	**123414184**	**96371687**	**5833553**	**84923956**	**73498823**	**7984979**
按市(州)分	**Grouped by Region**						
成都市	Chengdu	76317392	60869861	2994891	56107076	50564491	4891786
自贡市	Zigong	2386637	2138764	78611	1722998	1555699	22971
攀枝花市	Panzhihua	3017381	2283120	149453	2432151	2216222	180799
泸州市	Luzhou	4396031	3560167	250426	2713213	2169474	145029
德阳市	Deyang	2991373	2555282	108194	2185127	2014260	104290
绵阳市	Mianyang	5627491	4309810	169536	3617816	2785663	683785
广元市	Guangyuan	1600115	1267600	115202	963836	842705	71894
遂宁市	Suining	2377801	1772311	123269	1377775	912013	359390
内江市	Neijiang	1370720	1030156	87427	744462	657151	20353
乐山市	Leshan	2447041	1607516	164107	1519714	1067097	130160
南充市	Nanchong	3364791	2485204	295931	1703505	1341233	98680
眉山市	Meishan	2260116	1694628	88917	1300427	831441	328111
宜宾市	Yibin	3604882	2658046	242292	2006024	1541757	136845
广安市	Guangan	2794061	1807821	227750	1422797	1256411	49376
达州市	Dazhou	1907435	1302907	197828	967380	794746	21892
雅安市	Yaan	731812	405927	35423	397734	243867	133247
巴中市	Bazhong	3041934	2089163	318576	1887197	1050182	536382
资阳市	Ziyang	880323	715880	46591	518339	489469	10334
阿坝藏族羌族自治州	Aba	495295	372159	34764	237309	207204	10280
甘孜藏族自治州	Ganzi	271459	234584	19688	170200	132928	934
凉山彝族自治州	Liangshan	1530095	1210784	84681	928879	824812	48441
按资质等级分	**Grouped by Qualification Grade**						
总承包企业	The General Contractor	114731620	89577075	5337332	79062923	68282097	7686542
特级企业	The Special Grade	31354997	22902285	1591438	24354499	21866974	2446559
一级企业	The First Grade	39310906	32137258	1233312	28592286	25490826	2628941
二级企业	The Second Grade	29054645	23590255	1413805	17462058	14686121	1341798
三级企业	The Third Grade	15011072	10947277	1098777	8654080	6238176	1269244
专业承包企业	The Specialized Contractor	8682565	6794611	496222	5861033	5216726	298436
一级企业	The First Grade	3809192	3422359	155459	3025039	2966873	50957
二级企业	The Second Grade	2931340	2088649	186652	1787055	1428679	117856
三级企业及其他	The Third Grade & Others	1942033	1283603	154110	1048939	821174	129624

15-15 各市(州)总承包和专业承包建筑业企业所有者权益和利税(2018年)
Owners' Equities and Pre-tax Profits of General and Professional Contractor Construction Enterprises by Region(2018)

单位：万元 (10 000 yuan)

市(州)及分组	Region and Group	所有者权益 Owners' Equities	利税总额 Total Pre-tax Profits	利润总额 Total Profits	税金总额 Total Taxes	#工程结算税金及附加 Taxes and Extra Charges on Project Settlement Accounts
全　省	**Sichuan**	**38400054**	**9544086**	**4848110**	**4695976**	**1364917**
按市(州)分	**Grouped by Region**					
成都市	Chengdu	20120142	3010293	1442903	1567390	279560
自贡市	Zigong	663639	253761	136711	117050	30703
攀枝花市	Panzhihua	585231	93921	43524	50397	12230
泸州市	Luzhou	1682818	646300	312014	334287	87515
德阳市	Deyang	806246	145141	59686	85455	19885
绵阳市	Mianyang	2009675	491043	261769	229274	64228
广元市	Guangyuan	636279	218037	92567	125469	42139
遂宁市	Suining	1000025	266528	121553	144975	65434
内江市	Neijiang	626258	185435	65882	119553	54871
乐山市	Leshan	927327	315025	207818	107207	23026
南充市	Nanchong	1661287	890711	463192	427519	191690
眉山市	Meishan	959689	305332	149557	155775	49833
宜宾市	Yibin	1598858	444394	250138	194255	60368
广安市	Guangan	1371264	526423	321432	204991	87070
达州市	Dazhou	940055	597535	291671	305864	109432
雅安市	Yaan	334079	44374	24620	19754	6168
巴中市	Bazhong	1154737	516636	220084	296552	120197
资阳市	Ziyang	361984	144231	59316	84915	29391
阿坝藏族羌族自治州	Aba	257986	25798	5867	19931	5791
甘孜藏族自治州	Ganzi	101259	43897	23884	20013	2456
凉山彝族自治州	Liangshan	601216	379271	293920	85351	22932
按资质等级分	**Grouped by Qualification Grade**					
总承包企业	The General Contractor	35578522	8952521	4514763	4437758	1277992
特级企业	The Special Grade	7000498	727402	488220	239182	41262
一级企业	The First Grade	10696121	2559929	1152344	1407584	257565
二级企业	The Second Grade	11524911	3580050	1739620	1840430	638787
三级企业	The Third Grade	6356992	2085141	1134579	950562	340379
专业承包企业	The Specialized Contractor	2821532	591565	333347	258218	86926
一级企业	The First Grade	784154	160744	93057	67686	18011
二级企业	The Second Grade	1144284	244972	135773	109199	42884
三级企业及其他	The Third Grade & Others	893094	185850	104517	81332	26031

15-16 各市(州)按登记注册类型分建筑业企业劳动生产率(2018年)
Labor Productivity of Construction Enterprises by Region and Registered Types (2018)

单位:元/人 (yuan/person)

市(州)及分组	Region and Group	按总产值计算的劳动生产率 Overall Labor Productivity in Terms of Total Output Value	国有企业 State -owned	中央企业 Central	地方企业 Local	集体企业 Colle-ctive owned	其他企业 Others	#股份有限公司 Share-holding Corporations	#其他有限责任公司 Other Ltd. Company
全　省	**Sichuan**	**317145**	**379670**	**625578**	**355236**	**259340**	**311996**	**311756**	**354415**
按市(州)分	**Grouped by Region**								
成都市	Chengdu	384663	428707	730277	399067	219458	377259	396974	452490
自贡市	Zigong	324748	284314		284314	340066	331660	322665	376570
攀枝花市	Panzhihua	448261	485429	607785	459390	175733	447722		608713
泸州市	Luzhou	258805	239316		239316	267019	259280	304423	283101
德阳市	Deyang	301532	589768	383133	1308723	215706	291479	582365	311219
绵阳市	Mianyang	303430	423774	508517	327261	185328	292961	286012	315711
广元市	Guangyuan	234460	97608		97608	285370	251391	243597	285373
遂宁市	Suining	280926	461893		461893	209085	286435	242554	270537
内江市	Neijiang	286694	332469		332469	225629	287714	278049	252557
乐山市	Leshan	279749	238634		238634		280415	144964	302680
南充市	Nanchong	315304	389365		389365	336752	310129	377310	296705
眉山市	Meishan	288086	233070		233070	286476	292777		298221
宜宾市	Yibin	242936	267563		267563	296399	241084	179830	259597
广安市	Guangan	292350	342579		342579	308167	288000	244017	216018
达州市	Dazhou	309932	322230		322230	239558	313518	273423	308340
雅安市	Yaan	149883	323782		323782	254839	133615	195726	178791
巴中市	Bazhong	237750	243588	183734	244572	292908	234130	238612	229659
资阳市	Ziyang	233315	238348		238348	195965	235128	370136	236620
阿坝藏族羌族自治州	Aba	281795	346224		346224	180690	280005	140778	266040
甘孜藏族自治州	Ganzi	193284	197145		197145	261352	190037	92534	198593
凉山彝族自治州	Liangshan	326066	351735		351735	9369	336136	278915	359946
按资质等级分	**Grouped by Qualification Grade**								
总承包企业	The General Contractor	321715	386880	632958	361841	260017	316019	312311	358970
特级企业	The Special Grade	611976	279965	2364514	268642		798210	469995	1015144
一级企业	The First Grade	377558	467296	614883	433858	306126	359785	377832	356940
二级企业	The Second Grade	267370	268776		268776	266485	267340	245338	284231
三级企业	The Third Grade	266287	437449	362119	438550	234450	257811	257402	264721
专业承包企业	The Specialized Contractor	293761	207972	253041	205923	264387	300487	310069	334607
一级企业	The First Grade	385321	174559		174559	187016	409821	299416	503940
二级企业	The Second Grade	265969	258361	253041	259672	270336	265900	746012	276007
三级企业及其他	The Third Grade & Others	236275	222487		222487	355710	236191	211047	234486
劳务分包企业	The Subcontractor of Labour Services	138294				65466	139015	262805	137633
一级企业	The First Grade								
二级企业	The Second Grade								
不分等级	Not Classified by Grade	138294				65466	139015	262805	137633

主要统计指标解释

建筑业统计单位 指从事房屋、构筑物建造和设备安装活动的法人企业。建筑业法人企业应具有建筑业资质并能够独立核算，同时还应具备以下条件：①依法成立，有自己的名称、组织机构和场所，能够承担民事责任；②独立拥有和使用资产，承担负债，有权与其他单位签订合同；③独立核算盈亏，能够编制资产负债表。

建筑业总产值 是以货币形式表现的建筑业企业在一定时期内生产的建筑业产品和提供服务的总和。建筑业总产值包括：

(1)建筑工程产值：指列入建筑工程预算内的各种工程价值。

(2)安装工程产值：指设备安装工程价值，不包括被安装设备本身的价值。

(3)其他产值：指建筑业总产值中除建筑工程、安装工程以外的产值。包括房屋构筑物修理产值、非标准设备制造产值、总包企业向分包企业收取的管理费以及不能明确划分的施工活动所完成的产值。

建筑业增加值 指建筑业企业在报告期内以货币形式表现的建筑业生产经营活动的最终成果。

房屋施工面积 指在报告期内施工的全部房屋建筑面积，包括本期新开工的房屋建筑面积、上期跨入本期继续施工的房屋建筑面积、上期停缓建在本期恢复施工的房屋建筑面积、本期竣工的房屋建筑面积及本期施工后又停缓建的房屋建筑面积。

房屋竣工面积 指报告期内房屋建筑按照设计要求已全部完工，达到住人和使用条件，经验收鉴定合格或达到竣工验收标准，可正式移交使用的各栋房屋建筑面积的总和。

Explanatory Notes on Main Statistical Indicators

Statistical Unit in Construction refers to a corporate enterprise engaged in the construction of buildings and structures and in the installation of equipment. A corporate construction enterprise should have qualification certificates with independent accounting system, and should meet the following 3 requirements: a) being set up in line with relevant legal basis, having its full name, organization and location, and capable of taking civil liabilities; b) independently possessing and using its assets and assuming its liabilities, and entitled to sign contracts with other institutions; and c) making independent accounts of its profits and losses, and capable of compiling its own balance sheet.

Gross Output Value of Construction refers to total of construction products, expressed in money terms, completed by construction and installation enterprises during a given period of time. It includes:

(1) Output value of construction projects, that is the value of projects covered by the project budgets;

(2) Output value of installation projects, that is the value of the installation of equipment, (excluding the value of the equipment to be installed);

(3) Output value of others, that is the output value of construction industry excluding that of construction projects and installation projects. It includes: output value of repair of buildings and structures; output value of non-standard equipment manufacturing; overhead expenses received by contracted enterprises to the sub-contracted enterprises and the completed output value of construction activities that have no clear definition.

Value-added of Construction refers to the final result of the activities of production and management of construction industry in monetary terms in the reference period.

Floor Space of Buildings refers to floor space of buildings under construction in the reference period, including the space of buildings for which construction has newly started; buildings for which construction has started earlier and is continuing during the reference period; and buildings for which construction has been suspended earlier but has restarted during the reference period; buildings completed during the reference period; and buildings under construction but construction has subsequently been during the reference period.

Floor Space of Buildings Completed refers to the total floor space of each building that has been completed in the reference period in accordance with the requirements of the design, up to the standard for being resided in and put into use, or has been checked and accepted by departments concerned as qualified ones or up to the standard of buildings completed and can be handed over for putting into use.

16 交通运输和邮电业

Chapter 16 Transportation and Post

16-1 交通运输业基本情况
Basic Conditions of Transport

指　标		Item		2010	2014	2015	2016	2017	2018
运输线路长度	(万公里)	**Length of Transport Routes**	**(10 000 km)**						
铁路营业里程		Railways in Operation		0.4	0.4	0.4	0.5	0.5	0.5
公路里程		Highways		26.6	31.0	31.5	32.4	33.0	33.2
内河航道里程		Navigable Inland Waterways		1.1	1.2	1.1	1.1	1.1	1.1
航空里程		Civil Aviation		56.1	85.1	97.2	112.4	102.6	121.4
客运量总计	(万人)	**Total Passenger Traffic**	**(10 000 persons)**	**242732**	**141899**	**140044**	**128220**	**113937**	**103918**
铁路		Railways		6829	8778	9078	11321	12499	14982
公路		Highways		230988	126691	124014	109716	94098	81461
水运		Waterways		2733	2677	2748	2574	2364	1991
民用航空		Civil Aviation		2182	3752	4204	4609	4976	5484
旅客周转量总计	(亿人公里)	**Total Passenger-Kilometers**	**(100 million passenger-km)**	**1392**	**1532**	**1663**	**1686**	**1698**	**1802**
铁路		Railways		221	272	272	302	318	380
公路		Highways		802	630	672	598	521	466
水运		Waterways		2	3	3	2	2	2
民用航空		Civil Aviation		366	628	717	784	856	954
货运量总计	(万吨)	**Total Freight Traffic**	**(10 000 tons)**	**133364**	**157730**	**153270**	**159689**	**171398**	**185473**
铁路		Railways		7093	7192	5893	5452	5397	5223
公路		Highways		121017	142132	138622	146046	158190	173324
水运		Waterways		5218	8361	8688	8131	7750	6862
民用航空		Civil Aviation		36	45	67	60	61	64
货物周转量总计	(亿吨公里)	**Total Freight Ton-kilometers**	**(100 million ton-km)**	**1711**	**2366**	**2290**	**2406**	**2583**	**2820**
铁路		Railways		643	690	614	605	637	721
公路		Highways		985	1511	1481	1565	1677	1815
水运		Waterways		75	154	183	223	256	270
民用航空		Civil Aviation		8	11	12	13	14	14
民用汽车拥有量	(万辆)	Possession of Civil Motor Vehicles	(10 000 units)	355.0	668.2	768.5	882.4	991.8	1099.6
#私人汽车	(万辆)	Private Vehicles	(10 000 units)	281.0	577.2	677.3	787.5	886.3	976.7
载客汽车拥有量	(万辆)	Possession of Buses and Cars	(10 000 units)	281.6	572.3	674.0	785.3	890.6	988.8
载货汽车拥有量	(万辆)	Possession of Trucks	(10 000 units)	70.4	91.0	89.6	91.9	96.0	105.2
其他机动车拥有量	(万辆)	Possession of Other Motor Vehicles	(10 000 units)	5.9	4.9	5.0	5.2	5.2	5.6
公路部门营运车辆	(万辆)	Number of Motor Vehicles Owned by Highway Departments	(10 000 units)	62.0	65.3	57.1	57.7	69.9	75.7
民用运输船舶拥有量	(艘)	Possession of Civil Transport Vessels	(unit)	8414	7642	7489	7265	6466	5316
机动船	(艘)	Motor Vessels	(unit)	7350	6564	6435	6216	5524	4431
驳船	(艘)	Barges	(unit)	1064	1078	1054	1049	941	885

注：①从2014年开始，公路货运量和货物周转量由抽样调查改变为根据高速公路计重收费数据推算，公路客运量和旅客周转量中的出租车和公交车统计范围作了较大调整，故2014年相关数据与往年不可比；②2015年起，航空货运量及货物周转量由双流机场提供改变为由航空公司提供，故数据与往年不可比；③公路数据由四川省交通运输厅道路运输管理局提供，铁路数据由成都铁路局提供，水运数据由四川省交通运输厅航务管理局提供，航空数据由四川航空公司、国航西南分公司、东航四川分公司、成都航空公司提供。

a)Beginning in 2014, freight traffic and ton-kilometers of highways are changed from the sample survey to highway toll collection data, statistics range of taxi and bus in highway passenger traffic and passenger-kilometers made a big adjustment, so data of 2014 are not comparable with previous years.
b)Data of air cargo volume and cargo turnover, which was provided by Sichuan Airlines, have been provided by Shuangliu Airport since 2015. Therefore, Southwest branch, Sichuan branch of China Eastern Airlines and Chengdu airlines. the data cannot be compared with previous years.
c)Highway data are provided by Road Transport Administration of Sichuan Provincial Transportation Bureau, railway data are provided by Chengdu Railway Bureau, waterway data are provided by the Shipping Administration of Sichuan Provincial Communications Department, air data are provided by Sichuan Airlines, Air China Southwest branch, Sichuan branch of China Eastern Airlines and Chengdu airlines.

16-2 各市(州)公路运输情况(2018年)
Main Indicators of Highway Transportation by Region(2018)

市(州)	Region	公路总里程(公里) Total Length of Highways (km)	#等级公路里程 Expressway and Class I to IV Highways	#高速公路 Expressway	民用汽车拥有量(万辆) Possession of Civil Motor Vehicles (10 000 units)	#私人汽车 Private Vehicles	公路旅客周转量(万人公里) Passenger-kilometers of Highways (10 000 passenger-km)	公路货物周转量(万吨公里) Freight Ton-kilometers of Highways (10 000 ton-kilometers)
全　省	**Sichuan**	**331592.26**	**304830.31**	**7131.37**	**1099.60**	**976.70**	**4661427**	**18149502**
成都市	Chengdu	27729.19	27070.22	956.50	487.72	420.28	885490	2840229
自贡市	Zigong	6550.74	6144.62	234.22	66.15	61.95	119560	666082
攀枝花市	Panzhihua	4812.22	3929.29	195.39	25.52	23.39	59718	622082
泸州市	Luzhou	14628.85	12470.57	467.68	18.29	16.29	353549	1528217
德阳市	Deyang	8341.12	7856.92	201.44	40.52	36.23	231148	657353
绵阳市	Mianyang	20146.05	17249.89	412.27	49.92	46.28	228547	842133
广元市	Guangyuan	19970.09	15908.98	391.09	24.40	22.86	99350	778442
遂宁市	Suining	8985.21	8162.27	358.50	25.28	23.79	126431	561262
内江市	Neijiang	12666.16	10299.51	306.84	25.15	22.94	406637	423368
乐山市	Leshan	12162.00	11664.30	259.28	39.28	35.27	149931	1284454
南充市	Nanchong	22689.61	21661.39	543.17	17.92	16.16	305224	1110073
眉山市	Meishan	7931.57	6510.79	403.16	37.98	34.91	127382	652635
宜宾市	Yibin	19336.11	18306.32	258.55	51.82	46.10	182061	680288
广安市	Guangan	13865.63	13310.53	367.76	35.73	31.95	94478	304937
达州市	Dazhou	19573.35	17702.28	423.59	18.06	15.93	267287	1442170
雅安市	Yaan	6711.46	6356.50	346.82	11.15	9.90	64991	749925
巴中市	Bazhong	17155.70	17069.91	313.60	9.07	8.07	171587	474178
资阳市	Ziyang	12345.90	11705.12	277.40	31.00	28.41	118469	388922
阿坝藏族羌族自治州	Aba	13526.07	13139.51	155.92	24.24	22.36	166264	617663
甘孜藏族自治州	Ganzi	34879.44	33629.84	45.45	23.31	21.49	154386	223945
凉山彝族自治州	Liangshan	27585.77	24681.54	212.74	35.10	32.18	348936	1301143

16-3 邮电业务基本情况
Basic Conditions of Postal and Telecommunication Services

指标		Item		2014	2015	2016	2017	2018
邮电业务总量	**(亿元)**	**Business Volume of Postal and Telecommunication Services**	**(100 million yuan)**	**1027.1**	**1281.1**	**1870.5**	**1509.9**	**3643.8**
邮政业务总量	(亿元)	Business Volume of Postal Services	(100 million yuan)	117.4	138.6	199.0	269.2	348.4
电信业务总量	(亿元)	Business Volume of Telecommunication Services	(100 million yuan)	909.7	1142.5	1671.5	1240.7	3295.4
邮政业务		**Postal Services**						
营业网点	(处)	Number of Offices	(unit)	5880	6117	6108	6109	6114
邮路长度	(万公里,单程)	Length of Postal Routes	10 000 km,one way)	10.00	10.15	11.96	13.55	15.88
邮运汽车	(辆)	Postal Cars	(unit)	732	739	792	899	886
函件	(万件)	Number of Letters	(10 000 pcs)	10510	6335	3755	3265	2776
包裹	(万件)	Number of Parcels	(10 000 pcs)	231	170	103	95	89
报刊期发数	(万份)	Issue of Newspapers and Magazines	(10 000 copies)	660	698	661	675	688
特快专递	(万件)	Pieces of Express Mail Services	(10 000 pcs)	37942	48797	80148	110796	145992
电信业务		**Telecommunication Services**						
年末固定电话用户	(万户)	Number of Fixed Telephone Subscribers at Year-end	(10 000 subscribers)	1294	1353	1490	1636	1721
城市固定电话	(万户)	Urban Fixed Telephone Subscribers	(10 000 subscribers)	917	939	981	1028	1041
农村固定电话	(万户)	Rural Fixed Telephone Subscribers	(10 000 subscribers)	377	414	509	608	680
年末移动电话用户	(万户)	Number of Mobile Telephone Subscribers at Year-end	(10 000 subscribers)	6609	6872	7295	7694	9069
互联网宽带接入用户数	(万户)	Number of Broad Band Subscribers of Internet	(10 000 subscribers)	883	1026	1851	2168	2625
长途交换机容量	(万路端)	Capacity of Long-distance Telephone Exchanges	(10 000 lines)	37.4	37.4	37.4	37.4	23.0

注：①2010年起邮路长度不含邮政速递公司自营邮路；特快专递包括邮政公司和其他快递公司数据。②邮政业务数据由四川省邮政管理局、中国邮政集团四川省分公司提供；电信业务数据由四川省通信管理局提供。

a)Postal routes exclude express delivery company's own length postman since 2010. The data of pieces of express mail services comes from the post offices and other express delivery companies. b)Data of the postal service are provided by the Sichuan Provincial Post Office and China Post Group's Sichuan branch. Data from the telecommunication services are provided by the Sichuan Provincial Communications Administration Bureau.

主要统计指标解释

铁路营业里程 又称营业长度，指投入客货运输营业或临时营业的线路长度。

公路里程 指报告期末公路的实际长度。统计范围：包括城间、城乡间、乡（村）间能行驶汽车的公共道路，公路通过城镇街道的里程，公路桥梁长度、隧道长度、渡口宽度。不包括城市街道里程，断头路里程，农（林）业生产用道路里程，工（矿）企业等内部道路里程。统计原则：按已竣工验收或交付使用的实际里程计算；两条或多条公路共同经由同一路段的重复里程，只计算一次。

内河航道里程 指在一定时期内，能通航运输船舶及排筏的天然河流、湖泊水库、运河及通航渠道的长度。包括全年季节性通航累计三个月以上的航道，不包括仅供零散流放竹、木排的河道。两省以河为界的航道里程，双方均按一半计算，以免重复。

定期航班航线里程 指定期航班营运里程的总长度，以万公里为计算单位。航线里程的统计分为按重复距离计算和按不重复距离计算两种形式。“按重复距离计算”是指不同航线的相同航段距离可以重复累加；“按不重复距离计算”则不同航线相同航段只统计一次。

货(客)运量 指在一定时期内，各种运输工具实际运送的货物重量(旅客数量)。货运按吨计算，客运按人计算。货物不论运输距离长短、货物类别，均按实际重量统计。旅客不论行程远近或票价多少，均按一人一次客运量统计；半价票、小孩票也按一人统计。

货物(旅客)周转量 指在一定时期内，由各种运输工具运送的货物(旅客)数量与其相应运输距离的乘积之总和。该指标反映运输业生产的总成果，也是编制和检查运输生产计划，计算运输效率、劳动生产率以及核算运输单位成本的主要基础资料。计算货物周转量通常按发出站与到达站之间的最短距离，也就是计费距离计算。计算公式为：

货物(旅客)周转量=Σ〔货物(旅客)运输量×运输距离〕

民用汽车拥有量 指报告期末，在公安交通管理部门按照《机动车注册登记工作规范》，已注册登记领有民用车辆牌照的全部汽车数量。汽车拥有量统计的主要分类：根据汽车结构分为载客汽车、载货汽车及其他汽车；根据汽车所有者不同分为个人(私人)汽车、单位汽车；根据汽车的使用性质分为营运汽车、非营运汽车；根据汽车大小规格不同，载客汽车分为大型、中型、小型和微型，载货汽车分为重型、中型、轻型和微型。

邮政、电信业务总量 指以货币形式表示的邮电通信企业为社会提供各类邮电通信服务的总数量。计算方法为各类业务的实物量分别乘以相应的不变单价，求出各类业务的货币量加总求得。没有不变单价的业务按其业务收入直接相加。

移动电话用户 指在电信运营企业营业网点办理开户登记手续，通过移动电话交换机进入移动电话网，占用移动电话号码的各类电话用户。包括各类签约用户、智能网预付费用户、无线上网卡用户。

固定电话用户 指在电信企业营业网点办理开户登记手续并已接入固定电话网上的全部电话用户。包括普通电话用户、无线市话用户、公用电话用户、窄带综合业务数字网（N—ISDN）用户、智能网专用接入终端用户等。

城市电话用户 指按行政区划属于中央直辖市、省辖市、地级市、县级市的市区、市郊区及县城区范围内的电话用户数。包括分布在农村地区但以县团级以上建制的独立工矿区、林区、驻军的电话用户。

农村电话用户 指按行政区划属于城市范围以外的乡（镇）、村电话用户。

住宅电话用户 指私人付费或安装在居民住宅并按照私人或住宅电话用户登记注册和收费的各类电话用户。

Explanatory Notes on Main Statistical Indicators

Length of Railways in Operation refers to the total length of the trunk line for passenger and freight transportation in full operation or temporary operation.

Length of Highways refers to the actual length of highways at the end of reference period. It covers public roads running vehicles among cities, city and rural areas, township (villages), highways passing through streets at small cities and towns, length of bridges and tunnels, width of ferry piers. It does not include the length of streets in cities, dead end highways, the length of streets built for agricultural (forest) production and inside factories (mines). It can only be calculated with the actual mileage having been completed, checked and accepted or put into operation. If two or more highways go the same section of the way, the length of the section is only calculated for once.

Length of Navigable Inland Waterways refers to the length of natural rivers, lakes, reservoirs and canals that are open to navigation for ships and rafts during a given period. It includes the channels with annual seasonal navigation for more than three months other than the waterways only for scattered bamboo and wooden rafts. If two provinces share one river as the border, the length of waterways will be half divided for each province to avoid duplication.

Length of Routes with Scheduled Flights refers to the total length of all routes for scheduled flights, which is calculated using million kilometres as the unit. There are usually two ways to calculate the route length: duplicated calculation and non-duplicated calculation. Duplicated calculation means that the same segment of different routes can be added duplicately, while the non-duplicated calculation allows the same segment of different routes be counted once only.

Freight (Passenger) Traffic refers to the weight of freight (number of passenger) transported with various means within a specific period of time. Freight transport is calculated in tons and passenger traffic is calculated in terms of number of persons. Freight transport is calculated in terms of the actual weight of the goods and takes no account of the type of freight and distance of travel. Passenger traffic is calculated by the principle that one person can be counted only once in one trip and takes no account of the travelling distance and ticket price. The passengers who travel with a half price ticket or a child's ticket is also calculated as one person.

Freight Ton-kilometers (Passenger-kilometers) refer to the sum of the products of the volume of transported cargo (passengers) multiplying by the transport distance. It is an important indicator to reflect the achievement of transportation industry. Normally, the shortest distance between the departure station and the destination station (i.e., the payable distance) is the basis to calculate the freight ton-kilometers. This is an important indicator to show the total results of the transport industry, to prepare and examine the transport plan and to measure the efficiency, the labor productivity and the unit cost of transport. The formula is as follows:

$$\frac{\text{Freight ton - kilometres}}{\text{(passenger - kilometres)}} = \sum \frac{\text{freight}}{\text{(passenger)traffic}} \times \frac{\text{distance of}}{\text{transportation}}$$

Possession of Civil Motor Vehicles refer to the total numbers of vehicles that are registered and received vehicles license tags according to the Work Standard for Motor Vehicles Registration formulated by the Transport Management Office under the department of public security at the end of the reference period. They are divided into categories. According to the structure of motor vehicles, they are divided into passenger vehicles, trucks and others; according to ownership into private vehicles and vehicles for the unit's use; according to kind of usage into working vehicles and non-working vehicles; and according to size of vehicles into large passenger vehicles, medium-sized passenger vehicles, small passenger vehicles and mini passenger vehicles, heavy trucks, light-heavy trucks, light trucks and mini-trucks.

Business Volume of Post and Telecommunications refers to the total amount of postal and telecommunication services, expressed in value terms, provided by the post and telecommunications departments for society. Business volume of post and telecommunications is the sum of each service in kind multiplying with its correspondent unit price (constant price). Business without constant price add their business revenue directly.

Mobile Telephone Subscribers refer to persons who have gone through registration procedures in the operation points of enterprises engaged in telecommunications and are hence connected with the mobile telephone communication network through the mobile telephone switchboards and occupy mobile phone numbers. Included are various types of subscriber, prepaid users for intelligent network and wireless network card users.

Local Telephone Subscribers refer to all subscribers who have gone through registration procedures in the operation points of enterprises engaged in telecommunications and are hence connected to the local telecommunications service provider through fixed line network. Included are general subscribers, wireless local telephone subscribers, public telephones subscribers, N-ISDN subscribers and intelligent network terminal subscribers.

Urban Telephone Subscribers refer to the number of telephone subscribers, located at the municipalities directly under the Central Government, cities under the jurisdiction of province, cities at prefecture level, downtown and suburb of city at county level town and county towns according to the administrative division, including subscribers in rural mineral area, forest area, military area that are at or above county level.

Rural Telephone Subscribers refer to telephone subscribers, located at the towns and villages outside the coverage of urban areas according to the administrative division.

Household Telephone Subscribers refer to all kinds of subscribers with telephone sets paid privately or installed in the dwelling units of residents, and registered as private subscribers or residence subscribers for payment.

国内贸易

Chapter 17 Domestic Trade

17-1 社会消费品零售总额
Total Retail Sales of Consumer Goods

单位：亿元 (100 million yuan)

年份 Year	社会消费品零售总额 Total Retail Sales of Consumer Goods	年份 Year	社会消费品零售总额 Total Retail Sales of Consumer Goods
1990	348.60	2005	3003.49
1991	399.85	2006	3472.61
1992	470.63	2007	4105.61
1993	572.18	2008	4944.82
1994	742.17	2009	5779.89
1995	958.98	2010	6884.84
1996	1137.34	2011	8290.84
1997	1292.50	2012	9622.00
1998	1409.39	2013	11001.00
1999	1516.65	2014	12459.99
2000	1671.43	2015	13961.40
2001	1880.24	2016	15601.87
2002	2070.14	2017	17480.53
2003	2293.72	2018	18254.54
2004	2615.24		

17-2 按各项分组的社会消费品零售总额
Total Retail Sales of Consumer Goods by the Grouping

单位：万元 (10 000 yuan)

指　标	Item	2012	2013	2014	2015	2016	2017	2018
全　省	**Sichuan**	**96219957**	**110010000**	**124599878**	**139614039**	**156018675**	**174805305**	**182545393**
按销售单位所在地分	Grouped by Location of Retailers							
城镇	Retail Sales in Town	77827312	88806253	100523024	112353161	125353584	140441299	143901259
乡村	Retail Sales in Rural	18392645	21203747	24076855	27260878	30665091	34364006	38644134
按消费形态分	Grouped by Consumption Patterns							
餐饮收入	Catering Revenue	14124591	15895439	17425532	19560345	22140353	24878060	28073863
商品零售	Retail Sale	82095366	94114561	107174346	120053695	133878322	149927245	154471530
按行业分	Grouped by Industry of Retailers							
批发业	Wholesale Trade	8063497	9806160	11208135	12636121	14132570	15774491	15403148
零售业	Retail Trade	73825201	84083290	95931052	107136995	119410241	133832218	138753320
住宿业	Lodge Trade	980679	1005950	1057944	1172542	1318049	1439093	1464546
餐饮业	Catering Trade	13350581	15114600	16402747	18668381	21157815	23759504	26924379

17-3 各市(州)社会消费品零售总额
Total Retail Sales of Consumer Goods by Region

单位：万元 (10 000 yuan)

市(州)	Region	2010	2011	2012	2013	2014	2015	2016	2017	2018
全　省	**Sichuan**	**68848429**	**82908366**	**96219957**	**110010000**	**124599878**	**139614039**	**156018675**	**174805305**	**182545393**
成都市	Chengdu	24934379	30197889	35087160	39911842	46925855	52017311	57423661	64035285	68018100
自贡市	Zigong	2505517	3007572	3476849	3979292	4476763	5016314	5558073	6240353	6262553
攀枝花市	Panzhihua	1434435	1723640	1996790	2286067	2560949	2861953	3169046	3524076	3612644
泸州市	Luzhou	2665362	3216359	3749188	4321029	4913963	5596624	6371529	7220721	7639610
德阳市	Deyang	3014577	3610694	4190912	4817544	5448356	6159572	6988068	7907827	8205977
绵阳市	Mianyang	4333278	5211136	6047567	6885157	7782856	8791555	9884783	11124769	11494767
广元市	Guangyuan	1494330	1777164	2050950	2345748	2642250	2966232	3310685	3717899	4053316
遂宁市	Suining	2032614	2426599	2809061	3229511	3664807	4154086	4703892	5269662	5707262
内江市	Neijiang	2012745	2423564	2807571	3227264	3636429	4085847	4605438	5118750	5385158
乐山市	Leshan	2784017	3287558	3772877	4333646	4873825	5520094	6242618	7052509	6672670
南充市	Nanchong	3421459	4116787	4778015	5502990	6242112	6988210	7856249	8882684	9599826
眉山市	Meishan	1916985	2303242	2673399	3059866	3454790	3887558	4380662	4869349	4964250
宜宾市	Yibin	3285181	3977228	4627980	5311215	6044421	6806018	7683995	8679138	9306732
广安市	Guangan	2148443	2457018	2822286	3244311	3670594	4135312	4687869	5249640	5000091
达州市	Dazhou	3210238	3881178	4530071	5216404	5926020	6724721	7617181	8603660	8896991
雅安市	Yaan	1029859	1222858	1409247	1569382	1777624	2001515	2231816	2480685	2429073
巴中市	Bazhong	1233687	1488566	1729804	1986735	2241153	2544679	2874218	3242269	3214471
资阳市	Ziyang	2140442	2675872	3123841	3594078	4071420	2951711	3260373	3656535	3789801
阿坝藏族羌族自治州	Aba	363218	438949	522128	600245	680678	760132	838777	858069	792688
甘孜藏族自治州	Ganzi	391742	470671	542898	617617	694327	742038	815920	908642	1003637
凉山彝族自治州	Liangshan	2495920	2993824	3471364	3970056	4478224	4972454	5513824	6162785	6495777

17-4 限额以上批发和零售业法人企业基本情况
Basic Conditions of Enterprises above Designated Size in Wholesale and Retail Trades

指 标		Item		2010	2011	2012	2013	2014	2015	2016	2017	2018
批发和零售业		**Wholesale and Retail Trades**										
法人企业数	(个)	Number of Corperation Units	(unit)	3001	4435	5252	6039	6600	6537	6819	6637	6930
年末从业人数	(人)	Persons Engaged	(person)	302200	366573	397758	449177	485604	477833	479270	452861	463018
商品购进额	(亿元)	Total Purchases	(100 million yuan)	4729.6	6423.0	8946.5	10036.6	11450.0	10895.7	11883.4	12218.5	14258.8
商品销售额	(亿元)	Total Sales	(100 million yuan)	5563.7	7897.9	9697.1	11038.5	12358.9	12185.8	13313.8	13702.9	15626.9
期末商品库存额	(亿元)	Total Stock at Year-end	(100 million yuan)	440.1	768.4	899.8	826.8	913.3	893.8	851.8	885.7	943.7
批发业		**Wholesale Trade**										
法人企业数	(个)	Number of Corperation Units	(unit)	1134	1732	1949	2201	2421	2292	2330	2305	2545
年末从业人数	(人)	Persons Engaged	(person)	101525	130141	134176	144586	159482	154078	151524	150874	153857
商品购进额	(亿元)	Total Purchases	(100 million yuan)	2846.8	4027.6	5574.2	6012.7	6663.6	6057.4	6694.2	7345.0	8960.0
商品销售额	(亿元)	Total Sales	(100 million yuan)	3348.4	4841.8	6003.8	6676.3	7287.2	6789.8	7437.9	8211.4	9522.5
期末商品库存额	(亿元)	Total Stock at Year-end	(100 million yuan)	275.8	489.9	488.3	492.7	531.9	459.1	458.4	473.3	516.6
零售业		**Retail Trade**										
法人企业数	(个)	Number of Corperation Units	(unit)	1867	2703	3303	3838	4179	4245	4489	4332	4385
年末从业人数	(人)	Persons Engaged	(person)	200675	236432	263582	304591	326122	323755	327746	301987	309161
商品购进额	(亿元)	Total Purchases	(100 million yuan)	1882.8	2395.4	3372.3	4023.9	4786.4	4838.3	5189.3	4873.5	5298.7
商品销售额	(亿元)	Total Sales	(100 million yuan)	2215.3	3056.1	3693.3	4362.1	5071.7	5396.0	5875.9	5491.5	6104.3
期末商品库存额	(亿元)	Total Stock at Year-end	(100 million yuan)	164.3	278.5	411.5	334.1	381.4	434.7	393.3	412.4	427.1

17-5 限额以上批发零售贸易、住宿餐饮业基本情况(2018年)
Basic Conditions of Enterprises above Designated Size in Wholesale and Retail Trades, Hotels and Catering Services (2018)

单位：个、人 (unit, person)

指标	Item	法人企业 Number of Corporation	产业活动单位和个体数 Number of Individual and Active	从业人数 Persons Engaged
总计	**Total**	**9615**	**4216**	**754680**
一、批发业合计	**Wholesale Trades**	**2545**	**90**	**156108**
内资企业	Domestic-Funded Enterprises	2522	3	152075
国有企业	State-owned Enterprises	66	2	15823
集体企业	Collective-owned Enterprises	10		572
股份合作企业	Cooperative Enterprises	2		196
联营企业	Joint Ownership Enterprises			
有限责任公司	Limited Liability Corporations	821	1	63800
股份有限公司	Share-holding Corporations Ltd.	63		12629
私营企业	Private Enterprises	1536		57890
其他企业	Others	24		1165
港、澳、台商投资企业	Enterprises with Investment from Hong Kong, Macao and Taiwan	8		1309
外商投资企业	Enterprises with Foreign Investment	15		1354
二、零售业合计	**Retail Trades**	**4385**	**1778**	**338681**
内资企业	Domestic-Funded Enterprises	4300	29	271765
国有企业	State-owned Enterprises	33	3	1232
集体企业	Collective-owned Enterprises	24		405
股份合作企业	Cooperative Enterprises	14	1	448
联营企业	Joint Ownership Enterprises	5		115
有限责任公司	Limited Liability Corporations	1140	7	105554
股份有限公司	Share-holding Corporations Ltd.	81	1	29665
私营企业	Private Enterprises	2995	13	134066
其他企业	Others	8	4	280
港、澳、台商投资企业	Enterprises with Investment from Hong Kong, Macao and Taiwan	43		15996
外商投资企业	Enterprises with Foreign Investment	42	4	23741
三、住宿餐饮业合计	**Lodging and Catering Trades**	**2685**	**2348**	**259891**
内资企业	Domestic-Funded Enterprises	2649	145	180440
国有企业	State-owned Enterprises	36	16	5877
集体企业	Collective-owned Enterprises	7	2	728
股份合作企业	Cooperative Enterprises	8	2	1916
联营企业	Joint Ownership Enterprises		1	15
有限责任公司	Limited Liability Corporations	668	55	69377
股份有限公司	Share-holding Corporations Ltd.	51	4	5424
私营企业	Private Enterprises	1879	55	96400
其他企业	Others		10	703
港、澳、台商投资企业	Enterprises with Investment from Hong Kong, Macao and Taiwan	18	5	10127
外商投资企业	Enterprises with Foreign Investment	18	2	15712

注：产业活动单位指非批发零售业法人企业附营的批发零售业产业活动单位。
a) Active units refer to the wholesale and retail trades activie units of the legal entity of the non wholesale and retail units.

17-6 各市(州)限额以上批发零售贸易、住宿餐饮业法人企业基本情况(2018年)
Basic Conditions of Incorporated Enterprises above Designated Size in Wholesale and Retail Trades, Hotels and Catering Services by Region(2018)

单位：个、人 (unit,person)

市(州)	Region	合计 Total		批发业 Whlesale Trade		零售业 Retail Trade		住宿业 Lodging Trade		餐饮业 Catering Trade	
		企业数 Number of Corporations	从业人数 Persons Engaged	企业数 Number of Corporations	从业人数 Persons Engaged	企业数 Number of Corporations	从业人数 Persons Engaged	企业数 Number of Corporations	从业人数 Persons Engaged	企业数 Number of Corporations	从业人数 Persons Engaged
全　省	**Sichuan**	**9615**	**649771**	**2545**	**153857**	**4385**	**309161**	**1141**	**80112**	**1544**	**106641**
成都市	Chengdu	2406	315363	887	63928	734	158339	337	30831	448	62265
自贡市	Zigong	337	13965	91	3775	156	5557	23	2489	67	2144
攀枝花市	Panzhihua	213	12523	87	4282	77	5273	24	1886	25	1082
泸州市	Luzhou	686	35827	288	19929	276	10830	43	2346	79	2722
德阳市	Deyang	425	21830	151	7863	177	7615	33	2398	64	3954
绵阳市	Mianyang	651	32092	144	8256	307	13727	63	4681	137	5428
广元市	Guangyuan	224	10395	35	2705	125	3964	51	3293	13	433
遂宁市	Suining	331	16736	75	5261	179	7803	24	1221	53	2451
内江市	Neijiang	382	14725	72	3569	179	5888	32	2077	99	3191
乐山市	Leshan	342	18146	58	2844	215	11101	41	2605	28	1596
南充市	Nanchong	547	24265	69	3642	342	12770	44	2726	92	5127
眉山市	Meishan	222	12373	42	1840	117	6241	29	2402	34	1890
宜宾市	Yibin	663	23549	182	6117	337	12154	59	3079	85	2199
广安市	Guangan	387	13443	68	2488	222	6902	30	1828	67	2225
达州市	Dazhou	486	29615	52	3079	311	19047	49	4201	74	3288
雅安市	Yaan	147	6506	29	1099	69	3303	38	1904	11	200
巴中市	Bazhong	458	16236	58	2490	267	8122	38	2460	95	3164
资阳市	Ziyang	194	10457	70	4375	90	3822	15	754	19	1506
阿坝藏族羌族自治州	Aba	128	4091	3	514	45	1243	69	2049	11	285
甘孜藏族自治州	Ganzi	85	3368	5	675	36	931	38	1603	6	159
凉山彝族自治州	Liangshan	301	14266	79	5126	124	4529	61	3279	37	1332

17-7 分行业限额以上批发零售贸易法人企业商品购、销、存总额(2018年)
Total Purchases, Sales and Inventory of Enterprises above Designated Size in Wholesale and Retail Trades by Sector(2018)

单位：万元 (10 000 yuan)

指　　标	Item	购进总额 Total Purchases	销售总额 Total Sales	年末库存总额 Inventory (year-end)
总　计	**Total**	**142587694**	**156268509**	**9437029**
一、批发企业合计	**Wholesale Trades**	**89600215**	**95225299**	**5165669**
食品、饮料、烟草批发业	Food, Beverages and Tobaccos	19047616	18939693	1881334
#米、面制品及食用油批发	Grains and Edible Oil	6318588	1350947	126574
烟草制品批发	Tobaccos	5921450	9245001	887665
纺织、服装及家庭用品批发	Textiles, Garments, Shoes and Hats	2339246	2565200	227949
#服装批发	Garments	559141	614415	49669
文化、体育用品及器材批发业	Cultural and Sports Goods and Appliances	2865195	2957481	170823
医药及医疗器材批发业	Medicines and Medical Appliances	9972945	11278071	969309
矿产品、建材及化工产品批发	Mineral Products	44921592	47697928	1097398
#煤炭及制品批发业	Coal and Related Products	2715390	2851249	57836
石油及制品批发业	Petroleum and Related Products	13620452	14297467	276779
金属及金属矿批发业	Metal Materials and Mineral	13427573	14480866	381351
建材批发业	Building Materials	7950353	8515795	128824
化肥批发业	Chemical Fertilizers	2030427	2175545	91477
机械设备、五金产品及电子产品批发	Machinery, Hardware and Electronic Equipment	8091776	9233665	625267
#汽车、摩托车及零配件批发	Motor Vehicles, Motorcycles and Parts	1024400	1156421	82463
电气设备批发	Electrical Equipment	305622	381553	17559
计算机、软件及辅助设备	Computers, Software and Assistant Equipment	3718783	4112762	235822
其他批发业	Others not Classified	782919	820803	39850
二、零售企业合计	**Retail Trades**	**52987479**	**61043210**	**4271360**
综合零售业	General Retail	8326405	10111776	675376
#百货零售业	Daily Consumer Goods	4114156	5195470	268983
超级市场零售业	Super Market	3839662	4457113	373930
食品、饮料及烟草制品专门零售	Food, Beverages and Tobaccos	1395066	1742610	154689
纺织、服装及日用品专门零售业	Textiles, Garments, Shoes and Hats	1085201	1584539	261935
#服装零售业	Garments	429216	624377	126070
文化、体育用品及器材专门零售	Cultural and Sports Goods and Appliances	1211233	1323332	218442
医药及医疗器材专门零售业	Medicines and Medical Appliances	1212242	1576715	177418
汽车、摩托车燃料及零配件	Motor Vehicles, Motorcycles and Parts	29107554	32656835	2289331
#汽车零售业	Motor Vehicles	18566303	20539392	2070347
机动车燃料零售业	Mobile Fuel	10249856	11783083	192162
家用电器及电子产品专门零售	Household Appliance and Electronic Product	3722165	4122232	291717
五金、家具室内装饰材料专门零售	Hardware, Furniture and Domestic Decoration Material	808972	934229	36703
货摊、无店铺及其他零售业	Without Shop and Other Retail Trades	6118641	6990942	165749

17-8 各市(州)限额以上批发零售贸易法人企业商品购、销、存总额(2018年)
Total Purchases, Sales and Inventory of Enterprises above Designated Size in Wholesale and Retail Trades by Region(2018)

单位: 万元 (10 000 yuan)

市(州)	Region	购进总额 Total Purchases	销售总额 Total Sales	批 发 Wholesale Trade	零 售 Retail Trade	年末库存总额 Inventory (year-end)
全 省	**Sichuan**	**142587694**	**156268509**	**94230691**	**62037818**	**9437030**
成都市	Chengdu	85996819	90280520	57881568	32398952	5195058
自贡市	Zigong	3561044	3790587	2742495	1048092	115426
攀枝花市	Panzhihua	3324302	3712988	3064147	648841	202562
泸州市	Luzhou	8317907	9916259	5854490	4061770	637420
德阳市	Deyang	3568744	4122324	2311334	1810990	282894
绵阳市	Mianyang	8346278	9359919	6226667	3133251	661114
广元市	Guangyuan	1280618	1491488	667443	824045	86173
遂宁市	Suining	1917182	2241141	1113993	1127148	128227
内江市	Neijiang	2089416	2368095	1228251	1139844	142803
乐山市	Leshan	2761867	3247856	1524793	1723063	195963
南充市	Nanchong	3458542	3907848	1038129	2869719	184887
眉山市	Meishan	2062327	2388776	1168808	1219968	137773
宜宾市	Yibin	4125186	5011166	2930017	2081149	532598
广安市	Guangan	1277515	1484753	670271	814483	82768
达州市	Dazhou	4250452	4978376	1418687	3559689	220097
雅安市	Yaan	731786	826380	438975	387405	52394
巴中市	Bazhong	1700870	2023420	672964	1350456	102461
资阳市	Ziyang	1078940	1323707	724858	598849	78390
阿坝藏族羌族自治州	Aba	278394	324172	178130	146042	15541
甘孜藏族自治州	Ganzi	315926	397831	239335	158496	21463
凉山彝族自治州	Liangshan	2143581	3070903	2135336	935567	361018

17-9 限额以上批发零售贸易法人企业主要商品分类销售额(2018年)
Total Sales of Enterprises above Designated Size in Wholesale and Retail Trades by Category of Main Commodities(2018)

单位：万元 (10 000 yuan)

项目	Item	合计 Total	批发 Wholesale	零售 Retail Trade
粮油、食品类	Food	9161358	3810218	5351140
#肉禽蛋类	Meat, Poultry and Eggs	1221530	342765	878765
饮料类	Beverages	1551401	546651	1004750
烟酒类	Tobacco and Liquor	17000340	14544134	2456205
服装、鞋帽类	Garments, Footwear and Hats	5369776	503596	4866180
针、纺织品类	Knitwear and Textiles	890355	232081	658274
化妆品类	Cosmetics	1295674	241522	1054152
金银珠宝类	Gold, Silver and Jewelry	2907937	2162278	745659
日用品类	Articles for Daily Use	3523222	596110	2927112
#儿童玩具类	Toy for children Articles	123427	929	122499
五金、电料类	Hardware and Electrical Materials	344017	102789	241228
体育、娱乐用品类	Sports and Recreation Articles	312313	6579	305734
书报杂志类	Newspapers and Magazines	1191812	138876	1052936
电子出版物及音像制品类	E-journal and Video Products	19664		19664
家用电器和音像器材类	Household Appliances and Video Appliances	6458759	1201762	5256997
中西药品类	Traditional Chinese and Western Medicines	11522360	9845022	1677339
文化办公用品类	Cultural and Official Goods	5383133	4208562	1174570
家具类	Furniture	1604558	37482	1567076
通讯器材类	Communication Appliances	3233490	1558256	1675235
煤炭及制品类	Coal and Related Product	2331522	2324185	7336
木材及制品类	Wood and Wooden Product	142168	141148	1021
石油及制品类	Petroleum and Related Product	24111476	12075185	12036291
化工材料及制品类	Raw Chemical Materials	7650177	7518047	132130
金属材料类	Metals	16096708	16094757	1952
建筑及装潢材料类	Building and Decoration Materials	3156466	2132468	1023999
机电产品设备类	Mechanical and Electrical Products	2752711	2340643	412069
#农机类	Agricultural Machinery	379498	378689	809
汽车类	Automobile	20838434	1069569	19768865
种子饲料类	Seed and Feedstuff	315343	315238	104
棉麻类	Cotton, Hemp and Local livestock	233653	228856	4797
其他类	Others	2784290	2501063	283227

17-10 限额以上批发零售贸易法人企业主要财务指标(2018年)

Main Financial Indicators of Incorporated Enterprises above Designated Size in Wholesale and Retail Trades(2018)

单位：万元 (10 000 yuan)

指 标	Item	资产合计 Total Assets	#流动资产 Current Assets	#固定资产 Fixed Assets	负债合计 Total Liabilities	所有者权益 Total Owners' Equities	#实收资本 Paid-up Capital
总 计	**Total**	**65012725**	**49923894**	**5274032**	**45824939**	**19187787**	**13307445**
一、批发企业合计	**Wholesale Trades**	**41318830**	**34441999**	**2063954**	**30484705**	**10834125**	**5655175**
#国有及国有控股	State-owned & State-holding Majority Shares	15481922	12216169	1115357	10545699	4936223	1755695
按登记注册类型分	Grouped by Registration						
内资企业	Domestic-funded	40496200	33726544	2029359	29850904	10645296	5596695
国有企业	State-owned	3685266	3094862	379277	942939	2742326	156245
集体企业	Collective-owned	312937	181939	15002	209433	103503	11856
股份合作企业	Cooperative	12450	11677	321	12065	385	653
联营企业	Joint-owned						
有限责任公司	Limited Liability	22953323	19338711	867644	18906747	4046576	3515019
股份有限公司	Share-holding	3692934	2574339	224146	2498965	1193969	422835
私营企业	Private	9811650	8503029	536367	7274208	2537442	1477354
其他企业	Others	27642	21987	6602	6547	21096	12733
港澳台商投资企业	Funded by Hongkong, Macao and Taiwan	616112	570879	11975	460919	155193	30723
外商投资企业	Foreign-funded	206519	144576	22620	172882	33637	27756
二、零售企业合计	**Retail Trades**	**23693895**	**15481895**	**3210078**	**15340234**	**8353661**	**7652270**
#国有及国有控股	State-owned & State-holding Majority Shares	5039129	2542664	773511	2644986	2394144	1410490
按登记注册类型分	Grouped by Registration						
内资企业	Domestic-funded	21211761	13853253	2825170	13697418	7514344	6959516
国有企业	State-owned	95086	55320	18062	53399	41686	9558
集体企业	Collective-owned	19976	14615	3450	8569	11407	3019
股份合作企业	Cooperative	11488	8491	2475	6476	5012	1657
联营企业	Joint-owned	4028	1949	1583	811	3216	979
有限责任公司	Limited Liability	9869310	6230240	1267334	6711677	3157632	3196871
股份有限公司	Share-holding	3370897	1977253	504867	1605165	1765732	409143
私营企业	Private	7826205	5558152	1024682	5309095	2517111	3332171
其他企业	Others	14773	7234	2717	2225	12548	6119
港澳台商投资企业	Funded by Hongkong, Macao and Taiwan	758638	499903	161415	495683	262955	255146
外商投资企业	Foreign-funded	1723496	1128739	223493	1147133	576363	437608

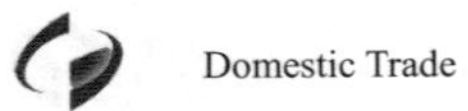

17-10 续表 continued

单位：万元 (10 000 yuan)

指 标	Item	主营业务收入 Revenue from Principal Business	主营业务成本 Cost of Principal Business	主营业务税金及附加 Tax and Extra Charges from Principal Business	管理费用 Cost of Management	财务费用 Cost of Finance	营业利润 Business Profits	利润总额 Total Profits
总 计	**Total**	**138397998**	**########**	**1319660**	**2489352**	**575658**	**3827588**	**3870088**
一、批发企业合计	**Wholesale Trades**	**84141298**	**76644471**	**1116272**	**1156390**	**315281**	**2369795**	**2393714**
#国有及国有控股	State-owned & State-holding Majority Shares	38577502	34856166	983809	496083	96739	1156054	1165004
按登记注册类型分	Grouped by Registration							
内资企业	Domestic-funded	81772892	74406267	1113926	1134205	311082	2303812	2326737
国有企业	State-owned	8000587	5686297	900285	333068	-36944	928084	922263
集体企业	Collective-owned	596065	583146	624	6293	6108	5003	7666
股份合作企业	Cooperative	17227	14903	30	152	25	37	-31
联营企业	Joint-owned							
有限责任公司	Limited Liability	46077432	43458996	112773	372527	215563	582556	602807
股份有限公司	Share-holding	4744242	4263449	12841	40917	23728	129662	130138
私营企业	Private	22255721	20329142	86520	379605	102295	653916	660496
其他企业	Others	81617	70334	852	1642	307	4554	3398
港澳台商投资企业	Funded by Hongkong, Macao and Taiwan	1910519	1845181	1349	12183	6415	36998	37603
外商投资企业	Foreign-funded	457887	393023	997	10002	-2216	28985	29373
二、零售企业合计	**Retail Trades**	**54256700**	**47852273**	**203388**	**1332962**	**260377**	**1457793**	**1476375**
#国有及国有控股	State-owned & State-holding Majority Shares	11255620	10329657	15186	172348	7183	263183	251126
按登记注册类型分	Grouped by Registration							
内资企业	Domestic-funded	49373482	43871886	178685	1147925	245366	1315335	1331306
国有企业	State-owned	82823	68326	166	6646	497	3698	6909
集体企业	Collective-owned	83308	72130	537	3637	146	4127	4024
股份合作企业	Cooperative	64152	56410	565	2061	141	2132	2135
联营企业	Joint-owned	10233	8997	108	119	9	657	897
有限责任公司	Limited Liability	21579144	19258740	63106	521711	116776	469897	485451
股份有限公司	Share-holding	6992886	6321403	12681	159583	13764	169894	155696
私营企业	Private	20524908	18055288	101427	453641	113789	660982	672545
其他企业	Others	36028	30593	97	528	244	3948	3648
港澳台商投资企业	Funded by Hongkong, Macao and Taiwan	1747844	1456021	7681	73738	4889	38886	44135
外商投资企业	Foreign-funded	3135375	2524366	17022	111299	10122	103572	100934

17-11 各市(州)限额以上批发零售贸易法人企业主要财务指标(2018年)

Main Financial Indicators of Incorporated Enterprises above Designated Size in Wholesale and Retail Trades by Region(2018)

单位：万元 (10 000 yuan)

市(州)	Region	资产合计 Total Assets	负债合计 Total Liabilities	主营业务收入 Revenue from Principal Business	主营业务成本 Cost of Principal Business	销售费用 Cost of Saling	主营业务税金及附加 Tax and Extra Charges from Principal Business	营业利润 Business Profits
全 省	**Sichuan**	**65012725**	**45824939**	**138397998**	**124496744**	**5938932**	**1319660**	**3827588**
成都市	Chengdu	39894438	29968595	79737018	73097883	3502602	444471	1242565
自贡市	Zigong	829076	550110	3307868	3095055	67928	35639	64124
攀枝花市	Panzhihua	1233774	872337	3299169	3086899	101430	20886	44893
泸州市	Luzhou	4662792	3548735	8718857	7712830	382509	103814	333357
德阳市	Deyang	2494681	1608079	3603405	3043228	214066	54244	176426
绵阳市	Mianyang	3134909	2164527	8241613	7628512	229561	68899	216469
广元市	Guangyuan	473267	240858	1299400	1097788	51091	31103	81138
遂宁市	Suining	946308	588576	1983934	1703588	107035	34184	80810
内江市	Neijiang	750396	480347	2081994	1831924	65364	47496	86898
乐山市	Leshan	1194309	785190	2988783	2562805	108394	7123	204770
南充市	Nanchong	1024391	604053	3672594	3309769	107839	67318	98495
眉山市	Meishan	760835	380649	2157818	1888844	111536	47164	89089
宜宾市	Yibin	2455262	1255049	4379075	3552503	293443	76398	349237
广安市	Guangan	555244	338792	1324714	1147930	50675	34631	49752
达州市	Dazhou	1296120	690276	4568780	3782065	220941	74433	280601
雅安市	Yaan	327066	193450	719957	616702	35520	17845	32221
巴中市	Bazhong	702997	408800	1839227	1557135	79037	44113	99143
资阳市	Ziyang	464974	250548	1170671	1018431	61622	25640	32118
阿坝藏族羌族自治州	Aba	108997	49616	271615	224920	12612	11567	9654
甘孜藏族自治州	Ganzi	130635	44974	343190	289383	17058	13017	12954
凉山彝族自治州	Liangshan	1572254	801377	2688316	2248551	118670	59676	242873

17-12 限额以上住宿餐饮法人企业主要财务指标(2018年)
Main Financial Indicators of Incorporated Enterprises above Designated Size in Hotels and Catering Services(2018)

单位：万元 (10 000 yuan)

指 标	Item	资产合计 Total Assets	#流动资产 Current Funds	#固定资产 Fixed Asset	负债合计 Total Liabilities	主营业务收入 Revenue of Principal Business
总 计	**Total**	**7951138**	**3435928**	**2577592**	**5758553**	**3772592**
#国有及国有控股	State-owned & State-holding Majority Shares	873396	331106	398407	494589	270597
按登记注册类型分	Grouped by Registration					
内资企业	Domestic-funded	7445870	3263252	2350391	5462387	3259087
国有企业	State-owned	188423	71915	66145	127736	63389
集体企业	Collective-owned	9057	5610	428	7680	10588
股份合作企业	Cooperative	80083	53108	19336	50399	40423
联营企业	Joint-owned					
有限责任公司	Limited Liability	3691435	1675707	1051847	2663722	1106368
股份有限公司	Share-holding	297082	168929	66396	238394	76303
私营企业	Private	3179791	1287984	1146240	2374457	1962017
其他企业	Others					
港澳台商投资企业	Funded by Hongkong, Macao and Taiwan	195590	103167	33375	204663	232980
外商投资企业	Foreign-funded	309678	69509	193826	91504	280524

17-12 续表 continued

单位：万元 (10 000 yuan)

指 标	Item	主营业务成本 Cost of Principal Business	管理费用 Cost of Management	主营业务税金及附加 Tax and Extra Charges from Principal Business	营业利润 Business Profits	利润总额 Total Profits
总 计	**Total**	**1918826**	**599257**	**46713**	**271807**	**292062**
#国有及国有控股	State-owned & State-holding Majority Shares	111084	73699	5461	-6780	1725
按登记注册类型分	Grouped by Registration					
内资企业	Domestic-funded	1684540	546180	44666	201867	222561
国有企业	State-owned	24351	17953	1079	-2924	-2857
集体企业	Collective-owned	3575	2608	131	621	706
股份合作企业	Cooperative	20669	5018	499	2528	6538
联营企业	Joint-owned					
有限责任公司	Limited Liability	509361	221395	15789	69445	80151
股份有限公司	Share-holding	31987	14833	1448	3954	4307
私营企业	Private	1094597	284373	25720	128243	133717
其他企业	Others					
港澳台商投资企业	Funded by Hongkong, Macao and Taiwan	69648	16582	622	33830	32209
外商投资企业	Foreign-funded	164638	36495	1425	36110	37292

17-13　各市(州)限额以上住宿餐饮法人企业主要财务指标(2018年)
Main Financial Indicators of Incorporated Enterprises above Designated Size in Hotels and Catering Services by Region(2018)

单位: 万元　　(10 000 yuan)

市(州)	Region	资产合计 Total Assets	负债合计 Total Liabilities	主营业务收入 Revenue from Principal Business	主营业务成本 Cost of Principal Business	销售费用 Cost of Saling	主营业务税金及附加 Tax and Extra Charges from Principal Business	营业利润 Business Profits
全　省	**Sichuan**	**7951138**	**5758553**	**3772592**	**1918826**	**909493**	**46713**	**271807**
成都市	Chengdu	3660050	2841548	1785350	784536	587950	15032	129736
自贡市	Zigong	118761	78952	61806	32459	12934	388	3233
攀枝花市	Panzhihua	189394	178975	35372	17730	10902	1029	-7341
泸州市	Luzhou	356218	290555	166122	93415	23863	2733	19433
德阳市	Deyang	254875	144339	112172	60431	21638	1638	2261
绵阳市	Mianyang	361971	215415	182222	99553	42212	2796	9598
广元市	Guangyuan	151061	97240	58825	32568	11272	1173	3475
遂宁市	Suining	298836	179707	65763	39989	6599	1278	4354
内江市	Neijiang	117034	82218	131495	87977	14095	1721	13981
乐山市	Leshan	176150	130548	106626	49508	21431	1154	14153
南充市	Nanchong	331322	271072	212535	128598	24799	3809	16440
眉山市	Meishan	191053	109506	61562	28604	14795	1111	2389
宜宾市	Yibin	215766	152769	146830	77534	19526	2929	19107
广安市	Guangan	228864	199176	69858	41083	12658	1331	2348
达州市	Dazhou	253581	139522	193973	116570	23137	2869	22740
雅安市	Yaan	132234	103661	23329	13226	6243	269	-2666
巴中市	Bazhong	199665	100697	146026	97245	16194	2535	17319
资阳市	Ziyang	82081	64525	42099	22952	9095	372	960
阿坝藏族羌族自治州	Aba	204919	133528	32851	15602	5852	503	-3671
甘孜藏族自治州	Ganzi	149475	73765	33316	15783	5134	613	1492
凉山彝族自治州	Liangshan	277833	170836	104459	63466	19163	1430	2467

主要统计指标解释

社会消费品零售总额 指企业（单位、个体户）通过交易直接售给个人、社会集团非生产、非经营用的实物商品金额，以及提供餐饮服务所取得的收入金额。个人包括城乡居民和入境人员，社会集团包括机关、社会团体、部队、学校、企事业单位、居委会或村委会等。

批发业 指向其他批发或零售单位（含个体经营者）及其他企事业单位、机关团体等批量销售生活用品、生产资料的活动，以及从事进出口贸易和贸易经纪与代理的活动，包括拥有货物所有权，并以本单位(公司)的名义进行交易活动，也包括不拥有货物的所有权，收取佣金的商品代理、商品代售活动；还包括各类商品批发市场中固定摊位的批发活动，以及以销售为目的的收购活动。

零售业 指百货商店、超级市场、专门零售商店、品牌专卖店、售货摊等主要面向最终消费者（如居民等）的销售活动，以互联网、邮政、电话、售货机等方式的销售活动，还包括在同一地点，后面加工生产，前面销售的店铺（如面包房）；谷物、种子、饲料、牲畜、矿产品、生产用原料、化工原料、农用化工产品、机械设备（乘用车、计算机及通信设备除外）等生产资料的销售不作为零售活动；多数零售商对其销售的货物拥有所有权，但有些则是充当委托人的代理人，进行委托销售或以收取佣金的方式进行销售。

批发和零售业商品购进、销售、库存额 指各种登记注册类型的批发和零售业企业(单位)以本企业(单位)为总体的，从国内、国外市场购进的商品总量、销售和出口的商品总量、库存的商品总量等情况。

商品购进额 指从本企业以外的单位和个人购进(包括从国外直接进口)作为转卖或加工后转卖的商品金额（含增值税）。

商品销售额 指对本企业以外的单位和个人出售的商品金额（包括售给本单位消费用的商品，含增值税）。

商品库存额 对于批发和零售业法人单位和个体经营户，是指报告期末取得所有权的全部商品金额（含增值税）；对于批发和零售业产业活动单位，是指报告期末实际在库且归属法人具有所有权的全部商品金额（含增值税）。

住宿业 指为旅行者提供短期留宿场所的活动，有些单位只提供住宿，也有些单位提供住宿、饮食、商务、娱乐一体的服务，不包括主要按月或按年长期出租房屋住所的活动。

餐饮业 指通过即时制作加工、商业销售和服务性劳动等，向消费者提供食品和消费场所及设施的服务。

营业额 指住宿和餐饮业单位在经营活动中因提供服务或销售商品等取得的收入（含增值税）。收入主要来源于提供客房、餐费服务、商品销售和其他服务，如商务服务。不包括多产业法人企业附营的其他行业产业活动单位的餐费收入、商品销售收入等各项收入。其中，客房收入指住宿和餐饮业单位在经营活动中因提供住宿服务取得的收入（含增值税）。不包括多产业法人企业附营的其他行业产业活动单位的客房收入。餐费收入指本单位为顾客提供就餐服务取得的收入（含增值税），包括：经烹饪、调制加工后出售的各种食品，如主食、炒菜、凉拌菜等的收入。不包括多产业法人企业附营的其他行业产业活动单位的餐费收入。

限额以上批发和零售业统计单位 指年主营业务收入2000万元及以上的批发业和年主营业务收入500万元及以上的零售业。

限额以上住宿和餐饮业统计单位 指年主营业务收入200万元及以上的住宿和餐饮业。

Explanatory Notes on Main Statistical Indicators

Total Retail Sales of Consumer refer to the amount obtained by enterprises (units, self-employed individuals) through direct sales of non-production and non-business physical commodity to individuals, social institutions, and revenue from providing catering services. Individuals include rural and urban households, population from abroad, social institutions include government agencies, social organizations, military units, schools, institutions, neighbourhood (village) committees.

Wholesale Trade refers to the activities of selling wholesale commodities for daily use and capital goods to enterprises of wholesale and retail trades (including self-employed individuals) and other enterprises, institutions and government organs and organizations, and the activities of engaging in import and export and acting as a trade agent. The wholesaler may have the ownership of the commodities for wholesale and trade in the name of its own (a company), and the wholesaler can act as commission agent or commodity broker without the ownership of commodities. Also included are the wholesale activities at the fixed stalls in wholesale market and the acquisition for sales purpose.

Retail Trade refers to the activities of department store, supermarket, franchised store, brand store, retail stall and on-the-spot-making-selling store selling commodities to the final consumers (residents) by any means including internet, post, telephone, sales machine. It also includes shops with sales and production localted in the same places (such as bakeries). Retail trade excludes the activities of sales of capital goods such as grain, seed, feed, livestock, mineral products, raw material for production, industrial chemicals, chemical products for agricultural use, machine and equipment (excluding vehicles, computers and communication equipment). Most retailers have the ownership of commodities to sell, but some are acting as agents or brokers to make transactions for a commission.

Purchase, Sales and Stock of Commodities by Wholesale and Retail Trade refer to the total volume of commodities purchased, total volume of sales and exports , and the stock of commodities by wholesale and retail enterprises (establishments) of different status of registration from domestic and overseas markets.

Total Purchases of Commodities refer to the total value of purchases of commodities by the enterprises (establishments) from other establishments or individuals (including direct import from abroad) for the purpose of re-selling, either with or without further processing of the commodities purchased.

Total Sales of Commodities refer to value of commodities sold by the establishments to other establishments and individuals (including goods sold for self consumption, including the value-added tax).

Total Stock of Commodities For the legal entities and self-employed individuals engaged in wholesale and retail trade, it refers to total value (including VAT) of commodities possessed at the end of the reference period; and for wholesale and retail establishments, it refers to the value (including VAT) of all commodities actually in stock and owned by their legal persons at the end of reference period.

Hotel Services refer to the accommodation services provided to visitors. Some units may provide only accommodation while others provide a combination of accommodation, meals, business services and/or recreational facilities. It excludes activities related to the provision of long-term primary residences in facilities such as apartments typically leased on a monthly or annual basis.

Catering Services refer to the activities of providing foods, serving locations and facilities to customers through instant processing, commercial sales and service-type labor.

Business Revenue refers to total revenue (including VAT) of hotels and catering services received from providing services or selling commodities through business activities, income comes mainly from providing hotels, catering services, selling of commodities and other services, such as commodity services. It does not include revenue such as meal fees, selling of commodities of other industrial units affiliated with multi industrial legal entities. Income from hotels refers to income (including VAT) of hotels and catering services by providing lodging services through business activities. Income from catering services refers to income (including VAT) from providing catering services, including selling of cooked or prepared foods, such as staple food, cooked dishes, or cold dishes. It does not include meal fees of other industrial units affiliated with multi industrial legal entities.

Wholesale and Retail Trade Units above Designated Size refer to wholesale trade of which annual main business income are more than 20 million yuan(RMB) , and retail corporate units of which the main business income are more than 5 million yuan(RMB).

Accommodation and Catering Trade Units above Designated Size refer to accommodation and catering corporate units of which the main business income are more than 2 million yuan(RMB).

18

对外经济贸易和旅游

Chapter 18 Foreign Trade and Economic Cooperation and Tourism

18-1 对外经济贸易
Foreign Trade and Economic Cooperation

单位：万美元 (USD 10 000)

指 标	Item	2005	2010	2014	2015	2016	2017	2018
进出口总额	**Total Imports and Exports**	**790476**	**3270396**	**7020297**	**5118856**	**4934941**	**6810677**	**8993788**
出口总额	Total Exports	470089	1884064	4483913	3309290	2795498	3755394	5039827
进口总额	Total Imports	320387	1386332	2536384	1809566	2139443	3055283	3953961
进出口差额	Balance	149702	497732	1947529	1499724	656055	700111	1085866
进出口总额	**Total Imports and Exports of Goods**	**790476**	**3270396**	**7020297**	**5118856**	**4934941**	**6810677**	**8993788**
出口总额	Total Exports	470089	1884064	4483913	3309290	2795498	3755394	5039827
初级产品	Primary Goods			84486	85878	71820	80380	87334
工业制成品	Manufactured Goods			4399427	3223412	2723678	3675014	4952493
进口总额	Total Imports	320387	1386332	2536384	1809566	2139443	3055283	3953961
初级产品	Primary Goods			183449	137945	126160	204725	260025
工业制成品	Manufactured Goods			2352935	1671621	2013283	2850558	3693936
对外签订利用外资协议(合同)金额	**Total Amount of Foreign Capital to be Utilized in the Signed Agreements and Contracts**	**205576**	**621470**	**301965**	**363904**	**431879**	**623793**	**637007**
外商直接投资	Foreign Direct Investment	200303	611651	294663	356592	425072	617751	630972
外商其他投资	Other Foreign Investment	5273	9819	7302	7312	6807	6042	6035
实际利用外资额	**Total Amount of Foreign Capital Actually Used**	**110206**	**701299**	**1065328**	**1043681**	**854381**	**869862**	**1103664**
企业境外中长期融资回调资金	Overseas Medium and Long-term Financing Callback Funds of Enterprises							192700
对外借款	Foreign Loans	19505	35000	19672	17661	45117	46753	
外商直接投资	Foreign Direct Investment	88686	602517	1028764	999607	797687	810135	896375
外商其他投资	Other Foreign Investment	2015	9782	7215	7013	5438	5521	5735
国外优惠贷款	Foreign Preferential Loans							8854
港澳援建资金	Reconstruction Funds from Hong Kong and Macao		54000	9677	19400	6139	7453	
对外承包工程	**Foreign Contracted Projects**							
新签合同额	ValueofNewlySignedContracts	138397	684878	362002	453003	700000	791610	1026598
完成营业额	Completed Turnover	57274	399299	709398	546020	447400	393093	610791

注：进出口统计资料由成都海关提供。
a) Import and export statistics are provided by Chengdu Customs.

18-2 出口商品分类金额
Exports Value by Category of Commodities

单位：万美元 (USD 10 000)

商品类别	Category of Commodities	2014	2015	2016	2017	2018
总　额	**Total Value**	**4483913**	**3309290**	**2795498**	**3755394**	**5039827**
初级产品	**Primary Goods**	**84486**	**85878**	**71820**	**80380**	**87334**
食品及活动物	Food and Live Animals	29568	24174	26761	29115	26076
饮料及烟类	Beverages and Tobacco	8592	17861	16257	15801	24523
非食用原料(燃料除外)	Nonedible Raw Materials(Except Fuels)	43515	28455	26442	26337	27142
矿物燃料、润滑油及有关原料	Mineral Fuels,Lubricants and Related Materials	509	80	129	3920	2162
动植物油、脂及蜡	Animal and Vegetable Oils,Fats and Waxes	2302	3206	2231	5207	7431
工业制成品	**Manufactured Goods**	**4399427**	**3223412**	**2723678**	**3675014**	**4952493**
化学成品及有关产品	Chemicals and Related Procucts	304349	255292	223308	267795	328608
按原料分类的制成品	Manufactured Goods Classified by Material	556817	444222	255456	282485	326069
机械及运输设备	Machinery and Transport Equipment	2571964	1918757	1853546	2771439	3836523
杂项制品	Miscellaneous Products	774532	511869	299076	330687	440159
未分类的商品	Products Not Clssified	191765	93272	92292	22608	21134

18-3 进口商品分类金额
Imports Value by Category of Commodities

单位：万美元 (USD 10 000)

商品类别	Category of Commodities	2014	2015	2016	2017	2018
总　额	**Total Value**	**2536384**	**1809566**	**2139443**	**3055283**	**3953961**
初级产品	**Primary Goods**	**183449**	**137945**	**126160**	**204725**	**260025**
食品及活动物	Food and Live Animals	31580	19746	17408	30550	36635
饮料及烟类	Beverages and Tobacco	1418	1255	1995	2359	3574
非食用原料(燃料除外)	Nonedible Raw Materials(Except Fuels)	132245	115080	105114	163806	203331
矿物燃料、润滑油及有关原料	Mineral Fuels,Lubricants and Related Materials	17504	1320	953	7347	14607
动植物油、脂及蜡	Animal and Vegetable Oils,Fats and Waxes	702	544	690	663	1878
工业制成品	**Manufactured Goods**	**2352935**	**1671621**	**2013283**	**2850558**	**3693936**
化学成品及有关产品	Chemicals and Related Procucts	203144	57374	54534	67747	84755
按原料分类的制成品	Manufactured Goods Classified by Material	91420	89977	63777	79124	93306
机械及运输设备	Machinery and Transport Equipment	1724475	1316895	1708665	2516806	3284124
杂项制品	Miscellaneous Products	145954	92641	96490	163404	219553
未分类的商品	Products Not Clssified	187942	114734	89817	23477	12198

18-4 各市(州)进出口总额
Total Imports and Exports by Region

单位：万美元 (USD 10 000)

市(州)	Region	2010	2011	2012	2013	2014	2015	2016	2017	2018
全　省	**Sichuan**	**3270396**	**4772328**	**5914360**	**6457884**	**7020297**	**5118856**	**4934941**	**6810677**	**8993788**
成都市	Chengdu	2468476	3796119	4761327	5070576	5592156	3942361	4102173	5830149	7536217
自贡市	Zigong	54127	70447	87374	101373	67150	49015	39353	45378	49364
攀枝花市	Panzhihua	25389	26586	26342	18714	30128	25643	20993	38706	46691
泸州市	Luzhou	13331	15193	18608	22654	27563	31343	31331	205717	276333
德阳市	Deyang	221420	288096	309231	339060	388352	305107	176354	153574	191518
绵阳市	Mianyang	159755	185142	221323	280998	291780	262710	176907	169832	391266
广元市	Guangyuan	20729	29692	33844	35019	42146	6953	2262	2522	7620
遂宁市	Suining	28150	39681	46507	56505	62808	63078	41029	34830	38169
内江市	Neijiang	16845	25696	31360	36298	31495	14115	13253	14204	21524
乐山市	Leshan	97609	79841	94539	111963	111031	88223	88772	102967	111977
南充市	Nanchong	30866	32794	41776	67249	28088	11044	16090	29065	15291
眉山市	Meishan	9985	13580	19458	28843	33376	20517	20812	27580	66267
宜宾市	Yibin	64936	81230	77648	81588	88989	95163	93128	84923	146859
广安市	Guangan	29275	44618	75377	98938	110634	106776	50852	29648	41154
达州市	Dazhou	7070	15298	18470	32106	32610	37078	15983	6909	8660
雅安市	Yaan	1333	3261	4269	6887	7696	7907	4645	4428	6356
巴中市	Bazhong	4863	2577	12475	14360	16680	19043	12151	3988	7860
资阳市	Ziyang	9662	12394	23552	41683	43254	19068	19780	16909	19614
阿坝藏族羌族自治州	Aba	1475	3853	3234	3927	4758	3600	3534	3337	3263
甘孜藏族自治州	Ganzi	1305	646	911	1042	1334	1469	919	1193	1929
凉山彝族自治州	Liangshan	3793	5582	6735	8098	8263	8642	4622	4817	5852

18-5 各市(州)出口总额
Total Exports by Region

单位：万美元 (USD 10 000)

市(州)	Region	2010	2011	2012	2013	2014	2015	2016	2017	2018
全 省	**Sichuan**	**1884064**	**2902697**	**3846907**	**4194906**	**4483913**	**3309290**	**2795498**	**3755394**	**5039827**
成都市	Chengdu	1392152	2300135	3042462	3198381	3390833	2390406	2193971	3055922	4150657
自贡市	Zigong	24869	34450	51746	61555	30902	26611	22496	25889	32863
攀枝花市	Panzhihua	18760	17549	22006	12306	17032	21923	13806	16537	19202
泸州市	Luzhou	10576	10335	15805	20459	25028	28422	27874	196438	254813
德阳市	Deyang	94137	139341	182412	235255	310129	234883	134598	104493	139943
绵阳市	Mianyang	82668	97375	137332	180331	207234	192082	103517	90760	99016
广元市	Guangyuan	17380	26246	27266	30838	41635	6522	1865	1928	5049
遂宁市	Suining	22703	33340	38368	41183	42014	43312	25257	17715	20929
内江市	Neijiang	16757	23330	27012	31546	27778	11755	10173	11316	17614
乐山市	Leshan	67581	49860	65871	82644	83959	68796	68273	75750	88169
南充市	Nanchong	28195	31231	39787	65446	27541	9868	15574	27789	10222
眉山市	Meishan	9048	11191	15639	19998	20865	17414	18861	22082	28504
宜宾市	Yibin	44170	54635	54180	56247	60693	63571	55226	47176	91780
广安市	Guangan	28011	42014	70245	98205	107457	106355	50512	28184	39064
达州市	Dazhou	6327	7302	9424	13705	27439	33469	15738	6427	8265
雅安市	Yaan	1226	1884	3787	6524	6982	7043	3670	3726	4820
巴中市	Bazhong	4863	2577	12475	14360	16680	19026	12126	3969	6629
资阳市	Ziyang	8693	11175	21351	14679	27459	15097	13807	10946	12504
阿坝藏族羌族自治州	Aba	856	2521	2120	2277	2685	2655	2622	2352	2248
甘孜藏族自治州	Ganzi	1299	646	911	1042	1332	1468	919	1193	1929
凉山彝族自治州	Liangshan	3792	5559	6708	7924	8233	8610	4615	4802	5606

18-6 各市(州)进口总额
Total Imports by Region

单位：万美元 (USD 10 000)

市(州)	Region	2010	2011	2012	2013	2014	2015	2016	2017	2018
全 省	**Sichuan**	**1386332**	**1869631**	**2067453**	**2262978**	**2536384**	**1809566**	**2139443**	**3055283**	**3953961**
成都市	Chengdu	1076324	1495984	1718865	1872195	2201323	1551955	1908202	2774227	3385560
自贡市	Zigong	29258	35997	35628	39818	36248	22404	16857	19489	16501
攀枝花市	Panzhihua	6629	9037	4336	6408	13096	3720	7187	22169	27489
泸州市	Luzhou	2755	4858	2803	2195	2535	2921	3457	9279	21520
德阳市	Deyang	127283	148755	126819	103805	78223	70224	41756	49081	51575
绵阳市	Mianyang	77087	87767	83991	100667	84546	70628	73390	79072	292250
广元市	Guangyuan	3349	3446	6578	4181	511	431	397	594	2571
遂宁市	Suining	5447	6341	8139	15322	20794	19766	15772	17115	17240
内江市	Neijiang	88	2366	4348	4752	3717	2360	3080	2888	3910
乐山市	Leshan	30028	29981	28668	29319	27072	19427	20499	27217	23808
南充市	Nanchong	2671	1563	1989	1803	547	1176	516	1276	5069
眉山市	Meishan	937	2389	3819	8845	12511	3103	1951	5498	37763
宜宾市	Yibin	20766	26595	23468	25341	28296	31592	37902	37747	55079
广安市	Guangan	1264	2604	5132	733	3177	421	340	1464	2090
达州市	Dazhou	743	7996	9046	18401	5171	3609	245	482	395
雅安市	Yaan	107	1377	482	363	714	864	975	702	1536
巴中市	Bazhong						17	25	19	1234
资阳市	Ziyang	969	1219	2201	27004	15795	3971	5973	5963	7110
阿坝藏族羌族自治州	Aba	619	1332	1114	1650	2073	945	912	985	1015
甘孜藏族自治州	Ganzi	6				2	1			
凉山彝族自治州	Liangshan	1	23	27	174	30	32	7	15	246

18-7 旅游发展情况
Development of Tourism

指 标		Item		2015	2016	2017	2018
旅行社数	(个)	**Number of Travel Agencies**	**(unit)**	**910**	**988**	**965**	**952**
星级饭店数	(个)	**Number of Star-rated Hotels**	**(unit)**	**449**	**427**	**398**	**382**
入境游客	(万人次)	**Number of Overseas Visitor Arrivals**	**(10 000 person-times)**	**273.20**	**308.79**	**336.17**	**369.82**
外国人		Foreigners		193.44	219.23	241.29	276.47
港澳同胞		Chinese Compatriots From Hong Kong and Macao		43.49	48.48	51.83	49.65
台湾同胞		Chinese Compatriots From Taiwan Province		36.27	41.08	43.05	43.70
国内游客	(万人次)	**Number of Domestic Visitors**	**(10 000 person-times)**	**58500.63**	**63025.00**	**66924.00**	**70198.44**
旅游收入	(亿元)	**Tourism Earnings**	**(100 million yuan)**	**6210.50**	**7705.54**	**8923.06**	**10112.75**
国际旅游(外汇)收入	(万美元)	Foreign Exchange Earnings from International Tourism	**(USD 10 000)**	118087.06	124596.98	144653.62	151164.79
国内旅游收入	(亿元)	Earnings from Domestic Tourism	(100 million yuan)	6137.60	7600.52	8825.39	10012.72

18-8 接待入境游客情况
Basic Conditions of Overseas Visitor Arrivals

单位：万人次 (10 000 person-times)

项 目	Item	2005	2010	2015	2016	2017	2018
总计	**Total**	**106.28**	**104.93**	**273.20**	**308.79**	**336.17**	**369.82**
外国人	**Foreigners**	**68.27**	**74.97**	**193.44**	**219.23**	**241.29**	**276.47**
亚洲	Asia	47.50	40.95	83.83	94.16	97.35	104.64
日本	Japan	15.45	20.23	17.18	20.29	21.20	24.69
马来西亚	Malaysia	6.80	3.18	12.62	14.65	16.12	14.46
新加坡	Singapore	7.39	3.62	12.37	13.97	15.18	18.72
泰国	Thailand	5.80	2.13	6.45	7.81	8.13	17.73
欧洲	Europe	9.50	17.44	53.30	61.70	71.11	86.39
英国	United Kingdom	1.86	5.24	17.41	20.46	23.16	27.35
德国	Germany	1.95	2.42	9.70	11.22	13.23	15.43
法国	France	1.77	2.80	7.47	8.73	10.13	7.47
意大利	Italy	0.80	0.72	2.72	3.07	3.48	4.26
北美洲	North America	8.49	11.93	39.83	45.76	52.21	48.34
加拿大	Canada	1.12	2.20	7.12	33.64	9.70	8.84
美国	United States	6.99	8.91	28.78	8.29	37.97	33.02
澳大利亚	Australia	1.02	2.31	8.95	10.29	11.87	15.89
非洲	Africa	0.29	0.40	2.29	2.44	2.92	3.55
其他	Others	1.18	1.09	2.73	2.32	2.86	11.03
港澳同胞	**Chinese Compatriots From Hong Kong and Macao**	**13.99**	**15.11**	**43.49**	**48.48**	**94.88**	**49.65**
台湾同胞	**Chinese Compatriots from Taiwan Province**	**24.02**	**14.85**	**36.27**	**41.08**	**43.05**	**43.70**

18-9　各市(州)旅游发展情况(2018年)
Development of Tourism by Region(2018)

市(州)	Region	星级饭店数(个) Number of Star-rated Hotels (unit)	入境游客人数(万人次) Number of Overseas Visitor Arrivals (10 000 person-times)	#外国人 Foreigners	国际旅游外汇收入(万美元) Foreign Exchange Earnings from International Tourism (USD 10 000)	国内旅游人数(万人次) Number of Domestic Visitors (10 000 person-times)	国内旅游收入(亿元) Earnings from Domestic Tourism (100 million yuan)
全　省	**Sichuan**	**382**	**369.82**	**276.47**	**151164.79**	**70198.44**	**10012.72**
成都市	Chengdu	91	340.61	257.54	144660.88	24017.29	3616.87
自贡市	Zigong	11	0.12	0.08	40.14	4620.41	391.69
攀枝花市	Panzhihua	18	0.15	0.05	33.29	2566.36	337.47
泸州市	Luzhou	19	0.24	0.11	74.70	5198.37	512.75
德阳市	Deyang	13	0.34	0.15	202.39	4332.50	385.17
绵阳市	Mianyang	25	0.85	0.53	375.59	6383.40	647.40
广元市	Guangyuan	17	0.09	0.01	25.66	5028.86	419.53
遂宁市	Suining	17	0.01	0.01	5.28	4971.36	467.21
内江市	Neijiang	6	0.02	0.01	9.07	4286.88	311.02
乐山市	Leshan	26	23.32	15.62	4734.48	5710.22	889.47
南充市	Nanchong	19	0.06	0.01	13.38	5736.50	578.61
眉山市	Meishan	12	0.05	0.04	24.39	4790.71	404.28
宜宾市	Yibin	13	0.09	0.04	29.61	6535.10	687.26
广安市	Guangan	13	0.80	0.33	184.10	4052.12	403.09
达州市	Dazhou	7	0.02	0.01	3.88	2831.08	208.86
雅安市	Yaan	19	0.33	0.15	76.05	3740.58	320.42
巴中市	Bazhong	7	0.00	0.00	0.20	2936.81	248.54
资阳市	Ziyang	7	1.08	0.70	273.13	2549.97	189.91
阿坝藏族羌族自治州	Aba	16	0.24	0.09	48.55	2369.47	165.59
甘孜藏族自治州	Ganzi	7	1.32	0.93	330.01	2212.47	220.80
凉山彝族自治州	Liangshan	19	0.05	0.03	20.01	4651.14	436.66

注：国内旅游人数全省合计对重复统计人数进行了剥离，国内旅游收入全省合计根据平均系数进行了调整，故各市州加总不等于全省合计。

a) The data of domestic visitors stripped the number of repeated statistics, and the data of earnings from domestic tourism was adjusted according to the average coefficient, so the sum number of cities and states is not equal to the total of the province.

主要统计指标解释

货物进出口总额　指实际进出我国国境的货物总金额。包括对外贸易实际进出口货物，来料加工装配进出口货物，国家间、联合国及国际组织无偿援助物资和赠送品，华侨、港澳台同胞和外籍华人捐赠品，租赁期满归承租人所有的租赁货物，进料加工进出口货物，边境地方贸易及边境地区小额贸易进出口货物，中外合资企业、中外合作经营企业、外商独资经营企业进出口货物和公用物品，到、离岸价格在规定限额以上的进出口货样和广告品(无商业价值、无使用价值和免费提供出口的除外)，从保税仓库提取在中国境内销售的进口货物，以及其他进出口货物。该指标可以观察一个国家在对外贸易方面的总规模。我国规定出口货物按离岸价格统计，进口货物按到岸价格统计。

实际利用外资　指批准的合同外资金额的实际执行数，外国投资者根据批准外商投资企业的合同(章程)的规定实际缴付的出资额和企业投资总额内外国投资者以自己的境外自有资金实际直接向企业提供的贷款。

对外借款　指通过对外正式签订借款协议，从境外筹措的资金，包括外国政府贷款、国际金融组织贷款、外国银行商业贷款、出口信贷以及对外发行债券等。

外商直接投资　是指外国投资者在我国境内通过设立外商投资企业、合伙企业、与中方投资者共同进行石油资源的合作勘探开发以及设立外国公司分支机构等方式进行投资。外国投资者可以用现金、实物、无形资产、股权等投资，还可以用从外商投资企业获得的利润进行再投资。

对外承包工程　根据《对外承包工程管理条例》，对外承包工程是指中国的企业或者其他单位承包境外建设工程项目的活动。

对外劳务合作　指组织劳务人员赴其他国家或地区为国外的企业或机构工作的经营性活动。

入境游客　指报告期内来中国（大陆）观光、度假、探亲访友、就医疗养、购物、参加会议或从事经济、文化、体育、宗教活动的外国人、港澳台同胞等游客（即入境旅游人数）。统计时，入境游客按每入境一次统计 1 人次。入境旅游人数包括入境过夜游客和入境一日游游客。

国内游客　指报告期内在中国（大陆）观光游览、度假、探亲访友、就医疗养、购物、参加会议或从事经济、文化、体育、宗教活动的中国（大陆）居民人数，其出游的目的不是通过所从事的活动谋取报酬。统计时，国内游客按每出游一次统计 1 人次。

国际旅游收入　指入境游客在中国（大陆）境内旅行、游览过程中用于交通、参观游览、住宿、餐饮、购物、娱乐等全部花费。

国内旅游收入　指国内游客在国内旅行、游览过程中用于交通、参观游览、住宿、餐饮、购物、娱乐等全部花费。

Explanatory Notes on Main Statistical Indicators

Total Import and Export of Goods refer to the real value of commodities imported and exported across the border of China. They include the actual imports and exports through foreign trade, imported and exported goods under the processing and assembling trades and materials, supplies and gifts as aid given gratis between governments and by the United Nations and other international organizations, and contributions donated by overseas Chinese, compatriots in Hong Kong and Macao and Chinese with foreign citizenship, leasing commodities owned by tenant at the expiration of leasing period, the imported and exported commodities processed with imported materials, commodities trading in border areas, the imported and exported commodities and articles for public use of the Sino-foreign joint ventures, cooperative enterprises and ventures with sole foreign investment. Also included is import or export of samples and advertising goods for which CIF or FOB value are beyond the permitted ceiling (excluding goods of no trading or use value and free commodities for export), imported goods sold in China from bonded warehouses and other imported or exported goods. The indicator of the total imports and exports at customs can be used to observe the total size of external trade in a country. In accordance with the stipulation of the Chinese government, imports are calculated at CIF, while exports are calculated at FOB.

The actual utilization of foreign capital refers to the actual number of execution of the approved contractual foreign capital amount, the actual amount of foreign investment paid by foreign investors in accordance with the provisions of the contract (articles of association) for the approval of foreign-funded enterprises, and the total amount of enterprise investment actually provided by foreign investors to enterprises directly with their own overseas funds.

Foreign Borrowings refer to funds borrowed from abroad through formal signing of borrowing agreements with foreign institutions, including loans of foreign governments, loans of international financial institutions, commercial loans of foreign banks, export credit , and funds raised by Chinese bonds issued abroad.

Foreign Direct Investment refers to foreign investment in China through the establishment of foreign invested enterprises, cooperative exploration and development of petroleum resources with domestic investors and the establishment of branch organizations of foreign enterprises. Foreign investment can be made in forms of cash, physical investment, intangible assets and equity, in addition with reinvestment of the foreign enterprises with the profits gained from the investment.

Overseas Contracted Project refers to activities of contracting overseas construction projects by Chinese enterprises or any other units, which are stipulated in the Regulations on Administration of Foreign Contracted Project.

Overseas Labor Services refer to operational activities of organizing labor force to go abroad providing services to foreign enterprises or agencies.

International Visitor Arrivals refer to the number of tourists of foreigners, Chinese compatriots from Hong Kong, Macao and Taiwan who come to China (mainland) within the reference period for sight-seeing, vacation, visiting relatives, medical treatment, shopping, attending conference, or to engage in economic, cultural, sports and religious activities (namely the number of overseas visitor arrivals). In compiling statistics, each arrival is counted as one person-time. The number of overseas visitor arrivals includes inbound overnight tourists and one-day tourists.

Number of Domestic Tourists refers to the number of Chinese (mainland) residents who travel within China (mainland) for sight-seeing, vacation, visiting relatives, medical treatment, shopping, attending conference, or to engage in economic, cultural, sports and religious activities. In compiling statistics, each time of travelling is counted as one person-time.

Foreign Exchange Earnings from International Tourism refer to the total expenditure of foreigners, overseas Chinese, Chinese compatriots from Hong Kong, Macao and Taiwan during their stay in the mainland of China on transportation, sighting, accommodation, food, shopping and entertainment.s

Income from Domestic Tourism refer to expenditure of domestic tourists on transportation, sighting, accommodation, food, shopping and entertainment while they travel.

金融业

Chapter 19 Financial Intermediation

19-1　金融机构(含外资)本外币信贷收支表(资金来源)

Balance Sheet of Local and Foreign Credit Funds of Financial Institutions (Funds Sources)

单位：亿元　　　　(100 million yuan)

项　　目	Item	2018	比年初增减数 amount over the beginning of the year
资金来源总计	**All Sources**	**78885.25**	**4703.05**
各项存款	Deposits	77391.02	4311.63
非金融企业存款	Deposits of Non-financial Enterprises	19069.96	-177.50
住户存款	Deposits of Households	38629.52	3605.35
#活期存款	Demand Deposits	12602.70	765.03
广义政府存款	Broad Deposits of Government	16366.69	1489.86
非银行业金融机构存款	Deposits of Non-banking Financial Institutions	3199.28	-580.86
金融债券	Financial Bonds	308.86	-5.93
卖出回购资产	Assets Sold for Repurchase	51.05	-65.61
借款及非银行业金融机构拆入	Borrowing and Non-banking Financial Institutions Borrowing	161.73	-56.91
联行往来(净)	Inter-branche Exchange (net)		
应付及暂收款	Account Payable and Temporary Collection	1724.35	174.58
各项准备	Reserves	1931.38	193.31
所有者权益	Owners' Equities	3069.36	345.03
其他	Others	-5752.50	-193.05

注：本表金融机构包括中国人民银行、中资全国性大型银行、中资全国性中小型银行、中资区域性中小型银行、城市信用社、农村信用社、财务公司、信托投资公司、租赁公司、外资金融机构和汽车金融公司(后同)。

a) Financial institution of balance sheet includes the People’s Bank of China, large,small and medium-sized Chinese-funded national banks, small and medium-sized regional and Chinese-funded banks,urban and rural credit cooperative banks,finance companies,financial trust and investment companies,financial leasing companies,Foreign financial institutions and auto finance company (the same as the follows) .

19-2 金融机构(含外资)本外币信贷收支表(资金运用)

Balance Sheet of Local and Foreign Credit Funds of Financial Institutions (Funds Uses)

单位：亿元 (100 million yuan)

项　目	Item	2018	比年初增减数 amount over the beginning of the year
资金运用总计	**All Uses**	**78885.25**	**4703.05**
各项贷款	Loans	55390.86	6376.17
住户贷款	Loans of Households	17484.93	2379.24
短期贷款	Shot-term Loans	2466.17	244.61
中长期贷款	Medium-term & Long-term Loans	15018.76	2134.63
非金融企业及机关团体贷款	Loans of Non-financial Enterprises & Government Agencies and Organizations	37331.49	3723.26
短期贷款	Shot-term Loans	8156.92	-48.89
中长期贷款	Medium-term & Long-term Loans	27312.77	3253.40
票据融资	Bill Financing	1725.14	463.27
各项垫款	Various Money Paid Back Later	41.55	-0.64
债券投资	Bond Investment	6127.60	525.90
股权及其他投资	Equity and Other Investment	4173.81	-487.75
买入返售资产	Redemptory Capital for Sale	539.52	-69.37
存放非银行业金融机构款项	Due from Non-banking Financial Institutions	38.80	8.61
联行往来(净)	Inter-branche Exchange (net)	11340.18	-1789.24
应收及预付款	Account Receivable and Advanced Payment	707.10	132.40
固定资产	Fixed Assets	564.54	6.64
外汇占款	Position for Foreign Purchase		
投资性房地产	Investment Property	2.86	-0.31

19-3 各市(州)金融机构各项存款和贷款(2018年底)
Deposits and Loans of Financial Institutions by Region at Year-end of 2018

单位：亿元 (100 million yuan)

市(州)	Region	本外币各项存款 RMB and Foreign Currency Deposits	人民币各项存款 RMB Deposits	#住户存款 Household Savings	本外币各项贷款 RMB and Foreign Currency Loans	人民币各项贷款 RMB Loans	#短期贷款 Short-term Loans	#中长期贷款 Medium and Long-term Loans
全　省	**Sichuan**	**77391.02**	**76088.75**	**38402.77**	**55390.86**	**54097.84**	**10098.10**	**42124.97**
成都市	Chengdu	38004.67	36820.23	13168.73	33294.70	32057.77	5197.79	26110.56
自贡市	Zigong	1711.75	1708.76	1145.90	1011.46	1010.40	381.69	611.60
攀枝花市	Panzhihua	1043.79	1041.79	658.90	807.02	804.70	240.02	418.64
泸州市	Luzhou	2653.66	2634.80	1631.83	1714.39	1714.16	376.04	1263.75
德阳市	Deyang	2720.06	2694.37	1703.84	1459.44	1442.31	413.52	870.06
绵阳市	Mianyang	3860.39	3848.78	2242.62	2173.71	2167.25	702.26	1298.22
广元市	Guangyuan	1479.82	1478.55	979.68	796.13	795.37	158.85	607.00
遂宁市	Suining	1574.42	1571.98	1117.10	1040.75	1040.67	213.13	806.51
内江市	Neijiang	1652.02	1649.36	1265.67	902.79	901.69	247.37	595.91
乐山市	Leshan	2223.45	2217.55	1574.30	1560.93	1558.88	356.74	1104.69
南充市	Nanchong	3313.93	3292.66	2397.37	1979.42	1961.17	385.56	1518.37
眉山市	Meishan	2094.55	2087.24	1467.72	1043.10	1042.89	163.74	867.78
宜宾市	Yibin	2985.57	2976.12	1424.08	1642.40	1636.91	358.06	1228.54
广安市	Guangan	1868.29	1867.48	1398.36	809.61	809.57	157.97	642.36
达州市	Dazhou	2928.87	2927.09	2055.08	1502.95	1502.91	199.39	1239.12
雅安市	Yaan	1126.86	1125.73	669.47	657.86	657.82	107.94	529.62
巴中市	Bazhong	1247.90	1247.59	913.97	716.43	716.43	96.69	614.34
资阳市	Ziyang	1419.72	1418.75	967.07	707.70	706.89	135.72	561.31
阿坝藏族羌族自治州	Aba	652.76	652.71	257.07	299.56	299.56	36.30	257.94
甘孜藏族自治州	Ganzi	698.41	698.35	247.36	353.62	353.62	16.56	306.79
凉山彝族自治州	Liangshan	2130.12	2128.87	1116.65	916.88	916.87	152.76	671.86

19-4 各市(州)金融机构人民币各项存款(年底余额)
Deposits of Financial Institutions by Region at Year-end

单位：亿元 (100 million yuan)

市(州)	Region	2010	2011	2012	2013	2014	2015	2016	2017	2018
全　省	**Sichuan**	**30299.67**	**34734.69**	**41130.79**	**47667.28**	**53282.03**	**59184.83**	**65638.43**	**71591.42**	**76088.75**
成都市	Chengdu	15277.25	17098.02	20354.17	23662.21	26797.50	29474.92	31597.50	34581.17	36820.23
自贡市	Zigong	559.32	676.80	821.51	974.97	1075.20	1319.76	1524.05	1723.67	1708.76
攀枝花市	Panzhihua	570.72	661.26	765.69	784.18	802.87	856.81	938.59	981.36	1041.79
泸州市	Luzhou	827.23	1000.48	1212.63	1409.46	1611.60	1829.88	2179.23	2459.19	2634.80
德阳市	Deyang	1388.03	1509.93	1663.30	1793.35	1918.54	2066.30	2307.72	2455.34	2694.37
绵阳市	Mianyang	1784.47	1932.66	2126.34	2410.27	2621.72	2882.91	3181.69	3588.52	3848.78
广元市	Guangyuan	717.15	750.03	833.32	933.80	1005.82	1134.41	1302.22	1417.40	1478.55
遂宁市	Suining	523.16	625.87	745.53	893.29	989.44	1187.12	1376.76	1554.82	1571.98
内江市	Neijiang	599.86	727.13	888.65	1077.59	1134.36	1202.20	1366.90	1512.92	1649.36
乐山市	Leshan	867.41	1033.20	1264.58	1524.56	1709.12	1723.96	1858.89	2080.04	2217.55
南充市	Nanchong	1100.50	1362.36	1668.78	1916.56	2154.46	2561.43	3047.30	3216.07	3292.66
眉山市	Meishan	615.24	761.90	931.07	1115.04	1253.85	1432.08	1670.36	1961.14	2087.24
宜宾市	Yibin	945.60	1199.82	1464.38	1573.67	1685.23	1911.25	2322.47	2646.64	2976.12
广安市	Guangan	638.85	769.69	937.31	1114.68	1265.03	1424.65	1662.73	1828.89	1867.48
达州市	Dazhou	901.08	1098.82	1317.17	1588.05	1752.37	2086.42	2624.98	2801.93	2927.09
雅安市	Yaan	454.34	516.81	592.57	842.89	974.25	1008.95	1042.06	1104.51	1125.73
巴中市	Bazhong	354.91	468.16	568.61	678.61	777.13	921.73	1145.80	1247.67	1247.59
资阳市	Ziyang	674.99	787.53	925.73	1083.87	1245.84	1377.85	1673.02	1355.97	1418.75
阿坝藏族羌族自治州	Aba	425.96	419.70	424.51	435.15	473.60	535.36	568.00	594.92	652.71
甘孜藏族自治州	Ganzi	243.70	312.62	374.86	442.28	499.03	588.24	595.64	631.30	698.35
凉山彝族自治州	Liangshan	699.04	869.67	1078.02	1271.89	1386.67	1490.66	1652.53	1847.95	2128.87

19-5 各市(州)金融机构人民币住户存款(年底余额)
Household Deposits of Financial Institutions by Region at Year-end

单位：亿元 (100 million yuan)

市(州)	Region	2010	2011	2012	2013	2014	2015	2016	2017	2018
全　省	**Sichuan**	**13650.83**	**16189.15**	**19567.57**	**22956.68**	**25731.62**	**28575.90**	**31950.42**	**34800.89**	**38402.77**
成都市	Chengdu	5071.37	5980.01	7157.04	8408.79	9280.25	9922.18	10831.38	11995.87	13168.73
自贡市	Zigong	383.69	444.57	543.29	639.49	718.51	819.38	923.57	1033.62	1145.90
攀枝花市	Panzhihua	281.42	312.14	368.02	411.91	431.79	462.44	522.97	575.92	658.90
泸州市	Luzhou	517.19	617.39	758.32	880.83	1000.65	1140.17	1313.47	1475.96	1631.83
德阳市	Deyang	685.49	784.38	931.33	1074.21	1188.39	1292.47	1425.36	1531.40	1703.84
绵阳市	Mianyang	803.22	932.87	1125.95	1328.09	1479.82	1640.86	1838.25	2028.73	2242.62
广元市	Guangyuan	323.74	387.25	474.09	557.47	641.05	733.00	811.44	891.97	979.68
遂宁市	Suining	358.61	423.50	508.96	577.96	649.28	788.08	910.44	1005.90	1117.10
内江市	Neijiang	437.78	524.17	641.20	749.61	836.39	935.67	1045.62	1144.95	1265.67
乐山市	Leshan	522.37	634.06	773.08	931.54	1057.43	1161.20	1277.37	1407.65	1574.30
南充市	Nanchong	753.62	905.92	1122.38	1306.68	1467.24	1723.13	2009.68	2175.10	2397.37
眉山市	Meishan	427.95	521.78	649.59	778.44	907.67	1020.38	1156.75	1275.28	1467.72
宜宾市	Yibin	466.25	560.26	674.28	770.04	886.63	1010.17	1150.62	1277.47	1424.08
广安市	Guangan	480.51	560.58	682.02	795.90	902.15	1061.78	1198.60	1316.29	1398.36
达州市	Dazhou	665.75	800.36	952.50	1139.67	1304.62	1505.90	1739.52	1917.50	2055.08
雅安市	Yaan	221.19	258.35	310.31	379.84	447.05	505.29	543.35	596.13	669.47
巴中市	Bazhong	241.45	312.52	404.08	482.26	557.00	634.06	741.94	828.99	913.97
资阳市	Ziyang	467.71	566.11	691.67	806.05	938.20	1060.43	1211.38	884.28	967.07
阿坝藏族羌族自治州	Aba	97.44	113.94	132.92	148.26	164.64	186.67	215.71	233.12	257.07
甘孜藏族自治州	Ganzi	74.93	95.71	117.74	139.72	163.93	186.06	209.67	226.66	247.36
凉山彝族自治州	Liangshan	351.04	435.11	528.48	627.81	687.43	764.83	873.33	978.10	1116.65

19-6 各市(州)金融机构人民币各项贷款(年底余额)
Loans of Financial Institutions by Region at Year-end

单位：亿元 (100 million yuan)

市(州)	Region	2010	2011	2012	2013	2014	2015	2016	2017	2018
全 省	**Sichuan**	**19129.79**	**22033.21**	**25560.36**	**29542.74**	**33884.06**	**38011.83**	**42828.13**	**48124.44**	**54097.84**
成都市	Chengdu	12139.43	13766.85	15630.39	17617.51	19778.93	21970.64	25522.23	28870.55	32057.77
自贡市	Zigong	248.24	303.33	371.19	449.33	520.81	614.57	708.35	825.98	1010.40
攀枝花市	Panzhihua	380.31	445.72	532.19	608.93	658.19	697.15	738.63	795.54	804.70
泸州市	Luzhou	406.72	507.85	629.59	766.70	919.42	1092.70	1281.64	1451.30	1714.16
德阳市	Deyang	592.39	717.98	849.28	956.40	1065.81	1075.92	1190.04	1292.54	1442.31
绵阳市	Mianyang	858.31	968.98	1086.78	1252.78	1398.50	1532.85	1667.43	1864.71	2167.25
广元市	Guangyuan	236.21	280.65	331.81	406.87	472.32	531.18	610.20	703.84	795.37
遂宁市	Suining	276.37	329.47	399.92	499.02	615.01	740.81	820.20	922.72	1040.67
内江市	Neijiang	266.90	313.69	406.08	514.11	608.07	688.15	731.65	782.70	901.69
乐山市	Leshan	585.87	695.04	807.45	931.75	1086.79	1230.91	1308.83	1431.65	1558.88
南充市	Nanchong	424.82	519.63	653.62	824.66	1038.07	1293.89	1479.68	1684.34	1961.17
眉山市	Meishan	281.58	344.17	427.63	531.99	625.17	683.76	747.19	864.31	1042.89
宜宾市	Yibin	447.67	523.08	625.43	760.64	900.79	1054.48	1223.82	1390.60	1636.91
广安市	Guangan	251.60	286.99	341.19	424.53	514.94	582.13	639.09	725.86	809.57
达州市	Dazhou	363.46	439.79	531.89	655.58	801.71	929.32	1077.62	1277.93	1502.91
雅安市	Yaan	238.90	279.69	330.68	412.44	474.98	510.09	527.85	594.84	657.82
巴中市	Bazhong	129.22	155.95	203.60	264.93	345.03	457.83	542.50	641.40	716.43
资阳市	Ziyang	281.77	333.82	414.77	525.02	642.08	716.90	735.29	597.15	706.89
阿坝藏族羌族自治州	Aba	136.87	151.70	165.89	186.44	205.68	221.63	252.47	269.70	299.56
甘孜藏族自治州	Ganzi	111.61	131.33	149.80	167.60	194.05	230.49	273.62	317.17	353.62
凉山彝族自治州	Liangshan	345.31	409.74	499.90	575.47	655.43	700.41	749.78	819.60	916.87

19-7 金融机构存款基准利率
Official Interest Rates of Deposits of Financial Institutions

单位：年利率% (Annual Interest Rate %)

项目	Item	2010.10.20 Oct.20 2010	2010.12.26 Dec.26 2010	2011.02.09 Feb.9 2011	2011.04.06 Apr.6 2011	2011.07.07 July.7 2011	2012.06.08 June.8 2012	2012.07.06 July.6 2012	2014.11.22 Nov.22 2014	2015.03.01 Mar.1 2015	2015.05.11 May.11 2015	2015.06.28 June.28 2015	2015.08.26 Aug.26 2015	2015 10.24 Oct.24 2015
个人人民币储蓄存款	**Household Deposits**													
活期	Demand Deposits	0.36	0.36	0.40	0.50	0.50	0.40	0.35	0.35	0.35	0.35	0.35	0.35	0.35
定期	Time Deposits													
三个月	3 Months	1.91	2.25	2.60	2.85	3.10	2.85	2.60	2.35	2.10	1.85	1.60	1.35	1.10
半年	6 Months	2.20	2.50	2.80	3.05	3.30	3.05	2.80	2.55	2.30	2.05	1.80	1.55	1.30
一年	1 Year	2.50	2.75	3.00	3.25	3.50	3.25	3.00	2.75	2.50	2.25	2.00	1.75	1.50
二年	2 Years	3.25	3.55	3.90	4.15	4.40	4.10	3.75	3.35	3.10	2.85	2.60	2.35	2.10
三年	3 Years	3.85	4.15	4.50	4.75	5.00	4.65	4.25	4.00	3.75	3.50	3.25	3.00	2.75

19-8 金融机构贷款利率
Official Interest Rates of Loans of Financial Institutions

单位：年利率% (Annual Interest Rate %)

项目	Item	2010.10.20 Oct.20 2010	2010.12.26 Dec.26 2010	2011.02.09 Feb.9 2011	2011.04.06 Apr.6 2011	2011.07.07 July.7 2011	2012.06.08 June.8 2012	2012.07.06 July.6 2012	2014 11.22 Nov.22 2014	2015.03.01 Mar.1 2015	2015.05.11 May.11 2015	2015.06.28 June.28 2015	2015.08.26 Aug.26 2015	2015.10.24 Oct.24 2015
短期贷款	**Short-term Loans**													
六个月以内（含六个月）	6 Months Or Less	5.10	5.35	5.60	5.85	6.10	5.85	5.60	5.60	5.35	5.10	4.85	4.60	4.35
六个月至一年（含一年）	12 Months Or Less	5.56	5.81	6.06	6.31	6.56	6.31	6.00	5.60	5.35	5.10	4.85	4.60	4.35
中长期贷款	**Mediun-term & Long-time Loans**													
一至三年（含三年）	Three Years Or Less	5.60	5.85	6.10	6.40	6.65	6.40	6.15	6.00	5.75	5.50	5.25	5.00	4.75
三至五年（含五年）	5 Years Or Less	5.96	6.22	6.45	6.65	6.90	6.65	6.40	6.00	5.75	5.50	5.25	5.00	4.75
五年以上	Above 5 Years	6.14	6.40	6.60	6.80	7.05	6.80	6.55	6.15	5.90	5.65	5.40	5.15	4.90
个人住房公积金贷款	**Loans For Public Accumulation Funds Of Housing**													
五年以下（含五年）	5 Year Or Less	3.50	3.75	4.00	4.20	4.45	4.20	4.00	3.75	3.50	3.25	3.00	2.75	2.75
五年以上	Above 5 Years	4.05	4.30	4.50	4.70	4.90	4.70	4.50	4.25	4.00	3.75	3.50	3.25	3.25

注：2014年11月22日之后，人民银行对存贷款基准利率期限档次进行了简并，贷款基准利率期限档次简并为一年以内(含一年)、一至五年(含五年)和五年以上三个档次。

a)Since November 22,2014,The People's Bank of China has simplified and merged the term classes of deposit and loan interest rates.The classes of loan interest base rates were turned to 3 grades of "less than 1 year (including 1 year)", "1 to 5 years (including 5 years)" and "more than 5 years".

19-9 人民币汇率（年平均价）
RMB Exchange Rate (Annual Average)

单位：人民币元 (RMB yuan)

年份 Year	100美元 $100	100日元 100 yen	100港元 HK $ 100	100欧元 € 100
1981	170.50	0.7735	30.41	
1982	189.25	0.7607	31.15	
1983	197.57	0.8318	27.36	
1984	232.70	0.9780	29.71	
1985	293.67	1.2457	37.57	
1986	345.28	2.0694	44.22	
1987	372.21	2.5799	47.74	
1988	372.21	2.9082	47.70	
1989	376.51	2.7360	48.28	
1990	478.32	3.3233	61.39	
1991	532.33	3.9602	68.45	
1992	551.46	4.3608	71.24	
1993	576.20	5.2020	74.41	
1994	861.87	8.4370	111.53	
1995	835.10	8.9225	107.96	
1996	831.42	7.6352	107.51	
1997	828.98	6.8600	107.09	
1998	827.91	6.3488	106.88	
1999	827.83	7.2932	106.66	
2000	827.84	7.6864	106.18	
2001	827.70	6.8075	106.08	
2002	827.70	6.6237	106.07	800.58
2003	827.70	7.1466	106.24	936.13
2004	827.68	7.6552	106.23	1029.00
2005	819.17	7.4484	105.30	1019.53
2006	797.18	6.8570	102.62	1001.90
2007	760.40	6.4632	97.46	1041.75
2008	694.51	6.7427	89.19	1022.27
2009	683.10	7.2986	88.12	952.70
2010	676.95	7.7279	87.13	897.25
2011	645.88	8.1050	82.97	900.11
2012	631.25	7.9037	81.38	810.67
2013	619.32	6.3323	79.85	822.19
2014	614.28	5.8196	79.22	816.51
2015	622.84	5.1543	80.34	691.41
2016	664.23	6.1243	85.58	734.26
2017	675.18	6.0244	86.64	763.03
2018	661.74	5.9890	84.43	780.16

19-10 保险业务经济技术指标
Economic and Technical Indicators of Insurance Business

单位：万元 (10 000 yuan)

项 目	Item	2013	2014	2015	2016	2017	2018
保费收入合计	**Premium Income Total**	**9146769**	**10606332**	**12673045**	**17120774**	**19393937**	**19580848**
财产保险	**Property Insurance**	**3151222**	**3717618**	**4214379**	**4572146**	**4963608**	**5424358**
企业财产保险	Enterprise Property Insurance	120850	127969	125462	130541	124654	130097
机动车辆保险	Automobile Insurance	2497479	3007648	3462691	3749762	3923080	3073062
货物运输保险	Cargo Transportation Insurance	22542	20954	15524	13333	13923	16629
责任保险	Liability Insurance	113555	138383	169309	186878	218753	285056
信用保证保险	Credit and Guarantee Insurance	27888	12277	14686	19332	32972	39561
其他财产保险	Others	368907	410387	426706	472301	650227	1249953
人身保险	**Life Insurance**	**5995547**	**6888714**	**8458666**	**12548628**	**14430329**	**14156489**
人寿保险	Life Insurance Business						
非分红产品	Non-participating	610129	2401216	3601751	6476327	7480289	5158949
分红产品	Participating	4564934	3398221	3268583	3393194	4090501	6344701
投资连接产品	Unit-link	725	705	611	561	543	540
万能产品	Universal	34062	35944	37380	42944	44849	45017
健康险	Health Insurance						
短期健康险	Short-term Health Insurance	254462	363569	451923	526781	744711	873179
长期健康险	Long-term Health Insurance	264200	391329	769516	1730729	1603716	1725761
意外伤害险	Personal Accident Insurance	267034	297730	328902	378093	465720	511860
赔款给付支出合计	**Claim Total**	**3146178**	**3739403**	**4540817**	**5543581**	**5833192**	**6327362**
财产保险	**Property Insurance**	**1671196**	**1958958**	**2188599**	**2168841**	**2411127**	**3103449**
企业财产保险	Enterprise Property Insurance	70007	74235	51575	46160	50036	99156
机动车辆保险	Automobile Insurance	1390131	1635895	1833642	1801011	1973086	2215797
货物运输保险	Cargo Transportation Insurance	7468	8061	6618	4995	6850	7016
责任保险	Liability Insurance	45265	54204	60195	72068	82785	110996
信用保证保险	Credit and Guarantee Insurance	7898	5678	8985	18747	16584	11151
其他财产保险	Others	150427	180885	227585	225860	281785	659333
人身保险	**Life Insurance**	**1474982**	**1780445**	**2352218**	**3374740**	**3422065**	**3224724**
人寿保险	Life Insurance Business						
非分红产品	Non-participating	144543	141833	208261	335344	566454	594569
分红产品	Participating	1054397	1250732	1652058	2469916	2129803	1994973
投资连接产品	Unit-link	76	84	368	612	125	102
万能产品	Universal	8248	7936	9349	10211	10418	10505
健康险	Health Insurance						
短期健康险	Short-term Health Insurance	145212	232140	312715	356824	459970	572261
长期健康险	Long-term Health Insurance	36132	53349	67861	91049	132634	191031
意外伤害险	Personal Accident Insurance	86374	94373	101606	110784	122660	71601

19-11 各财产保险公司和人身保险公司四川省分公司保费收入

Premium Income of Property Insurance Companies (Sichuan Branch) and Life Insurance Companies (Sichuan Branch)

单位：万元 (10 000 yuan)

公司名称	Company Name	2017	2018
合　计	**Total**	**19393937**	**19580848**
财产保险公司	**Property Insurance Companies**	**5339943**	**5424358**
中国人民财产保险股份有限公司	PICC Property & Casualty Insurance Company Limited	1870204	1767835
中国太平洋财产保险股份有限公司	China Pacific Insurance (Group) Co.,Ltd	359378	495442
中国平安财产保险股份有限公司	Ping An Insurance (Group) Company of China , Ltd.	1339502	1167297
永安财产保险股份有限公司	Yong An Insurance Co,.Ltd.	60195	100981
华泰财产保险股份有限公司	Huatai Insurance Co., Ltd.	54674	58113
中华联合财产保险股份有限公司	China United Property Insurance Company	252477	289916
天安财产保险股份有限公司	Tanan Property Insurance Co., Ltd.	49889	63839
太平保险有限公司	TaiPing Insurance Company Ltd.	182049	126954
中国大地财产保险股份有限公司	China Continent Property & Casualty Insurance Company	120640	145784
华安财产保险股份有限公司	Sinosafe Insurance	48734	52124
中航安盟财产保险有限公司	Groupama-Avic Property Insurance Co.,Ltd	78933	83249
中国出口信用保险公司	China Export & Credit Insurance Corporation (SINOSURE)	29909	37761
安邦财产保险股份有限公司	Anbang Property & Casualty Insurance Co.,Ltd	15914	15556
永诚财产保险股份有限公司	Alltrust Insurance Company of China ,Co., Ltd	74527	72204
安盛天平财产保险股份有限公司	AXA Tianping P&C Insurance Co., Ltd.	28021	21614
阳光财产保险股份有限公司	Sunshine Property & Casualty Insurance Company of China ,Co.,Ltd.	113970	134619
都邦财产保险股份有限公司	Dubang Property & Casualty Insurance Company of China ,Co.,Ltd.	17579	18217
渤海财产保险股份有限公司	Bohai Property & Casualty Insurance Company of China ,Co.,Ltd.	9464	5817
中银保险有限公司	China Bank Property & Casualty Insurance Company of China ,Co.,Ltd.	30065	34324
华农财产保险股份有限公司	Huanong Property & Casualty Insurance Co.,Ltd.	5216	10218
安诚财产保险股份有限公司	Ancheng Property & Casualty Insurance Co.,Ltd.	19691	24513
亚太财产保险有限公司	Asia Pacific Property Insurance Company Limited	15360	20110
浙商财产保险股份有限公司	Zheshang Property & Casualty Insurance Co.,Ltd.	14343	18666
鼎和财产保险股份有限公司	Dinghe Property & Casualty Insurance Company of China ,Co.,Ltd.	12949	13620
英大泰和财产保险股份有限公司	Yingda Taihe Property & Casualty Insurance Co.,Ltd.	43208	43560
锦泰财产保险股份有限公司	JinTai Property Insurance Co.,Ltd.	138418	156386
紫金财产保险股份有限公司	Zijin Property and Casualty Insurance Co.,Ltd.	12988	16425
中国人寿财产保险股份有限公司	China Life Property & Casualty Insurance Co.,Ltd.	214116	243600
信达财产保险股份有限公司	Cinda Property Insurance Co.,Ltd.	4029	6260
国泰财产保险有限责任公司	Cathay Insurance Co., Ltd.	677	409
富德财产保险股份有限公司	Fund Property&Casualty Insurance Co.,Ltd.	29609	38269

19-11 续表 1 continued

单位：万元 (10 000 yuan)

公司名称	Company Name	2017	2018
安华农业保险股份有限公司	Anhua Agricultural Insurance Co.,Ltd	4803	2591
中意财产保险有限公司	Generali China Insurance Co., Ltd.	7311	7032
鑫安汽车保险股份有限公司	Sanguard Automobile Insurance Co., Ltd.	8293	12002
利宝保险有限公司	Liberty Insurance Co., Ltd.	7699	15191
诚泰财产保险份有限公司	Cheng Tai Property Insurance Company Limited	8548	7656
富邦财产保险有限公司	Fubon Property Insurance Co., Ltd.	4806	5974
珠峰财产保险股份有限公司	Everest Property Insurance Co., Ltd.	14731	18520
中煤财产保险股份有限公司	China Coal Property Insurance Co., Ltd.	5995	11068
长江财产保险股份有限公司	Changjiang Property Insurance Co., Ltd.	1470	3462
众安在线财产保险股份有限公司	Zhongan Online Property Insurance Co., Ltd.	18965	30807
中国铁路财产保险自保有限公司	China Railway Property Insurance Holding Co., Ltd.	2913	1844
阳光渝融信用保证保险股份有限公司	Sunshine Yurong Credit and Guarantee Insurance Co., Ltd.	8	252
泰康在线财产保险股份有限公司	Taikang Online Property Insurance Co., Ltd.	7651	23614
易安财产保险股份有限公司	Yi An Property Insurance Co., Ltd.	1	
安心财产保险有限责任公司	Answern Property & Casualty Insurance Co.,Ltd.	21	666
人身保险公司	**Life Insurance Companies**	**14053994**	**14156489**
中国人寿保险股份有限公司	China Life Insurance(Group) Company	2491147	2459673
中国太平洋人寿保险股份有限公司	China Pacific Insurance(group)Co.,Ltd	528159	628430
中国平安人寿保险股份有限公司	Ping An Insurance (Group) Company of China , Ltd.	1238697	1444668
新华人寿保险股份有限公司	New China Insurance Co., Ltd.	393210	437839
泰康人寿保险股份有限公司	Taikang Life Insurance Company	869013	823356
太平人寿保险有限公司	Taiping Life Insurance Co.,Ltd.	1186923	1270649
民生人寿保险股份有限公司	Minsheng Life Insurance Co.,Ltd.	68676	74383
中英人寿保险有限公司	Aviva Cofco Life Insurance Co.,Ltd.	169753	184286
富德生命人寿保险股份有限公司	Sino Life Insurance Co.,Ltd.	360571	292231
北大方正人寿保险有限公司	Founder Meiji Yasuda Life Insurance Co.,Ltd	33431	35861
长城人寿保险股份公司	Great Wall Life Insurance Co.,Ltd.	60272	59581
中宏人寿保险股份公司	Manulife-Sinochem Insurance Co.,Ltd.	62293	78324
中德安联人寿保险有限公司	Allianz China Life Insurance Co.,Ltd.	28145	31615
农银人寿保险股份有限公司	ABC Life Insurance Co., Ltd	169940	131722
中国人民人寿保险股份有限公司	PICC Life Insurance Co.,Ltd.	701070	704360
华泰人寿保险有限公司	Huatai Life Insurance Co.,Ltd.	37588	41836
人保健康保险有限公司	PICC Health Insurance Co.,Ltd.	47645	27397
恒安标准人寿保险有限公司	Heng'an Standard Life Co.,ltd.	9440	13036

19-11 续表 2 continued

单位：万元 (10 000 yuan)

公司名称	Company Name	2017	2018
招商信诺保险有限公司	CIGNA&CMC Insurance Co.,Ltd.	37412	43282
合众人寿保险有限公司	Union Life Insurance Co.,Ltd.	118061	50054
阳光人寿保险有限公司	Sunshine Life Insurance Co.,Ltd.	179800	171280
中意人寿保险有限公司	General China Insurance Co.,Ltd.	46305	41924
华夏人寿保险有限公司	Huaxia China Insurance Co.,Ltd.	670831	1275640
中国平安养老保险股份有限公司	Ping An Insurance (Group) Company of China , Ltd.	62354	68451
太平养老保险股份有限公司	TaiPing Pension Company Limited	15270	18456
恒大人寿保险有限公司	Evergrande Life Insurance Company Limited	469721	522178
中邮人寿保险有限公司	China Post Lift Insurance Co.,Ltd.	268989	387789
幸福人寿保险有限公司	Happy Life Insurance Co.,Ltd.	126386	37713
中美联泰大都会人寿保险有限公司	Sino-US United Metlife Insurance Co.,Ltd.	27990	37293
国华人寿保险股份有限公司	Guohua Life Insurance Co.,Ltd.	272526	194455
和谐健康保险股份有限公司	Harmony Health Insurance Company Limited	381402	704360
安邦人寿保险股份有限公司	Anbang Life Insurance Co.,Ltd.	919616	6975
光大永明人寿保险有限公司	Sun Life Everbright Life Insurance Co.,Ltd.	53795	147653
工银安盛人寿保险有限公司	ICBC-AXA Assurance Co., Ltd.	202936	192017
百年人寿保险股份有限公司	Aeon Life Insurance Co.,Ltd.	157624	237747
中融人寿保险股份有限公司	Zhongrong Life Insurance Co.,Ltd.	42541	157671
英大泰和人寿保险股份有限公司	Yngda Taihe Life Insurance Co.,Ltd.	5529	12176
中银三星人寿保险有限公司	BOC Samsung Life Insurance Company Limited	53615	30233
建信人寿保险有限公司	CCB Life Insurance Company Limited	212966	159343
泰康养老保险股份有限公司	Taikang Pension Insurance Co.,Ltd.	16920	20125
同方全球人寿保险有限公司	Aegon THTF Life Insurance Co.,Ltd.	9545	14284
天安人寿保险股份有限公司	Tianan Life Insurance Company Limited of China Co.,Ltd.	567686	596413
东吴人寿保险股份有限公司	SooChow Life Insurance Company Limited Co.,Ltd.	65258	12368
利安人寿保险股份有限公司	Lian Life Insurance Co.,Ltd.	26612	40063
交银康联人寿保险有限公司	Bocomm Life Insurance Co.,Ltd.	47158	29470
前海人寿保险股份有限公司	Foresea Life Insurance Co.,Ltd.	466846	732772
长生人寿保险有限公司	Great Wall Changsheng Life Insurance Co.,Ltd.	42875	80787
安邦养老保险股份有限公司	Ampang Pension Insurance Co.,Ltd.	19660	24356
陆家嘴国泰人寿保险有限责任公司	Cathay Lujiazui Life Insurance Company Limited	8493	16846
太保安联健康保险股份有限公司	CPIC Allianz Health Insurance Co., Ltd.	14	173
平安健康保险股份有限公司	Ping An Health Insurance Company of China, Ltd.	919	12344
中信保诚人寿保险有限公司	CITIC Prudential Life Insurance Company Limited	368	8190

主要统计指标解释

信贷资金 指金融机构以信用方式积聚和分配的货币资金。金融机构信贷资金的来源有各项存款、金融债券、对国际金融机构负债、流通中现金、其他项目等；信贷资金的运用有各项贷款、有价证券及投资、黄金占款、外汇买卖、财政借款及在国际金融机构中的资产等。

存款 指企业、机关、团体或居民把货币资金存入银行或其他信贷机构保管，可随时或按约定时间支取款项并取得一定利息的一种信用活动形式。根据存款对象或性质的不同可划分为住户存款、非金融企业存款、政府存款、非银行业金融机构存款等科目。它是银行信贷资金的主要来源。

贷款 指银行或其他信贷机构根据资金必须归还的原则，按一定利率，为企业、个人等提供资金的一种信用活动形式。我国银行贷款分为短期贷款、中长期贷款、融资租赁、票据融资、各项垫款、境外贷款等。

保险公司 在中国境内的、经过保险监督管理部门批准设立，并依法登记注册的各类商业保险公司。

保险金额 指保险人承担赔偿或者给付保险金责任的最高限额。

保费 指投保人为取得保险人在约定范围内所承担赔偿责任而支付给保险人的费用。

赔款 指保险人根据保险合同的规定，向被保险人支付的赔偿保险责任损失的金额。

给付 包括死伤医疗给付和满期给付。死伤医疗给付是指保险人根据人寿保险及长期健康保险合同的规定，因被保险人在保险期内发生保险责任范围内的保险事故支付给被保险人(或受益人)的金额。满期给付是指被保险人生存期满，保险人按人寿保险合同规定支付给被保险人的满期保险金额。

Explanatory Notes on Main Statistical Indicators

Credit Funds refer to the monetary funds accumulated and distributed in the means of credit by the financial institutions. The sources of credit funds include various deposits, financial bonds, liabilities to international financial institutions, currency in circulation, other items. The uses of credit funds include loans, securities and investment, position for bullion purchase, foreign exchange trading, advances to treasury, and assets with international financial institutions.

Deposit is a form of credit by which enterprises, institutions, organizations or households can put money into banks and other credit institutions for safekeeping and interest earning and can withdraw anytime or at appointed time.l. According to different depositors, deposits are divided into household deposits, non financial enterprise deposits, government deposits, non banking financial institutions deposits. Deposits are major sources of the credit funds of banks.

Loan is a form of credit by which banks and other credit institutions provide funds at certain interest rate to enterprises and individuals in the light of the principle of unconditional repayment. Loans from Chinese banks include short-term loan, medium-term and long-term loans, financial lease, bill financing, various money advanced, foreign loans.

Insurance Companies refer to commercial insurance companies of various forms registered by law and established in China with the approval of insurance regulatory agencies.

Amount Insured refers to the maximum that the insurant will get for the claim of the case insured.

Premium is the fee paid by the insurant to the insurer to obtain the obligation of compensation from the insurance within the agreed terms.

Settled Claim is the compensation paid by the insurer to the insurant in accordance with the insurance contract.

Payment including payment for death, injury or medical treatment and mature payment. Payment for death, injury or medical treatment refers to the money paid to the insurant (or the beneficiary) in accordance with the life or health insurance contract when the insurant encounters accidents within the insured period covered in the contract. Mature payment refers to the mature payment to the insurant in accordance with the life insurance contract at the end of the insured period.

20

教育、科技和专利

Chapter 20 Education, Science, Technology and Patents

20-1 各类学校数
Number of Schools by Type

单位：所 (unit)

年份 Year	普通高等学校 Regular Institutions of Higher Education	中等职业学校 Secondary Vocational Schools	普通中学 Regular Secondary Schools	小学 Primary Schools	幼儿园 Kindergartens	特殊教育学校 Special Education Schools
1952	10		306	35373	609	
1957	13		488	43665	612	
1962	17		866	44683	305	
1965	20		3693	108974	1349	5
1970	18		2769	70263	687	3
1975	17		3287	86254	2397	3
1978	28		4605	72563	35306	3
1980	29		4524	67659	24814	3
1985	39		4017	61953	13280	9
1990	40		4332	55047	13831	22
1991	40		4433	53792	10478	27
1992	40		4460	53011	11148	45
1993	41		4545	52280	10216	52
1994	42		4572	51498	12079	52
1995	42		4578	55799	12485	53
1996	42		4506	48911	11602	59
1997	42		4420	46917	11223	55
1998	43		4448	46092	11385	62
1999	43		4375	45133	12016	63
2000	42		4321	43326	12780	63
2001	49		5154	31447	7875	69
2002	59		5093	25972	7935	68
2003	62		5000	24573	8388	70
2004	68		4965	21935	7602	73
2005	72		4995	19305	8875	83
2006	76		5181	17372	8596	88
2007	76		5093	15834	8580	88
2008	78		4937	13993	8425	93
2009	92		4809	12437	8562	95
2010	93	679	4738	9282	9483	100
2011	94	656	4704	8847	10162	107
2012	99	630	4643	8586	10794	113
2013	103	595	4630	7257	11759	119
2014	107	568	4633	6959	12111	122
2015	109	550	4590	6487	12365	124
2016	109	526	4555	5981	12903	125
2017	109	520	4476	5721	13243	127
2018	119	508	4484	5730	13396	128

注：中等职业学校中包括技工学校。各类学校基本情况由四川省教育厅提供(后同)。

a) Secondary vocational schools include Technical Schools.The basic statistics of schools is provided by the Provincial Department of Education (the same as follows).

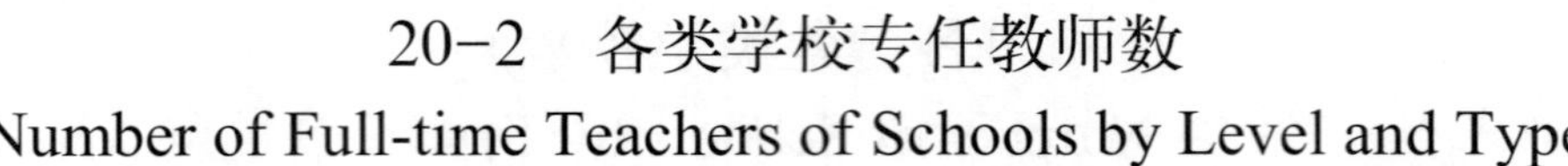

20-2 各类学校专任教师数
Number of Full-time Teachers of Schools by Level and Type

单位：人 (person)

年份 Year	普通高等学校 Regular Institutions of Higher Education	中等职业学校 Secondary Vocational Schools	普通中学 Regular Secondary Schools	小 学 Primary Schools	幼儿园 Kindergartens	特殊教育学校 Special Education Schools
1952	1228		5953	111229	1556	
1957	3238		11873	132141	4679	
1962	5675		18597	146639	4523	
1965	6125		29097	225914	4720	35
1970	6414		55788	213151	3992	53
1975	7487		92015	334794	1858	20
1978	9047		167540	342661	39245	25
1980	10562		152660	343175	39028	44
1985	14577		145715	340164	32284	115
1990	16058		176179	321087	43573	322
1991	16056		180737	314747	45528	416
1992	15767		185790	312380	49970	565
1993	16216		183492	313597	49873	610
1994	16208		186224	320196	54504	647
1995	16439		190184	320923	55420	728
1996	16799		193942	323713	56052	730
1997	16786		196636	330212	56107	837
1998	17228		199357	334999	57738	987
1999	17891		207305	336356	58165	1148
2000	18418		217039	331551	58128	1113
2001	21984		227035	325123	30956	942
2002	26852		237425	321193	30591	973
2003	31372		247098	316029	32515	994
2004	39306		253358	307940	33997	1068
2005	44854		258924	307113	36654	1174
2006	52211		265540	306886	37530	1318
2007	55903		269967	306149	39337	1407
2008	59174		273559	307687	41827	1478
2009	61772		279414	306528	45136	1572
2010	64991	44051	284962	305741	51909	1711
2011	67448	48873	285755	305508	57528	1784
2012	73137	48186	290366	304899	65403	1941
2013	76795	45952	292629	305619	77336	2055
2014	81404	46767	292967	304909	86414	2211
2015	84430	46869	293165	308059	96885	2355
2016	85832	46621	294676	314406	105592	2503
2017	83949	46314	298805	325016	117052	2798
2018	86997	46046	304586	329927	122972	2970

20-3 各类学校在校学生数

Number of Enrollments of Formal Education by Level and Type

单位：人 (person)

年份 Year	普通高等学校 Regular Institutions of Higher Education	中等职业学校 Secondary Vocational Schools	普通中学 Regular Secondary Schools	小 学 Primary Schools	幼儿园 Kindergartens	特殊教育学校 Special Education Schools
1952	9104		155252	3807776		
1957	19565		320254	4574044		
1962	36587		324216	3962046		
1965	28236		669901	7859341	127921	398
1970			1481952	6341703	95325	503
1975	21203		2085366	11013460	199412	345
1978	35715		3838846	10745859	1389229	339
1980	48497		2974390	11441551	957632	347
1985	72812		2516824	10418664	833754	623
1990	91866		2892023	6873322	1062885	1422
1991	91365		2853499	6500936	1375654	1846
1992	96678		2724618	6424068	1572526	3133
1993	113465		2481484	6662850	1576287	3261
1994	125944		2561995	7020619	1689081	3972
1995	126280		2705466	7350179	1777728	509
1996	131459		2765730	7797611	1793653	7400
1997	140451		2748214	8270885	1779648	9444
1998	151905		2908894	8438446	1860762	10104
1999	180256		3364576	8270859	1923949	10771
2000	235470		3919813	8026506	1892626	8224
2001	316701		4282666	7948490	1658864	14616
2002	412357		4568419	7785414	1595534	13390
2003	512663		4810712	7554308	1588575	15839
2004	637340		4909216	7365754	1527298	17354
2005	775436		4855390	7145093	1526827	24788
2006	860640		5014951	7217750	1562466	28621
2007	918438		5054691	6965306	1560935	39900
2008	991072		5026261	6488221	1597919	41739
2009	1035934		4990033	6170471	1707263	41767
2010	1086215	1399557	4900896	5921080	1887545	41839
2011	1139316	1407636	4778133	5798017	2110148	40898
2012	1223680	1398563	4558398	5607407	2192890	44287
2013	1270818	1302260	4233225	5259536	2314907	43731
2014	1328329	1195396	4073109	5313193	2407717	42289
2015	1387889	1107828	3934438	5417353	2481681	43251
2016	1446559	1019183	3895408	5495234	2593131	47780
2017	1499715	973974	3904323	5518361	2625168	53461
2018	1564710	941636	4007635	5554589	2608595	56851

注：普通高等学校学生数为普通本专科学生数；特殊教育在校生数含随班就读、送教上门等人数(后同)。

a) Number of students in regular institutions of higher education is the number of ordinary college students. Number of students in special education schools includes the number of students enrolled in the class. (the same as follows)

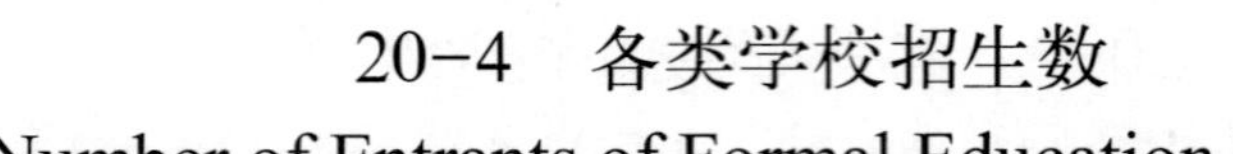

20-4 各类学校招生数

Number of Entrants of Formal Education by Type

单位：人 (person)

年份 Year	普通高等学校 Regular Institutions of Higher Education	中等职业学校 Secondary Vocational Schools	普通中学 Regular Secondary Schools	小学 Primary Schools	特殊教育学校 Special Education Schools
1952	2353		81221		
1957	4823		116364	128678	
1962	4895		121261	1544971	
1965	6570		316756	2302127	
1970			747057	1899719	
1975	7569		1200679	2800872	33
1978	14916		1609352	2649457	34
1980	11610		1106948	2519225	87
1985	26069		943009	1455993	281
1990	26962		1019786	999538	485
1991	26919		971091	994759	536
1992	33613		947724	1179830	1047
1993	42058		883979	1364953	671
1994	40259		981989	1459974	992
1995	41714		1041585	1479126	1423
1996	43774		948623	1412690	1210
1997	46196		964969	1397645	1386
1998	49035		1176141	1293404	1232
1999	65481		1427007	1240217	1163
2000	95565		1527602	1256880	1182
2001	119470		1595486	1338908	2676
2002	152754		1717062	1320396	2157
2003	180308		1746751	1223734	2550
2004	215243		1696131	1169163	2726
2005	267198		1684360	1092214	3916
2006	266491		1767927	1151856	4503
2007	297566		1758759	1083015	6169
2008	328341		1754692	1006479	6333
2009	307127		1692325	945131	6483
2010	337892	575964	1641724	1231433	6684
2011	351846	575321	1593466	996827	6767
2012	381519	543472	1510249	1009618	8398
2013	376806	531212	1390078	950346	8230
2014	408941	482493	1332203	929667	8014
2015	436467	441280	1297254	934786	8096
2016	439286	414212	1322169	930103	9579
2017	460776	395511	1335486	911391	10361
2018	484148	376168	1385397	952217	10298

20-5 各类学校毕业生数

Number of Graduates of Formal Education by Type

单位：人 (person)

年份 Year	普通高等学校 Regular Institutions of Higher Education	中等职业学校 Secondary Vocational Schools	普通中学 Regular Secondary Schools	小 学 Primary Schools	特殊教育学校 Special Education Schools
1952	2742				
1957	1773		75254	739606	
1962	5317		80499	303087	
1965	8489		104984	399595	
1970	4796		142279	829050	
1975	5701		626880	1279795	35
1978	5884		1268232	1782504	35
1980	7130		934730	1603760	82
1985	13592		728872	1446826	57
1990	27672		746250	1408170	66
1991	27041		763298	1187057	8
1992	28348		813783	1074324	148
1993	26088		793429	940854	212
1994	28826		707196	999601	229
1995	40915		644932	1018463	336
1996	37872		719950	897863	445
1997	35658		818628	875741	552
1998	36672		868089	1069005	1036
1999	35465		804529	1327862	943
2000	40104		818595	1397579	1190
2001	44602		992309	1347390	1824
2002	52405		1224114	1361854	1677
2003	74307		1299710	1324117	2090
2004	100998		1385780	1221872	2131
2005	139328		1510287	1187842	2160
2006	173287		1527428	1221708	2953
2007	228028		1554082	1247914	4565
2008	247707		1575017	1253417	5312
2009	252214		1571659	1166577	5933
2010	278577	357279	1587603	1113444	5817
2011	289165	387422	1606332	1042069	5486
2012	286756	405599	1571830	1001656	7969
2013	318407	447222	1512136	886816	9191
2014	338643	498424	1422928	830744	9004
2015	361510	452593	1379237	803044	8634
2016	362127	433944	1329596	842414	8192
2017	386145	386220	1293825	869517	9557
2018	393689	363828	1262078	919381	10094

20-6 高等学校基本情况(2018年)
Basic Statistics on Institutions of Higher Education(2018)

单位：所、人 (unit, person)

项 目	Item	学校数(所) Number of Institutions	毕业生数 Graduates	招生数 Entrants	在校学生数 Enrollment	教职工数 Staff and Workers	#校本部 Main Campus
合 计	**Total**	**120**	**393689**	**484148**	**1564710**	**125535**	**120431**
#女	Female		215734	258294	834748	61114	58785
一、普通高等学校	Regular Institutions of Higher Education	119	393543	484148	1564620	125535	120431
综合大学	Comprehensive University	38	136519	169898	524371	40295	37695
理工院校	Science and Engineering College	38	119357	151133	483189	40998	39917
农业院校	Agriculture College	2	11890	12573	48612	4240	3635
医药院校	Medicine College	8	22873	26641	96199	8084	7997
师范院校	Teacher Training College	12	47626	57521	195649	13463	12982
财经院校	Economics and Finance College	7	18642	21652	67199	5917	5870
政法院校	Politics and Law College	2	2702	3000	9867	755	747
体育院校	Physical Culture College	2	2147	2361	9534	1248	1245
艺术院校	Art Institues	6	16067	22358	67208	6434	6302
民族院校	College of Nationalities	2	8982	9352	36814	2646	2586
语文院校	Chinese College	2	6738	7659	25978	1455	1455
二、成人高等学校	Adult Institutions of Higher Education	1	146		90		

注：毕业生数、招生数、在校学生数合计中含成人高等学校普通本、专科学生的情况。
a) The sum of graduates,entrants and enrollment includes the data of students in regular college course and specialized subjects of adult institutions of higher education.

20-6 续表 continued

单位：所、人 (unit, person)

项 目	Item	专任教师数 Full-time Teachers	正高级 Senior	副高级 Sub-senior	中级 Middle	初级 Junior	未定职称 No Rank
合 计	**Total**	**86997**	**9666**	**23447**	**33201**	**14987**	**5696**
#女	Female	42924	2682	10466	17589	8980	3207
综合大学	Comprehensive University	27615	3058	7541	10169	4750	2097
理工院校	Science and Engineering College	27582	3091	7789	10932	4454	1316
农业院校	Agriculture College	3050	354	673	1266	554	203
医药院校	Medicine College	6102	758	1628	2559	993	164
师范院校	Teacher Training College	10114	1218	2814	3893	1635	554
财经院校	Economics and Finance College	3973	426	1105	1328	678	436
政法院校	Politics and Law College	510	41	127	193	95	54
体育院校	Physical Culture College	747	83	181	185	212	86
艺术院校	Art Institues	4302	332	890	1312	1230	538
民族院校	College of Nationalities	1895	267	568	839	100	121
语文院校	Chinese College	1107	38	131	525	286	127

20-7 普通本科分学科学生数(2018年)
Number of Regular Students for Normal Courses in Higher Education Institutions by Discipline(2018)

单位: 人 (person)

项 目	Item	毕业生数 Graduates	招生数 Entrants	在校学生数 Enrollment
合 计	**Total**	**186361**	**242838**	**913215**
#女	Female	102045	131593	492773
哲 学	Philosophy	27	38	132
经济学	Economics	7457	9113	35822
法 学	Law	6025	7428	28062
教育学	Education	7912	12049	41631
文 学	Literature	17079	24295	89671
历史学	History	932	1122	4314
理 学	Science	12456	16113	60029
工 学	Engineering	60948	79233	295216
农 学	Agriculture	2629	3353	11399
医 学	Medicine	12832	14629	66235
管理学	Management	35080	43077	162200
艺术学	Art	22984	32388	118504

20-8 分学科研究生数(2018年)
Number of Postgraduates by Academic Field(2018)

单位: 人 (person)

项 目	Item	毕业生数 Graduates	#攻读博士学位 Study in Doctor Degree	招生数 Entrants	#攻读博士学位 Study in Doctor Degree	在校学生数 Enrollment	#攻读博士学位 Study in Doctor Degree
合 计	**Total**	**26981**	**2249**	**39003**	**3804**	**128271**	**16787**
#女	Female	13257	849	20223	1585	59760	6118
哲 学	Philosophy	178	22	201	24	683	124
经济学	Economics	1725	105	2122	190	5715	1087
法 学	Law	1505	74	2069	149	6258	666
教育学	Education	1459	4	2038	34	6213	124
文 学	Literature	1295	73	1509	110	4630	570
历史学	History	243	28	265	44	913	270
理 学	Science	2014	295	2649	447	8069	1817
工 学	Engineering	10360	893	15115	1648	56645	7935
农 学	Agriculture	1105	76	2007	128	6887	506
医 学	Medicine	2884	545	4182	764	11406	2270
军事学	Strategics	2		1		14	
管理学	Management	3336	118	5770	251	17548	1310
艺术学	Art	875	16	1075	15	3290	108
专业学位	**Professional Degree**	**11184**	**172**	**20666**	**345**	**68028**	**813**

注：不含在职人员攻读硕士学位人数。
a)Data in this table does not include the number of on-the-job personnel studying for master's degree.

20-9 中等职业学校基本情况(2018年)
Basic Statistics on Secondary Vocational Schools(2018)

单位：人 (person)

项　目	Item	毕业生数 Graduates	招生数 Entrants	在校学生数 Enrollment	专任教师数 Full-time Teachers
合　计	**Total**	**327834**	**325773**	**820060**	**37892**
#女	Female	163238	147142	383349	19485
#专业课	Speciality Course				19733
农林牧渔类	Farming,Forestry,Animal Husbandry and Fishery	15389	12260	28757	702
资源环境类	Resouces and Environment	380	69	471	12
能源与新能源类	Energy and New Energy	531	331	1296	89
土木水利类	Civil Engineering and Water Conservancy	12806	11848	27491	808
加工制造类	Machining and Manufacture	47247	39375	95687	2632
石油化工类	Petroleum Chemical	686	498	1358	80
轻纺食品类	Textile Food	2341	2552	5373	200
交通运输类	Transportation	45830	52290	142165	2052
信息技术类	Information Technology	63375	70658	153239	3804
医药卫生类	Medicine and Sanitation	38541	29054	95625	1672
休闲保健类	Leisure Care	1176	1093	2048	72
财经商贸类	Fanancial Business	25009	24046	60784	1605
旅游服务类	Tourism Service	23956	25824	58269	1581
文化艺术类	Culture and Art	10183	10442	22506	1004
体育与健身	Sports and Fitness	924	1074	2923	281
教育类	Education	33713	36567	105663	2375
司法服务类	Judicial Service	538	435	1055	27
公共管理与服务类	Public Management and Service	5209	7059	14782	358
其他	Others		298	568	379
文化基础课	Basic Courses				16312
实习指导课	Practice Guidance Section				1847

注：专任教师中含文化基础课和实习指导课教师，以上数据不包含技工学校。
a) Full-time teachers include basic cultural courses and practical guidance section teachers,but exclude teachers in technical schools.

20-10 技工学校基本情况
Basic Statistics on Technical Schools

单位：所、人 (unit, person)

年份 Year	学校数 Schools	毕业生数 Graduates	招生数 Entrants	在校学生数 Enrollment	教职工数 Staff and Teachers	培训社会人员数 Number of Training for Social Personnel	#失业人数 Unemployed	#农村劳动者 Rural Laborers
1990	387	37673	46334	119125	25778	23049		
1995	407	60392	54438	130896	26504			
2000	186	20177	16753	40147	9843	54335	6830	
2005	121	28326	47042	101037	8992	141836	14470	36156
2006	122	37684	53857	120462	9821	129603	19098	36935
2007	112	40946	65242	136395	9671	131459	18164	49701
2008	120	40816	68771	144608	10080	153200	16114	53324
2009	121	43214	64335	162614	10404	227563	18741	66781
2010	116	46910	52019	141407	10136	181246	12921	57617
2011	115	46500	42362	136347	9368	204035	19838	58244
2012	92	33009	41243	107175	8064	181758	9923	63233
2013	87	30804	39157	113406	8354	180313	14542	39216
2014	85	30337	38651	116168	8324	132163	9752	33996
2015	83	29507	40500	120337	9589	130328	11112	29498
2016	81	30136	39632	106669	10480	117333	14350	36776
2017	84	32730	46180	113961	10775	127922	7561	29794
2018	89	35994	50395	121576	11694	137377	9921	28713

注：①本表由四川省人力资源和社会保障厅提供；②1996年以前的数据包括重庆市部分；③2009年开始，原指标“培训社会人员结业数”调整为“培训社会人员数”。

a) Data of the table are provided by Sichuan Provincial Department of Human Resources and Social Security; b)The data before 1996 included ChongQing; c) Since 2009,indicator "number of training personnel exit" is adjusted to indicator "number of training for social personnel".

20-11　成人教育基本情况(2018年)
Basic Statistics on Adult Education(2018)

单位：所、人 (unit, person)

项　目	Item	学校数 Schools	毕(结)业生数 Graduates	招生数 Entrants	在校学生数 Enrollment	教职工数 Teachers and Staff	#专任教师 Full-time Teachers
成人高等教育	**Adult Education Schools**	**91**	**123537**	**130979**	**307365**	**1597**	**925**
职工高等学校	Schools of Higher Education for Staff and Workers	11	3612	4972	9611	981	616
管理干部学院	Colleges for Management Cadres						
教育学院	Pedagogical Colleges						
广播电视大学	Radio and TV Universities	2	4920	5040	14550	616	309
普通高校成人教育	Adult Higher Education	78	115005	120967	283204		
成人中学	**Secondary Schools for Adults**						
农民中学(初中)	Secondary Schools for Peasants						
成人技术培训学校	**Technical Training Schools for Adults**	**4147**	**1996286**		**2117485**	**18268**	**10949**
职工技术培训学校	Technical Training Schools for Staff and Workers	122	298036		315271	4450	3270
农村成人文化技术培训学校(机构)	Technical Training Schools for Peasants	3555	1513987		1607944	9391	4577
教育部门办	Sponsored by Education Department	3409	1413326		1501595	8888	4179
其他部门办	Sponsored by other Department	92	83797		87285	58	35
民办	Sponsored by Private	54	16864		19064	445	363
其他培训机构	Other Training Schools for Adults	470	184263		194270	4427	3102
教育部门办	Sponsored by Education Department	30	81190		81220	1040	770
其他部门办	Sponsored by other Department	81	14465		17826	657	179
民办	Sponsored by Private	359	88608		95224	2730	2153

注：成人技术培训学校数据中含其它培训机构数据。
a) Data of adult technical training schools include data of other training institutions.

20-12　各类学校女学生和女教师数
Number of Female Students and Teachers of School by Type

单位：人　(person)

指　标	Item	2010	2013	2014	2015	2016	2017	2018
女学生	**Number of Female Students**							
普通高等学校	Regular Institutions of Higher Education	543727	664566	701944	740606	773424	801108	834748
中等职业学校	Secondary Vocational Schools	674900	612327	547630	495967	454105	417361	383349
普通中学	Regular Secondary Schools	2371942	2074412	1992167	1924574	1907230	1915578	1968154
高中	Senior	724940	772875	760445	749832	738709	724463	714093
初中	Junior	1647002	1301537	1231722	1174742	1168521	1191115	1254061
小学	Primary Schools	2799856	2504884	2530725	2586309	2628154	2648104	2669666
特殊教育	Special Schools	14002	15656	15451	15894	17957	20171	21984
女教师	**Number of Female Teachers**							
普通高等学校	Regular Institutions of Higher Education	29297	35473	38056	39740	41121	40966	42924
中等职业学校	Secondary Vocational Schools	15680	18765	19075	19085	19069	19253	19485
普通中学	Regular Secondary Schools	120391	130296	133632	136332	140003	145893	151549
高中	Senior	32636	38945	40884	42558	44096	45644	47370
初中	Junior	87755	91351	92748	93774	95907	100249	104179
小学	Primary Schools	158241	166311	172094	179892	189238	202473	210586
特殊教育	Special Schools	1166	1423	1558	1679	1795	2042	2168

注：中等职业学校中不包括技工学校。
a) Female teachers in secondary vocational schools don't include technical schools.

20-13　各市(州)普通高等学校基本情况(2018年)
Basic Statistics on Regular Senior Secondary Schools by Region(2018)

单位：所、人　(unit, person)

市(州)	Region	学校数 Number of Schools	毕业生数 Graduates	招生数 Entrants	在校学生数 Enrollment	专任教师数 Full-time Teachers
全　省	**Sichuan**	**119**	**393543**	**484148**	**1564620**	**86997**
成都市	Chengdu	57	212486	250680	840297	49448
自贡市	Zigong	2	9132	13079	39868	2000
攀枝花市	Panzhihua	2	6500	7712	26513	1221
泸州市	Luzhou	6	14110	15144	47978	2664
德阳市	Deyang	8	21889	27136	80224	4283
绵阳市	Mianyang	10	33462	46566	145055	7151
广元市	Guangyuan	2	4510	5681	14939	642
遂宁市	Suining	1	4387	4631	13389	608
内江市	Neijiang	3	7923	10914	34741	1724
乐山市	Leshan	3	11536	14468	47087	2509
南充市	Nanchong	4	19344	22341	78078	4094
眉山市	Meishan	6	5930	9872	27843	1507
宜宾市	Yibin	2	7787	9805	28200	1414
广安市	Guangan	1	3123	4771	11635	588
达州市	Dazhou	2	7051	8881	26167	1330
雅安市	Yaan	2	12050	14016	51388	3199
巴中市	Bazhong	1	1544	2026	5454	209
资阳市	Ziyang	1	2014	2241	4370	218
阿坝藏族羌族自治州	Aba	2	1773	4028	10076	506
甘孜藏族自治州	Ganzi	1	2374	2449	8877	393
凉山彝族自治州	Liangshan	3	4618	7707	22441	1289

20-14 各市(州)中等职业教育基本情况(2018年)
Basic Statistics on Secondary Vocational Schools by Region(2018)

单位：所、人 (unit, person)

市(州)	Region	学校数 Number of Schools	毕业生数 Graduates	招生数 Entrants	在校学生数 Enrollment	教职工数 Teacher and Staff	#专任教师 Full-time Teachers
全 省	**Sichuan**	**419**	**327834**	**325773**	**820060**	**48342**	**37892**
成都市	Chengdu	86	75254	65414	199494	13122	9453
自贡市	Zigong	19	10054	12056	24241	1466	1189
攀枝花市	Panzhihua	4	4073	3789	10337	727	571
泸州市	Luzhou	17	27593	21133	60550	2612	2226
德阳市	Deyang	18	10453	10827	25827	1772	1238
绵阳市	Mianyang	23	21877	19183	42194	1998	1716
广元市	Guangyuan	12	8431	7892	18843	1298	1141
遂宁市	Suining	14	10485	10082	21364	1572	1397
内江市	Neijiang	22	14402	14721	30682	1837	1318
乐山市	Leshan	19	11738	11251	31399	2020	1444
南充市	Nanchong	37	22841	22841	57632	3682	2737
眉山市	Meishan	17	11949	10523	24683	1854	1269
宜宾市	Yibin	19	21628	30540	68766	3021	2685
广安市	Guangan	23	16794	18022	40515	1732	1486
达州市	Dazhou	33	22255	27177	62819	3879	3285
雅安市	Yaan	8	4130	4736	12561	511	409
巴中市	Bazhong	18	13069	11558	27239	1627	1314
资阳市	Ziyang	7	9629	9764	19855	989	857
阿坝藏族羌族自治州	Aba	4	1047	1034	3354	399	311
甘孜藏族自治州	Ganzi	3	1667	2041	5969	358	301
凉山彝族自治州	Liangshan	16	8465	11189	31736	1866	1545

注：以上数据不含技工学校。
a) Data in this table exclude technical schools.

20-15 各市(州)普通高中基本情况(2018年)
Basic Statistics on Regular Senior Secondary Schools by Region(2018)

单位：所、人 (unit, person)

市(州)	Region	学校数 Number of Schools	毕业生数 Graduates	招生数 Entrants	在校学生数 Enrollment	专任教师数 Full-time Teachers
全　省	**Sichuan**	**768**	**479939**	**461665**	**1389515**	**99647**
成都市	Chengdu	149	70203	67726	200476	18744
自贡市	Zigong	22	13248	13568	41153	2691
攀枝花市	Panzhihua	8	8761	7081	23829	1622
泸州市	Luzhou	30	26075	30486	83283	5409
德阳市	Deyang	23	17683	16685	49502	3576
绵阳市	Mianyang	36	36209	35096	105140	7486
广元市	Guangyuan	27	19201	15797	51099	3986
遂宁市	Suining	29	19831	17555	54556	4287
内江市	Neijiang	39	18847	19529	56772	3465
乐山市	Leshan	25	13911	13411	40453	3606
南充市	Nanchong	64	45012	37930	119800	7469
眉山市	Meishan	29	16631	14610	45482	3360
宜宾市	Yibin	34	27000	28069	82202	5966
广安市	Guangan	40	28138	24405	77331	5346
达州市	Dazhou	46	34816	38172	110560	6317
雅安市	Yaan	15	6844	7456	21928	1519
巴中市	Bazhong	47	29905	25991	82780	5380
资阳市	Ziyang	28	13460	14233	41490	2518
阿坝藏族羌族自治州	Aba	18	5351	5182	16025	1403
甘孜藏族自治州	Ganzi	20	4905	4924	14545	978
凉山彝族自治州	Liangshan	39	23908	23759	71109	4519

20-16 各市(州)普通初中基本情况(2018年)
Basic Statistics on Regular Junior Secondary Schools by Region(2018)

单位：所、人 (unit, person)

市(州)	Region	学校数 Number of Schools	毕业生数 Graduates	招生数 Entrants	在校学生数 Enrollment	专任教师数 Full-time Teachers
全　省	**Sichuan**	**3716**	**782139**	**923732**	**2618120**	**204939**
成都市	Chengdu	460	118912	141002	399699	33032
自贡市	Zigong	117	24664	31865	87579	6089
攀枝花市	Panzhihua	44	12737	12291	38206	3529
泸州市	Luzhou	191	58262	77735	219917	12772
德阳市	Deyang	123	25061	28060	80204	7386
绵阳市	Mianyang	183	41689	48040	136437	11034
广元市	Guangyuan	127	21092	23204	65847	6456
遂宁市	Suining	129	23519	26223	73847	7027
内江市	Neijiang	137	33227	44268	122800	8457
乐山市	Leshan	167	24926	29507	84017	7411
南充市	Nanchong	424	54762	62955	179131	15945
眉山市	Meishan	162	22348	23270	68530	6750
宜宾市	Yibin	246	57475	65689	189158	13513
广安市	Guangan	236	41682	42798	124264	11079
达州市	Dazhou	347	68119	75132	217798	15807
雅安市	Yaan	73	13773	16472	46092	3786
巴中市	Bazhong	170	37891	33434	103324	9595
资阳市	Ziyang	167	25649	36212	100881	7017
阿坝藏族羌族自治州	Aba	37	9279	9509	27630	2734
甘孜藏族自治州	Ganzi	31	11860	13977	39282	2951
凉山彝族自治州	Liangshan	145	55212	82089	213477	12569

20-17 各市(州)普通小学基本情况(2018年)
Basic Statistics on Primary Schools by Region(2018)

单位：所、人 (unit, person)

市(州)	Region	学校数 Number of Schools	毕业生数 Graduates	招生数 Entrants	在校学生数 Enrollment	专任教师 Full-time Teachers
全 省	**Sichuan**	**5730**	**919381**	**952217**	**5554589**	**329927**
成都市	Chengdu	590	141437	188396	991803	53673
自贡市	Zigong	121	31572	26781	173007	9635
攀枝花市	Panzhihua	60	11666	11029	67922	4891
泸州市	Luzhou	224	76534	51715	357281	18851
德阳市	Deyang	203	27435	32113	185068	11137
绵阳市	Mianyang	409	42808	49000	280470	16207
广元市	Guangyuan	264	23204	25170	154143	11555
遂宁市	Suining	196	25634	31535	177921	11537
内江市	Neijiang	273	43713	33305	213472	12742
乐山市	Leshan	227	29623	31581	181100	11348
南充市	Nanchong	265	61335	60396	360652	23588
眉山市	Meishan	172	23086	29070	159705	9969
宜宾市	Yibin	306	65250	61827	377401	21349
广安市	Guangan	192	42721	39779	239306	14848
达州市	Dazhou	283	73543	62680	396299	25551
雅安市	Yaan	158	17108	14310	88088	6059
巴中市	Bazhong	203	32737	34443	196797	15620
资阳市	Ziyang	180	35399	26131	176225	9675
阿坝藏族羌族自治州	Aba	243	10196	11298	63334	6531
甘孜藏族自治州	Ganzi	376	15667	23871	108303	7615
凉山彝族自治州	Liangshan	785	88713	107787	606292	27546

20-18 各市(州)幼儿园基本情况(2018年)
Basic Statistics on Kindergartens by Region(2018)

单位：所、个、人 (unit, person)

市(州)	Region	园数 Number of Kindergartens	班数 Number of Classes	幼儿数 Children Enrollment	教职工数 Teachers and Staff	#教师 Teachers
全　省	**Sichuan**	**13396**	**88344**	**2608595**	**217286**	**122972**
成都市	Chengdu	2528	18604	565180	79715	39198
自贡市	Zigong	429	2362	67971	5560	3155
攀枝花市	Panzhihua	194	1122	31738	3643	1894
泸州市	Luzhong	723	4488	136813	8732	5483
德阳市	Deyang	337	2811	89262	6855	3795
绵阳市	Mianyang	792	5281	144589	14207	7422
广元市	Guangyuan	308	2469	68554	4320	2728
遂宁市	Suining	512	3244	94042	7811	5132
内江市	Neijiang	673	3079	91791	7115	4212
乐山市	Leshan	732	3452	93903	8700	5177
南充市	Nanchong	793	5458	164262	9629	6474
眉山市	Meishan	454	2990	90301	7143	4086
宜宾市	Yibin	928	5089	153128	11574	7258
广安市	Guangan	688	3726	112295	7584	4867
达州市	Dazhou	741	6443	179367	10129	6136
雅安市	Yaan	268	1498	42019	3205	2046
巴中市	Bazhong	260	3522	89742	3926	2586
资阳市	Ziyang	748	2518	71272	4991	3244
阿坝藏族羌族自治州	Aba	308	1139	30670	1795	1319
甘孜藏族自治州	Ganzi	400	1245	36391	1531	1180
凉山彝族自治州	Liangshan	580	7804	255305	9121	5580

20-19　研究与试验发展(R&D)经费构成情况
Basic Statistics on Research and Development Activities

指　　标		Item		2005	2010	2015	2016	2017	2018
研究与试验发展(R&D)经费	(万元)	Funds for R&D	(10 000 yuan)	962450	2706452	5028761	5614193	6378500	7370813
地区生产总值(GDP)	(亿元)	GDP	(100 million yuan)	7385.10	17185.48	30053.10	32934.54	36980.20	40678.13
R&D经费占地区生产总值（GDP)比例	(%)	R&D Funds as Percentage of GDP	(%)	1.30	1.57	1.67	1.72	1.72	1.81
R&D经费按执行部门分组		**Grouped by Executive Departments**							
科研机构	(万元)	Scientific Research Institutions	(10 000 yuan)	384195	1239870	2116421	2173686	2211427	2391390
高等院校	(万元)	Institutions of Higher Education	(10 000 yuan)	145941	363509	465250	478284	558042	662684
企业	(万元)	Enterprises	(10 000 yuan)	422936	1061086	2402691	2915165	3558715	4257561
#工业企业	(万元)	Industrial Enterprises	(10 000 yuan)	397645	879858	2238051	2572607	3010846	3423923
其他	(万元)	Others	(10 000 yuan)	9378	41987	44399	47058	50316	59179
R&D经费按资金来源分组		**Grouped by Funding Sources**							
政府资金	(万元)	Government Appropriation Func	(10 000 yuan)	438399	1512528	2302223	2404210	2455639	2909491
企业资金	(万元)	Funds Raised by Enterprises	(10 000 yuan)	456173	1136088	2439994	2930224	3602613	4234597
境外资金	(万元)	Foreign Funds	(10 000 yuan)	3966	5958	12915	10611	5505	8863
其他资金	(万元)	Other Funds	(10 000 yuan)	63912	51878	273629	269147	314742	217862

20-20　研究与试验发展(R&D)情况
Basic Statistics on Research and Development by Region

年　份	R&D人员折合全时人员(人年) Full-time Equivalent of R&D Personnel (man-year)	#研究人员 Researchers	R&D经费内部支出(万元) Internal Expenditure on R&D (10 000 yuan)	#日常性支出 Routine Expenses
2001	48180	35325	574712	506285
2002	61312	44957	619233	571565
2003	57867	43995	794211	736462
2004	60201	46373	780066	713398
2005	65747	51403	962450	894850
2006	67932	53552	1075659	984546
2007	78452	62595	1391130	1273338
2008	87557	63130	1622607	1537790
2009	85921	48786	2144590	1755258
2010	83506	45205	2706452	2031519
2011	82485	44005	2941010	2371221
2012	98010	52059	3508589	2747195
2013	109708	57956	3999702	3133297
2014	119676	62756	4493285	3577596
2015	116842	67516	5028761	4274116
2016	124614	70834	5614193	4857028
2017	144821	77241	6378500	5546985
2018	158847	81071	7370813	6483823

注：R&D人员折合全时人员中的研究人员，在2009年及以前为科学家和工程师。

a) Indicator of researchers in the full-time equivalent of R&D personnel is the indicator of scientists and engineers before 2009.

20-21 各市(州)研究与试验发展(R&D)情况(2018年)

Basic Statistics on Research and Development by Region(2018)

市(州)	Region	R&D人员折合全时人员(人年) Full-time Equivalent of R&D Personnel (man-year)	#研究人员 Researchers	R&D经费内部支出(万元) Internal Expenditure on R&D (10 000 yuan)	#日常性支出 Routine Expenses
全　省	**Sichuan**	**158847**	**81071**	**7370813**	**6483823**
成都市	Chengdu	88811	49427	3923101	3504387
自贡市	Zigong	2850	1294	109506	98141
攀枝花市	Panzhihua	2717	1018	144439	140379
泸州市	Luzhou	3144	1394	122896	93120
德阳市	Deyang	10394	4926	572636	500168
绵阳市	Mianyang	28480	14041	1523706	1283309
广元市	Guangyuan	1172	546	41830	36560
遂宁市	Suining	2019	568	86082	75749
内江市	Neijiang	1918	830	57641	52875
乐山市	Leshan	2238	837	150290	119058
南充市	Nanchong	2802	1503	103588	93379
眉山市	Meishan	1421	390	50898	44576
宜宾市	Yibin	5245	1848	244450	221975
广安市	Guangan	630	186	15196	13596
达州市	Dazhou	1763	606	67787	62343
雅安市	Yaan	1227	742	63378	58051
巴中市	Bazhong	406	127	17288	14114
资阳市	Ziyang	492	183	19236	16376
阿坝藏族羌族自治州	Aba	319	168	9915	9649
甘孜藏族自治州	Ganzi	214	132	3657	3364
凉山彝族自治州	Liangshan	586	307	43296	42657

20-22 各市(州)县级以上政府部门属研究与开发机构及情报文献机构数、人员数(2018年)

Number and Personnel of State-owned Research and Development Institutions and Information and Literature Institutions at and above County Level by Region(2018)

单位：个、人 (unit, person)

市(州)	Region	合 计 Total Number		自然科学技术领域 Field of Natural Sciences and Technology			社会、人文科学技术领域 Field of Social Sciences and Humanities			科技情报和文献机构 Scientific-Technical Information and Literature Institutions		
		机构 Institutions	从业人员 Employees	机构 Institutions	从业人员 Employees	#科技活动人员 S & T Personnel	机构 Institutions	从业人员 Employees	#科技活动人员 S & T Personnel	机构 Institutions	从业人员 Employees	#科技活动人员 S & T Personnel
全 省	**Sichuan**	**139**	**15147**	**96**	**13126**	**9606**	**19**	**1226**	**1071**	**24**	**795**	**728**
成都市	Chengdu	72	11901	51	10281	7448	12	1069	932	9	551	490
自贡市	Zigong	5	318	3	260	249	1	33	28	1	25	25
攀枝花市	Panzhihua	4	212	3	193	136				1	19	19
泸州市	Luzhou	3	72	2	52	37				1	20	20
德阳市	Deyang	3	157	1	112	112	1	28	22	1	17	17
绵阳市	Mianyang	1	117	1	117	110						
广元市	Guangyuan	5	122	4	107	38				1	15	15
遂宁市	Suining	1	9							1	9	9
内江市	Neijiang	3	280	2	263	240				1	17	17
乐山市	Leshan	2	86	2	86	60						
南充市	Nanchong	5	365	4	348	286				1	17	14
眉山市	Meishan											
宜宾市	Yibin	7	510	6	496	213				1	14	12
广安市	Guangan	1	14				1	14	12			
达州市	Dazhou	5	175	3	133	112	1	26	25	1	16	16
雅安市	Yaan	2	56	1	26	20				1	30	30
巴中市	Bazhong	1	5							1	5	5
资阳市	Ziyang	1	65	1	65	65						
阿坝藏族羌族自治州	Aba	8	214	5	173	152	2	32	28	1	9	8
甘孜藏族自治州	Ganzi	5	215	4	197	155				1	18	18
凉山彝族自治州	Liangshan	5	254	3	217	173	1	24	24	1	13	13

注：县级以上政府部门属研究与开发机构及情报文献机构资料由四川省科技厅提供。

a) Information of research and development institutions and the literature of intelligence agencies in government departments above the county level are provided by Sichuan Provincial Science and Technology Department.

20-23 各市(州)县级以上政府部门属研究与开发机构及情报文献机构经费收入总额(2018年)

Total Funds of State-owned Research and Development Institutions and Information and Literature Institutions at and above County Level by Region(2018)

单位:千元 (1 000 yuan)

市(州)	Region	合 计 Total	自然科学技术领域 Field of Natural Sciences and Technology	#政府拨款 Government Approp-riations	社会、人文科学技术领域 Field of Social Sciences and Humanities	#政府拨款 Government Approp-riations	科技情报和文献机构 Scientific-Technical Information and Literature Institutions	#政府拨款 Government Approp-riations
全 省	**Sichuan**	**6890077**	**6197939**	**3965151**	**449584**	**323581**	**242554**	**198419**
成都市	Chengdu	6012313	5413446	3282170	401654	285320	197213	154147
自贡市	Zigong	109059	95412	78276	9267	9267	4380	4380
攀枝花市	Panzhihua	65767	61494	53201			4273	4272
泸州市	Luzhou	14712	10426	7837			4286	4164
德阳市	Deyang	88682	75466	72276	9959	348	3257	3257
绵阳市	Mianyang	52340	52340	50607				
广元市	Guangyuan	12495	12005	11540			490	490
遂宁市	Suining	599					599	599
内江市	Neijiang	60847	57149	54142			3698	3698
乐山市	Leshan	20155	20155	20035				
南充市	Nanchong	107145	103439	78079			3706	3706
眉山市	Meishan							
宜宾市	Yibin	80122	77507	55228			2615	2548
广安市	Guangan	1277			1277	1277		
达州市	Dazhou	38509	28480	25848	6637	6610	3392	3392
雅安市	Yaan	7440	3703	2828			3737	2858
巴中市	Bazhong	720					720	720
资阳市	Ziyang	9566	9566	9566				
阿坝藏族羌族自治州	Aba	78684	67473	60859	8840	8809	2371	2371
甘孜藏族自治州	Ganzi	61036	57498	50279			3538	3538
凉山彝族自治州	Liangshan	68609	52380	52380	11950	11950	4279	4279

20-24 各市(州)县级以上政府部门属研究与开发机构及情报文献机构经费支出总额(2018年)

Total Expenditures of State-owned Research and Development Institutions and Information and Literature Institutions at and above County Level by Region(2018)

单位:千元 (1 000 yuan)

市(州)	Region	合 计 Total	自然科学技术领域 Field of Natural Sciences and Technology	#科技经费支出 Scientific-Technical Expenditures	社会、人文科学技术领域 Field of Social Sciences and Humanities	#科技经费支出 Scientific-Technical Expenditures	科技情报和文献机构 Scientific-Technical Information and Literature Institutions	#科技经费支出 Scientific-Technical Expenditures
全 省	**Sichuan**	**6426496**	**5727698**	**4478697**	**465192**	**385072**	**233606**	**206508**
成都市	Chengdu	5560313	4954744	3815088	417575	352657	187994	163201
自贡市	Zigong	87217	73515	69951	9267	5158	4435	4133
攀枝花市	Panzhihua	64888	60639	52278			4249	3949
泸州市	Luzhou	17482	13196	5505			4286	4260
德阳市	Deyang	97220	84104	81802	9859	55	3257	3125
绵阳市	Mianyang	52340	52340	48864				
广元市	Guangyuan	13460	13220	7500			240	240
遂宁市	Suining	599					599	599
内江市	Neijiang	64480	60846	58031			3634	3634
乐山市	Leshan	18867	18867	17340				
南充市	Nanchong	109437	105607	78816			3830	3405
眉山市	Meishan							
宜宾市	Yibin	75646	73323	66636			2323	1986
广安市	Guangan	1346			1346	1277		
达州市	Dazhou	37781	28556	25104	6490	6490	2735	2735
雅安市	Yaan	10001	4713	1186			5288	5230
巴中市	Bazhong	720					720	720
资阳市	Ziyang	7393	7393	7393				
阿坝藏族羌族自治州	Aba	82375	70573	58574	9218	7998	2584	2012
甘孜藏族自治州	Ganzi	57222	53297	44483			3925	3883
凉山彝族自治州	Liangshan	67709	52765	40146	11437	11437	3507	3396

20-25 高等学校科技人力资源和研究机构情况(2018年)
Basic Statistics on Human Resources for Scientific and Technological Activities and Research Institution of Higher Education(2018)

单位：个、人、万元 (person, unit, 10 000 yuan)

项 目 市(州)	Item Region	科技活动人员 S&T Personnel	#大学本科及以上学历 Bachelor's Degree and above	研究机构数 Number of Research Institutions	R&D人员 R&D Personnel	#博士毕业 Doctor's Degree	#硕士毕业 Master's Degree	R&D经费内部支出 Expenditure on R&D
合 计	**Total**	**91135**	**84585**	**614**	**9391**	**4428**	**3034**	**86987**
理 科	Science	55332	49593	406	6396	3251	1763	82957
文 科	Liberal arts	35803	34992	208	2995	1177	1271	4030
成都市	Chengdu	51270	48273	369	6757	3510	1943	76857
自贡市	Zigong	2148	2052	17	394	107	181	2111
攀枝花市	Panzhihua	1457	1417	35	63	17	11	138
泸州市	Luzhou	8667	6880	29	332	65	188	336
德阳市	Deyang	3866	3181	7	123	9	81	1363
绵阳市	Mianyang	5755	5561	47	254	55	68	1100
广元市	Guangyuan	595	581	1	6		6	
遂宁市	Suining	662	629					
内江市	Neijiang	1621	1537	7	123	51	55	101
乐山市	Leshan	1874	1797	15	159	45	83	284
南充市	Nanchong	4574	4339	46	670	350	235	2041
眉山市	Meishan	1221	1209					
宜宾市	Yibin	958	947	14	217	58	112	146
广安市	Guangan	483	468					
达州市	Dazhou	1072	1038	4	24	4	16	27
雅安市	Yaan	2309	2236	9	200	153	20	2352
巴中市	Bazhong	287	277					
资阳市	Ziyang	182	180					
阿坝藏族羌族自治州	Aba	569	532	1	3	1	1	3
甘孜藏族自治州	Ganzi	501	448	1	5		3	7
凉山彝族自治州	Liangshan	1064	1003	12	61	3	31	123

20-26 科技成果水平及应用情况(2018年)
Level and Utility of Achievement in Scientific and Technical Research(2018)

单位：项 (item)

指 标	Item	合计 Total	科研机构 Research Institutions	大专院校 Universities and Colleges	企业 Enterprises	其他 Others
基本情况	**Basic Condition**					
登记项目数	Number of Projects Registered	3702	408	760	2412	122
鉴定项目数	Number of Projects Appraised	119	12	14	84	9
奖励项目数	Number of Projects Praised	287	48	98	125	16
成果计划	**Achievements Plan**					
国家计划项目	Projects of Country Plans	158	26	77	29	26
部门计划项目	Projects of Department	42	14	8	11	9
地方计划项目	Projects of Local Government	174	51	30	67	26
部门基金项目	Projects of Department Foundation	8		3		5
地方基金项目	Projects of Local Government Foundation	12	2	4	2	4
其他	Others	3308	315	638	2303	52
成果类别	**Achievements Type**					
基础理论	Basic Theory	53	5	35	3	10
应用技术	Applied Technology	3637	401	721	2405	110
软科学	Soft Science	12	2	4	4	2
成果水平	**Achievements Level**					
国际领先	International Original	71	8	16	36	11
国际先进	International Advanced	223	26	46	134	17
国内领先	Domestic Original	329	25	37	243	24
国内先进	Domestic Advanced	131	17	11	78	25
应用项目	**Projects Applied**					
农、林、牧、渔业	Farming, Forestry, Animal Husbandry and Fishery	250	95	61	85	9
工业	Industry	2655	235	464	1930	26
建筑业	Construction	89	9	11	69	
交通运输、邮电通讯业	Transportation, Postal and Telecommunication Services	59	2	11	44	2
信息传输、计算机服务和软件业	Information Transmission, Computer Services and Software	348	22	126	197	3
批发和零售业	Wholesale and Retail Trades					
住宿和餐饮业	Hotels and Catering Services	14		8	6	
金融、保险业	Banking and Insurance	1			1	
房地产业	Real Estate	5		3	2	
租赁和商务服务业	LeasingAndBusinessServices					
科学研究、技术服务和地质勘查业	Scientific Research,Technic Services and Geological Prospecting	65	24	11	22	8
水利、环境和公共设施管理业	Management of Water Conservancy.Environment and Public Facilities	26	6	4	15	1
居民服务和其他服务业	Residental Service And Others					
教育	Education	6			6	
卫生、社会保障和社会福利业	Health Care, Social Security and Social Welfare	102	6	19	18	59
文化、体育和娱乐业	Culture, Sports and Entertainment	5			5	
公共管理和社会组织	Public Management and Social Organizations	11	2	3	4	2
其他行业	Others	1			1	
未应用项目	**Projects not Applied**	**19**	**4**	**6**	**5**	**4**

注：科技成果水平及应用资料由四川省科学技术厅提供。
a) Data of achievement and application of information technology are provided by Provincial Science and Technology Department.

20-27 专利申请量及授权量
Patent Applications Accepted and Granted

单位：项 (item)

项 目	Item	2013	2014	2015	2016	2017	2018
全省专利申请量合计	**Total Applications Examined**	**82453**	**91167**	**110746**	**142522**	**167484**	**152987**
1. 发明	I. Creations and Inventions	23510	29926	40437	54277	64642	53805
实用新型	Utility Models	33488	32085	41859	58088	73789	73167
外观设计	Designs	25455	29156	28450	30157	29053	26015
2. 个人	II.Individuals	21994	22664	25599	30468	28334	28992
大专院校	Universities and Colleges	6144	6593	8991	14333	18782	19192
科研单位	Research Institutions	1997	2436	3565	4052	3975	4338
工矿企业	Industrial and Mineral Enterprises	51429	58770	71181	91647	113103	97062
机关团体	Government Agencies and Organizations	889	704	1410	2022	3290	3403
全省专利授权量合计	**Total Applications Granted**	**46171**	**47120**	**64953**	**62445**	**64006**	**87372**
1. 发明	I. Creations and Inventions	4566	5682	9105	10350	11367	11697
实用新型	Utility Models	24730	24060	31420	31813	33613	53121
外观设计	Designs	16875	17378	24428	20282	19026	22554
2. 个人	II.Individuals	13699	8124	12750	12097	11274	13232
大专院校	Universities and Colleges	2539	3060	4693	6297	8165	10102
科研单位	Research Institutions	1093	1173	1469	1854	2133	2370
工矿企业	Industrial and Mineral Enterprises	28334	34153	45042	41064	41097	60199
机关团体	Government Agencies and Organizations	506	610	999	1133	1337	1469

注：专利资料由四川省知识产权服务促进中心提供。
a) Data of patent information are provided by Intellectual Property Service Promotion Center of Sichuan Provincial.

20-28 各类技术合同签订及执行情况
Concluded and Fulfilled Technical Contracts

单位：项、万元 (item, 10 000 yuan)

项 目	Item	合同数 Number of Contracts		合同成交额 Value of Contracts		技术交易额 Technology Business Value	
		2017	2018	2017	2018	2017	2018
全 省	**Total**	**12853**	**15192**	**4196804**	**10041758**	**3399348**	**4109940**
技术开发	Technical Development	8414	10246	1577033	1881831	1420739	1778214
技术转让	Technical Transfer	488	613	337271	405493	206606	334207
技术咨询	Technical Consultation	368	286	150595	142507	149790	88951
技术服务	Technical Services	3583	4047	2131905	7611927	1622213	1908568

注：各类技术合同签定及执行情况由四川省科学技术厅提供。
a) Data of various types of technology and the implementation of the contract signed are provided by Provincial Science and Technology Department.

主要统计指标解释

普通高等学校 指通过国家普通高等教育招生考试，招收高中毕业生为主要培养对象，实施高等学历教育的全日制大学、独立设置的学院、独立学院和高等专科学校、高等职业学校及其他机构。

大学、独立设置的学院主要实施本科及本科层次以上的教育。独立学院主要实施本科层次的教育。高等专科学校、高等职业学校实施专科层次的教育。其他机构是指承担国家普通招生计划任务不计校数的机构，包括普通高等学校分校、大专班等。

成人高等学校 指通过国家成人高等教育招生考试，招收具有高中毕业或同等学力的人员为主要培养对象，利用函授、业余、脱产等多种形式，对其实施高等学历教育的学校。包括：职工高等学校、农民高等学校、管理干部学院、教育学院、独立函授学院、广播电视大学、其他机构。其他机构是指承担国家成人招生计划任务不计校数的机构。

科技活动 指在自然科学、农业科学、医药科学、工程与技术科学、人文与社会科学领域(简称科学技术领域)中与科技知识的产生、发展、传播和应用密切相关的有组织的活动。为核算科技投入的需要，可分为研究与试验发展(R&D)、科学研究与试验发展成果应用及相关的科技服务三类活动。

科技活动人员 指直接从事科技活动、以及专门从事科技活动管理和为科技活动提供直接服务，累计的实际工作时间占全年制度工作时间 10%及以上的人员。(1)直接从事科技活动的人员包括：在独立核算的科学研究与技术开发机构、高等学校、各类企业及其他事业单位内设的研究室、实验室、技术开发中心及中试车间(基地)等机构中从事科技活动的研究人员、工程技术人员、技术工人及其它人员；虽不在上述机构工作，但编入科技活动项目(课题)组的人员；科技信息与文献机构中的专业技术人员；从事论文设计的研究生等。(2)专门从事科技活动管理和为科技活动提供直接服务的人员，包括：独立核算的科学研究与技术开发机构、科技信息与文献机构、高等学校、各类企业及其他事业单位主管科技工作的负责人，专门从事科技活动的计划、行政、人事、财务、物资供应、设备维护、图书资料管理等工作的各类人员，但不包括保卫、医疗保健人员、司机、食堂人员、茶炉工、水暖工、清洁工等为科技活动提供间接服务的人员。该指标用来反映投入科技活动人力的规模。

研究与试验发展(R&D) 指在科学技术领域，为增加知识总量，以及运用这些知识去创造新的应用进行的系统的创造性的活动，包括基础研究、应用研究、试验发展三类活动。国际上通常采用 R&D 活动的规模和强度指标反映一国的科技实力和核心竞争力。

R&D 人员 指参与研究与试验发展项目研究、管理和辅助工作的人员，包括项目(课题)组人员，企业科技行政管理人员和直接为项目(课题)活动提供服务的辅助人员。反映投入从事拥有自主知识产权的研究开发活动的人力规模。

R&D 经费支出合计 指调查单位用于内部开展 R&D 活动（基础研究、应用研究和试验发展）的实际支出。包括用于 R&D 项目（课题）活动的直接支出，以及间接用于 R&D 活动的管理费、服务费、与 R&D 有关的基本建设支出以及外协加工费等。不包括生产性活动支出、归还贷款支出以及与外单位合作或委托外单位进行 R&D 活动而转拨给对方的经费支出。

专利 是专利权的简称，是对发明人的发明创造经审查合格后，由专利局依据专利法授予发明人和设计人对该项发明创造享有的专有权。包括发明、实用新型和外观设计。反映拥有自主知识产权的科技和设计成果情况。

发明（专利） 指对产品、方法或者其改进所提出的新的技术方案。是国际通行的反映拥有自主知识产权技术的核心指标。

实用新型（专利） 指对产品的形状、构造或者其结合所提出的适于实用的新的技术方案。反映具有一定技术含量的技术成果情况。

外观设计（专利） 指对产品的形状、图案、色彩或者其结合所作出的富有美感并适于工业上应用的新设计。反映拥有自主知识产权的外观设计成果情况。

Explanatory Notes on Main Statistical Indicators

Regular Institutions of Higher Education refer to educational establishments recruiting graduates from senior secondary schools as the main target through National Matriculation TEST. They include full-time universities, independently established colleges, colleges, and institutions of higher professional education, institutions of higher vocational education and others.

Universities and independently established colleges primarily provide undergraduate and above courses; colleges mainly impart undergraduate courses, institutions of higher professional education and institutions of higher vocational education primarily provide professional trainings; and others refer to educational establishments, which are responsible for enrolling higher education students under the State Plan but not enumerated in the total number of schools, including: branch schools of universities and colleges and junior colleges.

Institutions of Higher Education for Adults refer to educational establishments, enrolling personnel with senior secondary school or equivalent education through National Matriculation TEST for Adult, and providing higher education courses in forms of correspondence, spare time, or full time for adults. Institutions of higher learning for adults include schools of higher education for staff and workers, schools of higher education for peasants, colleges for management cadres, pedagogical colleges, independent correspondence colleges, radio and television universities and other educational establishments. Other educational establishments refer to undertaking adult students enrolment but not enumerated in the number of schools under the State Plan.

Scientific and Technological Activities (S&T Activities) refer to organized activities which are closely related with the creation, development, dissemination and application of the scientific and technical knowledge in the fields of natural sciences, agricultural science, medical science, engineering and technological science, humanities and social sciences (referred to as scientific and technological fields). To account for the needs of scientific and technological investment, S&T activities can be classified in to 3 categories: research and development (R&D) activities, application of R&D results, and related S&T services.

Personnel Engaged in S&T Activities refer to personnel directly engaged in S&T activities, in the management of S&T activities, and in providing direct service to S&T activities, who spend over 10% of the total working hours in a year in S&T activities. (1) Personnel directly engaged in S&T activities include researchers, engineers, technicians and other related personnel engaged in S&T activities in independent-accounting R&D institutions, institutions of higher learning, and in research institutes, laboratories, technology development centers and central experiment workshops under enterprises and institutions. Also included are people working in S&T research project teams, professional and technical personnel working in S&T information archiving institutes, and graduate students working on the design of their thesis. (2) Personnel engaged in the management of S&T activities and in providing direct service to S&T activities include senior management people responsible for S&T activities in independent -accounting R&D institutions, S&T information archiving institutes, institutions of higher learning, and in enterprises and institutions where S&T activities are undertaken. Also included are people responsible for the planning, administration, personnel management, financial management, logistics supply, equipment maintenance, information and library management that are related with S&T activities. People providing indirect services are excluded, such as security, medical service, drivers, plumbers, cleaners and those providing catering and related service. This indicator reflects the size of personnel engaged in S&T activities.

Research and Development (R&D) refers to systematic and creative activities in the field of science and technology aiming at increasing the knowledge and using the knowledge for new application. R&D includes 3 categories of activities: basic research, applied research and experiments and development. The scale and intensity of R&D are widely used internationally to reflect the strength of S&T and the core competitiveness of a country in the world.

R&D Personnel refer to persons engaged in research, management and supporting activities of R & D, including persons in the project teams, persons engaged in the management of S&T activities of enterprises and supporting staff providing direct service to the research projects. This indicator reflects the size of personnel engaged in R&D activities with independent intellectual property.

Total Expenditure of Funds on R&D refers to the real expenditure of surveyed units on their own R&D activities (basic research, application study, test and development) including direct expenditure on R&D activities, indirect expenditure of management and services on R&D activities, expenditure on capital construction and material processing by others. Excluding the expenditure on production activities, return of loan, and fees transferred to cooperated and entrusted agencies on R&D activities.

Patent is an abbreviation for the patent right and refers to the exclusive right of ownership by the inventors or designers for the creation or inventions, given from the patent offices after due process of assessment and approval in accordance with the Patent Law. Patents are granted for inventions, utility models and designs. This indicator reflects the achievements of S&T and design with independent intellectual property.

Patented Inventions refer to the new technical proposals to the products or methods or their modifications. This is universal core indicator reflecting the technologies with independent intellectual property.

Patented Utility Models refer to the practical and new technical proposals on the shape and structure of the product or the combination of both. This indicator reflects the condition of technological results with certain technical content.

Designs refer to the aesthetics and industrially applicable new designs for the shape, pattern and color of the product, or their combinations. This indicator reflects the appearance design achievements with independent intellectual property.

21 文化、体育和卫生

Chapter 21 Culture, Sports and Public Health

21-1 文化艺术、文物事业机构数
Number of Institutions for Culture, Art and Cultural Relics

单位：个 (unit)

年份 Year	艺术表演团体 Art Performance Troupes	公共图书馆 Public Libraries	文化馆 Cultural Centers	文化站 Cultural Stations	博物馆 Museums
1952	126	4	148	146	1
1957	148	21	163	115	2
1962	205	36	161	76	11
1965	198	36	167	31	13
1970	169	36	171	16	13
1975	190	36	178	13	13
1978	193	57	178	8	12
1980	183	71	177	656	11
1985	148	82	172	5196	24
1990	109	109	168	4957	34
1991	106	112	168	4973	37
1992	105	117	169	4329	37
1993	103	117	169	3745	37
1994	101	118	170	3634	42
1995	101	123	171	3613	42
1996	101	125	172	3384	44
1997	101	127	170	3574	44
1998	100	129	170	3689	47
1999	99	129	171	3666	47
2000	98	129	171	3667	50
2001	89	129	174	3720	51
2002	89	131	173	3525	51
2003	89	132	181	3722	51
2004	84	137	180	3701	54
2005	85	141	180	4515	54
2006	81	146	202	3600	59
2007	84	151	202	3795	62
2008	83	154	203	3873	85
2009	84	156	203	4019	89
2010	82	161	204	4448	108
2011	75	169	205	4593	144
2012	63	188	205	4595	152
2013	52	197	207	4595	188
2014	51	198	207	4601	206
2015	52	203	207	4578	225
2016	50	203	207	4574	239
2017	52	204	207	4578	255
2018	52	204	207	4574	252

注：文化艺术、图书馆、博物馆等资料由四川省文化和旅游厅提供。
a) Data of culture and art, libraries, museums and other information are provided by the Provincial Department of Culture and Tourism.

21-2 各市(州)文化艺术、文物事业机构和人员数(2018年)
Institutions and Personnel of Culture, Art and Cultural Relics by Region(2018)

单位：个、人、千册 (unit,person, 1 000 volumes)

市(州)	Region	艺术表演团体 Art Performance Troupes		公共图书馆 Public Libraries			文化馆 Cultural Centers		博物馆 Museums	
		机构数 Institutions	从业人员 Employed Persons	机构数 Institutions	从业人员 Employed Persons	藏书量 Collections	机构数 Institutions	从业人员 Employed Persons	机构数 Institutions	从业人员 Employed Persons
全 省	**Sichuan**	**52**	**3136**	**204**	**2313**	**39484**	**207**	**3004**	**252**	**6201**
成都市	Chengdu	12	1282	23	789	16219	23	559	102	2450
自贡市	Zigong	6	298	7	63	571	7	75	4	263
攀枝花市	Panzhihua	2	145	6	41	862	6	79	3	88
泸州市	Luzhou	1	14	9	78	1598	8	105	11	120
德阳市	Deyang	1	17	7	79	1190	7	119	10	445
绵阳市	Mianyang	3	131	10	86	2130	10	120	14	357
广元市	Guangyuan	2	28	8	75	1427	9	88	13	284
遂宁市	Suining	1	52	6	60	907	6	78	5	139
内江市	Neijiang	5	116	4	72	765	6	115	4	59
乐山市	Leshan	2	145	12	82	996	12	122	9	170
南充市	Nanchong	4	195	10	103	1940	10	131	8	286
眉山市	Meishan	1	44	7	57	549	7	76	6	127
宜宾市	Yibin	1	100	10	77	1366	11	174	9	92
广安市	Guangan			7	95	2158	7	125	4	300
达州市	Dazhou	2	187	8	115	1445	8	216	7	119
雅安市	Yaan			9	64	969	9	80	9	132
巴中市	Bazhong	2	46	6	66	1091	6	111	11	296
资阳市	Ziyang	2	36	4	52	523	4	60	1	118
阿坝藏族羌族自治州	Aba	1	88	14	77	790	14	106	10	184
甘孜藏族自治州	Ganzi	2	82	19	76	727	19	239	5	67
凉山彝族自治州	Liangshan	2	130	18	106	1259	18	226	7	105

注：全省合计中含省直属单位数。
a) The provincal data includes those of unites directly under the province.

21-3 各市(州)文化站基本情况(2018年)
Basic Statistics on Cultural Stations by Region(2018)

市(州)	Region	文化站(个) Cultural Stations (unit)	#乡镇文化站 Township Cultural Stations	从业人员(人) Employed Persons (person)	举办展览(个) Number of Exhibitions (unit)	组织文艺活动次数(次) Art Performances & Cultural Sessions (time)	藏书量(千册) Collections (1 000 copies)
全　省	**Sichuan**	**4574**	**4257**	**8408**	**10426**	**61971**	**17851**
成都市	Chengdu	372	246	1446	1723	17374	2625
自贡市	Zigong	108	96	184	135	1982	200
攀枝花市	Panzhihua	60	44	115	115	1294	228
泸州市	Luzhou	143	127	275	380	1148	684
德阳市	Deyang	127	119	212	244	1680	959
绵阳市	Mianyang	291	273	566	673	3273	1748
广元市	Guangyuan	238	230	337	652	1809	914
遂宁市	Suining	115	105	230	223	1711	427
内江市	Neijiang	121	107	243	263	1027	525
乐山市	Leshan	218	211	582	412	2341	666
南充市	Nanchong	424	393	483	1017	4002	944
眉山市	Meishan	131	127	229	197	1539	291
宜宾市	Yibin	185	172	346	380	2384	841
广安市	Guangan	179	170	382	195	1104	509
达州市	Dazhou	312	310	510	936	1535	1563
雅安市	Yaan	142	138	312	325	2138	475
巴中市	Bazhong	200	187	379	1141	3190	1315
资阳市	Ziyang	120	116	280	246	1546	537
阿坝藏族羌族自治州	Aba	219	219	267	202	1389	354
甘孜藏族自治州	Ganzi	325	325	344	56	6480	478
凉山彝族自治州	Liangshan	544	542	686	911	3025	1567

21-4 群众艺术馆、文化馆(站)业务活动及经费情况(2018年)
Basic Statistics on Activities and Expenditures of Mass Art Centers and Cultural Centers (Stations)(2018)

项　目		Item		总　计 Total	群众艺术馆(文化馆) Mass Art Centers Cultural Centers	文化站 Cultural Stations
单位数	(个)	Number of Units	(unit)	4781	207	4574
举办展览	(个)	Number of Exhibitions	(unit)	12112	1686	10426
组织文艺活动	(次)	Art Performances and Cultural Sessions	(time)	77221	15250	61971
举办训练班		Training Courses				
班次	(次)	Number of Classes	(time)	38642	8710	29932
培训人次	(万人次)	Number of Persons Completing Courses	(10 000 person-times)	204	48	156
群众业余演出团(队)	(个)	Part-time Art Groups	(unit)	25005	3517	21488
总支出	(万元)	Total Expenses	(10 000 yuan)	148850	70162	78688
#基本支出	(万元)	Basic Expenses	(10 000 yuan)	75477	42375	33102

注:本表各项指标仅指文化部门系统内的。
a) Data in this table only refers to those under the administration of cultural departments.

21-5 公共图书馆业务活动及经费情况(2018年)
Business Activities and Expenditures of Public Libraries(2018)

项 目		Item		总计 Total	省级公共图书馆 Public Libraries at Provincial Level	市(州)级公共图书馆 Public Libraries at Prefecture Level	县级公共图书馆 Public Libraries at County Level
总藏量	(千册、件)	Total Collections	(1 000 volumes)	39484	5555	12427	21502
书架总长度	(千米)	Total Length of Bookshelves	(km)	1618	40	988	589
有效借书证个数	(千个)	Number of Library Cards Distributed	(1 000 units)	2407	134	1058	1215
书刊外借情况		Condition of Books Borrowed by the Readers					
人次	(千人次)	Total Number of Circulation	(1 000 person-times)	9753	178	3272	6302
册次	(千册次)	Number of Books Borrowed by the Readers	(1 000 volume-times)	17849	400	5973	11475
为读者举办各种活动		Service Activities Provided for Readers					
次数	(次、个)	Number of Activities	(time,unit)	6169	92	1450	4627
参加人数	(千人次)	Number of Readers Involved	(1 000 person-times)	4001	519	781	2702
总支出	(万元)	Total Expenditures	(10 000 yuan)	66352	15826	17302	33224
基本支出	(万元)	Basic Expenses	(10 000 yuan)	29479	3945	8814	16721
#新增藏量购置费	(万元)	Purchase of New Reserves	(10 000 yuan)	5288	1295	1596	2398
本年新增藏量	(万册)	New Reserves this Year	(10 000 volumes)	191	17	39	135
阅览室座席	(千个)	Seating Capacity of Reading Rooms	(1 000 seats)	58	3	13	42

注：总藏量从2013年起不包括电子图书。
a) Total collections don't include electronic books since 2013.

21-6 博物馆、文物机构业务活动及经费情况(2018年)
Business Activities and Expenditures of Museums and Cultural Relic Agencies(2018)

项 目		Item		博物馆 Museums	文物保护管理机构 Cultural Relic Agencies
藏品	(件)	Number of Collections	(piece)	4026271	136040
#一级品	(件)	Grade One	(piece)	4615	851
本年支出	(万元)	Total Expenses	(10 000 yuan)	148874	63820
#基本支出	(万元)	Basic Expense	(10 000 yuan)	51878	14230
#商品和服务支出	(万元)	Goods and Sevices Expenses	(10 000 yuan)	61807	25806

21-7 图书、杂志和报纸出版情况
Number of Books, Magazines and Newspapers Published

年份 Year	图书 Books Published 种数 (种) Number of Publications (kind)	#新出版 New Publications	总印数 (万册) Total Printed Copies (10 000 copies)	总印张数 (万印张) Total Printed Sheets (10 000 sheets)	杂志 Magazines Published 种数 (种) Number of Publications (kind)	每期平均印数 (万册) Average Printed Copies per Issue (10 000 copies)	总印数 (万册) Total Printed Copies (10 000 copies)	总印张数 (万印张) Total Printed Sheets (10 000 sheets)	报纸 Newspapers Published 种数 (种) Number of Newspaper Published (kind)	每期平均印数 (万份) Average Printed Copies per Issue (10 000 copies)	总印数 (万份) Total Printed Copies (10 000 copies)	总印张数 (万印张) Total Printed Sheets (10 000 sheets)
1952	53	20	1481	3195	25	45	565	540	14	34	6799	5150
1957	52		909	1783					15	35	8109	6005
1962	86		2484	5256								
1965	65		6280	15006								
1970	24		4225	10677								
1975	292	233	17184	48499								
1978	277	241	24993	83916	13	57	562	1173	15	170	51889	43758
1980	549	502	31370	119063	71	341	3036	8699	22	214	50627	42305
1985	1273	1151	28023	99516	224	690	5532	17810	69	859	92878	64138
1990	2676	1896	21152	82360	226	324	3257	9149	66	818	94657	64642
1991	2769	1730	16634	71891	234	362	3192	9443	70	869	101753	68660
1992	3022	2063	22903	99185	249	404	4030	11697	75	818	97368	72598
1993	2459	1795	17666	72266	256	456	4674	12491	80	823	104000	73974
1994	3840	2818	21650	105849	275	412	4067	11865	91	885	102319	72532
1995	3017	1876	15438	83894	287	487	4993	14898	93	710	100500	122632
1996	3833	2256	27975	138772	289	409	4339	12025	95	680	109084	138292
1997	4510	2005	33272	153193	289	405	4336	12484	95	763	126818	227065
1998	4436	2369	31491	151112	284	403	4508	13211	100	757	124922	235944
1999	4306	2254	29852	147862	287	419	4754	14944	100	782	127708	240359
2000	3855	2134	27315	157672	275	451	4950	16238	91	711	133590	366840
2001	3820	2104	26032	158031	334	362	4172	16233	84	671	136737	394553
2002	3895	2244	25932	165312	256	440	5572	20688	92	654	135163	319004
2003	4131	2315	25889	170470	267	352	4767	21421	93	634	139266	357423
2004	4059	1911	21690	154980	225	293	5269	32515	107	651	155972	498494
2005	4836	2975	23643	193903	330	459	7502	60933	130	659	155865	671830
2006	4873	3070	19643	149609	335	509	8215	59996	136	618	155800	685570
2007	5150	3287	19591	146591	335	496	9514	74788	136	660	168638	656104
2008	5021	2885	19490	142562	336	475	8237	53222	136	670	164273	737694
2009	6719	3878	17492	127321	336	494	8303	52759	136	613	155286	797707
2010	6645	3396	19493	147325	340	498	10593	74892	136	687	170176	999545
2011	8081	3951	24787	179489	343	471	9293	67424	136	670	174021	1019233
2012	7794	4235	23587	176618	343	470	9066	63236	136	661	172573	865664
2013	8554	4946	23416	186771	346	417	7499	54658	137	687	170457	833132
2014	9095	5252	19623	156848	349	376	6382	44033	136	653	167699	752920
2015	10097	6074	24805	193337	352	330	5655	35616	134	642	162781	647618
2016	10878	6332	24264	196767	354	316	5045	29000	132	636	162153	646976
2017	13329	8287	29195	224165	355	282	5128	28702	130	551	141828	368846
2018	14456	8746	32520	254859	356	278	4997	28352	130	543	133057	327443

注：图书、杂志、报纸、音像制品出版资料由中共四川省委宣传部提供。
a) Data of books, magazines, newspapers, audio-visual products published are provided by Propaganda Department of the Sichuan Provincial Party Committee of the Communist Party in China.

21-8 录像制品出版情况 Publication of Video Products

年份 Year	录像制品合计 Total 种数(种) Kind	数量(万盒、万张) Volume (10 000 pieces)	录像带 Audio-tapes 种数(种) Kind	数量(万盒) Volume (10 000 cassettes)	数码激光视盘 VCD 种数(种) Kind	数量(万张) Volume (10 000 pieces)	高密度激光视盘 DVD-V 种数(种) Kind	数量(万张) Volume (10 000 pieces)
2000	172	97.72			172	97.72		
2001	260	391.98	48	24.60	210	365.38	2	2.00
2002	446	501.51	18	64.25	401	424.61	27	12.65
2003	490	310.23	57	34.00	380	205.63	53	25.60
2004	241	198.36			216	184.54	25	13.82
2005	294	171.80			240	147.94	54	23.87
2006	542	240.82	3	1.10	243	122.99	296	116.73
2007	491	164.01	1	0.30	288	99.38	202	64.33
2008	343	153.23	1	0.80	163	83.37	179	69.06
2009	250	124.30			106	53.26	144	72.04
2010	191	108.46			58	24.01	133	84.45
2011	96	73.13	1	0.25	22	10.58	73	62.30
2012	91	80.35			6	1.70	85	78.65
2013	77	45.54			10	3.03	67	42.51
2014	54	47.85			5	0.70	49	47.15
2015	48	67.45			2	0.30	46	67.15
2016	73	54.52			8	2.35	65	52.17
2017	53	61.25					53	61.25
2018	91	54.23					91	54.23

21-9 录音制品出版情况 Publication of Audio Products

年份 Year	录音制品合计 Audio Products 种数(种) Kind	数量(万盒、万张) Volume (10 000 pieces)	#盒式音带 Cassettes Audio-tapes 种数(种) Kind	数量(万盒) Volume (10 000 cassettes)	#激光唱片 CD 种数(种) Kind	数量(万张) Volume (10 000 pieces)
1998	85	123.53	56	96.83	29	26.70
1999	178	89.31	80	56.74	98	32.57
2000	92	64.03	40	37.73	52	26.30
2001	114	93.53	61	42.27	53	51.26
2002	210	95.39	117	53.44	93	41.95
2003	158	127.27	56	38.52	102	88.75
2004	42	61.96	1	0.40	41	36.52
2005	177	88.20	69	33.70	108	54.50
2006	139	70.45	44	15.60	95	54.85
2007	164	71.73	48	13.74	114	55.99
2008	72	25.40	13	8.05	59	16.99
2009	75	40.58	12	15.30	63	25.28
2010	47	28.38	15	14.28	32	14.09
2011	32	25.77	4	4.00	28	21.77
2012	12	5.03	3	2.50	9	4.78
2013	35	19.70	1	0.20	34	19.50
2014	38	17.34	3	6.00	35	11.34
2015	15	8.65	2	4.00	13	4.65
2016	14	1.77			14	1.77
2017	17	3.80			17	3.80
2018	11	3.20			10	1.60

21-10 广播电视事业发展情况
Basic Statistics on Development of Broadcasting and Television

年份 Year	广播电台 (座) Broadcasting Stations (set)	中短波发射台及转播台 (座) Transmission Stations and Relaying Stations of Medium and Short Wave (set)	中短波发射机功率 (部/千瓦) Power of Transmitters of Medium and Short Wave (unit / kw)	电视台 (座) Television Stations (set)	调频、电视发射台及转播台 (座) FM, TV Transmitting and Relay Stations (set)	电视发射机功率 (部/千瓦) Power of Television Transmission (unit / kw)	广播综合人口覆盖率 (%) Comprehensive Population Coverage Rate of Broadcasting (%)	电视综合人口覆盖率 (%) Comprehensive Population Coverage Rate of Television (%)	广播电视台(站) (个) Broadcasting and Television Stations of County Level (set)
1952	3	2	2 / 2				20.06		
1957	1	1	2 / 2				20.06		80
1962	3	4	3 / 23.8	1	1	1 / 1	30.18	3.87	129
1965	3	4	3 / 123.8	1	1	1 / 1	30.09	3.87	141
1970	3	4	5 / 260.6	1	1	1 / 1	35.28	5.29	150
1975	3	9	10 / 327.6	1	14	15 / 5.50	43.13	18.73	157
1978	3	9	11 / 413.3	1	82	76 / 6.74	46.91	38.60	165
1980	3	11	15 / 488.0	1	208	235 / 21.39	49.91	45.69	168
1985	5	13	20 / 442.5	3	865	921 / 73.05	52.37	58.70	169
1990	14	18	29 / 453.0	15	2100	2577 / 183.38	64.46	71.46	166
1991	13	19	30 / 462.0	16	2244	2775 / 186.89	64.75	71.78	171
1992	15	19	32 / 514.0	21	2438	3106 / 199.05	64.84	71.88	169
1993	19	20	35 / 533.1	23	2518	3289 / 194.78	70.21	76.12	165
1994	25	20	34 / 632.0	27	2950	3757 / 202.80	75.40	80.50	150
1995	52	27	43 / 515.1	31	3114	4036 / 218.38	80.40	85.50	134
1996	58	27	40 / 521.1	32	3303	3952 / 207.09	84.47	83.57	161
1997	67	27	48 / 556.1	34	3227	3959 / 230.62	86.34	87.37	162
1998	17	29	48 / 556.1	23	3264	4009 / 235.94	88.90	88.97	44
1999	18	30	47 / 654.2	23	2626	3244 / 185.04	91.05	91.98	46
2000	19	28	52 / 673.1	23	4779	5636 / 266.82	92.85	93.61	42
2001	20	35	68 / 482.5	20	4839	5598 / 267.37	93.66	94.46	42
2002	20	34	69 / 558.0	22	4428	5353 / 260.53	94.07	95.08	110
2003	20	34	69 / 558.0	22	4385	5696 / 263.36	94.83	95.54	111
2004	20	34	69 / 558.0	22	4308	4546 / 250.77	95.34	96.39	111
2005	20	35	96 / 658.0	21	3849	5044 / 262.29	95.41	96.74	113
2006	20	35	96 / 658.0	21	2471	5524 / 280.14	95.70	96.77	113
2007	20	37	112 / 711.0	21	2469	5757 / 376.57	95.92	97.05	114
2008	16	37	114 / 710.0	16	4434	5644 / 505.59	95.97	97.10	119
2009	15	37	96 / 680.0	15	3944	5323 / 600.38	96.19	97.27	152
2010	10	37	101 / 687.0	10	3482	4810 / 587.11	96.22	97.33	156
2011	8	37	102 / 787.0	8	3001	4121 / 628.24	96.60	97.69	158
2012	7	36	96 / 747.0	7	3056	4173 / 644.52	96.78	97.75	159
2013	1	36	96 / 747.0	1	2187	2906 / 661.39	96.98	97.89	165
2014	1	40	104 / 701.5	1	566	944 / 638.77	97.04	98.07	165
2015	1	36	95 / 659.2	1	403	942 / 1260.95	97.14	98.24	165
2016	1	36	104 / 774.0	1	338	934 / 978.76	97.19	98.29	165
2017	1	39	108 / 645.0	1	345	1059 / 656.74	97.42	98.54	165
2018	1	42	109 / 780.0	1	303	969 / 623.81	97.84	98.79	171

注：广播电视资料由四川省广播电视局提供。

a) Data of radio and TV broadcast information are provided by Broadcasting and Television Bureau of Sichuan Provincial.

21-11 广播电视播放情况(2018年)
Basic Statistics on Broadcasting and Television(2018)

项目	Item	节目套数(套) Number of Programs (set)	公共广播(电视)节目播出时间(小时) Broadcasting Hours of Public Broadcasting (Television) (hour)	新闻资讯类节目 News and Referrence Programs	专题服务类节目 Special Subject and Services Programs	综艺类节目 Omnibus Enter-tainment Programs	广播(影视)剧类节目 Broadcast Movies And TV	广告类节目 Advertis-ement	其他类节目 Others
广播播出合计	**All Radio Broadcasting**	**144**	**710807**	**167437**	**144895**	**147676**	**39089**	**50326**	**161382**
省级广播电台	Provincial Level	9	64057	12222	18129	16636	189	6756	10123
市(州)级广播电台	Prefecture Level	45	274250	56832	60887	57968	13045	23573	61942
县级广播电视台	County Level	90	372499	98382	65878	73071	25855	19996	89316
电视播出合计	**All Television Broadcasting**	**213**	**1157815**	**172499**	**120268**	**69399**	**538519**	**119099**	**138029**
省级电视台	Provincial Level	9	73800	10762	7163	5467	30473	11793	8141
市(州)级电视台	Prefecture Level	49	323551	48470	47789	20808	120956	49619	35907
县级广播电视台	County Level	155	760462	113266	65314	43124	387089	57686	93981

21-12 各市(州)有线广播电视基本情况(2018年)
Basic Statistics on Cable Broadcasting and Television by Region(2018)

单位: 户、公里 (household,kilometer)

市(州)	Region	有线广播电视用户 Cable Broadcasting and Television Users	#数字电视用户 Digital Television Users	#付费数字电视用户 Pay Digital Television Users	有线广播电视传输网络干线总长 Total Length of Main Link of Cable Broadcasting and Television Transmission
全　省	**Sichuan**	**11816272**	**11238253**	**5280336**	**27462.39**
省本级	**Shengbenji**				
成都市	Chengdu	5791038	5562064	1514509	10812.71
自贡市	Zigong	245875	219610	159384	297.30
攀枝花市	Panzhihua	69040	66187	46234	319.82
泸州市	Luzhou	194664	194664	137219	619.97
德阳市	Deyang	463331	419599	289057	340.70
绵阳市	Mianyang	475801	470045	387394	1029.00
广元市	Guangyuan	308814	308808	214224	735.00
遂宁市	Suining	531171	531171	301025	549.64
内江市	Neijiang	439302	433467	309508	342.00
乐山市	Leshan	408347	407833	242759	1141.40
南充市	Nanchong	599298	563000	335780	873.20
眉山市	Meishan	233043	231178	153712	395.00
宜宾市	Yibin	258673	248060	228295	703.76
广安市	Guangan	367297	322728	166261	433.07
达州市	Dazhou	527261	420044	336930	649.76
雅安市	Yaan	199032	179221	141732	1104.50
巴中市	Bazhong	203320	194320	181211	513.00
资阳市	Ziyang	180651	180651	44098	423.00
阿坝藏族羌族自治州	Aba	62772	54594	23509	2594.20
甘孜藏族自治州	Ganzi	37768	30641		1090.36
凉山彝族自治州	Liangshan	219774	200368	67495	2495.00

21-13 各市(州)农村广播电视有线传输情况(2018年)
Basic Statistics on Rural Radio and Television Cable Transmission by Region(2018)

单位：户、% (household, %)

		农村有线广播电视用户数 Rural Cable radio and Television Users	农村有线广播电视入户率 Rural Households on Cable TV Rate	农村广播覆盖率 Rural Radio Coverage	农村电视覆盖率 Rural Television Coverage
全 省	**Sichuan**	**3372841**	**16.85**	**97.24**	**98.57**
成都市	Chengdu	620690	29.77	99.99	99.99
自贡市	Zigong	93369	15.46	99.61	99.50
攀枝花市	Panzhihua	7045	4.64	98.19	98.93
泸州市	Luzhou	68067	6.32	98.72	99.42
德阳市	Deyang	246924	28.38	99.41	99.30
绵阳市	Mianyang	275500	19.22	99.60	99.58
广元市	Guangyuan	233153	31.24	98.54	98.72
遂宁市	Suining	300259	32.38	99.82	99.26
内江市	Neijiang	198969	17.13	96.69	98.06
乐山市	Leshan	100443	13.80	99.41	99.57
南充市	Nanchong	260853	14.33	99.07	99.21
眉山市	Meishan	84800	10.05	100.00	100.00
宜宾市	Yibin	56543	6.42	94.91	97.42
广安市	Guangan	143126	11.91	99.57	99.68
达州市	Dazhou	209893	13.25	96.97	95.83
雅安市	Yaan	121357	36.97	94.95	99.31
巴中市	Bazhong	104601	11.11	98.26	99.51
资阳市	Ziyang	111396	10.85	96.44	99.10
阿坝藏族羌族自治州	Aba	22828	10.19	91.50	98.10
甘孜藏族自治州	Ganzi	6457	2.85	97.07	96.89
凉山彝族自治州	Liangshan	106568	9.20	82.63	94.26

21-14 体育事业情况(2018年)
Basic Conditions of Sports Cause(2018)

项 目		Item		2018
国家级体育传统项目学校	(所)	Traditional Sports Events Schools of National Level	(unit)	21
省级体育传统项目示范学校	(所)	Traditional Sports Events Schools of Provincial Level	(unit)	312
#本年度新命名	(所)	Newly Named at the Current Year	(unit)	12
国家级青少年体育俱乐部	(所)	Youth Sports Clubs of National Level	(unit)	264
#本年度新命名	(所)	Newly Named at the Current Year	(unit)	0
国家级高水平体育后备人才基地	(个)	National High Level Sports Talented Reserve Bases	(unit)	18
四川省高水平体育后备人才基地	(个)	Provincial High Level Sports Talented Reserve Bases	(unit)	27
四川省县级业余训练重点单位	(个)	County-level Key Units of Amateur Training	(unit)	28
四川省幼儿体育基地	(个)	Provincial Children's Sports Bases	(unit)	50
城市街道体育组织累计	(个)	Sports Organizations in the Urban Streets	(unit)	2499
#本年度新增	(个)	Newly Added at the Current Year	(unit)	79
农村乡镇体育组织累计	(个)	Sports Organizations in the Rural Villages and Towns	(unit)	3936
#本年度新增	(个)	Newly Added at the Current Year	(unit)	144
健身站(点)累计	(个)	Fitness Stations (points)	(unit)	16907
#本年度新增	(个)	Newly Added at the Current Year	(unit)	414
社区体育健身俱乐部累计	(个)	Community Sports Fitness Clubs	(unit)	1586
#本年度新增	(个)	Newly Added at the Current Year	(unit)	76
行政村农民体育健康工程累计	(个)	Farmer Sports Health Projects in Administrative Village	(unit)	29776
#本年度新建	(个)	Newly Added at the Current Year	(unit)	2597
乡镇农民体育健身工程累计	(个)	Farmer Sports Fitness Projects in Villages and Towns	(unit)	1689
#本年度新建	(个)	Newly Added at the Current Year	(unit)	98
本年底国民体质测试站(点)累计	(个)	National Physical Fitness Test Station (points) at the End of This Year	(unit)	174
#本年度新增	(个)	Newly Added at the Current Year	(unit)	10
本年度接受国民体质监测人数	(人)	Number of People Receiving National Physical Fitness Monitoring	(person)	246369
本年度举办全民健身科学知识宣传讲座次数	(次)	Number of Lectures on Scientific Knowledge of National Fitness	(time)	448
本年度编印科学健身知识书籍册数	(册)	Copies of Books Published Scientific Knowledge of Fitness	(volume)	200950
审批社会体育指导员人数累计	(人)	Approval of the Number of Social Sports Instructors	(person)	191124
#本年度审批人数	(人)	Number of Annual Examination and Approval	(person)	15323
本年度培训社会体育指导员人数	(人)	Number of People Receiving Social Sports Instructor Training	(person)	20496
世界级比赛获得奖牌数	(枚)	Number of Medals Won in the World Competition	(piece)	15
#金牌	(枚)	Gold Medals	(piece)	7
亚洲级比赛获得奖牌数	(枚)	Number of Medals Won in Asian Games	(piece)	28
#金牌	(枚)	Gold Medals	(piece)	11
全国比赛获得奖牌数	(枚)	Number of Medals Won in the National Competition	(piece)	65
#金牌	(枚)	Gold Medals	(piece)	23

注：体育事业情况由四川省体育局提供。
a) Data in thie table are provided by the Sports Bureau of Sichuan Province.

21-15 各市(州)体育彩票发行情况(2018年)

Sports Lottery Distribution by Region(2018)

单位：万元 (10 000 yuan)

市(州)	Region	当年体育彩票发行额 Sports Lottery Issuance in Current Year	#足彩 Soccer Betting	#竞彩 Race Lottery	#即开型 Open-Type	当年提取公益金 Public Welfare FundDrawn from Sports Lottery(year-end)
全 省	**Sichuan**	**848504**	**40738**	**504924**	**26363**	**201366**
成都市	Chengdu	391903	21008	235709	11300	92527
自贡市	Zigong	21073	881	12221	537	5074
攀枝花市	Panzhihua	20244	752	11753	678	4814
泸州市	Luzhou	19879	1346	11219	302	4838
德阳市	Deyang	40867	1089	26788	975	9411
绵阳市	Mianyang	49604	2216	33771	1548	11143
广元市	Guangyuan	24175	1123	16662	430	5410
遂宁市	Suining	17692	398	9922	801	4328
内江市	Neijiang	18278	995	10622	480	4388
乐山市	Leshan	35415	1833	19529	1487	8612
南充市	Nanchong	31835	1712	18702	912	7617
眉山市	Meishan	25033	1542	14605	1074	5935
宜宾市	Yibin	38891	1084	24994	721	8936
广安市	Guangan	14977	893	10232	313	3351
达州市	Dazhou	24738	1299	12511	608	6269
雅安市	Yaan	11499	809	5897	522	2831
巴中市	Bazhong	13230	452	4663	759	3671
资阳市	Ziyang	12788	583	7942	386	2977
阿坝藏族羌族自治州	Aba	5239	134	2024	474	1384
甘孜藏族自治州	Ganzi	6045	140	3254	385	1473
凉山彝族自治州	Liangshan	25099	448	11901	1670	6377

注：当年提取公益金合计中含中央、省级提取数据。

a) Pubic welfare funds drawn from sport lottery include state and provincial data.

21-16 卫生机构基本情况(2018年)
Basic Statistics on Health Institutions(2018)

机构类别	Item	机构数(个) Health Institutions (unit)	实有床位数(张) Beds (bed)	人员合计(人) Personnel (person)	#卫生技术人员 Medical Technical Personnel	#管理人员 Administrative Personnel
全　省	**Total**	**81539**	**598842**	**747160**	**563086**	**34910**
医院合计	Total Number of Hospitals	2343	442215	438202	354778	23898
城市	Hospitals at Prefecture Level	1155	244446	265022	212385	15761
农村	Hospitals at County Level	1188	197769	173180	142393	8137
综合医院	General Hospitals	1485	284637	298596	244909	15960
中医医院	Hospitals of Chinese Medicine	232	60316	61259	51785	2611
中西医结合医院	Hospital Combining Traditional Chinese and Western Medicine	33	8431	8624	7393	382
民族医院	Minority Nationality Hospital	35	1565	1423	1175	69
专科医院	Specialized	550	86731	67896	49209	4856
#口腔	Stomatological	48	887	3126	2400	268
眼科	Ophthalmological	46	2850	4085	2415	482
耳鼻喉	Otoraryngology	15	1014	959	639	64
肿瘤	Oncological	10	3262	3696	3020	126
心血管病	Cardiovascular System Diseases	5	973	673	556	30
胸科	Chest Hospital	1	60	42	32	1
妇产(科)	Gynaecological and Obstetrical	43	2157	5334	3469	404
儿童	Paediatrics	5	512	697	505	58
精神病	Psychiatrical	90	46408	16894	12918	1057
传染病	Epidemiological	8	1982	2153	1781	115
皮肤病	Dermatology	16	656	760	551	63
麻风病	Leprological	3	243	77	46	5
职业病	Occupational disease	2	375	690	533	94

注：卫生机构资料由四川省卫生健康委员会提供。

a) Data of health agencies are provided by Health Commission of sichuan provincial.

21-16 续表 continued

机构类别	Item	机构数(个) Health Institutions (unit)	实有床位数(张) Beds (bed)	人员合计(人) Personnel (person)	#卫生技术人员 Medical Technical Personnel	#管理人员 Administrative Personnel
骨科	Orthopaedics	60	6687	6144	4762	331
康复	Recuperation	44	4189	2627	1990	240
整形外科医院	Orthopetic Survey	2	56	163	61	18
美容医院	Beauty Hospital	26	553	3998	1453	538
其它专科	Other Specialized Hospital	126	13867	15778	12078	962
护理院	Nursing Home	8	535	404	307	20
疗养院	Nurse Hospital					
社区卫生服务中心	Community Health Care Centre	424	10649	19684	16432	940
社区卫生服务站	Community Health Service Stations	557	1112	3547	3045	283
卫生院	Sanitation Station	4437	131644	112784	93767	5452
门诊部	Outpatient Department	523	441	8955	6290	737
诊所	Clinics	15663		36908	36072	
卫生所、医务室	Healthy Centre	804		2174	2047	
村卫生室	Village Clinics	56019		76741	13834	
急救中心(站)	First-aid Centre	18		431	280	51
采供血机构	Blood Collection and Supply Institution	35		2393	1757	186
妇幼保健院(所、站)	Maternity and Child Care Centre	201	12499	26133	21361	1489
专科疾病防治院(所、站)	Specialized Prevention Station	24	282	458	357	26
疾病预防控制中心(防疫站)	Epidemic Prevention and Control Centre	206		12812	9435	954
卫生监督所	Sanitary Supervision Station	202		3199	2483	309
医学科学研究机构	Research Institution of Medical Sciences	7		660	243	118
医学在职培训机构	Medical On the Job Training Institution	13		226	48	29
健康教育所(站、中心)	Healthy Education Centre	11		90	25	37
其他卫生机构	Other Health Care Institutions	52		1763	832	401

21-17 卫生机构数
Number of Health Institutions

单位：个 (unit)

年份 地区	Year Region	机构数 Number of Health Care Institutions	#医院 Hospitals	#社区卫生服务中心 Community Health Care Centres	#卫生院 Sanitation Stations	#疾病预防控制中心 Epidemic Prevention and Control Centres	#妇幼保健院(所、站) Maternity and Child Care Centres
2002		72768	1173	44	6280	214	200
2003		72810	1164	50	6048	208	198
2004		70944	1144	63	5369	209	196
2005		72399	1155	68	5179	207	197
2006		75262	1178	213	5012	207	202
2007		72862	1162	214	4845	208	201
2008		71195	1143	234	4817	208	201
2009		72907	1187	257	4745	207	202
2010		74311	1260	306	4688	207	203
2011		75814	1393	344	4619	206	203
2012		76555	1542	361	4607	204	200
2013		80039	1716	379	4595	207	202
2014		81081	1822	397	4575	207	202
2015		80114	1942	397	4511	206	202
2016		79516	2067	412	4493	206	202
2017		80480	2219	417	4476	206	203
2018		81539	2343	424	4437	206	201
成都市	Chengdu	10755	605	123	286	23	21
自贡市	Zigong	2245	72	16	96	7	7
攀枝花市	Panzhihua	1056	31	21	43	6	6
泸州市	Luzhou	4616	147	18	129	8	8
德阳市	Deyang	2819	90	15	132	7	6
绵阳市	Mianyang	4674	117	23	274	11	10
广元市	Guangyuan	3540	80	13	248	8	7
遂宁市	Suining	3779	73	15	104	6	6
内江市	Neijiang	3297	76	15	110	6	6
乐山市	Leshan	3259	102	15	207	12	12
南充市	Nanchong	8583	165	36	440	10	10
眉山市	Meishan	2040	88	11	126	7	7
宜宾市	Yibin	5260	135	14	177	11	11
广安市	Guangan	3446	73	12	174	7	7
达州市	Dazhou	4293	109	13	303	7	8
雅安市	Yaan	1456	43	4	144	9	9
巴中市	Bazhong	3274	78	27	230	6	6
资阳市	Ziyang	3438	47	8	117	4	3
阿坝藏族羌族自治州	Aba	1683	41	8	220	14	14
甘孜藏族自治州	Ganzi	2777	44	2	332	19	19
凉山彝族自治州	Liangshan	5249	127	15	545	18	18

21-18 各市(州)卫生机构数
Number of Health Institutions by Region

单位：个 (unit)

市(州)	Region	2010	2011	2012	2013	2014	2015	2016	2017	2018
全　省	**Total**	**74311**	**75814**	**76555**	**80039**	**81081**	**80114**	**79516**	**80480**	**81539**
成都市	Chengdu	7194	7401	7605	7976	8190	8481	9853	10183	10755
自贡市	Zigong	2125	2346	2377	2460	2409	2346	2274	2333	2245
攀枝花市	Panzhihua	1020	1025	1024	1044	1079	1064	1060	1064	1056
泸州市	Luzhou	4733	4778	4351	4633	4619	4566	4560	4628	4616
德阳市	Deyang	2732	2816	2765	2795	2774	2717	2708	2738	2819
绵阳市	Mianyang	3976	4173	4325	4436	4494	4417	4371	4449	4674
广元市	Guangyuan	3371	3285	3313	3531	3554	3545	3460	3557	3540
遂宁市	Suining	3713	3724	3750	3798	3762	3735	3846	3822	3779
内江市	Neijiang	2971	3126	3119	3246	3228	3195	3096	3259	3297
乐山市	Leshan	2957	3026	3062	3286	3277	3098	3100	3206	3259
南充市	Nanchong	8040	8269	8399	8856	8780	8712	8703	8696	8583
眉山市	Meishan	2064	1989	1919	2059	2107	2057	2044	2068	2040
宜宾市	Yibin	4158	4137	4180	4389	5136	4963	5025	5062	5260
广安市	Guangan	3072	3347	3362	3561	3561	3500	3447	3446	3446
达州市	Dazhou	4068	4063	4172	4406	4397	4413	4172	4191	4293
雅安市	Yaan	1279	1367	1369	1520	1518	1494	1334	1426	1456
巴中市	Bazhong	3053	3062	3086	3305	3299	3164	3234	3218	3274
资阳市	Ziyang	5004	4912	4829	4969	4956	4902	3485	3460	3438
阿坝藏族羌族自治州	Aba	1557	1562	1570	1624	1683	1649	1642	1656	1683
甘孜藏族自治州	Ganzi	2292	2359	2701	2722	2776	2725	2706	2719	2777
凉山彝族自治州	Liangshan	4932	5047	5277	5423	5482	5371	5396	5299	5249

21-19 卫生机构床位数
Number of Beds in Health Institutions

单位：张 (bed)

年 份 地 区	Year Region	床位数 Number of Beds in Health Care Centre	#医院 Hospitals	#社区卫生服务中心 Community Health Care Centres	#卫生院 Sanitation Stations	#妇幼保健院（所、站） Maternity and Child Care Centres
2002		187179	119976	206	56467	4289
2003		187741	120173	144	56671	4501
2004		191523	123995	304	56945	4786
2005		194940	127129	1053	57460	5016
2006		201854	130677	2270	59707	5301
2007		214329	136757	3149	66063	5838
2008		244119	149289	4526	80697	6390
2009		275555	167271	5170	92403	7050
2010		302061	185459	6812	98252	7843
2011		335151	212282	8299	102544	7892
2012		390122	257333	8636	111550	8759
2013		426378	289022	9003	114412	9682
2014		459588	319155	9046	117090	10152
2015		488719	345791	8995	119156	10681
2016		519149	375708	9388	120387	11122
2017		563419	411911	10135	127419	11794
2018		598842	442215	10649	131644	12499
成都市	Chengdu	143248	118128	4140	17684	3088
自贡市	Zigong	22014	16868	285	3859	655
攀枝花市	Panzhihua	10398	9404	56	663	236
泸州市	Luzhou	31839	22407	618	7642	625
德阳市	Deyang	24254	16496	219	6863	610
绵阳市	Mianyang	38559	25937	381	11515	683
广元市	Guangyuan	22091	15895	364	5186	572
遂宁市	Suining	20139	13822	391	5612	286
内江市	Neijiang	24106	17520	83	6219	261
乐山市	Leshan	24063	17644	564	5073	745
南充市	Nanchong	41694	31167	712	8708	1032
眉山市	Meishan	19693	12978	361	5654	642
宜宾市	Yibin	33454	25106	541	7347	457
广安市	Guangan	19777	13982	423	5114	246
达州市	Dazhou	32943	20959	466	10863	503
雅安市	Yaan	12344	10415	71	1780	78
巴中市	Bazhong	21769	14253	494	6566	434
资阳市	Ziyang	19004	12145	52	6391	333
阿坝藏族羌族自治州	Aba	4899	3710	29	1006	136
甘孜藏族自治州	Ganzi	5207	3576		1375	256
凉山彝族自治州	Liangshan	27347	19803	399	6524	621

21-20 各市(州)卫生机构床位数
Number of Beds in Health Institutions by Region

单位：张 (bed)

市(州)	Region	2010	2011	2012	2013	2014	2015	2016	2017	2018
全　省	**Total**	**302061**	**335151**	**390122**	**426378**	**459588**	**488719**	**519149**	**563419**	**598842**
成都市	Chengdu	69459	79780	92062	100957	108031	114726	128058	134507	143248
自贡市	Zigong	10533	11757	14304	15249	16396	17644	18832	20064	22014
攀枝花市	Panzhihua	7321	7972	8578	9254	9599	10097	9867	10004	10398
泸州市	Luzhou	13321	15277	20451	21897	22666	24548	26612	29256	31839
德阳市	Deyang	14144	15725	16895	17785	19118	19968	21190	22570	24254
绵阳市	Mianyang	20046	22236	25913	28755	30756	32110	33708	36322	38559
广元市	Guangyuan	11853	12392	14292	15567	16753	18211	19778	21233	22091
遂宁市	Suining	10277	11468	13421	14110	15825	17197	18174	19543	20139
内江市	Neijiang	12615	13744	17153	18399	19825	20326	20769	22605	24106
乐山市	Leshan	13703	14764	15807	17282	18979	19290	20553	22390	24063
南充市	Nanchong	19810	21883	24522	26779	29670	32634	36222	40193	41694
眉山市	Meishan	9393	10462	12429	14376	15830	16296	16687	19170	19693
宜宾市	Yibin	17123	18006	21070	23611	25061	26408	29437	32122	33454
广安市	Guangan	9349	9828	11033	12080	13213	14729	15940	18186	19777
达州市	Dazhou	15247	16913	20277	22225	22495	23998	25447	29915	32943
雅安市	Yaan	7181	8027	8649	9738	10812	11759	11861	12382	12344
巴中市	Bazhong	9338	9868	12160	13459	14608	15546	16767	19174	21769
资阳市	Ziyang	13037	15067	18423	19553	20847	22269	16302	17815	19004
阿坝藏族羌族自治州	Aba	3026	3292	3700	3883	4272	4435	4447	4551	4899
甘孜藏族自治州	Ganzi	2909	3280	3681	4136	5063	4918	5054	4955	5207
凉山彝族自治州	Liangshan	12376	13410	15302	17283	19769	21610	23444	26462	27347

21-21 卫生机构人员数
Number of Persons Engaged in Health Institutions

单位：人 (person)

年 份 市(州)	Year Region	人员合计 Total	#卫生技术人员 Medical Technical Personnel	#执业医师 Licensed Doctor	#执业助理医师 Licensed Assistant Doctor	#注册护士 Licensed Nurse	#管理人员 Administrative Personnel
2002		378830	248470	86978	33378	60098	20070
2003		373628	245326	86101	34124	59494	17960
2004		363179	242255	84785	34531	60871	17392
2005		362014	244367	86205	35832	61237	15825
2006		378374	255140	87944	41446	63730	15903
2007		388644	264206	91273	34848	73485	19467
2008		400248	277112	96460	25324	78062	18500
2009		437758	303050	109090	29594	91164	18456
2010		467774	323915	114734	29843	104930	23288
2011		505113	353561	122525	31489	121319	25632
2012		549866	389001	130106	33272	139811	26850
2013		595645	426597	139037	34805	157459	29675
2014		627159	451747	145026	34494	175522	32091
2015		647577	472816	149101	33110	190643	30778
2016		671305	496343	153859	32171	207691	31480
2017		710787	530935	162995	32590	228608	32747
2018		747160	563086	171554	34056	247322	34910
成都市	Chengdu	215863	168682	56116	5432	78395	11628
自贡市	Zigong	24861	19614	5826	1220	8829	1427
攀枝花市	Panzhihua	13130	10651	3590	352	4890	648
泸州市	Luzhou	36642	27507	7922	1884	12911	1665
德阳市	Deyang	30425	23625	7455	1758	9858	1106
绵阳市	Mianyang	42343	32996	10395	2443	14226	1762
广元市	Guangyuan	24382	18173	5237	1106	7696	1113
遂宁市	Suining	23256	17333	5894	1068	7174	1000
内江市	Neijiang	26184	19776	6023	1625	8889	1415
乐山市	Leshan	26858	20555	6182	1625	9271	1043
南充市	Nanchong	49793	34870	11895	1910	13883	2764
眉山市	Meishan	23026	17122	4864	1311	7539	791
宜宾市	Yibin	38141	28827	7447	2237	13225	1323
广安市	Guangan	22957	15774	4538	1017	6599	1182
达州市	Dazhou	37522	26107	7439	2152	11294	1326
雅安市	Yaan	14723	11940	3254	903	5008	733
巴中市	Bazhong	23551	16783	4624	1919	6744	863
资阳市	Ziyang	19756	14421	4226	1176	5993	881
阿坝藏族羌族自治州	Aba	9228	6723	1568	524	2078	365
甘孜藏族自治州	Ganzi	9931	6556	1252	439	1994	477
凉山彝族自治州	Liangshan	34588	25051	5807	1955	10826	1398

21-21 续表 continued

单位：人 (person)

年 份 市(州)	Year Region	人员合计 Total	#医院 Hospitals	#社区卫生服务中心 Community Health Care Centres	#卫生院 Sanitation Stations	#疾病预防控制中心 Epidemic Prevention and Control Centres	#妇幼保健院(所、站) Maternity and Child Care Centres
2002		378830	144086	556	79247	11219	10053
2003		373628	142945	509	77447	10944	8672
2004		363179	142017	709	72939	10518	8674
2005		362014	142955	1487	70403	10410	8648
2006		378374	147122	2672	69172	10491	8856
2007		388644	167432	5918	73729	10450	10588
2008		400248	175472	7813	76405	10444	11188
2009		437758	195099	9370	82778	10352	11950
2010		467774	215902	11658	84200	10431	13153
2011		505113	243520	13773	88075	10638	14297
2012		549866	277344	14393	93287	11035	15656
2013		595645	309129	15091	95886	11307	16950
2014		627159	336694	15532	97671	11552	18096
2015		647577	359411	16003	100127	11593	20071
2016		671305	383958	17788	104809	12307	22440
2017		710787	412759	18699	109238	12697	24678
2018		747160	438202	19684	112784	12812	26133
成都市	Chengdu	215863	148879	9729	14538	2872	7138
自贡市	Zigong	24861	14847	462	3798	505	1428
攀枝花市	Panzhihua	13130	8676	592	992	253	510
泸州市	Luzhou	36642	20697	714	6120	487	1010
德阳市	Deyang	30425	17006	524	5412	505	1070
绵阳市	Mianyang	42343	24527	710	8063	611	1452
广元市	Guangyuan	24382	13455	501	4836	378	1029
遂宁市	Suining	23256	12227	459	4066	331	574
内江市	Neijiang	26184	14871	187	4633	420	564
乐山市	Leshan	26858	15094	671	4285	574	1269
南充市	Nanchong	49793	27516	967	7299	558	1691
眉山市	Meishan	23026	12184	614	4938	437	1266
宜宾市	Yibin	38141	21648	683	6445	585	1154
广安市	Guangan	22957	11553	542	5090	451	675
达州市	Dazhou	37522	18448	752	8066	674	1035
雅安市	Yaan	14723	9726	168	2416	394	328
巴中市	Bazhong	23551	10961	514	5220	358	955
资阳市	Ziyang	19756	9581	257	4717	320	641
阿坝藏族羌族自治州	Aba	9228	4318	107	2039	576	487
甘孜藏族自治州	Ganzi	9931	3934	19	2415	463	519
凉山彝族自治州	Liangshan	34588	18054	512	7396	1060	1338

21-22 各市(州)卫生机构人员数

Number of Persons Engaged in Health Institutions by Region

单位：人 (person)

市(州)	Region	2010	2011	2012	2013	2014	2015	2016	2017	2018
全　省	**Total**	**467774**	**505113**	**549866**	**595645**	**627159**	**647577**	**671305**	**710787**	**747160**
成都市	Chengdu	117401	130490	143410	153962	164273	173167	190236	200739	215863
自贡市	Zigong	16565	17485	19114	20598	21570	22318	22799	23899	24861
攀枝花市	Panzhihua	10482	11272	11283	12035	12683	12689	12776	12901	13130
泸州市	Luzhou	21062	22940	25008	27965	29513	30722	31196	34524	36642
德阳市	Deyang	19834	22030	23187	24803	25826	27038	28024	29404	30425
绵阳市	Mianyang	27662	29964	32803	35932	37303	37180	38265	39971	42343
广元市	Guangyuan	16882	17356	18689	20155	21006	21733	21979	22924	24382
遂宁市	Suining	16675	17245	18452	19195	19830	20634	21174	22718	23256
内江市	Neijiang	18343	19350	21431	23030	23486	23495	24017	25305	26184
乐山市	Leshan	18446	20093	21295	22671	23516	23790	24523	25762	26858
南充市	Nanchong	30741	33008	36264	39455	41401	42864	44833	47840	49793
眉山市	Meishan	15055	15805	17866	18784	20432	20077	20639	22705	23026
宜宾市	Yibin	22387	24507	26230	29572	31183	31702	33793	36343	38141
广安市	Guangan	14800	15575	16394	17459	18917	19835	20942	22295	22957
达州市	Dazhou	26555	27917	29878	32888	33415	33814	33435	36205	37522
雅安市	Yaan	8568	9092	10086	11435	12470	12758	13269	13983	14723
巴中市	Bazhong	15319	16297	18289	20502	21328	20891	21820	22523	23551
资阳市	Ziyang	19466	21204	23050	24593	25470	26113	18478	19138	19756
阿坝藏族羌族自治州	Aba	5466	5670	6306	7164	7736	8030	8498	8774	9228
甘孜藏族自治州	Ganzi	6977	7617	8151	8482	8711	9064	9387	9622	9931
凉山彝族自治州	Liangshan	19088	20196	22680	24965	27090	29663	31222	33212	34588

21-23 前十大类病伤死亡原因及构成(2018年)
Death Rate of 10 Major Diseases Categories(2018)

顺位 No.	病伤死亡原因	Cause of Death	死亡率(1/10万) Death Rate (per 100 000 persons)	构成(%) As % of Total Deaths
1	循环系统	Diseases of the Circulatory System	227.91	35.57
2	肿瘤	Tumour	161.27	25.17
3	呼吸系统	Diseases of the Respiratory System	118.71	18.53
4	损伤和中毒	Trauma and Toxicosis	48.79	7.62
6	消化系统	Diseases of the Digestive System	19.91	3.11
7	内分泌、营养、代谢、免疫	Endocrine, Nutritional, Metabolic and Immune Diseases	16.30	2.54
5	传染病和寄生虫病	Infectious Disease and Verminosis	8.76	1.37
8	泌尿和生殖系统	Diseases of the Genitourinary System	8.14	1.27
9	神经系统疾病	Nervous System Diseases	6.77	1.06
10	精神障碍	Mental Disorders	2.55	0.40

21-24 前十位单病种死亡原因及构成(2018年)
Death Rate of 10 Single-species Major Diseases(2018)

顺位 No.	前十位单病种类目	10 Single-species Major Diseases	死亡率(1/10万) Death Rate (per 100 000 persons)	构成比(%) As % of Total Deaths
1	脑血管病	Cerebrovascular Disease	119.71	18.68
2	慢性阻塞性肺病	Chronic Obstructive Pulmonary Disease	112.96	17.63
3	缺血性心脏病	Ischemic Heart Disease	79.50	12.41
4	肺癌	Malignant Tumour	46.77	7.30
5	肝癌	Malignant Liver Tumour	25.29	3.95
6	食管癌	Malignant Oesophagus Tumour	19.25	3.00
7	胃癌	Malignant Stomach Tumour	15.81	2.47
8	高血压性心脏病	Hypertensive Heart Disease	15.66	2.44
9	交通事故	Traffic	15.16	2.37
10	糖尿病	Diabetes mellitus	14.81	2.31

21-25 国家免疫规划疫苗基础免疫接种率(2018年)
Basis Inoculability Rate of National Immunization Vaccine Planning(2018)

种 类	Item	常规报告接种率(%) Inoculability Rate of Conventional Report (%)
卡介苗	Bcg Vaccine	99.71
脊灰疫苗	Poliomyelitis Vaccine	99.66
百白破三联	Chincough, Diphtheria and Tetanus Joint Vaccine	99.22
麻疹疫苗	Measles Vaccine	98.96
乙肝疫苗全程	Hepatitis-B Vaccine Full Process	99.63

21-26 法定报告传染病发病及死亡情况(2018年)
Incidence and Death from Infectious Diseases(2018)

病 种	Item	发病率(1/10万) Incidence Diseases Rate (per 100 000 persons)	死亡率(1/10万) Death Rate (per 100 000 persons)	病死率(%) Mortality Rate per 100 Infectous Disease Patients
甲乙丙合计	**Total of Category A, B and C**	**428.8677**	**4.9819**	**1.1616**
一.甲乙类合计	**I. Total of Category A and B**	**188.9762**	**4.9771**	**2.6337**
鼠疫	The Plague	-	-	-
霍乱	Cholera	-	-	-
传染性非典型肺炎	SARS	-	-	-
艾滋病	AIDS	17.4657	4.7121	26.9792
H I V	HIV	31.7562	7.6704	24.1540
病毒性肝炎	Hepatitis	63.8906	0.0349	0.0546
甲肝	A	2.1826	0.0012	0.0550
乙肝	B	46.4298	0.0253	0.0545
丙肝	C	13.1258	0.0084	0.0640
丁肝	D	0.0205	-	-
戊肝	E	1.4611	-	-
肝炎(未分型)	Hepatitis (Not Classified)	0.6709	-	-
脊髓灰质炎	Poliomyelitis	-	-	-
人感染高致病性禽流感	People Avian Flu	-	-	-
麻疹	Measles	0.165	-	-
流行性出血热	Hemorrhage Fever	0.3505	0.0036	1.0271
狂犬病	Hydrophobia	0.0253	0.0253	100.0000
流行性乙型脑炎	Encephalitis B	0.1759	0.0036	2.0466
登革热	Dengue Fever	0.059	-	-
炭疽	Anthrax	0.106	0.0012	1.1321
细菌性和阿米巴性痢疾	Dysentery	5.8492	-	-
肺结核	Pulmonary Tuberculosis	57.3368	0.1891	0.3298
伤寒和副伤寒	Typhoild and Paratyphoid Fever	0.4397	-	-
流行性脑脊髓膜炎	Epidemic Encephalitis	0.0072	-	-
百日咳	Pertussis	1.5575	0.0012	0.0770
白喉	Diphtheria	-	-	-
新生儿破伤风 *	Newborn Baby Tetanus	0.0024	-	-
猩红热	Scarlet Fever	2.2139	-	-
布鲁氏菌病	Brucellosis	0.0771	-	-
淋病	Gonorrhea	3.8015	-	-
梅毒	Syphilis	35.1542	0.006	0.0171
钩端螺旋体病	Leptospirosis	0.0289	-	-
血吸虫病	Schistosomiasis	0.006	-	-
疟疾	Malaria	0.2638	-	-
人感染H7N9禽流感	Human Infection with H7N9 Avian Influenza	-	-	-
二.丙类合计	**Ⅱ. Total of Category C**	**239.8916**	**0.0048**	**0.0020**
流行性感冒	Influenza	10.2758	0.0036	0.0350
流行性腮腺炎	Epidemic Mumps	18.2089	-	-
风疹	Rubella	0.2313	-	-
急性出血性结膜炎	Acute Haemorrhagic Conjunctivitis	0.7576	-	-
麻风病	Leprosy	0.0265	-	-
流行性和地方性斑疹伤寒	Typhus Fever	0.1156	-	-
黑热病	Kala-Azar	0.0181	-	-
包虫病	Echinococcosis	0.5529	-	-
丝虫病	Filariasis	-	-	-
其它感染性腹泻病	Other Infectious Diarrhoea	44.7145	-	-
手足口病	Hand-foot-mouth Disease	164.9904	0.0012	0.0007

注：新生儿破伤风发病率＝当年发病数÷当年0岁组人口数×1000‰；新生儿破伤风死亡率＝当年死亡数÷当年0岁组人口数×1000‰。
a) Incidence diseases rate of newborn baby tetanus=Number of incidence diseases in current year÷Number of population of 0 age group in current year×1000‰.Death rate of newborn baby tetanus=Number of death in current year÷Number of population of 0 age group in current year×1000‰.

主要统计指标解释

艺术表演团体 指由文化部门主办或实行行业管理(经文化行政部门审批或已申报登记并领取相关许可证)，专门从事表演艺术等活动的各类专业艺术表演团体，含民间职业剧团。不包括群众业余文艺表演团体。

广播/电视节目综合人口覆盖率 指根据原国家广电总局制定的《广播电视人口覆盖率统计技术标准和方法》进行统计调查的，在对象区内能接收到由中央、省、地市或县通过无线、有线或卫星等各种技术方式转播的各级广播/电视节目的人口数占全省总人口数的百分比。

医疗卫生机构 指从卫生(卫生计生)行政部门取得《医疗机构执业许可证》、《计划生育技术服务许可证》，或从民政、工商行政、机构编制管理部门取得法人单位登记证书，为社会提供医疗服务、公共卫生服务或从事医学科研和医学在职培训等工作的单位。医疗卫生机构包括医院、基层医疗卫生机构、专业公共卫生机构、其他医疗卫生机构。

医院 包括综合医院、中医医院、中西医结合医院、民族医院、各类专科医院和护理院，不包括专科疾病防治院、妇幼保健院和疗养院，包括医学院附属医院。

卫生人员 指在医院、基层医疗卫生机构、专业公共卫生机构及其他医疗卫生机构工作的职工，包括卫生技术人员、乡村医生和卫生员、其他技术人员、管理人员和工勤人员。一律按支付年底工资的在岗职工统计，包括各类聘任人员(含合同工)及返聘本单位半年以上人员，不包括临时工、离退休人员、退职人员、离开本单位仍保留劳动关系人员、本单位返聘和临聘不足半年人员。

卫生技术人员 包括执业医师、执业助理医师、注册护士、药师（士）、检验技师（士）、影像技师、卫生监督员和见习医（药、护、技）师（士）等卫生专业人员。不包括从事管理工作的卫生技术人员(如院长、副院长、党委书记等)。

甲乙类法定报告传染病发病率 指某年某地区每 10 万人口中甲、乙类法定报告传染病发病数。即:

甲乙类法定报告传染病发病率=甲、乙类法定报告传染病发病数/人口数 × 100000

甲乙类法定报告传染病死亡率 指某年某地区每 10 万人口中甲、乙类法定报告传染病死亡数。即:

甲乙类法定报告传染病死亡率=甲、乙类法定报告传染病死亡数/人口数 × 100000

甲乙类法定报告传染病病死率 指某年某地区甲、乙类法定报告传染病死亡数与发病数之比。即:

甲乙类法定报告传染病病死率=甲、乙类法定报告传染病死亡数/发病数 × 100%

Explanatory Notes on Main Statistical Indicators

Arts Performance Troupes refer to the various professional performing arts groups, which sponsored by the cultural sectors or guided by the cultural society (approved by the cultural administration authority, or registered and permitted with the relative certificate), including non-governmental troupes. The mass amateur arts performance troupes are not included.

The Population Coverage Rate of Radio/Television refers to the percentage of the provincial population who can receive radio/television programs transmitted by national, provincial, municipal or county stations through wireless, cable or satellite techniques, according to Statistical Standard and Method on Television and Radio Coverage of Population established by the former State Administration of Broadcasting, Film and Television.

Medical and Health Care Institutions refer to the units which have been qualified the Certification of Health Care Institution, certification of family planning technical service by the administration of public health (family planning), or qualified the Certification of Corporate Unit by the civil affairs, administration for industry and commerce, commission office for public sector reform, and engaging in medical health care services, public health services, or medicine research and on-job training, etc., including: hospitals, health care institutions at grass-root level, specialized public health institutions, and other medical and health care institutions.

Hospitals include general hospitals, hospitals specialized in traditional Chinese medicine, hospitals of integrated traditional Chinese and western medicine, ethnic hospitals, specialized hospitals and nursing hospitals, excluding specialized disease prevention and treatment institutes, maternal and child health care hospitals and convalescent hospitals, including affiliated hospital of medical college.

Health Care Employee refer to all employees engaged in the health care institutions, such as hospitals, health care institutions at grass-root level, specialized public health institutions, and other medical and health care institutions, including medical technical personnel, village doctors and assistants, other technical personnel, managerial and service staff. The data is based on the year end payroll, including personnel hired (including contract labour) and re-employed after retirement by the institution for over half a year and excluding temporary workers, retired personnel, resigned personnel, personnel who have left the institution but kept the contract relation and personnel who are re-employed after retirement or temporarily employed for less than half a year.

Medical Technical Personnel refer to the professional staff engaged in health care, including licensed doctors, licensed assistant doctors, registered nurses, pharmacists, laboratory technicians, imaging staff, health care supervisors and intern doctors, pharmacists, nurses, and technical personnel, excluding the medical technical personnel engaged in managerial job (e.g. president, vice president and secretary of the party committee, etc.).

Incidence Rate of A and B Type of Notifiable Infectious Diseases refer to the incidence cases notifiable class A and class B infectious diseases per 100 thousand population in the reference region in the reference year. The formula is:

$$\frac{\text{Incidence Rate of A and B of}}{\text{Notifiable Infectious Diseases}} = \frac{\text{Incidence Cases Notifiable Class A and Class B Infectious Diseases}}{\text{Population}} \times 100000$$

Death Rate of A and B Type of Notifiable Infectious Diseases refer to the death cases notifiable class A and class B infectious diseases per 100 thousand population in the reference region in the reference year. The formula is:

$$\frac{\text{Death Rate of A and B Type of}}{\text{Notifiable Infectious Diseases}} = \frac{\text{Death Cases Notifiable Class A and Class B Infectious Diseases}}{\text{Population}} \times 100000$$

Mortality Rate of A and B Type of Notifiable Infectious Diseases refer to the ratio of death cases notifiable class A and class B infectious diseases to the incidence cases in the reference region in the reference year. The formula is:

$$\frac{\text{Mortality Rate of A and B Type}}{\text{Notifiable Infectious Diseases}} = \frac{\text{Death Cases Notifiable Class A and Class B Infectious Diseases}}{\text{Incidence Cases}} \times 100\%$$

其他社会活动

Chapter 22 Other Social Activities

22-1 收养类单位基本情况
Basic Statistics on Adoption Units

项 目		Item		2018
单位数	(个)	Number of Units	(unit)	2572
工商部门登记	(个)	Registered in Business Administration	(unit)	167
编制部门登记	(个)	Registered in Establishment Departments	(unit)	1825
民政部门登记	(个)	Registered in Civil Administration	(unit)	435
未登记	(个)	Unregistered	(unit)	145
床位数	(张)	Number of Beds	(bed)	319579
工商部门登记	(张)	Registered in Business Administration	(bed)	24454
编制部门登记	(张)	Registered in Establishment Departments	(bed)	225454
民政部门登记	(张)	Registered in Civil Administration	(bed)	59175
未登记	(张)	Unregistered	(bed)	10496
工作人员	(人)	Persons Engaged	(person)	24699
工商部门登记	(人)	Registered in Business Administration	(person)	2470
编制部门登记	(人)	Registered in Establishment Departments	(person)	15222
民政部门登记	(人)	Registered in Civil Administration	(person)	6123
未登记	(人)	Unregistered	(person)	884

注：收养类单位情况由四川省民政厅提供。
a) Data of adoption units are provided by Sichuan Provincial Civil Affairs Department.

22-2 收养类单位床位数及收养人员数
Number of Beds and Persons Housed in Adoption Units

项 目	Item	床位数(张) Number of Beds (bed)		收养人数(人) Person Housed (person)	
		2017	2018	2017	2018
合 计	**Total**	**54082**	**52549**	**32575**	**31242**
优抚收养性单位	Units for Arranging the Family Members of Martyrs and Disabled Veterans	8235	4155	5632	996
荣誉军人康复医院	Convalescent Homes for Honored Ex-servicemen	1110	596	861	122
复员军人疗养院	Sanatoriums for Ex-servicemen	330	198	89	32
复退军人精神病院	Mental Hospitals for Ex-servicemen	3378	1520	3320	200
光荣院	Homes for Disabled Veterans	3417	1841	1362	642
福利收养性单位	Welfare Adoption Units	45847	48394	26943	30246
社会福利院	Social Welfare Homes	28967	28507	14934	15228
儿童福利院	Children Welfare Homes	6456	6772	2818	2872
社会福利医院	Psychopathy Welfare Homes	10424	13115	9191	12146

22-3 社区服务机构基本情况
Basic Statistics on Community Service Organizations

项　目		Item		2018
社区服务机构单位数	(个)	Number of Community Service Organizations	(unit)	24599
#农村社区服务机构	(个)	Rural Community Service Organization	(unit)	11807
#可以为居民提供便民办事服务的机构	(个)	Institutions to Provide Convenience Services for Residents	(unit)	9376
#可以为居民提供活动场所的机构	(个)	Mechanism for Providing Active Sites for Residents	(unit)	1265
#可以为居民提供养老等服务的机构	(个)	Institutions to Provide Pension Services for Residents	(unit)	649
#农村	(个)	Countryside	(unit)	
年末职工人数	(人)	Number of Employees at the end of this Year	(person)	76532
#女性	(人)	Female	(person)	26531
机构床位数	(张)	Number of Beds in Organizations	(bed)	218051
日间照料床位数	(张)	Day Care Beds	(bed)	86307
#农村	(张)	Countryside	(bed)	40661
住宿收养床位数	(张)	Accommodation & Adoption Beds	(bed)	131744
#农村	(张)	Countryside	(bed)	84778
年末收养人数	(人)	Number of Adoption at the End of this Year	(person)	66041
日间照料人数	(人)	Number of People under Day Care	(person)	18518
#农村	(人)	Countryside	(person)	13420
住宿收养人数	(个)	Number of Accommodation & Adoption	(unit)	47523
#农村	(人)	Countryside	(person)	35940
社区服务志愿者组织数	(个)	Volunteer Organizations of Community Service	(unit)	352
注册社区志愿者人数	(人)	Registered Community Volunteers	(person)	43795

22-4 婚姻登记和离婚情况
Basic Statistics on Marriages and Divorces

项　目		Item		2010	2015	2016	2017	2018
按居住地分		By Residence						
内地居民登记结婚	(对)	Registered Marriages of Mainland	(couple)	713263	740186	725628	688133	667559
涉外及华侨、港澳台居民登记结婚	(对)	Registered Marriages with Foreigner and the Citizen of Hongkong, Macao, Taiwan	(couple)	1580	1340	1490	1397	1483
按婚前状况分		By Premarital Situation						
初婚	(人)	First Marriages	(person)	1197122	1138435	1093585	1029904	986278
再婚	(人)	Remarriages	(person)	232564	344617	360651	349156	351806
再婚中恢复结婚	(对)	Remarriages of Divorced Couple	(couple)	8594	29669	33747	31898	33330
内地居民离婚数	(对)	Registered Divorces of Mainland	(couple)	173824	241133	254928	269070	269511

22-5 各市(州)内地居民婚姻登记和离婚情况
Basic Statistics on Marriage and Divorces of Mainland by Region

单位：对 (couple)

市(州)	Region	内地居民登记结婚 Registered Marriages of Mainland					内地居民登记离婚 Registered Divorces of Mainland				
		2010	2015	2016	2017	2018	2010	2015	2016	2017	2018
全　省	**Sichuan**	**713263**	**740186**	**725628**	**688133**	**667559**	**173824**	**241133**	**254928**	**269070**	**269511**
成都市	Chengdu	119408	125085	131802	131111	132891	43236	52726	60686	68820	63760
自贡市	Zigong	24959	24349	23000	21764	19978	6369	9259	9734	10321	9904
攀枝花市	Panzhihua	9780	10064	9437	8494	8127	3946	4344	4307	4247	4177
泸州市	Luzhou	38260	35798	37392	33839	31514	8331	11388	12070	12723	12727
德阳市	Deyang	26303	30978	29357	26701	24669	10157	12165	12554	12975	12596
绵阳市	Mianyang	46778	43988	41748	37679	36582	13033	15931	16475	16519	15802
广元市	Guangyuan	19400	23257	21321	19782	19760	4462	5735	6886	6743	6607
遂宁市	Suining	25423	31339	28931	25830	25145	4552	9395	9921	10470	10526
内江市	Neijiang	36061	32677	29955	26887	25688	8898	14161	14357	14258	14469
乐山市	Leshan	27988	29105	28322	25882	24324	9547	11438	11737	11787	11899
南充市	Nanchong	60430	57118	56934	44973	48680	9612	14884	16032	14050	17975
眉山市	Meishan	37337	30658	29716	28503	26616	10337	11454	11958	12522	12148
宜宾市	Yibin	40138	45466	43772	39396	37627	10830	15171	15836	16785	17510
广安市	Guangan	33873	34607	33772	31116	30594	5533	10169	10767	11370	11948
达州市	Dazhou	55942	56163	49864	45401	42684	7964	13322	14049	15136	15177
雅安市	Yaan	12715	13400	13406	12555	12632	3731	5371	5136	5494	5738
巴中市	Bazhong	40540	33497	33187	29705	28146	2757	5585	6058	6615	6870
资阳市	Ziyang	37014	35376	22739	22416	20346	7502	12479	8843	9341	9350
阿坝藏族羌族自治州	Aba	6145	7648	8691	7475	7214	381	1138	1504	1449	1476
甘孜藏族自治州	Ganzi	3949	12516	13416	13186	11101	458	1171	1294	1556	1583
凉山彝族自治州	Liangshan	10820	27097	38866	55441	53241	2188	3847	4724	5889	7269

注：婚姻登记情况由四川省民政厅提供。离婚数不包括法院判决数。

a) Data of marriage registration are provided by Sichuan Provincial Civil Affairs Department. The number of divorces mediated by the count are not included in that of divorces.

22-6 律师、公证、调解工作基本情况
Basic Statistics on Lawyers, Notarization and Mediation

项 目		Item		2005	2010	2014	2015	2016	2017	2018
律师工作		**Lawyers**								
律师事务所	(所)	Number of Law Offices	(unit)	615	802	1032	1130	1233	1329	1458
律师工作者	(人)	Number of Lawyers	(person)	6331	9297	13974	15526	16683	19505	21206
#专职律师	(人)	Full-time Lawyers	(person)	6025	8504	13207	14519	15314	17794	19424
担任法律顾问的单位	(家)	Number of Units with Permanent Legal Advisors	(unit)	12704	15530	31595	35510	36430	35260	43150
民事诉讼代理	(件)	Agent of Civil Cases	(case)	35310	49772	80952	96880	98127	176024	135415
刑事诉讼辩护及代理	(件)	Defender and Agent of Criminal Cases	(case)	15852	33845	46024	41613	35168	35635	29084
非诉讼法律事务	(件)	Agent of Non-Litigious Legal Affairs	(case)	44558	42463	35794	39122	38530	32331	58785
咨询和代写法律文书	(次)	Agent of Advise and Legal Documents Written for	(copy)	283976	502229	323666	315901	338018	353454	386082
公证工作		**Notarization**								
公证处	(个)	Number of Notary Offices	(unit)	207	205	208	208	208	209	209
公证人员	(人)	Notarial Personnel	(person)	1165	1720	2169	2221	2302	2356	2414
#公证员	(人)	Notaries	(person)	679	723	836	839	860	923	946
受理国内公证	(件)	Internal Notarization	(case)	150854	732398	901910	832457	963057	1026940	1077254
受理涉外公证	(件)	Foreign-related Notarization	(case)	18322	65775	110032	101597	110387	108434	120524
受理涉台、港、澳公证	(件)	Notarization of Hong Kong Macao & Taiwan	(case)	2366	6886	5631	6087	6192	7922	5862
出证	(件)	Number of Notarized Documents	(copy)	170028	802173	1015655	943074	1022941	1143296	1203640
人民调解工作		**People's Mediation**								
专职司法助理员	(人)	Number of Full-time Judicial Assistants	(person)	1053	2739	3862	3862	3862	3862	3862
人民调解委员会	(个)	Number of People's Mediation Committees	(unit)	64879	63912	63414	63587	63623	63370	62433
调解员	(人)	Number of Mediators	(person)	524428	429763	37539	376748	375771	340030	321345
基层法律服务所调解纠纷	(件)	Mediation of Grassroots Legal Service	(case)	42060	39282	38453	44755	52497	26381	44487

注：律师、公证和调解资料由四川省司法厅提供。
a) Data of lawyers, notarization and mediation information are provided by the Provincial Department of Justice.

22-7 调解民间纠纷情况
Statistics on Mediation of Civil Disputes

项 目	Item	调解纠纷(件) Mediation of Disputes (case)		各类纠纷所占比重(%) Percentage of Disputes (%)	
		2017	2018	2017	2018
合 计	**Total**	**423099**	**425767**	**100.0**	**100.0**
婚姻家庭纠纷	Marriage and Family Disputes	101451	95063	24.0	22.3
邻里纠纷	Neighbourhood Disputes	115783	117856	27.4	27.7
房屋宅基地纠纷	Homestead Housing Disputes	13942	11290	3.3	2.7
合同纠纷	Contracts Disputes	17148	15481	4.1	3.6
生产经营纠纷	Production and Management Disputes	9982	9156	2.4	2.2
损害赔偿	Damage Disputes	32410	33662	7.7	7.9
劳动争议	Labor Disputes	9322	8947	2.2	2.1
村务管理纠纷	Village Services ManagementDisputes				
山林土地纠纷	Forest Land Disputes	19571	19774	4.6	4.6
征地拆迁纠纷	Land Acquisition and Resettlement Disputes	8425	7078	2.0	1.7
计划生育纠纷	Family Planning Disputes				
环境保护	Environmental Protection	3798	3325	0.9	0.8
道路交通事故	Road Traffic Accidents	44949	52676	10.6	12.4
物业纠纷	Property Disputes	4943	5718	1.2	1.3
医疗纠纷	Medical Malpractice	2845	2537	0.7	0.6
其他纠纷	Other Disputes	38530	43204	9.1	10.1

22-8 各市(州)检察机关审查批准、决定逮捕犯罪嫌疑人和提起公诉被告人情况

Arrests of Criminal Suspects and Defendants under Public Prosecution Approved by People's Procuratorate by Region

单位：件、人 (case, person)

案件分类 市(州)	Case Item Region	批捕、决定逮捕合计 Total of Approval and Arrest 2017		2018		决定起诉合计 Total of Pubilc Prosecutions 2017		2018	
合 计	**Total**	**31508**	**42304**	**30283**	**43003**	**53999**	**72903**	**50353**	**71208**
公安、安全、监狱机关提请小计	**Sub-total of Requests by Departments of State and Public Security and Prisons**	**30884**	**41633**	**29923**	**42600**	**52632**	**70998**	**49468**	**70059**
危害国家安全、公共安全案	Offences Against State Security	1417	1541	1339	1444	14148	14473	13871	14224
破坏社会主义市场经济秩序案	Offences Against Socialist Economic Order	1401	2358	1329	2498	2053	3889	2104	4528
侵犯公民人身、民主权利案	Offences Against Citizens' Personal and Democratic Rights	3381	4201	3514	4449	**17032**	23611	4893	6505
妨害社会管理秩序案	Offences Against Social Management of Order	11290	15664	11806	18334	14418	22274	13921	24190
侵犯财产案	Offences Against Properties	13381	17850	11923	15861	4972	6738	14667	20585
危害国防利益案	Offences Against National Defense	14	19	12	14	9	13	12	27
检察机关直接立案侦查案件小计	**Sub-total of Cases Handled Directly by Procuratorate's Offices**	**624**	**671**	**360**	**403**	**1367**	**1905**	**883**	**1147**
贪污贿赂案	Offences on Corruption and Bribery	585	625	341	380	1215	1695	812	1044
渎职侵权案	Offences on Abuse and Dereliction of Duty	39	46	19	23	152	210	71	103
按市(州)分	**Grouped by Region**								
四川省人民检察院	Provincial Procuratorate	90	91	9	40				
成都市	Chengdu	11764	15858	10711	14988	18084	23874	16808	22840
自贡市	Zigong	892	1096	800	1071	1568	2135	1385	1983
攀枝花市	Panzhihua	563	765	505	730	1449	1902	1217	1641
泸州市	Luzhou	1194	1528	1310	1782	2444	3160	2343	3115
德阳市	Deyang	983	1205	929	1238	2115	2655	1893	2443
绵阳市	Mianyang	1257	1643	1201	1661	2746	3878	2650	3814
广元市	Guangyuan	630	919	548	840	1614	2281	1258	1857
遂宁市	Suining	812	1069	784	1086	1574	2149	1457	2043
内江市	Neijiang	898	1175	920	1258	1886	2607	1652	2323
乐山市	Leshan	1008	1308	1085	1643	1686	2310	1642	2399
南充市	Nanchong	1619	2256	1813	2598	2642	3696	2735	4090
眉山市	Meishan	965	1306	929	1328	1810	2535	1677	2489
宜宾市	Yibin	1538	2003	1500	2049	2886	3787	2766	3765
广安市	Guangan	779	1129	927	1424	1473	2123	1540	2458
达州市	Dazhou	1155	1467	1308	1889	1774	2318	1714	2545
雅安市	Yaan	611	824	631	928	1079	1559	955	1531
巴中市	Bazhong	593	856	600	876	1338	1792	1291	1877
资阳市	Ziyang	537	725	576	802	1218	1758	1146	1694
阿坝藏族羌族自治州	Aba	255	390	316	499	475	697	532	780
甘孜藏族自治州	Ganzi	377	544	447	692	416	596	466	771
凉山彝族自治州	Liangshan	2865	4003	2354	3487	3562	4892	3119	4628
四川省人民检察院成都铁路运输分院	Procuratorate of Chengdu Railroad Bureau	123	144	80	94	160	199	107	122

22-9 人民法院审理各类案件受理结案情况
Criminal Trial Cases Accepted and Settled by Courts

单位：件 (case)

项目	Item	受理 Cases Accepted		结案 Cases Settled	
		2017	2018	2017	2018
合计	**Total**	**1117113**	**1239142**	**1042776**	**1125076**
一审	**First Trial**	**623908**	**674360**	**584603**	**621327**
刑事	Criminal	55948	53560	53940	50702
民事	Civil	556541	607012	520396	558432
行政	Administrative	11419	13788	10267	12193
二审	**Second Trial**	**64885**	**69420**	**60535**	**63676**
刑事	Criminal	6795	6778	6483	6290
民事	Civil	52976	56783	49518	52362
行政	Administrative	5114	5859	4534	5024
审判监督	**Trial Oversight**	**2172**	**2606**	**1622**	**2053**
刑事	Criminal	119	146	87	115
民事	Civil	1966	2370	1490	1857
行政	Administrative	87	90	45	81
管辖	**Jurisdiction**	**8336**	**7306**	**8119**	**7138**
再审审查	**Retrial review**	**11683**	**14718**	**9793**	**11410**
国家赔偿与司法救助	**State Compensation and Judicial Assistance**	**2843**	**3553**	**2656**	**3186**
执行案件	**Enforcement cases**	**355798**	**401372**	**329941**	**353490**
刑罚与执行变更审查	**Punishment and Execution change review**	**14808**	**25736**	**14591**	**25496**
其他案件	Other Cases	32680	40071	30916	37300

22-10 人民法院执行案件标的和减、免、缓诉讼费情况
Subjects Implemented and Litigation Costs Reduced, Exempted and Deferred by Courts

项目	Item	2017	2018
申请执行标的 (亿元)	Subject matter of application for execution (100 million yuan)	2386.35	2648.20
执行到位标的 (亿元)	Subject matter of execution in place (100 million yuan)	465.90	621.50
减、免、缓诉讼费案件 (件)	Cases of Litigation Costs Reduced, Exempted and Defered (case)	15624	11123
减、免、缓诉讼费 (万元)	Litigation Costs Reduced, Exempted and Defered (10 000 yuan)	11098.94	13565.19
减交 (万元)	Reduction (10 000 yuan)	82.56	117.85
免交 (万元)	Exemption (10 000 yuan)	1046.62	1369.49
缓交 (万元)	Deferral (10 000 yuan)	9969.76	12077.85

注：人民法院审理案件等情况由四川省高级人民法院提供。
a) People's court cases are prepared and provided by Sichuan Provincial Higher People's Court.

22-11 公安机关受理查处治安案件情况(2018年)

Offense Cases Against Public Order Handled by Public Security Organs(2018)

单位：起 (case)

案件类别	Category of Cases	受理 Cases Accepted to be Treated	查处 Cases Investigated and Treated
合　计	**Total**	**250865**	**164857**
扰乱公共秩序	Disrupt Public Order	8271	7330
扰乱单位秩序	Disrupt Unit Order	2897	2559
扰乱公共场所秩序	Disrupt Public Place Order	4447	4004
扰乱公共交通工具秩序	Disrupt Public Transport Order	169	112
妨碍交通工具正常行驶	Impedes Normal Conditions of Transport	751	649
扰乱大型群众性活动秩序	Disrupt the order of large scale mass activities	7	6
妨害公共安全	Prejudice Public Safety	3568	2741
违反危险物质管理规定 非法携带枪支、弹药、管制刀	Violation of Hazardous Material Regulations Illegal Possession of Firearms. Ammunition. Knife Control	2454	2187
盗窃、损毁公共设施	Theft. Damage to Public Facilities	1114	554
侵犯他人人身权利、财产权利	Violations of the Personal Rights of Others. Property Rights	178261	96596
强迫他人劳动	Forced Labor	8	5
侮辱、诽谤、诬告陷害	Insult. Libel. Calumniation	3547	3107
发送信息干扰正常生活	Send Information Interfered with the Normal Life	240	153
殴打他人	Assault	61828	49666
盗窃	Theft	112638	43665
妨害社会管理	Prejudice and Social Management	60765	58190
阻碍执行职务	Impeding the Implementation of Duties	2925	2666
违反旅馆业管理	Hotel Management Violation	3000	2849
卖淫、嫖娼	Prostitution. Whoring	6154	5804
毒品违法活动	Drug-related activities	48686	46871

注：治安情况、火灾事故和交通事故资料由四川省公安厅提供。
a) Data of law and order, fire and accident are provided by the Provincial Public Security Bureau.

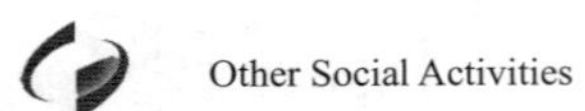

22-12 各市(州)查处治安案件和刑事案件立案、破案数

Number of Offense Cases Against Public Order Investigated and Prosecuted and Criminal Case Filed and Cracked by Region

单位：起 (case)

市(州)	Region	治安案件 Offense Cases Against Public Order				刑事案件立案 Criminal Case Filed		刑事案件破案 Criminal Case Cracked	
		发现 Discovered		查处 Investigated and Prosecuted					
		2017	2018	2017	2018	2017	2018	2017	2018
全　省	**Sichuan**	**476973**	**422322**	**342653**	**298661**	**282079**	**255558**	**102316**	**92180**
成都市	Chengdu	241469	203541	158008	131279	109417	104613	23388	23584
自贡市	Zigong	9088	9134	7679	7588	8784	6868	5277	3219
攀枝花市	Panzhihua	6839	5801	6699	5199	4153	3486	2241	1654
泸州市	Luzhou	13516	11537	12516	10701	11606	9900	6040	5012
德阳市	Deyang	19405	15481	12796	9860	14813	13453	6217	5908
绵阳市	Mianyang	15267	14224	10799	9355	15365	14254	4143	4769
广元市	Guangyuan	9971	9241	5797	5641	6233	5337	2434	2483
遂宁市	Suining	12123	12844	9930	10273	10743	9181	5143	4091
内江市	Neijiang	10644	9783	10466	9622	8320	7474	3321	3160
乐山市	Leshan	15913	18645	15913	18645	10462	9023	3824	3612
南充市	Nanchong	12876	13364	8329	7289	15385	13257	9143	8076
眉山市	Meishan	15314	15202	11574	12073	8959	7392	3518	2735
宜宾市	Yibin	26847	24198	11056	8371	13717	11383	6535	5531
广安市	Guangan	15759	13491	15724	13463	9817	9377	4651	3998
达州市	Dazhou	17273	15955	13935	12979	8446	7332	3543	3021
雅安市	Yaan	3112	3467	2556	2561	4658	3929	1813	1510
巴中市	Bazhong	7491	7373	7098	6970	6117	5681	3345	2699
资阳市	Ziyang	6619	5236	4993	3596	4494	4548	1970	1739
阿坝藏族羌族自治州	Aba	1924	1796	1875	1690	1099	1177	577	601
甘孜藏族自治州	Ganzi	397	936	316	766	380	691	185	357
凉山彝族自治州	Liangshan	15124	11073	14594	10740	9111	7202	5008	4421

22-13 火灾事故情况
Basic Statistics on Fire Accidents

指 标		Item	合计 Total		特大事故 Extraordinarily		重大事故 Serious		较大事故 major		一般事故 Ordinary	
			2017	2018	2017	2018	2017	2018	2017	2018	2017	2018
火灾事故发生起数	（起）	Number of Fires (case)	20541	16148				1	3	2	20538	16145
死亡人数	（人）	Number of Deaths (person)	84	87				1	10	10	74	76
受伤人数	（人）	Number of Injuries (person)	73	58							73	58
损失折款	（万元）	Losses Converted into Cash (10 000 yuan)	14097	21970				9210	40	94	14058	12666
平均每起事故损失	（万元）	Losses per Case(10 000 yuan)	0.69	1.36				9210.00	13.23	46.91	0.68	0.78

22-14 各市(州)火灾事故情况
Basic Statistics on Fire Accidents by Region

市(州)	Region	火灾事故(起) Number of Fire Accidents (case)		火灾伤亡人数(人) Number of Deaths (person)		火灾损失金额(万元) Losses Converted into Cash (10 000 yuan)	
		2017	2018	2017	2018	2017	2018
全 省	**Sichuan**	**20541**	**16148**	**157**	**145**	**14097.2**	**21970.2**
成都市	Chengdu	6280	4182	19	24	3453.6	2078.3
自贡市	Zigong	155	95	3	7	682.1	350.5
攀枝花市	Panzhihua	346	260		2	144.7	158.9
泸州市	Luzhou	1539	1711	11	6	775.3	461.2
德阳市	Deyang	1318	794	4	8	856.3	277.4
绵阳市	Mianyang	264	297	13	3	605.9	513.9
广元市	Guangyuan	812	734	5	4	266.6	423.1
遂宁市	Suining	1460	1434	8	8	548.3	949.6
内江市	Neijiang	957	885	16	7	488.0	420.5
乐山市	Leshan	1616	828	7	1	683.0	185.2
南充市	Nanchong	827	386	10	16	360.4	927.4
眉山市	Meishan	373	282		3	1548.9	320.5
宜宾市	Yibin	948	890	12	14	650.1	1784.6
广安市	Guangan	914	569	5	2	604.4	309.8
达州市	Dazhou	487	762	6	16	538.4	10780.1
雅安市	Yaan	458	433	4	3	193.5	147.3
巴中市	Bazhong	802	758	10	9	206.3	667.1
资阳市	Ziyang	556	442	5	9	66.8	60.0
阿坝藏族羌族自治州	Aba	30	6	1		400.0	157.5
甘孜藏族自治州	Ganzi	50	19	6		595.6	574.3
凉山彝族自治州	Liangshan	348	381	8	3	429.0	423.1

22-15 交通事故情况(2018年)
Basic Statistics on Traffic Accidents(2018)

项 目		Item		合计 Total	特大事故 Extraordinarily Serious	重大事故 Serious	一般事故 Ordinary	其它 Others
发生数	(起)	Number of Traffic Accidents	(case)	8908			33	8875
死亡人数	(人)	Number of Deaths	(person)	2367			125	2242
受伤人数	(人)	Number of Injuries	(person)	10553			75	10478
损失折款	(万元)	Losses Converted into Cash	(10 000 yuan)	7325			850	6475
平均每起事故损失	(元)	Losses Converted per Case	(yuan)	8223			257576	7296

22-16 各市(州)交通事故情况(2018年)
Basic Statistics on Traffic Accidents by Region(2018)

市(州)	Region	发生数 (起) Number of Traffic Accidents (case)	死亡人数 (人) Number of Deaths (person)	受伤人数 (人) Number of Injuries (person)	损失折款 (万元) Losses Converted into Cash (10 000 yuan)
全 省	**Sichuan**	**8908**	**2367**	**10553**	**7724.95**
成都市	Chengdu	1808	619	1390	665.46
自贡市	Zigong	182	67	203	44.52
攀枝花市	Panzhihua	135	31	148	56.04
泸州市	Luzhou	133	48	179	91.73
德阳市	Deyang	279	72	297	97.34
绵阳市	Mianyang	722	196	809	465.36
广元市	Guangyuan	330	68	466	164.94
遂宁市	Suining	123	41	131	65.31
内江市	Neijiang	161	42	199	45.57
乐山市	Leshan	554	164	602	444.56
南充市	Nanchong	312	52	373	96.93
眉山市	Meishan	183	64	161	27.87
宜宾市	Yibin	765	97	1029	241.18
广安市	Guangan	89	39	79	41.91
达州市	Dazhou	318	101	383	119.30
雅安市	Yaan	575	86	771	332.72
巴中市	Bazhong	169	57	248	100.76
资阳市	Ziyang	169	107	173	70.15
阿坝藏族羌族自治州	Aba	223	49	369	474.39
甘孜藏族自治州	Ganzi	104	91	200	654.53
凉山彝族自治州	Liangshan	1232	114	1671	488.16

注：合计中不含高速公路交通事故的数据。
a)The data of Sichuan exclude the data of Traffic Accidents on Expressway.

主要统计指标解释

社区服务机构数 指报告期末设立的社区服务指导中心、社区服务中心、社区服务站、社区养老机构、社区互助型养老机构及其他社区服务机构的总和数。具有面向老人，残疾人，儿童及其家庭的商品递送、医疗保健、家庭保洁、日间照料、陪伴服务等为社区居家养老服务的设施和突出综合服务的职能。包括党员活动室、就业保障网络、社区卫生服务站、文化活动室、图书室、“爱心超市”、社区捐助接收站点、警务站（室）、老年活动室、未成年人文化活动场所等具有综合服务功能的机构。

公证人员 指在公证处工作的人员总称，包括公证处主任、副主任、公证员、公证员助理(助理公证员)和其他从事辅助性工作的人员。

人民检察院直接立案侦查案件 指按照管辖的规定，由人民检察院直接立案侦查的贪污贿赂犯罪、渎职犯罪、国家机关工作人员利用职权实施的侵犯公民人身权利和民主权利的犯罪以及经省级人民检察院决定立案侦查的国家机关工作人员利用职权实施的其他重大犯罪案件。

受理 是指人民法院对符合诉讼法规定立案条件，决定立案审理的案件。受理包括上期“旧存”和本期“新收”案件两部分。

结案 是指人民法院依照诉讼法规定审理案件，案件审理结束已作出处理决定的案件。

特大火灾 指造成30人以上死亡，或者100人以上重伤，或者1亿元以上直接财产损失的火灾。

重大火灾 指造成10人以上30人以下死亡，或者50人以上100人以下重伤，或者5000万元以上1亿元以下直接财产损失的火灾。

较大火灾 指造成3人以上10人以下死亡，或者10人以上50人以下重伤，或者1000万元以上5000万元以下直接财产损失的火灾。

一般火灾 指造成3人以下死亡，或者10人以下重伤，或者1000万元以下直接财产损失的火灾。

特大交通事故 指一次造成死亡3人以上，或者重伤11人以上，或者死亡1人，同时重伤8人以上，或者死亡2人，同时重伤5人以上，或者财产损失6万元以上的交通事故。

重大交通事故 指一次造成死亡1至2人，或者重伤3人以上10人以下，或者财产损失3万元以上不足6万元的交通事故。

Explanatory Notes on Main Statistical Indicators

Number of Service Institutions in Communities refer to the total number of community service guidance centers, community service centers, community service stations, community pension institutions, community mutual aid pension facilities and other community service institutions at the end of the reporting period. These institutions offer home keeping and elderly care services for the elderly, handicapped people, children and their families, like commodity delivery, health care, cleaning, adult day care, companion and others.

Notary Personnel refers to people working for notary offices including: directors, deputy director, notaries, assistant notaries, and other people providing assistance.

Cases Registered and Handled Directly by People's Procuratorate Offices refer to those serious criminal cases that, according to the functional jurisdiction, are registered and handled by the People's Procuratorate Offices, including the ones on bribery and corruption, the ones on abuse and dereliction of duty, offences against citizens' personal and democratic rights by government officials abusing their powers; and that are registered and handled by the provincial Procuratorate offices in relation to other major crimes committed by government officials by abusing their powers.

Acceptance of Case refers to People's Court decide to accept in accordance with the Provisions of Procedural law .The cases include two parts: cases turned over from previous year and cases accepted this year.

Settlement of Case refers to People's Court decide to accept the case and make decision in accordance with the Provisions of Procedural law.

Extraordinarily Serious Fire Case refers to a case which has caused over 30 deaths; or over 100 serious injuries; or a direct property loss over 100 million yuan(RMB).

Serious Fire Case r efers to a case which has caused over 10 to 30 deaths; or over 50 to 100 serious injuries; or a direct property loss over 50 million to 100 million yuan(RMB).

Comparatively Serious Fire Case refers to a case which has caused over three to ten deaths; or over 10 to 50 serious injuries; or a direct property loss over 10 million to 50 million yuan(RMB).

Ordinary Fire Case refers to a case which has caused less than three deaths; or less than 10 serious injuries; or a direct property loss less than 10 million yuan(RMB).

Extraordinarily Serious Traffic Accident refers to an accident which has caused three or more deaths; or over 11 serious injuries; or one death and over 8 serious injuries; or two deaths and over 5 serious injuries; or a loss over 60 thousand yuan(RMB).

Serious Traffic Accident refers to an accident which has caused one or two deaths; or three to ten serious injuries; or a loss over 30 thousand yuan to 60 thousand yuan(RMB).

中国统计出版社有限公司最新图书简目

(仅供参考,以实际出版为准)

统计资料

中国统计年鉴　中国统计摘要　中国第三产业统计年鉴
中国第三次全国农业普查综合资料　国际统计年鉴　金砖国家联合统计手册
中国-东盟国家统计手册　中国农村统计年鉴　中国县域统计年鉴
中国农产品价格调查年鉴　中国城市统计年鉴　中国价格统计年鉴
中国贸易外经统计年鉴　中国零售和餐饮连锁企业统计年鉴　中国商品交易市场统计年鉴
大中型批发零售和住宿餐饮企业统计年鉴　中国住户调查年鉴　中国工业统计年鉴
中国环境统计年鉴　中国能源统计年鉴　中国建筑业统计年鉴
中国房地产统计年鉴　中国固定资产投资统计年鉴　中国对外直接投资统计公报
中国人口和就业统计年鉴　中国劳动统计年鉴　中国社会统计年鉴
中国科技统计年鉴　中国高技术产业统计年鉴　全国企业创新调查年鉴
中国文化及相关产业统计年鉴　2018年时间利用调查资料　中国妇女儿童状况统计资料
中国基本单位统计年鉴　中国教育统计年鉴　中国教育经费统计年鉴
中国民族统计年鉴　中国残疾人事业统计年鉴　长江经济带发展统计年鉴

省级综合统计年鉴系列

北京 天津 河北 山西 内蒙古 辽宁 吉林 黑龙江 上海 江苏 浙江 安徽 福建 江西 山东 河南 湖北 湖南 广东 广西 海南 重庆 四川 贵州 云南 西藏 陕西 甘肃 青海 宁夏 新疆 新疆生产建设兵团

市(县)级综合统计年鉴系列

滨海新区 石家庄 唐山 邯郸 保定 沧州 邢台 廊坊 承德 衡水 秦皇岛 张家口 太原 大同 阳泉 长治 晋城 朔州 晋中 运城 忻州 临汾 吕梁 呼和浩特 鄂尔多斯 包头 沈阳 大连 长春 延吉 四平 白山 通化 哈尔滨 齐齐哈尔 黑龙江垦区 上海浦东新区 南京 无锡 徐州 常州 苏州 南通 连云港 淮安 盐城 扬州 镇江 泰州 宿迁 江阴 丹阳 海门 张家港 杭州 宁波 温州 嘉兴 湖州 绍兴 金华 衢州 舟山 台州 丽水 合肥 安庆 福州 厦门 宁德 漳州 龙岩 莆田 泉州 三明 南平 南昌 九江 上饶 新余 抚州 赣州 景德镇 济南 青岛 枣庄 潍坊 聊城 郑州 洛阳 平顶山 三门峡 南阳 商丘 信阳 济源 汝州 武汉 十堰 荆州 宜昌 荆门 咸宁 黄冈 长沙 鹰潭 广州 深圳 惠州 东莞 汕尾 湛江 肇庆 南宁 柳州 桂林 贵港 梧州 来宾 河池 防城港 海口 三亚 儋州 成都 内江 贵阳 黔南 毕节 昆明 文山 德宏 西安 延安 安康 铜川 汉中 商洛 银川 兰州 庆阳 乌鲁木齐 昌吉 阿勒泰 兵团一师、二师、三师、四师、六师、七师、八师、十师、十三师、十四师

调查年鉴系列

天津 内蒙古 上海 河南 湖北 湖南 广东 广西 重庆 四川 云南 甘肃 宁夏 南宁 贵港 昆明

统计方法应用/实用手册

Python数据分析基础（第二版）　医用多元统计分析（第三版）　中华生物统计用表
中国国民经济核算体系（2016）基础知识　国民经济核算初级教程　医学统计学手册
全国统计专业技术资格考试系列考试用书：统计业务知识（第四版修订版）　统计业务知识学习指导与习题
全国统计专业技术资格考试系列考试用书：统计相关知识（第四版）　统计相关知识学习指导与习题

统计通俗读物/统计科普图书

领导干部统计知识问答　《防范和惩治统计造假、弄虚作假督察工作规定》辅导读本
统计新媒体运营指南　统计公文知识问答　理解国民账户　中国古代统计史简编

重点图书

辉煌70年　第三次全国农业普查农作物面积遥感测量图集　中国第四次经济普查年鉴
新编英汉汉英统计大词典　中国国民经济核算体系2016　国民经济行业分类注释
挑大学选专业2019—考研择校指南　挑大学选专业2019—高考志愿填报指南　中华医学统计百科全书